ACCOUNTING FOR MANAGERS

Text and Cases

3e

WILLIAM J. BRUNS, JR.

Henry R. Byers Professor of Business Administration, Emeritus
Harvard University
and
Visiting Professor
Northeastern University

THOMSON

SOUTH-WESTERN

Accounting for Managers: Text and Cases, 3/e

William J. Bruns, Jr.

VP/Editorial Director:
Jack W. Calhoun

Publisher:
Rob Dewey

Acquisitions Editor:
Julie Moulton

Developmental Editor:
Allison Rolfes

Marketing Manager:
Keith Chasse

Production Editor:
Margaret M. Bril

Technology Project Editor:
Sally Nieman

Media Editor:
Robin Browning

Manufacturing Coordinator:
Doug Wilke

Production House:
Cover to Cover Publishing, Inc.

Printer:
Quebecor World
Taunton, Massachusetts

Design Production:
Kathy Hemming

Internal and Cover Designer:
Justin Klefeker

Cover Images:
© Getty Images

For permission to use material
from this text or product, submit a
request online at
http://www.thomsonrights.com.

For more information
contact South-Western,
5191 Natorp Boulevard,
Mason, Ohio 45040.
Or you can visit our Internet site at:
http://www.swlearning.com

CONTENTS

PREFACE

Accounting systems, information, and reports have the potential to provide managers with critical data and information about their organizations and those of customers and competitors. Unfortunately, however, many managers never learn how to use and exploit that potential. The complexity of modern accounting systems and standards can be daunting in spite of the apparent simplicity of basic accounting frameworks. Untrained in the complexities, many managers retreat from accounting, content to leave it to the accountants, and never to admit their uneasiness with accounting information and reports.

Accounting for Managers was written with the belief that managers must learn to work with accounting and accountants, but they do not need to learn how to be accountants themselves. Managers need to know what accountants do and what they do not do. They need to know the vocabulary, perspectives, and bias that underlie accounting processes and reports. Managers need to know how to ask accountants for data and information they want, and they need to know how to use accounting as a strategic tool. But managers do not need to be accountants themselves.

In 1989, the faculty of the Harvard Business School established a new required course titled *Financial Reporting and Management Accounting* (now *Financial Reporting and Control*). Although the charter and objectives for the course were vague, the mandate was to create an accounting course that would focus on what accountants do and why they do it, rather than how they do it. The course was to focus on how managers could manage better because of what accountants do, and how managers could use accounting reports, systems, and information as effectively as possible.

Case studies are an ideal way to achieve these objectives because they illustrate and describe what accountants do and provide a basis for discussions about alternatives and implications of accounting standards, procedures, and reports. Cases allow the reader to understand that accountants make choices that determine what information managers, as well as outsiders, will see, and the form it will take. If the manager needs other information or wants to present another accounting picture, the manager needs to intervene and provide direction through questions or requests. By doing so, the manager uses accounting as a tool to accomplish his or her objectives.

Some of the case studies in *Accounting for Managers* look deceptively easy, while others look impossibly difficult. The former are usually more complex than they look because of the nuances that underlie any accounting. The latter can usually be broken into easy-to-understand parts because of the power of the basic accounting models that underlie financial reporting, product costing, and measurements for control.

The majority of cases are based on information gathered from actual organizations and present real problems managers have to solve.

Most case studies contain ambiguities and complexities that preclude any single correct answer. Individual study of cases is best followed by small group and class discussions. In these exchanges, learning is enhanced. The role of the instructor or discussion leader is to ensure that alternative analyses and conclusions are carefully considered along with their implications. The goal for everyone in a case discussion should be to improve his or her ability to approach, analyze, and reach conclusions about the next newspaper or magazine story about accounting or the next accounting problem or case study that he or she will encounter.

Accounting is too important to managers, organizations, and societies to be left to accountants alone. Accounting information is often a basis for decisions. Accounting reports are often the basis on which the effectiveness of stewardship, decisions, and actions are evaluated. Effective managers are always aware of the potentials and problems that accountants and accounting processes can create. Your study of this text and the case situations should help you to become more effective managers, and better management helps everyone.

ACKNOWLEDGEMENTS

Many people have helped to create and improve *Accounting for Managers*. More than 11,000 students in the Harvard Business School MBA Classes of 1990 through 2003 have commented, made suggestions, and corrected errors in many of the cases and chapters that comprise this book. Students since 1998 have made many suggestions that have improved this Third Edition.

The colleagues with whom I have been privileged to teach this material in a group-teaching, file-sharing environment have contributed much and have helped to improve it. These include Mary Barth, Sharon Bruns, Brian Bushee, James Chang, Chuck Christensen, Srikant Datar, Bala Dharan, Marc Epstein, Dave Hawkins, Paul Healy, Julie Hertenstein, Regi Herzlinger, Gerald Holtz, Ken Merchant, V.G. Narayanan, Chris Noe, Dick Nolan, Tom Piper, Donella Rapier, Ratna Sarkar, Bob Simons, Amy Hutton, Guy Weyns, Pete Wilson, and Karen Wruck. Many of these wrote material included in *Accounting for Managers*, and all others will find their influences in special places.

Other faculty contributors to this book include Bob Anthony, Robin Cooper, Bob Kaplan, Krishna Palepu, Peter Turney, and Dave Wilson. I appreciate their allowing me to include some of their cases and notes.

Six research associates contributed greatly to this project, and I acknowledge the great contributions of the late Jeremy Cott, Dave Ellison, Susan Harmeling, Terry Nichols, and Eric Petro.

The Harvard Business School and Deans John H. McArthur and Kim B. Clark provided encouragement and a supporting environment for what was one of the most satisfying teaching assignments in my career. *Business Horizons*, *The Wall Street Journal*, and the *Harvard Business Review* each agreed to allow me to reprint articles.

Finally, special thanks are due to the group who helped to put this material together. The staff of the Document Service Center at the Harvard Business School provided invaluable help in making the cases and notes readable, and their service went beyond that which I have any right to expect. My assistant, Janice Simmons, kept the project on schedule. Her cheerful acceptance of unreasonable demands for countless corrections on tight deadlines will not be forgotten. At Thomson Business and Professional Publishing, the contributions of Ken Martin, Marge Bril, and Allison Rolfes, also deserve special mention. Shannon Meadows of Cover to Cover Publishing provided invaluable editorial assistance and suggestions for improvement.

Finally, my wife Shay supported this project with affection, help, and needed criticism. She read drafts, improved presentations, contributed ideas, and taught several cases to her students before making suggestions about improvements. Her ideas are to be found throughout this book.

William J. Bruns, Jr.
Boston, Massachusetts

REVIEWERS

The following faculty and instructors have used *Accounting for Managers* or cases and notes from it in their courses and have provided valuable feedback and suggestions:

Robert D. Austin (Harvard)
Mary E. Barth (Stanford)
Sharon M. Bruns (Northeastern)
Brian J. Bushee (Harvard)
James Chang (Harvard)
Srikant M. Datar (Harvard)
Bala G. Dharan (Rice)
Marc J. Epstein (Rice)
David F. Hawkins (Harvard)
Paul M. Healy (Harvard)
Regina E. Herzlinger (Harvard)
Gerald Holtz (Harvard and Boston College)
Robert S. Kaplan (Harvard)
Alfred M. King
Kenneth A. Merchant (Harvard and University of Southern California)
V.G. Narayanan (Harvard)
Christopher F. Noe (Harvard)
Richard L. Nolan (Harvard)
Thomas R. Piper (Harvard)
Marjorie Platt (Northeastern)
Ratna G. Sarkar (Harvard)
Robert L. Simons (Harvard)
Amy P. Hutton (Harvard)
Kiran Verma (Harvard and University of Massachusetts—Boston)
Guy Weyns (Harvard)
G. Peter Wilson (Harvard and Boston College)
Karen Wruck (Harvard)

To Shay and Stacy

INTRODUCTION

Accounting for Managers is a text for managers who want to make the most of accounting information in the business environment. It is not a comprehensive accounting text. Instead, readers are broadly exposed to the way in which accountants contribute to organizations and to some of the things accountants do that every manager should know.

Why Managers Need to Know What Accountants Do

Accountants are the scorekeepers who observe, measure, and report on the economic aspects of organizations. Using the rules and procedures that have developed over many years, they measure the effects of economic activities. Managers have played important roles in the development of these rules and procedures, and they will continue to do so as those principles and practices evolve in the future. Managers who know something about the status and use of accounting standards will be more effective in telling their story and in getting the information they really need.

Accounting is a language system that facilitates efficient communication between managers about economic aspects of organizations. Standardized terminology developed and used by accountants facilitates discussion of complex aspects of economic conditions and the performance of organizations. If managers do not understand the vocabulary and accounting methodology, communication in the organization becomes awkward and inefficient. In turn, the possibility of confusion or mistakes increases.

Accountants maintain records that become the basis for financial reports. Such reports summarize the financial status and success of the organization at one or more points in time, and they may describe how the financial structure and strength of the organization has changed over a period of time.

Financial reports are important to managers for two reasons. First, they allow managers to evaluate how their strategies and discussions are affecting the economic status and viability of their organization. By comparing the expected results of those that have been reported by accountants, managers can judge their own success and decide whether changes in strategy or decisions are needed. Second, since external parties often have interests in the financial status and success of organizations, financial statements are commonly used to report on those interests. Managers need a basic understanding of the way in which accountants summarize economic activities and prepare financial reports, so they can assess how their actions will appear to others both inside and outside of the organization.

The structure of financial reports is part of the language that accounting brings into an organization. As managers try to anticipate how their decisions might affect the organization, the framework provided by financial reports is often a useful way of summarizing the possible effects and consequences of actions.

Accounting records are often the most comprehensive records that any organization maintains. As a result, those records often provide useful information to managers trying to solve problems or decide between alternative decisions or courses of action. By knowing what kind of information is kept in accounting records and by knowing where it is maintained, managers can more efficiently request needed information and understand the proper use of that information for decisions at hand.

An Overview of the Text

Accounting for Managers has seven parts:

Part I provides an overview of accounting and financial reporting. The accounting framework and some accounting concepts are introduced so that managers can immediately begin working with financial statements.

Part II is concerned with how accountants measure and report on the assets, liabilities, and equities different parties have in an organization. In this part, classifications and elements of financial statements are examined separately to give managers an understanding of some of the difficulties that both managers and accountants have in measuring and describing the economic substance of an organization.

Part III introduces the idea that managers can choose a reporting strategy in presenting their organization to those who may request and use financial statements. A combination of accounting policies that underlie a set of financial statements can be described as conservative or aggressive. By taking an active role in the financial reporting process, managers can minimize the risk that their strategic directions will be misunderstood by outsiders who seek to understand and appraise an organization based on financial statements alone.

Part IV introduces some of the concepts of cost used by managers in decision making, planning, and controlling operations.

Part V is concerned with procedures accountants use in estimating product costs and provides an introduction to cost management. Accounting for cost is primarily an activity that takes place for the benefit of managers. Product costs are useful for pricing and product line decisions. In addition, measurements of product costs can be compared against expectations in determining whether planned efficiencies have been attained.

Part VI introduces capital investment analyses. Capital investment analyses are a special kind of cost management problem because they affect the future of the organization for longer periods of time.

Part VII presents some of the ways in which accounting measurements are used by managers in planning and controlling organizational activities. Because of their expertise, accountants are often called upon by managers to make measurements, to communicate, to motivate, and to provide a basis for evaluating part of an organization and the products or services that it provides. The case studies in Part VII illustrate how some organizations have sought to improve their internal measurement and management systems to benefit from their knowledge that what gets measured matters.

A Brief Summary of Text Objectives

Six objectives have guided the development and selection of the text and case studies that comprise *Accounting for Managers*. When you have finished this text you should:

- Be familiar with the accounting framework and how it is used in evaluating economic conditions and success and in decision making in organizations.
- Have a sense for the conceptual basis of accounting as it is carried out in organizations today.
- Be familiar with financial statements, accounting reports, and the vocabulary found within them.
- Have a sense of how managers use a reporting strategy in communicating with each other and with parties external to their organization.
- Understand the complexity of determining and using information on the cost of products and services produced by an organization.
- Understand the power of measurements in coordinating, motivating, and evaluating the activities of employees and managers in modern organizations.

Some of the case studies are based on situations where managers are trying to solve one or more complex problems that may not have a solution that will satisfy the objectives and needs of all the affected parties. In other cases, complex problems have been greatly simplified using hypothetical situations and descriptions to allow students to discover why problems in accounting often demand extensive examination and discussion.

An Overview of Accounting and Financial Reporting

The Accounting Framework, Financial Statements, and Some Accounting Concepts

- *Maria Hernandez & Associates*

Introduction to Accounting Records

- *Chemalite, Inc.*
- *Hanson Ski Products*
- *Thumbs-Up Video, Inc.*
- *Monterrey Manufacturing Company*

Introduction to Financial Ratios and Financial Statement Analysis

- *Drivers of Industry Financial Structure*
- *The Financial Reporting Project*

The Accounting Framework, Financial Statements, and Some Accounting Concepts

Providing information for decisions about the deployment and use of resources in an organization and in the economy is one of the top objectives of accounting and accountants. Over many years, certain formats and procedures for presenting accounting information have come into wide use. Financial statements are based on a framework appropriately called *The Accounting Framework*.

THE BASIC ACCOUNTING FRAMEWORK

The accounting framework rests on two premises. The first is the idea that it is possible to distinguish an *accounting entity*—the person or organization for which a set of accounts is kept—from other persons or organizations that are associated with it. The second premise is that for any accounting entity, the resources available will be exactly equal to the resources provided by creditors and owners. This second assumption is usually called *the accounting equation*, and is written as follows:

Assets = Equities

The accounting processes of observing, measuring, and reporting are always carried out with an eye to maintaining this fundamental equality of assets and equities.

Assets

In general, assets may be thought of as all things of value that the organization has a right to use. They consist of financial resources, equipment and other physical resources, and other resources having value to the entity. Most business organizations have a wide variety of assets, which they may classify according to common characteristics. Some prevalent financial assets include cash and cash balances in banks, amounts owed to the organization by customers, and marketable securities held by

Professor William J. Bruns, Jr. prepared this case. HBS cases are developed solely as the basis for class discussion. Cases are not intended to serve as endorsements, sources of primary data, or illustrations of effective or ineffective management.

the firm. Operating assets often include land, buildings, equipment used in carrying out the activities of the organization, and inventories of unsold products. Other assets might include such intellectual property as copyrights or patents, conveying exclusive rights to profit from the use of property or process.

Equities

Equities in an organization represent claims on its resources or assets. In a crude way, equities reveal the suppliers of an organization's resources. Some parties provide resources and expect to be repaid; these are creditors. Others contribute resources and thereby become participants; these are owners. Equities of nonowners include amounts owed to employees or suppliers, amounts owed on short-term loans, and loans represented by other debts of one kind or another. Owners share in both the risks and whatever profits accrue. Equities of owners include the amount of resources that they originally contributed as well as some portion of the earnings that they have not withdrawn.

Assets = Equities

The accounting equation demands that, in accounting for an organization, the equality of assets and equities must be preserved. Thought of in another way, if the resources owned by an entity increase, the new resources had to have come from somewhere, and that source has a claim against them. If the things of value owned by an organization increase, the corresponding increase either in the amount of obligations or in the equities of owners must be recognized. Likewise, if the things of value owned by an entity decrease, obligations to nonowners may have been satisfied, or the equity of owners may have been reduced.

CLASSIFICATIONS OF ASSETS AND EQUITIES

Although there are decision situations in which information about total assets or total equities can be useful, in most cases greater detail is desired. Both assets and equities come in very different forms with very different characteristics, as we have already noted. For this reason, it is customary in accounting to adopt a scheme for classifying assets and equities of various types. The classifications can be as large or as small as necessary to achieve the objectives for measuring and reporting. As the number of classifications increases, the cost of measuring, record keeping, and reporting increases, so there is usually an economic constraint that limits the number of classifications actually employed.

The basic accounting equation is commonly expanded to highlight the two major equity classifications:

Assets = Liabilities + Owners' Equity

This expansion recognizes that there is a fundamental difference between the obligations the organization has to outsiders, or those who are not members or owners, and the obligation it has to owners, or shareholders—those who have invested capital in the organization. In the event the organization is dissolved, obligations to creditors must be met before assets are distributed to owners. This legal distinction provides the basis for this additional classification.

One reason why this expanded form of the accounting equation is used relates to the fundamental distinction between an organization or entity and its owners. The owners contribute capital, but they are not the entity. If the excess of assets over liabilities increases, owners' equity is increased. As long as owners do not make additional capital contributions or withdrawals from the assets of the firm, increases in owners' equity are usually associated with income-generating activities of an organization, whereas decreases usually result from losses.

BASIC FINANCIAL STATEMENTS

The nature and format of financial statements are derived directly from the basic accounting framework and the accounting equation. A *balance sheet* (or *statement of financial position*) lists the assets, liabilities, and owners' equity at a specified point in time. An asset-flow statement (the *statement of cash flows* is the most common) summarizes the reasons why a class of assets has increased or decreased over a period of time. A *statement of income* (or *earnings*) explains why the retained earnings classification within owners' equity has changed over a period of time, assuming owners have not taken assets from the firm in the form of dividends.

Although financial statements are prepared in many different formats and may use account classifications that differ substantially, a reader of financial reports who understands the basic accounting equation can usually figure out how to read the financial reports of an organization regardless of the particular reporting scheme that the organization has chosen. The consolidated financial statements of the Coca-Cola Company and Subsidiaries for 2003 provide an illustration of the relationship between the accounting equation and a set of financial reports for a corporation. The consolidated balance sheet (see **Exhibit 1**) illustrates the basic equality between assets and equities. The consolidated statement of income (see **Exhibit 2**) measures how retained earnings were affected by operations before the payment of cash dividends, and the consolidated statement of cash flows (see **Exhibit 3**) shows why the amount of cash and cash equivalents changed because of operating, investing, and financing activities.

These financial reports provide an outline for reviewing some of the elements that will be found in every set of financial reports of a corporation.

The Balance Sheet

The *balance sheet* (or *statement of financial position*) presents a company's financial position as of a specific date, based on measurements made in accordance with *generally accepted accounting principles (GAAP)* or some other reporting basis. By definition, the measured amount of total assets is always equal to the measured amount of liabilities and owners' equity. Except for monetary amounts such as cash, accounts receivable, and accounts payable, the measurements of each classification will rarely be equal to the actual current value or cash value shown. This is due to the fact that most measurements in accounting are made at the time a transaction took place in the past, and these historical measurements are retained in the accounts, even though the values of assets and some obligations may increase or decrease with the occurrence of events or passage of time. It is essential to remember that no statement of financial position will ever present the true financial value of an organization or the financial significance of the classifications used in the reports.

The classifications used by the Coca-Cola Company in its consolidated balance sheet (**Exhibit 1**) are typical of those that will be found in the balance sheets of other companies. *Current Assets* include cash and other assets used in operations during the normal operating cycle of the business, or within one year if the operating cycle is shorter than one year. The *normal operating cycle* of a company is that period of time required to acquire services and materials to create a product or service, which is sold to a customer, who then pays for the product or service, thus supplying the cash to begin the cycle again. *Cash and cash equivalents* are measured at their face amounts, whether they are in the possession of the company or deposited in banks. *Marketable securities* represent temporary investments, which can be easily converted to cash if more cash is needed. *Trade accounts receivable* are amounts that are due from customers who have purchased goods or services on credit. *Inventories* typically include materials that will be converted into product, work-in-process inventory, and finished goods that are ready for sale or have not yet been delivered to customers. *Prepaid expenses* include expenditures that have been made to acquire future benefits or services (an insurance policy would be an example), but for which the benefits have not been obtained at the date of the financial reports.

Following the current assets are a number of other assets that are *not* current; that is, they are not expected to be used up within a year or within the normal operating cycle of the business.

Many companies, particularly large companies, have assets that are not used directly in their operations or for which they do not have majority ownership. These are considered "nonoperating" assets and are usually called *Investments*. Coca-Cola has a number of such "investments." *Marketable securities* are securities of other companies similar to the marketable securities in the "Current Assets" section, except that *these* securities are expected to be held for a long-term period. *Equity method investments* are also investments in the securities of other companies, but these have to be accounted for somewhat differently (under the *equity method*) because the investor (here, Coca-Cola) owns enough of the companies to have "significant influence" over them (usually presumed to be 20% or more of their outstanding stock but less than 50%). The equity method of accounting essentially records the investor's pro rata share of all of the earnings of the investee and represents a more elaborate way of accounting for the investment than occurs with ordinary "marketable securities." Other kinds of "investments" (not represented here) might be the cash surrender value of life insurance or special-purpose funds that accumulate cash in a systematic way to meet some specific future needs.

Property, Plant and Equipment represents the cost of long-lived, tangible assets that are used in the company's operations. Land is almost always included at its original cost, while other assets are stated at their original cost less the proportion of original cost that has been included in the expenses of prior periods' operations as depreciation.

If a company has purchased another company for a price in excess of the fair market value of its identifiable assets, *goodwill* is assumed to have been acquired and will be recorded as an additional asset. Goodwill represents intangible things like the acquired company's excellent reputation or highly marketable brand names.

On the other side of the accounting equation are liabilities and the owners' equity. *Liabilities* are obligations that an organization must satisfy by transferring assets to or performing services for a person or organization at some time in the future. *Current liabilities* are those that an organization expects to satisfy either with assets that have been classified as current or in the course of normal operations or during the following year. Liabilities not falling within these categories are usually shown as *long-term debts* or *other liabilities*.

Shareowners' Equity (or *Stockholders' Equity*) represents the interest of the owners in the organization. Mathematically, its total is always equal to the amount that remains after deducting the total liabilities of the organization from its total assets. Only by coincidence would this amount be equal to the true value of the organization to its owners. Instead, the total is very much an artifact of the measurements and accounting procedures that have been used to record and account for assets and liabilities.

The amount of assets that owners originally committed to the organization (usually cash paid for stock) is usually shown separately in the owners' equity section of the Balance Sheet. In the case of the Coca-Cola Company, that amount consists of *Common stock* with a certain "par value" (which is a nominal, base value) plus *Capital surplus* (often called *Additional paid-in capital*), which represents the money that owners paid for stock in excess of the par value. Once these original assets are turned over to an organization, no further measurements are made, and the market value of the shares representing ownership may differ substantially from the original amount paid by the original owners.

Reinvested earnings (often referred to as *Retained earnings*) shows the accumulated net income of an organization from its origin to the present, after deducting dividends to shareholders.

Following this, Coca-Cola shows two additional, special components of Shareowners' Equity. *Unearned compensation on restricted stock* refers to the value of stock that has been awarded to certain officers of the company but not yet earned. Lastly, *Treasury stock* measures amounts that Coca-Cola has paid to reacquire its own stock. Although these shares have not been canceled, they are no longer outstanding and therefore do not represent any owners' interest at the date of the Balance Sheet.

The Statement of Income

The results of operations of business over a period of time are shown in the *statement of income*, or the *income statement*. Just as the balance sheet can be represented by the accounting equation, the income statement can be represented by the following equation:

Revenues – Expenses = Net Income (or Net Loss)

In actual reports, this equation is expanded considerably and usually includes details about the nature of important categories, particularly in footnotes to the statement.

Revenues result from selling products or services to customers. In its consolidated statement of income (see **Exhibit 2**), Coca-Cola shows a single figure for its "Net operating revenues" during the designated periods of time (that is, the years ending December 31, 2003, 2002, and 2001). Some companies might give figures for different kinds of revenue.

This is immediately followed by *Cost of goods sold*, which represents, for Coca-Cola, the direct, factory-related cost of producing the products it sold. (If Coca-Cola were a retailer rather than a manufacturer, cost of goods sold would represent the amount of money it paid to outside suppliers for the merchandise that it then resold to the public.) Coca-Cola's *Gross profit* represents simply the difference between revenues and cost of goods sold.

Following this is what Coca-Cola labels *Selling, administrative, and general expenses*. Other companies sometimes call it *Operating expenses* or will sometimes break it down into a few different categories. This represents general overhead expenses that the company incurred during the designated periods of time. Deducting these general overhead expenses from the gross profit figure yields the company's *Operating income*, which is thus a measure of the income derived from the principal operations of the company.

The consolidated statement of income of Coca-Cola is typical in that, in addition to operating income, other income and expense items must be added and subtracted before the *net income* total is measured. In many organizations, these nonoperating amounts are significant, but they are shown separately to enable a reader of the financial report to make alternative assumptions about the efficiency and success of operations in the current or future periods.

The Statement of Cash Flows

The *statement of cash flows* details the reasons why the amount of cash (and cash equivalents) changed during an accounting period. Just as the statement of income describes how retained earnings have changed during an accounting period, the statement of cash flows describes how the amount of cash and cash equivalents has changed during the accounting period. The statement's format reflects the three categories of activities that affect cash. Cash can be increased or decreased (1) because of *operations*, (2) because of the acquisition or sale of assets or *investments*, or (3) from changes in debt or stock or other *financial activities*.

Although it may not be self-evident from the consolidated statement of cash flows from the Coca-Cola Company (see **Exhibit 3**), the statement of cash flows can be thought of as containing much of the same kind of information as a checkbook register or bankbook. Sales or purchases of assets increase or decrease the amount of cash that can be deposited. Borrowing cash or payment of debt affects the balance similarly. Operations have similar effects on the balance of cash available. The reason this analogy to a bank balance is not obvious may be due to the most common form in which the statement of cash flows is presented. This common format reconciles the net income reported in the income statement to the net cash provided by operations. Upon further study, it will become apparent why statements of cash flows are often presented in this format rather than by showing directly the demands for cash made by operations and the receipts of cash provided by operations.

ACCOUNTING CONCEPTS

Four basic accounting concepts underlie the presentation in any statement of income. They are the *accounting period concept*, the *accrual concept*, the *realization* or *recognition concept*, and the *matching concept*.

A statement of income is always presented for a period of time. In fact, part of the heading of the statement of income must include a description of the time period for which the income has been measured. The *accounting period concept* covers the period over which a statement of income has been prepared. The accounting period can be of any length, but customarily it is related to a calendar period such as one year, one-half year, or perhaps one month. It is often useful to think of the accounting period as the time between the preparation and presentation of two successive statements of financial position by an organization. The statement of income presents the changes in owners' equity due to operations and other events between one balance sheet and the next.

The *accrual concept* supports the idea that income should be measured at the time major efforts or accomplishments occur rather than simply when cash is received or paid. Revenue and expenses can be recognized before or after cash flows. If revenue is recognized, but cash has not been received, then it will be recorded among current assets as accounts receivable. Correspondingly, if an expense has been incurred, but cash has not been paid, it will be recorded as a current liability.

What accountants call the *realization concept* is really a family of rules that might be more clearly labeled *recognition concepts*. These rules aid the accountant in determining that a revenue or expense has occurred, so that it can be measured, recorded, and reported in financial reports. There is actually a large number of these rules, many of which are conditional on circumstances affecting a particular organization at a particular point in time. For example, revenue is often realized (recognized) when a product is shipped to a customer. However, in other circumstances where a customer has contracted for a special product, some portion of revenue might be recognized at the end of an accounting period, even though the product is not complete and has not been delivered. In general, revenue is recognized along with associated expenses when an exchange has taken place, the earnings process is complete, the amount of income is determinable, and collection of amounts due is reasonably assured.

The amount of expenses to be deducted in each accounting period is determined by the *matching concept* through which the expenses associated with revenue are identified and measured. The accountant attempts to match the cost and expenses of producing a product or service with revenues obtained from its delivery to customers, so that net income can be measured. This matching of revenues and expenses allows readers to understand better the possible expenses of future revenues the organization will try to earn.

Our introduction to the accounting framework and financial reports illustrates four additional accounting concepts. These concepts include the *money measurement concept*, the *business entity concept*, the *going concern concept*, and the *cost concept*.

Accountants measure things in terms of money. The *money measurement concept* has the advantage of expressing all measurements in a common monetary unit that can be added, subtracted, multiplied, and divided to produce reports which themselves can become the subject of further analysis. Nevertheless, there are many things that affect an organization but are difficult or impossible to measure in terms of money. The knowledge and skills of members or employees of an organization have great value, but they are virtually impossible to measure in terms of money. Customer loyalty may ensure future profitability, but only past revenues will be shown in past reports. Because accountants employ the money measurement concept, readers of accounting reports should not expect to find a complete picture or all the facts about an organization.

The *business entity concept* delineates the boundaries of the organization for which accounts are kept and reports are made. The reports of the Coca-Cola Company that we have examined contain no information about who the owners or the managers of the Coca-Cola Company are. At the same time, because the accounts of many parts of the Coca-Cola Company have been consolidated, we cannot see the financial condition or financial success of a particular sales office or product line. Common sense tells us that within the Coca-Cola Company, accounts are probably maintained and reports prepared for each of those entities. The entity concept means that anyone who uses financial reports has to be sure that those reports are for the exact entity in which he or she is interested, whether it be the organization as a whole or a particular subset of it.

Financial reports assume that the entity is a *going concern*. Reports are not prepared on a basis that would show the liquidation value of an organization or what would happen if the organization was liquidated. Instead, the accountant works on the assumption that an entity will continue to operate much as it has been operating for an indefinitely long period in the future.

A fourth concept seen in the financial reports you have examined is the *cost concept*. Transactions provide the information necessary for measuring and recording assets in the accounts and subsequently reporting about them. Although a reader of a financial report may be interested in the value of assets or the value of an organization, the accountant is not. Assets are initially recorded by measuring the amount paid for them. When that cost is matched with revenues, it is matched at its historical amount rather than at the current value of the asset used to create a product or service. The cost concept means that as time passes asset measurements are not changed even if the current value of those assets is changing. Likewise, when coupled with the money measurement concept, no allowance is made for changes in the purchasing power of the currency that may have been used to acquire an asset. There can be no doubt that the cost concept greatly simplifies the accountant's job in maintaining a record that can become the basis for financial reports. But it does so by sacrificing the relevance of those reports to many kinds of economic decision making.

Three other concepts are important to financial reporting, even though they are somewhat less obvious. These are the concepts of *conservatism*, *consistency*, and *materiality*.

The *conservatism concept* operates as a safeguard to overstatement of asset values and owners' equity. It requires that accountants be slower to recognize revenues and gains and quicker to recognize expenses and losses. This potentially negative bias in the accountant's behavior is the basis for many jokes about the differences in the way accountants and other managers see things occurring in organizations.

The *consistency concept* requires that once an entity has selected an accounting method for a kind of event or a particular asset, that same method should be used for all future events of the same type and for that asset. The consistency concept enhances the comparability of accounting reports from one period to that of another. In that way, it enhances the usefulness of financial reports. Nevertheless, certain caution must be attached to any discussion of the consistency concept because accountants use the term consistency in a narrower sense than found in other uses. Consistency is required all the time, but there is no requirement for logical consistency at a moment in time. For example, assets that may appear identical may be accounted for using different accounting methods. All that is required is that the same method be used for the same asset over time, not that all like assets be accounted for using the same method. This means that financial statement users must be constantly alert for the specific accounting methods used in different parts of financial reports. Just because a reader of financial reports understands the way in which factory machinery has been measured and reported does not necessarily mean that the same reader will have any idea how trucks or delivery equipment have been measured and reported.

Finally, arching over the entire process of accounting and financial reporting is the *materiality concept*. This concept allows that the accountant does not need to attempt to measure and record events that are insignificant or to highlight events that differ from the usual or the norm. Events or assets judged to be insignificant can be ignored or disregarded. On the surface, this concept seems to make good sense, as it focuses both the accountant and the financial report reader's attention on important things. Unfortunately, the exact line between what is significant and what is insignificant is very difficult to define. Furthermore, something may seem insignificant to the accountant but might be regarded as very significant to a managing director. The materiality concept is both a strength and a weakness in financial reporting, and a wise reader of reports must be constantly on guard for its occasionally pernicious effects.

SUMMARY

The accounting equation

Assets = Equities

or in its expanded form

Assets = Liabilities + Owners' Equity

provides the basis for the accounting framework. The format for the statement of financial position derives directly from the accounting equation, and the assumed equality of assets and equities provides a basis for accounting record systems as well as the balance sheet.

Two additional financial reports stem directly from the accounting equation. The statement of income explains the change in the owners' equity that occurs during an accounting period by giving details of both revenues that increase owners' equity and expenses that decrease owners' equity. It provides a basis for analyzing the effectiveness of operations. The statement of cash flows explains why the amount of cash and equivalents has increased or decreased during a period of time. It details whether or not operations have provided additional cash or have themselves consumed cash. It also reveals cash that is provided by new loans or that has been used to pay off debts, and how cash has been invested or obtained by selling assets.

This brief overview of the accounting framework and financial reporting has served as an introduction to eleven important accounting concepts, financial reports, and the work of accountants. Only practice and further study can give real meaning to these accounting concepts, but understanding their existence is critical to studying the work of accountants, and some of the reasons why they operate as they do. The eleven concepts introduced here are accounting period, accrual, realization, matching, money measurement, business entity, going concern, cost, consistency, conservatism, and materiality. We will see in detail how these concepts are applied as we continue in our study of accounting principles.

EXHIBIT 1
The Coca-Cola Company and Subsidiaries
Consolidated Balance Sheets (in millions)

December 31	2003	2002
ASSETS		
CURRENT		
Cash and cash equivalents	$ 3,362	$ 2,260
Marketable securities	120	85
	3,482	2,345
Trade accounts receivable, less allowance		
of $61 in 2003 and $55 in 2002	2,091	2,097
Inventories	1,252	1,294
Prepaid expenses and other assets	1,571	1,616
TOTAL CURRENT ASSETS	8,396	7,352
INVESTMENTS AND OTHER ASSETS		
Equity method investments:		
Coca-Cola Enterprises, Inc.	1,260	972
Coca-Cola Hellenic Bottling Company S.A.	941	872
Coca-Cola FEMSA, S.A. de C.V.	674	347
Coca-Cola Amatil Limited	652	492
Other, principally bottling companies	1,697	2,054
Cost method investments, principally bottling companies	314	254
Other assets	3,322	2,694
	8,860	7,685
PROPERTY, PLANT AND EQUIPMENT		
Land	419	385
Buildings and improvements	2,615	2,332
Machinery and equipment	6,159	5,888
Containers	429	396
	9,622	9,001
Less allowances for depreciation	3,525	3,090
	6,097	5,911
TRADEMARKS AND INDEFINITE LIVES	1,979	1,724
GOODWILL	1,029	876
OTHER INTANGIBLE ASSETS	981	858
TOTAL ASSETS	$27,342	$ 24,406

EXHIBIT 1 (*continued*)
The Coca-Cola Company and Subsidiaries
Consolidated Balance Sheets (in millions)

December 31	2003	2002
LIABILITIES AND SHAREOWNERS' EQUITY		
CURRENT		
Accounts payable and accrued expenses	$ 4,058	$ 3,692
Loans and notes payable	2,583	2,475
Current maturities of long-term debt	323	180
Accrued income taxes	922	994
TOTAL CURRENT LIABILITIES	7,886	7,341
LONG-TERM DEBT	2,517	2,701
OTHER LIABILITIES	2,512	2,260
DEFERRED INCOME TAXES	337	304
SHAREOWNERS' EQUITY		
Common stock, $0.25 par value		
Authorized: 5,600,000,000 shares; issued: 3,494,799,258		
shares in 2003 and 3,490,818,627 shares in 2002	874	873
Capital surplus	4,395	3,857
Reinvested earnings	26,687	24,506
Accumulated other comprehensive income (loss)	(1,995)	(3,047)
	29,961	26,189
Less treasury stock, at cost (1,053,267,474 shares in 2003;		
1,019,839,490 shares in 2002)	(15,871)	(14,389)
	14,090	11,800
TOTAL LIABILITIES AND SHAREOWNERS' EQUITY	$27,342	$ 24,406

EXHIBIT 2
The Coca-Cola Company and Subsidiaries Consolidated Statements of Income (in millions, except share data)

Year Ended December 31	2003	2002	2001
NET OPERATING REVENUES	**$21,044**	$19,564	$17,545
Cost of goods sold	**7,762**	7,105	6,044
GROSS PROFIT	**13,282**	12,459	11,501
Selling, general and administrative expenses	**7,488**	7,001	6,149
Other operating changes	**573**	—	—
OPERATING INCOME	**5,221**	5,458	5,352
Interest income	**176**	209	325
Interest expense	**178**	199	289
Equity income—net	**406**	384	152
Other income (loss)—net	**(138)**	(353)	39
Gains on issuances of stock by equity investees	**8**	—	91
INCOME BEFORE INCOME TAXES AND CUMULATIVE EFFECT OF ACCOUNTING CHANGE	**5,495**	5,499	5,670
Income taxes	**1,148**	1,523	1,691
NET INCOME BEFORE CUMULATIVE EFFECT OF ACCOUNTING CHANGE	**4,347**	3,976	3,979
Cumulative effect of accounting change for SFAS No. 142, net of income taxes			
Company operations	—	(367)	—
Equity investees	—	(559)	—
Cumulative effect of accounting change for SFAS No. 133, net of income taxes	—	—	(10)
NET INCOME	**$ 4,347**	$ 3,050	$ 3,969
BASIC NET INCOME PER SHARE:			
Before accounting change	**$1.77**	$ 1.60	$1.60
Cumulative effect of accounting change	—	(0.37)	—
	$1.77	$ 1.23	$1.60
DILUTED NET INCOME PER SHARE:			
Before accounting change	**$1.77**	$ 1.60	$1.60
Cumulative effect of accounting change	—	(0.37)	—
	$1.77	$ 1.23	$1.60
AVERAGE SHARES OUTSTANDING	**2,459**	2,478	2,487
Effect of dilutive securities	**3**	5	—
AVERAGE SHARES OUTSTANDING ASSUMING DILUTION	**2,462**	2,483	2,487

EXHIBIT 3
The Coca-Cola Company and Subsidiaries
Consolidated Statements of Cash Flows (in millions)

Year Ended December 31	2003	2002	2001
OPERATING ACTIVITIES			
Net income	$4,347	$ 3,050	$ 3,969
Depreciation and amortization	850	806	803
Stock-based compensation expense	422	365	41
Deferred income taxes	(188)	40	56
Equity income or loss, net of dividends	(294)	(256)	(54)
Foreign currency adjustments	(79)	(76)	(60)
Gain on issuances of stock by equity investee	(8)	—	(91)
(Gains) losses on sales of assets,			
including bottling interests	(5)	3	(85)
Cumulative effect of accounting changes	—	926	10
Other operating charges	330	—	—
Other items	249	291	(17)
Net change in operating assets and liabilities	(168)	(407)	(462)
Net cash provided by operating activities	5,456	4,742	4,110
INVESTING ACTIVITIES			
Acquisitions and investments, principally			
trademarks and bottling companies	(359)	(544)	(651)
Purchases of investments and other assets	(177)	(141)	(456)
Proceeds from disposals of investments			
and other assets	147	243	455
Purchases of property, plant and equipment	(812)	(851)	(769)
Proceeds from disposals of property,			
plant and equipment	87	69	91
Other investing activities	178	159	142
Net cash used in investing activities	(936)	(1,065)	(1,188)
FINANCING ACTIVITIES			
Issuances of debt	1,026	1,622	3,011
Payments of debt	(1,119)	(2,378)	(3,937)
Issuances of stock	98	107	164
Purchases of stock for treasury	(1,440)	(691)	(277)
Dividends	(2,166)	(1,987)	(1,791)
Net cash used in financing activities	(3,601)	(3,327)	(2,830)
EFFECT OF EXCHANGE RATE CHANGES			
ON CASH AND CASH EQUIVALENTS	183	44	(45)
CASH AND CASH EQUIVALENTS			
Net increase during the year	1,102	394	47
Balance at beginning of year	2,260	1,866	1,819
Balance at end of year	$3,362	$ 2,260	$ 1,866

Maria Hernandez & Associates

In June 2004, Maria Hernandez found herself out of a job for the second time in six months. As she left the building that had housed her failed dot-com employer, carrying a small box of personal belongings, her mind was already embracing a plan that would have her start her own business. At least, in her own business she would control part of her own destiny instead of being subject to the decisions of others.

Hernandez was a graduate of the Massachusetts College of Art. After working three years for an advertising agency where she specialized in advertising layout, she used part of her savings to take a technical course in webpage design. Her first job after completing her training was with a startup retail dot-com that ran through its initial cash and loans in less that one year. It took her only one week to find her latest employer, but in less than six months it had folded, too. She loved her work as a webpage designer, and she had confidence in her own abilities and skill. Her art training allowed her to blend design, color, and webpage layout in attractive and effective ways. But having been burned twice by startup dot-com employers, she was also reluctant to go to work for a third.

Within days she had put together a simple business plan to create a webpage design consultancy to offer webpage designs to anyone. She would head the company and employ other designers as well to meet demand. There were plenty of potential customers in Boston, and she knew that several of her former colleagues from art school could be interested in the better pay that webpage design could support.

On June 20, 2004, she transferred all of her savings, $30,000, to a new bank account with the company name, and two days later she added $20,000 borrowed from her father to the account. After that things moved quickly as she rented a second floor office for $3,000 a month, paying one month's rent in advance as a security deposit to apply to the end of the lease, and $3,000 for July 2004. She purchased some used computer equipment with software from her last employer, and ordered stationary and office supplies that cost $5,000 when they were delivered on June 29.

Professor William J. Bruns, Jr. prepared this case. HBS cases are developed solely as the basis for class discussion. Cases are not intended to serve as endorsements, sources of primary data, or illustrations of effective or ineffective management.

Maria Hernandez & Associates opened for business on July 2, 2004. Although Maria was not an accountant, she took stock of her company's financial position as she began to seek her first contracts. The company had spent all but $12,000 of the cash that had been put into the bank account, but it had some assets as well.

Assets		Liabilities and Owner's Equity	
Cash in bank	$12,000	Loan	$20,000
Office supplies	5,000	Maria's equity	30,000
Equipment and software	27,000		
Prepaid rent	6,000		

Maria was a little worried that the cash had gone so quickly, but she also had confidence in herself and her willingness to work hard.

In the first few days, Maria lined up two webpage design projects from local businesses. She spent part of each day working on the projects, and the remainder of her time was spent looking for new clients. By early August she had four other designers at work and a steady stream of new work coming in by way of referrals. She also felt far too busy to attend to any financial aspects of the business. When clients paid, the money went into the bank account. The associates were paid weekly, and she paid rent and other bills when they were received. In the ninth week of operations, Maria's father telephoned her to ask how things were going, and she could not answer the question with any confidence. It was time for an accounting, and the end of August would be a good time to do it.

Hernandez found the following information she had accumulated during the two months of operations:

1. Clients had paid $40,000 for completed work, and two clients still owed a total of $7,000 for work that had been completed and delivered to them. There were no projects underway as the office closed on August 31 for the Labor Day weekend.

2. Additional office supplies had been purchased for cash of $900, and office supplies and stationery that had cost $4,200 were still on hand.

3. Rent of $6,000 for August and September was paid in cash. Utility bills, a repair of equipment, and the salaries paid to designers (including Maria Hernandez) were paid in cash totaling $33,000.

4. Additional equipment and software was purchased on August 27 for $11, 000, with half of that amount being paid in cash and the remainder due one month later.

As Maria Hernandez thought about the first two month's operations, she was perplexed by the fact that cash in the bank had decreased by $5,400 even though she was sure the business was operating profitably.

She also wondered how to account for the following:

1. She had agreed to pay her father interest on his loan of 6% per year, but no interest had been paid so far.

2. The equipment and software were working out well, but Hernandez knew that they had a technological life of no more than three years from the time that she had purchased them.

In brief, Maria Hernandez felt that the first two months had been successful, but she was puzzled about how to draft meaningful reports to mail to her father.

QUESTIONS

1. How would you have reported on operations of Maria Hernandez & Associates through August 31, 2004? Had the company made a profit as Maria Hernandez believed? If so, how would you explain why the cash in the bank has declined?

2. How would you report the status of the business on August 31, 2004?

Introduction to Accounting Records

Almost all accounting systems have two major components. One of these, called the journal, is a sequential listing of events that have had a measurable effect on an organization's economic condition. The journal is, in effect, a diary of the economic events that have taken place on a day-to-day basis. The second component, called accounts, consists of summaries by categories of all events that have occurred during a period or since the formation of the entity. A complete set of accounts is called a ledger. A set of accounts for assets, liabilities, and owners' equity is called a general ledger. The purpose of this note is to illustrate briefly the nature of a journal and a ledger and to describe some of the conventions used in maintaining them.

The development of electronic media, such as computers, has drastically changed the way records are kept in most organizations. The introduction of new technologies, however, has not displaced the terminology and basic record-keeping functions of the double-entry bookkeeping system originally developed before the end of the 15th century.

THE JOURNAL

The journal is a sequential record of events and their effects on the entity. The double-entry bookkeeping system is a means of ensuring that the accounting equation of assets = equities remains in balance. Entries are made in the journal using this system. It is labeled double entry because there will always be at least two parts to the entry. For example, if an asset increases, something else must occur to keep the equation in balance (such as an equity increase or another asset decrease).

January 2	Cash	100	
	Capital Stock		100

Professor William J. Bruns, Jr. prepared this note for class discussion. HBS cases are developed solely as the basis for class discussion. Cases are not intended to serve as endorsements, sources of primary data, or illustrations of effective or ineffective management.

The significance of the location of the parts of the entry will become clear shortly. At this point, simply note that one line has a different margin than the other. This left-versus-right format is a conventional way of describing whether these accounts have increased or decreased. Convention dictates that all lines with left margins are presented first with all indented lines following in each individual journal entry. **Exhibit 1** summarizes the nine classes of changes that can affect assets, liabilities, and owners' equity. Note that the above example is in the third category mentioned in **Exhibit 1** (Increase in assets, Increase in owners' equity). Cash, an asset, increases by $100 because an owners' equity account increases due to an owner's purchase of capital stock for $100.

Inspection of **Exhibit 1** reveals some important characteristics of almost all journals. Each event is dated. Where a date is not shown, it is presumed to be the same as that of the preceding entry. A description is included giving details about classifications that are increased or decreased. Finally, the amount of increase or decrease is listed in two columns labeled debit (dr.) or credit (cr.). The words debit and credit in accounting have no meaning other than left and right, and no attempt should be made to relate the meaning of these two words in other contexts to the way in which they are used in accounting records. An inspection of **Exhibit 1** will reveal that increases in assets and decreases in liabilities and owners' equity are always entered in the left-hand or debit column, and decreases in assets and increases in liabilities and owners' equity are always listed in the right-hand or credit column.

A journal may contain other information as well, as illustrated in the explanations in parentheses under several journal entries in **Exhibit 3**. This descriptive detail allows a reader to understand more quickly the journal entry.

ACCOUNTS

The entries for events or transactions listed in the journal are then transferred to accounts in a ledger and accumulated. An account is maintained for each classification of assets, liabilities, or owners' equity that has been established by a journal entry. No entry is made in an account until a record has been made in the journal, and every entry in the journal results in a change in the status of two or more accounts.

Many different forms of accounts are used. Typically, the form of account provides space for keeping a record of the date of a change and whether it represents an increase or decrease. In addition, space may be provided for maintaining a running balance and/or for entering a description of the type of event or transaction that resulted in the change. Entries in the accounts are almost always cross-referenced to the journal; that is, a page number or journal entry number is included so that the accountant can move from the account back to the record of original journal entry without difficulty.

In the study of accounting and in discussions of accounting problems by managers, a skeleton form of account—called a "T" account—is frequently used. The left-hand side is called the debit side, and the right-hand side is called the credit side. **Exhibit 2** illustrates T accounts and summarizes the general rules for entry of amounts of change in the accounts. These correspond exactly to the placement of amounts listed in the journal.

It is unusual to find accounts that are headed solely by the classification assets or liabilities and owners' equities. Subclassifications are used, that is, separate asset accounts for cash, amounts receivable from customers, amounts owed to creditors, amounts contributed by owners, and so forth. The number of accounts corresponds to the number of classifications that have been established by the accountant.

An important characteristic of conventional accounting records can now be pointed out. Because the amount of increase and decrease entered in each half of a journal entry is identical, the total amount of debits will always be equal to the total amounts of credits. When these amounts are transferred to accounts, the amount of debits and the amount of credits remain the same. Therefore, if a listing of all accounts in a general ledger is made showing their debit or credit balances, and these are summed, the amounts should be equal. A listing such as this is called a trial balance, and it provides a check on the clerical accuracy of the record. As indicated earlier, a group of accounts is called a ledger. The clerical accuracy of entries made in the general ledger is often "proven" by checking to see that the equality of debits and credits has been maintained.

SPECIALIZED RECORDS

The forms that are illustrated in **Exhibits 1** and **2** are general in character; many accounting systems use forms that are quite different. When a large number of entries of the same type is to be made in the journal, often a special journal will be established to simplify the clerical task involved in making that group of entries. In some cases, a variety of journals may be used to take advantage of special characteristics of the accounting task in a particular firm or situation.

For the same reasons that special journals are sometimes used, special ledgers are sometimes established. In particular, rather than maintain a separate account in the general ledger for each customer or creditor, subsidiary ledgers are established that relate in total to an account maintained in the general ledger of the accounting system. When a subsidiary ledger is used, the total of all debits and credits in the subsidiary ledger will be equal to the total amounts listed in the control account in the general ledger.

It is not within the scope of this note to illustrate all possible forms of journals or ledgers and the ways in which they are used. The design of an effective accounting record system depends upon the comprehension and ingenuity of the accountant and the needs of the business and its managers, who must develop and adopt an effective system from the generic forms illustrated herein.

AN ILLUSTRATION

To demonstrate the way in which the general journal form and T accounts can be used to record information about an entity, consider the following example:

> On September 1, 2004, Robert Greene opened a store, the Greene Paint Company. On preceding days he had taken $3,500 of his own cash and had placed it in a separate bank account, which he intended to use only for the store. In addition, he borrowed $2,000 from the local bank. He used some cash to acquire equipment, but he

was able to purchase on credit the rest of his equipment and some merchandise inventory. By the time he opened his doors for business on September 1, the business, the Greene Paint Company, could be represented by the following Statement of Financial Position:

TABLE A
Greene Paint Company—Statement of Financial Position, September 1, 2004

Assets		Liabilities and Owners' Equity	
Cash	$3,300	Amount owed to supplier	$1,500
Merchandise inventories	700	Loans owed	2,000
Equipment	3,000	Owners' equity	3,500
	$7,000		$7,000

During the month of September, business was much slower than Mr. Greene had hoped it would be. Nevertheless, four kinds of events took place. They were:

1. Additional merchandise was purchased at a cost of $1000, and Mr. Greene promised to pay the suppliers as soon as he could.

2. $900 cash was paid on accounts already owed to suppliers.

3. The merchandise that he had purchased at the beginning of the month for $1000 was sold for $1500, with the customer promising to pay within 30 days.

4. Mr. Greene estimated that his equipment had depreciated $100 during the month.

Exhibit 3 shows the journal of the Greene Paint Company for August and September, and **Exhibit 4** shows the accounts. Note that the accountant established some temporary accounts in September to keep track of details affecting Greene's equity, then closed those accounts to a new account called retained earnings. **Exhibit 5** shows the Statement of Financial Position for the Greene Paint Company at the end of September.

THE BOOKKEEPING CYCLE

As economic events are observed and measured by the accountant, their effects are measured and recorded sequentially in a journal. The journal tells the accountant which accounts have been affected and which need to be updated. Temporary accounts are usually established to keep track of details of events that affect owners' equity. At the end of each accounting period, the length of which is determined by the needs or interests of managers or owners, the accountant may adjust the balances in some accounts before summarizing the effects of entries in temporary accounts on retained earnings. Permanent accounts comprise the Statement of Financial Position. Information in the temporary accounts is used to prepare the Statement of Income. This exercise, repeated each accounting period, is known as the bookkeeping cycle.

EXHIBIT 1
A Journal Showing Nine Classes of Events

Date	Description	Dr.	Cr.
		(The left-hand column, or debit column, records amounts of increases of assets and decreases in equities.)	(The right-hand column, the credit column, records amounts of decreases of assets and decreases in equities.)
(Each event or transaction is dated.)	(Details about classifications increased or decreased are included in the description.)		

2004			
January 1	Increase in assets		
	Decrease in assets	XX	XX
January 2	Increase in assets		
	Increase in liabilities	XX	XX
	Increase in assets		
	Increase in owners' equity	XX	XX
January 3	Decrease in liabilities		
	Decrease in assets	XX	XX
	Decrease in owners' equity		
	Decrease in assets	XX	XX
January 4	Decrease in liabilities		
	Increase in liabilities	XX	XX
	Decrease in liabilities		
	Increase in owners' equity	XX	XX
	Decrease in owners' equity		
	Increase in liabilities	XX	XX
	Decrease in owners' equity		
	Decrease in owners' equity	XX	XX

EXHIBIT 2
T Accounts

Assets		Liabilities and Owners' Equity	
Increases in asset accounts are entered on the left-hand side	Decreases in asset accounts are entered on the right-hand side	Decreases in liability and owners' equity accounts are entered on the left-hand side	Increases in liability and owners' equity accounts are entered on the right-hand side

EXHIBIT 3
Journal of Greene Paint Company

Date		Description	Dr.	Cr.
2004				
August		Entries to record creation of equity		
	(A1)	Cash	$3,500	
		Owners' equity B. Greene (investment of cash)		$3,500
	(A2)	Cash	2,000	
		Loans owed		2,000
	(A3)	Merchandise inventory	700	
		Amount owed to suppliers (purchase of inventory)		700
	(A4)	Equipment	3,000	
		Amount owed to suppliers		800
		Cash (purchase of equipment)		2,200
September				
	(S1)	Merchandise inventory	1,000	
		Amounts owed to suppliers (purchase of more paint)		1,000
	(S2)	Amount owed to suppliers	900	
		Cash (payment to suppliers)		900
	(S3)	Amounts owed by customers	1,500	
		Sales (sales of merchandise)		1,500
	(S4)	Cost of goods sold	1,000	
		Merchandise inventory (cost of merchandise sold)		1,000
		An adjusting entry:		
	(S5)	Depreciation	100	
		Equipment		100
		A closing entry:		
	(S6)	Sales	1,500	
		Cost of goods sold		1,000
		Depreciation		100
		Retained earnings (to close three temporary accounts)		400

EXHIBIT 4
General Ledger of Greene Paint Company

Assets		Liabilities and Owners' Equity	

Cash

(A1)	$3500	(A4)	$2200
(A2)	2000		
Bal., Sept. 1	$3300	(S2)	$ 900
Bal., Sept. 30	$2400		

Amounts Owed to Suppliers

		(A3)	$ 700
		(A4)	$ 800
(S2)	$900	Bal., Sept. 1	$1500
		(S1)	1000
		Bal., Sept. 30	$1600

Amounts Owed by Customers

Bal., Sept. 1	$ 00	
(S3)	1500	
Bal., Sept. 30	$1500	

Loans Owed

		(A2)	$2000
		Bal., Sept. 1	$2000
		Bal., Sept. 30	$2000

Merchandise Inventory

(A3)	$ 700		
Bal., Sept. 1	$ 700	(S4)	$1000
(S1)	1000		
Bal., Sept. 30	$ 700		

Owners' Equity, B. Greene

		(A1)	$3500
		Bal., Sept. 1	$3500
		Bal., Sept. 30	$3500

Equipment

(A4)	$3000		
Bal., Sept. 1	$3000	(S5)	$100
Bal., Sept. 30	$2900		

Retained Earnings

		(S6)	$400

Temporary Accounts

Sales

(S6)	$1500	(S3)	$1500

Cost of Goods Sold

(S4)	$1000	(S6)	$1000

Depreciation

(S5)	$100	(S6)	$100

EXHIBIT 5
Greene Paint Company—Statement of Financial Position, September 30, 2004

Assets		Liabilities and Owners' Equity	
Cash	$2,400	Amounts owed to suppliers	$1,600
Amounts owed by customers	1,500	Loans owed	2,000
Merchandise inventory	700	Owners' equity	3,500
Equipment	2,900	Retained earnings	400
	$7,500		$7,500

Chemalite, Inc.

I n late 2002, Bennett Alexander, a consulting chemical engineer, applied for and received a patent for one of his inventions, a Chemalite. A small, fragile glass vial of one chemical was inserted into a plastic, translucent cylinder that was then filled with a second chemical and sealed. Bending the cylinder caused the glass vial inside to break, allowing the two chemicals to mix. When combined, the two chemicals gave off a bright yellow-green glow.

Alexander anticipated a substantial market for the Chemalite. It had the appeal of being readily available in case of emergencies, but yet it did not require any form of ignition. He anticipated a considerable demand from the armed forces and manufacturers of flares and similar safety equipment.

On January 2, 2003, Alexander, together with a number of relatives and friends, established Chemalite, Inc.; 500,000 shares were issued, of which Alexander received 125,000 in exchange for his patent, and the remainder were sold to the other investors at $1 per share. During the period January 2, 2003, through June 30, 2003, Chemalite, Inc., made the following expenditures:

- January 15—Paid $7,500 in legal fees, charter costs, and printing expenses associated with the incorporation of the company.

- June 15—Spent $62,500 building the machinery that would be used to produce the first commercial models of the Chemalite.

- June 24—Purchased $75,000 worth of plastics and chemicals for use in the production of commercial Chemalites.

Toward the end of June, Alexander, who had assumed a very active role in the management of Chemalite, Inc., met with the rest of the stockholders to present a state of the corporation report and to discuss strategies for the future marketing of the Chemalites. He was hopeful that the company would be producing Chemalites by the end of August. Susan Peterson, a friend of Alexander who had invested a substantial sum in the company, indicated at the meeting that she had received inquiries from an auto parts distributor about the availability of Chemalites and their

Visiting Professor David A. Wilson prepared this case and it was revised by Professor Charles Christensen. HBS cases are developed solely as the basis for class discussion. Cases are not intended to serve as endorsements, sources of primary data, or illustrations of effective or ineffective management.

expected price. The distributor wished to purchase a substantial number of the lights as part of a highway safety promotion and was interested in pursuing the possibility of private branding.

At this point in the meeting, Mr. Larson, one of the stockholders, but a man with very little business experience and even less understanding of financial statements, interjected: "All this discussion of what we are going to do is well and good, but all I can see is that six months ago we had $375,000 and now we have $230,000. By my reckoning, we've managed to lose $145,000 in six months and haven't much to show for it."

Some of the stockholders agreed with Larson. Indeed, between January 2 and June 30, the company's bank balance had fallen from $375,000 to $230,000. Ms. D'Cruz, a stockholder, suggested that since Chemalite's operations were not in full swing, these preoperating outlays should probably be considered more as investments in the business by the business rather than as losses. After considerable discussion by all the stockholders, it was agreed that they would meet again in early January 2004 to study the state of the corporation. It was generally felt that the company should be in full operation by then and that the problems created by the preoperating period spoken of would be overcome by year-end.

During the last half of 2003, Chemalite, Inc., did indeed go into full operation. To prepare for the shareholder's meeting in early January 2004, Bill Murray, the firm's recently hired bookkeeper, produced the following data:

1. In early July 2003, a consulting engineer delivered the prototypes of the Chemalite that he had been developing, and he was paid a total of $23,750.

2. During the six months from July to December 2003, Chemalite sold $754,500 of its product. The largest single purchaser, the auto parts distributor with whom Peterson had negotiated, still owed Chemalite, Inc., $69,500. All other customers' accounts were paid in full by year-end.

3. Additional chemicals and plastics were purchased for a total of $175,000. All of these purchases were paid for in cash.

4. Chemalite, Inc., spent $22,500 on television and trade journal advertising to introduce the product.

5. During the six months ended December 31, 2003, the company expended $350,000 on direct manufacturing labor, and on manufacturing-related overhead (rent, utilities, supervisory labor). An additional $80,000 was spent on corporate salaries and other corporate expenses.

6. In early July, a further $150,000 was spent on machinery to be used in the production of Chemalites.

7. During the period, the company had borrowed $50,000 for a short time and repaid the loan by year-end. The interest paid on the loan amounted to $750.

In preparing his state of the corporation report, Alexander noted with some anxiety that the company's bank balance had fallen a further $117,000 from the $230,000 reported in June to only $113,000. It bothered him because he believed that the company was really doing quite well, and he failed to understand why the bank account did not appear to reflect this condition. In surveying the cash outflows incurred by Chemalite, Inc., over the entire year, he noted the following:

1. There was still a stock at December 31 of $55,000 worth of plastics and chemicals in the warehouse; however, there were no finished or partially finished Chemalites at year-end.

2. Although the patent that the company had acquired from Alexander had a legal life of 20 years, he expected competitors to develop equivalent products that did not use the patented technique in about five years.

3. The machinery used in the production of the Chemalites was general purpose machinery, not restricted to Chemalite production, that might reasonably be expected to last for 10 years, six months of which had already passed.

4. Alexander was quite confused by the worth of the prototypes. They had directly resulted in the development of the product the company was presently selling, so perhaps their value had actually increased over the last six months of 2003.

5. The committee organizing The Olympic Games, Athens 2004, had placed a firm order with the company for 60,000 Chemalites at a price of $1.50 each. It was their intention to give a Chemalite to each person at the opening ceremony of the 2004 Olympic Games and to have athletes and fans light their Chemalites, symbolic of the Olympic flame.

Alexander was an inventor, not a businessperson, and he was perplexed about how to report the events of the year to the stockholders. He had a feeling that things were going well, but he did not know how to convey this message to his fellow stockholders.

QUESTIONS

1. Prepare a summary of the cash transactions for the six months ended June 30, 2003.

2. Prepare an income statement for the six months ended June 30, 2003. Did the company incur a loss as Mr. Larson suggested?

3. Prepare a statement of financial position at June 30, 2003, and a statement of cash flows for the six-month period.

4. Prepare a set of financial statements for the stockholders for the year 2003: a statement of financial position at December 31, 2003; an income statement; and a statement of cash flows for the year ended December 31, 2003.

5. How would you have reported to stockholders on the financial performance of Chemalite, Inc., for its first year, January 1, 2003 to December 31, 2003?

Hanson Ski Products

In early July 1986, Alden (Denny) Hanson, president and chief executive officer of Hanson Ski Products, was preparing for a meeting with his executive committee on the company's current and longer-term financing needs. For one thing, Mr. Hanson wanted to review the plans for fiscal year (FY) 1987.[1] Although the company's bankers had provided a $4.2 million line of credit to meet the year's seasonal cash needs, Denny wanted to recheck his figures to be sure that this credit would be sufficient, particularly since Hanson Ski Products was scheduled to repay stockholder loans of $841,000 in November.

COMPANY BACKGROUND

Hanson Ski Products was a leading manufacturer of high-quality ski boots located in Boulder, Colorado. Although it was a relatively new entrant to the market, its revenues ranked among the top 10 ski boot manufacturers worldwide by 1984. Hanson commanded a 20% share of the U.S. market for high-quality ski boots, which was growing at an estimated 10% per year. While the focus of operations was U.S. skiers, the international portion of the company's business was growing faster than the domestic portion. The company expected that in FY 1987, its international revenues would represent about 30% of total sales.

One of the keys to Hanson's successful penetration of this tough market was the unique design of its ski boots. The revolutionary patented rear-entry concept, designed by Chris Hanson, balanced the objectives of comfort and skiing performance sought by the experienced skier. In May 1977, *Fortune* named the specially engineered boot in a worldwide competition "one of the 25 best-designed products available in America." By 1986, Hanson was marketing four models of adult boots, and newer models were continually being added as older models were dropped.

[1] Fiscal year 1987 at Hanson Ski Products began on April 1, 1986, and ended on March 31, 1987.

PAST OPERATING PERFORMANCE

Hanson Ski Products was founded in 1973. The first year of operations, FY 1974, was devoted to development of boot design and preparation for production. In FY 1975, Hanson shipped 2,300 pairs of boots to retailers. By FY 1986, this figure had grown to 85,000 pairs, and revenues had reached $9.8 million (see **Exhibits 1** and **2**).

Hanson management expected net revenues to continue to grow at an impressive rate during FY 1987. Sales projections made early in the planning process had later been revised upward so that it was now expected that net sales would reach $12 million for the year. By FY 1991, Hanson predicted revenues from ski boots would approximate $26 million; beyond that point it was expected that unit volume of sales would only increase proportionately to the overall growth in the market.

THE ORDER CYCLE

Hanson's boot business was extremely seasonal and could be broken down into the ordering, shipment, and collection phases. The ordering phase was composed of two parts: the stocking order period and the reorder period. During the stocking order period from March through June, sales representatives conducted an intensive marketing campaign, commencing with the equipment dealers' annual Ski Show held in Las Vegas in March. The timing of this show was important in that it was held just after the end of the previous ski season when both manufacturers and equipment dealers were aware of past equipment sales performance and retail inventory levels. Hanson usually received 25% to 30% of its total orders at this ski show and another 55% to 60% of the orders between April and June, when its sales representatives contacted all dealers who had not attended the show. Discounts ranging from 4% to 12% were offered to customers, and accounts were typically payable on the tenth day of the second or third month following shipment, depending upon the date of their requested shipment. These terms were similar to and slightly tighter than the terms offered by Hanson's competitors.

The reorder period accounted for the remaining 10% to 20% of Hanson's sales and started in July, when dealers reordered to replenish their supplies. A 2% discount was available to these customers for payment by the tenth of the month following shipment.

Sparse snow years affected the order phase in two fiscal years. The first effect was felt almost immediately in the year there was no snow and manifested itself as a reduction in the reorders received. The second and more pronounced effect was felt during the stocking order period in the following spring. At that time, dealers' inventories were higher than their normal levels, and dealers were wary of placing large initial stocking orders for fear of experiencing two consecutive poor snow years and the consequent falloff in demand.

Shipments began in July, peaked in August, and remained at a high level until December, when they trailed off. The largest part of Hanson's collections of accounts receivable began in December following the shipment phase. In a normal business year, the collection period was about 75 days. However, a poor snow year had the effect of significantly stretching the collection period.

THE PRODUCTION AND FINANCING CYCLE

Manufacturing of the following season's products commenced in January, and production schedules were subsequently modified and adjusted as the shape and size of the order pattern became clearer. A level production policy was adopted for three reasons. Hanson did not want to lay off skilled workers (50% of their 123-person production force) who were key to the manufacture of the ski boots. In addition, the company did not have sufficient physical capacity to turn out an entire year's production after March, when the first orders were received. Finally, management had sufficient confidence in its sales forecasts to manufacture up to 60% of such forecasts in advance of firm orders.

Hanson's seasonal marketing efforts and level manufacturing operations created a substantial financial management challenge. Although by June the company had produced approximately 60% of the year's expected volume of finished boots, it was not until November that most of the year's finished goods inventory was converted to accounts receivable; it was December before the bulk of receivables collections began flowing in.

David Snyder, Hanson's treasurer, typically developed a preliminary cash budget in January, before the start of the fiscal year. On the basis of that projection, he made appropriate arrangements for funding the coming season's cash needs. Based on the results of sales efforts and orders received during the spring, the budget was reviewed in June, and revisions were made as necessary. The proposed final budgets for fiscal year 1987 are shown in **Exhibits 3** and **4**, which also include Snyder's estimates of the balance in each current asset and current liability category at the end of each quarter.

Hanson's management also practiced very tight internal cash management. In fact, Mr. Snyder believed that the optimum target for the firm's cash balances was zero, since Hanson was highly leveraged financially and would have had to pay interest to support any cash balances maintained at the bank. In practice, the cash balances averaged about $100,000.

Despite these efforts to conserve or stretch cash within the firm, Hanson had still found it necessary to arrange substantial short-term loans from banks, finance companies, and from principal stockholders. Although current seasonal financing was being handled exclusively with a group of commercial banks, Hanson had made use of some commercial financing in the past. Commercial financing companies made more frequent audits of the borrower's operations and finances than was typical for the banks and usually levied a higher interest charge. Because of frequent monitoring and higher interest rates, the commercial finance companies felt comfortable in extending a larger amount of funds against inventory and accounts receivable collateral than would normally be true for a commercial bank.

It was the company's goal, however, to move toward exclusive reliance on commercial bank funding, primarily because of the potentially lower cost of such borrowings to Hanson and secondarily because of the higher-quality corporate image it portrayed. In February 1986, Hanson had obtained approval of a $4.2 million revolving line of credit for fiscal 1987 at 3.75% over prime[2] with a group of three banks led by the United Bank of Denver, which was in a good geographical position to maintain day-to-day contact with Hanson. Hanson could draw against this line of credit to the extent of 70% of the cost of inventories and 80% of current accounts receivable.

The banks' reduction of the interest rate charge in FY 1987 was seen by Denny Hanson as an indication of the company's improved credit standing in the eyes of these lenders. That conviction was further strengthened when the banks informed Hanson that the personal guarantees of the major stockholders would not be required as a condition of the 1987 credit line.

As of June 15, 1986, Hanson Ski Products had no plans to issue more stock, and, because of growth, no liquidations of plant or equipment were contemplated. The company had never paid a cash dividend, and it did not plan to initiate dividend payments in fiscal year 1987.

The final element of financial plans for fiscal year 1987 about which Denny Hanson was concerned was the set of loans from shareholders. A total of $841,000 in loans would become due in November 1986. An estrangement had developed between a key shareholder of the group and Mr. Hanson, and only if the loans were paid could Mr. Hanson be sure of maintaining personal control of operations. He hoped the bank line of credit was sufficient to enable the company to pay the loans in full and on time.

QUESTIONS

1. Using the information in the balance sheet for March 31, 1986 (**Exhibit 2**), and the fiscal year 1987 budgets (**Exhibits 3** and **4**), prepare a projected balance sheet for Hanson Ski Products for March 31, 1987. (To do this, you will need to estimate the size of the commercial bank loan—"Notes–bank"—on that date.) Does your balance sheet tell you whether or not the plans on which the budgets are based are feasible?

2. Project the size of the commercial bank loan at the end of each quarter of FY 1987. Can Hanson stay within the commercial banks' line of credit of $4.2 million? Will the company have sufficient collateral?

3. Prepare quarterly balance sheets for Hanson Ski Products for June 30, 1986; September 30, 1986; and December 31, 1986. What do the four balance sheets you have prepared tell you about the financial structure and strength of Hanson Ski Products?

4. Denny Hanson was particularly concerned that the stockholder loans be paid off in November 1986 when they were due, and he asked Dave Snyder, treasurer, to prepare a cash budget by months for the third quarter of FY 1987 (**Exhibit 5**). Do you see any problems in paying off the loans on time? What could Hanson do to be sure the loans can be paid?

---

[2] In July 1986 the prime rate was 8%. The credit line for fiscal 1986 had also been $4.2 million but had carried an interest rate of 4% over prime.

EXHIBIT 1
Hanson Ski Products, Income Statements ($000)

	FY 1984	FY 1985	FY 1986
Net sales	$5,753	$7,671	$9,776
Cost of goods sold[a]	3,040	4,140	5,177
Gross margin	$2,713	$3,531	$4,599
Selling, general, and administration	1,585	2,109	2,519
Product development	152	189	260
Operating earnings	$ 976	$1,233	$1,820
Interest expense	436	428	507
Income before tax and extraordinary item	$ 540	$ 805	$1,313
Tax provision	314	468	400
Earnings before extraordinary item	$ 226	$ 337	$ 913
Extraordinary item tax benefit from utilization of operating loss carryforwards	314	468	251
Net earnings	$ 540	$ 805	$1,164
Earnings per common share:			
Earnings before extraordinary item	0.39	0.57	1.50
Extraordinary item	0.53	0.79	0.41
Net earnings	0.92	1.36	1.91
Weighted average number of common shares outstanding	585,889	590,566	607,761

[a] Depreciation and amortization for 1984, 1985, and 1986 was $341, $396, and $561, respectively.

Part 1 *An Overview of Accounting and Financial Reporting*

EXHIBIT 2
Hanson Ski Products, Consolidated Balance Sheets ($000)

	3/31/84	3/31/85	3/31/86
Current Assets			
Cash	$ 163	$ 81	$ 156
Receivables, net	692	1,378	1,556
Inventories	1,352	2,104	1,729
Prepaid expenses	99	124	262
Total current assets	$ 2,306	$3,687	$3,703
Fixed Assets			
Plant, property, and equipment	1,430	1,958	3,393
Less accumulated depreciation and amortization	569	836	1,255
Total net fixed assets	$ 861	$1,122	$2,138
Other assets	171	191	207
Total Assets	$ 3,338	$5,000	$6,048
Liabilities			
Accounts payable	$ 536	$ 967	$1,586
Notes payable—banks	1,100	2,082	1,547[a]
Income taxes payable	—	—	149
Current installments—long-term debt	109	35	1,010[b]
Total current liabilities	$ 1,745	$3,084	$4,292
Long-term debt			
Term loan	1,423	1,407	—
Notes payable to banks	506	—	
Total	$ 1,929	$1,407	$ —
Stockholders' Equity:			
Common stock	1,126	1,166	1,249
Additional paid-in capital	105	105	105
Retained earnings (deficit)	(1,567)	(762)	402
Total stockholders' equity	$ (336)	$ 509	$1,756
Total Equities	$ 3,338	$5,000	$6,048

[a] Borrowings under the revolving line of credit were personally guaranteed by the major stockholders and were secured by all of the accounts receivable, inventories, machinery and equipment, furniture, trademarks, and patent rights.

[b] Current installments on long-term debt (3/31/86):

Officers and stockholders	$ 841,000
Installment purchases	169,000
Capital leases	—
	$1,010,000

EXHIBIT 3
FY 1987 Final Budget (June 15, 1986—$000)

	1st Quarter	2nd Quarter	3rd Quarter	4th Quarter	
	April–June 1986	July–September 1986	October–December 1986	January–March 1987	TOTAL
Net revenues	$ 391	$5,893	$4,769	$ 832	$11,885
Cost of goods sold	344	2,630	2,176	491	5,641
Gross margin	$ 47	$3,263	$2,593	$ 341	$ 6,244
Operating expenses	779	1,204	1,256	926	4,165
Operating income	$(732)	$2,059	$1,337	$(585)	$ 2,079
Tax allowance	—	432	261	—	693
Net income (loss)	$(732)	$1,627	$1,076	$(585)	$ 1,386

EXHIBIT 4

FY 1987 Cash Budget and Selected Expense and Balance Sheet Items (June 15, 1986—$000)

	1st Quarter April–June 1986	2nd Quarter July–September 1986	3rd Quarter October–December 1986	4th Quarter January–March 1987
Cash receipts	$1,487	$1,764	$4,572	$3,800
Cash outflows				
For materials, labor, and operating expenses (except for interest but including income taxes)[a]	1,928	2,967	2,698	2,022
Interest	67	110	168	86
Capital expenditures for fixed assets	177	238	179	301
Pay back stockholder loans	—	—	841	—
Depreciation	143	166	179	195
Assets at end of quarter				
Planned cash balance	100	100	100	100
Receivables, net	507	4,580	4,739	1,741
Inventories	2,808	1,690	1,166	1,869
Prepaid expenses	241	294	198	283
Other assets	201	247	283	302
Liabilities at end of quarter				
Accounts payable	1,849	1,717	1,755	1,664
Income taxes payable	—	—	—	—
Current installments long-term debt	980	1,060	207	189
Notes payable—banks (to be determined)				

[a] In general, corporations must pay current year income taxes on a quarterly basis. However, the precise payment requirements are based on a complex set of rules that are different for large or small corporations.

EXHIBIT 5
Third Quarter FY 1987 Cash Budget by Months ($000)

	October	November	December
Cash receipts	$1,000	$1,054	$2,518
Cash outflow			
For materials, labor, and operating expenses			
(except for interest)	830	1,065	803
Interest	54	56	58
Capital expenditures	69	62	48
Pay back stockholder loans	—	841	—
Collateral for bank loans at end of month			
Receivables	5,420	5,517	4,739
Inventory	1,331	1,363	1,166

Thumbs-Up Video, Inc.

In October 1988, Linda Williams was determined to open a video cassette rental store that would have a wider selection of tapes and could operate more efficiently than the few small video rental stores located in and around her hometown of Mystic, Connecticut. Williams knew that more than one-half of the homes in Mystic were equipped with video cassette recorders, but based on informal discussions with her friends and neighbors, she learned that these recorders were infrequently used. She felt that with this installed base of recorders, a new, upscale, well-stocked video cassette rental store would surely succeed.

After preparing a business plan, Williams approached a long-time friend who she felt would invest in this new venture. After considerable thought, this friend was willing to invest $66,000 with Williams putting up the remaining $99,000 to purchase shares in the new corporation, which was to be called Thumbs-Up Video, Inc.

In November 1988, Williams left her job as a real estate broker and began to establish her new enterprise. She first consulted with a lawyer to have the business incorporated. Because this was a fairly simple organization, the legal fees incurred were only $2,700. Her next task was to find some land and a building in which to operate. Her connections in real estate allowed her to negotiate a favorable price of $48,000 for a building near the center of town. The building was old and needed renovation work. The purchase documents allocated $43,000 to the land and only $5,000 to the building, due to its age and run-down appearance. A mortgage of $33,600 was secured for the purchase, with the remaining $14,400 paid in cash. Williams felt that the current building was structurally sound and with renovation work, the life of the building could be extended to 25 years. She ordered the renovation work, costing $20,000, to begin immediately. The work lasted through December 1988. Williams paid $5,000 in advance for the renovations, with the remainder paid in full at completion of the work on December 31, 1988.

In anticipation of the store's opening on January 2, 1989, Williams began negotiations with the major film distribution companies for purchase of a rental tape inventory. By the end of December 1988, Williams had purchased 2,000 tapes (1,000

Eric J. Petro prepared this case under the supervision of Professor William J. Bruns, Jr., as the basis for class discussion rather than to illustrate either effective or ineffective handling of an administrative situation.

different titles) at an average cost of $50 per tape. Since Thumbs-Up Video was a new entity with no credit history, every vendor required a personal guarantee from Williams before they shipped the tapes "on account." All tapes were paid for by December 31, 1988. Although this represented a very large investment, Williams was certain that a wide selection of tapes would ensure the success of her new store.

In December 1988, equipment worth $6,700, including a computer priced at $3,000, was purchased for cash. Williams paid an additional $1,000 for a computer software package to be used by the company. The software, which was specifically designed for Thumbs-Up Video, would efficiently track those tapes out on rental and those on the shelves. All of the equipment had estimated useful lives of five years. Also at the end of December 1988, $500 of miscellaneous office supplies were ordered for delivery January 2, 1989, to be paid cash on delivery.

Williams then contracted with a local advertising agency to provide various forms of advertising for a period of one year. On January 2, 1989, $6,000 was paid for advertising through December 1989.

The new store opened as scheduled on January 2, 1989. During the subsequent months, Williams was pleased with the way the business was developing. Confident of the success of the store, Williams purchased another 250 tapes for $75 each on June 1, 1989. The entire amount remained unpaid at June 30. These tapes were considered new releases of feature films and multiple copies (10 copies each of 25 different titles) were purchased to satisfy expected initial demand.

For the six months ended June 30, 1989, sales amounted to $96,000. Due to the nature of the business, most of the sales were cash sales. A limited number of customers were allowed to charge their rentals, and at June 30, 1989, only $2,200 had not been collected from charge sales of the previous six months. Employees earned wages of $32,000 during this six-month period. Williams drew a salary of $30,000.

When Williams met with her accountant at the end of June 1989, she was pleased that the bank account showed a balance of $45,500, considering that significant expenditures were made just to get the business started. She wondered if she should declare a dividend as a signal to her investor friend that the business was doing well. The accountant reminded Williams that certain accruals, including interest on the mortgage of $2,900, still needed to be made before dividends could be declared.

While discussing the results of the business through June 30, 1989, Williams and her accountant puzzled over how to account for a certain item. They knew that the tapes held for rental had a physical life of three years, and the cost of the tapes should be amortized over that period. However, they were unsure how to account for the new release tapes. They had the same physical life, but the initial demand (which warranted 10 copies of each title to be purchased versus the usual 2) was sure to wane significantly after only one year on the shelves. Williams felt that most of the revenues from these new releases would occur in the first year, and thereafter the store would derive little or no benefit from 8 extra copies of the same title.

This matter of the amortization of new releases and several other concerns needed to be resolved before financial statements of Thumbs-Up Video, Inc., could be issued.

QUESTIONS

1. Construct a set of T accounts to record the transactions that occurred at Thumbs-Up Video, Inc., from November 1988 through June 1989.

2. Prepare a statement of financial position as of June 30, 1989, for Thumbs-Up Video, Inc.

3. Prepare an income statement for Thumbs-Up Video, Inc., from incorporation through June 30, 1989. Disregard any income taxes that might be due.

Monterrey Manufacturing Company

The management of the Monterrey Manufacturing Company prepared annually a budget of expected financial operations for the ensuing calendar year. The completed budget provided information on many aspects of the coming year's operations. It included summaries of the projected estimated transactions for the budget year, the resulting assets and liabilities as of the end of that year, the sales, expense, and profit forecast for the year.

The final preparation of statements was accomplished only after careful integration of detailed computations submitted by each department to insure that the operation of all departments were balanced with one another. For example, the finance department needed to base its schedules of loan operations and collections disbursements on figures that were dependent upon manufacturing, purchasing, and selling expectations. The scale of manufacture would, of course, be geared to the forecasts of the sales department, and purchasing would be geared to the proposed manufacturing schedule. In short, it was necessary to integrate the estimates of each department and to revise them in terms of the overall effect on operations to arrive at a well-formulated and profitable plan of operations for the coming year. The budget statements ultimately derived from the adjusted estimated transactions would then serve the company as a reliable guide and measure of the coming year's operations.

At the time the 2004 budget was being prepared in November of 2003, estimated 2003 financial statements were compiled for use as a comparison with the budgeted figures. These 2003 statements were based on nine months' actual and three months' estimated transactions. See **Exhibits 1** and **2**.

Below is the summary of expected operations for the budget year 2004 as it was finally accepted.

Professor William J. Bruns, Jr. prepared this case. HBS cases are developed solely as the basis for class discussion. Cases are not intended to serve as endorsements, sources of primary data, or illustrations of effective or ineffective management.

SUMMARY OF EXPECTED OPERATIONS
FOR BUDGET YEAR 2004

1. **Sales** (on credit) $2,442,000; sales returns and allowances, $18,000; sales discounts taken by customers, $48,000. (The sales figure is net of expected bad debts.)

2. **Purchases of goods and services:**

   a. New Assets:

   Purchased for cash: manufacturing plant and equipment, $120,000; prepaid manufacturing taxes and insurance, $36,000.

   Purchased on accounts payable: raw materials, $822,000; supplies, $78,000.

   b. Services used to convert raw materials into goods in process which will increase the "value" of goods in process inventory:[1] Purchased for cash: direct manufacturing labor, $420,000; indirect manufacturing labor, $174,000; social security taxes on labor, $61,200; power, heat, and light, $92,400. (Accrued payroll was ignored in these estimates.)

   c. Sales and administrative services: Purchased for cash, $402,000.

3. **Conversion of assets into goods in process:** This appears as an increase in the "value" of goods in process and a decrease in the appropriate asset accounts.

   Depreciation of plant and equipment, $80,400; expiration of prepaid taxes and insurance, $30,000; supplies used in manufacturing, $90,000; raw materials put into process, $786,000.

4. **Transfer of work in process into finished goods:** This appears as an increase in finished goods and a decrease in goods in process.

   Total cost accumulated on goods that are expected to be completed and transferred to finished goods inventory, $1,650,000.

5. **Cost of finished goods sold to customers:** $1,638,000.

6. **Financial transactions:**

   a. Borrowed, $462,000 on notes payable to bank.

   b. Retired bank loans, $528,000.

   c. Cash payment to bank of $7,200 for interest on loans.

7. **Cash receipts** from customers on accounts receivable, $2,425,800.

---

[1] In a merchandising company, the cost of goods sold is roughly equal to the purchase price of these goods. In a manufacturing company, however, the cost of goods sold is the sum of the raw material in these goods plus the "value-added by manufacture." Thus, inventory is assumed to increase in value by the amounts spent to convert raw materials into salable products. These amounts include the items listed in 2(b) plus the items listed in (3) below. Three inventory items are used to collect information about this process: (1) raw materials; (2) goods in process, which shows the value built up on goods that are in the factory; and (3) finished goods, showing the value of goods that have been completed and are awaiting sale. Values are transferred from one to another in the manner suggested by items 3 and 4.

8. **Cash payments of liabilities:**
    a.   Payment of accounts payable, $958,800.
    b.   Payment of accrued 2003 Federal Income Tax, $21,000.
9. **Estimated Federal Income Tax** on 2004 income, accrued but unpaid as of December 31, 2004, $94,200.
10. **Dividends** declared for year and paid in cash, $126,000.

This summary presents the complete cycle of the Monterrey Manufacturing Company's budgeted yearly operations from the purchases of goods and services through their various stages of conversion to completion of the finished product to the sale of this product. All costs and cash receipts and disbursements involved in this cycle are presented, including the necessary provision for federal income tax and the payment of dividends.

In preparing the budget the management was interested in an analysis of the effect of each of these transactions upon the balance sheet items as of January 1, 2004. T-accounts to facilitate this analysis are shown in **Exhibit 3**. The T-accounts are categorized into asset accounts, liability accounts, and owners' equity accounts. Temporary accounts for income and expenses are also included.

QUESTIONS

1. Enter the year's projections on the T-accounts. Entries should be coded as illustrated by the sample entry for sales of $2,442,000 (coded 1).

2. Prepare pro forma 2004 financial statements similar to **Exhibits 1** and **2**.

3. Prepare a pro forma Statement of Cash Flows for the Monterrey Manufacturing Company for 2004.

EXHIBIT 1

Monterrey Manufacturing Company—Estimated Statement of Financial Position, December 31, 2003

Assets

Current Assets

Cash		$ 153,000	
Accounts receivable (net of allowance for doubtful accounts)		363,000	
Inventories:			
Raw materials	$ 330,000		
Work in process	145,200		
Finished goods	85,800		
Supplies	99,000	660,000	
Prepaid taxes and insurance		34,200	
Total current assets			$1,210,200

Fixed Assets

Manufacturing plant and equipment (original cost)	$1,920,000		
Less accumulated depreciation	600,000		1,320,000
			$2,530,200

Liabilities and Capital

Current Liabilities

Notes payable		$ 198,000	
Accounts payable		120,000	
Unpaid estimated federal income taxes		21,000	
Total current liabilities			$ 339,000

Owners' Equity

Capital stock		$1,980,000	
Retained earnings		211,200	2,191,200
			$2,530,200

EXHIBIT 2

Monterrey Manufacturing Company—Estimated Statement of Income for Year Ended December 31, 2003

Sales			$2,184,000
Less: Sales returns and allowances		$ 16,800	
Sales discounts		42,600	59,400
			$2,124,600
Net Sales			
Cost of Goods Sold:			
Finished goods inventory, 1/1/03		$ 504,000	
Work in process inventory, 1/1/03		$ 156,000	
Raw materials inventory, 1/1/03	$270,000		
Raw materials purchased	600,000		
	$870,000		
Raw materials inventory, 12/31/03	330,000		
Raw materials used		540,000	
Direct manufacturing labor		294,000	
Factory overhead:			
Indirect manufacturing labor	$114,000		
Power, heat, and light	54,000		
Depreciation of plant and equipment	76,800		
Social security taxes	45,000		
Factory, insurance and taxes	30,000		
Supplies	47,400	367,200	
		$1,357,200	
Less: Work in process, inventory, 12/31/03		145,200	
Cost of goods manufactured (i.e., completed)		1,212,000	
		$1,716,000	
Less: Finished goods inventory, 12/31/03		85,800	
Cost of goods sold			1,630,200
Gross margin			$ 494,400
Sales and administrative expenses		$ 360,000	
Interest expense		7,200	367,200
New profit before federal income tax			$ 127,200
Estimated income tax			21,000
Net profit after federal income tax			$ 106,200

EXHIBIT 3

Asset T-Accounts

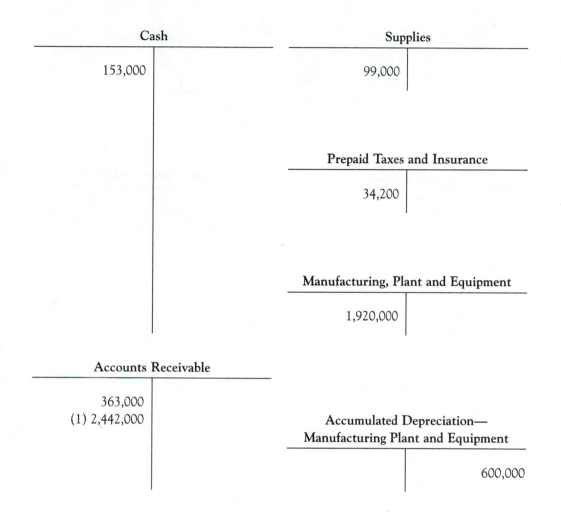

Cash	
153,000	

Supplies	
99,000	

Prepaid Taxes and Insurance	
34,200	

Manufacturing, Plant and Equipment	
1,920,000	

Accounts Receivable	
363,000	
(1) 2,442,000	

Accumulated Depreciation—Manufacturing Plant and Equipment	
	600,000

EXHIBIT 3 (*continued*)

Liability T-Accounts

Owner's Equity T-Accounts

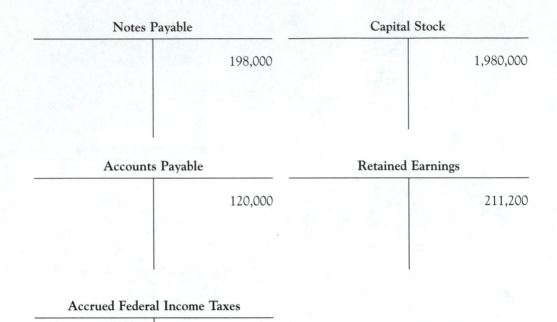

	Notes Payable		Capital Stock
	198,000		1,980,000

	Accounts Payable		Retained Earnings
	120,000		211,200

	Accrued Federal Income Taxes
	21,000

EXHIBIT 3 (*continued*)

Sales	Selling and Administrative Expenses
(1) 2,442,000	

Sales Returns and Allowances	Interest Expense

Sales Discount	Federal Income Taxes

Introduction to Financial Ratios and Financial Statement Analysis

There is almost always a reason why someone picks up an organization's financial statements and begins to analyze them. Lenders or creditors may be interested in determining whether they will be repaid money they have lent or may lend to the organization. Investors may be interested in comparing a potential investment in one organization with that of another. Employees may want to compare the current performance or financial status of their employer with earlier periods. Regulatory agencies often need to assess organizational or industry financial health and performance. Financial analysis is always based on a set of questions, and the specific questions requiring answers depend on who the financial statement user is and the reasons for his or her analysis.

Financial analyses based on accounting information consistently involve comparisons. Amounts or ratios may be compared with industry norms, the same measurement in a prior period, the same measurement in a competitor's organization, or with planned and budgeted amounts previously established. Figuring out which comparisons will best answer the questions motivating the analysis is one of the necessary steps in making the best use of accounting information.

Financial ratios can help describe the financial condition of an organization, the efficiency of its activities, its comparable profitability, and the perception of investors as expressed by their behavior in financial markets. Ratios often permit an analyst or decision maker to piece together a story about where an organization has come from, its current condition, and its possible future. In most cases, the story is incomplete, and important questions may remain unanswered.

Even though the analyst or decision maker is better informed as a result of doing the ratio analysis, the indiscriminate use of financial ratios can be extremely dangerous. Decision rules that rely on a specific or minimum value of a ratio can easily lead to missed opportunities or losses. Even the best ratio is not always indicative of the health, status, or performance of an organization. Ratios between apparently similar measurements in financial statements may be affected by differences in accounting classifications or by deliberate manipulation.

Professor William J. Bruns, Jr. prepared this case. HBS cases are developed solely as the basis for class discussion. Cases are not intended to serve as endorsements, sources of primary data, or illustrations of effective or ineffective management.

The ease with which ratios can be manipulated and the danger in using them as criteria lead many analysts to concentrate on trends in ratio measurements rather than on the absolute value or proportion expressed by the ratio itself. When a trend in the value of a ratio between financial attributes is observed, questions can be raised about why the trend is occurring. The answers to such questions provide new information, not necessarily contained in financial reports, but perhaps highly relevant and useful to the decision maker and the problem at hand.

Similarly, comparisons of firms only on the basis of ratios can lead to erroneous conclusions. The diversity inherent in available accounting practices and principles can lead to differences in ratios between organizations being compared. Comparisons between companies can be made, but they must be made with care and with full attention to the underlying differences in basic accounting methods used in the reports as well as in the companies themselves. With these cautions in mind, we can proceed to examine briefly some commonly used financial ratios.

PROFITABILITY RATIOS

Profitability ratios seek to associate the amount of income earned with either the amount of resources used or the amount of activity that has taken place. These correspond to efficiency measures often used in economic and engineering theory. Ideally, the firm should produce as much income as possible with a given amount of resources or a satisfactory amount of income using as few resources as possible.

Return on Investment (ROI)

Dividing net income by the amount of investment expresses the idea of economic efficiency. Return on assets (ROA), return on investment capital (ROIC), and return on owners' equity (ROE) are all used in financial analysis as measures of the effectiveness with which assets have been employed.

Return on assets (ROA) relates net income to the investment in all of the financial resources at the command of management. It is most useful as a measure of the effectiveness of resource utilization without regard to how those resources have been obtained and financed. The formula for this ratio is:

$$\text{Return on Assets (ROA)} = \frac{\text{Income}}{\text{Assets}}$$

The consolidated statement of earnings, consolidated balanced sheets, and consolidated statements of cash flows for the Gillette Company and Subsidiary Companies (hereafter the Gillette Company) are shown in **Exhibit 1**. These financial statements will be used as a basis for illustrating the calculation of each financial ratio in this introduction. For 2003 return on assets for the Gillette Company was:

$$\text{Return on Assets (ROA)} = \frac{\$1,385}{\$9,955} = 13.9\%$$

Return on invested capital (ROIC) relates all net income to all resources committed to the firm for long periods of time. It is calculated by dividing net income by the total amount of noncurrent liabilities and stockholders' equity. The formula for this ratio is:

$$\text{Return on Invested Capital (ROIC)} = \frac{\text{Net Income}}{\text{Total Liabilities and Stockholders' Equity} - \text{Current Liabilities}}$$

Return on invested capital in 2003 for the Gillette Company was:

$$\text{Return on Invested Capital (ROIC)} = \frac{\$1,385}{\$9,955 - \$3,658} = 22.0\%$$

Two variations in these two ratios are often observed. Because their purpose is to compare how efficiently a pool of capital has been used—a pool that includes long-term debt as well as stockholders' equity—the after-tax interest expense is often added back to income in the numerator. This can be easily calculated by the formula:

Interest expense $\times$ (1 – tax rate) = After-tax interest expense

The amount of the adjustment is the net interest cost. Interest expense is tax deductible, and the formula calculates the after-tax interest expense by multiplying the total interest expense by the complement of the tax rate. The rationale for this adjustment is that it is a better measure of the income flow generated by management, considering all of the sources of long-term financing it has chosen to use. Without the adjustment, the income understates the earnings generated by the total pool of capital.

A second variation is appropriate when the amount of assets or invested capital is changing. Since income is earned over a period of time, the appropriate denominator in the two ratios above is probably average assets or average invested capital. This is easily approximated by adding the beginning and ending measurements together and dividing by two. The analyst has to decide if these refinements to the ratios will improve his or her ability to answer the questions at hand.

Return on equity (ROE) relates net income to the amount invested by stockholders. It is a measure of the efficiency with which the stockholders' investment through their original capital contributions and earnings retained in the business have been used. The formula for this ratio is:

$$\text{Return on Equity (ROE)} = \frac{\text{Net Income}}{\text{Stockholders' Equity}}$$

Return on equity in 2003 for the Gillette Company was:

$$\text{Return on Equity (ROE)} = \frac{\$1,385}{\$2,224} = 62.3\%$$

Note that for this ratio stockholders' equity is the correct denominator because the ratio is an attempt to understand what the investment by the owners alone has earned. (For Gillette, the return on equity is higher than other companies often report, because Gillette has been buying its own stock, called treasury stock, for several years.)

Earnings per Share (EPS)

Because corporations have many owners, not all of whom own an equal number of shares, it is quite common to express earnings of a company on a per-share basis for those who wish to calculate their proportional share of earnings. The calculation of earnings per share can be complicated if there is more than one class of ownership, each with differing claims against the income of the firm. Preferred stock or other securities that are convertible into common shares are often treated as common stock equivalents in making this calculation. In published financial reports, this ratio is required to be presented, often in several variations such as "basic" or "diluted" (a very conservative form) EPS. Although the actual formulas for EPS are usually very complex, a simplified formula showing the basic common elements is:

$$\text{Earnings per Share (EPS)} = \frac{\text{Net Income} - \text{Preferred Stock Dividends}}{\text{Number of Shares of Common Stock} + \text{Equivalents}}$$

Net earnings per share for the Gillette Company for 2003 were $1.35.

Profit Margin

This ratio, which gives a rate of return on sales, relates two statement of income measurements to each other. For this reason, it is not a measure of efficiency, but instead, gives some indication of the sensitivity of income to price changes or changes in cost structure. The formula for this ratio is:

$$\text{Net Profit} = \frac{\text{Net Income}}{\text{Net Sales}}$$

It is important to note that neither a high nor low profit margin necessarily means good performance. A company with a high profit margin but high investment may not be returning a great amount to investors. A firm with a very low profit margin may have required only a very small investment so that it proves highly profitable to those who invest in it.

The profit margin in 2003 for Gillette was:

$$\text{Net Profit} = \frac{\$1,385}{\$9,252} = 15.0\%$$

ACTIVITY RATIOS

Activity ratios provide an indication of how well assets are utilized by the organization. Efficiency in using assets minimizes the need for investment by lenders or owners. Activity ratios provide measurements of how well assets or capital are being utilized.

Asset Turnover

This ratio measures the company's effectiveness in utilizing all of its assets. The formula for this ratio is:

$$\text{Asset Turnover} = \frac{\text{Net Sales}}{\text{Total Assets}}$$

For the Gillette Company in 2003, the asset turnover was:

$$\text{Asset Turnover} = \frac{\$9,252}{\$9,955} = .929$$

Since different industries require very different asset structures, comparing asset turnover ratios from one industry to those in another is potentially meaningless and must be done with caution. Likewise, when an organization participates in many industries, the exact meaning of an asset turnover ratio can be obscured, and the most valid comparisons of an asset turnover ratio at one date may be to that of the same firm at another recent date.

Asset turnover ratios can be calculated for any group of assets. Accounts receivable, inventory, and total working capital are all asset classifications for which comparison of turnover is potentially interesting and important.

Days' Receivables

Evidence about the amount of time that lapses between sales and receipt of payment from customers can be important information about the financial structure of a company. An approximation of the number of days that elapse can be obtained by dividing the amount of accounts receivable (and notes receivable if these are related to customer accounts) by the average day's sales. In cases where cash sales are a significant portion of the total, the amount of charge sales must be estimated for use in judging the length of collection.

The collection period for accounts receivable can be calculated by first dividing net sales by 365 days to determine average sales per day.

$$\text{Average Day's Sales} = \frac{\text{Net Sales}}{365}$$

Then calculate the collection period using the following formula:

$$\text{Day's Receivables} = \frac{\text{Accounts Receivable}}{\text{Average Day's Sales}}$$

Day's receivables in 2003 for the Gillette Company was:

$$\text{Average Day's Sales} = \frac{\$9,252}{365} = \$25.3 \text{ million}$$

$$\text{Day's Receivables} = \frac{\$920}{\$25.3} = 36 \text{ days}$$

Inventory Turnover

Determining the number of times that inventory is sold during the year provides some measure of its liquidity and the ability of the company to convert inventories to cash quickly if that were to become necessary. When turnover is slow, it may indicate that inventories are not a liquid asset and suggest they should be excluded from that category for analytical purposes. On the other hand, when turnover is quite rapid, that is when inventory is sold several times each year, the liquid character of inventory can provide funds if needed in the short term and may protect the firm against inventory obsolescence.

Inventory turnover is calculated by dividing the cost of goods sold by the inventory cost. The average inventory for the year should be calculated or approximated if there has been a significant change in inventory cost from the beginning to the end of the period. Usually it is sufficient simply to add the beginning and ending inventory amounts and to use one-half of that total as the average inventory for the year. Once the inventory is determined, it can be converted to days' inventory by dividing inventory turnover into 365 days.

$$\text{Inventory Turnover} = \frac{\text{Cost of Goods Sold}}{\text{Average Inventory}}$$

$$\text{Inventory Turnover Period in Days} = \frac{365}{\text{Inventory Turnover}}$$

In some financial reports issued for stockholders, the cost of goods sold is not revealed. In these cases, it is necessary to use sales as the numerator of the ratio, which gives the appearance of providing faster inventory turnover. If the relationship between price and cost does not change, the trend in turnover period would be approximately the same between two periods. Nevertheless, it is wise to use the ratio of sales to inventory with somewhat greater care.

Inventory turnover in 2003 for the Gillette Company was:

$$\text{Inventory Turnover} = \frac{\$3,708}{(\$1,094 + \$928) \div 2} = 3.6$$

$$\text{Days' Inventory} = \frac{365}{3.6} = 100 \text{ days}$$

Working Capital Turnover

Working capital turnover is a measure of the speed with which funds are provided by current assets to satisfy current liabilities. The formula for this ratio is:

$$\text{Working Capital Turnover} = \frac{\text{Net Sales}}{\text{Average Current Assets} - \text{Average Current Liabilities}}$$

Working capital turnover in 2003 for the Gillette Company was:

$$\text{Working Capital Turnover} = \frac{\$9,252}{(\$3,723.5 - \$3,573.0)} = 61.5\text{x}$$

SOLVENCY AND LEVERAGE RATIOS

When an organization is unable to meet its financial obligations, it is said to be insolvent. Because insolvency leads to organizational distress, or even to bankruptcy or organization extinction, ratios to test solvency are often used by investors and creditors. By measuring a company's ability to meet its financial obligations as they become current, solvency ratios give an indication of the liquidity of the company.

Current Ratio

This ratio is commonly used for testing liquidity or solvency. The formula for this ratio is:

$$\text{Current Ratio} = \frac{\text{Current Assets}}{\text{Current Liabilities}}$$

The size of the current ratio that a healthy company needs to maintain is dependent upon the relationship between inflows of cash and the demands for cash payments. A company that has a continuous inflow of cash or other liquid assets, such as a public utility or taxi company, may be able to meet currently maturing obligations easily despite the fact that its current ratio may be small. On the other hand, the manufacturing firm with a long product development and manufacturing cycle may need to maintain a larger current ratio.

The current ratio at the end of 2003 for the Gillette Company was:

$$\text{Current Ratio} = \frac{\$3,650}{\$3,658} = 1.0$$

Acid Test Ratio

In cases where there is a desire or a need to confirm the absolute liquidity of an organization, the current ratio is modified by eliminating from current assets all that cannot be liquidated on very short notice. Typically, then, this ratio consists of the ratio of so-called "quick" assets (cash, marketable security, and some forms of accounts receivable) to current liabilities.

$$\text{Acid Test Ratio} = \frac{\text{Quick Assets}}{\text{Current Liabilities}}$$

For 2003, add the cash, short-term investments, and receivables to calculate the acid test ratio for the Gillette Company.

$$\text{Acid Test Ratio} = \frac{\$1,952}{\$3,658} = .53$$

Debt Ratio

The degree to which the activities of a company are supported by liabilities and long-term debt as opposed to owner contributions is referred to as leverage. A firm that has a high proportion of debt to stockholder contributions would be referred to as being highly leveraged. The advantage to the owners of the firm of having high debt is that profits earned after payment of interest accrue to a smaller group of owners. On the other hand, when a firm is highly leveraged, risk rises when profits and cash flows fall. A company can be forced to the point of insolvency by the cost of interest on the debt.

The debt ratio is widely used in financial analysis because it reveals the effect of financial leverage. The debt ratio is calculated in different ways, and we will illustrate two here. First,

$$\text{Debt Ratio} = \frac{\text{Total Debt}}{\text{Total Assets}}$$

Alternatively, the debt-to-equity ratio is sometimes calculated by dividing total liabilities by the amount of stockholders' equity. The formula for this ratio would be:

$$\text{Debt-to-Equity Ratio} = \frac{\text{Total Liabilities}}{\text{Owners' Equity}}$$

Care must be taken in interpreting either of these ratios because there is no absolute level that can be referred to as being better than another. In general, as the ratio increases in size, returns to owners are higher but so also is risk higher. The trend in this ratio may reveal important management decisions about the financing of activities comparing two organizations. Differences in the size of the ratio may reveal management attitude toward risks and alternative strategies toward financing the activities of the respective entities.

Using the second of the two formulas above, the 2003 debt-to-equity ratio for the Gillette Company was:

$$\textbf{Debt-to-Equity Ratio} = \frac{\$9,955 - \$2,224}{\$2,224} = 3.5$$

Times Interest Earned

Almost every firm has continuing commitments that must be met by future flows if the company is to remain solvent. Interest payments are an example of such commitments. The common ratio that measures the ability of a company to meet its interest payments is times interest earned. The formula for this ratio is:

$$\textbf{Times Interest Earned} = \frac{\textbf{Pretax Operating Income + Interest Expense}}{\textbf{Interest}}$$

The number of times interest payments are covered by current earnings offers some measure of the degree to which income could fall without causing insolvency in this account. In many cases, this is not so much a test of solvency as a test of staying power under adversity. Times interest earned for 2003 for the Gillette Company was:

$$\textbf{Times Interest Earned} = \frac{\$1,964 + \$54}{\$54} = 37.4x$$

MARKET-RELATED AND DIVIDEND RATIOS

Two ratios are affected by the market price for shares of ownership in corporations. These are the price earnings ratio and the dividend yield ratio. In addition, analysts sometimes calculate a dividend payout ratio as a measure of the degree to which the firm is likely to be able to continue its dividend payments provided there is fluctuation in future income.

Price Earnings Ratio (PE)

The relationship of the market price of shares of stock to the earnings of the company is of great interest to investors. Companies that are growing rapidly and are thought to have good potential for future growth often find that their shares are traded at a multiple of earnings per share much higher than companies thought to have less promise. The price earnings ratio is often included in stock market tables in investment information prepared by analysts. The formula for this ratio is:

$$\text{Price Earnings Ratio (PE)} = \frac{\text{Market Price per Share of Stock}}{\text{Earnings per Share}}$$

Since the market price of shares frequently fluctuates, this ratio is sometimes calculated using an average market price for a period of time. If the average price of a share of Gillette stock in 2003 was $34.00, the price earnings ratio would have been 25.2%.

$$\text{2003 Price Earnings Ratio} = \frac{\$34.00}{\$1.35} = 25.2$$

Dividend Yield Ratio

The dividend yield to common shareholders is dependent upon the market price originally paid for the share and is calculated by dividing dividends received by the market price originally paid for the shares. For a prospective investor, dividend yield is the dividend per share divided by the current market price of the stock.

$$\text{Dividend Yield} = \frac{\text{Dividends per Share}}{\text{Market Price per Share}}$$

If the market price of shares in the Gillette Company was $34.00, the dividend yield in 2003 when dividends per share of $.65 were paid to shareholders would have been:

$$\text{Dividend Yield} = \frac{\$.65}{\$34.00} = 1.9\%$$

Dividend Payout

The dividend payout ratio shows the proportion of net income that was paid in dividends. Both the dividend yield and dividend payout ratio are useful for forecasting future dividend streams to investors in the company's common stock. The formula for this ratio is:

$$\text{Dividend Payout} = \frac{\text{Dividends}}{\text{Net Income (available to common shareholders)}}$$

For the Gillette Company in 2003, dividends paid to common stockholders totaled $666.0 million; therefore the dividend payout was:

$$\text{Dividend Payout} = \frac{\$666}{\$1,385} = 48\%$$

USING RATIOS TO THINK ABOUT MANAGEMENT STRATEGIES

Sometimes it is useful when conducting a financial analysis to think about the interrelationships between ratios and to use them to think about the strategies that management has adopted or might adopt. One well-known algebraic construction using ratios is known as the du Pont model because financial analysts at the E. I. du Pont de Nemours & Co. are credited with its development and use during the 1920s. The du Pont model multiplies profit margin times asset turnover times a ratio of assets over equity to calculate return on stockholders' equity. If we look at this algebraic construction, we can see why it is so useful.

$$\frac{\text{Income}}{\text{Sales}} \times \frac{\text{Sales}}{\text{Assets}} \times \frac{\text{Assets}}{\text{Owners' Equity}} = \text{Return on Owners' Equity}$$

The first ratio, profit margin, can be used to focus management's attention on the relationship between the price and cost of products or services sold. The second ratio, asset turnover, emphasizes the efficient use of resources in producing products and services. The third ratio, assets over equity, focuses on the ability of management to leverage the firm properly to provide maximum return to stockholders. Each of these major classes of decisions that managers must make can be examined in light of its ability to provide the overall objective of increasing return to stockholders.

COMMON SIZE FINANCIAL STATEMENTS

In order to examine the changing financial structure of a firm through time and the changing nature of operations, many analysts like to create common size financial statements in which the balance sheet and the statement of income are prepared in the percentage format. In a common size balance sheet, each asset, liability, and owners' equity amount is expressed as a percentage of total assets. In a common size statement of income, sales is set at 100%, and each item is expressed as a percentage of sales.

Common size financial statements facilitate the comparison of firms of a different size as well. Although firms may be in the same industry, they may be of significantly different sizes, and common size statements allow an analyst to focus on the efficiency with which managements of different firms have created a capital structure and have achieved efficient operations.

Common size balance sheets and statements of income for the Gillette Company are presented in **Exhibit 2**.

EXHIBIT 1

The Gillette Company and Subsidiary Companies—Consolidated Statement of Income for Years Ended December 31, 2003, 2002, and 2001 (dollars in millions, except per share amounts)

	Year Ended December (millions, except per share amounts)		
	2003	2002	2001
Net Sales	$9,252	$8,453	$8,084
Cost of Sales	3,708	3,511	3,407
Gross Profit	5,544	4,942	4,677
Selling, General, and Administrative Expenses	3,541	3,172	3,007
Restructuring, Asset Impairment and Other	—	(39)	172
Profit from Operations	2,003	1,809	1,498
Nonoperating Charges (Income)			
Interest income	(12)	(25)	(4)
Interest expense	54	84	145
Other charges (income)—net	(3)	(2)	15
	39	57	156
Income from Continuing Operations before Income Taxes	1,964	1,752	1,342
Income Taxes	589	543	432
Income from Continuing Operations	1,375	1,209	910
Income from Discontinued Operations, net of tax	10	7	—
Net Income	$1,385	$1,216	$ 910
Net Income Per Common Share, Basic			
Continuing Operations	$1.35	$1.15	$.86
Discontinued Operations	.01	—	—
Net Income	$1.36	$1.15	$.86
Net Income Per Common Share, Assuming Full Dilution			
Continuing Operations	$1.34	$1.14	$.86
Discontinued Operations	.01	.01	—
Net Income	$1.35	$1.15	$.86
Adjusted Net Income, assuming the adoption of SFAS 142 for 2001	$1,385	$1,216	$934
Adjusted Net Income per Common Share, assuming the adoption of SFAS 142 for 2001			
Basic	$1.36	$1.15	$.89
Assuming full dilution	$1.35	$1.15	$.88
Weighted average number of common shares outstanding			
Basic	1,021	1,055	1,055
Assuming full dilution	1,024	1,059	1,058

EXHIBIT 1 (*continued*)
The Gillette Company and Subsidiary Companies— Consolidated Balance Sheets, December 31, 2003 and 2002 (dollars in millions except per share amounts)

At December 31	2003	2002
Assets		
Current Assets		
Cash and cash equivalents	$ 681	$ 801
Trade receivables, less allowances: 2003—$53; 2002—$73	920	1,202
Other receivables	351	311
Inventories	1,094	928
Deferred income taxes	322	380
Other current assets	282	175
Total current assets	3,650	3,797
Property, plant and equipment, net	3,642	3,565
Goodwill	1,023	962
Intangible assets, net	496	400
Other assets	1,144	1,139
Total assets	$ 9,955	$ 9,863
Liabilities and Shareholders' Equity		
Current Liabilities		
Loans payable	$ 117	$ 673
Current portion of long-term debt	742	527
Accounts payable and accrued liabilities	2,506	2,054
Income taxes	293	234
Total current liabilities	3,658	3,488
Long-term debt	2,453	2,457
Deferred income taxes	626	692
Other long-term liabilities	929	920
Minority Interest	65	46
Stockholders' Equity		
Common stock, par value $1 per share		
Authorized: 2,320 shares		
Issued 2003—1,374 shares; 2002—1,370 shares	1,374	1,370
Additional paid-in capital	1,273	1,197
Earnings reinvested in the business	7,333	6,608
Accumulated other comprehensive loss	(1,088)	(1,523)
Treasury stock, at cost		
2003—367 shares; 2002—326 shares	(6,665)	(5,392)
Deferred stock-based compensation	(3)	—
Total stockholders' equity	2,224	2,260
Total liabilities and stockholders' equity	$ 9,955	$ 9,863

EXHIBIT 1 (*continued*)
The Gillette Company and Subsidiary Companies—
Common Size Balance Sheets, December 2003 and 2002 (%)

At December 31	2003	2002
Assets		
Current Assets		
Cash and cash equivalents	6.8	8.1
Trade receivables, less allowances: 2003—$53; 2002—$73	9.2	12.2
Other receivables	3.5	3.2
Inventories	11.0	9.4
Deferred income taxes	3.2	3.9
Other current assets	2.8	1.8
Total current assets	36.5	38.6
Property, plant and equipment, net	36.6	36.1
Goodwill	10.3	9.8
Intangible assets, net	5.0	4.1
Other assets	11.5	11.5
Total assets	100.0	100.0
Liabilities and Shareholders' Equity		
Current Liabilities		
Loans payable	1.2	6.8
Current portion of long-term debt	7.5	5.3
Accounts payable and accrued liabilities	25.2	20.8
Income taxes	2.9	2.4
Total current liabilities	36.8	35.3
Long-term debt	24.6	24.9
Deferred income taxes	6.3	7.0
Other long-term liabilities	9.3	9.3
Minority Interest	.7	.5
Stockholders' Equity		
Common stock, par value $1 per share		
Authorized: 2,320 shares		
Issued 2003—1,374 shares; 2002—1,370 shares	13.8	13.9
Additional paid-in capital	12.8	12.1
Earnings reinvested in the business	73.7	67.0
Accumulated other comprehensive loss	(10.9)	(15.4)
Treasury stock, at cost		
2003—367 shares; 2002—326 shares	(67.0)	(54.7)
Deferred stock-based compensation	0.0	0.0
Total stockholders' equity	22.3	22.9
Total liabilities and stockholders' equity	100.0	100.0

Note: Columns do not add because of rounding.

EXHIBIT 1 (*continued*)
The Gillette Company and Subsidiary Companies—Consolidated Statements of Cash Flows for Years Ended December 31, 2003, 2002, and 2001 (dollars in millions)

Years Ended December 31	2003	2002	2001
Operating Activities			
Income from continuing operations	$ 1,375	$ 1,209	$ 910
Adjustments to reconcile income from continuing operations to net cash provided by operating activities:			
Restructuring and asset impairment charge (recovery)	—	(9)	172
Depreciation and amortization	578	500	509
Funding of company pension loans	(72)	(525)	(35)
Pension expense	143	70	46
Deferred income taxes	(49)	162	45
Other	7	8	(18)
Changes in assets and liabilities, excluding effects of acquisitions and divestitures:			
Accounts receivable	286	364	622
Inventories	(43)	123	101
Accounts payable and accrual liabilities	334	188	(191)
Other working capital items	38	(137)	(20)
Other noncurrent assets and liabilities	43	124	(49)
Net cash provided by operating activities	2,640	2,077	2,092
INVESTING ACTIVITIES			
Additions to property, plant and equipment	(408)	(405)	(624)
Disposals of property, plant and equipment	45	43	59
Acquisition of business, net of cash acquired	(161)	—	—
Other	6	—	1
Net cash used in investing activities	(518)	(362)	(564)

EXHIBIT 1 (*continued*)
The Gillette Company and Subsidiary Companies—
Consolidated Statements of Cash Flows for Years Ended
December 31, 2003, 2002, and 2001 (dollars in millions)

Years Ended December 31	2003	2002	2001
FINANCING ACTIVITIES			
Purchase of treasury stock	(1,273)	(427)	(12)
Proceeds from sale of put options	—	15	9
Proceeds from exercise of stock option and purchase plans	80	57	53
Proceeds from long-term debt	709	1,174	525
Repayment of long-term debt	(534)	(458)	(684)
Increase (decrease) in loans payable	(567)	(1,565)	56
Dividends paid	(666)	(685)	(686)
Settlements of debt-related derivative contracts	1	45	4
Net cash used in financing activities	(2,250)	(1,844)	(735)
Effect of Exchange Rate Changes on Cash	8	5	(1)
Net Cash Provided (Used) by Discontinued Operations	—	(22)	93
Increase (Decrease) in Cash and Cash Equivalents	(120)	(146)	885
Cash and Cash Equivalents at Beginning of Year	801	947	62
Cash and Cash Equivalents at End of Year	$ 681	$ 801	$ 947
Supplemental disclosure of cash paid for:			
Interest	$ 59	$ 83	$ 154
Income taxes	$ 563	$ 345	$ 232

EXHIBIT 2
The Gillette Company and Subsidiary Companies—Common Size Statement of Income for Years Ended December 31, 2003, 2002, and 2001 (%)

	2003	2002	2001
Net Sales	100.0	100.0	100.0
Cost of Sales	40.1	41.5	42.1
Gross Profit	59.9	58.5	57.9
Selling, General, and Administrative Expenses	37.3	37.5	37.2
Restructuring, Asset Impairment and Other	—	(.5)	2.1
Profit from Operations	21.6	21.5	18.5
Nonoperating Charges (Income)			
Interest income	(.1)	(.3)	0
Interest expense	.6	1.0	1.8
Other charges (income)—net	0	0	.2
Income from Continuing Operations before Income Taxes	21.2	20.7	16.6
Income Taxes	6.4	6.4	5.3
Income from Continuing Operations	14.9	14.3	11.3
Income from Discontinued Operations, net of tax	.1	0	0
Net Income	15.0	14.3	11.3

Note: Columns do not add because of rounding.

Drivers of Industry Financial Structure

Common-sized financial statements and selected ratios of 10 companies, along with an explanation of key items, are presented in the following pages. The companies were chosen because they consist of primarily one major business segment and the relationships between balance sheet items, profit, and operations are fairly typical of these industries.

To facilitate accounting comparisons, the companies are all headquartered in the United States. The financial statements are the latest annual financials for the respective fiscal years ending in 1999 or 2000.

The companies involved are:

- Developer of prepackaged software
- On-line retailer
- Warehouse club for food and general merchandise
- Major passenger airline
- International hotel chain
- Temporary staffing agency
- Supermarket grocery retailer
- Pharmaceutical company
- Manufacturer of electronic communications equipment
- Manufacturer and marketer of consumer products

Use the ratios, common-sized statements, and your knowledge of business operations and conditions at the time these data were generated to identify the companies.

Research Associate Indra A. Reinbergs prepared this case under the supervision of Professor Dwight B. Crane as the basis for class discussion rather than to illustrate either effective or ineffective handling of an administrative situation. The format of this case is based on HBS No. 198-017, "Identify the Industries—1996" and its predecessors.

EXPLANATION OF SELECTED ITEMS

Balance Sheet Items

Cash & Marketable Securities — Includes bank deposits and short-term, relatively risk-free, liquid investments such as U.S. Treasury bills.

Investments — Represents long-term equity investments in other companies.

Goodwill & Intangibles — Goodwill arises when one company acquires another for a price that exceeds the book value of the assets. The difference is put on the books of the acquiring company as goodwill or an intangible, such as brand value.

Current Portion of Long-Term Debt — The portion of long-term debt principal that must be paid within one year.

Total Long-Term Debt — Debt obligations with maturities beyond one year (e.g., bonds, notes, mortgages).

Preferred Stock — Carries a right to a fixed annual dividend payment (like interest on debt), but does not grant any voting rights. In liquidation it ranks behind debt obligations and ahead of common stock.

Financial Ratios

Gross Margin — Measures gross profits on goods sold. *Calculated as (Sales-Cost of Goods Sold)/Sales.*

Research & Development/Sales — A measure of how heavily a company is engaged in developing new products and services.

Net Income/Sales — Net profit margin measures "bottom-line" profitability after consideration of all expenses and revenues.

Days of Receivables — Measures how long customers take to pay invoices. *Calculated as Accounts Receivable/(Net Sales/365).*

Inventory Turnover — Measures the firm's efficiency in managing and selling inventory. *Calculated as Cost of Goods Sold/Inventories.*

Part 1 An Overview of Accounting and Financial Reporting

Financial Ratios (continued)

Fixed Asset Turnover	Indicates the capital intensity of the business. *Calculated as Sales/Net Property, Plant and Equipment.*
Total Asset Turnover	Indicates the asset intensity of the business. *Calculated as Sales/Total Assets.*
Net Income/Assets	"Return on Assets" (ROA) measures the firm's overall efficiency in managing assets.
Net Income/Equity	"Return on Equity" (ROE) measures the rate of return on the shareholders' common stock investment.
Assets/Equity	A measure of how much the firm has leveraged or geared its shareholders' equity to provide higher returns to shareholders (owners). *Calculated as Total Assets/Common Stock.*
Debt/Equity	*Calculated as (Short-Term Debt + Current Portion of L/T Debt + L/T Debt)/Common Stock.* Another frequently used measure of leverage.
Long-Term Debt/Total Capital	Calculated as L/T Debt/(Preferred Stock + Common Stock + L/T Debt). Measures the extent to which long-term debt is used as part of the capital structure or long-term financing of the firm.

Note: See "Introduction to Financial Ratios and Financial Statement Analysis" for further reference, HBS No. 193-029.

EXHIBIT 1
Common-Sized Financial Statements

	A	B	C	D	E	F	G	H	I	J	Median
ASSETS											
Cash & Marketable Securities	28.6%	1.6%	1.1%	6.9%	8.7%	9.0%	10.8%	5.6%	5.8%	62.0%	7.8%
Receivables	—	3.5%	4.3%	3.6%	9.2%	11.5%	13.7%	4.8%	58.3%	9.8%	7.0%
Inventories	8.9%	21.9%	1.0%	—	10.4%	8.0%	9.2%	41.6%	—	—	8.5%
Other Current Assets	3.5%	3.8%	1.9%	5.6%	7.1%	3.1%	10.5%	2.0%	7.1%	5.7%	4.7%
Total Current Assets	41.0%	30.8%	8.2%	16.2%	35.4%	31.6%	44.2%	54.1%	71.2%	77.5%	38.2%
Net Plant & Equipment	12.9%	46.1%	44.4%	69.3%	39.3%	27.2%	24.8%	44.8%	18.1%	8.6%	33.2%
Investments	15.0%	—	14.1%	5.0%	—	13.4%	—	—	—	—	—
Goodwill & Intangibles	29.5%	20.9%	25.1%	5.4%	21.2%	21.3%	—	—	6.6%	—	13.8%
Other Noncurrent Assets	1.6%	2.2%	8.2%	4.2%	4.1%	6.6%	31.0%	1.1%	4.1%	13.9%	4.1%
Total Noncurrent Assets	59.0%	69.2%	91.8%	83.8%	64.6%	68.4%	55.8%	45.9%	28.8%	22.5%	61.8%
Total Assets	100.0%	100.0%	100.0%	100.0%	100.0%	100.0%	100.0%	100.0%	100.0%	100.0%	
LIABILITIES AND EQUITY											
Accounts Payable	18.7%	16.0%	6.6%	13.0%	7.2%	11.7%	8.1%	26.9%	7.1%	4.4%	9.9%
Short-term Debt	—	—	—	—	9.8%	8.0%	6.7%	—	4.6%	—	—
Current Portion of L/T Debt	0.6%	3.0%	0.1%	4.2%	—	—	—	0.0%	—	—	0.0%
Unearned Revenues	2.2%	—	—	11.0%	—	—	—	—	—	2.0%	—
Other Current Liabilities	8.4%	12.9%	0.1%	4.0%	16.5%	4.9%	18.5%	14.8%	32.0%	26.9%	13.9%
Total Current Liabilities	29.9%	31.9%	6.8%	32.2%	33.5%	24.6%	33.3%	41.7%	43.7%	33.3%	32.7%
Total Long-Term Debt	59.3%	44.8%	65.8%	11.8%	19.4%	8.8%	8.3%	0.2%	—	—	10.3%
Other Noncurrent Liabilities	—	8.4%	12.1%	27.9%	9.5%	29.4%	13.4%	4.4%	—	3.0%	9.0%
Total Liabilities	89.2%	85.1%	84.7%	71.9%	62.5%	62.8%	54.9%	46.2%	43.7%	36.3%	62.6%
Preferred Stock	—	—	—	1.2%	5.5%	—	1.3%	—	—	—	—
Common Stock	10.8%	14.9%	15.3%	26.9%	32.0%	37.2%	43.8%	53.8%	56.3%	63.7%	34.6%
Total Stockholders' Equity	10.8%	14.9%	15.3%	28.1%	37.5%	37.2%	45.1%	53.8%	56.3%	63.7%	37.4%
Total Liabilities & Equity	100.0%	100.0%	100.0%	100.0%	100.0%	100.0%	100.0%	100.0%	100.0%	100.0%	

Note: Columns do not add because of rounding.

EXHIBIT 1 (*continued*)
Common-Sized Financial Statements

	A	B	C	D	E	F	G	H	I	J	Median
SELECTED RATIOS											
Gross Margin	17.7%	26.5%	43.2%	38.3%	44.4%	46.4%	38.0%	11.4%	17.9%	90.7%	38.2%
R&D/Sales	9.7%	—	—	—	—	6.5%	11.1%	—	—	19.8%	—
Net Income/Sales	(43.9%)	1.4%	8.1%	7.4%	9.9%	18.1%	2.6%	2.6%	2.0%	23.4%	5.0%
Days of Receivables	—	5	N/M	15	28	46	60	5	52	28	28
Inventory Turnover	6.1	8.5	N/M	—	6.4	6.2	5.6	8.3	—	6.1	6.1
Fixed Asset Turnover	5.163	5.481	0.523	1.283	3.020	3.381	3.345	8.740	22.829	14.687	4.272
Total Asset Turnover	0.663	2.524	0.232	0.889	1.187	0.918	0.829	3.918	4.130	1.263	1.053
Net Income/Assets	(0.291)	0.035	0.019	0.066	0.117	0.166	0.022	0.104	0.082	0.296	0.074
Net Income/Equity	(2.704)	0.234	0.123	0.245	0.366	0.447	0.050	0.192	0.146	0.464	0.213
Assets/Equity	9.282	6.696	6.539	3.719	3.125	2.691	2.284	1.859	1.775	1.569	2.908
Debt/Equity	5.561	3.198	4.307	0.596	0.913	0.453	0.342	0.004	0.081	—	0.525
L/T Debt/Total Capital	0.846	0.750	0.811	0.296	0.341	0.192	0.155	0.004	—	—	0.244

Notes: "—" = Category not reported separately on financial statements. "N/M" = Category not meaningful.
Columns do not add because of rounding.

The Financial Reporting Project[1]

This project involves an in-depth analysis of a publicly traded company, and a comparison to its peers in the industry. The project should be completed in groups of four participants. You are free to form your own groups. If you are unable to form/find a group, your professor will help.

Each group should provide its top two choices from the following list of companies your professor will provide. The Professor will approve companies on a first-come, first-served basis and hence it is important for your group to decide on your top two choices as soon as possible and communicate it to the Professor.

As soon as you receive approval from the Professor, your group must obtain a copy of your company's latest Annual Report, 10-K, and Proxy Statement. You can do this by downloading and printing the documents from your company's website or from the EDGAR database at the Securities & Exchange Commission (http://www.sec.gov).

The project is completed in three phases. The first phase emphasizes a basic understanding of the company and the business and economic environment in which it operates. The second phase requires that you obtain an understanding of the information provided in the Annual Report, 10-K, and Proxy Statement of your company. The third and final phase involves computation of ratios and financial analysis, including an investment recommendation.

The report is completed in three phases so that the entire work on the project is not deferred until the end of the term. Further, by turning in three reports, you will obtain timely feedback from your professor that will help you improve your performance in each successive report. Each progress report requires a group leader to coordinate the work. Rotate your group leader for each progress report.

Based on past experience, the following procedures will help you maximize your performance in the project:

- Each group member should independently complete the assignments required for each progress report before meeting with other members of the group.

- The group meetings should review all of the individual work, investigate and resolve disagreements, and work together to prepare written reports.

- After the draft of each report is completed, each person in the group should review the draft to ensure that the writing is concise and clear, and that the

---

[1] This exercise was developed by Professor Ganesh Krishnamoorthy at Northeastern University. Used with permission of the author.

spelling and grammar are appropriate, before turning in the final draft to the professor.

The quality of the project will be judged on the basis of a *collective*, not an allocated effort. Experiencing the challenges and the rewards of working as a group in a business setting is an integral part of the learning process in this course.

A major objective of the project is to help develop your communication skills, including the ability to communicate clearly and concisely. Hence each report is restricted to the following maximum page length.

PROGRESS REPORT 1   3 pages maximum
PROGRESS REPORT 2   3 pages maximum
PROGRESS REPORT 3   5 pages maximum (excluding appendix)

Your report must be typewritten (word-processed) and double-spaced. To ensure consistency, you must use a 12-point font and a 1" margin throughout (left, right, top and bottom).

SELECTED RESEARCH RESOURCES

The following internet resources may be helpful in completing the Financial Reporting Project. Note that these are not exhaustive and you should feel free to explore other websites on your own.

http://www.hoovers.com: This site helps you locate your company's website.

http://www.bigcharts.com: A very good site to chart company stock price and find basic information.

http://bamboo.tc.pw.com: An excellent site for inter-company analysis. You can use this site to prepare graphs and to compare results with other companies.

http://www.sec.gov/edgarhp.htm: Website of the Securities & Exchange Commission—provides important SEC filings (e.g., 10K) online.

http://www.rutgers.edu/Accounting/raw.htm: A comprehensive site that provides links to a number of important accounting sites.

http://www.nasdaq.com: A comprehensive website providing useful information about companies listed on NASDAQ as well as the NYSE.

http://www.reportgallery.com: Contains the Annual Report of many companies downloadable in pdf format.

THE FINANCIAL REPORTING PROJECT
PROGRESS REPORT 1

The purpose of this report is help you develop a basic understanding of your company and the business environment in which it operates. The Annual Report, 10-K, and the Proxy Statement of your company, along with other readings and resources, will help you complete this report.

Company Background

A. What is the ticker symbol of your company? Identify the stock exchange(s) where your company stock trades.
B. Read the auditor's report included in the annual report of the company and explain its purpose. Identify the name of the auditing firm.
C. Briefly explain the major operations of your company. What products does it sell and/or services does it render? Identify the major competitors of the company.

Developments relating to the Company

Identify two recent events of significance (e.g., layoffs, reorganizations) that have affected the company. [Hint: You can obtain this information using the company's website. Alternatively, you may use other financial news services available in print or on the internet, such as Yahoo Finance, *Fortune*, *Forbes*, and the *Wall Street Journal*]. **Note: You need not include a copy of the Press Releases or the articles with your report.**

Developments relating to the Industry

A. Is the demand for the products and services provided by this industry increasing, decreasing, or staying stable? Briefly explain the factors that are influencing the demand for products and services in this industry.
B. Identify and briefly explain significant events (technological breakthroughs, regulatory changes) that may have affected the industry recently.

Ethical Issues

Ensuring ethical conduct is a core objective that every company should strive for. Identify one or more recent ethical issue(s) faced by the company and/or its industry (e.g., financial fraud, management integrity) and explain how your company/industry responded to the issues.

THE FINANCIAL REPORTING PROJECT
PROGRESS REPORT 2

The objective of this report is for you to develop a general understanding of the information contained in your company's 10K, Annual Report, and the Proxy Statement. Based on your research, prepare a well-written, concise report that covers the following issues. **(Note: Unless otherwise noted, all questions must be answered with reference to the latest financial statements reported in the Annual Report):**

1. How does current year's net income (i.e., earnings) compare with that in previous years? Compute the annual growth rate in earnings for the last five years. [For example, if earnings in Year 1 and 2 are 100 and 125 respectively, the growth rate from Year 1 to Year 2 is 25%]. What earnings trend do you observe and what factors may be causing this trend?

2. Calculate the gross margin percentage (Gross Profit divided by Net Sales) for each period presented in the income statement. What trend in gross margin do you observe and what factors may be causing this trend?

3. Where are the resources of your company employed (i.e., what percentage of the total assets of the company are invested in current assets, long-term assets, etc.)?

4. Some companies have intangible resources (e.g., brand recognition) that they do not report on their balance sheet. Does your company have such resources? If so, why doesn't your company record them on their balance sheet?

5. What method(s) of depreciation does your company use? Does the company use the same method of depreciation for all types of long-lived assets?

6. What method(s) does your company use to value its inventory? Compute the inventory turnover ratio for the last three years. Comment briefly on the trend observed.

7. Provide a breakdown of the liabilities of the company in percentage terms (i.e., what percentage of the total liabilities of the company are current liabilities, long-term liabilities, etc.?).

8. Identify the major components of stockholders' equity. Did the stockholders' equity change significantly during the year? If so, briefly explain the cause(s) for the change.

9. The 10K and Proxy Statements provide important information to the stockholders and others. Briefly explain the nature of the information contained in these two statements.

THE FINANCIAL REPORTING PROJECT
PROGRESS REPORT 3

The objective of this final report is for you to analyze the company in terms of its profitability, liquidity, and provide your investment and credit recommendations. You will also have an opportunity to learn about executive compensation and corporate governance. Based on your research, prepare a well-written, concise report that covers the following issues.

1. Compute the following ratios for the most recent year and include them in an Appendix to this report.
   a. Return on Equity (Return on Owners' Investment)
   b. Return on Assets (Return on Total Investment)
   c. Earnings per Share
   d. Profit Margin
   e. Current Ratio
   f. Quick Ratio
   g. Receivable Turnover
   h. Inventory Turnover
   i. Times interest earned
   j. Debt to Equity ratio
   k. Price/Earnings (P/E) ratio

2. Identify a company that you believe is the closest competitor ("competitor") to your company. Compute the ratios in (1) above for the competitor and include them in the Appendix.

Based on your computations in (1) and (2) above, address the following:

Profitability:
1. What is your assessment of the profitability of your firm in recent years? How does your firm's profitability compare with that of the competitor?
2. Compare the cash flows from operating activities for your firm with the net income for the most recent year. What factors have contributed to the difference between these two numbers?

Liquidity and Capital Structure:
1. Will the company be able to meet its obligations as they become due? How does your firm's liquidity compare with that of the competitor?
2. What is the capital structure of your company (i.e., what percentage of the total assets of the company are financed through liabilities and what percentage through stockholders' equity)? Identify two stakeholders and explain why the capital structure of the company is important to them.
3. Is the capital structure of the competitor significantly different from that of your company? Briefly explain your answer.

Corporate Governance and Executive Compensation (From Proxy Statement)
1. What issues were addressed at the most recent shareholders' meeting?
2. How many individuals serve on the Board of Directors of your company? Does your company's board consist of majority independent, outside directors? Explain your answer.

3. List the various committees of the board of directors. In particular, explain the rights, duties and obligations of the audit committee of the board of directors.

4. What was the total compensation earned by the Chief Executive Officer of your company in the most recent fiscal year? Did it increase/decrease over the prior year?

Recommendations

1. Based on your analysis, would you loan money to this company short-term? Would you loan money to this company long-term? Explain your answer.

2. Provide a recommendation as to whether an individual should buy, sell, or hold (if they already own it) the stock of this company. Your recommendation should be supported by an adequate explanation.

Note that the quality of the arguments you provide in support of your position for (1) and (2) above is more important than your final recommendation.

How Accountants Measure and Report

Accounting for Current Assets

- *The Question of LIFO or FIFO; Which Is Preferable?*

Recognizing Revenues and Expenses: When Is Income Earned?

- *Circuit City Stores, Inc. (A)*

Accounting for Property, Plant, and Equipment and Other Assets

- *Depreciation at Delta Air Lines and Singapore Airlines (A)*

- *Kansas City Zephyrs Baseball Club, Inc.*

- *Buying Time*

Liabilities and Time

- *Laurinburg Precision Engineering*

- *Accounting for Frequent Fliers*

Introduction to Owners' Equity

Solving the Puzzle of the Cash Flow Statement

- *Crystal Meadows of Tahoe, Inc.*

Accounting for Current Assets

Current assets are those resources that are expected to benefit the organization within the next operating cycle. Current assets reported by the Gillette Company and Subsidiary Companies in their 2003 Annual Report are typical (see **Exhibit 1**). *Cash and cash equivalents* and *short-term investments* always head the list of current assets, and they are the means by which current operating expenses can be met. Other current assets are usually listed in an order that approximates their nearness to cash; *inventories* are available for sale to customers, whose accounts then become *accounts receivable*, which when paid become cash to replenish the inventory pool to start the cycle again. These flows are going on continuously, and the balance sheet merely provides a view at one moment in time.

CASH, CASH EQUIVALENTS, AND OTHER TEMPORARY INVESTMENTS

The title *Cash and Cash Equivalents* has become very prevalent as more and more organizations engage in cash management techniques. Since idle cash provides no return, financial managers try to invest any temporary excess amounts of cash in highly liquid, short-term investments. Money market funds, government securities, certificates of deposit, or high-grade commercial paper are some of the investments that may be used for this purpose. Because they can be readily resold and converted into cash, accounting treats them as if they are cash.

Forecasting cash receipts and disbursements is an important part of the treasury function in most corporations. Since the yield (interest earned) on investments tends to be higher on marketable securities that are less liquid, many organizations invest a part of their excess cash in other marketable securities, which are shown separately as temporary investments. For most purposes, the distinction between cash equivalents and other temporary investments in marketable securities is unimportant, except as an indication of the investment horizon in a cash management program.

Professor William J. Bruns, Jr. prepared this case. HBS cases are developed solely as the basis for class discussion. Cases are not intended to serve as endorsements, sources of primary data, or illustrations of effective or ineffective management.

ACCOUNTS RECEIVABLE

When a sale to a customer is made on terms other than cash, an account receivable is created. Accounts receivable from customers are reported at the amount that is expected to be received from customers in settlement of their obligations. This may differ from the total of stated selling prices for two reasons. First, as an inducement for prompt payment, customers may be offered a *cash discount* if they pay within a short period of time. Second, although there is an assumption at the time of every sale that customers will pay, in practice not all do. For this reason, a valuation adjustment, or *allowance for doubtful accounts*, is normally recorded to recognize that some accounts will become *bad debts* and to bring the accounts receivable balance to a more realistic level.

Cash discounts are normally anticipated at the time of sale and deducted from sales, creating an allowance for cash discounts that is deducted from the total amount owed by customers to arrive at the amount of accounts receivable included in the balance sheet. The amount of the allowance is almost always based on the company's past experience with cash discounts taken by customers.

The problem in estimating the amounts that customers will not pay (bad debts) is somewhat more complex. Most organizations know from experience that some customers will be unable or unwilling to pay the amounts they owe. The problem is that at the time a sale is made and a receivable is recorded, managers do not know which customers will pay and which will not. The solution to this problem lies in making an estimate that is based on past experience of the portion of accounts receivable that will not be paid in full either at the time it is due or within some reasonable time thereafter.

A number of methods are used to estimate the *allowance for doubtful accounts*, also called the *allowance for bad debts*. Sometimes a percentage of the total amount of sales is charged to expense during the period in which sales are made, and that amount is established as an allowance against which bad accounts are offset when they are finally identified. The percentage of sales taken is customarily based on the experience of the firm with its particular group of customers, and it may vary with the type of customer to which sales are made.

Alternatively, an examination could be made of the distribution of accounts according to how long they have been outstanding. The percentage used to estimate default on accounts already overdue can be different from that applied to accounts that have not reached the point where payment is expected. Estimating the amount of accounts that will not be collected is an important aspect of reporting realistic figures for accounts receivable. If no allowance for doubtful accounts is made, the amount of accounts receivable may be overstated.

INVENTORIES

Inventories are considered a significant current asset in many firms. By holding an inventory of finished product, an organization can fill orders more quickly and provide better customer service. Even when products or services have to be created after a customer order is received, inventories of raw materials speed the process of satisfying customer demands.

Accounting for inventories has two important aspects. First, the cost of inventory that is purchased or manufactured has to be determined. That cost is then held in the inventory accounts of the firm until the product is sold. Once the product has been shipped or delivered to a customer, the cost becomes an expense to be reported in the income statement as the cost of goods sold.

To understand the process of inventory accounting, you have to imagine costs flowing into the inventory account and then being removed from that account and charged to cost of goods sold in the income statement. Just as products are physically moved onto shelves or into a warehouse and then physically removed as they are delivered to customers, so too is the cost of inventory moved into an account and later removed from it. It is important to recognize, however, that the flows need not be parallel, that is, the flow of costs into and out of the inventory account need not be in the same order as the flow of goods into and out of the warehouse.

Inventory Cost Flows

At first glance, it seems there is no need to make an assumption about how costs flow through the inventory account. The cost of each item placed in the physical inventory can be entered into the account, and then, as the item is physically taken from inventory, the cost can be removed from the account. In this way, the costs accumulated in the account can match perfectly with the items physically held, and the costs of goods sold can be equal to the sum of the cost of each item actually delivered to a customer. Such an inventory cost system can be identified as a *specific identification* system.

Specifically identifying each item in inventory is relatively easy if each item is unique, such as an art object, expensive jewelry, or custom-made furniture, or if each item has an identification number, such as an automobile. However, specific identification is not practical for a company having a large number of inventory items that are not easily identifiable individually. In these cases, it is common for accountants to assume a flow of cost through the inventory account that is unrelated in any way to the actual physical flow of goods.

Three common assumptions used in accounting for inventory cost are: (1) average cost, (2) first-in, first-out (FIFO), and (3) last-in, first-out (LIFO). A company can choose any of these three assumptions and use them consistently for each classification of inventory regardless of the way in which goods physically move into and out of inventory.

Using the *average-cost method* requires calculation of the average cost of items in the beginning inventory plus purchases made during the accounting period to determine the cost of goods sold and the cost of inventory on hand at the end of the period. The average cost is assumed to be a representative cost of all the items available for sale during the accounting period. Rather than wait until the end of an accounting period to calculate the average cost, some companies use a predetermined unit cost of all transactions that take place during the accounting period. This is a *standard-cost system* and is a variation of the average-cost method. Any difference between the actual average unit cost and the predetermined standard cost during a period is usually added to or subtracted from the cost of goods sold for that period.

If the *first-in first-out*, or *FIFO*, assumption is used, the oldest costs in the inventory account are the first to be transferred to cost of goods sold when merchandise is sold. Using this assumption means that the costs retained in the inventory account will always be those most recently incurred for the purchase or manufacture of inventory. For this reason, the FIFO assumption produces an inventory account balance that usually comes the closest of the three methods to approximating the replacement cost of the inventory.

The *last-in first-out*, or *LIFO*, assumption is the opposite of FIFO. Cost of goods sold is measured using the cost of the most recent additions to inventory, and the inventory account always retains the oldest cost of items purchased or manufactured. *This assumed cost flow may be quite different from the actual physical flow of goods, and it usually is when the LIFO method is used.* If older costs are retained in the inventory account for some time because the inventory is never depleted, and if prices change substantially in the accounting periods during which these old costs are retained, the LIFO inventory balance will likely bear little relation to the current value of the same amount of inventory recently purchased.

Use of the LIFO assumption is not permitted in some countries. It is, however, permitted in the United States and is quite popular. The reasons for this popularity are rooted in the fact that the United States has experienced fairly continuous inflation and cost increases for many commodities and goods. Since the LIFO assumption can be used in reporting income for income taxation purposes, firms choose to use it to reduce income taxes that are due in the current period. For most accounting methods, there is no requirement under U.S. tax law that the same method be employed in financial reports issued to shareholders and in financial reports on which taxes are based. However, LIFO is an exception. A company that chooses to save taxes by using the LIFO assumption must also use the LIFO method in its reports to shareholders. For this reason, the cost associated with paying lower taxes comes from the fact that management must then report to shareholders lower earnings than might be the case if an alternative inventory assumption were used.

These three common assumptions—average cost, LIFO, and FIFO—are illustrated in **Exhibit 2**. The differences caused by the differing flow assumptions are a function of the rate at which prices have changed during the period as well as the length of time old costs have been retained in the account because of the LIFO assumption. The important thing to remember is that the inventory cost flow assumption has an impact on cost of goods sold, reported net income, and the inventory value that will be shown among the current assets in the statement of financial position. The amount of difference between cost of goods sold reported under one assumption and cost of goods sold reported under another will depend on the speed with which costs of inventory are changing.

A reader of financial reports also has to be alert for situations in which the LIFO assumption has been used and inventory costs acquired many periods beforehand have been allowed to flow into cost of goods sold. Assuming the costs of inventory have risen, dipping into these old inventory costs by reducing the size of inventory on hand (called a LIFO liquidation) will give a burst of net income, which may not be sustainable in future periods.

We can sum up our discussion of inventory accounting to this point quite simply. Inventory accounting consists of measuring the cost of items that are added to inventory and then choosing the flow assumption to determine which of those costs are moved first to cost of goods sold when inventory is sold and delivered to customers. In organizations that only purchase items for their own use or for resale to others, the only other issue that arises is whether a perpetual record of inventory purchases and deliveries is kept or whether the firm relies on a periodic inventory count to determine the quantity of inventory on hand at the end of an accounting period that will be carried forward as the beginning inventory in the subsequent period. However, many organizations buy materials, expend labor on changing their character, and manufacture products or create services, which all add cost to the products eventually delivered to customers. These firms require additional records and account classifications in order to record and report properly their inventories.

ACCOUNTING FOR MANUFACTURED INVENTORIES

The record keeping required to maintain control of inventory items as their form and character change is often complex and voluminous. A branch of accounting known as *cost accounting* is devoted to analysis and study of the type of problems encountered in measuring and recording information necessary to determine the cost of inventories and the effects of expenditures and expenses incurred during the manufacturing process.

In the case of manufactured inventory, it is necessary to choose a flow assumption just as we would in a case where inventory was only purchased and sold. Since inventories are typically in several different forms in the manufacturing firm—raw materials, work in process, and finished goods—the record-keeping task is necessarily more complex. Labor and supplies may be used to alter raw materials, increasing the amount and cost of work in process. Raw materials and labor may be necessary to create finished goods. Costs now flow not only within classifications of the inventory according to assumptions (FIFO, LIFO and so on), but the amount used becomes the input for another class of inventory. In a typical manufacturing firm, the flow is like that depicted in **Exhibit 3**. **Exhibit 4** is a numerical illustration of the way in which costs might be assumed to flow through the inventory accounts in a simple manufacturing company. **Exhibit 5** shows how the cost of goods sold can be detailed in a comprehensive statement of income for the same firm.

Although the application of particular flow assumptions used in the manufacturing firm demands care (and occasionally ingenuity) on the part of the accountant, the problems of inventory accounting are essentially the same in all organizations. As inventories become a relatively larger portion of the total working capital or total assets of a firm, issues of inventory costing and measurement become more and more important and demand more attention of management.

OTHER CURRENT ASSETS

The major category of other current assets that you are likely to encounter in financial reports is *prepaid expenses*. In most cases, these are expenditures that have not yet become expenses because they have future value to the firm. They will be matched with revenue in subsequent accounting periods as their usefulness has been realized. Typical examples might be rents paid in advance for machinery or facilities that will be used in future months, amounts paid as insurance premiums at the beginning of insurance coverage, and travel-expense advances to employees for trips to be subsequently taken. These deferred expenses are typically used up over a short period of time, and for this reason, they are classified as current assets.

SUMMARY

Because the items classified as current assets are so important to current operations, they tend to turn over fairly quickly. The amounts shown on the balance sheet are usually fairly close to the amount that would be paid for a replacement asset of the same classification. The major exception to this is the inventory account during periods of rapid price changes, or if the LIFO inventory flow assumption is used.

In most organizations, there is a logical flow through those assets reported as current assets. Cash is used to purchase or create inventory. Inventory is delivered to customers, and their accounts become receivables. Receivables are collected, making cash available for operations. This flow is what operations are about. These operating assets are what demand management's day-to-day attention as inventories are turned into more liquid assets to finance the creation of more inventories ready to satisfy customer orders.

EXHIBIT 1
The Gillette Company and Subsidiary Companies

Excerpts from Consolidated Balance Sheets

At December 31,	2003	2002
	(millions)	
Cash and cash equivalents	$ 681	$ 801
Trade receivables, less allowances 2003—$53; 2002—$73	920	1,202
Other receivables	351	311
Inventories	1,094	928
Deferred income taxes	322	380
Other current assets	282	175
Total current assets	3,650	3,797

Notes to Consolidated Financial Statements

Cash and Cash Equivalents

Cash and cash equivalents include cash, time deposits, and marketable securities that are highly liquid and have maturities of three months or less at the date of purchase.

Allowances for Doubtful Accounts

Years ended December 31,	2003	2002	2001
		(millions)	
Balance at beginning of year	$ 73	$ 69	$ 81
Additions	19	37	30
Deductions	(39)	(33)	(42)
Balance at end of year	$ 53	$ 73	$ 69

Inventories

Years ended December 31,	2003	2002
	(millions)	
Raw materials and supplies	$ 114	$115
Work in process	196	191
Finished goods	784	622
Total	$1,094	$928

Inventories are stated at the lower of cost or market. Cost is determined on a first-in, first-out (FIFO) basis.

EXHIBIT 2
Inventory Cost-Flow Assumptions Illustrated

The Xitan Plumbing Supply Company maintained an inventory of standard brass faucets for sale to plumbers. In 2004, because of increasing copper prices, the price paid to suppliers increased significantly. A record of purchases in 2004 showed the following:

February 1	50 @ $ 6.00	$ 300
April 1	50 @ 7.50	375
May 1	50 @ 8.50	425
July 1	50 @ 9.00	450
October 1	50 @ 10.50	525
		$2,075

Prices had been stable prior to 2004. On January 1, 2004, there were 29 faucets on hand, each of which had cost $5.00. At the end of the year on December 31, there were 54 faucets on hand.

If inventories are valued periodically, the value of inventory in terms of historical prices and the cost of faucets sold depends on the inventory flow assumption adopted, as shown below:

Xitan Plumbing Supply Company—Expense Standard Brass Faucets—2004

	Assumed Flow of Costs		
	First-in, First-Out	Average Cost	Last-in, First-Out
Brass faucets, January 1, 2004			
29 @ $5.00	$ 145	$ 145	$ 145
Purchases, 2004	2,075	2,075	2,075
Available for sale, 2004	$2,220	$2,220	$2,220
Brass faucets, December 31, 2004			
FIFO: 50 @ $10.50 = $525			
4 @ 9.00 = 36	561		
Average cost: 54 @ $7.96[a]		430	
LIFO: 29 @ $5.00 = $145			
25 @ 6.00 = 150			
			295
Cost of faucets sold, 2004	$1,659	$1,790	$1,925

[a] Average cost is measured here by taking the total cost of brass faucets purchased and dividing it by the total number of faucets purchased.

EXHIBIT 3
Inventory Flows in Manufacturing

1. Materials and parts are purchased for use in manufacturing

   Raw Materials at Beginning of Period
   + Purchases
   − To work in process

2. Cost flow of raw materials into manufacturing processes is assumed as labor and other costs are assumed to add to value

   Work in Process at Beginning of Period
   + Raw materials used
   + Cost of labor
   + Other manufacturing costs (cost of management; heat, power, and light; supplies used; depreciation
   − To finished goods

3. Cost flow of goods finished is assumed as products are completed and ready for sale

   Finished Goods at Beginning of Period
   + Goods completed
   + Goods purchased ready for sale
   − Cost of products sold

EXHIBIT 4
Manufactured Inventory Accounting Illustrated

The Astroweld Company produces and distributes an advanced technology home welding unit. From two suppliers, the company purchases two parts assemblies—one electrical and one mechanical—for each finished welding unit. These are assembled by company employees using company-owned equipment in a rented factory building. The firm uses *LIFO* flow assumptions for all inventories except work in process.

During May of last year these inventory accounts showed the following conditions and events:

Raw Materials—Electrical Parts Assemblies

On hand, May 1	15 @ $33	$ 495
May purchases	10 @ $39	390
		$ 885
On hand, May 31	13 @ $33	429
May usage (10 @ $39, 2 @ $33)	12	$ 456

Raw Materials—Mechanical Parts Assemblies

On hand, May 1	19 @ $10	$ 190
May purchases	10 @ $11	110
		$ 300
On hand, May 31	14 @ $10	140
May usage (10 @ $11, 5 @ $10)	15	$ 160

Manufacturing Costs for May

Assembly labor	$ 650
Supervisory salaries	220
Heat, light, and power	56
Depreciation of equipment	120
Supplies used	32
Total	$1,078

Work in Process

In process, May 1		None
Processing in May		
12 electrical parts	$ 456	
15 mechanical parts	160	
Manufacturing costs	$1,078	
		$1,694
In process, May 31		
3 mechanical parts (3 @ $10)	$ 30	
Labor cost	40	
Cost of supervision	10	
		80
Transferred to finished goods in May		$1,614

EXHIBIT 4 (*continued*)
Manufactured Inventory Accounting Illustrated

Finished Welders	
On hand, May 1 5 @ $127.50	$ 637.50
May production from work in process	1,614.00
On hand, May 31 2 @ $127.50	(255.00)
Cost of welders sold in May	$1,996.50

Since 12 welders were completed in May and transferred to finished goods at a total cost of $1,614, the average cost of each welder manufactured was $134.50.

An income statement for May for Astroweld might show expense of goods sold as shown in **Exhibit 5**.

EXHIBIT 5
Astroweld Company—Cost of Welders Sold—May

Raw Materials Cost

Raw materials—electrical, May 1	$495.00		
Purchases	390.00		
Total available	$885.00		
Raw materials—electrical, May 31	429.00		
To work in process		$ 456.00	
Raw materials—mechanical, May 1	$190.00		
Purchases	110.00		
Total available	$300.00		
Raw materials—mechanical, May 31	140.00		
To work in process		160.00	
Work in process, May 1		0	
Add: Manufacturing costs for May		1,078.00	
		$1,694.00	
Work in process, May 31			80.00
To finished welders			$1,614.00
Finished welders, May 1			637.50
Welders available for sale			$2,251.50
Finished welders, May 31			255.00
Cost of welders sold, May			$1,996.50

The Question of LIFO or FIFO; Which Is Preferable?

Accounting for inventories is a tricky business. This is particularly true because a company's level of inventories cannot be judged precisely short of an actual count, verification and appraisal of value. Because it is expensive to do this, companies maintain careful records of purchases and goods manufactured and sold. Record keeping requires choices about what to include in the cost of inventory purchased or manufactured and the flow of those costs through the inventory accounts as inventory is used or sold to customers.

It is rarely possible to associate the actual cost of a particular item with that item as it enters, resides in, and is removed from, an inventory account. Only if items are very expensive (such as precious gemstones) or have specific identifying numbers (such as automobiles) is the effort to keep track of particular items considered worth the effort by accountants. Instead, like items are classified in an account, and an assumption is made about the cost of items used or sold. If prices or costs are changing, the assumption about the cost of items removed from inventory will affect reported expenses or cost of goods sold.

Three common assumptions about the flow of costs through inventory accounts define the most widely used inventory accounting methods. If it is assumed that the oldest costs are matched with revenues first, the method is called the first-in, first-out, or FIFO, inventory valuation method. If it is assumed that the most recent costs are matched with revenues first, the method is called the last-in, first-out method, or LIFO.[1] The average cost method is based on the assumption that an "average cost" is matched with revenues. It is important to note that the actual physical flow of items does not need to correspond to the assumed flow of costs and it rarely does. In accounting for milk or bread in a retail grocery store, an accountant could use a LIFO assumption, even though the grocer would probably want to maintain a FIFO physical flow.

Professor Emeritus William J. Bruns, Jr. and Professor Sharon M. Bruns of Northeastern University, adapted this note from "LIFO or FIFO? *That* Is the Question," HBS No. 192-046, written by Susan S. Harmeling (MBA '91), under Professor William J. Bruns, Supervisor, as the basis for class discussion.

[1] Use of the LIFO method is not permitted in many countries.

It is useful to visualize layers of cost built up over time in the inventory account. FIFO always takes the cost from the oldest layer. LIFO always takes the cost from the most recent layer, with the result that the bottom layers may be costs measured well in the past.

In the United States, the Internal Revenue Code permits companies to use the LIFO assumption in calculating income subject to taxation. If costs and prices are rising, more recent high costs increase expenses and cost of goods sold, reduce income, and reduce tax payments if the LIFO assumption is used. A company that elects to use the LIFO assumption in accounting for all or part of its inventories for tax purposes must also use that assumption in its published financial reports. This LIFO conformity requirement is the only rule which dictates that financial reports prepared for shareholders must be based on the same accounting assumptions as those used in preparing tax returns.

If prices and costs are rising, the opportunity to save cash by reducing tax payments will look attractive to many managers and they will be attracted to using the LIFO assumption. However, by choosing LIFO they will also be forced to report lower income than they would have reported if they had used the FIFO or average cost method. Often the choice managers make is determined in part by their belief about whether shareholders, investors, or lenders will understand that even though reported income is lower when LIFO is used in a time of rising costs, cash flow has been improved because lower taxes were paid.

Companies rarely change inventory flow assumptions. But when they do, management and independent auditors are required to note and highlight the change. The general requirement for any change in accounting method is that the new method be preferable to the old one. A different inventory valuation method from that previously used can be preferable for many reasons, so there is little to keep a management that wants to change from doing so. Of course, if their present inventory valuation method had been adopted very recently, another change would cause readers to be suspicious about the new accounting and about what management was trying to show or conceal. It would also violate the concept of consistency, so important to the financial reporting process, and would probably not be allowed by independent auditors and tax authorities.

A change in accounting method for inventories frequently signals a change in management assumptions about the future of their company, their industry, or the economy. In other cases, managers may change accounting methods to use the same methods used by other companies to which they hope to be compared. For these reasons, when a change is made, it frequently pays a reader of financial statements to think carefully about the reasons why management chose to change accounting methods.

Exhibit 1 shows an example of the kinds of things an analyst should look for and consider when a company management elects to change from one inventory cost flow assumption to another. In the exhibit, Example Corporation begins Year 1 using a last-in, first-out (LIFO) cost flow during a period when inventory costs are rising. At the beginning of Year 2, they can make a choice whether to adopt a first-in, first-out (FIFO) cost flow or continue to use LIFO. FIFO will report a larger ending inventory and greater net income in Year 2, but Example Corporation would have to pay more income taxes. Continuing to use LIFO will lead to lower reported net income, but lower taxes as well.

QUESTIONS

1. What factors should the management of Example Corporation consider when deciding whether to switch from LIFO to FIFO at the beginning of Year 2? Would this change impact the balance sheet or income statement in a material way? Why or why not?

2. What would have happened if Example Corporation had been using FIFO at the beginning of Year 1, instead of using LIFO that year?

3. In this example, prices had been rising in each year. How would Example Corporation and their accounting choices have differed if inventory purchase prices had been stable or had been falling, over the two-year period?

EXHIBIT 1
Example Corporation

	Year 1 (LIFO)			Year 2 (LIFO)			Year 2 (FIFO)		
	Units	Per Unit	Cost	Units	Per Unit	Cost	Units	Per Unit	Cost
Beginning inventory	1,500	900	$1,350,000	1,500	900	$1,350,000	1,500	900	$1,750,000[a]
Purchase 1	1,000	1,000	1,000,000	1,000	1,300	1,300,000	1,000	1,300	1,300,000
Purchase 2	1,000	1,100	1,100,000	1,000	1,400	1,400,000	1,000	1,400	1,400,000
Purchase 3	1,000	1,200	1,200,000	1,000	1,500	1,500,000	1,000	1,500	1,500,000
Available for sale	4,500		$4,650,000	4,500		$5,550,000	4,500		$5,950,000
Sales	3,000			3,000			3,000		
Ending inventory	1,500		1,350,000	1,500		1,350,000	1,500		2,200,000
Cost of goods sold	3,000		$3,300,000	3,000		$4,200,000	3,000		$3,750,000
Income Statement									
Sales			$5,000,000			$5,500,000			$5,500,000
Cost of goods sold			3,300,000			4,200,000			3,750,000
Gross margin			$1,700,000			$1,300,000			$1,750,000
Selling & administrative expenses			1,000,000			1,000,000			1,000,000
Income before taxes			$ 700,000			$ 300,000			$ 750,000
Income taxes (35%)			245,000			105,000			262,500
Net income			$ 455,000			$ 195,000			$ 487,500

[a] When changing from LIFO to FIFO, the LIFO inventory must be restated to its FIFO equivalent. In this case for Year 2 this would require a journal entry:

DR	Inventory	400,000	
CR	Retained earnings		260,000
CR	Taxes payable		140,000

This journal entry restores the accounts in Year 2 to what they would have been if FIFO had been used in Year 1.

Source: Casewriters

Recognizing Revenues and Expenses: When Is Income Earned?

The *accrual concept* forces accountants and managers to focus on changes in owners' equity rather than merely reporting changes to the cash or other asset accounts. The *matching concept* relates revenues and expenses so that owners' equity is neither overstated nor understated at any point in the stream of events that constitutes operations. The *realization concept* underlies the decision rules that accountants use in determining when revenues should be recognized and expenses matched to them.

Questions about the time at which revenue should be measured and recognized in reports are not always easy to answer, particularly if the accountant seeks to provide reliable and verifiable information. At first glance, the easy answer would be to recognize revenue only when cash is received. Recognizing and measuring revenues when cash is received constitute the *cash basis for accounting*. Using the cash basis, expenses are recognized when cash is expended. In contrast, when revenues are recognized and measured on the *accrual basis*, delivery of product or service is one cue accountants use to know to measure and report revenues even if cash has not yet been received; expenses are measured and recognized in the same accounting period as the revenues to which they relate. When revenues or expenses have been earned so that they are recognizable and measurable, they are often said to have been *realized*.

The only reason for considering use of the cash basis for accounting for revenues and expenses is simplicity. By counting cash received, revenues are easily measured. By counting cash spent, expenses are easily measured. But cash is only one of the resources that most organizations employ in carrying out operations and seeking to enhance the wealth of owners. The accrual basis is usually assumed to provide better information to owners on the results of operations and better information to those who use information from financial reports in making decisions.

The advantages of cash accounting need not be completely lost when the accrual basis is used. A summary of the monetary transactions of an organization or a statement of cash flows can easily be prepared to supplement balance sheets and income statements prepared on an accrual basis. Because no information is lost, and because

Professor William J. Bruns, Jr. prepared this note as the basis for class discussion rather than to illustrate either effective or ineffective handling of an administrative situation.

there appear to be important reasons to favor the accrual basis for income determination, the accrual basis has become the standard for the measurement and recognition of revenues, expenses, and income within companies and other organizations and in public reports about them.

WHEN SHOULD REVENUE BE RECOGNIZED?

Revenues arise in events and from transactions, and if revenues exceed expenses, income is earned and the organization grows in value. For most business entities, the largest and most important source of revenues is sales of goods and services to customers.

There are many points when revenue may be recognized as a result of sale of goods or services to customers. Five of the most common are:

1. The point at which an order is obtained from a customer.
2. The point at which an order is accepted and the terms of the sale are finalized.
3. The point at which goods are delivered to a customer.
4. The point at which the customer is billed.
5. The point at which payment is received from the customer.

Managers, especially those in marketing and sales, will probably favor revenue recognition practices that use either point 1 or point 2 as cues to begin the matching process. On the other hand, the *concept of conservatism* draws accountants toward point 3 or point 4, or perhaps even some later point in time such as point 5. At those points, there has been an observable market exchange that satisfies the criteria of feasibility, reliability, freedom from bias, verifiability, and high probability of cash collection.

The accrual concept provides the counterbalance to the concept of conservation to support the revenue recognition rules most often used. In most cases, generally accepted accounting principles call for revenues to be recognized at the time goods or services are delivered to the customer. Depending upon the legal form of the sales contract, delivery can take place when goods or services are shipped by the seller or when they are received by the buyer. This is the earliest point at which an outsider can independently determine that a sale has been completed in the terminology of accounting practice. Revenues are "realized" and are measured and reported when a sale is completed by delivery of goods to a customer. At that point in time, most critical earnings events have taken place, and the pragmatic issues of probable collection of receivables can be addressed.

Applying the Revenue Recognition Rule

One advantage of using the rule that revenue should be recognized when goods or services are delivered is that recognizing revenue at that time is fairly simple. When a customer buys goods in a retail store and carries the goods out the door, it is clear that something has happened and easy to see that a sale has been completed. In other cases where goods or services are delivered to customers, these events can be observed, and revenue can be recognized and measured. The ease of applying the rule for recognizing revenue at the time of delivery does not mean, however, that there are not important judgments to be made by managers and accountants about revenue recognition. Some of these judgments involve deciding how much revenue should be recognized, and others stem from other events that might take place. What, for example, should be done if merchandise is returned? What if additional services are required to satisfy the customer?

Since it is inevitable that some merchandise will be returned for credit, the amount actually reported as revenue frequently is reduced by estimated or actual returns for credit or refund, or for discounts that have been offered for prompt payment. Thus, it is not uncommon for the first line of an income statement to be labeled *net sales*. If there are important timing differences between the delivery of merchandise and the time it is returned or cash discounts taken, allowances for returns and discounts may be established as accounts and may appear in the statement of financial position as liabilities.

Measuring Revenue Prior to Delivery

Sometimes recognizing revenue on delivery does not provide the best information concerning actual events. One example is when an item is created or manufactured over a long period of time under contract to a customer. Large buildings, ships, and special production facilities designed and constructed as a special order for a customer are examples of items that may take several accounting periods to complete. The entire effort of an organization may be spent working several periods completing one item. In these cases, deferring recognition of income until the contract work is completely satisfied and the customer accepts the finished outcome does not give readers of financial reports an adequate sense of what is really happening.

In cases where the production cycle is long and involves large items, and where the income pattern of the firm will be distorted by deferring all recognition of revenue and hence all income to the period of delivery, accountants use procedures by which some of the anticipated income from a project can be recognized as parts of it are completed. Using these *percentage-of-completion methods*, a portion of the total revenue on a project is recognized in each period over the life of the project, and an appropriate amount of expenses is matched to it. Although this method is a deviation from the general rule that revenues should be recognized at the time of delivery of goods or services, for some industries it provides a better picture of the pattern of earnings activities.

A second situation where recognition of revenue is sometimes not deferred until time of delivery occurs when there is a price fixed by law or a well-established market price for the product. Precious metals, grains and other agricultural products, and marketable securities have readily determinable prices and can sometimes be sold without significant effort. When this is true, revenues are sometimes recognized at the point the production process is complete and the product ready for delivery, or when prices of the assets change.

APPLYING THE MATCHING CONCEPT

Once revenues have been recognized, the cost of creating the goods and services that were sold and the expenses of supporting the organization during the accounting period are matched to the revenues. Many times there is a fairly obvious and straightforward relationship between expenditures that have been made to create the revenue-producing process and the revenues themselves. In other situations, such as expenditures for advertising or research and development, the relationship between expenditures and revenues is less clear, and expenditures for these efforts will be matched to revenues in the period in which the expenditure takes place.

Finally, there is a kind of expense which can be difficult to observe, measure, and recognize. These are commitments that arise because promises of future expenditures have been made during the period in which revenues have been earned. Promises to employees for pensions or other post-retirement benefits are examples of this kind of promise. In these cases, transactions do not provide information about the amount of expense. Instead, estimates of the amount of future liability must be made so that the current expense can be matched against the revenue that created the commitment and hence a future obligation.

A FINAL COMMENT

Within many organizations, there is continual conflict between managers and accountants on the proper ways in which revenues should be recognized. Although everyone in an organization is biased toward recognizing organizational success quickly, accounting conventions for recognizing revenue and the underlying accounting concept of conservatism operate as checks on early revenue recognition. Everyone in an organization may be thrilled when a large contract is signed and sure that the value of the organization has been enhanced, but until the products and services promised under the contract have been delivered to customers, or criteria of the percentage of completion process have been met, no revenue will be reported.

Circuit City Stores, Inc. (A)

Michael Chalifoux, the senior vice president and chief financial officer of Circuit City Stores, a discount specialty retailer, was disturbed about a problem that had been brewing for some time. The issue involved Circuit City's accounting practices, specifically regarding the recognition of revenue from the sale of extended warranty and product maintenance contracts.

Chalifoux had just learned that the Financial Accounting Standards Board (FASB) had released a proposed FASB technical bulletin that would require Circuit City Stores to change its accounting for extended warranty and product maintenance contracts. The proposed accounting change would delay full recognition of revenue and income until the warranty period had expired. As a result, reported income would be lower than if Circuit City's present accounting policies were continued.

Circuit City believed that revenue from sales of extended warranty contracts most closely matched costs under the Partial Revenue Recognition method. The FASB was proposing that the Deferral of Revenue Method was more appropriate, whereas Circuit City argued that this would result in a mismatch of revenues and expenses.

BACKGROUND

Circuit City Stores was one of the first consumer-electronics and major-appliance retailers to adopt the concept of low pricing, selection, and service. By 1990 the company operated 149 retail outlets, 125 of which were designated Circuit City superstores. These 32,000-square-foot stores were designed to display a broad product selection from 2,800 brand-name items sold by Circuit City. In a typical superstore, customers could choose from almost 150 color televisions, more than 50 video cassette recorders, 30 camcorders, 30 compact disc players, 45 refrigerators, and 25 washer-and-dryer pairs. In addition, the selections could include car stereos, microwaves, cellular phones, telephones, telephone answering machines, and facsimile machines. Large in-store warehouses provided instant product availability, and

Professor William J. Bruns, Jr. and Susan S. Harmeling, MBA '91, prepared this case. HBS cases are developed solely as the basis for class discussion. Cases are not intended to serve as endorsements, sources of primary data, or illustrations of effective or ineffective management.

mechanized distribution centers allowed overnight inventory replenishment. Complete delivery, installation, and service were offered for almost every item sold.

Circuit City had experienced rapid growth in sales and profitability. Net revenues had increased from $705 million in 1986 to $2.1 billion in 1990. During the same period, net earnings had increased from $22 million to $78 million. Financial statements included in the 1990 Annual Report of Circuit City Stores are shown in **Exhibit 1**.

Circuit City Stores and other discount retailers like it made substantial profit margins on extended warranty contracts. An example of a typical transaction would be the following scenario. A retailer would sell a stereo system with a cost of $900 for $1,000. At the same time, the retailer offered the customer the option to purchase a two-year service contract for $100. Under the terms of the service contract, the retailer would clean and inspect the stereo every six months and would cover the cost of parts and labor should it need repair. Future costs to perform under the contract were estimated at $20. The retailer generally sold service contracts only to customers who also purchased a stereo from that retailer. The transaction could be summarized as follows:

	Stereo	Contract	Total
Revenue	$1,000	$100	$1,100
Cost	900	20	920
Profit	100	80	180

The joint sale of equipment and service contracts was part of Circuit City's corporate strategy. By successfully selling extended warranty and service contracts to a substantial portion of equipment customers, Circuit City could price its merchandise more competitively and draw customers to its stores through advertising. Circuit City had had much experience with the combined sale of equipment and extended warranty contracts. They looked on the combined sale as one transaction because they could predict with great certainty the percentage of customers, between 40% and 70% depending on the product, who would purchase both the item for sale and the warranty contract.

ACCOUNTING FOR EXTENDED WARRANTY CONTRACTS

There were several approaches to accounting for extended warranty contracts:

Approach 1: Full revenue recognition Proponents of this approach would recognize total revenue of $1,100 and total cost of $920 at the date of the sale (that is, profit of $180). If actual costs under the service contract either fell short of or exceeded the $20 estimate, an adjustment would be made later during the contract period.

Proponents of Approach 1 used the FASB's Statement of Financial Accounting Concepts No. 5, "Recognition and Measurement in Financial Statements of Business Enterprises," to support their position. A summary of this reasoning is shown in **Exhibit 2**.

Approach 2: Deferral of revenue Proponents of Approach 2 viewed the sale of the stereo and the sale of the extended warranty contract as two distinctly separate transactions that should be accounted for separately. They would recognize only the revenue and cost associated with the stereo at the point of the sale. Therefore, profit of $100 on the sale of the stereo would be recognized at that time. The $100 contract revenue would be deferred and recognized as revenue over the two-year contract period using some systematic allocation method. Costs under the contract would be recognized as incurred.

Proponents of deferring the revenue from the service contract believed it was inappropriate to recognize revenue at the point of sale because none of the services associated with the contract had yet been rendered and, therefore, the revenue had not been earned.

Proponents of Approach 2 looked to a proposed Statement of Position of the American Institute of Certified Public Accountants (AICPA), "Accounting for Certain Service Transactions," for support. A summary of this reasoning is shown in **Exhibit 3**.

Approach 3: Partial revenue recognition Companies such as Circuit City Stores and Highland Superstores used and supported an approach whereby a portion of the total revenue on the combined transaction would be recognized at the time of sale, with the remainder deferred and recognized over the contract period. Costs under the extended warranty contract would be recognized as incurred. This treatment would be allowable for financial reporting in only very limited circumstances.

Sample calculation of Approach 3 On a sale of $1,100 for a stereo and warranty with a combined expected cost of $900 + $20, this approach would result in $1,076 of revenue recognized at the time of sale, with the remaining $24 deferred and recognized over the contract period, as calculated below.

$$\frac{\$900}{\$920} \times \$1,100 = \$1,076 \quad \text{Recognized at time of sale}$$

$$\frac{\$20}{\$920} \times \$1,100 = \$\underline{\quad 24} \quad \text{Deferred total}$$

Profit of $176 ($1,076 revenue less $900 cost) would be recognized at the time of sale. Costs under the contract would be recognized as incurred throughout the contract period.

Those who supported Approach 3 believed it was appropriate to consider the sale of the product and service contract as a package when the conditions outlined in **Exhibit 4** were met.

CIRCUIT CITY'S DILEMMA

The issue of how to account for the retail sale of an extended warranty contract had initially been addressed and was thought to have been resolved in discussions between the Securities and Exchange Commission (SEC) and Highland Superstores,

Inc. in March 1989. At that time, the SEC's staff required Highland to adopt the Partial Recognition Method for extended warranty contract revenues.

However, FASB's proposed technical bulletin had now reopened discussions on the proper accounting method for extended warranty contracts, and Mike Chalifoux was concerned. He felt that if Circuit City were required to adopt the Full Deferral Method, the negative impact on shareholder's equity of the largest companies in the merchandising industry would be significant.

Given the issue's importance to Circuit City Stores and its shareholders, Mr. Chalifoux wanted to be sure his reasoning on the proper accounting policies for extended warranties was correct and that he had properly explored all sides of the issue. If so, he had to decide how to make his argument clear and persuasive in a letter to FASB on the proposed bulletin. Finally, he had to consider how corporate strategy and policy might have to change if the proposed bulletin were issued as it stood at that time.

One possible way to avoid the adverse effects of the proposed accounting change would be to continue to sell extended warranty contracts but then to resell them to another party. The resale would "lock in" the profitability of the sale, but total margins would have to be reduced somewhat to allow the buyer of the contracts to earn a profit as well. Although this method might allow Circuit City to avoid the adverse effects of the proposed accounting change, it seemed at first glance to be choosing "form over substance" by letting the accounting method drive the selection of the firm's competitive strategy.

QUESTIONS

1. Which of the three approaches to accounting for extended warranty and service contracts is most consistent with the actual substance of a sales transaction involving equipment and an extended warranty contract? Explain your selection and your reasoning fully.

2. What should Mike Chalifoux do?

EXHIBIT 1
Independent Auditors' Report

The Board of Directors and Stockholders of Circuit City Stores, Inc.:

We have audited the accompanying consolidated balance sheets of Circuit City Stores, Inc. and subsidiaries as of February 28, 1990 and 1989, and the related consolidated statements of earnings, stockholders' equity, and cash flows for each of the years in the three-year period ended February 28, 1990. These consolidated financial statements are the responsibility of the Company's management. Our responsibility is to express an opinion on these consolidated financial statements based on our audits.

We conducted our audits in accordance with generally accepted auditing standards. Those standards require that we plan and perform the audits to obtain reasonable assurance about whether the financial statements are free of material misstatement. An audit includes examining, on a test basis, evidence supporting the amounts and disclosures in the financial statements. An audit also includes assessing the accounting principles used and significant estimates made by management, as well as evaluating the overall financial statement presentation. We believe that our audits provide a reasonable basis for our opinion.

In our opinion, the consolidated financial statements referred to above present fairly, in all material respects, the financial position of Circuit City Stores, Inc. and subsidiaries at February 28, 1990 and 1989, and the results of their operations and their cash flows for each of the years in the three-year period ended February 28, 1990, in conformity with generally accepted accounting principles.

KPMG Peat Marwick
Richmond, Virginia
April 5, 1990

EXHIBIT 1 (*continued*)
Circuit City Stores, Inc. Consolidated Statements of Earnings ($ in thousands, except per-share data)

Years Ended February 28 or 29	1990	1989	1988
Net sales and operating revenues (note 9)	$2,096,588	$1,721,497	$1,350,425
Cost of sales, buying and warehousing	1,477,502	1,219,570	961,345
Gross profit	619,086	501,927	389,080
Selling, general and administrative expenses (note 9)	482,229	379,045	291,489
Interest expense	8,757	8,382	8,391
Total expenses	490,986	387,427	299,880
Earnings before income taxes	128,100	114,500	89,200
Provision for income taxes	50,000	45,025	38,800
Net earnings	$ 78,100	$ 69,475	$ 50,400
Average common shares outstanding—primary	46,068	45,542	44,850
Net earnings per common share:			
Primary and fully diluted	**$1.70**	$1.52	$1.12

EXHIBIT 1 (*continued*)
Circuit City Stores, Inc. Consolidated Balance Sheets ($ in thousands)

At February 28	1990	1989
Assets		
Current assets:		
Cash and cash equivalents	$ 91,712	$ 46,124
Accounts and notes receivable	9,721	11,558
Merchandise inventory	331,244	302,596
Other current assets	9,531	6,615
Total current assets	442,208	366,893
Property and equipment, net	250,006	206,052
Deferred income taxes	6,460	3,023
Other assets	14,981	11,513
Total assets	$713,655	$587,481
Liabilities and stockholders' equity:		
Current liabilities:		
Current installments of long-term debt	$ 2,038	$ 2,002
Accounts payable	165,545	143,426
Accrued expenses and other liabilities	31,837	26,957
Accrued income taxes	22,823	19,765
Total current liabilities	222,243	192,150
Long-term debt	93,882	94,674
Other liabilities	66	79
Deferred revenue	38,178	26,961
Total liabilities	354,369	313,864
Stockholders' equity:		
Common stock of $1 par value	45,860	22,617
Capital in excess of par value	17,454	29,710
Retained earnings	295,972	221,290
Total stockholders' equity	359,286	273,617
Total liabilities and stockholders' equity	$713,655	$587,481

EXHIBIT 1 (*continued*)
Circuit City Stores, Inc. Consolidated Statements of Cash Flows ($ in thousands)

Years Ended February 28 or 29	1990	1989	1989
Operating activities:			
Net earnings	$ 78,100	$ 69,475	$ 50,400
Adjustments to reconcile net earnings to net cash provided by operating activities:			
Depreciation and amortization	21,890	16,981	13,592
Deferred revenue	11,217	8,086	7,266
Loss on sale of property and equipment	262	70	157
Decrease (increase) in accounts and notes receivable	1,837	(4,423)	5,184
Increase in merchandise inventory, deferred income taxes and other assets	(36,873)	(96,754)	(58,636)
Increase in accounts payable, accrued expenses, and other liabilities	30,044	75,309	16,448
Net cash provided by operating activities	106,477	68,744	34,411
Investing activities:			
Purchases of property and equipment	(110,879)	(81,948)	(74,186)
Proceeds from sale of property and equipment	43,177	14,091	52,404
Net cash used in investing activities	(67,702)	(67,857)	(21,782)
Financing activities:			
Additions to long-term debt	1,227	—	146
Principal payments on long-term debt	(1,983)	(1,359)	(4,378)
Proceeds from issuance of common stock	10,987	5,206	3,410
Dividends paid	(3,418)	(2,477)	(1,668)
Net cash provided (used) by financing activities	6,813	1,370	(2,490)
Increase in cash and cash equivalents	45,588	2,257	10,139
Cash and cash equivalents at beginning of year	46,124	43,867	33,728
Cash and cash equivalents at end of year	$ 91,712	$46,124	$43,867
Supplemental disclosures of cash-flow information:			
Cash paid during the year for:			
Interest	$ 11,928	$ 10,043	$ 11,129
Income taxes	49,007	32,173	38,561

1. *Summary of Significant Accounting Policies*

(G) Deferred Revenue: The Company sells extended warranty contracts beyond the normal manufacturers' warranty period, usually with terms of coverage (including the manufacturers' warranty period) between 12 and 60 months. A portion of the extended warranty contract revenue is recognized immediately, and the remainder is deferred and recognized in income in a systematic manner over the contract period. The portion deferred represents an estimate of future costs under the contract plus a profit margin based on the combined profit of the sale of the product and contract. Direct costs under the contract are charged to expenses as incurred.

9. *Supplementary Income Statement Information*

Net extended warranty contract revenue, which is included in net sales and operating revenues in the accompanying consolidated statements of earnings, amounted to $112,933,000, $92,808,000, and $70,800,000 (5.4%, 5.4%, and 5.2%, respectively, of net sales and operating revenues) in fiscal years 1990, 1989, and 1988, respectively.

Advertising expense, which is included in selling, general and administrative expenses in the accompanying consolidated statements of earnings, amounted to $129,177,000, $102,626,000, and $77,702,000 (6.2%, 6.0%, and 5.8%, respectively, of net sales and operating revenues) in fiscal years 1990, 1989, and 1988, respectively.

EXHIBIT 2
Support for Full Revenue Recognition in the Sale of an Extended Warranty Contract

Guidance for revenue recognition is provided in the Statement of Financial Accounting Concepts No. 5, "Recognition and Measurement in Financial Statements of Business Enterprises." Revenue must be both realized and earned prior to the recognition. In the case of the sale of an extended warranty, all the cash is received at the time the extended warranty is sold. Thus, the first criterion is met at the time of sale.

Further, revenue is considered to have been earned when the entity has substantially accomplished what it must do to be entitled to the benefits represented by the revenues. At the time of sale, an entity will be considered to have substantially completed the earning process if:

- It incurs the selling costs (the single largest cost).
- It has an established service network, which is there for the most part to provide the customer with the service associated with the manufacturer's warranty.
- Relatively few customers call for service during the extended period.
- There is a deductible (i.e., the customer must make a cash payment to obtain service), which in large part offsets the cost of the service to be provided.
- Estimates can be made with relative certainty as to future costs to be incurred under the extended warranty.

Thus the earning process is complete at the time of sale.

Appropriate revenue recognition principles require that all relevant tests as to certainty of revenue collection, relative risks associated with future anticipated costs, and the significance of such costs be considered.

Mike Chalifoux, for example, felt that deferral of revenue was not required because of uncertainties. In Circuit City's case, the revenues from extended warranties were collected at the time of the sale; the extended warranty was not subject to cancellation and prorated return of fee like an insurance policy. Thus no uncertainties existed as to realization. A long historical experience had shown that costs incurred to "perform under the contracts" after the year of sale could be estimated with great certainty and were small in relation to the extended-warranty-revenue amount. Costs were even smaller when considering the combined revenue from the sale of merchandise and the contract, thus representing an inconsequential future cost and low relative risk. These low uncertainties and low future costs were such that the deferral-of-revenue method would not be justifiable for Circuit City, and an argument might be made for using full revenue recognition.

EXHIBIT 3
Support for Deferral of Revenue on the Sale of an Extended Warranty Contract

The AICPA proposed Statement of Position (SOP), "Accounting for Certain Service Transactions," attempts to define criteria for determining when a service or product is incidental to a transaction.

The draft SOP acknowledges that determining when a service or product is incidental to a transaction can be difficult. According to the draft SOP, the following may indicate an incidental nature:

1. The inclusion of the product or service does not result in a variance in the total transaction price from what would be charged excluding that product or service.
2. The product is not sold or the service is not rendered separately in the seller's normal business.

(According to the draft SOP, "if a service is incidental to the sale of a product, the transaction would be accounted for as a product transaction.")

Proponents of Approach 2 believed that the draft SOP would support accounting for the sale of an appliance or electronic item, for example, a stereo, and an extended warranty contract was incidental and would be accounted for separately. Customers clearly had the option to purchase the stereo without the service contract. Both the stereo and service contract had distinctly separate prices. Therefore, two transactions had taken place that required different accounting treatments.

The draft SOP further stated that if separate service transaction accounting was warranted, revenue on the service contract would be recognized on the basis of the seller's performance of the transaction. The draft SOP stated that performance was "the execution of a defined act or acts or occurs with the passage of time." The draft SOP would support recognition of the revenue over the contract period. Direct costs of providing the service would be recognized as incurred.

Proponents of Approach 2 also looked to the FASB's Statement of Financial Accounting Standards No. 60, "Accounting and Reporting by Insurance Enterprises," which discussed accounting for short-duration insurance contracts. Short-duration insurance contracts provided insurance protection for a short fixed period and enabled the insurer to cancel the contract or adjust the provisions of the contract at the end of any contract period. Statement No. 60 said that premiums from such contracts ordinarily were earned and recognized as revenue over the period of the contract. Costs under the insurance contract were recognized as insured events occurred. Proponents of Approach 2 believed that service contracts were similar to insurance contracts. The seller insured that certain services would be provided and repair claims would be covered. Therefore, in their view the accounting for service contracts should follow Statement No. 60.

At least one automobile manufacturer that sold extended warranty contracts followed Approach 2, but it also attempted to spread costs out evenly over the contract period similar to the manner in which revenue was recognized.

EXHIBIT 4
Support for Partial Revenue Recognition on the Sale of an Extended Warranty Contract

It is appropriate to consider the sale of the product and extended warranty contracts as a package when the following conditions are met:

1. The pricing of the sale of an extended warranty contract is an integral part of pricing the related product (that is, a substantial portion of customers purchasing the product also purchase extended warranty contracts and, therefore, the retailer prices the product and contract assuming both will be sold).

2. The extended warranty contract relates to a product sold by the company (sales of contracts unaccompanied by product sales should be rare and only incidental to the company's business).

3. The profit margin on the extended warranty contract is unusually high in comparison to the profit margin on the product.

4. The estimated costs to be incurred to render services under the contract can be estimated with a high degree of reliability and are nominal in relation to the service contract sales price.

When the above conditions were met, supporters of Partial Revenue Recognition would recognize a portion of the combined revenue based on the relative costs of the product and extended warranty and service.

Accounting for Property, Plant, and Equipment and Other Assets

Expenditures for property and capital equipment represent a commitment of some of an organization's resources to investments that are likely to be utilized over several periods. The *matching concept* requires that the cost of such investments be matched with the revenues in the periods in which benefits are obtained by using the capital equipment. For buildings and equipment, the amount of expense matched with revenues is called *depreciation*. If the asset is a natural resource, such as forest land or mineral deposits, similar expenses might be called *depletion*. If the assets are intangible, the original cost is said to be *amortized* over the periods when benefits are obtained, or in some cases, over an arbitrary period.

In practice, accounting for the cost of assets that provide benefits over several periods (also called *fixed assets*) consists of three distinct phases: determining the cost of a fixed asset, amortizing the cost over the useful life of the asset, and removing it from the accounts at the end of the asset's life.

THE COST OF FIXED ASSETS

The cost of the fixed asset and the amount at which it will be initially measured in reports consist of the total amount of expenditures necessary to ready the asset for its intended use. To the price of acquiring legal title to ownership of an asset are added costs of delivery, installation, training of employees, and modification of facilities that are necessary in order to use the asset as planned. (**Exhibit 1** is an illustration of how the cost of a new asset might be measured.)

ESTIMATING DEPRECIATION

At the beginning of the life of an asset, an estimate of the asset's *salvage value* is made. The salvage value is the expected selling price of the asset less any removal costs at the end of its useful life to the organization. The difference between the cost and the salvage value is called the *depreciable cost*, and it is this cost that is to be

Professor William J. Bruns, Jr. prepared this case. HBS cases are developed solely as the basis for class discussion. Cases are not intended to serve as endorsements, sources of primary data, or illustrations of effective or ineffective management.

matched in some way to revenues earned in the accounting periods over which the asset will be used.

Determining depreciation expense using generally accepted accounting principles is not particularly difficult. Having determined depreciable cost, all that remains is to select a method for allocating that cost to periods when the asset will be used to generate revenues. The market prices provided by an asset purchase and an eventual sale provide information about an asset's value at those times. However, in between these points of time, when commonly used depreciation methods are employed, there is no assurance that the asset values are accurately estimated by the unamortized cost reported in the statement of financial position.

In allocating the depreciable cost, any one of several methods is acceptable. Although the methods may appear to be arbitrary, they meet two criteria. The most important criterion requires that the amount of depreciation charged is not subject to manipulation by management in such a way that income for any period can be capriciously distorted. The second criterion is that the amounts charged bear some resemblance to the decline in value of the asset measured on an historical cost basis. There are three methods of depreciation in common use with occasional variations in each: straight-line depreciation, declining balance depreciation, and sum-of-the-years' digits depreciation.

Straight-line Depreciation

Under the straight-line method of depreciation, an equal portion of the depreciable cost is charged according to some measure of the length of an asset's life. The measure may be periods of time, or it may be units of product. Under this method, as under any of the methods of depreciation commonly used, the amount charged to expense is usually accumulated and shown in statements of financial position as a deduction from the historical cost of the asset. This *accumulated depreciation* is called a *contra asset*. It is always associated with the asset to which it is related, and its balance offsets part of the original cost that has already been matched against revenues. **Exhibit 2** shows how depreciation can be estimated using the straight-line method.

Declining Balance Depreciation

In an attempt to reflect the fact that an asset is often most productive in the early years of its use in an organization, accountants often employ methods that charge a larger proportion of the total depreciation expense in the early years of life than in later periods. One common method for accomplishing this is to charge to each period a fixed percentage of the *original cost of the asset less any previously accumulated depreciation* (note the difference from straight-line depreciation in which the depreciation rate is applied to the entire depreciable cost of the asset each period). Commonly, this percentage will be 150% or 200% of the depreciation rate used under the straight-line method. Because the declining balance method will never completely amortize the original cost of an asset, it is customary not to deduct salvage value of the asset from the original cost prior to applying the depreciation percentage. **Exhibit 3** shows how depreciation can be estimated using the declining balance method.

GAIN OR LOSS ON DISPOSAL OF ASSET

A decision to sell or otherwise dispose of a fixed asset may come any time after it is acquired. In some cases, assets thought to be useful to the firm will prove not to be so useful. It may be that they are more valuable to the organization when sold for cash. For this reason, assets are sometimes sold before the end of their original expected useful life, so that the resources committed to them can be redeployed more effectively.

In other situations, assets may be held over a longer period of time than expected and employed in their intended uses very profitably. At some point, however, the cost of maintenance and repair necessary to maintain a favorable stream of income for the organization becomes prohibitive, and the asset must be sold or scrapped. In other cases, technological developments will cause an asset to become obsolete. Assets can also be sold or exchanged for another asset. Occasionally, however, an organization may have to pay to have a useless asset destroyed or hauled away.

When an asset is sold or otherwise disposed of, it is usually necessary to account for the fact that earlier estimates about the salvage value or life of the asset were not correct. Differences between the *book value* and the amount actually obtained upon disposal are shown either as a gain or loss in the period in which the asset disposal takes place. Although gains and losses resulting from the disposal of assets represent miscalculations made in other periods, it is usually not considered necessary to adjust estimates of income in those earlier periods except in the most extreme cases.

Typically, the used asset is sold, and the items relating to the asset disappear from the accounts of the firm. We use the difference between the book value of the assets and the amount of cash or other resources received to determine whether or not the gain or loss on disposal of the asset should be recognized. In either case, the cash received from the sale is not included in revenue, and the amount of gain or loss is usually reported separately in the income statement as gain or loss on sale of assets.

SOME FINAL COMMENTS ABOUT DEPRECIATION

This note has introduced in a cursory way three methods of allocating as expense all or part of the original cost of an asset over the life of that asset. Other methods have been proposed, and some are employed by business organizations. The importance of the depreciation estimate lies in its relationship to the proper determination of income. While the criterion of accurate estimation of periodic income should dictate the choice of depreciation method, in practice other criteria often dominate: simplicity of application, tax and other legal requirements, or the desire on the part of management to show earnings more favorable or less favorable than those that would be shown if another method were used. Estimates of depreciation expense, therefore, must be used and interpreted with great care.

One other aspect of depreciation accounting deserves mention. We have dealt with the depreciation of individual assets because this was the easiest way to illustrate different methods of depreciation. In practice, however, a large firm may have many assets of a certain type, for example, personal computers. The problems of accounting for acquisition, depreciation, and disposal of these types of assets may not be too different from those encountered when accounting for inventory. Sometimes, when there are large numbers of similar items, rather than keep track of each asset, accountants find it more feasible to depreciate them as a group. A full discussion of methods of *group depreciation* or *composite depreciation* is unnecessary, but you should be aware of the fact that such groupings are frequently used to simplify the recording and reporting tasks.

ACCOUNTING FOR LAND

Like other fixed assets, land is recorded in the accounting records at the cost needed to upgrade it to the condition necessary for its intended use. Purchase price, fees or taxes incurred in the purchase, the cost of clearing or grading land, or the cost of developing drainage would all be included in the amount of cost for purchase of a tract of land. In contrast to other fixed assets, land is not depreciated and is held at original cost until such time as it is sold, traded, or abandoned.

ACCOUNTING FOR LONG-TERM INVESTMENTS IN OTHER ORGANIZATIONS

Organizations often find it in their interest to acquire an investment in companies that they regard as subsidiaries. These investments in subsidiaries are considered long term. If the investment in a subsidiary is 20% or less of the total ownership of the subsidiary, the investment is usually accounted for using a *cost method*. The investment is carried at its original cost in the owning company's accounts, and any dividends are reported as current income.

If the investment in the affiliated company is greater than 20% but less than 50%, the parent company will usually account for the investment using a method known as the *equity method*. In this method, a share of the subsidiary's earnings proportional to the share of company ownership is added to the investment in the company accounts, whether the earnings have been distributed as dividends or not. If dividends are paid by the subsidiary, they reduce the equity investment shown in the parent company's account.

When ownership in a subsidiary exceeds 50% of the total ownership, consolidation of the accounts of both parent and subsidiary on a line-by-line basis is normally required. In these cases, other owners' interest may appear as a liability under the title *minority interest in subsidiaries*.

ACCOUNTING FOR INTANGIBLE ASSETS AND GOODWILL

In spite of their desire to produce the most useful information and reports, accountants frequently ignore many intangibles in statements of financial position. Unless intangibles have been purchased, it is difficult to estimate their value with any precision. Instead, expenditures for the purposes of developing trademarks or advertising programs which create customer loyalty, or research and development expenditures are expensed in the periods they are incurred. Current income is reduced during the period in which the expenditures are made, and no recognition is given to future benefits that may accrue from these expenditures.

One common intangible asset frequently found in financial reports is *goodwill*. When one company purchases another, paying more than fair value of the net assets of the acquired company, the difference is called goodwill and may be shown as an asset on the balance sheet of the purchasing firm. In the United States, management must test at least each year the reported amount of goodwill for impairment. If the goodwill is no longer worth the amount paid for it, the reported amount of goodwill must be reduced by the amount of the impairment.

If the tangible assets such as patents, trademarks, or software are purchased, they should be amortized over their estimated useful lives.

Plant assets, intangible assets, and other assets reported by the Gillette Company and Subsidiary Companies in its consolidated balance sheet for 2003 and 2004 are shown in **Exhibit 4**, along with the associated footnotes. In particular, the notes to financial statements illustrate several of the ideas and financial reporting concepts that have been discussed in this note.

EXHIBIT 1
Measuring the Cost of a New Asset

Western Metallurgical purchased a new laboratory furnace on January 1, 2004. The price of the new furnace was $13,000, but the manufacturer agreed to allow a trade-in of $3,000 for an old furnace and a $500 discount because Western agreed to pay $9,500 cash for the balance. To the $12,500 given in exchange for the new furnace, the following items were added to the cost of the new asset: $500 for freight charges for delivery, $2,000 paid to an electrician and engineer for installation, and $1,000 paid to reimburse two key employees for expenses incurred while visiting the manufacturer's plant in another city to receive instructions on operating the new equipment. The cost of the asset, and hence a measure of its value on the first day it was ready for operation, was estimated to be $16,000, as shown below.

Cost of New Laboratory Furnace—January 1, 2004

Cash paid for new furnace:		
Purchase price	$13,000	
Less: Trade-in allowance	3,000	
Less: Discount for cash	500	
	$ 9,500	
Value of old furnace		3,000
Total assets paid		$12,500
Freight charges for delivery		500
Installation costs		2,000
Training costs for employees		1,000
Total cost		$16,000

EXHIBIT 2
Estimating Straight-line Depreciation

Following the purchase of the new furnace, the management of Western Metallurgical turned to the problem of selecting a method of depreciation. It estimated that the furnace would have a salvage value of $6,000 at the end of its useful life of five years. Thus, the depreciable cost was estimated to be $10,000.

The accountant suggested that the $10,000 depreciable cost could be allocated on a straight-line basis at a rate of $2,000 per year over the five years the furnace would be used. As an alternative, he suggested that the firm might estimate the total number of pounds of metal that would be melted in the furnace over the five-year period and then charge depreciation expense in relation to the amount of metal melted as a proportion of the expected total. Management expected that it would melt about 250,000 pounds of metal in the next five years; therefore in each year, depreciation expense would be calculated by taking the number of pounds of metal melted and multiplying it by $.04. The depreciation expense that might be shown if the straight-line method were adopted is shown below:

Straight-Line Depreciation Schedule for Laboratory Furnace

Depreciable cost:

Price of furnace	$13,000
Less: Discount	500
	$12,500
Freight charge	500
Installation	2,000
Training expenses	1,000
Total cost	$16,000
Less: Salvage value	6,000
Depreciable cost	$10,000

Estimated life: 5 years
Expected metal melt: 250,000 pounds

Schedule of depreciation expense:

Year	Expected Melt (in pounds)	Time Base	Use Base
1	40,000	$ 2,000	$ 1,600
2	45,000	2,000	1,800
3	50,000	2,000	2,000
4	55,000	2,000	2,200
5	60,000	2,000	2,400
Total	250,000	$10,000	$10,000

EXHIBIT 3
Estimating Declining Balance Depreciation

Depreciable cost: $16,000
Estimated life: 5 years
Schedule of depreciation expense:

Year	Book Value at Beginning of Year	Depreciation Expense (40% of book value)	Book Value at End of Year
1	$16,000	$ 6,400	$9,600
2	9,600	3,840	5,760
3	5,760	2,304	3,456
4	3,456	1,382	2,074
5	2,074	829	1,245
Total		$14,755	

Management was disturbed by the fact that the use of this method would depreciate the asset by such an amount that the reported value after the second year would be less than the expected salvage value and that it would apparently show a large gain when the asset was sold at the end of its useful life. Its accountant explained that it would be possible to find a percentage rate that would exactly amortize the $10,000 depreciable cost over the five-year period if it preferred to do that rather than use an arbitrary 200% of the straight-line depreciation rate.

EXHIBIT 4
Noncurrent Assets, The Gillette Company and Subsidiary Companies

Excerpt from Consolidated Balance Sheets

At December 31,	2003	2002
	(millions)	
Property, plant and equipment, net	3,642	3,565
Goodwill	1,023	962
Intangible assets, net	496	400
Other assets	1,144	1,139

Notes to Consolidated Financial Statements

Property, Plant and Equipment

At December 31,	2003	2002
	(millions)	
Land	$ 79	$ 81
Buildings	929	844
Machinery and equipment	6,077	5,504
	7,085	6,429
Less accumulated depreciation	3,443	2,864
Total	$3,642	$3,565

Interest on funds used to finance construction of significant additions to tangible property and equipment is capitalized and recorded as part of the asset to which it relates and is amortized over the asset's estimated useful life. During 2003, 2002, and 2001, interest cost was capitalized in the amounts of $2 million, $4 million, and $11 million, respectively.

Property, Plant and Equipment

Property, plant and equipment are stated at cost. Depreciation is computed primarily on a straight-line basis over the estimated useful lives of assets: buildings and building equipment, five to 40 years, machinery and equipment, three to 20 years.

Intangible Assets

The Company accounts for intangible assets in accordance with Statement of Financial Accounting Standards (SFAS) 142, "Goodwill and Other Intangible Assets," which was adopted by the Company on January 1, 2002. In accordance with that statement, goodwill and intangible assets with indefinite lives are not amortized, but rather are tested for impairment, at least annually. Intangible assets with estimable useful lives, consisting primarily of patents, trademarks, software, and other similar items, are amortized on a straight-line basis over the estimated useful lives of three to 40 years, and are reviewed for impairment in accordance with SFAS No. 144, "Accounting for the Impairment of Long-Lived Assets."

For 2001, goodwill was amortized using the straight-line method, generally over a period of 40 years. Other intangible assets, consisting primarily of trademarks, trade names, patents, and other similar items, were amortized on the straight-line method over a period of 10 to 40 years, predominantly 40 years.

Impairment of Goodwill and Long-Lived Assets

Goodwill and intangible assets with indefinite lives are tested at least annually for impairment in accordance with the provisions of SFAS 142. The Company's impairment review is based on a discounted cash flow approach, at the segment reporting level that requires significant management judgment with respect to revenue and expense growth rates, changes in working capital, and the selection and use of an appropriate discount rate. The Company uses its judgment in assessing whether assets may have become impaired between annual impairment tests. Indicators such as unexpected adverse business conditions, economic factors, unanticipated technological change, or competitive activities, loss of key personnel, and acts by governments and courts, may signal that an asset has become impaired.

Intangible assets with estimable lives and other long-lived assets are reviewed for impairment whenever events or changes in circumstances indicate that the carrying amount of an asset or asset group may not be recoverable in accordance with SFAS 144. Recoverability of intangible assets with estimable lives and other long-lived assets is measured by a comparison of the carrying amount of an asset or asset group to future net undiscounted pretax cash flows expected to be generated by the asset or asset group. If these comparisons indicate that an asset is not recoverable, the impairment loss recognized is the amount by which the carrying amount of the asset or asset group exceeds the related estimated fair value. Estimated fair value is based on either discounted future pretax operating cash flows or appraised values, depending on the nature of the asset. The Company determines the discount rate for this analysis based on the expected internal rate of return for the related business and does not allocate interest charges to the asset or asset group being measured. Considerable judgment is required to estimate discount future operating cash flows.

Goodwill and Intangible Assets

In August 2003, the Company acquired a majority interest in Fujian Nanping Nanfu Battery Co., Ltd., a leading battery company in China. The Nanfu business is reported as part of the Duracell segment. The change between December 31, 2003, and December 31, 2002, goodwill and intangible balance is due mainly to the acquisition of Nanfu, and the impact of foreign currency translation. The Nanfu acquisition resulted in the capitalization of the Nanfu trademark as an indefinite-lived intangible asset, as well as other definite-lived intangible assets. The value of these intangibles, as well as the related goodwill, may be adjusted in future periods as the purchase price allocation for the acquisition is not yet final.

Total goodwill by segment follows.

At December 31,	2003	2002
	(millions)	
Blades & razors	$ 140	$140
Duracell	632	571
Oral care	191	191
Braun	60	60
Personal care	—	—
Total	$1,023	$962

The detail of intangible assets follows.

At December 31,	Weighted Average Amortization Period (Years)	2003		2002	
		Carrying Amount	Accumulated Amortization	Carrying Amount	Accumulated Amortization
Amortized Intangible Assets					
Patents	8	$101	$ 69	$101	$ 53
Trademarks	7	16	9	13	4
Software	5	14	12	12	9
Endorsements	—	61	61	61	61
Other	19	23	3	11	3
Total	7	$215	$154	$198	$130
Unamortized Intangible Assets					
Trademarks		$423		$317	
Pension		12		15	
Total		$435		$332	
Intangible Assets, net		$496		$400	

Aggregate Amortization Expense:
For the Years ended December 31:

2003	$21
2002	$20
2001	$56

Estimated Amortization Expense:
For the Years ended December 31:

2004	$21
2005	$9
2006	$5
2007	$5
2008	$4

Other Assets

At December 31,	2003	2002
	(millions)	
Pension	$ 747	$710
Benefit trusts	183	160
Derivatives (swaps and forward contracts)	83	135
Other	131	134
Total	$1,144	$1,139

Depreciation at Delta Air Lines and Singapore Airlines (A)

Property, plant, and equipment (PP&E) is a significant asset category of most airline companies. PP&E usually constitutes more than 50% of the total assets of an airline, and depreciation of these assets is a major operating expense.

However, unlike many expenses—for example, salaries, the cost of aircraft fuel, the cost of meals and beverages, all of which are significant operating expenses for airlines—depreciation of PP&E is different in that the methods and estimates used to determine the amount of this expense can vary widely among companies. Moreover, the methods and estimates used can have a significant impact on companies' reported earnings. Thus, unless the user of financial statements sifts through the footnotes to sort out the details, comparability among companies within an industry can be problematic.

Consider, for example, the depreciation practices of two major airlines—Delta Air Lines and Singapore Airlines—in 1993.

DELTA AIR LINES

Delta Air Lines was one of the major passenger airlines in the United States, with almost $12 billion in annual revenues. It served 161 cities in 44 states in the United States, and it also operated flights to 33 foreign countries. In terms of operating revenues and revenue passenger miles flown,[1] it was, in 1993, the third-largest U.S. airline. (American Airlines and United Airlines were the largest.)

Delta had been expanding its international operations. In fiscal year 1990 it entered a partnership with Singapore Airlines that was meant to coordinate some of their scheduling and marketing efforts. In November 1991, Delta purchased most of the transatlantic route authorities of Pan Am, which had gone bankrupt. Thus in fiscal year 1993, revenues from international flights represented 21% of total operat-

Research Associate Jeremy Cott prepared this case under the supervision of Professor William J. Bruns, Jr. as the basis for class discussion rather than to illustrate either effective or ineffective handling of an administrative situation.

[1] "Revenue passenger miles" is a widely used measurement of traffic volume in the airline industry. It represents the number of miles flown by all revenue-paying passengers.

ing revenues. This represented a large increase from earlier years, but it was still a smaller proportion of total revenues than what was the case for some other major carriers. (For example, in 1993, 38% of United's revenues, and 26% of American's, came from international flights.) Although Delta was the third-largest U.S. airline in terms of operating revenues and revenue passenger miles flown, it was the largest in terms of the number of airline departures and the number of passengers carried.

Exhibit 1 shows key financial and operational data for Delta for the years 1989 through 1993.

Delta was in the throes of difficulties affecting most American airlines. Deregulation of the industry in 1978 had led to increasing price competition; in the 1980s and early 1990s, airline fares didn't even remotely keep pace with inflation. Major carriers like Delta—with high cost structures left over from an earlier, regulated environment—were hit hard by competition from low-cost, no-frills airlines like Southwest and People's Express. In the late 1980s and early 1990s, the difficulties mounted: Iraq's invasion of Kuwait discouraged passenger travel and caused fuel prices to skyrocket; the American economy went into a recession; and fare wars intensified. In four years, 1990–1993, the American airline industry as a whole lost $12.8 billion. Delta went about reassessing its marketing programs and cutting back on staff in an effort to control costs. "The work we are doing to cut costs and raise revenues," the 1993 Annual Report stated, "fits within a comprehensive effort to transform our Company into a high performing organization."

Delta's property and equipment totaled $7.1 billion on its 1993 balance sheet. The largest part of this ($5.5 billion) consisted of aircraft and other flight equipment. (See **Exhibits 2** and **3**, which show the dollar values of Delta's fixed assets and the composition of its aircraft fleet.) The average age of Delta's aircraft was 8.8 years, which was relatively young by industry standards. Among other major airlines, the average age of aircraft varied a good deal. At American and United, the two largest passenger airlines in the United States, the average age of aircraft was 8.9 and 10.8 years, respectively. At Continental, the fifth-largest airline, it was 15.3. At TWA, the seventh largest, it was 18.7. (There was no necessary connection, however, between the average age of an airline's fleet and the assumption it made regarding the fleet's depreciable life.)

In April 1993 Delta announced a change in its depreciation assumptions regarding flight equipment. The last time Delta had made such a change had been in July 1986. (See the excerpts from the footnotes to Delta's financial statements, regarding this, in **Exhibit 4**.)[2]

SINGAPORE AIRLINES

Singapore Airlines was the largest private-sector employer in Singapore's booming economy. At the end of fiscal year 1993, its route network covered 70 cities in 40 countries. Singapore was a transit point for a good deal of travel in Asia, but the

---

[2] During fiscal year 1993 Delta also changed one of its assumptions regarding pension accounting. "Effective April 1, 1993, Delta increased from 9% to 10% its assumption regarding the expected return on plan assets associated with defined benefit pension plans. This change in accounting estimate resulted in a decrease in pension expense of $12.7 million in fiscal 1993, and is expected to reduce pension expense by an estimated $56 million in fiscal 1994." (1993 Annual Report)

airline also handled a lot of traffic to other continents: for example, it flew regularly to the United States across both the Atlantic and Pacific Oceans, and flew nonstop to and from London nine times a week. Of its total operating revenues, about 44% came from flights to Asia, 23% from flights to Europe, 22% from flights to North and South America, and 11% from flights to the Southwest Pacific. In fiscal year 1993 its total operating revenues ($5.1 billion in Singapore dollars, $3.1 billion in U.S. dollars) would have made it the seventh-largest airline in the United States—larger, for example, than Trans World Airlines and Southwest.[3]

Exhibit 5 shows key financial and operational data for Singapore for the years 1989 through 1993.

The airline was renowned for its high level of customer service, geared largely to business travelers. Year after year, it won awards from various trade associations and travel magazines for the quality of its service. The average age of its aircraft was 5.1 years, which was the youngest of any major airline in the world. (See **Exhibits 6** and **7**, which show the dollar values of Singapore's fixed assets and the composition of its aircraft fleet.) According to an industry publication, Singapore's exclusive MEGATOP 747-400, which it bought from Boeing, was "the largest, fastest long-haul aircraft in the world, offering state-of-the-art technology and comfort."[4]

Much of the Asian airline market was regulated. Moreover, slightly more than half of Singapore Airlines' common stock was owned by the Singapore government. However, the company received no government subsidy and operated under most of the usual pressures from international competition and the investment community. Its stock was followed by more than 20 investment analysts.

Asian airlines at this time were generally more profitable than American airlines, but they definitely did not feel immune to the problems in the industry. In 1993, Singapore Airlines' net profit dropped (in Singapore dollars) from $922 million to $741 million—or (in American dollars) from $555 million to $452 million. In its Annual Report for the year, the company said that the year had been "a difficult one for most airlines. The industry continued to be saddled with huge financial losses.... Singapore Airlines was not spared." As a result, the company's briefing for reporters was held at a much more modest hotel than usual, and staff bonuses were reduced from the 3.4 months of the previous year to a half-month. The company said that it was continuing with its expansion plans, expecting an eventual recovery in the business cycle. Its capital expenditures, however, were running about $2 billion a year (Singapore dollars), and, as a result, the company's Annual Report said, "it is possible that, in a few years' time, we shall have to incur debt."[5]

During fiscal year 1993, the company's assumptions regarding its depreciation of flight equipment remained unchanged. The last time Singapore had changed its depreciation policy regarding flight equipment had been in April 1989. (See the ex-

---

[3] Singapore Airlines was actually a wholly owned subsidiary of a holding company named SIA, 90% of whose revenues came from the airline operation. All of the financial and operating data cited in this case regarding Singapore Airlines, however, pertains solely to Singapore Airlines, not the holding company. (The holding company's other investments were in engineering and airport terminal services, a regional airline, and various hotel properties.)

[4] *Business Wire*, November 29, 1996.

[5] *Business Times* in Singapore reported on May 20, 1993, that "even with the lower earnings" in fiscal year 1993, Singapore Airlines "retained its position as the world's most profitable airline." The company's director of corporate affairs reported a conversation he had with an industry analyst in which "the analyst said that if an American airline had reported such figures, the market would have rejoiced at the news." In response, the company's director of corporate affairs said to the analyst, "You must forgive the local press because it is influenced by the performance of other Singapore companies."

cerpts from the footnotes to Singapore's financial statements, regarding this, in **Exhibit 8**.)

QUESTIONS

1. Calculate the annual depreciation expense that Delta and Singapore would record for each $100 gross value of aircraft.

    (a) For Delta, what was its annual depreciation expense (per $100 of gross aircraft value) prior to July 1, 1986; from July 1, 1986 through March 31, 1993; and from April 1, 1993 on?

    (b) For Singapore, what was its annual depreciation expense (per $100 of gross aircraft value) prior to April 1, 1989; and from April 1, 1989 on?

2. Are the differences in the ways that the two airlines account for depreciation expense significant? Why would companies depreciate aircraft using different depreciable lives and salvage values? What reasons could be given to support these differences? Is different treatment proper?

3. Assuming the average value of flight equipment that Delta had in 1993, how much of a difference do the depreciation assumptions it adopted on April 1, 1993 make? How much more or less will its annual depreciation expense be compared to what it would be were it using Singapore's depreciation assumptions?

4. Singapore Airlines maintains depreciation assumptions that are very different from Delta's. What does it gain or lose by doing so? How does this relate to the company's overall strategy?

5. Does the difference in the average age of Delta's and Singapore's aircraft fleets have any impact on the amount of depreciation expense that they record? If so, how much?

EXHIBIT 1
Delta Air Lines: Key Financial and Operational Data ($ millions)

	For the fiscal years ending June 30				
	1993	1992	1991	1990	1989
Total assets	11,871	10,162	8,411	7,227	6,484
Fixed assets	7,141	7,093	5,641	5,399	4,478
Fixed assets/Total assets	60.2%	69.8%	67.1%	74.7%	69.1%
Long-term debt (including capital leases)	3,717	2,833	2,058	1,315	703
Total debt/Total assets	31.3%	27.9%	24.5%	18.2%	10.8%
Total operating revenues	11,997	10,837	9,170	8,582	8,089
Total operating expenses	12,572	11,512	9,621	8,163	7,411
Depreciation expense for fixed assets	679	585	512	453	378
Depreciation expense/ Total operating expense	5.4%	5.1%	5.3%	5.5%	5.1%
Operating profit	(575)	(674)	(450)	420	678
Operating profit/Revenues	–4.8%	–6.2%	–4.9%	4.9%	8.4%
Gain on sale of flight equipment (pretax)	65	35	17	18	17
Net profit (excluding cumulative effect of accounting change)	(415)	(506)	(324)	303	461
Net profit/Revenues	–3.5%	–4.7%	–3.5%	3.5%	5.7%
Revenue passenger miles (millions)	82,406	72,693	62,086	58,987	55,904
Number of revenue passengers carried (millions)	85	77	69	67	64
Average passenger trip length (miles)	969	944	900	880	874
Available passenger miles (millions)	132,282	123,102	104,328	96,463	90,742
Capacity utilization	62.3%	59.1%	59.5%	61.1%	61.6%

Source: Company Annual Reports and 10-Ks; ratios calculated by casewriter.

Part 2 How Accountants Measure and Report

EXHIBIT 2
Delta Air Lines: Property and Equipment ($ millions)

| | June 30 | |
	1993	1992
Flight equipment owned	9,043	8,354
Less: Accumulated depreciation	(3,559)	(3,213)
	5,484	5,141
Flight equipment under capital leases	173	173
Less: Accumulated depreciation	(128)	(112)
	45	61
Ground property and equipment	2,373	2,211
Less: Accumulated depreciation	(1,143)	(983)
	1,230	1,228
Advance payments for equipment	383	663
Total	7,142	7,093

Source: Company Annual Reports.

EXHIBIT 3
Delta Air Lines: Aircraft Fleet as of June 30, 1993

Type of Aircraft	Average Seats per Aircraft	Owned	Leased	Total
A310-200	177	3	4	7
A310-300	178	—	15	15
B727-200	148	106	43	149
B737-200	107	1	57	58
B737-300	127	3	13	16
B757-200	182	43	41	84
B767-200	204	15	—	15
B767-300	254	2	23	25
B767-300ER	218	7	7	14
L1011-1	302	32	—	32
L1011-200	300	1	—	1
L-1011-250	266	6	—	6
L1011-500	223	17	—	17
MD-11	253	1	8	9
MD-88	142	59	57	116
MD-90	150	—	—	0
Total		296	268	564

Source: Company Annual Reports.

Note: All of the aircraft shown above as "leased" were being operated under "operating" leases.

EXHIBIT 4
Delta Air Lines' Depreciation Policy

Excerpt from Delta Air Lines' "Notes to Consolidated Financial Statements" (for fiscal year 1993)

Depreciation and Amortization—Prior to April 1, 1993, substantially all of the Company's flight equipment was being depreciated on a straight-line basis to residual values (10% of cost) over a 15-year period from the dates placed in service. As a result of a review of its fleet plan, effective April 1, 1993, the Company increased the estimated useful lives of substantially all of its flight equipment. Flight equipment that was not already fully depreciated is being depreciated on a straight-line basis to residual values (5% of cost) over a 20-year period from the dates placed in service.

Excerpt from Delta Air Lines' "Notes to Consolidated Financial Statements" (for fiscal year 1987)

Depreciation and Amortization—Prior to July 1, 1986, substantially all of the Company's flight equipment was being depreciated on a straight-line basis to residual values (10% of cost) over a 10-year period from dates placed in service. As a result of a comprehensive review of its fleet plan, effective July 1, 1986, the Company increased the estimated useful lives of substantially all of its flight equipment. Flight equipment that was not already fully depreciated is now being depreciated on a straight-line basis to residual values (10% of cost) over a 15-year period from dates placed in service. The effect of this change was a $130 million decrease in depreciation . . . for the year ended June 30, 1987.

Note: Delta's assumptions regarding the depreciable life and salvage value of fixed assets other than flight equipment were quite different and were, in any case, unchanged in 1993.

EXHIBIT 5
Singapore Airlines: Key Financial and Operational Data ($ millions, Singapore dollars)

	For the fiscal years ending March 31				
	1993	1992	1991	1990	1989
Total assets	9,417	9,366	8,516	7,708	6,365
Fixed assets	6,729	5,876	4,960	4,515	3,926
Fixed assets/Total assets	71.5%	62.7%	58.2%	58.6%	61.7%
Long-term debt (including capital leases)	0	421	450	518	624
Total debt/Total assets	0.0%	4.5%	5.3%	6.7%	9.8%
Total operating revenues	5,135	5,013	4,602	4,730	4,272
Total operating expenses	4,480	4,149	3,760	3,601	3,407
Depreciation expense for fixed assets	708	614	513	439	550
Depreciation expense/ Total operating expense	15.8%	14.8%	13.6%	12.2%	16.1%
Operating profit	655	863	842	1,129	865
Operating profit/Revenues	12.8%	17.2%	18.3%	23.9%	20.2%
Gain on sale of flight equipment (pretax)	42	129	208	195	96
Net profit (excluding cumulative effect of accounting change)	741	922	887	1,177	928
Net profit/Revenues	14.4%	18.4%	19.3%	24.9%	21.7%
Revenue passenger miles (millions)	23,663	21,808	19,582	19,210	17,991
Number of revenue passengers carried (millions)	8.7	8.1	7.1	6.8	6.2
Average passenger trip length (miles)	2,720	2,692	2,758	2,825	2,902
Available passenger miles (millions)	33,174	29,659	26,063	24,523	22,789
Capacity utilization	71.3%	73.5%	75.1%	78.3%	78.9%
Note: March 31 exchange rate for conversion of Singapore dollars to U.S. dollars	$1.64	$1.66	$1.80	$1.89	$1.96

Source: Company Annual Reports and 10-Ks; ratios calculated by casewriter.

EXHIBIT 6
Singapore Airlines: Fixed Assets ($ millions, Singapore dollars)

	March 31	
	1993	1992
Flight equipment	9,224	7,814
Less: Accumulated depreciation	(3,914)	(3,330)
	5,310	4,484
Ground property and equipment	1,020	1,018
Less: Accumulated depreciation	(549)	(589)
	471	429
Advance and progress payments	947	962
Total	6,728	5,875

Source: Company Annual Reports.

EXHIBIT 7
Singapore Airlines: Aircraft Fleet as of March 31, 1993

Type of Aircraft	In operation
B747-400 (MEGATOP)	18
B747-300 (BIG TOP)	11
B747-300 (COMBI)	3
B747-200	3
B747-200 Freighter	1
B737-200 Freighter	2
B737-300 Freighter	1
A310-300	12
A310-200	6
Total	57

Source: Company Annual Reports.

Note: Singapore owned all of its aircraft; it did not operate any under "operating leases." (Confirmed by company in June 6, 1997 phone conversation.)

EXHIBIT 8
Singapore Airlines' Depreciation Policy

Excerpt from Singapore Airlines' "Notes to the Accounts" (for fiscal year 1993)

Depreciation of Fixed Assets—The Company depreciates its new aircraft, spares and spare engines over 10 years to 20% residual values. . . . For used aircraft less than 5 years old, the Company depreciates them over the remaining life (10 years less age of aircraft) to 20% residual value. In the case of used aircraft more than 5 years old, they are depreciated over 5 years to 20% residual value.

Excerpt from Singapore Airlines' "Notes to the Accounts" (for fiscal year 1990)

Depreciation of Fixed Assets—[Prior to April 1, 1989], the operational lives of the aircraft fleet were estimated to be 8 years with 10% residual values. . . . [Effective] April 1, 1989, the Company depreciated its aircraft, spares and spare engines over 10 years to 20% residual values. . . . This arises from a review of the operational lives and residual values of the aircraft fleet.

Note: Singapore's assumptions regarding the depreciable life and salvage value of fixed assets other than flight equipment were quite different and were, in any case, unchanged in 1993.

Kansas City Zephyrs Baseball Club, Inc.

On April 17, 1985, Bill Ahern sat in his office and contemplated a difficult judgment he had to make in the next two days. Two weeks before, Bill had been asked to be an arbitrator in a dispute between the Owner-Player Committee (OPC, the representatives of the owners of the 26 major league baseball teams in collective bargaining negotiations) and the Professional Baseball Players Association (PBPA, the players' union).

A BASEBALL ACCOUNTING DISPUTE

The issue Ahern had to resolve was the profitability of the major league baseball teams. The players felt they should share in the teams' profits; the owners maintained, however, that most of the teams were actually losing money each year, and they produced financial statements to support that position. The players, who had examined the owners' statements, countered that the owners were hiding profits through a number of accounting tricks and that the statements did not accurately reflect the economic reality. Ahern's decision on the profitability issue was important because it would affect the ongoing contract negotiations, particularly in the areas of minimum salaries and team contributions to the players' pension fund.

On April 9, Ahern met with the OPC and the representatives of the PBPA. They explained they wanted him to focus on the finances of the Kansas City Zephyrs Baseball Club, Inc. This club was selected for review because both sides agreed its operations were representative, yet it was a relatively clean and simple example to study: the baseball club entity was not owned by another corporation, and it did not own the stadium the team played in. Furthermore, no private financial data would have to be revealed because the corporation was publicly owned. Ahern's task was to review the Zephyrs' financial statements, hear the owners' and players' arguments, and then reach a decision as to the profitability of the team by Friday, April 19.

Research Assistant Joseph P. Mulloy prepared this case under the supervision of Professors Kenneth A. Merchant and Krishna G. Palepu as the basis for class discussion rather than to illustrate either effective or ineffective handling of an administrative situation. The case is based on publicly available information.

MAJOR LEAGUE BASEBALL

Major league baseball in the United States was comprised of a number of components bound together by sets of agreements and contractual relationships. At the heart of major league baseball were the 26 major league teams. Each team operated as an independent economic unit in such matters as contracting for players, promoting games and selling tickets, arranging for the use of a stadium and other needed facilities and services, and negotiating local broadcasting of games. The teams joined together to establish common rules and playing schedules, and to stage championship games.

The business of most teams was limited exclusively to their major league activities. Very few integrated vertically by owning their own stadium or minor league teams. Most teams were organized as partnerships or privately held corporations, although a few were subunits of larger corporations. While baseball was often thought of as a big business, the individual teams were relatively small. For most of them, annual revenues were between $20 million and $30 million.

Each team maintained an active roster of 24 players during the playing season, plus 16 minor league players "on option," who might see major league action during the season. This made a total of 40 players on major league contracts for each team at any one time. Each team played a schedule of 162 games during the season, 81 at home and 81 away.

Collectively, the team owners established most of the regulations that governed the industry. The covenant that bound them was the Major League Agreement (MLA), to which was attached the Major League Rules. The rules detailed all the procedures the clubs agreed on, including the rules for signing, trading, and dealing with players.

Under the MLA, the owners elected a commissioner of baseball for a seven-year term. The commissioner acted as a spokesperson for the industry, resolved disputes among the clubs and the other baseball entities, policed the industry, and enforced the rules. The commissioner had broad powers to protect the best interests of the game. The commissioner also administered the Major Leagues Central Fund, under which he negotiated and received the revenues from national broadcast contracts for major league games. About one-half of the fund's revenues were passed on directly to the teams in approximately equal shares.

Within the overall structure of major league baseball, the 26 teams were organized into two leagues each with its own president and administration. The American League had 14 teams and the National League had 12 teams, of which one was the Kansas City Zephyrs. Each league controlled the allocation and movement of its respective franchises. In addition to authorizing franchises, the leagues developed the schedule of games, contracted for umpires, and performed other administrative tasks. The leagues were financed through a small percentage share of club ticket revenues and receipts from the World Series and pennant championship games.

In addition to the major league teams, U.S. baseball included about 150 minor league teams located throughout the United States, Canada, and Mexico. Minor league teams served a dual function: they were entertainment entities in their own right, and they were training grounds for major league players. Through Player Development Contracts, the major league teams agreed to pay a certain portion of their affiliated minor league teams' operating expenses and player salaries.

MEETING WITH THE ZEPHYRS' OWNERS

Bill Ahern spent Tuesday reviewing the history of major league baseball and the relationships among the various entities that make up the major leagues. Then he met with the Zephyrs owners' representatives on Wednesday.

The owners' representatives gave Ahern a short history of the team and presented him with the team's financial statements for the years 1983 and 1984 (**Exhibits 1** and **2**). The current owner was a corporation with five major shareholders, which bought the team on November 1, 1982, for $24 million. The Zephyrs did not own any of their minor league teams or their stadium, but two of the Zephyrs' owners were part owners of the private corporation that owned the baseball stadium.

Ahern studied the financial statements for a short time, and then he met with Keith Strong, the owners' lawyer. The conversation can be summarized by the following exchange:

Bill: I would like to know more about the controversial items in your financial statements. First, could you please explain your players' salaries expense entries?

Keith: Sure. Here is a list of our roster players and what we paid them last year [see **Exhibit 3**]. The number we show on our 1984 income statement is the total expense of $10,097,000. Most of the expense represents cash outflows in 1984. The only exception is shown in the last column of this exhibit. For our highest paid players, we have agreed to defer a portion of their salary for 10 years. That helps save them taxes and provides them with some income after their playing days are over.

Bill: What is the nonroster guaranteed contract expense?

Keith: That is also player salary expense, but we break it out separately because the salaries are paid to players who are no longer on our active roster. The salaries are amounts we owe to players whom we released who had long-term guaranteed contracts. The amount of $750,000 represents the amount we still owe at the end of 1984 to two players shown in Figure A. Joe Portocararo, one of our veteran pitchers, signed a four-year guaranteed contract last year, but before the season started he suffered a serious injury, and Joe and the team jointly decided it was best he retire. We released U. R. Wilson in spring training, hoping that another team would pick him up and pay his salary, but none did.

FIGURE A
Calculation of Nonroster Guaranteed Contract Expense ($000)

Player	1984	1985	1986	Total
		Amount Owed		
Joe Portocararo	$300.0	$350.0	$400.0	$1,050.0
U. R. Wilson	200.0			200.0
				$1,250.0

We still owe these players the amounts in their contracts. We decided to expense the whole amount in 1984 because they are not active players; they are not serving to bring in our current revenues. We felt it was more meaningful and conservative to recognize these losses now, as they result from the effects of past decisions that did not turn out well.

Bill: Okay. Let's move on to roster depreciation expense.

Keith: When the team was bought in 1982, 50 percent of the purchase price ($12 million) was designated as the value of the player roster at that time. This amount was capitalized and is being amortized over six years.

Bill: Why 50 percent?

Keith: That is the maximum percentage that the Internal Revenue Code will allow when purchasing a sports team.

Bill: I see. Is there anything else in the statements that the players dispute?

Keith: No, I don't think so. The rest of our accounting is very straightforward. Most of our revenues and expenses result directly from a cash inflow or outflow.

Bill: Well, that answers all my questions. Thank you.

Keith: I have just one more thing to say concerning baseball finances in general. People seem to think that we generate huge profits since we have a relative monopoly, but it should be obvious that the professional baseball leagues do not exist in order to carry out traditional cartel functions. The rules and regulations governing the clubs comprising the league are essential to the creation of the league as an entity and have virtually nothing to do with pricing policies of the individual clubs. The objective of the cooperative agreements is not to constrain the economic competition among them, but rather to create the league as a joint venture that produces baseball during a season of play. Without such rules of conduct, leagues would not exist.

When this meeting was completed, Bill Ahern felt he understood the owners' accounting methods well enough.

MEETING WITH THE PLAYERS

The following Monday, Ahern met with the PBPA representatives and their lawyer, Paul Hanrahan. They presented Ahern with income statements for the years 1983 and 1984 as they thought they should be drawn up (**Exhibit 4**). As Ahern studied them, he found the players' version of the financial statements showed profits before tax of $2.9 million for 1983 and $3.0 million for 1984 as compared to the losses of $2.4 million and $2.6 million on the owners' statements.

Ahern's conversation with Paul Hanrahan went approximately as follows:

Bill: The income statements you have given me are very similar to those of the owners except for a few items.

Paul: That's true; most of the expenses are straightforward. There are only a few areas we dispute, but these areas can have a significant impact on the overall profitability of the team. We feel that the owners have used three techniques to "hide" profits: (1) roster depreciation, (2) overstated player salary expense, and (3) related-party transactions.

Bill: Let's start with roster depreciation. Why have you deleted it?

Paul: We feel it gives numbers that aren't meaningful. The depreciation expense arises only when a team is sold, so you can have two identical teams that will show dramatically different results if one had been sold and the other had not. We also don't think the depreciation is real because most of the players actually improve their skills with experience, so if anything, there should be an increase in roster value over time, not a reduction as the depreciation would lead you to believe.

Bill: Okay. I understand your reasoning. I'll have to think about that. Let's move on to the next issue.

Paul: That's player salary expense. We think the owners overstate player expense in several ways. One is that they expense the signing bonuses in the year they're paid. We feel the bonuses are just a part of the compensation package, and that for accounting purposes, the bonuses should be spread over the term of the player's contract.

We gathered information on the bonuses paid in the last four years and the contract terms [**Exhibit 5**]. Then we adjusted the owners' income statements by removing the bonuses from the current roster salary expense and by adding an "amortization of bonuses" line. The net effect of this one adjustment on 1984, for example, was an increase in income of $373,000.[1]

Bill: But the owners have really paid out all the bonuses in cash, and there is no guarantee that the players will complete their contracts.

Paul: That's partly true. Some players get hurt and are unable to compete effectively. But the number of players who do not complete their contracts is very small, and we think it is more meaningful to assume that they will continue to play over the term of their contract.

Bill: Okay. What's next?

Paul: A second adjustment we made to the players' salary line was to back out the deferred portion of the total compensation. Many of the players, particularly those who are higher paid, receive only about 80% of their salaries in any given year. They receive the rest 10 years later [**Exhibit 3**]. We feel that since the team is paying this money over a long period of time, it is misleading to include the whole amount as a current expense. This adjustment increased 1984 income for the Zephyrs by $1,521,000. No salary expense deferred from prior years was added back in because that form of contract is a relatively recent phenomenon.

Bill: I've looked at some of the contracts, and it says very clearly that the player is to receive, say, $500,000, of which $100,000 is deferred to the year 1984. Doesn't that indicate that the salary expense is $500,000?

Paul: No. The team has paid only $400,000 in cash.

Bill: Doesn't the team actually set money aside to cover the future obligation?

---

[1] $1,320,000 less $947,000.

Paul: Some teams do, and in such cases, I think we would agree that it is appropriate to recognize that amount as a current expense. But the Zephyrs don't set any money aside.

Bill: Okay. You made a third adjustment to the players' salaries.

Paul: Yes, we think the salaries due to players who are no longer on the roster should be recognized when the cash is paid out, not when the players leave the roster. Unless that is done, the income numbers will vary wildly depending on when these players are released and how large their contracts are. Furthermore, it is quite possible that these players' contracts will be picked up by another team, and the Zephyrs would then have to turn around and recognize a large gain because the liability it has set up would no longer be payable.

Bill: Okay. Let's go to the last area: related-party transactions. You have listed Stadium Operations at about 80% of what the owners charged. Why is that?

Paul: You probably know that two of the Zephyrs' owners are also involved with the stadium corporation. But what you probably don't know is that they are the sole owners of that stadium company. We think that the stadium rent is set to overcharge the team and help show a loss for the baseball operations.

Bill: How did you get your numbers?

Paul: This wasn't easy, but we looked at what other teams pay for their stadiums. Every contract is slightly different, but we are sure that two of the five shareholders in the team are earning a nice gain on the stadium-pricing agreement.

Just for your own edification, this is not the only type of related-party transaction where the owners can move profits around. A few of the teams are owned by broadcasting organizations, and as a result, they report no local broadcasting revenues. Their individual losses are consolidated into the overall major league position, thus the overall loss is overstated. I know it's hard to do, but an objective look must be taken at all these related-party transactions if baseball's true position is to be fairly stated.

The overall effect of all these adjustments we have made to the Zephyrs' income statements changes losses to profits. In 1984, the change is from a loss of $1.7 million to a profit of $1.4 million. In the labor negotiations, the owners keep claiming that they're losing money and can't afford the contract terms we feel are fair. We just don't think that's true. They are "losing money" only because they have selected accounting methods to hide their profits.

Bill: Well, you've given me a lot to think about. There are a lot of good arguments on both sides. Thank you for your time. I'll have my answer for you soon.

BILL'S DECISION

By Wednesday, April 17, Bill was quite confused. To clarify the areas of disagreement, he prepared the summaries shown in Exhibit 6, but whereas the sets of numbers were clear, the answers to the conflicts were not. Bill had expected this arbitration to be rather straightforward, but instead he was mired in difficult issues involving the accounting unit, depreciation, amortization of intangibles, and related-party transactions. Now he was faced with a tight deadline, and it was not at all obvious to him how to define "good accounting methods" for the Zephyrs Baseball Club.

EXHIBIT 1
Income Statements
Owners' Figures (000s omitted)

| | Year Ending October 31 | |
	1983	1984
Operating Revenues:		
Game Receipts	$16,526.0	$18,620.0
National Television	2,360.8	2,730.8
Local Broadcasting	3,147.9	3,575.1
Concessions	2,886.3	3,294.3
Parking	525.1	562.0
Other	786.9	843.9
Total Revenues	$26,233.0	$29,626.1
Operating Expenses:		
Spring Training	$ 545.0	$ 594.0
Team Operating Expenses		
Players' Salaries		
Current Roster	9,111.0	10,097.0
Nonroster Guaranteed		
Contract Expense	0.0	1,250.0
Coaches' Salaries	756.9	825.7
Other Salaries	239.0	260.8
Miscellaneous	2,655.9	2,897.3
Player Development	2,996.0	3,269.0
Team Replacement:		
Roster Depreciation	2,000.0	2,000.0
Scouting	672.8	734.0
Stadium Operations	4,086.0	4,457.0
Ticketing and Marketing	1,907.0	2,080.0
General and Administrative	3,541.0	3,663.0
Total Operating Expense	$28,510.6	$32,127.8
Income from Operations	(2,277.6)	(2,501.7)
Other Income (Expense)	(96.0)	(101.0)
Income Before Taxes	(2,373.6)	(2,602.7)
Federal Income Tax Benefit	855.9	944.2
Net Income (Loss)	$(1,517.7)	$(1,658.5)

EXHIBIT 2
Balance Sheets
The Owners' Figures (000s omitted)

	Year Ending October 31	
	1983	1984
Assets		
Current Assets		
Cash	$ 488.0	$ 561.0
Marketable Securities	6,738.0	7,786.1
Accounts Receivable	598.0	681.2
Notes Receivable	256.0	234.0
Total Current Assets	8,080.0	9,262.3
Property, Plant & Equipment	1,601.0	1,892.0
Less Accumulated Depreciation	(359.0)	(511.0)
Net PP&E	1,242.0	1,381.0
Initial Roster	12,000.0	12,000.0
Less Accumulated Depreciation	(4,000.0)	(6,000.0)
Net Initial Roster	8,000.0	6,000.0
Other Assets	2,143.0	4,123.2
Franchise	6,500.0	6,500.0
Total Assets	$25,965.0	$27,266.5
Liabilities and Shareholders' Equity		
Current Liabilities		
Accounts Payable	$ 909.2	$ 1,020.2
Accrued Expenses	1,207.5	1,461.8
Total Current Liabilities	2,116.7	2,482.0
Long-Term Debt	7,000.0	8,073.7
Other Long-Term Liabilities	2,443.3	3,964.3
Shareholders' Equity:		
Common Stock, par value $1 per share,		
500,000 shares issued	500.0	500.0
Additional Paid-In Capital	10,000.0	10,000.0
Retained Earnings	3,905.0	2,246.5
Total Liabilities and Shareholders' Equity	$25,965.0	$27,266.5

EXHIBIT 3
Detailed Players' Salary Summary—1984 (000s omitted)

Roster Player	Signings Bonus	Base Salary	Performance and Attendance Bonuses	Total Compensation	Portion of 1984 Salary Deferred Until 1994
Bill Hogan	$ 500.0	$ 850.0	$ 250.0	$ 1,600.0	$ 250.0
Corby Megorden	300.0	600.0	225.0	1,125.0	200.0
Manuel Vasquez	200.0	500.0	100.0	800.0	150.0
Jim Showalter		600.0	100.0	700.0	200.0
Scott Van Buskirk	150.0	400.0	100.0	650.0	150.0
Jerry Hyde	150.0	400.0	50.0	600.0	150.0
Dave Schafer		355.0	50.0	405.0	130.0
Leslie Yamshita		300.0	37.5	337.5	100.0
Earl McLain		220.0	37.5	257.5	50.0
Shannon Saunders		210.0	37.5	247.5	50.0
Gary Blazin		190.0	37.5	227.5	40.0
Rich Hayes		160.0	25.0	185.0	30.0
Sam Willett		140.0	17.5	157.5	21.0
Chuck Wright	20.0	115.0	12.5	147.5	
Jim Urquart		115.0	12.5	127.5	
Bill Schutt		115.0	12.5	127.5	
Mike Hegarty		115.0	12.5	127.5	
Bruce Selby		110.0	12.5	122.5	
Dave Kolk		110.0	12.5	122.5	
Bill Kelly		110.0	12.5	122.5	
Dave Carr		110.0	12.0	122.0	
Tom O'Conner		110.0	5.0	115.0	
Jake Luhan		110.0		110.0	
Ray Woolrich		100.0		100.0	
John Porter		100.0		100.0	
Dusty Rhodes		100.0		100.0	
Lynn Novinger		100.0		100.0	
Bill Williams		95.0		95.0	
Jim Sedor		95.0		95.0	
Ralph Young		95.0		95.0	
Ed Marino		95.0		95.0	
Ray Spicer		90.0		90.0	
Eric Womble		90.0		90.0	
Ron Gorena		90.0		90.0	
Gene Johnston		90.0		90.0	
Jack Zollinger		90.0		90.0	
Ken Karr		90.0		90.0	
Tom Crowley		80.0		80.0	
Joe Matt		80.0		80.0	
Bill Brunelle		80.0		80.0	
Roster Player Salary	$1,320.0	$7,605.0	$1,172.0	$10,097.0	$1,521.0

EXHIBIT 4
Income Statements
Players' Figures (000s omitted)

| | Year Ending October 31 | |
	1983	1984
Operating Revenues:		
Game Receipts	$16,526.0	$18,620.0
National Television	2,360.8	2,830.8
Local Broadcasting	3,147.9	3,475.1
Concessions	2,886.3	3,294.3
Parking	525.1	562.0
Other	786.9	843.9
Total Revenues	$26,233.0	$29,626.1
Operating Expenses:		
Spring Training	$ 545.0	$ 594.0
Team Operating Expenses		
Players' Salaries		
Current Roster	5,897.4	7,256.5
Nonroster Guaranteed		
Contract Expense	0.0	500.0
Amortization of Bonuses	716.0	947.0
Coaches' Salaries	756.9	825.7
Other Salaries	239.0	260.8
Miscellaneous	2,655.9	2,897.3
Player Development	2,996.0	3,269.0
Team Replacement:		
Scouting	672.8	734.0
Stadium Operations	3,300.0	3,500.0
Ticketing and Marketing	1,907.0	2,080.0
General and Administrative	3,541.0	3,663.0
Total Operating Expenses	$23,227.0	$26,527.3
Income from Operations	3,006.0	3,098.8
Other Income (Expense)	(96.0)	(101.0)
Income Before Taxes	2,910.0	2,997.8
Provision for Federal Income Taxes[a]	1,338.6	1,379.0
City and State Taxes	236.0	253.0
Net Income	$ 1,335.4	$ 1,365.8

[a] Tax rate assumed to be 46%.

EXHIBIT 5
Summary of Signing Bonuses ($000)

Contract Length (Years)	Bonuses for Contracts Starting in			
	1981	1982	1983	1984
4	240	550	350	800
3	210	200	250	200
2	360	250	170	320

EXHIBIT 6
Summary of Items of Disagreement Between Owners and Players (000s)

Items of Dispute	1983			1984		
	Owners	Players	Difference	Owners	Players	Difference
Roster depreciation	2,000.0	0.0	2,000.0	2,000.0	0.0	2,000.0
Current roster salary	$9,111.0	$5,897.4	$3,213.6	$10,097.0	$7,256.5	$2,840.5
Amortization of signing bonuses	0.0	716.0	(716.0)	0.0	947.0	(947.0)
Nonroster guaranteed contract expense	0.0	0.0	—	1,250.0	500.0	750.0
Stadium operations	4,086.0	3,300.0	786.0	4,457.0	3,500.0	957.0
Total effect on net income			$5,283.6			$5,600.5

Effect on Net Income (Before Tax):	1983	1984
Income before tax per Owners' Financial Statements (Exhibit 1)	$(2,373.6)	$(2,602.7)
Total Items of Disagreement	5,283.6	5,600.5
Income before tax per Players' Financial Statements (Exhibit 4)	$ 2,910.0	$ 2,997.8

Buying Time

The concept of compound interest allows managers to connect money with time. Managers whose organizations lack the cash to pay for desirable projects can offer to pay interest to others for the use of their cash for a period of time. People with cash they do not currently need find the prospect of earning interest attractive because it means their claim to cash will be larger at a future date. Higher interest rates will make more money available to those who can use it most effectively over time periods of any length.

Suppose you need about $1,000 to purchase new computer software that you are sure will double your productivity. That increase in productivity leaves no doubt that you will have plenty of cash a year from now, even though you are a little short of cash today. The dealer who hopes to sell you the software proposes to lend you the cash you need for the purchase, provided you agree to pay interest at a rate of 10% per year. You agree to the deal, get the software, and repay the loan at the end of one year. You have used the dealer's cash, and you buy the use of that cash for one year's time. In money terms, the deal looks like this:

		To be Repaid at the End of Year
Original Loan	$1,000	$1,000
Interest Rate	× 10% per year	100
		$1,100

You paid $100 to use the cash you needed to improve your productivity. That was the interest on the dealer's cash.

Another dealer offers a new printer for about $1,000. With such a printer you would reproduce your productive results with greater clarity and effectiveness. This dealer will also lend you the money to buy this equipment, but the 10% interest is

Professor William J. Bruns, Jr. and Research Associate Susan S. Harmeling, MBA '91 prepared this case. HBS cases are developed solely as the basis for class discussion. Cases are not intended to serve as endorsements, sources of primary data, or illustrations of effective or ineffective management.

deducted from the loan when it is made. Again, you are using the dealer's cash, and you must buy the use of that cash for one year's time. In money terms, the deal looks like this:

		To be Repaid at the End of Year
Original Loan	$909	$ 909
Interest Rate	× 10% per year	91
		$1,000

Note that in this case you get less cash, but you still pay interest at 10%. The interest cost is less because you actually borrowed less.

We can view each of these loans using terms that managers use to describe the costs of buying time to use the cash that will be paid to others. The **present value** of the loan is the amount received or credited to the sale on the day we buy the software or equipment. The **future value** of the loan is the amount to which the loan has grown at the time payment is due. In our examples, these terms could be used as follows:

		Present Value		Future Value
Loan from dealer #1	$1,000	at 10% interest =		$1,100
Loan from dealer #2	$ 909	at 10% interest =		$1,000

The interest rate ties the present value of cash to its future value, and our example shows how we can look either forward or backward at a loan of "about $1,000." It is as if the present value and the future value represent the same amount of cash at two points in time, connected by an interest rate that determines what the borrower will pay for "buying time."

Two algebraic formulas provide bases for solving most business problems involving money and time. The future value of an amount earning **compound interest** can be calculated using the formula

$$PV\ (1 + i)^n = FV$$

where PV = present value of principal amount
      i = interest rate
      n = number of periods interest will compound
    FV = future value

Actually, most managers have no need to remember this or any other compound interest formula because compound interest tables have been constructed to ease the burden of computation of future or present values. Also, many calculators and computer software products are programmed to assist in such calculations.

Many business decisions involve a comparison of a present value of an amount of cash to be received in the future to the current price of the right to obtain the future payment. The present value of an amount to be received in n periods in the future can be calculated by rearranging the formula above:

$$PV = \frac{PV}{(1 + i)^n}$$

To facilitate the calculation of present values, tables are constructed based on this formula. An example is shown as **Table 1**.

TABLE 1
Present Value of $1

Period	8%	10%	12%
1	.9259	.9091	.8929
2	.8573	.8264	.7972
3	.7938	.7513	.7118
4	.7350	.6830	.6355
5	.6806	.6209	.5674
6	.6302	.5645	.5066

To use the table to find the present value of any future cash payment, you need only multiply the amount shown for the number of periods and chosen interest rate by the amount of the payment. For example, the present value of $1,000 to be paid or received in three years at 10% interest would be $751.30:

Present Value			**Future Value**
0	1	2	3

$751.30 ◄——————————————— $1,000

The process of calculating the present value of a future cash amount is called **discounting**.

Many investments generate a stream of cash receipts over a number of future periods. If the amount of cash to be received in each period is the same, it is sometimes called an **annuity**. The formula for calculating the present value of an annuity to be received for n periods is

$$PV = PMT \left[\frac{1 - \frac{1}{(1 + 1)^n}}{i} \right]$$

A table constructed to facilitate the calculation of the present value of an ordinary annuity, based on this formula, is shown as **Table 2**.

TABLE 2
Present Value of an Ordinary Annuity of $1

Period	8%	10%	12%
1	.9259	.9091	.8929
2	1.7833	1.7355	1.6901
3	2.5771	2.4869	2.4018
4	3.3121	3.1699	3.0373
5	3.9927	3.7908	3.6048
6	4.6229	4.3553	4.1114

Table 2 can be used to find the present value of a stream of equal future cash payments to be paid or received for a number of periods at a chosen interest rate. For example, the present value of $1,000 to be paid or received for three years at 10% interest would be $2,486.90. This is actually the sum of the present values of each of the three payments to be received over the waiting period for each. Using **Table 1** we could have calculated:

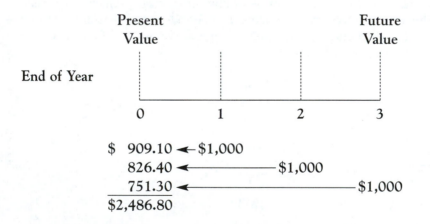

The small discrepancy in the two answers is the result of rounding within the **present value tables**. This often occurs, but it is rarely a problem in actual situations. If you want to be precise, use of a calculator or software program instead of present value tables is recommended.

THE USE OF COMPOUND INTEREST AND PRESENT VALUE IN ACCOUNTING

Companies make many contracts that call for the future receipt or payments of cash. Some examples of payments could include a loan to be repaid over several time periods, a financial contract calling for interest payments and repayment of borrowed principal after a time (a bond), payments due under a contract for leased equipment (a lease), or payments promised to employees after their retirement from active employment (a pension). When receipts or payments are due within a short period of time—trade accounts receivable or payable, for example—they are rarely discounted to their present value. However, almost all amounts due after a year or more would be discounted to their present value. Interest expense (or revenue) then accumulates at the rate of interest used in the original discounting.

PRACTICE EXAMPLE #1: RENT-A-LEMON, INC.

Hank Ford, founder of Rent-a-Lemon, Inc., needed to borrow some money, and he needed it fast. He was a pioneer in the business of buying older cars and renting them to college students visiting southern Florida on spring break. Rapid expansion of his rental locations was necessary to discourage competitors from entering the business. He hoped to open two new offices in Daytona Beach. To do this, Rent-a-Lemon would need about $2.5 million for location development and purchase of a fleet of well-used automobiles.

Ford's personal assistant, Ms. I. Countem, told him that he could get the money Rent-a-Lemon needed from Money-for-Nothing, Inc. (MFNI), a local loan broker. She suggested Rent-a-Lemon offer MFNI three annual payments of $1 million each, the first to be due one year from the date of the loan, and the second and third at subsequent one-year intervals. Ms. Countem said that Rent-a-Lemon would receive a loan of about $2,486,900 if MFNI would be satisfied with an interest rate of 10%. She also explained that during the first year, interest expense on the loan would total $248,690, and when the first $1 million payment was made, the principal owed to MFNI would be reduced by the difference between the $1 million paid and the interest expense.

Questions

1. How did Ms. Countem know that Rent-a-Lemon would get nearly $2.5 million if MFNI would lend at a 10% interest rate?

2. Assume Ms. Countem is right, and MFNI is willing to lend on Mr. Ford's promises to pay $1 million each year for three years. How much will Rent-a-Lemon owe on the day the loan is taken? How much will it owe one year later just before the first payment of $1 million is made to MFNI? What will be the liability of Rent-a-Lemon just **after** the first $1 million payment is made to MFNI?

3. Calculate the interest expense for Rent-a-Lemon for the second year of the loan and the liability at the end of that year after the annual $1 million payment is made? Repeat the exercise for the third year. What does MFNI mean when they say they want to earn a 10% interest rate?

4. Ms. Countem told Mr. Ford that she could be wrong about the interest rate MFNI might accept. It could be as low as 8% or as high as 12%. At these extremes, if Rent-a-Lemon offers the three annual payments of $1 million, how much will MFNI lend to Rent-a-Lemon, and what will be the interest expense in each year of the loan?

PRACTICE EXAMPLE #2:
I. COUNTEM'S ALTERNATIVE

Ms. Countem had suggested to Hank Ford that there was an alternative to dealing with the local Florida [loan] sharks. She thought Rent-a-Lemon could float a bond issue. She suggested selling 2,500 bonds with a face value of $1,000 each and a coupon interest rate of 10% to be paid annually. The principal amount of the bonds, $2.5 million, would be due and paid at the end of the third year.

Questions

5. If Rent-a-Lemon decides to issue the bonds suggested by I. Countem, and investors wish to earn exactly 10% interest on their investment, how much will Rent-a-Lemon get from selling the bonds? On the day the bonds are issued, is that the total amount of Rent-a-Lemon's liability? Why or why not?

6. What will Rent-a-Lemon's total liability be at the end of the first year just before the interest payment is made? Just after? At the end of the second year? The third year?

7. What will be the proceeds of the 10% bond issue if investors are content to earn an 8% interest rate? How will this affect interest expense each year? What if investors demand 12% interest?

Liabilities and Time

When an organization makes a commitment to an outside party to pay resources at some time in the future, the commitment is a *liability*. If the payment is due within one "operating cycle" (often assumed to be one year) of the organization's activities, the commitment will usually be classified as a *current liability*. *Noncurrent liabilities* are those that will be paid in a subsequent operating cycle or at a time beyond one year. The distinction between short-term liabilities and long-term liabilities is rarely precise. Likewise, the exact time period is rarely critical. Nevertheless, the distinction often determines how an accountant will measure the future burden of the liability, and how it will be reported in financial reports.

CURRENT LIABILITIES

Short-term or current liabilities of an individual or organization are created by exchanges or events that may involve a variety of sources. For example, accounts payable may be due to many different creditors. Current liabilities are usually labeled according to the party or class of creditor to which payments will be made. Classifications may be broad or narrow, depending upon the amount of detail that managers and their accountants wish to show in financial reports.

Exhibit 1 shows the liabilities reported for the Gillette Company and Subsidiary Companies at the end of 2003 and 2002. Additional detail on the amount of liabilities and debt is contained in the notes to financial statements, which are also shown in **Exhibit 1**. Gillette reports four classifications of current liabilities but groups all other liabilities into three classifications.

Many current liabilities arise from transactions involving employees and suppliers. These *accounts payable* report amounts owed to suppliers who have provided materials or services, but who have not yet been paid. This use of credit not only provides resources to the organization incurring a liability but also facilitates activity in that it is not necessary to pause and make payments continuously as transactions take place or services are rendered. Most organizations normally have a significant number of accounts payable. Gillette labels this item *Accounts Payable and Accrued*

Professor William J. Bruns, Jr. prepared this case. HBS cases are developed solely as the basis for class discussion. Cases are not intended to serve as endorsements, sources of primary data, or illustrations of effective or ineffective management.

Liabilities. These include amounts payable to suppliers for purchased goods and services, to employees for wages and salaries that were unpaid at the balance-sheet date, to government agencies as a result of payroll or property taxes, and so forth. If Gillette had wanted to show greater detail, it could have shown other categories in separate classifications.

Current liabilities are usually measured using the amount of cash or other assets that would currently satisfy the obligation if it were paid. If interest is associated with a liability, the amount of interest expense already incurred will be added to the original liability incurred. Measuring current liabilities is usually fairly straightforward, and understanding the future burden that they will place on the organization is usually simple, provided sufficient detail has been included in the statement of financial position.

Two kinds of liabilities, *unearned revenue* and *deferred credits*, are often found among current liabilities and deserve special mention. Each shows the obligation of the organization to customers or clients. In many types of businesses, customers pay in advance for services, and in return, the organization promises to provide future services or products. Magazine subscriptions are typically sold on this basis, as are tickets for artistic or athletic events and airline transportation. The amount of resources received in advance for services that have not as yet been provided is clearly a liability. The organization promises to provide a good or service in the future to the same degree of certainty as if it had promised to provide payment in the future. The fact that the obligation will not be settled by payment of cash or assets does not mean a liability does not exist.

These situations result in *unearned revenue*, which is included in current liabilities if the product or service is to be delivered within the next operating cycle. Then, when the product or service is delivered, the revenue previously unearned becomes revenue of that operating period. The expenses to provide the product or service are matched with the revenue recognized in measuring and reporting the income at the time the product or service is delivered.

Deposits received from customers can also create liabilities. Deposits are frequently called *deferred credits*. If the deposit is an advance payment for a product or service, the deposit will be added to other revenues obtained when the product or service is delivered and will be removed from the liability account at that time. Other types of deferred credits might include deposits on shipping containers or other items of value provided by the seller to a customer. The deposit serves as security, and when the container or other items are returned, the refund of the deposit reduces cash and eliminates the liability.

Finally, as time passes, liabilities once classified as long-term come within the reach of the next operating period when they will be satisfied. That portion to be paid in the subsequent operating period is transferred from long-term liability categories to current liabilities, where it may be identified as the *current portion of long-term debt*. Amounts that will not be paid in the next period will continue to be shown as long-term debts.

LONG-TERM DEBT

Agreements to pay at some future point of time or at intervals of time in the future represent an important source of resources to many organizations. Such agreements frequently take the form of loan contracts between the organization as a borrower and another individual or entity. They may take the form of debt security, such as debenture bonds, which lenders are free to trade among themselves and which are frequently traded in the securities markets. Loans can take other forms as well and may be known as mortgages, trust notes, or any of a number of other possible types of debt instruments. The characteristics that set these apart from other liabilities are their contractual nature and the extended period over which interest is to be accrued or payments are to be made.

Perhaps the simplest type of long-term debt is a contractual agreement to pay some specified amount at some time in the future. Consider the firm that has agreed to pay $1,000 in cash five years from today to another party.

At first glance, the $1,000 commitment might seem to have a value equal to cash or other resources the organization will have to give up when the debt falls due. Thus, we might simply say the liability has a value of $1,000. On the other hand, if we consider the investment decision of the person with whom we have made this agreement, the creditor, we would surely recognize that the value is less than the $1,000 amount stated in the liability agreement.

Suppose we were to go to the creditor and ask how much we would have to pay today to be released from our future obligation. Alternatively, we might go to a third party and ask it how much we would have to pay it to assume our promise to pay in the future.

Providing the creditor has alternative uses for the resources that we would offer today to cancel our future obligation, we should be able to settle for less than $1,000. If the market rate of interest is 10%, then we might expect that the creditor would accept the present value of $1,000 five years from now, or $620.92 today, and release us from our future commitment.[1] That is the amount that a person would have to invest today to have $1,000 five years hence if the available interest rate is 10%. Actually, we might have to pay slightly more than $620.92 to compensate the creditor for the inconvenience of locating another investment. The nature of the liability compels us to measure its value in terms of what we would have to pay to satisfy the creditor.

When an organization incurs a liability such as a promise of $1,000 to be paid at the end of five years, the proper measurement of the claim is never the amount promised in the future. Instead, it would be the present value considering alternative uses (for five years) of the resources that can be made by any other parties to the contract. Even if the creditor should reject the offer to settle a future commitment at a level reflecting the market rate of interest, there is no reason for concern. The entity committed to a future payment can invest resources at the market rate of interest and thus accumulate the amount necessary to satisfy its obligation when it finally falls due. **Exhibit 2** illustrates how the present burden of a liability can be estimated and related to the amount that will have to be paid when the settlement date of the obligation finally occurs.

Discounting future expenditures to their present value rather than observing only their contractual amount is important for valuing long-term liabilities. Although the same arguments could be applied to current liabilities, the fact that these liabilities

---

[1] The present value of $1,000 five years from now can be calculated by the formula:

Present Value = $1,000 ÷ (1 + .10)^5.

will be settled soon usually leads accountants to treat current liabilities as if the difference between the present value of the amount to be paid and the contractual amount is immaterial.

Bonds

The amounts that business firms and other organizations wish to borrow are sometimes quite large—larger than any single lender may be willing or able to provide. For this reason, securities are created. One general category of borrowing instruments is that of bond indentures. The terms of a loan are specified in a master contract between the entity, which is the borrower, and the bondholders, who are the lenders. Each bondholder receives a certificate showing the total indebtedness represented by the certificate and the terms of his or her contract with the firm.

All bond agreements have three basic features:

1. The *term* of the loan is specified.

2. A *face amount* of the loan is specified.

3. The *repayment schedule* is shown either in detailed amounts or as a percentage rate of interest to be paid at intervals based upon the face amount of the bond.

Other terms such as the privilege of conversion to other forms of securities may also be included in some bonds, but for simplicity we will ignore those complications here.

Bonds are typically issued in multiples of $1,000, so let us assume that an organization is offering to sell a bond with a term of 10 years, a face amount of $1,000, and annual payments based on an interest rate of 8%. Now what do these contractual terms mean?

The face amount of the bond determines the amount that the issuers will pay the holder at the end of the life of the bond. In this example, at the end of 10 years, the issuer of the bond will pay to whomever presents it, $1,000. The "nominal" interest rate, 8%, determines the amount of annual payments that will be made in addition to the terminal payment at the end of the bond term. Since that rate in our example is 8%, the annual payments on the $1,000 bond will be $80. For this reason, when the borrower firm offers this bond for sale, it is asking, "How much will you lend me for promises to pay $80 at the end of each year for 10 years and, in addition, for the promise that I will pay $1,000 at the end of 10 years?"[2]

The amount that a lender will be willing to offer for a bond is dependent upon the desired rate of interest, or *yield*, that the lender wishes to earn on the amount about to be invested. **Exhibit 3** illustrates the procedure that three investors might use to decide what to bid on a bond offering, assuming that each is willing to earn a different rate of interest on the investment. The lender willing to bid the highest amount determines the *prevailing market interest rate* for the bonds offered.

The difference between the face amount of the bond and the amount received by the borrower when the bond is initially issued is referred to as discount or premium.

---

[2] By convention, bond interest rates are quoted in annual terms, but one-half of the quoted interest rate is used to determine the amount of *semiannual* interest payments. However, for this illustration annual payments are assumed in order to simplify **Exhibits 3** and **4**.

If the amount received is *larger* than the face amount, the difference is called *premium*. If it is *smaller*, the difference is called *discount*. Premium or discount results whenever the nominal interest rate, that stated on the face of a bond, is different from the current market rate of interest demanded by lenders. Only after a bond is issued can the borrower determine the *effective interest rate* on the debt. The effective interest rate is the prevailing interest rate determined by the successful bid for the bonds.

The amount of the liability created by issuing a bond includes the premium (or excludes the discount), which will be amortized by the difference between the *interest expense* each period and the *interest payment* actually made. At any given time, the liability will be the face amount of the bond plus or minus the unamortized premium or discount created when the bond was first sold. From **Exhibit 4**, we can surmise that Investor A, who is willing to invest to earn 6% interest, would at any time be willing to allow Eastern Coast Company to buy back the bond for the amount of liability at the beginning of the year, plus current interest not yet paid, plus perhaps a small premium for inconvenience. Near the end of the tenth year, the amount would be about $1,000 plus current interest earned but not paid.

A similar analysis could be applied to bond discounts, except that the positions would be somewhat different. We can see by referring to **Exhibit 3** that if on the day after Eastern Coast had issued the bond to Investor C for $877, the company wished to cancel the agreement, Investor C probably would have been quite willing to accept $1,000 for it. On the other hand, if we assume that other investments offering a 10% interest rate are available and that Investor C would be able to reinvest at the same rate, it would not be surprising to find that Investor C would be willing to cancel the future obligations in return for a payment for something near $877.07 plus any current interest already earned but not yet paid.

In accounting for bonds, the reduction in liability due to the fact that the periodic payments on bonds issued at a premium exceed the effective interest is referred to as the *amortization of bond premium*. If bonds are issued at discount, the periodic payments will be less than the effective interest, and the liability will grow because of *amortization of bond discount*. When bonds are issued for exactly the face amount, there is no premium or discount to amortize, and since the effective rate of interest is equal to the stated rate, interest each period will be equal to the periodic payments. You should note that as the liability differs in each succeeding year due to amortization of premium or discount, so will the amount of interest expense change, even though the annual payment set by the contract will remain the same.

Exhibit 5 provides another illustration, somewhat more extensive than **Exhibits 3** and **4**, of a proposed bond issue.

If all bonds were as simple as those we have used here to illustrate the problems of accounting for long-term debt, observing, measuring, and reporting on liabilities of this type would be much easier than they frequently are in practice. As the number of conditions attached to a bond increases or the options open to either the bondholder (for example, the right to turn in the bond in return for ownership shares) or the borrower (for example, the right to pay off the bond at a specified sum at any point of time during its life) multiply, the more difficult become the problems of accounting for bonds.

Long-term Leases

Many organizations secure the future benefits of land, buildings, and equipment through lease agreements rather than through purchase. A lease agreement conveys to the organization the right to use a resource in return for a promise to pay a specified amount at some future time or at many times in the future. The owner of property or equipment who enters into such an agreement is called a *lessor*; the entity that secures the rights to use the resources in return for a promise to pay is called the *lessee*.

The terms of lease agreements vary widely. Some are for long periods, others are for short. Some demand that the lessee pay all expenses in maintaining and using the property, while others confer on the lessee the rights of use but leave the burdens of maintenance and replacement on the lessor.

Organizations that lease assets rather than purchase them may do so for a number of reasons. In many cases, leasing provides a type of financing. The products and benefits of using resources can be obtained through leasing without paying for them until receipts can be obtained from customers. This frees the firm from the necessity of other forms of borrowing and preserves liquid assets. In some instances, lease agreements are only veiled purchase agreements. This is particularly true when payments are to be made over a period of time, after which legal title to the leased property is transferred to the lessee.

Since a lease agreement requires the outflow of cash or other resources in the future, it has the essential characteristics of a liability. In many cases, this liability resembles long-term bonds, and the problem of accounting for the liability is quite similar to that for bonds. Because of their kinship to long-term liabilities, we might expect to find lease agreements included with long-term debts when reports on liabilities or the value of the firm are prepared. However, in practice, at least in public reports, long-term leases and their related obligations are often only reported in footnotes. Only when lease agreements are essentially agreements to purchase and simply provide a means for the buyer to delay payment for the assets do generally accepted accounting principles call for full disclosure of the liability inherent in the lease agreement.

CONDITIONAL LIABILITIES

An important class of liabilities to many business organizations is one in which the promises to pay are contingent upon the occurrence of other events. Product guarantees and pension payments are two important types of conditional liabilities. When an entity promises to expend resources if certain events occur, a *conditional liability* has been created.

The observation and measurement problems associated with conditional liabilities are somewhat more difficult than those for contractual liabilities, but not impossibly so. The accountant must consider what the probable payments may be and then calculate the present value of the expected future payments.

Product Guarantees

Often a business firm, in order to promote a product, will promise to refund the purchase price if the product fails to satisfy the customer. Alternatively, a replacement unit or cash refund based on use may be offered. Products returned under the guarantee rarely have any resale value. They have been used, and therefore they are often either given away or destroyed. The amount of liability created by such an agreement depends upon the frequency with which customers return the product and on the terms of the guarantee. The frequency will, in turn, be dependent upon factors, many of which are not easily measurable even when they are observed by the accountant. Product quality, product price, consumer expectations, and other factors all enter into the individual consumer's decision process in considering whether to return a product for refund. Despite the difficulty of projecting possible costs under product guarantees, it can be important in some circumstances. Thus, the accountant must employ as much ingenuity as possible in attempting to observe, measure, and report them.

Postretirement Benefits

Frequently, in order to increase the attractiveness of employment or to reward faithful service, an entity enters into an agreement with its employees to provide them with a pension or other benefits on their retirement. A pension is a promise to pay a specified amount periodically for a specified period of time. Typically, a pension agreement guarantees that a certain amount will be paid each month to an employee after he or she retires. The conditional nature of such a liability makes the measurement difficult, for many factors can change during the years that intervene before an employee's retirement date arrives and the payments begin. Furthermore, the period of time over which the payments must be made depends upon whether employees die before retirement, soon after, or live for many years.

A postretirement agreement consists in most cases of a fairly long list of promises with stipulations. Typically, it provides that a specified amount will be paid periodically or as a lump sum, provided that the employee has met certain conditions: that he or she has continued in the employment of the entity until his or her retirement; that he or she has served some minimum of time prior to retirement; and that he or she has contributed some proportion of the amount necessary to make payments. The amounts of payments may vary depending upon the salary earned for all employees.

In practice, liabilities for pensions are sometimes eliminated by paying premiums to insurance or other fiduciary or trust agencies which then assume the liability. Since the liability is transferred to another organization, the liability is no longer a liability of the organization that created it.

As in the case of any other long-term liability, the amount of pension liability can be affected by a change in the agreement, by a change in the work force resulting in older or younger employees, or by a change in the rate at which future payments are discounted. Environmental events can have an important impact on the amount of the liability and should be reflected in accounting for pension liabilities.

Deferred Taxes

When the amount of income taxes paid differs from the tax expense that should be reported in financial reports, the difference is recorded and reported as *deferred taxes*. Measuring and reporting deferred taxes create some of the most complicated reporting problems accountants face because of the complexity of income tax regulations and the conditional nature of income taxes not yet due.

SUMMARY

Liabilities are commitments to transfer resources to another person or organization at some time in the future. Current liabilities are usually measured and reported at the amount that will be paid to satisfy the claims of creditors. Long-term liabilities are usually reported at the present value of the amounts of claim or estimates of what will eventually be paid.

On a balance sheet, liabilities show the sources other than owners' contributions and retained earnings of the resources (assets) of the organization. Just as assets must be managed, liabilities need attention to make the best use of this important source of resources while preserving the credit worthiness of the organization.

EXHIBIT 1
The Gillette Company and Subsidiary Companies—Liabilities

Excerpt from Consolidated Balance Sheets

At December 31,	2003	2002
	(millions)	
Current Liabilities		
Loans payable	$ 117	$ 673
Current portion of long-term debt	742	527
Accounts payable and accrued liabilities	2,506	2,054
Income taxes	293	234
Total current liabilities	3,658	3,488
Long-term debt	2,453	2,457
Other long-term liabilities	626	692
Minority interest	65	46

Account Payable and Accrued Liabilities

At December 31,	2003	2002
	(millions)	
Accounts payable	$ 574	$ 581
Advertising and sales promotion	537	472
Payroll and payroll taxes	292	211
Dividends payable on common stock	163	170
Other	940	620
Total	$2,506	$2,054

Other Long-Term Liabilities

At December 31,	2003	2002
	(millions)	
Pensions	$ 404	$ 382
Postretirement medical	279	286
Deferred compensation	149	159
Other	97	93
Total	$ 929	$ 920

Loans Payable

At December 31,	2003	2002
	(millions)	
U.S. dollar commercial paper (interest at 0.9% and 1.5%)	$ 55	$ 549
Payable to bank (interest at 3.3% and 2.6%)	62	124
Total	$ 117	$ 673

Long-Term Debt

At December 31,	2003	2002
	(millions)	
2.23% Euro obligation due 2003	$ —	$ 297
6.25% Notes due 2003	—	154
Floating rate note due 2003	—	75
3.25% Euro note due 2004	379	312
3.75% Notes due 2004	255	259
5.75% Notes due 2005	213	219
4.00% Notes due 2005	361	373
5.25% Notes due 2006	133	142
5.00% Notes due 2006	323	325
4.125% Notes due 2007	253	254
3.50% Notes due 2007	495	499
2.875% Notes due 2008	299	—
2.50% Notes due 2008	300	—
Gillette CoreNotes due 2012	73	74
Gillette CoreNotes due 2013	3	—
Floating rate note due 2043	108	—
Other, multicurrency borrowings	—	1
Current portion of long-term debt	(742)	(527)
Total	$2,453	$2,457

The Company commercial paper program is supported by its revolving credit facility and other sources of liquidity. The Company has a revolving bank credit facility in the amount of $1.15 billion, of which $863 million is available on a 364-day basis and expires in October 2004, and $288 million expires October 2008. The revolving bank credit facility allows the Company to issue up to $1.53 billion in commercial paper in the U.S. and Euro markets. Under the agreement, the Company has the option to borrow at various interest rates, including the prime rate, and is required to pay a facility fee of .04% per annum for the 365-day facility and .06% per annum for the five-year facility, based on the Company's current

EXHIBIT 1 (*continued*)
The Gillette Company and Subsidiary Companies—Liabilities

credit rating. At December 31, 2003 and 2002, there were no borrowings under such agreements. In addition, there are other unused lines of credit amounting to $191 million at December 31, 2003.

Certain long-term debt instruments contain prepayment provisions at the option of either the holder of the instrument or the Company. The 3.50% notes due 2007 are redeemable at par at the Company's option, on any interest payment due on or after October 15, 2004. Under the Gillette $500 million CoreNotes program, the Company may periodically issue fixed and floating rate notes in $1,000 increments. At December 31, 2003, the coupon rates of the outstanding notes varied between 4.55% and 5.00%, and the interest payments are made quarterly. The notes mature on various dates in 2012 and 2013 and are redeemable at par, at the Company's option, on any interest payment date on or after one year from the date of issuance. The $108 million floating rate notes are redeemable at the option of the holder at various prices on a yearly basis from April 2004 to April 2014 and each third anniversary thereafter to maturity. The floating rate notes are also redeemable at the Company's option at various prices from April 2033 to maturity.

During 2002, two shelf registration statements were filed allowing the Company to issue up to $2.8 billion in debt securities in the U.S. At December 31, 2003, $1.54 billion was issued under the shelf registration, representing the 4.125% and 3.50% notes due 2007, the 2.875% and 2.50% notes due 2008, the floating rate notes due 2043, and the Gillette CoreNotes due 2012. At December 31, 2003, a total of $1.26 billion was available under these shelf registrations.

Long-term weighted average interest rates were 1.6% and 1.9% as of December 31, 2003 and 2002, respectively, after giving effect to interest rate hedging instruments. Aggregate maturities of total long-term debt, excluding $60 million in market value adjustments resulting from debt-related derivatives, for the five years after December 31, 2003, are $625 million in 2004, $550 million in 2005, $425 million in 2006, $750 million in 2007, and $600 million in 2008.

EXHIBIT 2
The Value of a Promise to Pay $1,000 at the End of Five Years (rate of interest = 10%)

End of Year	Total Liability, Which Is Equal to the Amount of Creditor's Investment	Interest Accumulated During Year
5	$1,000.00	$90.91
4	909.09	82.64
3	826.45	75.13
2	751.32	68.30
1	683.02	62.10
Now	620.92	

EXHIBIT 3
Analysis of a Bond by Three Investors

Eastern Coast Company—Analysis of Value of 10-Year, 8%, $1,000 Bonds to Three
Investors Who Seek 6%, 8%, and 10% Return, Respectively

Investor A demands 6%.
Investor B demands 8%.
Investor C demands 10%.

Bond contract ("indenture") promises:
a) Ten payments of $80 at end of each of 10 years.
b) One payment of $1,000 at end of 10 years.

Present Value of $1.00	At 6% Interest	At 8% Interest	At 10% Interest
Received annually for 10 years	7.3601	6.7101	6.1446
Received at end of 10 years	.5584	.4632	.3855

Value to Investors at Issue Date

A	B	C
7.3601 × $ 80 = $ 588.81	6.7101 × $ 80 = $ 536.80	6.1446 × $ 80 = $491.57
.5584 × 1,000 = __558.40__	.4632 × 1,000 = __463.20__	.3855 × 1,000 = __385.50__
Total $1,147.21[a]	Total $1,000.00	Total $877.07

A will pay a premium of
$147.21 over the face amount
of the bond.

B will pay the face amount
of $1,000.

C demands a discount of
$122.93 off the face
amount of the bond.

---

[a] The value of the liability and hence the amount that the business firm issuing this bond will receive are dependent on the rate
of return that the investors wish to earn on their investment. Because Investor A demands only 6% on his or her investment, he or
she is willing to lend more, given the fixed terms of the contract. The entity issuing these bonds would be foolish not to accept his
or her high bid of $1,147.21 for the bond.

EXHIBIT 4
A Investment in a Bond from the Investor's Point of View

Assume that the Eastern Coast Company issued the bond described in **Exhibit 3** to Investor A and received $1,147.21 from him or her. Investor A has accepted a yield rate of interest of 6%, which is the rate of interest Eastern Coast now will pay on the *actual* amount borrowed. Its original promises remain constant, however; it will make 10 payments of $80 at the end of each year for 10 years and 1 payment of $1,000 at the end of 10 years.

If the original liability of Eastern Coast is assumed to be equal to the amount received, the table below shows how that liability increases during each year because of the interest owed to Investor A, then falls as each $80 payment is made until at the end of 10 years it is exactly equal to the $1,000 terminal payment originally promised.

Year	Liability at Beginning of Year	Interest at 6% = Yield Rate	Liability at End of Year Before Payment	Payment	Liability at End of Year
1	$1,147.21	$ 68.83[a]	$1,216.04	$ 80.00	$1,136.04
2	1,136.04	68.16	1,204.20	80.00	1,124.20
3	1,124.20	67.45	1,191.65	80.00	1,111.65
4	1,111.65	66.69	1,178.34	80.00	1,098.34
5	1,098.34	65.90	1,164.24	80.00	1,084.24
6	1,084.24	65.05	1,149.29	80.00	1,069.29
7	1,069.29	64.16	1,133.45	80.00	1,053.45
8	1,053.45	63.21	1,116.66	80.00	1,036.66
9	1,036.66	62.20	1,098.86	80.00	1,018.86
10	1,018.86	61.14	1,080.00	80.00	1,000.00
10	—	—	1,000.00	1,000.00	0.00
Totals		$652.79		$1,800.00	

Total borrowed	$1,147.21
Add interest	652.79
Total paid	$1,800.00

[a] We can calculate the interest Investor A expects during the first year by multiplying the amount received by the interest rate used by Investor A (6.0%) originally to value the promised cash payments.

EXHIBIT 5
Proposed Bond Issue of Indet Corporation

The Indet Corporation is planning to issue bonds with a face value of $1,000,000, bearing a nominal interest rate of 5%, and payable at the end of 20 years. Interest is to be paid semiannually. The treasurer of the corporation has prepared three schedules to show the way in which the liability of the corporation will change over the life of the bonds under varying conditions with respect to yield rates. That is, if the prevailing market interest rate at the date the bonds are issued will be either 4%, 5%, or 6% interest return, the measurement of the liability will be affected as shown in these schedules (**Exhibits 5a, 5b,** and **5c**).

The schedules of liability prepared by the treasurer show some important features of long-term liabilities with contractual payments that have the same form as bonds. Until the last period, all payments remain the same. When payments are made semiannually, the annual rate of interest must be adjusted to reflect the time period stated for interest. In this case, since payments are to be made semiannually, the interest expense for each period is calculated using half the annual rate. The interest expense is based on the total outstanding liability at the beginning of the period. In cases where premium or discount has been created because the bonds sold at a yield rate different from the stated rate, the difference between the semiannual payment and the interest expense amortizes premium or discount as the case may demand. By the end of the last period of the life of the bonds, the liability is the amount equal to the terminal payment, which includes repayment of principle as well as payment of interest for the last period.

EXHIBIT 5A
Indet Corporation—Projected Liability at Selected Intervals Due to Sale of $1,000,000, 5%, 20-Year Bonds with Interest Due Semiannually, Sold to Yield 4% to Investors

Interest Period (6 months)	Total Liability at Beginning of Period	Unamortized Premiums	Interest Expense for Period at 4% (2% for 6 months)	Liability at End of Period before Payment	Payment at End of Period	Liability at End of Period after Payment
1	$1,136,787	$136,787	$22,735	$1,159,522	$ 25,000	$1,134,522
2	1,134,522	134,552	22,690	1,157,212	25,000	1,132,212
.	.	.	.	.	.	.
.	.	.	.	.	.	.
20	1,085,080	85,080	21,702	1,106,782	25,000	1,081,872
.	.	.	.	.	.	.
.	.	.	.	.	.	.
40	1,004,902	4,902	20,098	1,025,000	1,025,000	0

Indet Corporation—Projected Liability at Selected Intervals Due to Sale of $1,000,000, 5%, 20-Year Bonds with Interest Due Semiannually, Sold to Yield 5% to Investors

Interest Period (6 months)	Total Liability at Beginning of Period	Unamortized Premiums	Interest Expense for Period at 5% (2-1/2% for 6 months)	Liability at End of Period before Payment	Payment at End of Period	Liability at End of Period after Payment
1	$1,000,000	$0	$25,000	$1,025,000	$ 25,000	$1,000,000
2	1,000,000	0	25,000	1,025,000	25,000	1,000,000
.						
.						
20	1,000,000	0	25,000	1,025,000	25,000	1,000,000
.						
.						
40	1,000,000	0	25,000	1,025,000	1,025,000	0

Indet Corporation—Projected Liability at Selected Intervals Due to Sale of $1,000,000, 5%, 20-Year Bonds with Interest Due Semiannually, Sold to Yield 6% to Investors

Interest Period (6 months)	Total Liability at Beginning of Period	Unamortized Premiums	Interest Expense for Period at 6% (3% for 6 months)	Liability at End of Period before Payment	Payment at End of Period	Liability at End of Period after Payment
1	$884,470	$115,530	$26,534	$ 911,004	$ 25,000	$886,004
2	886,004	113,996	26,580	912,584	25,000	887,584
.						
.						
20	922,875	77,125	27,686	950,561	25,000	925,561
.						
.						
40	995,146	4,854	29,854	1,025,000	1,025,000	0

Laurinburg Precision Engineering

Oliver MacKinnon and Beacham McDougald founded Laurinburg Precision Engineering in 1997 to manufacture precision injection-molded parts for use in medical devices. After an uncertain start-up period, the company won contracts from several different manufacturers. Using special machinery and expertise in injection molding of specialty plastics, the company prospered.

In early 2004, the company was experiencing a cash crisis caused by rapid growth and the desire to extend capabilities through the acquisition of new molding machines. The partners had no additional capital to finance the expansions, and they were reluctant to sell equity to anyone else. A bank loan was considered, but financial projections indicated the loan could not be paid down for almost five years. Because of prevailing interest rates, local banks were unwilling to make a loan commitment of that duration.

Their local bank had introduced MacKinnon and McDougald to a small investment banking firm in Charlotte, North Carolina. After a consultation with MacKinnon and McDougald, Sheila Cox, a partner in the investment banking firm, suggested a $1 million bond issue with a term of five years. The bond issue would be secured by the new machinery and placed with private investors. Cox told MacKinnon and McDougald that she expected the bonds would have to be sold to yield almost 10% interest. She proposed setting the interest rate on the bonds at 10%, with semiannual interest payments and the principal due at the end of the fifth year, and she prepared a schedule of the interest and principal repayments that would be due if the bonds were sold to yield 10% interest exactly (see **Exhibit 1**).

Although the proposal seemed to be a reasonable solution to the problem facing MacKinnon and McDougald, both were worried about the semiannual interest payments in the early years. They expected operating cash flows would remain tight as Laurinburg Precision Engineering continued to grow. When they expressed this concern to Cox by telephone, she suggested a second alternative. Laurinburg Precision Engineering could issue zero-coupon bonds at the same interest rate and terms. On these bonds no interest payments would be made during the five years

Professor William J. Bruns, Jr. prepared this case. HBS cases are developed solely as the basis for class discussion. Cases are not intended to serve as endorsements, sources of primary data, or illustrations of effective or ineffective management.

Part 2 How Accountants Measure and Report

the bonds would be outstanding, and all interest and principal would be due on January 15, 2009, when the bonds matured. The principal amount of the zero-coupon bonds would be greater than that of the 10% bonds, but Laurinburg would have five years to prepare to pay interest and principal from either operations or additional financing.

QUESTIONS

1. Using the present-value tables in **Exhibits 2** and **3**, estimate the number of zero-coupon bonds (each with a face value of $1,000) that will have to be offered to provide the $1 million Laurinburg Precision Engineering needs for expansion, if investors seek a yield of 10%. Assume interest will compound on a semiannual basis over the life of the five-year-bond issue. Prepare a schedule similar to **Exhibit 1** that shows the interest expense and end-of-period bond liability for each semiannual compounding period. Why is the interest expense for the zero-coupon bonds different from the interest expense on the five-year bonds summarized in **Exhibit 1**?

2. Assume that MacKinnon and McDougald decide to issue bonds to finance the expansion of Laurinburg Precision Engineering. The terms of the $1,000 bonds to be due January 15, 2009, specify an interest rate of 10% with semiannual compounding or interest payments. However, Sheila Cox is able to find a group of investors who will accept a yield of 8% interest. How much will the investors be willing to pay for the 10% bonds? Prepare a schedule like **Exhibit 1** showing principal, interest payments, interest expense, and amortization of bond premium for these bonds. Why does the bond premium amortize to zero?

3. If zero-coupon bonds with semiannual compounding to be due January 15, 2009, are issued, what will be the amount due on that date if enough bonds are issued to provide $1 million on January 15, 2004, if the investors seek a yield of 8%? Prepare a schedule of interest expense and bond liabilities for each semiannual compounding period.

4. How should Oliver MacKinnon and Beacham McDougald decide which bonds to issue? What factors should they consider? Why?

EXHIBIT 1

Schedule of Interest Payments, Interest Expense,
and Bond Liability for a 10%, Five-year Bond with
Semiannual Interest Payments Issued to Yield 10% Interest

Date	Interest Payment	Interest Expense	Carrying Value	Principal to be Paid
1/15/2004	—	—	$1,000,000	—
7/15/2004	$50,000	$50,000	1,000,000	—
1/15/2005	50,000	50,000	1,000,000	—
7/15/2005	50,000	50,000	1,000,000	—
1/15/2006	50,000	50,000	1,000,000	—
7/15/2006	50,000	50,000	1,000,000	—
1/15/2007	50,000	50,000	1,000,000	—
7/15/2007	50,000	50,000	1,000,000	—
1/15/2008	50,000	50,000	1,000,000	—
7/15/2008	50,000	50,000	1,000,000	—
1/15/2009	50,000	50,000	1,000,000	$1,000,000

EXHIBIT 2

Present Value of $1

$$PV = \frac{1}{(1 + i)^{\eta}}$$

Period	3%	4%	5%	6%	7%	8%	10%
1	.9709	.9615	.9524	.9434	.9346	.9259	.9091
2	.9426	.9246	.9070	.8900	.8734	.8573	.8264
3	.9151	.8890	.8638	.8396	.8163	.7938	.7513
4	.8885	.8548	.8227	.7921	.7629	.7350	.6830
5	.8626	.8219	.7835	.7473	.7130	.6806	.6209
6	.8375	.7903	.7462	.7050	.6663	.6302	.5645
7	.8131	.7599	.7107	.6651	.6227	.5835	.5132
8	.7894	.7307	.6768	.6274	.5820	.5403	.4665
9	.7664	.7026	.6446	.5919	.5439	.5002	.4241
10	.7441	.6756	.6139	.5584	.5083	.4632	.3855

EXHIBIT 3
Present Value of Ordinary Annuity of $1

$$PV_A = \frac{1}{i}\left[1 - \frac{1}{(1 + i)^n}\right]$$

Period	3%	4%	5%	6%	7%	8%	10%
1	.9709	.9615	.9524	.9434	.9346	.9259	.9091
2	1.9135	1.8861	1.8594	1.8334	1.8080	1.7833	1.7355
3	2.8286	2.7751	2.7232	2.6730	2.6243	2.5771	2.4869
4	3.7171	3.6299	3.5460	3.4651	3.3872	3.3121	3.1699
5	4.5797	4.4518	4.3295	4.2124	4.1002	3.9927	3.7908
6	5.4172	5.2421	5.0757	4.9173	4.7665	4.6229	4.3553
7	6.2303	6.0021	5.7864	5.5824	5.3893	5.2064	4.8684
8	7.0197	6.7327	6.4632	6.2098	5.9713	5.7466	5.3349
9	7.7861	7.4353	7.1078	6.8017	6.5152	6.2489	5.7590
10	8.5302	8.1109	7.7217	7.3601	7.0236	6.7101	6.1446

Accounting for Frequent Fliers

By 1991, almost all U.S. airline companies offered frequent flier programs to their passengers. Under these programs, passengers could become members of a program where the miles they flew would be recorded and accumulated to earn free future flights. The proliferation and growth of frequent flier programs created concerns about the proper way to account for and report them in financial reports. The airlines, the Securities and Exchange Commission (SEC), the American Institute of Certified Public Accountants (AICPA), and the Financial Accounting Standards Board (FASB) had each voiced concerns about measuring the expenses and reporting airlines' obligations under frequent flier programs.

The percentage of revenue passenger miles (the number of miles flown by revenue passengers, including free-flight-award passengers, computed by multiplying the number of revenue passengers by the miles they have flown) flown under free travel awards was less than 5% for all U.S. airlines combined. However, on some routes for some airlines (U.S. mainland to Hawaii, for example) the percentage of revenue passenger miles represented by free flights exceeded 12%. And there was some evidence that the problem was growing.

BACKGROUND OF FREQUENT FLIER PROGRAMS

American Airlines first introduced frequent flier programs in 1981. Initially the program was meant to be a promotional gimmick designed to attract more customers. The program's immediate success in generating repeat business shocked the industry. This success forced other carriers to introduce their own free mileage programs, each promising better and better rewards to customers who would sign up. Through agreements with hotels, auto rental companies, and financial institutions, airlines made it possible for program participants to earn free miles by choosing where to stay, what auto to rent, or what credit card to use. By 1988, frequent flier programs were so popular that airlines owed more than 3 million round-trip domestic tickets to their free mileage program members. These tickets amounted to a minimum of 5.4 billion free miles according to one published report.

Susan S. Harmeling, MBA '91, prepared this case under the supervision of Professor William J. Bruns, Jr. as the basis for class discussion rather than to illustrate either effective or ineffective handling of an administrative situation.

The question was how, when, and whether participants would use their free miles. The worst scenario for the airline industry would have all their free fliers cashing in over a short period of time, taking up revenue-producing seats on many flights. In 1984, for example, Pan Am forced frequent fliers to use their awards or lose them, and the result was chaos at the check-in counter and a $50 million revenue loss. By 1991, all airlines limited the number of free travel award seats on some flights and used "blackout" dates during peak holiday travel periods when very limited or no free travel awards could be used. However, controls such as these had to be used cautiously to avoid diluting the promotional value of the programs. Members of a program who had earned a free flight but who then found it hard to schedule could easily switch their allegiance to another airline.

THE ACCOUNTING ISSUE

By 1990, all major airlines offered similar frequent flier programs. Members of a program would receive miles credited to their accounts based on the actual miles flown on the particular airline. In some cases, additional bonus miles were credited to members flying First or Business Class and, in certain circumstances, for flying certain routes or during periods when special promotions were offered.

The use of free mileage from frequent flier programs represented between 2% and 6% of total revenue passenger miles for each airline offering such awards in 1990. Based on the issuance of free travel awards to qualified members, coupled with program characteristics and the use of "blackout" dates during peak holiday periods, airlines generally did not consider the liability of free travel awards to be material.

In contrast, the airlines' auditors were concerned that growth of the programs might eventually force airlines to change the way in which they accounted for free miles. As more and more tickets were given away, and as paying passengers were replaced on flights by free fliers, a "new reality" might soon have to be reflected on the balance sheet and income statement.

The AICPA considered new rules that would likely force the airlines to change their accounting practices in 1988. When they did not take action, many observers thought the FASB might take up the problem, but the FASB did not add the issue to its agenda. Ultimately, the SEC issued a rule that required the airlines to disclose in their filings with the SEC, beginning in 1991, the number of free trips taken by frequent flier participants.

UNITED AIR LINES, INC.

One of the largest frequent flier programs was that of United Air Lines (United). Travel awards redeemed in 1990 by members of United's program totaled 1.2 million free trips, an increase of 200,000 over the prior year. By early 1991, United had enrolled more than 13.3 million members in its frequent flier program and was adding 130,000 new members each month. **Exhibits 1** and **2** contain some disclosures of financial and flight data taken from the 1990 Annual Report and Form 10K filed with the SEC by United in early 1991.

QUESTIONS

Part 1. The cost of United's frequent flier program:

    a.   What are the various methods United might use to measure the costs of its frequent flier program? What are the potential differences in dollars of the cost measured by each method?

    b.   What method should United use to measure the cost of its frequent flier program? Estimate the cost of the program using this method. Show all calculations and indicate the assumptions you make.

    c.   If you were the chief financial officer (CFO) of United, how would you determine if continuing the frequent flier program would be beneficial to United?

Part 2. Financial disclosure for United's frequent flier program:

    a.   Do you believe that United should account in its published financial statements for the frequent flier program or is "disclosure" in public filings with the SEC sufficient? Why?

    b.   In either case, what is it that should be accounted for or disclosed? Why?

    c.   What possible ways might United choose to account for the program in its published financial statements if it chooses to do so?

    d.   How do you believe United should account for the program in its published financial statements? Explain and support your chosen method and why you rejected other approaches. Show by some means (such as journal entries, T accounts, or pro forma statements) how your chosen method would be applied and all of the accounts that would be affected by the accounting you believe to be best.

    e.   If you were CFO of United, what would you do?

EXHIBIT 1
United Air Lines, Inc. Statement of Consolidated Financial Position (in thousands, except share data)

	December 31, 1990	December 31, 1989
Assets		
Current assets:		
Cash and cash equivalents	$ 221,401	$ 465,181
Short-term investments	973,695	957,312
Receivables, less allowance for doubtful accounts (1990—$13,129; 1989—$11,719)	912,663	888,015
Aircraft fuel, spare parts and supplies, less obsolescence allowance (1990—$57,406; 1989—$55,493)	322,866	248,581
Prepaid expenses	209,435	178,711
	2,640,060	2,737,800
Operating property and equipment:		
Owned—		
Flight equipment	5,677,428	5,217,535
Advances on flight equipment purchase contracts	641,281	427,616
Other property and equipment	1,747,415	1,537,401
	8,066,124	7,182,552
Accumulated depreciation and amortization	(3,565,590)	(3,557,440)
	4,500,534	3,625,112
Capital leases—		
Flight equipment	420,452	420,452
Other property and equipment	100,337	101,015
	520,789	521,467
Accumulated amortization	(272,394)	(248,117)
	248,395	273,350
	4,748,929	3,898,462
Other assets:		
Intangibles, less accumulated amortization (1990—$55,023; 1989—$42,074)	128,884	175,780
Deferred income taxes	49,193	71,022
Other	426,755	323,628
	604,832	570,430
	$7,993,821	$7,206,692

Notes are omitted.

EXHIBIT 1 (*continued*)
(In thousands, except share data)

| | December 31, | |
	1990	1989
Liabilities and Shareholders' Equity		
Current liabilities:		
Short-term borrowings	$ 447,260	$ 446,276
Long-term debt maturing within one year	61,607	60,928
Current obligations under capital leases	27,174	22,863
Advance ticket sales	842,665	660,639
Accounts payable	552,780	596,435
Accrued salaries, wages and benefits	675,547	585,983
Accrued aircraft rent	380,775	181,997
Accrued income taxes	86,945	62,656
Other accrued liabilities	682,514	606,046
	3,757,267	3,223,823
Long-term debt	**887,749**	945,667
Long-term obligations under capital leases	**361,246**	388,419
Other liabilities and deferred credits:		
Deferred pension liability	367,958	363,781
Deferred gains on sale and leaseback transactions	922,862	655,657
Other	24,493	62,945
	1,315,313	1,082,383
Redeemable preferred stock:		
5 1/2% cumulative prior preferred stock, $100 par value	**1,590**	2,067
Common shareholders' equity:		
Common stock, $5 par value; authorized, 125,000,000 shares; issued, 23,467,880 shares in 1990 and 23,419,953 shares in 1989	117,339	117,100
Additional capital invested	52,391	47,320
Retained earnings	1,620,885	1,526,534
Unearned compensation	(8,053)	(14,538)
Common stock held in treasury— 1,582,900 shares in 1990 and 1,585,400 shares in 1989	(111,906)	(112,083)
	1,670,656	1,564,333
Commitments and contingent liabilities		
	$7,993,821	$7,206,692

Notes are omitted.

EXHIBIT 1 (*continued*)
United Air Lines, Inc. Statement of Consolidated Operations (in thousands, except per share)

	Year Ended December 31,		
	1990	1989	1988
Operating Revenues:			
Passenger	$ 9,633,627	$8,536,000	$7,723,139
Cargo	592,872	521,274	509,639
Contract services and other	810,978	736,361	748,965
	11,037,477	9,793,635	8,981,743
Operating Expenses:			
Salaries and related costs	3,549,981	3,158,414	2,837,599
Aircraft fuel	1,811,417	1,352,511	1,179,571
Commissions	1,718,902	1,335,537	1,101,755
Depreciation and amortization	559,585	516,989	518,387
Purchased services	658,781	614,834	572,933
Rentals and landing fees	829,311	574,425	408,228
Aircraft maintenance materials and repairs	388,139	348,602	293,522
Food and beverages	241,583	213,693	193,367
Advertising and promotion	203,215	200,711	206,493
Personnel expenses	202,176	185,000	158,351
Other	910,663	828,379	846,609
	11,073,754	9,329,096	8,316,815
Earnings (loss) from operations	(36,277)	464,539	664,928
Other deductions (income):			
Interest expense	192,228	221,186	245,306
Interest capitalized	(71,323)	(51,884)	(30,983)
Interest income	(122,615)	(120,913)	(100,873)
Equity in earnings of Covia Partnership	(16,220)	(45,441)	(87,460)
Gain on sale of Covia Partnership interests	—	—	(393,006)
Net gains on disposition of property	(285,846)	(106,422)	(13,989)
Other, net	103,131	29,502	57,145
	(200,645)	(73,972)	(323,860)
Earnings from continuing operations before income taxes	164,368	538,511	988,788
Provision for income taxes	69,903	214,330	388,874
Earnings from continuing operations	94,465	324,181	599,914
Discontinued operations:			
Earnings from discontinued operations, less income taxes	—	—	457
Gain on sales of discontinued operations, less income taxes	—	—	523,929
Net earnings	$ 94,465	$ 324,181	$1,124,300
Net earnings per share:			
Continuing operations	$4.33	$14.96	$20.20
Discontinued operations	—	—	17.67
Net earnings	$4.33	$14.96	$37.87

Notes are omitted.

EXHIBIT 2
Selected Operating Statistics for United Air Lines, Inc.

	Year Ended December 31,				
	1990	1989	1988	1987	1986
Revenue aircraft miles (millions)[a]	597	552	543	553	507
Revenue aircraft departures	654,555	621,111	626,809	670,790	627,943
Available seat miles (millions)[b]	114,995	104,547	101,721	101,454	91,409
Revenue passenger miles (millions)[c]	76,137	69,639	69,101	66,348	59,312
Revenue passengers (thousands)	57,598	54,859	56,175	55,089	50,419
Average passenger journey (miles)	1,322	1,269	1,230	1,204	1,176
Average flight length (miles)	912	888	866	824	807
Passenger load factor[d]	66.2%	66.6%	67.9%	65.4%	64.9%
Breakeven load factor[e]	66.5%	63.0%	62.2%	63.0%	64.1%
Average yield per revenue passenger mile[f]	12.6¢	12.2¢	11.1¢	10.3¢	10.0¢
Cost per available seat mile[g]	9.6¢	8.9¢	8.2¢	7.9¢	7.7¢
Average price per gallon of jet fuel	80.4¢	63.6¢	56.0¢	57.8¢	56.2¢
Average fare per revenue passenger	$167.26	$155.60	$137.48	$124.45	$118.17
Average daily utilization of each aircraft (hours: minutes)[h]	8:14	8:09	8:29	9:04	8:46

[a] "Revenue aircraft miles" means the number of miles flown in revenue producing service.

[b] "Available seat miles" represents the number of seats available for passengers multiplied by the number of miles those seats are flown.

[c] "Revenue passenger miles" represents the number of miles flown by revenue passengers including frequent flier awards.

[d] "Passenger load factor" represents revenue passenger miles divided by available seat miles.

[e] "Breakeven load factor" represents the number of revenue passenger miles at which operating earnings would have been zero (based on the actual average yield) divided by available seat miles.

[f] "Average yield per revenue passenger mile" represents the average revenue received for each mile a revenue passenger is carried.

[g] "Cost per available seat mile" represents operating expenses divided by available seat miles.

[h] "Average daily utilization of each aircraft" means the average air hours flown in service per day per aircraft for the total fleet of aircraft.

Introduction to Owners' Equity

Almost all business organizations take one of three forms. The simplest form of organization is the *proprietorship*, or the business owned by a single individual. Typically, this individual has committed personal resources to the organization and has created the business entity. Whatever success the entity enjoys accrues to the owner as an individual. A *partnership* is a somewhat more sophisticated organization form, but it maintains several attributes of a single proprietorship. In this form, two or more persons agree to pool their resources and create a business entity, the success of which they will share equally or according to some agreement between them. The third widely used form of business organization is the *corporation*. In legal form, a corporation is more complex than either a proprietorship or partnership, but it is extremely popular for several reasons. One of the most important reasons is that it allows many investors to contribute their resources to one endeavor without the complication of agreements among them individually. Under the law, a corporation is a legal entity and as such assumes its own obligations. This frees the investor from having to use personal resources above the amount originally invested to satisfy claims against the entity, limiting liability. It also allows the use of ownership shares that can be exchanged for money or other securities should the shareholder wish to divest of ownership rights.

In terms of the aggregate amount of resources controlled by business organizations, the corporation is by far the most important form. It is for this reason that the remainder of this note will be concerned with corporation owners' equity.

ACCOUNTING FOR OWNERSHIP IN CORPORATIONS

Several technical complexities of accounting for ownership in corporations are the result of the laws that allow the creation of the corporation. The corporation must account to owners in the form required by the laws of the state or country in which the entity was formed; if securities issued by the corporation are traded publicly, regulations of applicable Company's Acts, the Securities & Exchange Commission,

Professor William J. Bruns, Jr. prepared this note as the basis for class discussion.

stock exchanges, and other regulatory agencies must also be heeded. Legal distinctions among classes of ownership, types of capital contributions, and the retention of the accumulated retained earnings are extremely important to the accountant maintaining records of corporate activity for management or public reporting. But from our point of view, they are important only insofar as some understanding is necessary if we are to read and use intelligently the accounting information in published financial reports.

Classification of Owners of Corporations

The owners of the common stock are the owners of the corporation. This group ultimately bears the risk of the operation of the business organization. It is also usually the last to receive distributions of income. In return for this assumption of risk not taken by others, it may receive higher returns than others if the entity is successful. It also usually has voting rights. In many respects, the common shareholder is analogous to the owner in a proprietorship.

Another important class of owners in some corporations is the preferred shareholders. The importance of the *preferred* designation usually revolves about the promise that dividends will be paid to this class of shareholders in a specified amount each period before any dividends are paid to common shareholders. Legal distinctions about payments in excess of this specified amount, or the effect of skipping a dividend payment on future dividend payments, can create a host of different legal subclassifications under the general category of preferred shareholders.

A third class of owners who may have some rights in particular situations within corporate operations, are those who hold certain classes of debt, such as mortgage bonds or debentures, which either give them a voice in the activities of the corporation or allow them to obtain a voice if certain contractual obligations are not satisfied. Some bond agreements allow holders to convert to an ownership interest at some time in the future or under specified conditions.

Rights and Responsibilities of Shareholders

The common shareholders are responsible for the management of the corporation. But due to the large number of shareholders typically represented, taking an active part in day-to-day management is usually impossible. This right is normally exercised through their election of a board of directors, which selects and directs the management of the corporation. While it is possible for shareholders to step forward and play a more active role in management by replacing those managers who have been selected by the board of directors with others, or even by replacing the board of directors itself, such action rarely occurs. Dissident shareholders are more apt to sell their interest in the corporation, thereby transferring their rights to others. They are then free to invest in situations in which they feel more comfortable, from which they feel they can receive a more satisfactory return, or through which they can accomplish other personal objectives.

It is important to note that the relationship between a corporation and common shareholders is not a direct one, but rather an indirect one through their acquisition of shares. The corporation sells shares originally in exchange for assets or services, usually cash, to shareholders. If original shareholders subsequently exchange their shares, transferring their rights to others, the corporation receives no added benefits. Records of current owners of shares are maintained by the company or its agents to ensure payment of dividends to current holders of shares. But the amount received by the corporation for a given share is determined only once—at the time the share is issued.

For many large corporations, shares are traded on a day-to-day basis on stock exchanges or through other electronic auction mechanisms. The prices for which shares are traded depend upon the evaluations and assessments of future corporate prospects by current shareholders and prospective investors. Except for those situations in which the corporation itself may acquire shares once held by shareholders (*treasury stock*), the owners' equity section in financial reports is unaffected by the day-to-day trading of ownership shares.

Accounting for Dividends

Cash or other assets are paid to shareholders as a dividend only when a dividend is declared by the board of directors. The decision to pay cash dividends normally rests on the availability of resources not essential to the continued operation of the corporation and the desire of the board of directors to provide some immediate and tangible return to those who have invested in the common shares of the corporation. A cash dividend is typically declared on a per-share basis; that is, the declaration may read "the Board of Directors of the X Corporation will pay a dividend of $.125 per share to each shareholder of record as of February 28, 2005." The effect of this declaration, which might be made at any time prior to the payment date, will be to cause a dividend check to be prepared and mailed to each owner whose name is registered as the owner of shares by the secretary or agent of the corporation. The check to each shareholder will represent the dividend payment appropriate to the number of shares owned.

At the time a dividend declaration is made, the effect on owners' equity should be apparent. A new obligation is created since the dividend declaration has a legal standing amongst the other obligations and liabilities of the corporation. Retained earnings, a part of owners' equity, is reduced, and the declared dividend becomes a liability to the corporation. The following are the journal entries when a dividend of $100,000 is declared and subsequently paid.

Date of Declaration: The date on which the Board of Directors declares the dividends.

Dr: Retained Earnings	$100,000	
Cr: Dividends Payable		$100,000

Date of Record: The date used to establish those stockholders who will receive the declared dividend. No journal entry is recorded.

Date of Payment: The date the dividend is paid to the shareholders of record.

Dr: Dividend Payable	$100,000	
Cr: Cash		$100,000

The Sale of Stock and Stock Distributions

When you examine the owners' equity section of a statement of financial position for a corporation, you are likely to find a minimum of three classifications. One of these is likely to be titled common stock; the second, paid-in-capital in excess of par or some equivalent phrase; and finally, a third, retained earnings.

Shares are typically issued by a corporation in exchange for resources, usually cash, that are given by the investor to the organization in exchange for the rights they obtain by owning shares. Usually the entire amount that an owner pays for shares is transferred to the corporation, except perhaps an amount for commissions to some selling agent for carrying out certain promotional activities related to the sales of shares. In the simplest form, sale of stock involves recognition that the resources of the organization have been increased without a related legal obligation to pay in the future. The effect of such an exchange is to increase owners' equity in the classification of common stock. However, legal distinctions required in accounting for owners' equity frequently complicate this simple procedure.

Common stock may be legally identified as par value stock or no par stock. Par value stock typically has a money figure quoted with it; that is, the corporation may be authorized to issue up to 1,000 shares of common stock with a par value of $5.00 per share. The mechanism of stated par value at one time was designed to protect investors and creditors, but today it has lost much of its significance. For this reason, many shares are now simply identified as no par common shares. However, to complicate the task of accounting for corporate equities, when no par shares are used, the laws of some countries and states require that a *stated value* per share be established, and that this be used in lieu of par value in recording the sale of shares. The use of par value or stated value means that not all the proceeds from the issuance of shares are credited to the common stock account. Those in excess of par or stated value are credited to a separate account called *paid-in-capital in excess of par* or sometimes *capital surplus*.

For example, XYZ sells 50,000 shares for $5 per share. Each share has a $1 par value. The journal entry that would be recorded is the following:

Dr: Cash	$250,000	
Cr: Common Stock		$ 50,000
Cr. Paid in Capital in Excess of Par		$200,000

Exhibit 1 shows the stockholders' equity of the Gillette Company and Subsidiary Companies at the end of 2003 and 2002. *Treasury stock* and *cumulative foreign currency translation adjustments*, will be discussed briefly below.

Amounts of paid-in-capital and common stock are usually subjected to some restrictions under the laws of the country or state in which the corporation is incorporated. These restrictions usually prevent dividend payments to common shareholders when the net worth of the corporation is less than the sum of par or stated values.

Sometimes shares are distributed in exchange for services or for resources other than cash. The basic principles for recording ownership rights remain the same. The valuation of shares issued rests in these cases on the market value of services or resources acquired, often measured by the market value of shares given in exchange. Thus, the owners' equity, as recorded in the common stock and related paid-in-capital accounts, should give the reader of a financial statement some impression of the amount contributed by shareholders to the corporation in the form of resources or services.

In addition to the distribution of shares through sale, other means have been established for increasing the number of shares outstanding. Stock distributions can take the form of *stock splits* or *stock dividends*. While a distinction is normally made between these two types of transactions, they are essentially the same. Both can be referred to as stock distributions.

Stock distribution takes place whenever the board of directors elects to send additional shares to each shareholder on a pro-rata basis. In the case of a stock split, no entry in the records or change to the monetary amounts is shown in the reports of the organization, except that the par value changes. A memorandum stating that the number of shares outstanding has been changed is appropriate. Accounting for stock dividends is somewhat different. Provided the stock dividend increases the number of shares outstanding by 20% or less, an amount equal to the market value of the shares distributed is transferred from retained earnings to the common stock and paid-in-capital account. Because the dividend results in the permanent transfer of retained earnings to paid-in-capital, the effect of a stock dividend transaction is sometimes referred to as *capitalizing retained earnings*.

Treasury Stock

When shares are traded on open financial markets, the corporation can purchase its own shares. Alternatively, some shareholders may express dissatisfaction with management action, and management may negotiate a purchase of the dissident shareholders' stock.

Sometimes shares are reacquired to reduce permanently the number of shares outstanding. If so, the shares are retired, and the records of their initial sale are updated to show that the shares are no longer in the shareholders' hands. Any apparent gain or loss in their cancellation affects the net worth of the remaining shares, but it has no income statement effect.

At other times, shares are reacquired and not canceled. Instead, they are held for future resale, distribution to officers or employees, used as gifts, or even to satisfy obligations to other persons or organizations. Shares so held are called *treasury shares* and reduce the amount of owners' equity shown in the accounts. Treasury shares are not an asset because the corporation cannot own itself or any part of itself. Even though the shares may have value because people may buy them at the market price, that value is not an asset, nor does it belong to the corporation and the holders of shares still outstanding. Shares held in treasury receive no dividends nor may they be voted in shareholders' meetings. Their purchase price appears as a reduction of stockholders' equity until they are resold.

Assume ABC acquires 1,000 of its own shares at $8 per share. Each share was initially sold for $5 and had a $1 par value. There are two methods to account for treasury stock: the par value method and the cost method. The cost method is more commonly used and is recorded in the following manner.

```
Dr: Treasury Stock                          $8,000
   Cr: Cash                                              $8,000
```

Alternatively, the recognition of the stock repurchase using the par value method will result in the following journal entry:

```
Dr: Treasury Stock                    $1,000   (1,000 shares at $1 par value)
Dr: Paid in Capital in excess of Par  $4,000   (1,000 shares * $4 excess of par)
Dr: Retained Earnings                 $3,000   (to balance)
   Cr: Cash                                   $8,000
```

Cumulative Foreign Currency Translation Adjustments

Many corporations own subsidiaries that operate in countries other than the domicile of the parent country. When the financial statements of these foreign subsidiaries are consolidated with those of the parent company, the foreign currency must be converted to the home country currency. The conversion process is referred to as *foreign currency translation*. Because exchange rates fluctuate over time, and because of the mechanics of translation, differences between the translated value of the subsidiaries' assets and liabilities and the translated value of the subsidiaries' owners' equity can arise. In order to maintain the equality of assets and total equities, these translation differences require recognition somewhere in the financial statements. In many circumstances, it seems inappropriate to include this difference as a gain or loss in the computation of net income, since it results only from the mechanics of the translation process. For this reason, cumulative foreign currency translation gains and losses are usually excluded from the computation of net income, but a record is maintained in the shareholders' equity section of the balance sheet to allow the integrity of the statement of financial position to be maintained with assets equaling liabilities and owners' equity.

MERGERS, ACQUISITIONS AND LEVERAGED BUYOUTS (LBOS)

Because a corporation is a separate entity, it is free to purchase another corporation. Sometimes such mergers occur with the approval of the acquired firm, and sometimes they do not. An unfriendly acquisition may occur when one firm acquires another by purchasing the stock of the company being acquired by paying cash or other securities to the shareholders of the targeted firm. Unfriendly acquisitions of this type are frequently called *takeovers*. In a friendly merger, managers usually agree, and terms are negotiated that allow one firm to acquire another by issuing stock of the surviving company to shareholders of the firm being acquired. In most cases, whether an acquisition or merger is friendly or unfriendly, it is undertaken in the belief that operating efficiencies in management and facilities utilization will result in performance superior to that which would have been obtained if the two firms had continued as separate entities.

A *leveraged buyout* takes place when the management of a firm elects to add debt in order to get the cash needed to buy the shares of public stockholders. Without shareholders (or at least nonmanagement shareholders), it is less likely that a corporation will be a target of an unfriendly acquisition. The burden of servicing the added debt and paying interest as it falls due affects both cash flow and profitability of the corporation.

In some cases, leveraged buyouts have taken place because a group of managers hope to leverage the performance of the corporation to their own benefit by eliminating other shareholders and by using financial leverage to the advantage of the shares they own. They hope the payoffs to themselves through share ownership and control of discretionary salaries and bonuses will justify the added risk of a heavily indebted corporation.

SUMMARY

Owners' equity is both the measure of the residual equity of the owners and a record of the sources of that entity. Corporations may have different classes of shareholders. When they do, separate records are needed to report the differential rights and capitalization of the classes. Shares can usually be transferred from one owner to another without the consent of the corporation and without additional payment to the company. Usually shares are sold by the corporation only once. The company keeps records to maintain the distinction between the capital directly contributed and earnings subsequently retained.

Dividends can be paid only if assets are available for distribution to shareholders, and legal restrictions for protection of creditors are met. When dividends are declared, they become a liability of the firm. Stock dividends are not dividends at all; they merely represent an increase in the number of shares of ownership having a claim on an unchanged equity. They do, however, reduce the amount of retained earnings by transferring a measured amount of retained earnings to the common stock and paid-in-capital accounts. Stock distributions or splits, which may be used to increase or decrease the number of shares outstanding, do not affect the value of owners' equity.

In recent years, the phenomenon of leveraged buyouts (LBOs) has led to a shift in the capital structure of many firms. Managers borrow money, thus leveraging the firm, and use the cash to acquire outstanding shares. This transaction reduces the amount of stockholders' equity outstanding and, at the same time, increases the amount of debt. After such an LBO, the debt-to-equity ratio increases, often substantially. Returns to the remaining shareholders can be leveraged dramatically if the company is able to meet the interest payments on debt issued to retire the outstanding stock.

EXHIBIT 1
Stockholders' Equity—The Gillette Company and Subsidiary Companies (Excerpt from Consolidated Balance Sheets) ($ millions)

At December 31,	2003	2002
Stockholders' Equity		
Common stock, par value $1 per share		
Authorized: 2,320 shares		
Issued 2003—1,374 shares; 2002—1,370 shares	1,374	1,370
Additional paid-in capital	1,273	1,197
Earnings reinvested in the business	7,333	6,608
Accumulated other comprehensive loss	(1,088)	(1,523)
Treasury stock, at cost:		
2003—367 shares; 2002—326 shares	(6,665)	(5,392)
Deferred stock-based compensation	(3)	—
Total Stockholders' Equity	2,224	2,260

Foreign Currency Translation

Financial statements of operating subsidiaries outside the U.S., other than those operating in highly inflationary environments, are measured using the local currency as the financial currency. Adjustments from translating these financial statements in U.S. dollars are accumulated in the equity section of the balance sheet under the caption "Accumulated other comprehensive loss." For those non-U.S. subsidiaries that are included in the Company's U.S. tax return, these adjustments are net of U.S. income tax.

Solving the Puzzle of the Cash Flow Statement

The cash flow statement is one of the most useful financial statements companies prepare. When analyzed in a rational, logical manner, it can illuminate a treasure trove of clues as to how a company is balancing its receivables and payables, paying for its growth, and otherwise managing its flow of funds. But many readers seem to bypass the cash flow statement and head only for the old, familiar, comfortable income statement and balance sheet—despite the fact that the cash flow statement may provide considerable information about what is really happening in a business beyond that contained in either of the other two statements.

There are several reasons why the cash flow statement may not get the attention it deserves. First, although it has been around in its present format since mid-1988, it is still considered the "new statement": many managers were not exposed to it during their business schooling in financial analysis. If they were, they may have been taught how to prepare one but not how to interpret the story it tells.

Second, the format of the "Cash Flow from Operating Activities" section of the statement can be challenging to follow if presented in what is known as the "indirect" method. But perhaps most daunting to many is the mistaken idea that it takes a very sophisticated analysis of complicated ratios and relationships to use a cash flow statement effectively.

Contributing to this notion are numerous business journal articles that have appeared in the past decade. They promote the value of the statement when appropriate cash flow ratios are used in statistical packages, such as those used to predict bankruptcy. Present day textbooks, when teaching students to prepare the statement, also concentrate on describing how ratios such as "free cash flow to net income" can be derived, but say little about what truly useful information these ratios or other information from the cash flow statement may provide.

Analyzing this statement should not present a formidable task when reviewed in the manner we are advocating here. Instead, it will quickly become obvious that the benefits of understanding the sources and uses of a company's cash far outweigh the costs of undertaking some very straightforward analyses. Executives want to know if the cash generated by the company will be sufficient to fund their expansion strategy; stockholders want to know if the firm is generating enough cash to pay dividends; suppliers want to know if their customers will be able to pay if offered credit; investors

Julie H. Hertenstein and Sharon M. McKinnon authored this article. Reprinted from Business Horizons, January–February 1997. Copyright 1997 by the Foundation for the School of Business at Indiana University. Used with permission.

want to evaluate future growth potential; and employees are interested in the overall viability of their employer as indicated by its ability to fund its operations. These are just a few of the valuable insights to be gained from the cash flow statement.

The method we suggest for studying this valuable statement contains several steps, with the preliminary step consisting of gaining a basic understanding of the format of the cash flow statement. Once a certain "comfort level" with the structure of the statement has been attained, individual companies' statements should be examined to gain practice in using the stepwise approach described shortly. These steps consist of:

1. scanning the big picture;
2. checking the power of the cash flow engine;
3. pinpointing the good news and the bad news; and
4. putting the puzzle together.

Pay attention, for you will be tested on your new expertise at the end of this article!

FORMAT OF THE CASH FLOW STATEMENT

The cash flow statement is divided into three sections: operating activities, investing activities, and financing activities. **Exhibit 1** presents an example of a simple cash flow statement with the three sections delineated in bold letters. Each section shows the cash inflows and outflows associated with that type of activity.

Cash flow from operating activities shows the results of cash inflows and outflows related to the fundamental operations of the basic line or lines of business in which the company engages. For example, it includes cash receipts from the sale of goods or services and cash outflows for purchasing inventory and paying rent and taxes. You will notice it does not show these items directly. It assumes that most of these cash inflows and outflows are already summarized in the "Net Income" figure, so it starts at that figure and makes an adjustment for everything that is not a true representation of "cash in and out" in net income. This approach is the "indirect format" of presenting cash flows from operating activities and is the one chosen by most companies. The indirect format can be confusing, and a longer explanation of "direct versus indirect" formats is provided in the **Appendix** for readers who desire more information.

Regardless of how the cash flow from operating activities is formatted, it is important to remember that this is the most important of the three sections because it describes how cash is being generated or used by the primary activities of the company. To picture activities that affect cash flow from operations, think of the cash receipts and payments that make most working capital accounts on the balance sheet increase or decrease. For example, accounts receivable decreases when cash is collected from customers, inventory increases when goods are purchased, and accounts payable decreases when suppliers are paid for their goods.

The next section is called *cash flow from investing activities*. Here you see the cash flows associated with purchases and sales of noncurrent assets, such as building and equipment purchases, or sales of investments or subsidiaries. An easy way to picture what activities would be here is to think again of a balance sheet. If you assume current assets are associated with operations, then the activities associated with all the rest of the assets are in this section.

The third section is called *cash flow from financing activities*. Again, the balance sheet provides a handy way of discerning what would be in this section. If you eliminate the current liabilities associated with operations, then the activities of all the rest of the liabilities and the stockholders' equity accounts are summarized here. These are all the flows associated with financing the firm, everything from selling and paying off bonds to issuing stock and paying dividends.

Warning! There are exceptions to everything, and the cash flow statement format has a few to watch out for. Two working capital accounts, one asset and one liability, are dealt with outside the cash flow from operating activities section. Short-term marketable securities are treated as long-term investments and appear in cash flow from investing activities; similarly, short-term debt is treated as long-term debt and appears in cash flow from financing activities.

Another anomaly is the treatment of interest and dividends. Although dividends are handled as a cash outflow in the cash flow from financing activities section, interest payments are considered an operating outflow, despite the fact that both are payments to outsiders for using their money! In some countries, such as the United Kingdom, interest payments are included in the financing activities section. But in the United States, the Financial Accounting Standards Board (FASB) voted that interest payments should be in the operating activities section instead. In such a situation, one might have to adjust somewhat if one were trying to compare a UK company like British Petroleum to a U.S. company like Exxon.

STEP 1: SCANNING THE BIG PICTURE

Now, sit back with your favorite company's annual report and follow these steps to understanding its cash flow picture. You can think of this as a big puzzle exercise. All the pieces are there in the statement; your task is to put them in the proper context to form a mosaic from which a picture of the firm's cash flow health emerges. If you don't have an annual report handy, you can use **Exhibit 2**, which shows the cash flow statements for the Colgate-Palmolive Company for the years ending 1992, 1993, and 1994. We chose Colgate-Palmolive because it represents one of the best annual reports in the country and the positive trends are clear for illustrative purposes. Other reports may not contain such "rosy scenarios," as you will discover shortly.

Scanning the big picture involves several substeps. The first is to place your company in context in terms of its age, industry, and size. We expect mature companies to have different cash flows from start-up companies, and service industries to look different from heavy manufacturing industries. Big corporations may experience declining cash flows in certain years, but the sheer immensity of their cash flows may ameliorate concerns, whereas the declining trend might be much more worrisome if they were small firms without such vast resources.

Colgate-Palmolive certainly qualifies as a mature company. It is huge (figures are rounded to millions), and it operates primarily in consumer product markets throughout the world. A firm like this should be involved in complex activities on a global scale. Colgate-Palmolive certainly is, but its cash flow statement is not much more complex than what one might expect from a much smaller, perhaps simpler, company.

Continue your big picture scan by flipping through the annual report to determine how management believes the year has progressed. Was it a good year? Perhaps a record-breaking year in terms of revenues or net income? Or is management explaining how the company has weathered some rough times?

A key part of the big picture scan is to look at a key summary figure of financial health—net income. If the cash flow statement has been prepared using the indirect method for operating cash flows, as Colgate-Palmolive's has, you can find this at the top of the cash flow statement. Otherwise you'll have to use the reconciliation of net income and operating cash flows that accompanies the cash flow statement, or take a peek at the income statement itself. What is the bottom line? Does it show income or losses over the past few years? Is income (or loss) growing or shrinking? Keep these points in mind as you examine the cash flows. In addition, scan the comparative numbers for the past three years for unusual items you'd like to have explained eventually.

Colgate-Palmolive shows positive net income for all three years—a promising start. The three year trend appears to be positive, but a big drop in 1993 raises a few questions. The statement also reveals a few items that need to be checked out. In the operating activities section, what is that "cumulative effect on prior years of accounting changes" in 1993? And what are those "restructured operations"? File those away to examine later. Note any line items that are vastly different from year to year. Colgate-Palmolive has a few of those, including changes in its working capital accounts, the proceeds from issuance of debt, and its purchases of treasury stock.

STEP 2: CHECKING THE POWER OF THE CASH FLOW ENGINE

The cash flow from operating activities section is the cash flow engine of the company. When this engine is working effectively, it provides the cash flows to cover the cash needs of operations. It also provides cash necessary for routine needs, such as the replacement of worn-out equipment and the payment of dividends. There are exceptions, of course. Start-up companies, for example, usually have negative cash flows from operating activities because their cash flow engines are not yet up to speed. Companies in cyclical industries might have negative operating cash flows in a "down" year; a company that has experienced an extensive strike could also be expected to have negative cash flow from operating activities. Although occasional years of negative cash flow from operating activities do not spell disaster, on the average we should expect it to be positive.

To check the cash flow engine, first observe whether cash flow from operating activities is greater than zero. Also check whether it is growing or shrinking. Assuming it is positive, the next question is whether or not it is adequate for important, routine expenditures. Just as we do not expect a start-up company to have positive cash flow from operating activities, we also do not expect a company still in a very rapid growth phase to generate enough cash flow from operating activities to cover the investments required to rapidly expand the firm. However, we do expect the operations of a mature company to generate enough cash to "keep the company whole." This would include the amount of investment required to replace those fixed assets that are used up, worn out, or technologically obsolete, as well as cash required to pay the annual dividend shareholders have come to expect.

It is difficult to know precisely how much cash is required to keep the company's fixed assets "whole," because the cash flow statement does not separate capital expenditures for replacement and renewal from those for expansion and growth. However, the annual depreciation amount provides a very rough surrogate for the amount of fixed assets that need to be replaced each year. In periods when prices are rising, the cost to replace assets should be somewhat greater than the cost of older assets that are being depreciated. So to ensure that the firm is kept whole and is not shrinking, we should expect the portion of investing activities related to the purchase of fixed assets to exceed depreciation.

Important information about the cash flow engine is also revealed by examining the operating working capital accounts. In the Colgate-Palmolive operating activities section, these are shown under "cash effects of these changes." In a healthy, growing company, we would expect growth in operating working capital accounts such as inventory and accounts receivable as well as in accounts payable and other operating payables. Obviously there can be quite a bit of variability in working capital accounts from period to period. Streamlining a collections policy or implementing a Just-In-Time inventory system could shrink accounts receivable or inventory in a growing company. But on the average, inventories, receivables, and accounts payable usually grow in expanding companies. Beware of situations in which all working capital accounts increase net cash from operating activities. This likely would not happen randomly in a healthy, growing company. It normally results from deliberate management action and could indicate a company in such a cash flow crisis that managers have been forced to raid the working capital accounts to survive.

With these ground rules, let's check Colgate-Palmolive's cash flow engine. In all three years, cash flow from operating activities is greater than zero, reaching over $800 million in 1994. It increases steadily every year, unlike net income. Annual depreciation is in the vicinity of $200 million each year, and the yearly dividend is also around $200 million. Colgate-Palmolive's cash flow engine is not only generating enough cash to cover "keeping the company whole," it is also able to throw off around $400 million annually for growth and investment, and the amount of excess cash has been increasing each year.

This is a powerful cash flow engine. A glance at the working capital account differences indicates that receivables, other assets, and payables have grown (net) over the three years, while inventories have shrunk slightly. This picture is consistent with a global company increasing its scope through acquisitions and new product development.

STEP 3: PINPOINTING THE GOOD NEWS AND THE BAD NEWS

This step involves looking at the total cash flow statement to find where the rest of the "good news" and "bad news" lie. What you are looking for is the story the statement is trying to tell you. It will not come simply by divine revelation, but by systematic observation of the items on the statement and their trends over the years presented for your comparison.

Begin with cash flow from investing activities. What is this section trying to tell you? One systematic observation is to check whether the company is generating or using cash in its investing activities. Whereas we expect positive cash flow from operating activities, we also expect a healthy company to invest continually in more plant, equipment, land, and other fixed assets to replace the assets that have been used up or have become technologically obsolete, as well as to expand and grow. Although companies often sell assets that are no longer of use to them, they would normally purchase more capital assets than they sell. As a result, we generally expect negative cash flows from investing activities. As with operating activities, exceptions do occur, especially if the firm divests a business or subsidiary. However, watch for companies that are beginning to shrink substantially because they are generating much of their cash by selling off chunks of the business!

Colgate-Palmolive exhibits the signs of a "good news from investing activities" company. Capital expenditures are nearly 1.5 times the amount of depreciation, so they are clearly at a level well beyond that required to keep the company whole. In addition, Colgate-Palmolive makes significant expenditures for acquisitions in each year—another growth indicator. These numbers remain consistent or increase from year to year and paint a picture of a steadily growing company, with enough cash flow from operating activities to cover these expenditures and more.

Cash flows from financing activities could as easily be positive as negative in a healthy company. Moreover, they are likely to change back and forth, so finding the "good" and "bad" is more challenging. It requires viewing the cash flows from financing activities in conjunction with other information on the cash flow statement and basing your conclusions on the weight of the evidence and your own judgment. Assume a company has borrowed cash or issued stock. A "good news" scenario might be that the firm has carefully analyzed its leverage and cost of capital and chosen to finance itself through debt or equity rather than from cash from operations. Another "good news" scenario might be that a new start-up is doing well enough to issue an Initial Public Offering. On the other hand, a "bad news" scenario might be that the company has low (or negative) cash flows from operations and is being forced to generate funds from other sources. You must look at the entire package to evaluate whether your cash flows from financing are in the "good news" or "bad news" categories.

One systematic way to begin is to compare borrowing and payments on debt with each other across the years and note the trends. Colgate-Palmolive has been consistently borrowing more than it has paid back, and to a very substantial degree in 1993. Good news or bad? We have already seen the incredible amount of cash being thrown off from operations, so this increase in debt financing is probably the result of a conscious management decision and not the actions of a company desperately borrowing to survive. Nevertheless, it might be worth another more detailed look if we wanted to consider whether continued borrowing provides a likely source of funds for future growth, or whether the firm is nearing its debt capacity.[1]

---

[1] This might be the time to go looking for clues in the rest of the annual report. Where to look? A footnote on long-term debt might seem logical, but it is often almost impossible to truly understand unless you are a Chief Financial Officer. Easier and sometimes more illuminating is to do some simple ratios on the balance sheet and income statement. How has debt changed as a percentage of total liabilities and stockholders' equity? For Colgate-Palmolive, the percentage of debt to total liabilities and stockholders' equity is quite high and has gotten higher, from 67% in 1993 to 70% in 1994. The company's income statement reveals that interest expense has almost doubled in the last year, and a quick ratio analysis of "number of times interest can be paid from income" shows a sharp decline from 7 times to about 4.5 times in one year. Further examination of the cash flow statement reveals that the company purchased large amounts of treasury stock. This helps explain why stockholders' equity is low in comparison to total equities, which may make that 70% debt-to-total equity ratio more understandable.

A second systematic step in uncovering the news in this section is to check the activities in the stock accounts. Colgate-Palmolive is not issuing much stock; instead, it seems to be buying back substantial amounts of treasury stock. In fact, that is the single largest use of cash outside of capital expenditures.[2] This is probably a "good news" scenario, because the company may be cashing in on what it considers a low price for its stock, or perhaps protecting itself from takeover attempts. In either event, Colgate-Palmolive appears to have sufficient cash available to make this large, non-routine investment. A little digging in the rest of the financial statements might present the whole story.

STEP 4: PUTTING THE PUZZLE TOGETHER

In evaluating the cash flow statement, you are evaluating many pieces of evidence to produce an overall picture. However, it would be rare to find a company in which all of the evidence is positive, or in which all of the evidence is negative. To make a balanced evaluation, you must use both the good news and the bad news identified in each section of the statement. To reach an overall conclusion, you need to judge the relative importance of each piece of evidence and assess its relationship to the overall picture. As in a legal case, your conclusion needs to be based on the "weight of the evidence."

Before proceeding with the overall evaluation, one loose end to tie up at this point might be any unusual line items you spotted in your scan of the big picture. Sometimes these demand that you ask an expert, but frequently you can think them through or search for illumination elsewhere in the annual report. Earlier we identified two unusual line items for Colgate-Palmolive. One was the "cumulative effect on prior years of an accounting change" in 1993. Without the deduction of this $358 million item from income in 1993, Colgate-Palmolive had a healthy income figure of $548 million. The explanation is that when Colgate-Palmolive made this accounting change, all of its effects prior to 1993 were charged to income in 1993. In reality, there was no actual expenditure of cash in 1993, which is why we added this back on the cash flow statement.[3] This is good to know, because if we ignore the accounting change and the associated charge, net income has steadily increased.

The other unusual line item was called "restructured operations," which Colgate-Palmolive subtracted from net income. This means that the cash flows associated with restructuring operations occurred in a different year from when these costs were expensed on the income statement. In all three years presented by Colgate-Palmolive, it had more cash outflows for restructuring than it expensed in the income statement.

Good news or bad news? When a company restructures some of its operations, there is both. The bad news is that there was some kind of problem that required the restructuring. The good news is that the company recognized the problem and took

---

[2] This contrasts with minor stock repurchases companies typically undertake to offer stock to employees in stock option plans; in such instances, modest treasury stock repurchases are offset by modest but comparable issuances of treasury stock.

[3] An accounting change is just a "paper decision"; it affects the way net income is presented, but it does not change the fundamental economic activity of the firm, so it does not affect cash receipts or cash expenditures.

action it hopes will be effective. Whether the restructuring cash costs are more or less than the restructuring expense is simply a timing issue. Because expenses are recognized as soon as reasonably possible, it typically requires several years after the expense has been recorded for all of the cash costs to be incurred. Colgate-Palmolive probably recognized these restructuring expenses in prior years and this is just the anticipated cash outflows catching up with them. Moreover, the amount on the cash flow statement is declining each year.

Whether or not to chase down explanations for unusual or unknown items is a subjective call. For example, if Colgate-Palmolive's restructuring charge differences were bigger or growing, it might be worthwhile to search for more information. However, the "weight of the evidence" so far indicates that this issue is not particularly relevant in getting at the big picture. If you encounter something you do not understand, consider its materiality. If it has a major effect on cash flow from operating activities, or if it ranks as one of the major sources or uses of cash, you should probably search for an explanation. Otherwise it may be more efficient to ignore it and concentrate on the many items you know.

Now let's summarize what we've learned by examining Colgate-Palmolive's cash flow statement. First, the good news. Net income has been positive for all three years and, if we eliminate the effects of the accounting change, has been steadily increasing. Operating cash flows have also been positive for three years; they, too, have been steadily increasing. Operating cash flows have significantly exceeded the sum of depreciation and dividends, so Colgate-Palmolive is generating enough cash from operations to expand the business. The working capital accounts are growing, consistent with the expectations for a growing business. By making capital expenditures that significantly exceed depreciation, and also by making fairly large acquisitions, Colgate-Palmolive shows that it is grooming the business for the future. There are no large-scale sales of fixed assets or divestitures that indicate any downsizing or shrinking of the business. The company has increased its dividend payments annually, an expression of management's confidence in the firm's future cash-generating capability. It also has sufficient excess cash to repurchase large amounts of its stock.

Now the bad news. The presence of charges for "restructured operations" indicates that Colgate-Palmolive has experienced problems in some portions of the business. It has borrowed significantly, in excess of repayment, which could increase leverage. The repurchase of stock could indicate management concerns with possible takeovers. And acquisitions sometimes create problems for firms; it is difficult to integrate them successfully into the company's business to ensure adequate returns.

The good news in the Colgate-Palmolive cash flow story is quite compelling. The bad news is more at the level of "concerns" rather than major cash flow problems. So considering the weight of the evidence, Colgate-Palmolive appears to have a strong positive cash flow story.

Now it's your turn. The best way to learn about cash flow statements is to study some carefully using the four steps described above. You may not become an expert but you will be able to spot the big trends and important issues involved with the management of cash in most companies.

Exhibit 3 provides you with the opportunity to test your newfound skills. It is similar to the puzzles you encountered as a child in which you spot the things that are wrong with the picture. Poor Jones Company is having some rough times, as illuminated by their cash flow statements for 1993, 1994, and 1995. See how many of these troubling developments you can identify by putting together the Puzzle of the Cash Flow Statement! (Some possible answers are listed in footnote 4.)

Opportunities for applying your new expertise are many. As an employee curious about your company's ability to cover your paycheck, you can check out the health of cash flow from operating activities. Or suppose you are a supplier whose customer has just announced a loss for the year and you are wondering whether to continue to extend credit. An analysis of the customer's cash flow from operating activities can provide you with evidence that the firm does or does not have strong enough cash flows from operating activities to pay its bills despite losses on the income statement.

If you are a stockholder, you may be interested in whether cash flow from operating activities is large enough to invest in the capital expenditures required to keep the company whole and make it grow while still paying the dividend you have come to expect. As an executive, you might examine the cash flow statement to determine whether it is likely that all of the major sources of cash—operating activities, issuing stock, and borrowing—will be sufficient to fund a major expansion program you plan to undertake. As your expertise increases, many other useful applications may appear to you.

The information contained in a cash flow statement cannot replace the information from the traditional income statement and balance sheet. But it does provide valuable input for understanding the relationships between income and its short- and long-term ability to generate cash.

REFERENCES

Mohamed A. Rujoub, Doris M. Cook, and Leon E. Hay, "Using Cash Flow Ratios To Predict Business Failures," *Journal of Managerial Issues*, Spring 1995, pp. 75–90.
"The Top 8 Reports," *Institutional Investor*, September 1995, pp. 123–129.

---

[4] Some possible answers are: (1) there have been losses in all three years; (2) depreciation charges have decreased; (3) capital expenditures are less than depreciation; (4) capital expenditures are less than disposals; (5) a big accounts receivable increase needs to be investigated; (6) inventories are decreasing; (7) segments of the business are being sold off; (8) the company has stopped paying dividends; (9) debt needs to be paid off with cash flow from operations; (10) there is much borrowing; and (11) there is less borrowing this year. Are creditors trusting the company less?

EXHIBIT 1
Statement of Cash Flows

Cash Flow from Operating Activities

Net Income	xxx,xxx
Adjustments to reconcile net income to net cash provided by operating activities	
Depreciation and amortization	xx,xxx
Changes in other accounts affecting operations	
(Increase)/Decrease in accounts receivable	x,xxx
(Increase)/Decrease in inventories	x,xxx
(Increase)/Decrease in prepaid expenses	x,xxx
Increase/(Decrease) in accounts payable	x,xxx
Increase/(Decrease) in taxes payable	x,xxx
Net cash provided by operating activities	xxx,xxx

Cash Flow from Investing Activities

Capital expenditures	(xxx,xxx)
Proceeds from sales of equipment	xx,xxx
Proceeds from sales of investments	xx,xxx
Investment in subsidiary	(xxx,xxx)
Net cash provided by (used in) investing activities	(xxx,xxx)

Cash Flow from Financing Activities

Payments of long-term debt	(xx,xxx)
Proceeds from issuance of long-term debt	xx,xxx
Proceeds from issuance of common stock	xxx,xxx
Dividends paid	(xx,xxx)
Purchase of treasury stock	(xx,xxx)
Net cash provided by (used in) financing activities	(xx,xxx)

Increase/Decrease in Cash   xx,xxx

EXHIBIT 2
Consolidated Statements of Cash Flows: Colgate-Palmolive

(in millions)	1994	1993	1992
Operating Activities			
Net Income	$ 580.2	$ 189.9	$ 477.0
Adjustments to reconcile net income to cash provided by operations			
Cumulative effect on prior years of accounting changes	—	358.2	—
Restructured operations, net	(39.1)	(77.0)	(92.0)
Depreciation and amortization	235.1	209.6	192.5
Deferred income taxes and other, net	64.7	53.6	(25.8)
Cash effects of these changes			
(Increase) in receivables	(50.1)	(103.6)	(38.0)
(Increase)/decrease in inventories	(44.5)	31.7	28.4
(Increase)/decrease in other current assets	(7.8)	(4.6)	10.6
Increase/(decrease) in payables	90.9	52.6	(10.0)
Net cash provided by operations	829.4	710.4	542.7
Investing Activities			
Capital expenditures	(400.8)	(364.3)	(318.5)
Payment for acquisitions	(146.4)	(171.2)	(170.1)
Investments	(1.9)	(12.5)	(6.6)
Sale of securities and investments	58.4	33.8	79.9
Other, net	33.0	61.7	17.4
Net cash used for investing activities	(457.7)	(452.5)	(397.9)
Financing Activities			
Principal payments on debt	(88.3)	(200.8)	(250.1)
Proceeds from issuance of debt	316.4	782.1	262.6
Proceeds from outside investors	15.2	60.0	—
Proceeds from exercise of stock options	18.5	21.8	22.6
Dividends paid	(246.9)	(231.4)	(200.7)
Purchase of treasury stock	(357.9)	(657.2)	(20.5)
Net cash used for financing activities	(343.0)	(225.5)	(186.1)
Effect of exchange rate changes on cash	(2.9)	(6.2)	(9.3)
Net increase (decrease) in cash	$ 25.8	$ 26.2	$ (50.6)

EXHIBIT 3
Jones Company: Statements of Cash Flows for Year Ending December 31

(in millions)	1995	1994	1993
Cash Flow from Operating Activities			
Net income (loss)	$ (43)	$(189)	$(134)
Depreciation	230	271	350
(Increase) in receivables	(121)	(25)	(4)
Decrease in inventories	50	42	30
Changes in other current accounts	16	(8)	(12)
Net cash provided by operating activities	132	91	230
Cash Flow from Investing Activities			
Capital expenditures	(200)	(260)	(300)
Disposal of plant assets	204	200	180
Disposal of business segment	134	51	—
Net cash (used in)/provided by investing activities	138	(9)	(120)
Cash Flow from Financing Activities			
Proceeds of long-term debt	200	450	215
Reductions of long-term debt	(460)	(480)	(322)
Dividends paid	—	—	(30)
Net cash used for financing activities	(260)	(30)	(137)
Increase (decrease) in cash	$ 10	$ 52	$ (27)

APPENDIX
Cash Flow from Operating Activities: Direct and Indirect Formats

The cash flow from operating activities section of a cash flow statement can be presented using the direct format or the indirect format. The bottom line is the same, but the two begin at different points. Companies are free to choose either format. In the example below, **A** is an income statement, followed by **B**, the cash flow from operating activities section for the same company presented in the two different formats.

The direct method is just like a cash tax return: how much cash came in the door for sales and how much cash went out the door for the inventory and other operating expenditures. Many believe the direct format is better, because it is easier to understand at first glimpse. However, if companies choose the direct format, they must also present a reconciliation between cash flows from operating activities and net income—which is precisely what the indirect format shows! Consequently, most firms simply choose to present the indirect format.

The indirect method starts with net income as a figure that summarizes most of the cash transactions for operating activities in a firm. However, net income also includes transactions that were not cash, so we must eliminate the noncash transactions from the net income figure to arrive at an accurate presentation of cash flows from operating activities.

A common, typically major expense that does not involve the expenditure of any cash at all is depreciation. Depreciation is always added back to net income under the indirect method. Do not be confused by this presentation into thinking depreciation somehow provides cash. It is only added back because it was subtracted to get to net income in the first place, and it must now be added back to get to cash. If there are other expenses that did not involve cash, these too will be added back to net income.

A. Income Statement

Sales	$ 412,000
Cost of goods sold	(265,000)
Other expenses	(117,000)*
Net income	$ 30,000

* Other expenses includes $25,000 depreciation expense.

B. Cash Flow from Operating Activities (two formats)

Direct

Cash received from customers	$ 400,000
Cash paid to suppliers	(260,000)
Cash paid to employees	(70,000)
Other cash operating expenditures	(30,000)
Net cash provided by operating activities	$ 40,000

Indirect

Net Income	$ 30,000
Adjustments to reconcile net income to net cash provided by operating activities:	
Depreciation	25,000
Changes in other accounts affecting operations:	
(Increase) in receivables	(12,000)
Decrease in inventory	5,000
(Decrease) in payables	(8,000)
Net cash provided by operating activities	$ 40,000

APPENDIX (*continued*)

For most income statement items, the cash paid (or received) could be a little more, or a little less, than the income statement item. For example, cash received from customers could be a little more than revenues, especially if we collected large amounts owed to us from prior years, or it could be a little less if we made significant credit sales this year. Changes in operating working capital accounts reveal whether or not the amounts included in net income for sales, inventory costs, and other expenses really reflect the actual cash inflows and outflows. Changes in these accounts are added back to or subtracted from net income to reveal the true cash inflows and outflows.

Say the total sales number on our income statement was $412,000. But if we examined accounts receivable, we would find that receivables increased by $12,000, which customers essentially "put on their bill," and only $400,000 was actually collected in cash. So the deduction of $12,000 for "increase in receivables" in the indirect format adjusts the sales number of $412,000 down to $400,000, the actual cash received.

The inventory decrease reveals that we used some inventory purchased in prior years for sales this year. Our cost of goods sold figure in net income is therefore too high as an indicator of cash paid this year for inventory. Similarly, it looks as if we paid some of last year's bills this year, because our payables went down by $8,000. So we must subtract an additional $8,000 to adjust the net income figure for the additional, actual cash expenditures.

There is a simple rule by which accounts should be added to or subtracted from net income: *Increases in current assets are subtracted and increases in current liabilities are added.* The simplest approach to remember this is to pick a single account that is easy to figure out when it changes in one direction. For example, you might remember that increases in accounts receivable represent goods sold on account, but not for cash; so increases in accounts receivable must be subtracted from net income to reflect cash flows from operating activities. Once you know this, you know that a decrease in accounts receivable must be treated the opposite way: it will be added. Now you can deduce the remaining working capital accounts. The asset accounts will be treated just like accounts receivable. And the liability accounts will be exactly the opposite. Once you know one working capital account, you know them all.

Although initially it takes practice to become familiar with the indirect format, you will discover that it actually shows quite a bit of useful information you might need to search for otherwise. The quickest way to find the company's total depreciation, for example, is on the cash flow statement. In addition, it directly displays the changes in the working capital accounts. If you were to use the balance sheet for this information, you would have to perform the subtraction yourself.

Crystal Meadows of Tahoe, Inc.

Crystal Meadows of Tahoe (CMOT) was a holding company for two different alpine (downhill) ski resorts. The company had operated Crystal Meadows near Lake Tahoe, California, since 1962 and had purchased Lake Ridge in Utah in 1975. In addition, the company was involved in the development of a new ski resort in Nevada through a limited partnership in the Toiyabe Resort Company.

The ski business was both highly cyclical and highly seasonal. For the U.S. ski industry, on average 94% of revenues were received during the winter ski season. CMOT employed 100 people year round, but its employment swelled to 850 during the operating season. Because snowfall at given areas varied from year to year, the industry was cyclical as well. A string of several years of low snowfall at a given area could cause severe financial distress in order to cover fixed obligations.

Revenues at ski areas came primarily from the sale of lift tickets and related items such as ski rentals, ski lessons, and food and refreshments. **Exhibit 1** outlines the revenue sources for the average U.S. ski area. In addition, some ski areas were involved in the sale or rental of residential and commercial real estate around the ski area.

Costs for ski areas included labor for operating lifts, patrolling slopes, selling tickets, teaching lessons, and staffing cafeterias and shops. While some ski areas owned the land on which they operated, many leased land from the U.S. Forest Service or from other private owners. Ski areas typically invested significant sums in buildings, lifts, and snowmaking and snow grooming equipment. Other expenses included administration, marketing, and advertising, which typically were spread through the year.

CMOT owned both Crystal Meadows and Lake Ridge, two different types of ski areas. Crystal Meadows, with a capacity of 6,500 skiers per day, was a day and weekend ski area. Its clientele consisted primarily of skiers from Northern California, particularly Sacramento and the greater San Francisco Bay area. Crystal Meadows did not operate lodging at the ski area, although many of its skiers would stay somewhere

This case is an update of Alpine Meadows of Tahoe, Inc. originally written by David J. Ellison under the supervision of Professor William J. Bruns, Jr., as the basis for class discussion rather than to illustrate either effective or ineffective handling of an administrative situation. Some information taken from public documents has been reclassified, combined, or disguised for classroom use.

in the Lake Tahoe area. Crystal Meadows competed with the other 18 ski areas in the greater Lake Tahoe area. On the other hand, Lake Ridge, with a capacity of 10,000 skiers per day, was primarily a destination resort, attracting people from all over the country. As a consequence, Lake Ridge competed with ski resorts all over the world including locations in California, Idaho, Colorado, Wyoming, and Europe. As a holiday resort, Lake Ridge also competed with other vacation alternatives such as sun and beach resorts.

CMOT was a partner in the Toiyabe Resort Company, which was developing a year-round ski and recreational resort in the Lake Tahoe area. CMOT had invested $5.3 million in capital and capitalized interest costs in the venture by 1991. The project to that time had involved the designing, planning, and filing of applications for necessary permits. Construction of the resort was expected to start in 1992.

In addition to its ski operations, CMOT held some real estate that it would sell from time to time. This land was reported in a separate asset account in its financial statements.

Results from operations in fiscal year 1991, which ran from June 1, 1990 to May 31, 1991, were very positive for the company. Aftertax income was $.41 per share, more than twice that of 1990. Weather conditions at both ski areas were good, resulting in 839,000 skier days, the largest number in CMOT's history. Financial statements for fiscal years 1990 and 1991 are summarized in **Exhibits 2** and **3**.

During the year, the company had invested $2.7 million in new snowmaking equipment, as well as $2.6 million in other improvements. The 1992 capital expenditure plan was the most ambitious in company history at $8.2 million ($5.6 million at Lake Ridge and $2.6 million at Crystal Meadows). The planned expenditures included the replacement of two lifts at Lake Ridge and one lift at Crystal Meadows.

At the request of Julie Barnes, chief financial officer of CMOT, the accounting department had prepared a summary of some financial transactions affecting cash and cash balances during fiscal year 1991. A copy of the summary is shown in **Exhibit 4**.

QUESTIONS

1. Prepare a statement of cash flows for CMOT for fiscal year 1991 using the indirect method. Organize the cash flows into cash flows from operating activities, cash flows from investing activities, and cash flows from financing activities. Does your statement explain the change in cash and cash equivalents between the beginning and end of 1991?

2. Prepare a schedule of cash flows from operations using the direct method. Is this schedule more or less informative about the company's operations than the one prepared by the indirect method in Question 1?

3. What does the analysis of cash flows reveal about CMOT that was not evident from analysis of the income statements and balance sheets?

EXHIBIT 1
Average U.S. Ski Area Revenues (percent of total revenues)

Winter Season:

Ski lift department	55.0%
Ski school	5.9
Food service	9.0
Bar	2.7
Retail store	4.0
Rental shop	3.7
Accommodations	3.9
Other	2.5
Subtotal	86.7%

Year-Round:

Real estate	5.3%
Utility	0.6
Miscellaneous	1.5
Subtotal	7.4%

Summer Season:

Lift department	0.9%
Food service	1.7
Retail store	0.4
Sports department	0.7
Accommodations	1.1
Slide	0.7
Other	0.3
Subtotal	5.8%
Total	100.0%

Based on data included in *Economic Analysis of North American Ski Areas* (Boulder, Colorado, 1990). Does not add due to rounding.

EXHIBIT 2

Crystal Meadows of Tahoe, Inc., Consolidated Statements
of Operations, Years Ended May 31 (thousands of dollars)

	1991	1990	Change from 1990 to 1991
Operating revenues:			
Ticket sales	$19,274	$16,319	$2,955
Ski school revenue	2,623	2,281	342
Other operating revenues	3,246	2,636	610
Total operating revenues	$25,143	$21,236	$3,907
Operating expenses:			
Salaries and wages	9,063	7,702	1,361
Depreciation and amortization	2,637	2,376	261
Land rent	1,447	1,412	35
Other operating expenses	9,702	8,360	1,342
Total operating expenses	$22,849	$19,850	$2,999
Income (loss) from operations	$ 2,294	$ 1,386	$ 908
Other income:			
Interest income	$ 279	$ 182	$ 97
Commercial property rent	274	311	(37)
Gain on sales of real estate	329	0	329
Miscellaneous income	26	34	(8)
Total other income	$ 908	$ 527	$ 381
Other expenses:			
Interest expense	$ 1,073	$ 956	$ 117
Miscellaneous expense	132	101	31
Total other expenses	$ 1,205	$ 1,057	$ 148
Income (loss) before taxes	$ 1,997	$ 856	$1,141
Income tax (provision) benefit	(579)	(185)	(394)
Net income (loss)	$ 1,418	$ 671	$ 747

EXHIBIT 3
Crystal Meadows of Tahoe, Inc., Consolidated Balance Sheets, Years Ended May 31 (thousands of dollars)

	1991	1990	Change from 1990 to 1991
Assets:			
Current assets:			
Cash and equivalents	$ 4,097	$ 3,272	$ 825
Accounts receivable	140	199	(59)
Prepaid expenses and other current assets	337	343	(6)
Total current assets	$ 4,574	$ 3,814	$ 760
Real estate held for sale	772	977	(205)
Notes receivable	967	927	40
Plant & equipment, net	17,826	15,317	2,509
Investment in development stage resort	5,299	4,883	416
Other assets	265	288	(23)
Total Assets	$29,703	$26,206	$3,497
Liabilities and Shareholders' Equity:			
Current liabilities:			
Long-term debt due within one year	$ 2,123	$ 2,294	$ (171)
Accounts payable	864	619	245
Accrued land rent	1,544	1,525	19
Accrued compensation	614	462	152
Deferred revenue	607	363	244
Income taxes payable	100	0	100
Other accrued liabilities	465	286	179
Total current liabilities	$ 6,317	$ 5,549	$ 768
Long-term debt	10,698	10,003	695
Deferred income taxes	1,041	562	479
Other deferred credits	570	354	216
Total liabilities	$18,626	$16,468	$2,158
Shareholders' equity:			
Voting preferred stock, $.25 par value: 1,750,000 shares authorized, 738,708 shares issued and outstanding (839,069 in 1990)	$ 185	$ 210	$ (25)
Common stock, $.25 par value: 5,250,000 shares authorized, 2,783,385 shares issued and outstanding (2,657,024 in 1990)	696	664	32
Capital in excess of par value	2,611	2,585	26
Retained earnings	7,585	6,279	1,306
Total shareholders' equity	$11,077	$ 9,738	$1,339
Total Liabilities and Shareholders' Equity	$29,703	$26,206	$3,497

EXHIBIT 4
Partial Summary of Cash and Other Financial Transactions During Fiscal Year 1991

1. Cash received in the course of operations during 1991 included:

From customers and concessions	$25,446,000
Interest on investments	279,000
Commercial property rental	274,000
Other cash receipts	26,000

2. Cash paid in the course of operations during 1991 included:

Salaries and wages	$8,911,000
Land rentals	1,428,000
Interest paid	1,073,000
Other operating and miscellaneous expenses	9,188,000

3. Cash dividends of $112,000 were paid in 1991.

4. CMOT made no tax payments in 1991 but expected to make an income tax payment of $100,000 early in fiscal year 1992.

5. From its inventory of real estate, CMOT sold land that had cost $221,000, resulting in a gain of $329,000. Of the total sales price, $110,000 was received in cash and the remainder in the form of a note receivable.

6. CMOT purchased plant and equipment with a total cost of $5,146,000 during 1991.

7. CMOT paid $416,000 in interest on funds borrowed to finance its investment in the Toiyabe resort, all of which was capitalized by adding the interest to prior CMOT investments in Toiyabe. Other investments in 1991 included:

A loan (note receivable) to the Toiyabe Resort Company	$85,000
Capital expenditures relating to real estate held for sale	16,000

Notes receivable that were paid in full to CMOT during 1991 totaled $485,000, and $23,000 was received for miscellaneous other assets sold during the year.

8. Seasonal cash needs required CMOT to borrow $1,200,000 on a bank line of credit, all of which had been repaid by the end of the fiscal year.

9. CMOT borrowed an additional $3,344,000 in long-term debt during 1991. Some of the proceeds were used to repay $2,820,000 in long-term debt that had been outstanding at the beginning of the year.

10. During the year, a voting preferred stockholder exchanged 100,361 preferred shares for 100,361 shares of common stock. An additional 26,000 shares of common stock were issued for $33,000.

Managing Financial Reporting

PART 3

Auditors and Their Opinions

Accounting's Global Rule Book; When It Comes to the Numbers, Why Can't the World Agree?

- *WPP Group and Its Acquisitions*

Diversity in Accounting Principles: A Problem, a Strategic Imperative, or a Strategic Opportunity?

- *Kendall Square Research Corporation (A) (Abridged)*
- *Harnischfeger Corporation*

Auditors and Their Opinions

How believable is the financial information that businesses—or any other organizations—make available to the public? There is a great deal in society that depends on this. If people are going to invest money in organizations, lend money to them, sell and buy things to and from them, even make contributions to them, they need to feel some confidence about what those organizations' resources are and how well they are being used. One job of auditors is to give people some confidence about financial information.

Making organizations' financial information believable is accomplished in different countries in different ways—with varying degrees of success. In the United States the primary mechanism for this was established in the aftermath of the stock market crash of 1929: Congress passed securities laws requiring almost all businesses whose stock is publicly traded to file with a governmental agency, on a regular basis, financial statements that have been examined by an independent auditor. These securities laws also gave that governmental agency (the Securities and Exchange Commission, or SEC) the authority to set accounting standards—that is, the way in which organizations' financial information is reported. For the most part, the SEC has outsourced this work of standard-setting to a nonprofit organization in the private sector, but it retains ultimate oversight over it.[1]

There is a very serious social purpose behind all this—to reduce "information risk" and thus promote the efficient allocation of resources in society. No one knows whether a given business or organization is going to do well or badly in the future, but if people don't have reasonably believable information about an organization in the first place, they are not going to be able to allocate resources very well. At the very least, they will—if they want to invest in a business, for example—demand a "risk premium." Thus, setting up certain information rules and requirements ulti-

Research Associate Jeremy Cott prepared this case under the supervision of Professor William J. Bruns, Jr. as the basis for class discussion rather than to illustrate either effective or ineffective handling of an administrative situation.

[1] Many organizations, both for-profit and not-for-profit, that are not legally required to have their financial statements audited do so nevertheless because potential investors, creditors, or vendors demand it.

mately reduces the risk premium that businesses have to pay and lowers their overall cost of capital.

Auditors express an "opinion" about whether an organization's financial statements present a fair picture of what is going on financially in that organization. The wording of their report is prescribed by a formal "statement of auditing standards" (published by the American Institute of Certified Public Accountants). An example is shown in **Exhibit 1**. The wording of the report may, on its surface, appear fairly bland and innocuous, but it is really a distillation of a great deal of thinking and history, with individual words chosen with great care—analogous to the wording of certain statutes or contracts. There is a lot riding on the auditor's report, including the assumption of legal responsibility.

TITLE AND ADDRESS

The title of the report always includes the word "independent." This is meant to convey that the report is coming not from the company's managers but from accountants who are independent of them and who therefore wouldn't (presumably) be biased in what they say or do not say. (If, for example, an auditor owned some of the company's stock or held a seat on its Board of Directors, that person wouldn't be considered "independent."[2]) It has become customary, in fact, for the Board of Directors of a public corporation to assign the responsibility for hiring the auditors and responding to any concerns they may have to a special "audit committee," consisting entirely of outside directors. This is meant to provide even greater assurance of the auditors' independence, to provide a "buffer" between them and management. Moreover, the auditor's report is addressed not to the company's management but to its Board of Directors and stockholders.

The independent auditor's report contains three main sections: an *Introductory Paragraph*, which indicates the degree of responsibility that the auditor is taking; a *Scope Paragraph*, which indicates the scope of the auditor's work; and an *Opinion Paragraph*, which expresses the auditor's opinion about the validity of the financial statements in question.

INTRODUCTORY PARAGRAPH

This indicates who is responsible for what. The company is responsible for preparing the financial statements; the auditor is not. The auditor is carrying out more of an oversight function and is expressing an "opinion" about what people in the company have done. Furthermore, the auditor's report covers only the financial statements (and the related notes that are, as is often said, "an integral part of the financial statements"). But a company's Annual Report often contains much more than financial statements—for example, a letter from the Chief Executive, President, or Chairperson of the Board of Directors to stockholders; management's "discussion and analysis" of results; information about stock prices—and the audit has nothing to do with those other things.

---

[2] These are the expectations in the United States. In some other countries, however, an auditor may sit on a company's Board of Directors or own some of the company's stock.

SCOPE PARAGRAPH

This indicates essentially what the auditor has done. A few words in the paragraph are really loaded:

- The audit is designed to obtain "reasonable" assurance, but not absolute assurance.

- The audit examines evidence on a "test basis," but not on a comprehensive basis. That is, it relies on a statistical sampling of the data; it doesn't examine every transaction and amount.

- The audit is designed to search for "material" misstatements, but not misstatements that are immaterial. What does "material" mean? Something that "matters," in a relative sense. For example, $10,000 may be material for a small business but completely immaterial for General Motors. The nature of an item is also a factor: a misstatement of $1,000,000 in a company's Cash balance is far more significant than a misstatement of $1,000,000 in the balance of Accumulated Depreciation. Auditing standards are ultimately quite practical in suggesting what is material: something is "material" if it is significant enough to influence the decision of a reasonable user of the financial statements (e.g., an investor or creditor or regulatory agency).

The implicit decision of society, reflected in the scope paragraph, is that there are costs as well as benefits to information and that an auditor can do only so much. What goes on in most public corporations is complicated. To require auditors to examine every financial transaction and amount—even if it were possible to do so—would cost too much, and investors wouldn't pay for it. The audit can provide only "reasonable assurance" of the validity of a company's financial statements. But that nevertheless represents a great deal: a company cannot give out whatever financial information it wants to in whatever form it wants. There are standards against which its financial information will be judged.

OPINION PARAGRAPH

The opinion paragraph typically consists of only one sentence. It is the most important part of the report, however, and, for that reason, the entire report is sometimes referred to as "the auditor's opinion."

The sentence begins "In our opinion…." This means that the auditor is reasonably sure of his or her conclusions. Earlier in the century, the typical auditor's report "certified" the company's financial statements as being "correct." That kind of language was eventually dropped, however, because it gave the reader the incorrect impression that things could be measured exactly and without any ambiguity. The auditor's opinion is an informed opinion, and it is extremely serious, but—like a doctor's opinion—it involves an exercise of judgment and doesn't provide any guarantees.

The key issue is whether the company's financial statements conform with "generally accepted accounting principles" (often referred to as "GAAP" in both the general business press and the accounting profession). What *are* "generally accepted accounting principles"? In fact, there isn't any official, definitive list of them. In the United States, the SEC has the legal authority to specify acceptable accounting practices, and, for the most part, it has delegated that authority to a nonprofit organization in the private sector.[3] What that organization says, however, is supplemented by the pronouncements and interpretations of various other professional organizations as well as by practices that become commonly accepted within certain industries. Thus when an auditor decides whether or not a company's financial statements conform with "generally accepted accounting principles," that person not only has to consider a certain amount of ambiguity in the principles themselves but also has to exercise judgment about how general principles apply to very specific situations. It is not a straightforward task.

The report shown in **Exhibit 1** is the standard auditor's report. It represents an "unqualified" opinion (sometimes called a "clean" opinion). This is what a company wants. The report is saying essentially that the *quality* of the financial statements is fine (that is, they conform with GAAP), and there has been no problem with the *scope* of the audit (that is, nothing has prevented the auditors from gathering the evidence needed to support their opinion).

Sometimes the auditors will add some explanatory language to their report, even when they are expressing an unqualified opinion. This is a way of drawing attention to some special circumstance—for example, if part of the audit was carried out by other auditors, or if a legitimate change in accounting principles has occurred.

There are, however, three serious *exceptions* to an unqualified report:

- *Qualified opinion.* This means that the financial statements contain some "material" departure from GAAP, or that there has been some "material" limitation placed on the scope of the auditors' work, but these problems do not overshadow the *overall* fairness of the statements. For example, a significant misstatement in the value of fixed assets might affect someone's willingness to lend money to the company if the assets were to be used as collateral, but the overall financial picture given of the company might still be fair. The wording of a qualified opinion would be similar to that of an unqualified opinion but would add the phrase "except for" and a brief explanation of what the problem is.

- *Adverse opinion.* This is more serious. This means that the financial statements contain departures from GAAP that are so material or so pervasive that the financial statements as a whole are misleading.

- *Disclaimer of opinion.* This means that the limitations placed on the scope of the auditors' work have been so material or so pervasive that the auditors simply do not have an adequate basis for expressing an opinion.

In practice, adverse opinions are rare because they would be of virtually no use to the client: potential investors wouldn't invest in the company, and potential lenders wouldn't lend money to the company. If auditors feel that a client's financial statements contain such material departures from GAAP as to warrant an adverse opinion, this situation would be discussed with the company's audit committee or management, and management would probably agree to make the necessary changes

---

[3] Since 1973, the organization that has been primarily responsible for issuing accounting standards for the private sector (both for-profit and not-for-profit organizations) is the Financial Accounting Standards Board (FASB), located in Norwalk, Connecticut. To date, it has issued over 120 "Statements of Financial Accounting Standards." Another organization, called the Government Accounting Standards Board (or GASB) issues accounting standards for the public sector (that is, governmental entities).

because not doing so would carry intolerable implications. Auditing standards, moreover, prohibit auditors from sidestepping an adverse opinion by disclaiming an opinion.

LEGAL IMPLICATIONS

What, however, happens in the real world? In the real world, auditors' opinions have come under increasing scrutiny and have provoked a good deal of litigation and scandal. Even harsh critics of the auditing profession in the United States acknowledge that, in the vast majority of cases, auditors' opinions are reliable.[4] In the 1980s and 1990s, however, there has been an enormous number of business failures, most significantly in the savings and loan industry, and many people—including some members of Congress—believe that auditors have not provided adequate warning to the public. People are astonished to see businesses file for bankruptcy not long after their auditors gave them a "clean" opinion. As a result, auditors in the United States have faced literally billions of dollars in damage claims.

Defenders of the profession regard many of the lawsuits as unjustified: when businesses fail, the auditors are sometimes seen as the only party left with "deep pockets," and investors and creditors may try to recoup their losses any way they can.

On the other hand, there clearly have been problems with the way in which auditors go about their work. A study by the federal government's General Accounting Office found that the audits of more than half of a sample number of bankrupt savings and loans failed "to meet professional standards." The National Commission on Fraudulent Financial Reporting, staffed by representatives of major accounting organizations, acknowledged that revenue and profit pressures in the auditing firms themselves detracted from the quality of their audits. The fact is that, even though auditing firms have a responsibility to provide independent judgments about the believability of organizations' financial information—to be, in effect, a guardian of the public interest—they also have a private interest in making money. Naturally, they want to retain clients; they don't want to offend them. "As all accounting firms are well aware, clients determined to have their way on critical issues will often shop for the 'right' audit opinion, using the competition among the firms to find a 'cooperative' auditor. Those that fail to cooperate often lose the business."[5]

In response, expectations have been formally raised. Auditors used to be required to plan their search for material misstatements "within the limitations of the audit process."[6] Now, they are required to be more pro-active: auditors have to provide "reasonable assurance" of detecting material misstatement based on a documented assessment of specific risk factors for misstatement.[7] They first set up an audit plan, but if the risks of material misstatement appear to be greater than anticipated, they have to modify the plan. They may even have to modify it several times. A similar

---

[4] Mark Stevens, *The Big Six: The Selling Out of America's Top Accounting Firms* (Simon & Schuster, 1991), p. 254.

[5] Ibid., p. 87.

[6] Statement of Auditing Standards 16 (effective in 1977).

[7] Statements of Auditing Standards 53 and 58 (effective in 1989) and 82 (effective in 1997). The second sentence of the "Scope Paragraph" in **Exhibit 1** ("[Generally accepted auditing standards] require that we plan and perform the audit to obtain reasonable assurance about whether the financial statements are free of material misstatement") is new to the standard auditor's report (as of 1989). The previous version of the standard auditor's report (in use since the late 1940s) contained no such assertion.

change has occurred regarding the possibility of bankruptcy. Auditors used to assume that their clients had the ability to continue as a "going concern."[8] Now, they are required to be more pro-active on this issue as well.[9]

Finally, auditors used to assume that their clients were honest,[10] even though they were expected to carry out their work with an attitude of "professional skepticism." Now they are expected to assume that their clients are neither honest nor dishonest.[11]

---

[8] Statement of Auditing Standards 34 (effective 1981).
[9] Statement of Auditing Standards 59 (effective 1989).
[10] Stevens, op. cit., p. 60.
[11] Statement of Auditing Standards 53 (effective in 1989).

EXHIBIT 1
Standard Auditor's Report

[Title]

Report of Independent Auditors

[Addressed to:]

Board of Directors and Stockholders

of XYZ Corporation

[Introductory Paragraph}

We have audited the accompanying balance sheets of XYZ Company as of June 30, 1997 and 1996, and the related statements of income, retained earnings, and cash flows for the fiscal years then ended. These financial statements are the responsibility of the Company's management. Our responsibility is to express an opinion on these financial statements based on our audits.

[Scope Paragraph]

We conducted our audits in accordance with generally accepted auditing standards. Those standards require that we plan and perform the audit to obtain reasonable assurance about whether the financial statements are free of material misstatement. An audit includes examining, on a test basis, evidence supporting the amounts and disclosures in the financial statements. An audit also includes assessing the accounting principles used and significant estimates made by management, as well as evaluating the overall financial statement presentation. We believe that our audits provide a reasonable basis for our opinion.

[Opinion Paragraph]

In our opinion, the financial statements referred to above present fairly, in all material respects, the consolidated financial position of XYZ Company as of June 30, 1997 and 1996, and the results of its operations and its cash flows for the years then ended in conformity with generally accepted accounting principles.

R. Smith & Co.
Certified Public Accountants

August 15, 1997

Source: Statement of Auditing Standards 58 (effective in 1989).

Accounting's Global Rule Book; When It Comes to the Numbers, Why Can't the World Agree?

The U.S. and countries overseas can't even agree on what set of measurements to use in the kitchen. So how will they ever "harmonize" international standards on accounting?

Well, that is just what accounting rule makers are trying to do. They're stepping up efforts for a convergence of U.S. and international standards, a move that took on urgency after the Enron Corp.-led rash of accounting scandals shook investor confidence in the superiority of American standards.

The remaining huge differences will probably take years to solve—if they're even solvable.

Nevertheless, U.S. companies soon will start to feel the effect, just like international peers that already are grappling with numerous rule changes. Within the next few weeks, officials at the Financial Accounting Standards Board plan to propose changes to bring U.S. rules in line with the approach of its overseas counterpart, the International Accounting Standards Board.

It is a rare time when accounting-rule makers in the U.S. have expressly altered rules to take into account the international way of doing things—instead of expecting their overseas counterparts to conform to U.S. standards.

"Europe will be impressed that the U.S. is prepared to take the pain," says David Tweedie, IASB chairman.

Standard setters both in the U.S. and overseas envision the financial statements of a company—say, in Germany—one day being comparable with those of a U.S. rival, simplifying cross-border investment and international stock listings at exchanges in the U.S. and elsewhere.

"If we think the international approach is better or equal, we will propose moving" in that direction, says Robert Herz, the FASB's chairman. Mr. Herz anticipates resistance from corporate executives in instances where they perceive such changes would damage their companies' financial statements, adding that the board already has begun to hear from some companies with worries.

In Brussels, the seat of the European Union, a spokesman for the 15-nation European Commission trade bloc says, "Let's wait and see what they do," referring to the

Cassell Bryan-Low. *Wall Street Journal.* (Eastern edition). New York, N.Y.: Nov 28, 2003. pg. C.1

David Reilly contributed to this article.

FASB and its proposal. He adds it is important to see that convergence "implies movement in both directions."

Among the most notable changes that the FASB proposal probably will include is a general requirement for companies to apply accounting changes retroactively. Currently, U.S. companies typically make a one-time cumulative catch-up adjustment in the year of a change, while international rules call for companies to adjust prior years' statements as if the change had been in effect then. The FASB hopes to issue a final standard by the middle of next year.

The IASB was set up with the help of the Securities and Exchange Commission and the FASB in April 2001 to develop a single set of high-quality international standards. The attitude of many in the U.S. at the time was that their standards were generally superior. The collapse of Enron in late 2001 forced U.S. regulators and standard setters to rethink the matter.

To speed up efforts, the FASB and the IASB now will meet formally twice a year. The EU has agreed to adopt the IASB's standards by 2005; as many as 91 countries in total by that date will require or allow their companies to adopt international standards. "The point isn't really about arguing over arcane accounting," says Mr. Tweedie. "This is really about growth, investment and trade."

Delivering a unified approach "will be pretty difficult," says Robert Willens, an accounting analyst at Lehman Brothers. It isn't that the differences are "insuperable," he says; the obstacles lie instead in matters of prestige. "I don't think FASB wants to sacrifice its pre-eminent position as the setter of accounting standards." The group isn't "going to be willing to compromise that much," he predicts.

The FASB, for its part, acknowledges the size of the task ahead, but says it fully supports attempts to bring together the two sets of standards. The standard-setting body also notes that support from corporate officers will be essential.

And it isn't just U.S. executives who must throw their weight behind the effort; European counterparts also face change, and resistance already has cropped up. For instance, big banks in Europe, with the French government and the European Commission by their side, have objected to the international board's proposals on the financial instruments known as derivatives. The IASB believes that derivatives should be valued at their current market value, similar to the U.S. approach. European countries, under current rules, typically allow derivatives to be valued at the cost at which they were acquired. That approach is favored by the big banks there, the main users of derivatives. The banks have argued that the IASB's approach would cause unnecessary volatility in earnings.

The IASB, which has issued several proposals in this area and expects to release some final standards in December, is reluctant to compromise on a fair-value approach, in part because that could jeopardize convergence with the U.S.

Among the trickiest areas to reconcile is pension accounting. Current U.S. standards attempt to smooth short-term fluctuations in earnings by allowing companies to calculate the return on their pension-fund investments using an assumed rate, rather than the actual return on a pension fund's stocks, bonds and other assets.

The IASB's Mr. Tweedie is determined that international rules should reflect a plan's actual value, and he says the international standard likely will go even further than current U.K. rules, which require companies to give a more real-time snapshot of the value of assets than in the U.S. Given the discomfort that the U.K. standard already has caused in that country, Mr. Tweedie admits his proposals will probably "go down like a rat sandwich."

Another fundamental difference lies in re-evaluations of the value of property, plants and equipment. Overseas, it is common for countries to permit periodic re-evaluation of such assets, either up or down. The U.S. doesn't allow for such upward re-evaluations. As a result, real estate owned by American companies is often worth a lot more than is reflected in the books.

Among the next wave of projects that the boards plan to tackle: concurrent efforts to overhaul the income statement. Both boards have agreed they want to see "comprehensive income" on the income statement. Comprehensive income would include certain items that affect shareholders' equity but that aren't currently run through the income statement, such as unrealized gains and losses on certain securities. Still, there are differences between the two boards. The IASB, for instance, wants to remove net income from the income statement, while the FASB hasn't yet reached a conclusion on the matter.

Other planned projects: addressing differences in accounting for acquisitions of companies and creating a conceptual model for when revenue is booked.

WPP Group and Its Acquisitions

Martin Sorrell, chief executive officer (CEO) of London's WPP Group, supervised his firm's acquisition of New York's JWT Group, parent company of J. Walter Thompson, in 1987. Goodwill of $465 million was recognized on the deal and WPP took this amount out of its shareholders' equity account, leaving the company with a negative £64 million net worth at the end of that year. But in 1988, WPP said that the brand-name value of J. Walter Thompson and JWT's Hill and Knowlton public relations firm was £175 million. At the end of 1988, WPP reported shareholders' equity of positive £61 million. To outsiders, this change in value seemed impossible to explain, but the explanation could be found in a discrepancy between standard accounting procedures in the United States and the United Kingdom.

A year later, in mid-1989, Sorrell bought Ogilvy & Mather (O&M) for $862 million, bringing the controversy to the forefront again. The O&M brand name was also valued at £175 million. Now, even with the controversial accounting policy, WPP's balance sheet carried £600 million in long-term debt and negative stockholders' equity of £330 million. (See **Exhibit 1** for WPP 1987, 1988, and 1989 financial statements.)

BACKGROUND

WPP Group PLC was an enormous communications empire with revenues of nearly £1 billion in 1989. WPP's six service sectors included strategic marketing, media advertising, public relations, market research, nonmedia advertising, and specialist communications.

Martin Sorrell had built WPP from nothing. From 1977, after earning his MBA from the Harvard Business School, until 1986, he was chief financial officer to the leading British advertising agency, Saatchi & Saatchi. But Sorrell's responsibilities there went beyond financial matters. He helped Maurice and Charles Saatchi build their small shop into an international firm touting the virtues of "global marketing," which to them meant selling a product the same way in every country.

Susan S. Harmeling, MBA '91, prepared this case under the supervision of Professor William J. Bruns, Jr. as the basis for class discussion rather than to illustrate either effective or ineffective handling of an administrative situation.

Sorrell explained, "Maurice and Charles Saatchi used global marketing to differentiate themselves from others."[1] Eventually, Sorrell came to believe that global marketing could work for a few choice brands like Coca-Cola and Marlboro, but in reality only a small portion of an advertising agency's revenues could realistically come from such products.

So in 1986, when Sorrell left Saatchi & Saatchi, he pursued a very different strategy. He set out to acquire a number of small shops in specialty areas of marketing services. He began by purchasing a British maker of grocery baskets and used it to acquire several small marketing firms.

At that time, in early 1986, Sorrell claimed that he was "three or four years away"[2] from making a big advertising agency purchase. But at the end of 1986, a New York analyst mentioned JWT to Sorrell. JWT, along with its affiliated public relations group Hill and Knowlton, had suffered two quarters of losses, the company's CEO and chairman had left, and major clients were putting their accounts up for review.

Meanwhile, Sorrell discovered that about 30% of JWT's business came from marketing services other than advertising in fast-growing sectors like public relations and market research. In February 1987, Sorrell decided to acquire JWT, and with JWT's disappointing record on Wall Street, he had every reason to believe his bid would succeed. WPP quietly accumulated just under 5% of JWT at an average price of $31 per share between March and June 1987. On June 10, Sorrell surprised everyone with his $45 per share cash bid for JWT. Five days later, he raised the bid to $50.50 per share as rumors of rival bidders surfaced. After meeting with his advisers at First Boston Corp. on June 25, Sorrell delivered his clinching bid of $55.50 per share. With the generous earnings multiples awarded to ad agencies in Britain, some $340 million of the $566 million purchase price came from a new stock offering and the remainder from long-term debt.

This acquisition marked the beginning of a heated debate over how to account for brand names and goodwill on the balance sheet and on income statements. After the acquisitions were completed, the two brand names together were valued at £175 million, with JWT representing £150 million and Hill and Knowlton £25 million. Such substantial valuation of brand names as intangible assets had many observers questioning WPP's accounting.

Two years later, Sorrell and WPP bought O&M for $862 million—26 times O&M's earnings. Sorrell rationalized the high prices he paid for both companies in the following three ways:

1. The pound was strong against the dollar, making U.S. properties relative bargains.
2. His stock was strong. When Sorrell bought JWT, WPP traded at about 35 times earnings, versus a multiple of about 15 for most U.S. ad companies.
3. U.K. accounting rules allowed goodwill to be written off as a charge to owners' equity when purchased, rather than capitalized to be expensed as a charge against earnings in future years (as practiced according to U.S. rules).[3]

---

[1] Marcia Berss, "The Bad Boy of Advertising," *Forbes*, 8 July 1991, 49.

[2] Richard A. Melcher and Mark N. Vamos, "Hang On, Madison Avenue, Martin Sorrell Isn't Finished," *Business Week*, 13 July 1987, 81.

[3] Berss, *Forbes*, loc. cit.

With respect to Sorrell and WPP valuing the brand names and capitalizing them, in effect reversing part of the goodwill write-off, he said, "I see no difference between valuing a brand and valuing a piece of property. Advertising agencies' names can be brands in the same way as KitKat or Polo."[4] He was unmoved by the protests of accountants that such intangibles should not be taken into account on balance sheets. He observed, "I wanted our balance sheets to reflect a true and fair view of the value of the assets. It is unfortunate that accounting systems were designed for manufacturing companies and not for service companies."[5]

THE GOODWILL CONTROVERSY

For the sake of debate, the issue of brands was "inextricably linked to the goodwill issue in the minds of most finance directors:"[6]

> British firms used brand values primarily to boost their balance sheets; by recording brand values as intangible assets, they could magically increase their assets while drawing attention to their important brands. U.S. accounting rules didn't allow any such advantages.
>
> Brand valuations made sense for companies that were potential takeover targets, too. A company thinking that its stock was undervalued might make its brand values public in order to prompt an increase in the share price and thwart potential raiders. . . .[7]

Many other companies, such as Grand Metropolitan and Ranks Hovis MacDougall, also put high brand values on their balance sheets.

Goodwill was treated very differently in the United States and the United Kingdom. In fact, the problem of goodwill was dealt with differently around the world. (See **Exhibit 2** for a chart on international goodwill procedures.) In the United States, the goodwill issue only arose when a purchaser was paying some amount in excess of the fair market value of identifiable assets of the target firm. This excess could arise, for example, because of a particularly strong brand name that was expected to be of some mutually agreed-upon value in the future. In the United States, goodwill was capitalized on the balance sheet and written off against the income statement over a maximum period of 40 years.

In the United Kingdom, goodwill was written off against shareholders' equity at the time of purchase. It was **not** charged as an expense item against income, so that companies in the United Kingdom did not have to burden their future earnings by charging goodwill against the income statement.

In certain firms, advertising agencies, for example, where tangible assets (desks, paper, office equipment) were quite small relative to intangible assets (the good reputation of the company, intellectual property, etc.), this discrepancy in accounting practices was significant indeed. For such firms in the United States, the write-off of these large intangible assets as an expense on the income statement had a greater impact on future earnings relative to firms in the United Kingdom, where the entire transaction was completed at the time of purchase.

---

4 "The Art of Valuing Agency Brands," *Sunday Times*, London, 2 July 1989.

5 Ibid.

6 David Waller, "Gloves Will Soon Come Off in Goodwill Battle," *Financial Times*, 3 August 1989.

7 Joanne Lipman, "British Value Brand Names—Literally," *Wall Street Journal*, 9 February 1989, B4.

THE BRAND VALUATION PROCESS

In order to measure the value of a given brand name, it was necessary to develop a system that was both "objective and scientific." This was easier to do for consumer goods than for the "brand name" of a service firm such as an advertising agency. For consumer goods, the procedure, developed at the Henley Centre, an economic forecasting consultancy in London owned by WPP Group, worked as follows: First, the level of income arising from sales of a brand was split conceptually into two categories—those sales due to short-run marketing influences and those sales due to loyalty to the brand. The aim of this approach was to isolate short-run marketing influences by obtaining a mathematical formula based on statistical analysis to explain the sales of the brand in the recent past.

Once brand loyalty sales had been isolated, the profit element attributed to brand loyalty could be assessed. At any point in time, however, many factors could operate in determining the total level of sales of a brand. This range of factors likely to exercise a systematic and important influence on sales included: spending power of consumers, demographics, price, competitors' price, advertising, competitors' advertising, promotion, and distribution. For each brand, a unique mathematical formula was generated, and the appraisers were allowed to choose which factors were important in a particular case. Once the formula was derived and tested, the level of brand loyalty sales could be calculated.

Although this technique was proven to work well for consumer goods, there were practical problems in obtaining information on these factors and especially in obtaining information on competitors, in the case of service firms. But even before consideration of those problems, there was a further point related to services that needed to be examined. This was the extent to which loyalty to the service depended upon the individual providing the service rather than the brand. (See **Exhibit 3** for a more detailed description of these problems.)

In addition, there was a major difference in auditing standards between the United States and the United Kingdom. In the United States, an auditor, working with the firm he or she was to represent, had to follow strict guidelines, the Generally Accepted Accounting Principles (GAAP). It was the responsibility of the auditor to follow these guidelines or risk prosecution for material misstatement or fraud (from *The New Auditor's Report* of the AICPA).

In the United Kingdom, the overriding requirement was to give a "true and fair view" of the value of the assets of any given company. The British philosophy was that rules alone could not necessarily result in a complete measure of value. Thus, all relevant information regarding value had to be weighed and taken into account in each specific case.

This approach was difficult to define and thus gave auditors in the United Kingdom more discretion in deciding what the "true and fair" value really was for each firm. In addition, while GAAP restricted U.S. auditors from certain "liberal" practices, the "true and fair" approach allowed U.K. auditors to measure value in closer accordance with the wishes of each firm's management team.

EXHIBIT 1
Excerpts from Annual Reports of the WPP Group PLC for the
Years 1987, 1988, and 1989 (including the Consolidated Profit
and Loss Accounts, End-of-Year Consolidated Balance Sheets,
Selected Notes from the Annual Reports, and Auditors' Reports).

Consolidated Profit and Loss Account (for the year ended 31 December 1987)

	1987 £000	1986 £000	1987 $000	1986 $000
Turnover	£ 284,082	£ 23,685	$ 477,258	$ 39,791
Cost of sales	(65,160)	(17,761)	(109,469)	(29,839)
Gross Profit	£ 218,922	£ 5,924	$ 367,789	$ 9,952
Other operating expenses	(197,468)	(4,502)	(331,746)	(7,563)
Operating Profit	£ 21,454	£ 1,422	$ 36,043	$ 2,389
Interest receivable	3,739	530	6,282	891
Interest payable and similar charges	(11,076)	(195)	(18,608)	(328)
Profit on Ordinary Activities before Taxation	£ 14,117	£ 1,757	$ 23,717	$ 2,952
Tax on profit on ordinary activities	(6,810)	(613)	(11,441)	(1,030)
Profit on Ordinary Activities after Taxation	£ 7,307	£ 1,144	$ 12,276	$ 1,922
Minority interests	(222)	(75)	(373)	(126)
Profit before Extraordinary Items	£ 7,085	£ 1,069	$ 11,903	$ 1,796
Extraordinary items	—	32	—	54
Profit for the Financial Year	£ 7,085	£ 1,101	$ 11,903	$ 1,850
Dividends paid and proposed	(2,337)	(352)	(3,926)	(592)
Retained Profit for the Year	£ 4,748	£ 749	$ 7,977	$ 1,258
Earnings per share	32.1p	13.2p	$ 0.54	$ 0.22

The main reporting currency of the group is the pound sterling and the accounts have been prepared on this basis. Solely for convenience, the accounts set out are also presented expressed in U.S. dollars using the approximate average rate for the year for the profit and loss account ($1.68 = £1), the rate in effect on 31 December 1987 for the balance sheets ($1.8785 = £1), and a combination of these for the statement of source and application of funds. This translation should not be construed as a representation that the pound sterling amounts actually represent or could be converted into U.S. dollars at the rates indicated.

EXHIBIT 1 (*continued*)
Consolidated Balance Sheet (as at 31 December 1987)

	1987 £000	1986 £000	1987 $000	1986 $000
Fixed Assets				
Tangible assets	£ 79,184	£ 4,801	$ 148,747	$ 9,019
Investments	3,464	—	6,507	—
	£ 82,648	£ 4,801	$ 155,254	$ 9,019
Current Assets				
Stocks and work-in-progress	£ 37,920	£ 1,810	$ 71,233	$ 3,400
Debtors	247,836	11,852	465,560	22,263
Assets held for resale and investments	115,273	1,040	216,540	1,954
Cash at bank and in hand	72,616	8,554	136,409	16,069
	473,645	23,256	$ 889,742	$ 43,686
Creditors: amounts falling due within one year	(454,733)	(21,510)	(854,216)	(40,407)
Net Current Assets	£ 18,912	£ 1,746	$ 35,526	$ 3,279
Total Assets less Current Liabilities	101,560	6,547	190,780	12,298
Creditors: amounts falling due after more than one year	(91,333)	(2,725)	(171,568)	(5,119)
Provisions for Liabilities and Charges	(74,719)	(300)	(140,360)	(563)
Net Assets (Liabilities)	£ (64,492)	£ 3,522	$(121,148)	$ 6,616
Capital and Reserves				
Called-up share capital	£ 3,670	£ 1,139	$ 6,894	$ 2,139
Share premium	—	8,396	—	15,772
Merger reserve	(89,423)	(9,388)	(167,981)	(17,635)
Other reserves	13,233	646	24,858	1,213
Profit and loss account	6,963	2,027	13,080	3,808
Shareholders' Funds	£ (65,557)	£ 2,820	$(123,149)	$ 5,297
Minority interests	1,065	702	2,001	1,319
Total Capital Employed	£ (64,492)	£ 3,522	$(121,148)	$ 6,616

Signed on behalf of the Board on 6 May 1988

R.E. Lerwill and M.S. Sorrell, Directors

The main reporting currency of the group is the pound sterling and the accounts have been prepared on this basis. Solely for convenience, the accounts set out are also presented expressed in U.S. dollars using the approximate average rate for the year for the profit and loss account ($1.68 = £1), the rate in effect on 31 December 1987 for the balance sheets ($1.8785 = £1), and a combination of these for the statement of source and application of funds. This translation should not be construed as a representation that the pound sterling amounts actually represent or could be converted into U.S. dollars at the rates indicated.

EXHIBIT 1 (*continued*)
Notes to the Accounts (31 December 1987)

Note 11—Tangible Fixed Assets

a) Group

The movement in the year was as follows:

	Land and Buildings			Plant and Machinery	Fixtures and Fittings	Motor Vehicles	Total
	Freehold	Long Leasehold	Short Leasehold				
Cost or valuation:							
Beginning of year	2,147	88	569	1,905	1,615	929	7,253
New subsidiaries	7,878	4,094	40,580	1,668	25,345	1,325	80,890
Additions	1,486	316	1,726	574	4,045	1,131	9,278
Disposals	(429)	(112)	(883)	(322)	(1,949)	(635)	(4,330)
Exchange adjustments	130	(155)	(5,481)	(155)	(2,985)	(103)	(8,749)
Revaluation	1,474	—	—	—	—	—	1,474
End of year (see below)	12,686	4,231	36,511	3,670	26,071	2,647	85,816
Depreciation:							
Beginning of year	35	4	93	1,044	891	385	2,452
Charge	190	389	1,744	728	3,287	487	6,825
Disposals	(225)	(14)	(558)	(300)	(1,158)	(390)	(2,645)
End of year (see below)	—	379	1,279	1,472	3,020	482	6,632
Net book value:							
31 December 1987	12,686	3,852	35,232	2,198	23,051	2,165	79,184
31 December 1986	2,112	84	476	861	724	544	4,801

Leased assets included above have a net book value of £322,000 (1986: £142,000).

Basis of valuations: Plant and machinery (including fixtures and fittings) are shown at cost. Land and buildings include certain properties professionally revalued during 1987, by Messrs. James Andrew Badger (Surveyors & Valuers), on an open market, existing use basis. The historic gross cost of such land and buildings is £1,859,000 (1986: £333,000).

Auditor's Report

To the members of WPP Group plc:

We have audited the accounts set out on pages 87 to 109 in accordance with approved Auditing Standards.

In our opinion, the accounts, which have been prepared under the historical cost convention, as modified by the revaluation of land and buildings, give a true and fair view of the state of affairs of the Company and of the Group at 31st December 1987 and of the Group profit and source and application of funds for the year then ended, and comply with the Companies Act 1985.

Arthur Andersen & Co.

London

6th May 1988

EXHIBIT 1 (*continued*)
Consolidated Profit and Loss Account
(for the year ended 31 December 1988)

	1988 (£000)	1987 (£000)	1988 ($000)	1987 ($000)
Turnover[a]	£2,251,306	£1,097,775	$4,010,702	$1,844,262
Revenue	£ 547,129	£ 284,082	$ 974,710	$ 477,258
Cost of sales	(105,313)	(65,160)	(187,615)	(109,469)
Gross Profit	£ 441,816	£ 218,922	$ 787,095	$ 367,789
Other operating expenses (net)	(390,380)	(197,468)	(695,462)	(331,746)
Operating Profit	£ 51,436	£ 21,454	$ 91,633	$ 36,043
Interest receivable	7,926	3,739	14,120	6,282
Interest payable and similar charges	(19,044)	(11,076)	(33,926)	(18,608)
Profit on Ordinary Activities before Taxation	£ 40,318	£ 14,117	$ 71,827	$ 23,717
Tax on profit on ordinary activities	(18,930)	(6,810)	(33,724)	(11,441)
Profit on Ordinary Activities after Taxation	£ 21,388	£ 7,307	$ 38,103	$ 12,276
Minority interests	(266)	(222)	(474)	(373)
Profit for the Financial Year	£ 21,122	£ 7,085	$ 37,629	$ 11,903
Dividends paid and proposed	(7,033)	(2,337)	(12,529)	(3,926)
Retained Profit for the Year	£ 14,089	£ 4,748	$ 25,100	$ 7,977
Earnings per share	55.0p	32.1p	$ 0.98	$ 0.54

The main reporting currency of the group is the pound sterling, and the accounts have been prepared on this basis. Solely for convenience, the accounts set out are also presented expressed in U.S. dollars using the approximate average rate for the year for the profit and loss account (1988: $1.7815 = £1; 1987: $1.6800 = £1), the rate in effect on 31 December for the balance sheets (1988: $1.8090 = £1; 1987: $1.8785 = £1), and a combination of these for the statement of source and application of funds. This translation should not be construed as a representation that the pound sterling amounts actually represent, or could be converted into, U.S. dollars at the rate indicated.

---

[a] Note on the difference between Turnover and Revenue:

"Turnover comprises the gross amounts billed to clients in respect of commission based income together with the total of other fees earned. Revenue comprises commissions and fees earned in respect of turnover."

"Turnover and revenue are stated exclusive of VAT, sales taxes and trade discounts."

EXHIBIT 1 (*continued*)
Consolidated Balance Sheet (as at 31 December 1988)

	1988 £000	1987 £000	1988 $000	1987 $000
Fixed Assets				
Intangible assets (Note 10)	£ 175,000	£ —	$ 316,575	$ —
Tangible assets (Note 11)	86,378	79,184	156,258	148,747
Investments	4,678	3,464	8,463	6,507
	£ 266,056	£ 82,648	$ 481,296	$ 155,254
Current Assets				
Stocks and work-in-progress	£ 34,340	£ 37,920	$ 62,121	$ 71,233
Debtors	266,405	247,836	481,927	465,560
Investments and assets held for resale	13,912	115,273	25,167	216,540
Cash at bank and in hand	92,591	72,616	167,497	136,409
	£ 407,248	£ 473,645	$ 736,712	$ 889,742
Creditors: amounts falling due within one year	(437,079)	(454,733)	(790,676)	(854,216)
Net Current Assets (Liabilities)	£ (29,831)	£ 18,912	$ (53,964)	$ 35,526
Total Assets less Current Liabilities	236,225	101,560	427,332	190,780
Creditors: amounts falling due after more than one year	(140,761)	(91,333)	(254,637)	(171,568)
Provisions for Liabilities and Charges	(34,603)	(74,719)	(62,597)	(140,360)
Net Assets (Liabilities)	£ 60,861	£ (64,492)	$ 110,098	$(121,148)
Capital and Reserves				
Called-up share capital	£ 3,973	£ 3,670	$ 7,187	$ 6,894
Merger reserve	(150,603)	(89,423)	(272,441)	(167,981)
Other reserves	185,259	13,233	335,134	24,858
Profit and loss account	21,052	6,963	38,083	13,080
Shareholders' Funds	£ 59,681	£ (65,557)	$ 107,963	$(123,149)
Minority interests	1,180	1,065	2,135	2,001
Total Capital Employed	£ 60,861	£ (64,492)	$ 110,098	$(121,148)

Signed on behalf of the Board on 9 May 1989

R.E. Lerwill and M.S. Sorrell, Directors

The main reporting currency of the Group is the pound sterling and the accounts have been prepared on this basis. Solely for convenience, the accounts set out are also presented expressed in U.S. dollars using the approximate average rate for the year for the profit and loss account (1988: $1.7815 = £1; 1987: $1.6800 = £1), the rate in effect on 31 December for the balance sheets (1988: $1.8090 = £1; 1987: $1.8785 = £1), and a combination of these for the statement of source and application of funds. This translation should not be construed as a representation that the pound sterling amounts actually represent, or could be converted into, U.S. dollars at the rate indicated.

EXHIBIT 1 (*continued*)
Notes to the Accounts (31 December 1988)

Note 10—Intangible Fixed Assets

	1988 £000	1987 £000
Corporate brand names	175,000	—

Corporate brand names represent the directors' valuation of the brand names J. Walter Thompson and Hill and Knowlton, which were acquired in 1987 as part of JWT Group, Inc. These assets have been valued under the Alternative Accounting Rules of the Companies Act 1985 in accordance with the group's accounting policy for intangible fixed assets. The directors in the course of their valuation have consulted their advisers Samuel Montagu & Co. Limited.

Note 11—Tangible Fixed Assets

(a)   Group

The movement in the year was as follows:

(£000)	Land and Buildings			Plant and Machinery	Fixtures and Fittings	Motor Vehicles	Total
	Freehold	Long Leasehold	Short Leasehold				
Cost or valuation:							
Beginning of year	£12,686	£ 4,231	£36,511	£ 3,670	£26,071	£2,647	£ 85,816
New subsidiaries	1,099	163	507	719	1,856	441	4,785
Reclassification	—	(2,523)	2,523	—	—	—	—
Additions	2,122	325	1,776	1,493	8,244	3,055	17,015
Disposals	(5,732)	(26)	(2,022)	(1,274)	(2,188)	(990)	(12,232)
Exchange adjustments	649	494	2,117	185	1,435	52	4,932
Revaluation	3,202	—	1,350	—	—	—	4,552
End of year	£14,026	£ 2,664	£42,762	£ 4,793	£35,418	£5,205	£104,868
Depreciation:							
Beginning of year	£ —	£ 379	£ 1,279	£ 1,472	£ 3,020	£ 482	£ 6,632
Charge	275	154	3,896	599	5,572	1,123	11,619
Disposals	(204)	(20)	(42)	(208)	(521)	(402)	(1,397)
Exchange adjustments	40	31	677	110	760	18	1,636
End of year	£ 111	£ 544	£ 5,810	£ 1,973	£ 8,831	£1,221	£ 18,490
Net book value:							
31 December 1988	£13,915	£ 2,120	£36,952	£ 2,820	£26,587	£3,984	£ 86,378
31 December 1987	£12,686	£ 3,852	£35,232	£ 2,198	£23,051	£2,165	£ 79,184

Leased assets (other than leasehold property) included above have a net book value of £1,373,000 (1987: £322,000).

Basis of valuation: Plant and machinery (including fixtures and fittings) are shown at cost. Land and buildings include certain properties professionally revalued during 1987 and 1988, by James Andrew Badger (Surveyors & Valuers), on an open market, existing use basis. The historic net book value of such land and buildings is £6,511,000 (1987: £1,859,000).

EXHIBIT 1 (*continued*)
Notes to the Accounts (31 December 1988)

Auditors' Report

To the members of WPP Group plc:

We have audited the accounts set out on pages 63 to 84 in accordance with approved Auditing Standards.

In our opinion, the accounts, which have been prepared under the historical cost convention, as modified by the revaluation of land and buildings and corporate brand names, give a true and fair view of the state of affairs of the Company and of the Group at 31 December 1988 and of the Group profit and source and application of funds for the year then ended, and comply with the Companies Act 1985.

Arthur Andersen & Co.

London

9 May 1989

EXHIBIT 1 (continued)
Consolidated Profit and Loss Account (for the year ended 31 December 1989)

	1989 (£000)	1988 (£000)	1989 ($000)	1988 ($000)
Turnover[a]	£4,406,898	£2,251,306	$ 7,190,735	$4,010,702
Revenue	£1,005,453	£ 547,129	$ 1,640,598	$ 974,710
Gross Profit	£ 843,032	£ 441,816	$ 1,375,575	$ 787,095
Other operating expenses (net)	(740,550)	(390,380)	(1,208,355)	(695,462)
Operating Profit	£ 102,482	£ 51,436	$ 167,220	$ 91,633
Interest receivable	16,072	7,926	26,224	14,120
Interest payable and similar charges	(43,515)	(19,044)	(71,003)	(33,926)
Profit on Ordinary Activities before Taxation	£ 75,039	£ 40,318	$ 122,441	$ 71,827
Tax on profit on ordinary activities	(34,532)	(18,930)	(56,346)	(33,724)
Profit on Ordinary Activities after Taxation	£ 40,507	£ 21,388	$ 66,095	$ 38,103
Minority interests	(2,306)	(266)	(3,763)	(474)
Profit for the Financial Year	£ 38,201	£ 21,122	$ 62,332	$ 37,629
Preference dividends	(8,413)	—	(13,727)	—
Profit Attributable to Ordinary Shareholders	£ 29,788	£ 21,122	$ 48,605	$ 37,629
Ordinary dividends	(9,913)	(7,033)	(16,175)	(12,529)
Retained Profit for the Year	£ 19,875	£ 14,089	$ 32,430	$ 25,100
Earnings per Share				
Basic	73.0p	54.3p	$ 1.19	$ 0.97
Fully diluted	71.2p	NA	$ 1.16	NA

The main reporting currency of the Group is the pound sterling and the accounts have been prepared on this basis. Solely for convenience, the accounts set out are also presented expressed in U.S. dollars using the approximate average rate for the year for the profit and loss account (1989: $1.6317 = £1; 1988: $1.7815 = £1), the rate in effect on 31 December for the balance sheets (1989: $1.6125 = £1; 1988: $1.8090 = £1), and a combination of these for the statement of source and application of funds. This translation should not be construed as a representation that the pound sterling amounts actually represent, or could be converted into, U.S. dollars at the rate indicated.

[a] Note on the difference between Turnover and Revenue:

"Turnover comprises the gross amounts billed to clients in respect of commission based income together with the total of other fees earned. Revenue comprises commissions and fees earned in respect of turnover."

"Turnover and revenue are stated exclusive of VAT, sales taxes and trade discounts."

EXHIBIT 1 (*continued*)

Consolidated Balance Sheet (as at 31 December 1989)

	1989 £000	1988 £000	1989 $000	1988 $000
Fixed Assets				
Intangible assets (Note 9)	£ 350,000	£ 175,000	$ 564,375	$ 316,575
Tangible assets	156,583	86,378	252,490	156,258
Investments	19,774	4,678	31,886	8,463
	£ 526,357	£ 266,056	$ 848,751	$ 481,296
Current Assets				
Stocks and work-in-progress	£ 91,004	£ 34,340	$ 146,744	$ 62,121
Debtors	648,778	266,405	1,046,155	481,927
Investments and assets held for resale	6,759	13,912	10,899	25,167
Cash at bank and in hand	233,617	92,591	376,707	167,497
	£ 980,158	£ 407,248	$ 1,580,505	$ 736,712
Creditors: amounts falling due within one year	(1,149,858)	(437,079)	(1,854,146)	(790,676)
Net Current Assets (Liabilities)	£ (169,700)	£ (29,831)	$ (273,641)	$ (53,964)
Total Assets less Current Liabilities	356,657	236,225	(575,110)	427,332
Creditors: amounts falling due after more than one year	(535,618)	(140,761)	(863,684)	(254,637)
Provisions for Liabilities and Charges	(151,170)	(34,603)	(243,762)	(62,597)
Net (Liabilities) Assets	£ (330,131)	£ 60,861	$ (532,336)	$ 110,098
Capital and Reserves				
Called-up share capital	£ 25,505	£ 3,973	$ 41,127	$ 7,187
Share premium	192,721	—	310,763	—
Goodwill reserve	(797,811)	(150,603)	(1,286,470)	(272,441)
Other reserves	196,247	185,259	316,447	335,134
Profit and loss account	40,927	21,052	65,995	38,083
Shareholders' Funds	£ (342,411)	£ 59,681	$ (552,138)	$ 107,963
Minority interests	12,280	1,180	19,802	2,135
Total Capital Employed	£ (330,131)	£ 60,861	$ (532,336)	$ 110,098

Signed on behalf of the Board on 9 May 1989

R.E. Lerwill and M.S. Sorrell, Directors

The main reporting currency of the Group is the pound sterling and the accounts have been prepared on this basis. Solely for convenience, the accounts set out are also presented expressed in U.S. dollars using the approximate average rate for the year for the profit and loss account (1989: $1.6317 = £1; 1988: $1.7815 = £1), the rate in effect on 31 December for the balance sheets (1989: $1.6125 = £1; 1988: $1.8090 = £1), and a combination of these for the statement of source and application of funds. This translation should not be construed as a representation that the pound sterling amounts actually represent, or could be converted into, U.S. dollars at the rate indicated.

EXHIBIT 1 (*continued*)
Notes to the Accounts (31 December 1989)

Note 9—Intangible Fixed Assets

	£000
Corporate brand names:	
Beginning of year	£175,000
Additions at fair value to the group—Ogilvy & Mather	175,000
End of year	£350,000

Corporate brand names represent the directors' valuation of the brand names J. Walter Thompson and Hill and Knowlton which were valued in 1988 and Ogilvy & Mather acquired in 1989 as part of The Ogilvy Group, Inc. These assets have been valued in accordance with the group's accounting policy for intangible fixed assets and in the course of this valuation the directors have consulted their advisers, Samuel Montagu & Co. Limited.

EXHIBIT 1 (*continued*)
Notes to the Accounts

Note 10—Tangible Fixed Assets

a) Group

The movement in the year was as follows:

(£000)	Land and Buildings		Fixtures, Fittings, and Equipment	Total
	Freehold	Leasehold		
Cost or valuation:				
Beginning of year	14,026	45,426	45,416	104,868
New subsidiaries	3,969	24,060	30,181	58,210
Additions	139	7,108	19,112	26,359
Disposals	(851)	(1,665)	(4,134)	(6,650)
Exchange adjustments	419	4,974	5,334	10,727
Revaluation	2,445	(350)	—	2,095
End of year	20,147	79,553	95,909	195,609
Depreciation:				
Beginning of year	111	6,354	12,025	18,490
Charge	146	4,780	14,903	19,829
Disposals	(12)	(100)	(1,073)	(1,185)
Exchange adjustments	34	411	1,447	1,892
End of year	279	11,445	27,302	39,026
Net book value:				
31 December 1989	19,868	68,108	68,607	156,583
31 December 1988	13,915	39,072	33,391	86,378

Leasehold land and buildings comprises £3,485,000 (1988: £2,120,000) held on long leasehold and £64,623,000 (1988: £36,952,000) held on short leasehold. Leased assets (other than leasehold property) included above have a net book value of £1,812,000 (1988: £1,373,000).

Basis of valuation: Fixtures, fittings, and equipment are shown at cost. Land and buildings include certain properties professionally revalued during 1989, by messrs. James Andrew Badger (Surveyors & Valuers), on an open market, existing use basis. Other properties are included at historic cost. The amount included in respect of revalued properties is £16,444,000 (1988: £12,314,000); the historic net book value of such land and buildings is £8,542,000 (1988: £6,511,000).

Auditors' Report

To the members of WPP Group plc:

We have audited the accounts set out on pages 41 to 63 in accordance with Auditing Standards.

In our opinion, the accounts give a true and fair view of the state of affairs of the Company and of the Group at 31 December 1989 and of the profit and source and application of funds of the Group for the year then ended, and have been properly prepared in accordance with the Companies Act 1985.

Arthur Andersen & Co.

London

EXHIBIT 2
Goodwill[a]

Country	Predominant Method	Comments
U.S.	Capitalize.	Amortize to expense over Useful Life—not to exceed 40 years.
U.K.	Direct write-off versus reserves (i.e., Retained Earnings) in the year of acquisition.	Capitalization is permitted. If capitalized amortized to earnings over Useful Life, if determinable. If Useful Life is not reasonably determinable, the Goodwill should not be written off. There is no stated maximum Useful Life restriction.
Canada	Capitalize.	Similar to U.S.
Japan	Capitalize the amount by which the purchase price exceeds the **Book Value** of net assets acquired (not Fair Value).	If capitalized, amortize to expense over Useful Life—not to exceed five (5) years. Expense is tax-deductible.
France	Capitalize.	Amortize to expense over a 5 to 20-year period.
Germany	Capitalize.	Amortize to expense over a 4-year period (can be extended if justified in the circumstances). Expense is tax-deductible on a straight line basis over 15 years.
Switzerland	Option to write off versus reserves in the year of acquisition or to capitalize.	Goodwill purchased as a pre-existing asset of an acquired company is capitalizable and the amortization of this Goodwill is tax deductible.
Netherlands	Options: (1) Capitalize. (2) Write-off to expense in the year of acquisition. (3) Write-off vs. equity in the year of acquisition.	If capitalized, amortize over 5 years (can be extended to 10 years if justified in the (2) circumstances).
Hong Kong	Similar to the Netherlands.	If capitalized, amortize to expense **Only if, and to the extent,** that value has diminished.
Australia	Capitalize.	Amortize to expense over Useful Life—not to exceed 20 years.
Malaysia	Capitalize.	Amortize to expense over Useful Life with no stated maximum.

Description: Goodwill arises from Business Combinations accounted for under the purchase method. It is defined as the amount by which the purchase price of the Acquired Company exceeds the fair value of the Acquired Company's net assets. Goodwill may either be capitalized by the Acquiror and amortized ratably over its Estimated Useful Life (with stated maximums) or written off in the year of acquisition. Such a direct write-off normally is directly against Shareholders' Equity (called Reserves in the United Kingdom). The amortization of Goodwill is not a tax-deductible expense excepts as noted above.

[a] Reprinted with the permission of Mr. John Fawls, CPA, Merrill Lynch Capital Markets, Copyright 1989.

EXHIBIT 3

In thinking along the lines of corporate versus personalized loyalty it might be useful to introduce a simple analogy. If one thinks of a football team this is clearly a case of corporate loyalty. Individual players and managers may come and go, but the fans' loyalty is predominantly with that abstract corporate notion—the "team." On the other side of the coin, one can imagine a consultant's (e.g., a doctor's) relationship with a client—a relationship based primarily upon personal factors. Should the consultant in question leave his present firm it's quite conceivable that he will take his clients with him. The question now is where along this corporate-loyalty, personal-loyalty continuum lies the world of the advertising agency.

In approaching this question the following general factors need to be considered:

A People Profession

Undoubtedly the advertising world is grounded upon a considerable degree of personal interaction. Within such an environment individual relationships and loyalties naturally flourish—even more so given the need for confidentiality and campaign consistency. The exact extent of the "personal factor" is difficult to quantify since it will vary from case to case and depend upon the influence of the person in question. There is no doubt, however, that in some cases a client's loyalty is primarily to their contact within an agency rather than with the agency itself. There have been some notable examples of this, through clients following key individuals when they leave the agency. A famous example in 1981 was a number of clients who followed Frank Lowe from Collet Dickenson Pearce to Lowe Howard-Spink. Recent examples include:

Dec 1988— David Harrison leaves Leo Burnett Direct and formed RSCG Direct. He takes with him the Bankers Clearing Services Consortium account which he brought to the company when he joined.

Dec 1988— David Pasley leaves FCB Pasley Woods and takes clients with him.

1988— Malcolm Gaskin leaves TBWA to form WMGO and takes the Wolverhampton and Dudley Breweries Account with him.

Nov 1987— John Collington joins CTMC from Hilton Consumer and takes the Answercall account with him.

June 1987— Chris Davis seems set to leave AHH and industry sources suggest that if he leaves, a number of clients with whom he has worked will be prompted to review.

A Capricious Profession

Given the advertising world's dependence upon creativity, there is an inherent danger of it becoming a hostage to fads and novelty. The continual quest for innovation makes it a volatile environment and can at times dictate against a lasting client-agency relationship. This tendency was demonstrated recently upon the transferral of H.R. Owen's account to Leagas Shafron, during which their Marketing Manager stated that "it wasn't that we were unhappy with Connell May and Stevenson, but it was felt that the time was right for a change." This type of philosophy can clearly impinge upon the loyalty of an agency's client-base.

A Predatory Profession

The advertising world is, in a client sense, a highly acquisitive environment. *Advertising Age*, for example, found that 72% of its sample of company advertising directors had been approached within the previous 3 months by agencies trying to acquire their business. In such a competitive arena corporate (and individual) loyalty is put under a strain.

EXHIBIT 3 (*continued*)

This volatility is further increased by the prevalence of new agencies; in the case of Britain an average of 20 a year (in 1981 there were 43 new agencies launched). The disruptive effect of these new players is increased by the fact that their very newness may, for the creative reasons alluded to earlier, be perceived as attractive in itself.

Agency Size (Client Base)

To set against the above, the size of the agency is a very important fact. The larger the agency, the easier it is to replace important individuals with others of similar standing in the profession. Obviously in the case of JWT, its list of accounts is among the most comprehensive of all agencies on a world scale. Just as important though is the quality of the client base. Here, JWT is again impressive with names such as Kellogg, Rowntree Mackintosh, and Kraft on its books. The strength of these brands is in part attributable to JWT's own guidance, and it can be said that some of their brand strength has rubbed off on to JWT itself. This will be particularly true where the relationship is long-standing. In this sense JWT again looks good with an average length of service for its present clients standing at 13 years—with many accounts going back much further, e.g., Kraft 1926, Lever 1927, and Kellogg 1938. This evidence would suggest that to a large extent, JWT transcends the erratic nature of the advertising game. Moreover, this duration of client relationship would also imply that JWT's clients do not easily transfer their loyalty from the corporate body to individuals within it.

Most examples of accounts moving with individuals relate to the smaller agencies rather than to the major players in the game.

To illustrate this latter point, advertising agencies are categorized according to their age. This is most commonly expressed in the form of 3 separate "waves" of agencies. This corruption of Toffler's term represents a rather obtuse form of description, although it does provide a reasonably convenient way of approaching the subject.

Although exact definitions vary, the "first wave" is generally used to refer to those agencies, such as JWT, which existed prior to 1970. Those agencies which emerged in the next decade and a half tend to constitute the "second wave," and include such names as Lowe Howard-Spink and Saatchi and Saatchi. Finally, there is the "third wave" which goes back to the mid-1980s and is used to refer to new agencies such as Devito, Butterfield, Day, and Hockney.

Upon the basis of this schema we can make some general comments relating to the likely balance of corporate versus individual influences within the different categories of agency. In the case of the "first wave" for example, their client loyalty will have accrued over a long period of time and will be relatively independent of the qualities and influences of existing members of staff. This will be less true in the case of the "second wave," since it's likely that their founders will still be in control and will be personally responsible for much of the goodwill enjoyed by the agency. Finally, in the case of the "third wave" agencies, their brand value will tend to be heavily skewed towards their high profile founders and other key personnel.

Following on from the above approach it is clear that the names of the newer agencies tend to be synonymous with the name of their founders or other key personnel. In the event that one of these key personnel leaves the agency, then the agency's own name and state of continuity, may be disrupted. In short this type of agency is extremely susceptible to the mutilation of its brand image.

This will also tend to be the case with the second wave of agencies, although to a lesser extent since their longer existence will have imbued some level of brand value independent of those individuals of whom the agency is the namesake. Nevertheless, it would still be inconceivable to imagine that the likes of Saatchi and Saatchi could survive the departure of

EXHIBIT 3 (*continued*)

their founders with their reputation intact. Again, to a large extent these agencies are their key personnel.

In the case of the "first wave" agencies such as JWT though, the situation is entirely different. Put simply, the name JWT is not a derivative of any existing individuals within the agency. As such, its future brand value is not contingent upon its continued association with certain high profile individuals. In discussing brands in general, Professor John Quelch of the Harvard Business School has stated that "brands of the highest stature are likely to be those coincidental with the companies' own name" (e.g., Heinz soup rather than "Head and Shoulders"). Adapting this to the case of advertising agencies, the opposite can seem to be the case; that is, the strongest and most secure brands are those where the product (i.e., the personnel) do not share the companies' name.

To conclude then, it appears from this analysis that JWT satisfies all those criteria which would suggest the existence of a strong client loyalty; a loyalty which is grounded upon corporate rather than individual allegiance.

In the case of the United States this strength would seem to be confirmed by the results of the *Advertising Age's* Agency Watch poll which has consistently placed JWT in the number one position in terms of industry perceptions. This consistency, moreover, was not disrupted by the personnel problems experienced by JWT over the last few years: as the *Advertising Age* (May 1988) itself expressed it, "JWT seems to be surviving the management turmoil of the past 18 months with its reputation intact."

In the British context this same strength is demonstrated by the high level of continuity of JWT's accounts. In 1986 and 1987 for example around 96% of JWT's clients kept their business with the agency for the following year—an impressive level of retention given the possibility of "one off" campaigns (e.g., Government flotations) and the erratic nature of the industry.

As mentioned above, a practical problem with carrying out the brand valuation for an agency in the same way as for a consumer product arises from a lack of data. A more oblique way of approaching the question is required.

An extensive literature exists in economic theory relating to dominant firms and the likelihood of their decline. (See, for example, Geroski in Hay and Vickers (1987), *The Economics of Market Dominance*, for a recent critical survey.) In other words, given a firm which has a large market share, what is the likelihood of this declining substantially and by what processes will this decline come about? There is a presumption in theory that competitive forces will erode monopoly power and lead to the decline of even the most dominant firm. In practice, the theory is not supported all that well and powerful firms exercising dominance over markets can persist for a very long time.

Source: *Valuing the JWT Brand*, a Henley Centre Report, Jan. 1989, 3-7.

Diversity in Accounting Principles: A Problem, a Strategic Imperative, or a Strategic Opportunity?

I n our study of accounting decision making, we have been reading and discussing situations in which managers have had choices about the way in which they would report on the results of operations and the financial condition of their organizations. We have shown that managers must choose between using LIFO or FIFO in measuring and reporting on inventories, or between straight-line depreciation or accelerated depreciation in reporting on plant, property, and equipment. For almost every classification of assets, liabilities, shareholders' equity, and revenue and expenses, alternative conventions, practices, and principles exist from which managers and their accountants can choose. With such an array of methods and practices available, what is the meaning of "generally accepted accounting principles"?

GENERALLY ACCEPTED ACCOUNTING PRINCIPLES

In general, when managers prepare reports for use by outsiders such as lenders, investors, regulatory authorities, or other interested groups, they must choose among accounting conventions, practices, and principles, which become bases for making the measurements necessary to prepare financial reports. Once a choice is made, the concept of consistency demands that similar conventions and practices be used in subsequent periods unless there is a reason that an alternative method would be preferred. We have seen how auditors refer to the use of "generally accepted" accounting principles in expressing their opinions on many financial statements prepared for the use of outsiders.

The use of the word "principles" is perhaps unfortunate, for it connotes something more basic than, in fact, most accounting principles are. Accounting principles are not fundamental truths or even necessarily rules of conduct. They are methods used in observing, measuring, and reporting which are widely used or which have substantial, authoritative support. A generally accepted accounting principle is created whenever a method, practice, concept, or convention is widely used by those who prepare reports, or whenever an official pronouncement is made by a group such as the Financial Accounting Standards Board in the United States, the International

Professor William J. Bruns, Jr. prepared this note as the basis for class discussion.

Accounting Standards Committee, by a change to a Company's Act, or by a regulator with authority to influence reporting and securities trading.

The fact that wide use leads to general acceptance in accounting principles makes it critical to understand the accounting process and the way in which it operates. In preparing and distributing their reports, managers and their accountants participate in the development of accounting principles. Through the criteria its managers adopt in deciding which measurements should be made and reported, an organization supports and advances the development of principles that may be used even more widely in the future.

The idea of a set of generally accepted accounting principles is very important historically. When there were fewer constraints on the accounting practices that could be employed by managers in preparing reports, unscrupulous entrepreneurs often took advantage of investors, creditors, and other interested groups by rendering misleading reports about income and financial position. In an effort to avert such practices, professional accountants, regulators, independent authorities, and government agencies in most countries have sought to limit the kinds of practices that fall within the guidelines that generally accepted accounting principles provide.

Nevertheless, there is no definitive list of practices and principles that are "generally accepted." It is much easier to find lists or regulations of methods or practices that are not generally accepted. This means that in spite of all the efforts to reduce diversity in reporting practices, great diversity still remains, and anyone who seeks to use financial reports has to pay close attention to the methods used by the managers and accountants who prepared them.

Unfortunately, diversity in accounting principles presents an important problem to anyone who wants to compare the economic performance or financial position of an organization at two points in time, or with that of another organization, or to some normative standard or model. To merely look at the numbers that are reported without considering the methods that lie behind them creates the risk of faulty conclusions or errors in judgment. The next section demonstrates why this is so.

DIVERSITY IN ACCOUNTING PRINCIPLES

The diversity in accounting principles is so great that it would be impossible to summarize in brief form all of the concepts, methods, and procedures that are at the present time acceptable in accounting practice. It is important at least to realize how many diverse practices are acceptable and the way in which the possibilities are multiplied if combinations of different principles and practices relating to assets, liabilities, shareholders' equity, revenues, and expenses are considered. **Exhibit 1** lists some selected examples of diverse generally accepted accounting principles for presentation of financial information about important classifications.

It would be helpful if there were some normative standard against which diverse practices and their effect on financial reports might be compared. If there were a normative standard, then accounting principles producing reports that were closest to the normative standard would be preferred. By estimating the difference between a report in hand and one based on the normative standard, a financial report reader could make a judgment about the quality of information available in the financial report. In the absence of a standard, each person who seeks to use accounting information needs to create his or her own reference point. This is harder to do than it appears at first glance. Consider the simple example that follows.

How is Diversity a Problem?

Assume that two identical companies start business at the same time, and that the events and transactions in which they engage during the first year of their operations are identical. If managers of each company choose alternative accounting principles in preparing their reports, those reports may be quite different, even after only one year. **Exhibit 2** shows the statement of financial position for each of the two companies to be the same when they begin operations. **Exhibit 3** shows the events and transactions that affect both companies identically. **Exhibit 4** shows the accounting methods used by the managers of each company in reporting those identical events and transactions. **Exhibit 5** shows the statements of income and financial position that each company will prepare at the end of one year of operations. And finally, **Exhibit 6** shows how the income of the two identical companies might be reconciled.

While this example is quite simple and is obviously hypothetical, differences like these arise in actual financial reporting. Anyone who attempts to compare financial statements from two or more entities is faced with the task of identifying the accounting methods used. Then, the impact that particular methods might have had on the reports must be estimated before any comparison of the two organizations can be made. Even when examining the financial statements of a single company through time, attention must be given to possible changes in accounting principles and the impact these changes may have had before information contained in the financial reports can be used for many purposes.

DIVERSITY: STRATEGIC IMPERATIVE VS. STRATEGIC OPPORTUNITY

Financial reports are a showcase through which managers can fulfill their obligations to provide information to shareholders and other interested parties. The fact that periodic financial reporting is required shows how important the economic community and society think reporting by managers is in facilitating the free flow of capital and preventing one group from taking advantage of another because of the information available to it. It is difficult to imagine how a modern free-enterprise economy could function without a financial reporting system that is somewhat effective.

The role that financial reporting plays in a modern economy requires that managers should be trying to report about the operations and financial condition of their organizations as accurately and informatively as possible. Those who fear that managers might withhold information to use to their own advantage would argue that some minimum set of disclosure and reporting requirements is necessary to get managers to report effectively. Whichever points of view you have about the environment in which financial reporting occurs, you must consider what managers should do if they discover that the accounting methods and principles that they are using and reporting are not the right ones, and that a change is needed.

Why might managers or an organization be using accounting methods and principles that are incorrect or ineffective? There are at least three obvious reasons. First, it may be that the initial choice of an accounting method or principle was a poor one. Since many initial choices of accounting principles or methods are made when a firm is small or when a problem is first encountered, the implications of those choices may not be obvious. As the organization grows and develops, or as its activities stabilize, it may become obvious that the method or principle initially chosen does not provide as much or as good information as an alternative might.

A second reason why managers or an organization may need to change accounting methods or principles may be because conditions have changed. The environment in which the organization is operating, or the relationships with various suppliers, investors, or financing sources, or a change in the product mix or strategy of the firm all may dictate that an alternative method or principle would be more informative than one previously employed.

A third reason why change may be necessary may be due to the actions of management itself. In developing new strategies, in taking the organization in new directions, and in adopting new tactics to deal with the action of competitors, managers may want to signal that the old accounting methods supported the old strategy, but new accounting principles and methods are needed given the chosen change in strategic direction.

Regardless of which of these three reasons creates a need for change in the accounting method or principles used in reporting, management may view the need for change as imperative. It is simply impossible to report effectively using the old method when it is obvious that a new method or principle would be more appropriate or effective.

Despite the demands for consistency that are created by the accountant's concept of consistency, an accounting change is permitted and even encouraged when it can be demonstrated that another method or principle would be preferable. In other case studies, we have seen that auditors must note a change in accounting method, but they do not need to deny an unqualified auditor's opinion simply because managers have changed accounting methods or principles. In fact, in many circumstances, the auditors append to their notice of change some phrase like "with which we concur" to signal that they are in agreement with and support the change that management has made in preparing its reports.

Unfortunately, the strategic imperative also creates the opportunity to use changes as a strategic opportunity. Selecting new accounting methods means that managers can present things differently. The results of operations or financial position can be presented in a light different than they would have been presented had the old methods or principles been retained. Because modern organizations and economic activities are so complex, what may to some managers be a strategic imperative to report things as clearly as possible, may open the door to strategic opportunities to other managers who are less scrupulous or who desire to present things in a light particularly advantageous to themselves or their organization.

Diversity in accounting principles is unlikely to be eliminated by policy, law, or practice. Diversity exists because the arena in which financial communication, accounting measurement, and financial reporting takes place is a complex one. Those who use financial reports prepared in an atmosphere where accounting diversity is the norm must examine the accounting principles and methods used, consider what alternatives might have been available, and then decide how to use the information in reports. Those who prepare financial reports and are responsible for them must consider how to balance the strategic imperative to report as accurately and honestly as possible with the strategic opportunity to present information in such a way that some who see and use the information might be misled into drawing erroneous conclusions and taking undesirable actions.

EXHIBIT 1
Selected Examples of Diversity in Generally Accepted Accounting Principles

Cash

1. Include all cash on hand and in banks as one item.
2. Use separate captions for cash on hand, and/or cash in banks, and/or cash in banks that cannot be easily withdrawn, and/or separate currencies.

Receivables

1. Show receivables at gross amount.
2. Show receivables at gross amount less allowances for unearned interest and doubtful accounts.
3. Show receivables classified by type (accounts, notes, etc.), and/or by time, and/or by source (customers, employees, government, etc.).
4. Exclude receivables unless earned and due, as in lease payments receivable.

Marketable securities (temporary investments)

1. Show securities at cost.
2. Show securities at market value when below cost.
3. Show securities at cost plus interest earned but not yet paid.
4. Show securities at approximate market value.

Inventories

1. Show inventories at gross cost and/or by classes (supplies, raw materials, work in process, finished goods ready for sale).
2. Show inventories at cost or market, whichever is lower.
3. Show inventories at market or selling price.
4. Determine "cost" or "price" by assuming average costs or standard costs.
5. Report flow of costs and value of goods remaining by assuming last-in first-out, or first-in first-out, or average costs in and out, or standard costs in and out, etc. (Also see **Cost of goods sold** below.)

Land, plant, and equipment

1. Show land, plant, and equipment at original cost, and/or adjusted original cost, and/or cost or market value, whichever is lower.
2. Show plant and equipment at current value.
3. Show plant and equipment at cost less accumulated depreciation calculated by assuming straight-line allocation of cost to periods, or by an accelerated or decelerated rate of depreciation.
4. Charge all purchases of plant and equipment as expense in period purchased.
5. Show land at original cost less depletion caused by mining, harvesting, or extraction of gases or fluids.

EXHIBIT 1 (*continued*)

Investments

1. Show investments in other companies at cost.
2. Show investments in other companies at cost or market value, whichever is lower.
3. Show investments in other companies at cost plus any proportional share of earnings on investment not received.
4. Show investments at market value.

Intangible assets

1. Exclude intangible assets, charging all costs related thereto as expense in the period of expenditure.
2. Show all intangible assets at cost.
3. Show intangible assets at cost but allocate costs over a few periods until only a nominal value remains.
4. Show intangible assets at cost but allocate cost to all periods of expected value.
5. Show intangible assets at cost but do not charge costs to periods unless value has clearly fallen.
6. Show intangible assets at estimated value at time of acquisition, adjusted for subsequent charges.

Current liabilities

1. Show liabilities at face amount.
2. Show liabilities at amount at which obligations could be satisfied plus any costs of doing so.

Long-term liabilities

1. Show long-term liabilities at face amount.
2. Show long-term liabilities at face amount adjusted for discounts or premiums given at acceptance and amortized over period of the liability.
3. Show liabilities, including commitments on leases, pensions, and other contractual agreements, at face amount or adjusted for effects of interest.

Owners' equity

1. Show owners' equity as the amount of assets less the amount of liabilities.
2. Show owners' equity classified to show original source.
3. Show owners' equity classified by original source but modified by transactions between the entity and shareholders, and/or extraordinary reclassifications or adjustments.
4. Within owners' equity, segregate earnings retained by implied use of resources earned.

Revenues

1. Recognize revenue in period when products or services are delivered.
2. Recognize revenue in period when product is ready for delivery (as in case of precious gems or metals).
3. Recognize revenue in period when payment is received from customer or client.

EXHIBIT 1 (*continued*)

Cost of goods sold

1. Recognize expense in the period and at purchase of product delivered.
2. Recognize expense in the period and at purchase cost of some assumed unit of product delivered.
3. Recognize expense in the period and at cost of replacement of the product delivered. (Also see **Inventories** above.)

Expenses

1. Recognize, as expenses of the period, all or selected cash payments.
2. Recognize, as expenses of the period, all expenditures related to products or services sold in the period. All expenditures are assets or in satisfaction of obligations.
3. Recognize, as expenses in the period, all estimated declines in assets value and estimated increases in obligations not related to cost of goods sold.

Net income

1. Show all increases or decreases in net value of owners' equity as net income, regardless of source.
2. Exclude from net income all adjustments relating to prior period reports, and/or extraordinary events.

EXHIBIT 2
Statements of Financial Position, January 1, 1992

	Company A		Company B	
Assets				
Cash		$ 500		$ 500
Marketable securities		1,000		1,000
Inventories (100 units @ $10)		1,000		1,000
Building and equipment				
(estimated life 10 years)	$2,000		$2,000	
Less: Accumulated depreciation	—		—	
		2,000		2,000
Total assets		$4,500		$4,500
Equities				
Accounts payable		$ 200		$ 200
Bank loans		1,000		1,000
Total liabilities		$1,200		$1,200
Owners' equity:				
Common Stock		3,300		3,300
Total equities		$4,500		$4,500

EXHIBIT 3
Events and Transactions of Companies A and B[a] for the Year 1992

Sales of merchandise (200 units @ $40 each)		$8,000
Purchase of inventory on account		
(a 3% discount is available if paid within 10 days):		
March 31	50 units @ $10	500
June 30	50 units @ $12	600
September 30	50 units @ $15	750
December 31	50 units @ $20	1,000
Paid accounts payable:		
April 30		500
July 31		600
October 31		750
Paid salaries		$2,500
Increased bank loan		$2,000
Purchased new equipment (estimated life, 4 years)		$2,000
Paid for research on new product not yet introduced		$ 500
Value of marketable securities, December 31, 1992		$ 950

[a] Assumed to be identical for each company

EXHIBIT 4
Accounting Methods Used in Preparing Financial Reports by Companies A and B

Item	Company A	Company B
Cash	Report face amount on hand and in bank.	Report face amount on hand and in bank.
Marketable securities	Report at cost unless market is "materially" lower and sale contemplated.	Report at lower of market cost or market.
Inventory	Report at cost, assuming first-in, first-out.	Report at cost, assuming last-in, first-out.
Buildings and equipment	Report at cost less accumulated straight-line depreciation.	Report at cost less accumulated depreciation accelerated at two times straight-line rate.
Intangible assets	Hold as asset at cost until related revenues are realized.	Charge against revenues when cash expended.
Accounts payable	Report at amount due less discounts available.	Report at face amount.
Bank loan	Report at amount due.	Report at amount due.
Owners' equity	Assets – Liabilities	Assets – Liabilities

EXHIBIT 5
Financial Reports of Companies A and B

Statement of Income

For the Year 1992	Company A		Company B	
Sales revenues		$ 8,000		$8,000
Less cost of goods sold:				
Beginning inventory	$1,000		$1,000	
Add: purchases	2,850		2,850	
Available	$3,850		$3,850	
Ending inventory	1,750		1,000	
		2,100		2,850
Gross margin		$ 5,900		$5,150
Less expenses:				
Salaries	$2,500		$2,500	
Depreciation	700		1,400	
Research on new product	—		500	
		3,200		4,400
Operating income:		$ 2,700		$ 750
Add: Discount available		30		—
Less: Loss on securities held		—		50
Net Income		$ 2,730		$ 700

Statements of Financial Position,

December 31, 1992	Company A		Company B	
Assets				
Cash		$ 3,650		$3,650
Marketable securities		1,000		950
Inventories		1,750		1,000
Building and equipment:				
Cost	$4,000		$4,000	
Accumulated depreciation	700		1,400	
		3,300		2,600
Research on new product		500		—
Total assets		$10,200		$8,200
Equities				
Accounts payable		$ 1,170		$1,200
Bank loans		3,000		3,000
Total liabilities		$ 4,170		$4,200
Owners' equity:				
Common stock		3,300		3,300
Retained earnings		2,730		700
		6,030		4,000
Total equities		$10,200		$8,200

EXHIBIT 5 (*continued*)

Statement of Cash Flows For the Year 1992	Company A	Company B
Cash from Operations:		
Net income	$ 2,730	$ 700
Add: Depreciation	700	1,400
Decrease in marketable securities	—	50
Increase in inventories	(750)	—
Increase in Accounts Payable	970	1,000
Total cash from operations	$ 3,650	$ 3,150
Cash from Inventories:		
Purchase of new equipment	$(2,000)	$(2,000)
Research on new product	(500)	—
Total cash from Inventory	$(2,500)	$(2,000)
Cash from financing:		
New bank loan	$ 2,000	$ 2,000
Total changes in cash	$ 3,150	$ 3,150
Cash, January 1, 1992	500	500
Cash, December 31, 1992	$ 3,650	$ 3,650

EXHIBIT 6
Reconciliation of Income for Companies A and B

Company B income	$ 700
Add $50 because Company A does not reduce value of marketable securities to market value of $950	50
Add $750 because Company A uses FIFO instead of LIFO for inventory values and determining cost of goods sold	750
Add $700 because Company A uses straight-line depreciation instead of an accelerated method	700
Add $500 because Company A retains research costs as an asset	500
Add $30 because Company A reduced liabilities to discounted amount	30
Company A income	$2,730

Kendall Square Research Corporation (A) (Abridged)

Kendall Square Research Corporation (KSR) was founded in 1986. KSR was the third computer company established by its co-founders. At KSR, they chose a radical design for a supercomputer that would make the machines attractive for both government and university laboratories and for commercial users. The company delivered its first machine to the Oak Ridge National Laboratory in the fall of 1991, and Kendall Square Research reported that it reached break-even volume before the end of 1992.

From its beginning KSR funded its development and the design of its products through private placements of its equity and debt securities and an initial public stock offering in April 1992. A subsequent stock offering in April 1993 brought the total financing of the start-up to about $150 million—more than $80 million of which had come in two offerings of stock to the public. Shares in the first of the public offerings had more than doubled in price in less than 18 months. By October 1993, the market capitalization of the shares was about five times estimated 1993 sales and 45 times estimated 1993 earnings.[1]

From the time of its first sale, some critics questioned the criteria used by KSR to determine when revenue would be recognized. The company recognized revenue on product sales upon written customer acceptance of the product. Acceptance often occurred before the configuration of a particular system was finalized or any payment had been received from a customer. Kendall Square Research fully disclosed its policy on revenue recognition in its financial reports to shareholders. (See **Exhibit 1** for excerpts from the 1992 Kendall Square Research Corporation Annual Report to Shareholders.)

In mid-September 1993, George McClelland, an early-round investor in the firm and a former associate of the founders, joined Kendall Square as Chief Administrative Officer.

This case derives from an earlier case, "Kendall Square Research Corporation (A)," HBS No. 194-068, prepared by Professor William J. Bruns, Jr. This version was prepared by Professor F. Warren McFarlan. HBS cases are developed solely as the basis for class discussion. Cases are not intended to serve as endorsements, sources of primary data, or illustrations of effective or ineffective management.

---

[1] John R. Dorfman and William M. Bulkeley, "Heard on the Street: Supercomputer Maker Kendall Square's Effort to Crack Business Markets Has Some Skeptics," *The Wall Street Journal*, October 11, 1993, p. C2.

KENDALL SQUARE RESEARCH AND SUPERCOMPUTING

Kendall Square Research[2] recognized at its founding that a key to its success would be its ability to deliver more computing power at lower cost per computation than its competitors. Its approach was based on linking many low-cost minicomputers and dividing the computer task among them, rather than building larger mainframe computers or trying to improve programming and software to wring more performance from the computer architectures that were available. The concept of massively parallel processing had first surfaced in the 1980s, and several competitors felt that it had tremendous potential.

A large-scale parallel computer was potentially faster and less expensive than traditional mainframes or available supercomputers. In addition to lower cost per computation or transaction, large-scale parallel computers were theoretically scaleable; bigger and more powerful machines could be assembled merely by adding processors and the memory and input and output devices to support them. However, as processors were added, programming became more difficult and cumbersome.

Kendall Square's founders believed that a highly successful parallel computer could succeed only if it could take advantage of the library of applications and languages that were already standard in the mainframe and supercomputer worlds. Their goal was to develop a standards-based multi-user system that could run multiple applications simultaneously, so that a sufficiently powerful system could serve an entire technical or business enterprise. Their ideal system would even be able to run scientific and business applications at the same time.

The technology that was needed to develop such a computer did not exist in 1986 when KSR was founded. For six years Kendall Square scientists and engineers invested in chip development technology that they hoped would turn their insight into a working computer. By 1992 they were sure they had succeeded. They had developed a large-scale parallel computer which combined the power of massively parallel, distributed memory machines with the familiar shared-memory programming environment of conventional mainframes. The KSR1 family of computers was designed for high performance computing requirements typical of scientific environments, for decision support and complex database query applications, and for on-line transaction-intensive environments such as automatic teller machines or airline reservation systems.

The KSR1 family of systems scaled from 16 to 1088 processors. A $975,000 model with 16 processors could handle 1,200 transactions per second, a measure of commercial computer speed. Scalability allowed users to add computer resources in incremental and cost-effective steps without changes in software and without performance degradation. Therefore, a customer could add to an installation at a later date without the need to replace all software or to reprogram operating systems. While the scaling up of processors in massive parallel processing computer systems was not fully reliable, reports from users of KSR machines seemed to support the company's contention that they scale up more effectively than those of some other competitors.

---

[2] This section is based on information taken from the 1992 Annual Report of Kendall Square Research Corporation.

In 1993 supercomputers with massively parallel processing were more commonly found in scientific applications than in commercial applications. One reason for this was the tendency for supercomputers to crash as users pushed their limits. In scientific applications, users were often willing to sacrifice reliability for performance, but most commercial applications required computers to work reliably for months at a time. The business market for supercomputers had been estimated to be about $31 billion—far larger than the scientific and research market, which had been estimated to be about $4 billion.[3] In 1992, Kendall Square signed contracts with Neodata, a direct-mail company working with Electronic Data Systems (EDS), and AMR, the parent company of American Airlines, to work together to develop systems using KSR computers.

REVENUE RECOGNITION AT KENDALL SQUARE RESEARCH CORP.

Critics of the revenue recognition practices used by KSR claimed that the company was far too liberal in what it called a sale of a machine or system. They cited cases in which laboratories had ordered or received equipment which was subsequently accepted but for which there was no prospective funding, or for which research grants had been requested but not yet granted. In such cases there was no assurance that the research grant would be received and, even if it was, there could be significant delays before the customer would pay KSR.

Other analysts thought that the liberal accounting practices used by KSR were not uncommon in the computer industry, but such practices were less visible in the financial statements of more mature companies such as IBM or Digital Equipment Corporation. These analysts pointed out that terms requiring payment in six or nine months after a customer had received a grant from a government agency—often very slow payers—were not unusual. Such terms might be appropriate for the typical university or research laboratory that was the base of early KSR users.

> Terms of Kendall's supercomputer deliveries were often extremely attractive to researchers. For example, Edward Lazowska, chairman of the department of computer science at the University of Washington, said that it has two KSR1 computers with a total of 60 processors. He said, "We paid $1 million for half of it, and the rest was a loan of equipment against future grants." Kendall . . . treated the entire shipment as a sale.
>
> William Goddard, a physicist at the California Institute of Technology, said he paid for 32 processors in September 1992 using a National Science Foundation grant. He liked it so much that last spring he wanted to double the size of the system and applied for more grant money. Kendall shipped him the computer immediately, but he and Kendall are still waiting for the grant award. "I'm committed to buying it," he said. "I am applying for two very large grants."[4]

Other contracts included one for $1.5 million that could be canceled if the second of two phases was not completed. Still others involved distributors that had the right to cancel the contract if a customer could not be found.

---

[3] Dorfman and Bulkeley, loc. cit.

[4] William M. Bulkeley, "Kendall Square . . . " *The Wall Street Journal*, December 2, 1993, p. A3.

A second sales practice added to the concerns of critics of KSR's accounting policies. Some users purchased machines with fewer processors than were eventually thought to be needed. In these cases the processors purchased were booked as revenue and accounts receivable, but KSR had delivered additional processors to the customer for installation and use by the customer. The additional processors remained on KSR's balance sheet as inventory pending the customer's decision to keep the processors, apply for grants to buy them, or to otherwise make arrangements to pay for the loaned processors.

As a result of these practices, revenues recognized had exceeded cash collected from customers by significant amounts. Some critics thought this indicated that revenue was being recognized too early. Other observers thought this was normal for a new, growing company in the process of ramping up sales.

Of additional concern was the practice of KSR giving research grants to some users of its systems. Such grants had been reported to range between $5,000 and $50,000 or more. The CEO was reported to have agreed that grants ". . . sometimes do run into substantial amounts, but are legitimate expenses to foster software development, not disguised sales incentives. . . ."[5]

Kendall Square Research in 1993

In August 1993, *The Wall Street Journal* reported:

> **WALTHAM, Mass** Kendall Square Research Inc. is "quite comfortable" with analysts' estimates that it will earn 45 cents to 50 cents a share for the year,

The article stated that the company's president said, he is comfortable with estimates that revenue for the year will top $60 million, up from $20.7 million. And he said he is comfortable with third-quarter earnings estimates of 9 cents to 13 cents a share. For the year-earlier quarter, Kendall Square reported a net loss of 29 cents a share on revenue of $5.3 million.[6]

---

[5] William M. Bulkeley, "Kendall Square . . . "

[6] "Kendall Square Agrees with Profit Estimates for Quarter and Year," *The Wall Street Journal*, August 13, 1993, p. B5A.

EXHIBIT 1
Excerpts from 1992 Annual Report of Kendall Square Research Corporation

Management's Discussion and Analysis of Financial Condition and Results of Operations

Introduction

The Company was incorporated in February 1986 and sold its first computer system in September 1991. As of December 26, 1992, the Company had sold 22 systems, of which 11 were sold to customers in the United States and 11 to customers in Europe. Several of these customers have enlarged the size of their system configuration since initial installation. The Company's revenue for the fiscal year ended December 26, 1992, was $20.7 million. The Company has not been profitable on an annual basis since its inception and no assurance can be given that the Company will be able to operate on a profitable basis. As of December 26, 1992, the Company's accumulated deficit was approximately $69.7 million.

The Company's future operating results will depend on many factors, including the demand for the Company's products for both technical and commercial applications, the level of competition faced by the Company and the ability of the Company to develop and market new products and control costs. The Company's sales and marketing strategy contemplates sales of its computer systems for both technical and commercial applications. To date, however, all of the computer systems have been sold for technical applications.

Results of Operations

Years Ended December 28, 1991, and December 26, 1992

The Company does not believe that the year-to-year comparison of various items of expense as a percentage of revenue is meaningful due to the significant growth in the Company's revenue from 1991 to 1992.

Revenue

Revenue increased from $904,000 to $20,729,000. The Company shipped its first computer system in September 1991 and recorded its first revenue in the third quarter of 1991. The Company recorded revenue growth in each of the four quarters in 1992 as it increased the number of systems shipped. There can be no assurance that the Company will continue to achieve quarterly revenue growth in future periods. See "Quarterly Results." Sales to customers in Europe accounted for approximately 44% of revenue in 1992.

Cost of Revenue

Cost of revenue increased from $332,000 to $9,189,000, or from 37% to 44% of revenue. These expenses include actual material, labor, and indirect costs associated with the manufacture of systems for which revenue has been recognized. The Company does not believe that the year-to-year comparison is meaningful due to the low level of revenues in fiscal 1991 as well as the allocation of certain start-up manufacturing costs in 1991 to other operating costs.

Research and Development

Research and development expenses decreased by 11% from $15,786,000 to $14,113,000. Additionally, in 1992 the Company capitalized $3,506,000 of costs attributable to software license fees and software development. No such costs were capitalized in 1991. The Company increased research and development staffing levels from 79 to 115 persons from 1991 to 1992. In order to establish a competitive position and to develop new and enhanced products, the Company intends to continue to devote substantial resources to research and development. The Company expects that research and development expenses will fluctuate from quarter to quarter but will generally increase over time.

Selling, General and Administrative

Selling, general and administrative expenses increased by 63% from $6,441,000 to $10,475,000. These expenses were comprised primarily of selling and marketing expenses, reflecting significant increases in sales, marketing, and support staffing levels from 49 to 66 persons from 1991 to 1992. These expenses are expected to continue to increase as the Company expands its selling and marketing efforts.

Other Operating Costs and Expenses

Other operating costs in 1991 of $850,000 resulted from costs incurred in the establishment of the Company's manufacturing facilities and procedures and other initial manufacturing costs, including depreciation of test equipment. The manufacturing facilities and procedures became operational during the fourth quarter of 1991. There were no such costs incurred in 1992.

Other Income (Expense), Net

The Company recorded other income of $326,000 in 1992, compared to other expense of $2,000 in 1991. Interest income increased by 104% from $380,000 to $775,000 which was partially offset by an 18% increase in interest expense from $382,000 to $449,000. The Company's average cash and investments balances were higher in 1992 than in 1991 as a result of the receipt of proceeds from convertible debt financings and the Company's initial public offering. All of the convertible debt was converted into shares of common stock upon the closing of the Company's initial public offering on April 3, 1992.

To date, inflation has not had a material impact on the Company's revenue or results of operations.

Years Ended December 29, 1990, and December 28, 1991

Revenue

Revenue for the year ended December 28, 1991, of $904,000 resulted from the Company's first shipment and customer acceptance of one KSR1-20 system. There were no shipments in the year ended December 29, 1990.

Cost of Revenue

Cost of revenue of $332,000 includes actual material, labor, and indirect costs associated with the manufacture of systems for which revenue was recognized.

Research and Development

Research and development expenses increased by 49% from $10,575,000 to $15,786,000. This increase resulted primarily from materials and other costs incurred in the design and development of product prototypes, as well as an increase in research and development staffing levels from 77 to 79 persons from 1990 to 1991.

Selling, General and Administrative

Selling, general and administrative expenses increased by 108% from $3,099,000 to $6,441,000. These expenses were comprised primarily of selling and marketing expenses, reflecting an increase in sales, marketing and support staffing level from 24 to 49 persons from 1990 to 1991. These expenses were incurred as part of the Company's strategy to market its computer systems concurrently with its development efforts.

Other Operating Costs and Expenses

Other operating costs increased by 134% from $363,000 to $850,000. This increase resulted from costs incurred in the establishment of the Company's manufacturing facilities and procedures and other initial manufacturing costs, including depreciation of test equipment.

Other Income (Expense), Net

The Company recorded other expense of $2,000 in 1991 compared to other income of $687,000 in 1990. The Company had more proceeds from private equity and convertible subordinated debt financings in 1990 available for investment than in 1991 and earned higher average interest rates thereon. Additionally, interest expense was higher in 1991 as a result of higher capital lease obligations and the issuance in 1991 of $12,820,000 in convertible subordinated notes.

Quarterly Results

The following table presents unaudited quarterly financial information for the four fiscal quarters ended December 26, 1992. This information has been prepared by the Company on a basis consistent with the Company's audited consolidated financial statements and includes all adjustments (consisting only of normal recurring adjustments) which management considers necessary for a fair presentation of the results for such periods. The operating results for any quarter are not necessarily indicative of the results for any future period.

	3 Months Ended			
(In thousands)	March 28, 1992	June 27, 1992	September 26, 1992	December 26, 1992
Revenue	$ 1,954	$ 2,297	$ 5,310	$11,168
Cost of revenue	896	1,058	2,466	4,769
Gross profit	1,058	1,239	2,844	6,399
Cost and expenses:				
Research and development	3,407	4,312	3,444	2,950
Selling, general and administrative	1,890	2,160	2,859	3,566
	5,297	6,472	6,303	6,516
Loss from operations	(4,239)	(5,233)	(3,459)	(117)
Other income (expense):				
Interest income	30	348	249	148
Interest expense	(323)	(61)	(40)	(25)
	(293)	287	209	123
Net income (loss)	$(4,532)	$(4,946)	$(3,250)	$ 6

Revenue in the first full year of shipments demonstrated successive quarterly growth, highlighted by fourth quarter revenue of $11,168,000 from the sale of systems to 13 new customers. The Company sold systems to eight new customers during the first three quarters of the year. Gross profit was approximately 54% of revenue throughout the first three quarters and improved to approximately 57% in the fourth quarter as revenues increased more rapidly than fixed costs. Research and development expenses increased in the second quarter primarily due to the shifting of development efforts to new products. The reduction in fourth quarter expenses was attributable to the capitalization of certain patents and trademarks and to increased capitalization of software development costs. Selling, general and administrative expenses reflect the increasing investment in the expansion of sales offices in Europe and the United States, staffing increases in sales, marketing and support staffing level and marketing programs. Interest income increased in the second quarter as a result of the investment of the proceeds from the Company's initial public offering. Interest expense in the first quarter was primarily attributable to the outstanding convertible debt, which was converted into shares of common stock early in the second quarter. The balance of the year reflects the interest expense on capital leases.

Selected Consolidated Financial Data

The following data has been derived from audited financial statements. The consolidated balance sheet at December 28, 1991 and December 26, 1992 and the related consolidated statements of operations, of stockholders' equity and of cash flows for the three years ended December 26, 1992 and the notes thereto appear elsewhere in this Annual Report.

			Year Ended		
(In thousands except per share data)	December 31, 1988	December 30, 1989	December 29, 1990	December 28, 1991	December 26, 1992
Statement of Operations Data:					
Revenue				$ 904	$ 20,729
Cost of revenue				$ 332	$ 9,189
Gross profit				572	11,540
Costs and expenses:					
Research and development	$ 6,348	8,253	10,575	15,786	14,113
Selling, general and administrative	902	2,494	3,099	6,441	10,475
Other operating costs and expenses			363	850	
	7,250	10,747	14,037	23,077	24,588
Loss from operations	(7,250)	(10,747)	(14,037)	(22,505)	(13,048)
Other income (expense), net	499	425	687	(2)	326
Net loss	(6,751)	(10,322)	(13,350)	(22,507)	(12,722)
Pro forma net loss per share[a]	(2.31)	(2.92)	(2.77)	(3.90)	(1.22)
Weighted average shares outstanding[a]	2,925	3,531	4,814	5,712	10,171

			Year Ended		
(in thousands)	December 31, 1988	December 30, 1989	December 29, 1990	December 28, 1991	December 26, 1992
Balance Sheet Data:					
Working capital	$ 7,112	$5,471	$10,674	$ 4,463	$ 33,473
Total assets	10,298	9,226	15,959	13,129	48,733
Long-term capital lease obligations		114	942	892	599
Stockholders' equity[a]	9,316	7,523	12,812	6,408	40,427

[a] Assumes the conversion of all outstanding shares of all series of convertible preferred stock and convertible subordinated notes outstanding prior to the closing of the Company's initial public offering on April 3, 1992 into common stock. See Notes 1 and 4 of Notes to Consolidated Financial Statements.

Price Range of Common Stock

The Company's common stock is traded in the Over-the-Counter market on the National Association of Securities Dealers, Inc. Automated Quotation ("NASDAQ") National Market System under the symbol "KSRC." The following table sets forth the range of high and low sale prices for the common stock for the periods indicated, as reported on the NASDAQ National Market System. Quotations represent prices between dealers and do not reflect retail mark-ups, markdowns or commissions. There was no market for the Company's common stock prior to its initial public offering effective on March 27, 1992.

Price Range of Common Stock

	High	Low
First quarter	$12	$11
Second quarter	13 1/4	7 1/2
Third quarter	11 1/2	7 1/2
Fourth quarter	19 1/2	5 1/2

As of February 10, 1993, there were approximately 1,500 individual participants in security position listings for the Company's common stock.

Report of Independent Accountants

To the Board of Directors and Stockholders of

Kendall Square Research Corporation

In our opinion, the accompanying consolidated balance sheet and the related consolidated statements of operations, of stockholders' equity and of cash flow present fairly, in all material respects, the financial position of Kendall Square Research Corporation and its subsidiaries at December 26, 1992 and December 28, 1991, and the results of their operations and their cash flows for each of the three years in the period ended December 26, 1992, in conformity with generally accepted accounting principles. These financial statements are the responsibility of the Company's management; our responsibility is to express an opinion on these financial statements based on our audits. We conducted our audits of these statements in accordance with generally accepted auditing standards which require that we plan and perform the audit to obtain reasonable assurance about whether the financial statements are free of material misstatement. An audit includes examining, on a test basis, evidence supporting the amounts and disclosures in the financial statements, assessing the accounting principles used and significant estimates made by management, and evaluating the overall financial statement presentation. We believe that our audits provide a reasonable basis for the opinion expressed above.

Major accounting firm

February 8, 1993,

except as to Note 4, which is as of April 1, 1993

EXHIBIT 1 (*continued*)
Consolidated Balance Sheet

(In thousands, except per share data)	December 28, 1991	December 26, 1992
Assets		
Current assets:		
Cash and cash equivalents	$ 4,035	$ 7,392
Short-term investments		10,372
Accounts receivable	804	13,328
Inventories	4,316	8,939
Prepaid expenses and other current assets	1,137	1,149
Total current assets	10,292	41,180
Fixed assets, net	2,635	3,108
Software development cost, net		3,451
Other assets, net	202	994
	$ 13,129	$ 48,733
Liabilities and Stockholders' Equity		
Current liabilities:		
Accounts payable	$ 2,885	$ 3,001
Accrued payroll costs	1,019	1,575
Other accrued expenses	612	2,047
Deferred revenue	428	196
Current portion of long-term capital lease obligations	885	888
Total current liabilities	5,829	7,707
Long-term capital lease obligations	892	599
Stockholders' equity:		
Convertible preferred stock	50,098	
Convertible subordinated notes, converted into common stock upon the closing of the initial public offering	13,029	
Common stock. $.01 par value; 35,000,000 shares authorized; 375,578 and 11,356,517 shares issued at December 28, 1991 and December 16, 1992, respectively	4	114
Additional paid-in capital	215	109,987
Accumulated deficit	(56,938)	(69,660)
	6,408	40,441
Less 1,263 shares of common stock held in treasury, at cost		(14)
Total stockholders' equity	6,408	40,427
Commitments	$ 13,129	$ 48,733

The accompanying notes are an integral part of the financial statements.

EXHIBIT 1 (*continued*)
Consolidated Statement of Operations

(In thousands, except per share data)	Year Ended		
	December 29, 1990	December 28, 1991	December 26, 1992
Revenue		$ 904	$ 20,729
Cost of revenue		332	9,189
Gross profit		572	11,540
Costs and expenses:			
Research and development	$ 10,575	$ 15,786	$ 14,113
Selling, general and administrative	3,099	6,441	10,475
Other operating costs and expenses	363	850	—
	14,037	23,077	24,588
Loss from operations	(14,037)	(22,505)	(13,048)
Other income (expense):			
Interest income	755	380	775
Interest expense	(68)	(382)	(449)
	687	(2)	326
Net losses	$(13,350)	$(22,507)	$(12,722)
Unaudited proforma net loss per share assuming conversion of convertible preferred stock and convertible subordinated notes (Note 1)	$ (2.77)	$ (3.90)	$ (1.22)
Weighted average shares outstanding	4,814	5,712	10,171

The accompanying notes are an integral part of the financial statements.

EXHIBIT 1 (*continued*)
Consolidated Statement of Cash Flows Increase (decrease) in Cash and Cash Equivalents

(In thousands, except per share data)	Year Ended		
	December 29, 1990	December 28, 1991	December 26, 1992
Cash flows from operating activities:			
Cash received from customer		$ 527	$ 8,533
Cash paid to suppliers and employees	$(13,538)	(23,192)	(36,231)
Interest received	636	530	681
Interest paid	(68)	(173)	(177)
Net cash used for operating activities	(12,970)	(22,308)	(27,194)
Cash flows from investing activities:			
(Purchase) sale of short-term investments	(2,888)	2,888	(10,372)
Payment for capitalized software development costs			(3,506)
Purchase of fixed assets	(1,561)	(710)	(879)
Proceeds from sale of fixed assets	242		
Net cash provided for (used for) investing activities	(4,207)	2,178	(14,757)
Cash flows from financing activities:			
Proceeds from sale and leaseback of equipment	961		
Principal payments on capital lease obligations	(325)	(666)	(1,156)
Issuance of convertible subordinated notes		12,820	6,451
Debt issuance costs			(288)
Issuance of convertible preferred stock	18,817	3,059	
Convertible preferred stock issuance costs	(195)	(47)	
Initial public offering of common stock			44,000
Initial public offering issuance costs			(3,964)
Proceeds from exercise of common stock options, warrants, and employee stock purchases	17	64	279
Repurchase of common stock			(14)
Net cash provided by financing activities	19,275	15,230	45,308
Net increase (decrease) in cash and cash equivalents	2,098	(4,900)	3,357
Cash and cash equivalents, beginning of period	6,837	8,935	4,035
Cash and cash equivalents, end of period	$ 8,935	$ 4,035	$ 7,392

The accompanying notes are an integral part of the financial statements.

EXHIBIT 1 (*continued*)

Consolidated Statement of Cash Flows (*continued*)— Reconciliation of Net Loss to Net Cash Used for Operating Activities

	Year Ended		
(In thousands)	December 29, 1990	December 28, 1991	December 26, 1992
Net loss	$ (13,350)	$ (22,507)	$ (12,722)
Adjustments to reconcile net loss to cash used for operating activities:			
Depreciation and amortization	1,526	1,786	2,115
Gain on sale of fixed assets	(114)		
Interest accrued on convertible subordinated notes		209	277
Change in assets and liabilities:			
Increase in accounts receivable		(804)	(12,524)
Increase in inventories		(4,316)	(5,411)
Increase in prepaid expenses and other current assets	(860)	(81)	(12)
(Increase) decrease in other assets	(183)	10	(792)
Increase (decrease) in accounts payable	(161)	2,190	116
Increase in accrued payroll costs	107	509	556
Increase in other accrued expenses	65	268	1,435
Increase (decrease) in deferred revenue		428	(232)
Net cash used for operating activities	$ (12,970)	$ (22,308)	$ (27,194)

The accompanying notes are an integral part of the financial statements.

EXHIBIT 1 (continued)
Notes to Consolidated Financial Statements

Note 1: Nature of Business and Summary of Significant Accounting Policies

Kendall Square Research Corporation (the "Company") was incorporated on February 4, 1986. The Company develops, manufactures, markets, and supports a family of high performance, general purpose parallel computer systems for a broad range of mainstream applications, including numerically intensive computation, on-line transaction processing and database management and inquiry.

Principles of consolidation The consolidated financial statements include the accounts of the Company and its wholly-owned subsidiaries. All significant intercompany transactions are eliminated in consolidation.

Fiscal year The Company's fiscal year ends on the last Saturday of December.

Cash equivalents and short-term investments The Company considers all highly liquid debt instruments purchased with original maturities of three months or less to be cash equivalents. Short-term investments, which include treasury bills with original maturities of greater than three months, are recorded at cost which approximates market.

Revenue recognition The Company recognizes revenue from product sales upon written customer acceptance. Warranty costs are accrued as product sales revenue is recognized.

Inventories Inventories are stated at the lower of cost or market. Cost is determined by the first-in, first-out (FIFO) method.

Fixed assets Fixed assets are recorded at cost and depreciated by use of the straight-line method over their estimated useful lives. Repair and maintenance costs are expensed as incurred.

Software development costs Certain software development costs incurred subsequent to the establishment of technological feasibility are capitalized and amortized under straight-line and units-shipped methods over the lesser of the estimated economic life of the products or three years commencing when the products are available for general release. Amortization of software development costs is included in cost of revenue and in 1992 totaled $55,000.

Note 2: Inventories

Inventories consist of the following (in thousands):

	December 28, 1991	December 26, 1992
Raw materials and manufactured assemblies	$1,337	$4,808
Work in process	1,906	1,272
Finished goods	1,073	2,859
	$4,316	$8,939

Deposits on inventory purchases at December 28, 1991 and December 26, 1992 totaled $543,000 and $164, respectively and are included in prepaid expenses and other current assets.

EXHIBIT 1 (*continued*)
Notes to Consolidated Financial Statements

Note 3: Fixed Assets

Fixed assets consist of the following (in thousands):

	Useful Life in Years	December 28, 1991	December 26, 1992
Computer equipment and purchased software	3	$ 7,151	$ 8,916
Office furniture and equipment	3–5	778	1,274
Leasehold improvements	Lease term	345	617
		8,274	10,807
Less accumulated depreciation and amortization		(5,639)	(7,699)
		$ 2,635	$ 3,108

The Company incurred capital lease obligations of $1,757,000, $844,000 and $866,000 in 1990, 1991, and 1992, respectively. Accumulated depreciation on equipment under capital leases totaled $1,229,000 and $2,219,000 at the end of 1991 and 1992, respectively.

In 1992, inventories totaling $788,000 were transferred to fixed assets.

The Company has a $2,600,000 lease line with a commercial lender for the leasing of fixed assets. At December 26, 1992, the Company has $1,734,000 available under the lease line.

Note 4: Stock Option and Purchase Plans

During 1991, the board of directors adopted the 1991 Stock Option Plan (the "Plan") under which it may issue both incentive and nonqualified stock options. The exercise price of incentive stock options will be no less than the fair market value of the common stock on the date of grant. The Plan allows for a maximum of 1,211,250 common shares to be granted under options over a ten-year period expiring in 2001. The options generally vest between three to five years. Options for the purchase of 210,625 common shares vest in seven years, however, the vesting may be accelerated based on the Company achieving certain revenue levels. All options to date have been issued at fair market value. At December 26, 1992, options for 181,492 shares were available for future grants. On February 8, 1993, the board of directors, subject to stockholder approval, authorized an increase of an additional 1,500,000 shares issuable under the Plan.

EXHIBIT 1 (*continued*)
Notes to Consolidated Financial Statements

A summary of activity in the Plan is as follows:

Incentive Stock Options	Incentive Stock Options		Nonqualified Stock Options	
	Number of Shares	Option Price	Number of Shares	Option Price
Balance at December 30, 1989	320,421	$ .16–$ 1.60	48,750	1.60
Granted	50,656	1.60– 4.00		
Exercised	(22,646)	.16– 1.60		
Canceled	(32,031)	.80– 1.60		
Balance at December 29, 1990	316,400	.80– 4.00	48,750	1.60
Granted	91,500	4.00– 9.00	23,125	4.00
Exercised	(42,916)	.80– 4.00		
Canceled	(77,772)	.80– 4.00		
Balance at December 28, 1991	287,212	.80– 9.00	71,875	1.60–4.00
Granted	432,099	9.00– 11.00		
Exercised	(26,986)	.80– 4.00	(4,125)	1.60
Canceled	(22,946)	1.60– 11.00	—	
Balance at December 26, 1992	669,379	.80– 11.00	67,750	1.60–4.00

At December 26, 1992, options for the purchase of 149,384 shares were exercisable.

On December 14, 1991, the Company's board of directors adopted the 1991 Employee Stock Purchase Plan (the "Purchase Plan") which provides for the issuance of up to 262,500 shares of common stock to participating employees of the Company through a series of four six-month offerings, beginning May 1, 1992. The Purchase Plan covers substantially all employees, subject to certain limitations. Each employee may elect to have up to 11% of base pay withheld and applied toward the purchase of shares in such offering. The price at which the shares of common stock may be purchased in an offering is 85% of the fair market value of the common stock on the date such offering commences or the date such offering terminates, whichever is lower. In 1992, 33,395 shares were purchased under the Purchase Plan.

The Company has reserved 1,412,892 shares of common stock for issuance upon the exercise of warrants (Note 4) and for use in the Plan and Purchase Plan.

EXHIBIT 1 (*continued*)
Notes to Consolidated Financial Statements

Note 6: Income Taxes

Certain items of expense, primarily research and development, are recognized for income taxes in different periods than for financial reporting purposes. Certain research and development costs are capitalized for tax reporting purposes. Beginning in 1992, the Company is amortizing these costs over a period of 60 months. At December 26, 1992, unamortized research and development costs totaled $34,100,000.

At December 26, 1992, the Company has net operating loss carryforwards of approximately $64,100,000 and $26,500,000 for financial and tax reporting purposes, respectively. The net operating loss carryforwards expire through 2007. In addition, the Company has research and development tax credit carryforwards which expire through 2007 of approximately $2,900,000 available to offset future regular income tax liabilities. Under the Internal Revenue Code, certain substantial changes in the Company's ownership could result in an annual limitation on the amount of the carryforwards which could be utilized.

Note 8: Major Customers and Export Sales

Sales to one and three major customers accounted for $904,000 and $7,763,000, or 100% and 37% of revenue, for 1991 and 1992, respectively. In 1992, revenue from European customers totaled $9,173,000.

Note 10: Line of Credit

The Company has a bank line-of-credit which provides for borrowings of up to $2,500,000. Borrowings under the line-of-credit bear interest at the bank's base rate plus 2%. In the event that the Company's quarterly net income exceeds $250,000, borrowings under the line of credit may increase to $5,000,000 and the interest will decrease to the bank's base rate plus 3/4%. All borrowings are secured by accounts receivable and inventories. At December 26, 1992, there were no borrowings outstanding under the line of credit.

Harnischfeger Corporation

In February 1985, Peter Roberts, the research director of Exeter Group, a small Boston-based investment advisory service specializing in turnaround stocks, was reviewing the 1984 annual report of Harnischfeger Corporation (**Exhibit 4**). His attention was drawn by the $1.28 per share net profit Harnischfeger reported for 1984. He knew that barely three years earlier the company had faced a severe financial crisis. Harnischfeger had defaulted on its debt and stopped dividend payments after reporting a hefty $7.64 per share net loss in fiscal 1982. The company's poor performance continued in 1983, leading to a net loss of $3.49 per share. Roberts was intrigued by Harnischfeger's rapid turnaround and wondered whether he should recommend the purchase of the company's stock (see **Exhibit 3** for selected data on Harnischfeger's stock).

COMPANY BUSINESS AND PRODUCTS

Harnischfeger Corporation was a machinery company based in Milwaukee, Wisconsin. The company had originally been started as a partnership in 1884 and was incorporated in Wisconsin in 1910 under the name Pawling and Harnischfeger. Its name was changed to the present one in 1924. The company went public in 1929 and was listed on the New York Stock Exchange.

The company's two major segments were the P&H Heavy Equipment Group, consisting of the Construction Equipment and the Mining and Electrical Equipment divisions, and the Industrial Technologies Group, consisting of the Material Handling Equipment and the Harnischfeger Engineers divisions. The sales mix of the company in 1983 consisted of Construction Equipment, 32%; Mining and Electrical Equipment, 33%; Material Handling Equipment, 29%; and Harnischfeger Engineers, 6%.

Harnischfeger was a leading producer of construction equipment. Its products, bearing the widely recognized brand name P&H, included hydraulic cranes and lattice boom cranes. These were used in bridge and highway construction and for cargo and other material handling applications. Harnischfeger had market shares of about

Professor Krishna Palepu prepared this case as the basis for class discussion rather than to illustrate either effective or ineffective handling of an administrative situation.

20% in hydraulic cranes and about 30% in lattice boom cranes. In the 1980s the construction equipment industry in general was experiencing declining margins.

Electric mining shovels and excavators constituted the principal products of the Mining and Electrical Equipment Division of Harnischfeger. The company had a dominant share of the mining machinery market. The company's products were used in coal, copper, and iron mining. A significant part of the division's sales were from the sale of spare parts. Because of its large market share and the lucrative spare parts sales, the division was traditionally very profitable. Most of the company's future mining product sales were expected to occur outside the United States, principally in developing countries.

The Material Handling Equipment Division of Harnischfeger was the fourth-largest supplier of automated material handling equipment with a 9% market share. The division's products included overhead cranes, portal cranes, hoists, monorails, and components and parts. The demand for this equipment was expected to grow in the coming years as an increasing number of manufacturing firms emphasized cost reduction programs. Harnischfeger believed that the material handling equipment business would be a major source of its future growth.

Harnischfeger Engineers was an engineering services division engaged in design, custom software development, and project management for factory and distribution automation projects. The division engineered and installed complete automated material handling systems for a wide variety of applications on a fee basis. The company expected such automated storage and retrieval systems to play an increasingly important role in the "factory of the future."

Harnischfeger had a number of subsidiaries, affiliated companies, and licensees in a number of countries. Export and foreign sales constituted more than 50% of the total revenues of the company.

FINANCIAL DIFFICULTIES OF 1982

The machinery industry experienced a period of explosive growth during the 1970s. Harnischfeger expanded rapidly during this period, growing from $205 million in revenues in 1973 to $644 million in 1980. To fund this growth, the company relied increasingly on debt financing, and the firm's debt/equity ratio rose from 0.88 in 1973 to 1.26 in 1980. The worldwide recession in the early 1980s caused a significant drop in demand for the company's products starting in 1981 and culminated in a series of events that shook the financial stability of Harnischfeger.

Reduced sales and the high interest payments resulted in poor profit performance leading to a reported loss in 1982 of $77 million. The management of Harnischfeger commented on its financial difficulties:

> There is a persistent weakness in the basic industries, both in the United States and overseas, which have been large, traditional markets for P&H products. Energy-related projects, which had been a major source of business of our Construction Equipment Division, have slowed significantly in the last year as a result of lower oil demand and subsequent price decline, not only in the U.S. but throughout the world. Lack of demand for such basic minerals as iron ore, copper and bauxite have decreased worldwide mining activity, causing reduced sales for mining equipment, although coal mining remains relatively strong worldwide. Difficult economic conditions have caused many of

our normal customers to cut capital expenditures dramatically, especially in such depressed sectors as the steel industry, which has always been a major source of sales for all P&H products.

The significant operating losses recorded in 1982 and the credit losses experienced by its finance subsidiary caused Harnischfeger to default on certain covenants of its loan agreements. The most restrictive provisions of the company's loan agreements required it to maintain a minimum working capital of $175 million, consolidated net worth of $180 million, and a ratio of current assets to current liabilities of 1.75. On October 31, 1982, the company's working capital (after reclassification of about $115 million long-term debt as a current liability) was $29.3 million, the consolidated net worth was $142.2 million, and the ratio of current assets to current liabilities was 1.12. Harnischfeger Credit Corporation, an unconsolidated finance subsidiary, also defaulted on certain covenants of its loan agreements, largely due to significant credit losses relating to the financing of construction equipment sold to a large distributor. As a result of these covenant violations, the company's long-term debt of $124.3 million became due on demand, the unused portion of the bank revolving credit line of $25.0 million became unavailable, and the unused short-term bank credit lines of $12.0 million were canceled. In addition, the $25.1 million debt of Harnischfeger Credit Corporation also became immediately due. The company was forced to stop paying dividends and began negotiations with its lenders to restructure its debt to permit operations to continue. Price Waterhouse, the company's audit firm, qualified its audit opinion on Harnischfeger's 1982 annual report with respect to the outcome of the company's negotiations with its lenders.

CORPORATE RECOVERY PLAN

Harnischfeger responded to the financial crisis facing the firm by developing a corporate recovery plan. The plan consisted of four elements: (1) changes in the top management, (2) cost reductions to lower the break-even point, (3) reorientation of the company's business, and (4) debt restructuring and recapitalization. The actions taken in each of these four areas are described below.

To deal effectively with the financial crisis, Henry Harnischfeger, then chairman and chief executive officer of the company, created the position of chief operating officer. After an extensive search, the position was offered in August 1982 to William Goessel, who had considerable experience in the machinery industry. Another addition to the management team was Jeffrey Grade, who joined the company in 1983 as senior vice president of finance and administration and chief financial officer. Grade's appointment was necessitated by the early retirement of the previous vice president of finance in 1982. The engineering, manufacturing, and marketing functions were also restructured to streamline the company's operations (see **Exhibits 1** and **2** for additional information on Harnischfeger's current management).

To deal with the short-term liquidity squeeze, the company initiated a number of cost reduction measures. These included (1) reducing the workforce from 6,900 to 3,800; (2) eliminating management bonuses and reducing of benefits and freezing wages of salaried and hourly employees; (3) liquidating excess inventories and stretching payments to creditors; and (4) permanent closure of the construction equipment plant at Escanaba, Michigan. These and other related measures improved the company's cash position and helped to reduce the rate of loss during fiscal 1983.

Concurrent with the above cost reduction measures, the new management made some strategic decisions to reorient Harnischfeger's business. First, the company entered into a long-term agreement with Kobe Steel, Ltd., of Japan. Under this agreement, Kobe agreed to supply Harnischfeger's requirements for construction cranes for sale in the United States as Harnischfeger phased out its own manufacture of cranes. This step was expected to significantly reduce the manufacturing costs of Harnischfeger's construction equipment, enabling it to compete effectively in the domestic market. Second, the company decided to emphasize the high technology part of its business by targeting for future growth the material-handling equipment and systems business. To facilitate this strategy, the Industrial Technologies Group was created. As part of the reorientation, the company stated that it would develop and acquire new products, technology, and equipment, and would expand its abilities to provide computer-integrated solutions to handling, storing, and retrieval in areas hitherto not pursued—industries such as distribution warehousing, food, pharmaceuticals, and aerospace.

While Harnischfeger was implementing its turnaround strategy, it was engaged at the same time in complex and difficult negotiations with its bankers. On January 6, 1984, the company entered into agreements with its lenders to restructure its debt obligations into three-year term loans secured by fixed as well as other assets, with a one-year extension option. This agreement required, among other things, specified minimum levels of cash and unpledged receivables, working capital, and net worth.

The company reported a net loss of $35 million in 1983, down from the $77 million loss the year before. Based on the above developments during the year, in the 1983 annual report the management expressed confidence that the company would return to profitability soon.

> We approach our second century with optimism, knowing that the negative events of the last three years are behind us, and with a firm belief that positive achievements will be recorded in 1984. By the time the corporation celebrates its 100th birthday on December 1, we are confident it will be operating profitably and attaining new levels of market strength and leadership.

During 1984 the company reported profits during each of the four quarters, ending the year with a pre-tax operating profit of $5.7 million, and a net income after tax and extraordinary credits of $15 million (see **Exhibit 4**). It also raised substantial new capital through a public offering of debentures and common stock. Net proceeds from the offering, which totaled $150 million, were used to pay off all of the company's restructured debt. In the 1984 annual report the management commented on the company's performance as follows:

> 1984 was the Corporation's Centennial year and we marked the occasion by rededicating ourselves to excellence through market leadership, customer service and improved operating performance and profitability.

> * * * * * *

> We look back with pride. We move ahead with confidence and optimism. Our major markets have never been more competitive; however, we will strive to take advantage of any and all opportunities for growth and to attain satisfactory profitability. Collectively, we will do what has to be done to ensure that the future will be rewarding to all who have a part in our success.

EXHIBIT 1 Board of Directors, Harnischfeger Corporation, 1984

Name	Director Since	Current Term	Shares Owned	
Edward W. Duffy	1981	1985	100	Chairman of the Board and Chief Executive of United States Gypsum Company, manufacturer of building materials and products used in industrial processes, since 1983. Former Vice Chairman from 1981 to 1983; President and Chief Operating Officer from 1971 to 1981. Director American National Bank and Trust Company of Chicago, Walter E. Heller International Corporation, W. W. Grainger, Inc., and UNR Industries, Inc. Age 64.
Herbert V. Kohler, Jr.	1973	1985	700	Chairman, Chief Executive Officer, and Director of Kohler Company, manufacturer of plumbing and specialty products, engines and generators, since 1972; President since 1974. Age 44.
Taisuke Mori	1981	1985	None	Executive Vice Chairman and Director of Kobe Steel, Ltd., a Japanese manufacturer of steel and steel products, industrial machinery, construction equipment, aluminum, copper and alloy products, and welding equipment and consumables. Age 63.
William W. Goessel	1982	1986	15,000	President and Chief Operating Officer of the Corporation since 1982. Executive Vice President of Beloit Corporation from 1978, Director to 1982. Goulds Pumps, Inc. Age 56.
Henry Harnischfeger	1945	1986	611,362	Chairman of the Board and Chief Executive Officer of the Corporation since 1970; President from 1959 to 1982. Director, First Wisconsin Corporation and First Wisconsin National Bank of Milwaukee. Age 60.
Karl F. Nygren	1964	1986	2,000	Partner in Kirkland & Ellis, attorneys, since 1959. Age 56.
John P. Gallagher	1979	1987	500	Senior lecturer, Graduate School of Business, University of Chicago. Director, IC Industries, Inc., Stone Container Corporation, UNR Industries, Inc., American National Bank and Trust Company of Chicago, and Walter E. Heller International Corporation. Age 67.
Jeffrey T. Grade	1983	1987	3,750	Senior Vice President Finance and Administration and Chief Financial Officer of the Corporation since August 1, 1983. Vice President Corporate of IC Industries from 1981 to 1983; Assistant Vice President from 1976 to 1981. Age 40.
Donald Taylor	1979	1987	100	President, Chief Operating Officer, and Director of Rexnord, Inc., a major manufacturer of industrial components and machinery, since 1978. Director, Johnson Controls, Inc., Marine Corporation, and Marine Bank, N.A. Age 56.
Frank A. Lee	1983	1987	None	Director of Foster Wheeler Corporation since 1971; Chairman of the Board from 1981 to 1982; President and Chief Executive from 1978 to 1981. Director, Belco Pollution Control Corporation, International General Industries, Inc., and Banker's Life Insurance Co. Age 59.

EXHIBIT 2
Executive Compensation, Harnischfeger Corporation

The following table sets forth all cash compensation paid to each of the Corporation's five most highly compensated executive officers and to all executive officers as a group for services rendered to the Corporation and its subsidiaries during fiscal 1984.

Cash Compensation

Henry Harnischfeger	Chairman of the Board and Chief Executive Officer	$ 364,004
William W. Goessel	President and Chief Operating Officer	280,000
C. P. Cousland	Senior Vice President and group executive, P&H Heavy Equipment	210,000
Jeffrey T. Grade	Senior Vice President Finance and Administration and Chief Financial Officer	205,336
Douglas E. Holt	President, Harnischfeger Engineers, Inc.	152,839
All persons who were executive officers during the fiscal year as a group (14 persons)		2,159,066

1985 Executive Incentive Plan
In December 1984, the board of directors established an Executive Incentive Plan for fiscal 1985 which provides an incentive compensation opportunity of 40% of annual salary for 11 senior executive officers only if the Corporation reaches a specific net after-tax profit objective and it provides an additional incentive compensation of up to 40% of annual salary for seven of those officers if the corporation exceeds the objective. The Plan covered the chairman, president, senior vice presidents; president, Harnischfeger Engineers, Inc.; vice president, P&H World Services; vice president, Material Handling Equipment; and secretary. Awards made regarding fiscal year 1984 are included in the Compensation Table above.

EXHIBIT 3
Selected Stock Price and Market Data

A. Stock Prices

	Harnischfeger's Stock Price			S&P 400 Industrials Index		
	High	Low	Close	High	Low	Close
January 4, 1985	9 1/8	8 6/8	9	186.4	181.8	182.2
January 11, 1985	10 6/8	8 7/8	10 5/8	188.2	182.2	182.8
January 18, 1985	11	10	10 4/8	191.9	186.9	191.3
January 25, 1985	11 2/8	10 1/8	11	199.7	191.3	198.6
February 1, 1985	11 5/8	10 7/8	11 2/8	201.8	198.6	200.0

Harnischfeger's stock beta = 0.95 (Value Line estimate)

B. Market Data

	February 1985
Median P/E ratio of Dow Jones Industrials	10.9
Median P/E ratio of Value Line stocks	11.3
Median P/E ratio of machinery industry (construction and mining equipment)	10.0
Prime rate	10.5%
91-day Treasury bill rate	8.4%
30-year Treasury bond yield	11.4%
Moody's Aaa corporate bond yield	12.0%

EXHIBIT 4
1984 Annual Report—Edited

To Our Shareholders

The Corporation recorded gains in each quarter during fiscal 1984, returning to profitability despite the continued depressed demand and intense price competition in the world markets it serves.

For the year ended October 31, net income was $15,176,000 or $1.28 per common share, which included $11,005,000 or 93¢ per share from the cumulative effect of a change in depreciation accounting. In 1983, the Corporation reported a loss of $34,630,000 or $3.49 per share.

Sales for 1984 improved 24% over the preceding year, rising to $398.7 million from $321 million a year ago. New orders totaled $451 million, a $101 million increase over 1983. We entered fiscal 1985 with a backlog of $193 million, which compared to $141 million a year earlier.

All Divisions Improved

All product divisions recorded sales and operating improvements during 1984.

Mining equipment was the strongest performer with sales up over 60%, including major orders from Turkey and the People's Republic of China. During the year we began the implementation of the training, engineering and manufacturing license agreement concluded in November, 1983 with the People's Republic of China, which offers the Corporation long-term potential in modernizing and mechanizing this vast and rapidly developing mining market.

Sales of material handling equipment and systems were up 10% for the year and the increasingly stronger bookings recorded during the latter part of the year are continuing into the first quarter of 1985.

Sales on construction equipment products showed some signs of selective improvement. In the fourth quarter, bookings more than doubled from the very depressed levels in the same period a year ago, although the current level is still far below what is needed to achieve acceptable operating results for this product line.

Financial Stability Restored

In April, the financial stability of the Corporation was improved through a public offering of 2.15 million shares of common stock, $50 million of 15% notes due April 15, 1994, and $100 million of 12% subordinated debentures due April 15, 2004, with two million common stock purchase warrants.

Net proceeds from the offering totaled $149 million, to which we added an additional $23 million in cash, enabling us to pay off all of our long-term debt. As a result of the refinancing, the Corporation gained permanent long-term capital with minimal annual cash flow requirements to service it. We now have the financial resources and flexibility to pursue new opportunities to grow and diversify.

Furthermore, should we require additional funds, they will be available through a $52 million unsecured three-year revolving credit agreement concluded in June with ten U.S. and Canadian banks. An $80 million product financing capability was also arranged through a major U.S. bank to provide financing to customers purchasing P&H products.

EXHIBIT 4 (*continued*)
1984 Annual Report—Edited

Outlook

Throughout 1985 we believe we will see gradual improvements in most of our U.S. and world markets.

For our mining excavator product line, coal and certain metals mining are expected to show a more favorable long-term outlook in selected foreign requirements and our capability to source equipment from the U.S., Japan or Europe places us in a strong marketing position. In the U.S., we see only a moderate strengthening in machinery requirements for coal, while metals mining will remain weak.

Continuing shipments of the Turkish order throughout 1985 will help to stabilize our plant utilization levels and improve our operating results for this product line.

In our material handling and systems markets, particularly in the U.S., we are experiencing a moderately strong continuation of the improved bookings which we began to see in the third and fourth quarters of last year.

In construction lifting equipment markets, we expect modest overall economic improvement in the U.S., which should help to absorb the large numbers of idle lifting equipment that have been manufacturer, distributor and customer inventories for the last three years. As this overhang on the market is reduced we will see gradual improvement in new sales. Harnischfeger traditionally exports half of its U.S.-produced lifting products. However, as with mining equipment, the continued strength of the U.S. dollar severely restricts our ability to sell U.S.-built products in world markets.

In addition to the strong dollar and economic instability in many foreign nations, overcapacity in worldwide heavy equipment manufacturing remains a serious problem in spite of some exits from the market as well as consolidations within the industry.

The Corporation continues to respond to severe price competition through systematic cost reduction programs and through expanded sourcing of P&H equipment from our European operation and, most importantly, through our 30-year association with our Japanese partner, Kobe Steel, Ltd. P&H engineering and technology have established world standards for quality and performance for construction cranes and mining equipment, which customers can expect from every P&H machine regardless of its source. More than a dozen new models of foreign-sourced P&H construction cranes will be made available for the first time in the U.S. during 1985, broadening our existing product lines and giving competitive pricing to our U.S. distributors and customers.

To improve our future operating results, we restructured our three operating divisions into two groups. All construction and mining related activities are in the new "P&H Heavy Equipment Group." All material handling equipment and systems activities are now merged into the "Industrial Technologies Group." More information on these Groups is reported in their respective sections.

We are pleased to announce that John P. Moran was elected Senior Vice President and Group Executive, Industrial Technologies Group, and John R. Teitgen was elected Secretary and General Counsel.

In September Robert F. Schnoes became a member of our Board of Directors. He is President and Chief Executive Officer of Burgess, Inc. and of Ultrasonic Power Corporation, and a member of the Board of Signode Industries, Inc.

EXHIBIT 4 (*continued*)
1984 Annual Report—Edited

Beginning Our Second Century

1984 was the Corporation's Centennial year and we marked the occasion by rededicating ourselves to excellence through market leadership, customer service and improved operating performance and profitability.

Our first century of achievement resulted from the dedicated effort, support and cooperation of our employees, distributors, suppliers, lenders, and shareholders, and we thank all of them.

We look back with pride. We move ahead with confidence and optimism. Our major markets have never been more competitive; however, we will strive to take advantage of any and all opportunities for growth and to attain satisfactory profitability. Collectively, we will do what has to be done to ensure that the future will be rewarding to all who have a part in our success.

Henry Harnischfeger
Chairman of the Board

William W. Goessel
President

January 31, 1985

Management's Discussion & Analysis

Results of Operation

1984 Compared to 1983

Consolidated net sales of $399 million in fiscal 1984 increased $78 million or 24% over 1983. Sales increases were 62% in the Mining and Electrical Equipment Segment, and 10% in the Industrial Technologies Segment. Sales in the Construction Equipment Segment were virtually unchanged reflecting the continued low demand for construction equipment worldwide.

Effective at the beginning of fiscal 1984, net sales include the full sales price of construction and mining equipment purchased from Kobe Steel, Ltd. and sold by the Corporation, in order to reflect more effectively the nature of the Corporation's transactions with Kobe. Such sales aggregated $28.0 million in 1984.

The $4.0 million increase in Other Income reflected a recovery of certain claims and higher license and technical service fees.

Cost of Sales was equal to 79.1% of net sales in 1984 and 81.4% in 1983; which together with the increase in net sales resulted in a $23.9 million increase in gross profit (net sales less cost of sales). Contributing to this increase were improved sales of higher-margin replacement parts in the Mining Equipment and Industrial Technologies Segments and a reduction in excess manufacturing costs through greater utilization of domestic manufacturing capacity and economies in total manufacturing costs including a reduction in pension expense. Reductions of certain LIFO inventories increased gross profit by $2.4 million in 1984 and $15.6 million in 1983.

EXHIBIT 4 (*continued*)
1984 Annual Report—Edited

Product development selling and administrative expenses were reduced, due to the funding of R&D expenses in the Construction Equipment Segment pursuant to the October 1983 Agreement with Kobe Steel, Ltd., to reductions in pension expenses and provision for credit losses, and to the absence of the corporate financial restructuring expenses incurred in 1983.

Net interest expense in 1984 increased $2.9 million due to higher interest rates on the outstanding funded debt and a reduction in interest income.

Equity in Earnings (Loss) of Unconsolidated Companies included 1984 income of $1.2 million of Harnischfeger Credit Corporation, an unconsolidated finance subsidiary, reflecting an income tax benefit of $1.4 million not previously recorded.

The preceding items, together with the cumulative effect of the change in depreciation method described in Financial Note 2, were included in net income of $15.2 million or $1.28 per common share, compared with net loss of $34.6 million or $3.49 per share in 1983.

The sales orders booked and unshipped backlogs of orders of the Corporation's three segments are summarized as follows (in millions of dollars):

Orders Booked	1984	1983
Industrial Technologies	$132	$106
Mining and Electrical Equipment	210	135
Construction Equipment	109	109
	$451	$350
Backlogs at October 31		
Industrial Technologies	$ 79	$ 71
Mining and Electrical Equipment	91	50
Construction Equipment	23	20
	$193	$141

1983 Compared to 1982

Consolidated net sales of $321 million in fiscal 1983 were $126 million or 28% below 1982. This decline reflected, for the second consecutive year, the continued low demand in all markets served by the Corporation's products, with exports even more severely depressed due to the strength of the dollar. The largest decline was reported in the Construction Equipment Segment down 34%; Mining and Electrical Equipment Segment, shipments were down 27%, and the Industrial Technologies Segment, 23%.

Cost of Sales was equal to 81.4% of net sales in 1983 and 81.9% in 1982. The resulting gross profit was $60 million in 1983 and $81 million in 1982, a reduction equal to the rate of sales decrease.

The benefits of reduced manufacturing capacity and economies in total manufacturing costs were offset by reduced selling prices in the highly competitive markets. Reductions of certain LIFO inventories increased gross profits by $15.6 million in 1983 and $7.2 million in 1982.

EXHIBIT 4 (*continued*)
1984 Annual Report—Edited

Product development, selling and administrative expenses were reduced as a result of expense reduction measures in response to the lower volume of business and undertaken in connection with the Corporation's corporate recovery program, and reduced provisions for credit losses, which in 1982 included $4.0 million in income support for Harnischfeger Credit Corporation.

Net interest expense was reduced $9.1 million from 1982 to 1983, due primarily to increased interest income from short-term cash investments and an accrual of $4.7 million in interest income on refundable income taxes not previously recorded.

The Credit for Income Taxes included a federal income tax benefit of $5 million, based upon the recent examination of the Corporation's income tax returns and refund claims. No income tax benefits were available for the losses of the U.S. operations in 1983.

The losses from unconsolidated companies recorded in 1983 included $0.5 million in Harnischfeger Credit Corporation; $2.1 million in Cranatex, Inc., a Corporation-owned distributorship in Texas; and $0.8 million in ASEA Industrial Systems Inc., then a 49%-owned joint venture between the Corporation and ASEA AB and now 19%-owned with the investment accounted for on the cost method.

The preceding items were reflected in a net loss of $34.6 million or $3.49 per share.

Liquidity and Financial Resources

In April 1984, the Corporation issued in public offerings 2,150,000 shares of Common Stock, $50 million principal amount of 15% Senior Notes due in 1994, and 100,000 Units consisting of $100 million principal amount of 12% Subordinated Debentures due in 2004 and 2,000,000 Common Stock Purchase Warrants.

The net proceeds from the sales of the securities of $149 million were used to prepay substantially all of the outstanding debt of the Corporation and certain of its subsidiaries.

During the year ended October 31, 1984, the consolidated cash balances increased $32 million to a balance of $96 million, with the cash activity summarized as follows (in millions of dollars):

Funds provided by operations	$ 10
Funds returned to the Corporation upon restructuring of the Salaried Employees' Pension Plan	39
Debt repayment less the proceeds of sales of securities	(9)
Plant and equipment additions	(6)
All other changes—net	(2)
	$ 32

In the third quarter of fiscal 1984 the Corporation entered into a $52 million three-year revolving credit agreement with ten U.S. and Canadian banks. While the Corporation has adequate liquidity to meet its current working capital requirements, the revolver represents another step in the Corporation's program to strengthen its financial position and provide the required financial resources to respond to opportunities as they arise.

EXHIBIT 4 (*continued*)
Consolidated Statement of Operations
(Dollar amounts in thousands except per share figures)

	Year Ended October 31		
	1984	1983	1982
Revenues			
Net sales	$398,708	$321,010	$447,461
Other income, including license and technical service fees	7,067	3,111	5,209
	405,775	324,121	452,670
Cost of sales	315,216	261,384	366,297
Operating Income	90,559	62,737	86,373
Less:			
Product development, selling and administrative expenses	72,196	85,795	113,457
Interest expense—net	12,625	9,745	18,873
Provision for plant closing	—	—	23,700
Income (Loss) before provision (credit) for income taxes, equity items and cumulative effect of accounting change	5,738	(32,803)	(69,657)
Provision (Credit) for income taxes	2,425	(1,400)	(1,600)
Income (Loss) before equity items and cumulative effect of accounting change	3,313	(31,403)	(68,057)
Equity items			
Equity in earnings (loss) of unconsolidated companies	993	(3,397)	(7,891)
Minority interest in (earnings) loss of consolidated subsidiaries	(135)	170	(583)
Income (loss) before cumulative effect of accounting change	4,171	(34,630)	(76,531)
Cumulative effect of change in depreciation method	11,005	—	—
Net income (loss)	$ 15,176	$ (34,630)	$(76,531)
Earnings (loss) per common and common equivalent share:			
Income (loss) before cumulative effect of accounting change	$ .35	$(3.49)	$(7.64)
Cumulative effect of change in depreciation method	.93	—	—
Net income (loss)	$1.28	$(3.49)	$(7.64)
Pro forma amounts assuming the changed depreciation method had been applied respectively:			
Net (loss)		$ (33,918)	$(76,695)
(Loss) per common share		$(3.42)	$(7.65)

EXHIBIT 4 (*continued*)
CONSOLIDATED BALANCE SHEET
(Dollar amounts in thousands except per share figures)

	October 31, 1984	1983
Assets		
Current Assets		
Cash and temporary investments	$ 96,007	$ 64,275
Accounts receivable	87,648	63,740
Inventories	144,312	153,594
Refundable income taxes and related interest	1,296	12,585
Other current assets	5,502	6,023
Prepaid income taxes	14,494	14,232
	349,259	314,449
Investments and Other Assets		
Investments in and advances to:		
Finance subsidiary, at equity in net assets	8,849	6,704
Other companies	4,445	2,514
Other assets	13,959	6,411
	27,253	15,629
Operating Plants		
Land and improvements	9,419	10,370
Buildings	59,083	60,377
Machinery and equipment	120,949	122,154
	189,451	192,901
Accumulated depreciation	(93,259)	(107,577)
	96,192	85,324
	$472,704	$ 415,402

EXHIBIT 4 (*continued*)
CONSOLIDATED BALANCE SHEET
(Dollar amounts in thousands except per share figures)

	October 31,	
	1984	1983
Liabilities and Shareholders' Equity		
Current Liabilities		
Short-term notes payable to banks by subsidiaries	$ 9,090	$ 8,155
Long-term debt and capitalized lease obligations payable		
within one year	973	18,265
Trade accounts payable	37,716	21,228
Employee compensation and benefits	15,041	14,343
Accrued plant closing costs	2,460	6,348
Advance payments and progress billings	20,619	15,886
Income taxes payable	1,645	3,463
Account payable to finance subsidiary	—	3,436
Other current liabilities and accruals	29,673	32,333
	117,217	123,457
Long-Term Obligations		
Long-term debt payable to:		
Unaffiliated lenders	128,550	139,092
Finance subsidiary	—	5,400
Capitalized lease obligations	7,870	8,120
	136,420	152,612
Deferred Liabilities and Income Taxes		
Accrued pension costs	57,611	19,098
Other deferred liabilities	5,299	7,777
Deferred income taxes	6,385	134
	69,295	27,009
Minority Interest	2,400	2,405
Shareholders' equity		
Preferred stock $100 par value—authorized 250,000 shares:		
Series A $7.00 cumulative convertible preferred shares:		
authorized, issued and outstanding 117,500 shares in 1984		
and 100,000 shares in 1983	11,750	10,000
Common stock, $1 par value—authorized 25,000,000 shares:		
issued and outstanding 12,283,563 shares in 1984 and		
10,133,563 shares in 1983	12,284	10,134
Capital in excess of par value of shares	114,333	88,332
Retained earnings	19,901	6,475
Cumulative translation adjustments	(10,896)	(5,022)
	147,372	109,919
	$472,704	$ 415,402

| | Year Ended October 31, | | |
	1984	1983	1982
Funds Were Provided by (Applied to):			
Operations:			
Income (loss) before cumulative effect of accounting change	$ 4,171	$ (34,630)	$(76,531)
Cumulative effect of change in depreciation method	11,005	—	—
Net income (loss)	15,176	(34,630)	(76,531)
Add (deduct)—			
Items included not affecting funds:			
Depreciation	8,077	13,552	15,241
Unremitted (earnings) loss of unconsolidated companies	(993)	3,397	7,891
Deferred pension contributions	(500)	4,834	—
Deferred income taxes	6,583	(3,178)	1,406
Reduction in accumulated depreciation resulting from change			
in depreciation method	(17,205)	—	—
Other—net	(2,168)	(67)	2,034
Decrease in operating working capital (see below)	7,039	11,605	72,172
Add (deduct) the effects on operating working capital of:			
Conversion of export and factored receivable sales to debt	—	23,919	—
Reclassification to deferred liabilities:			
Accrued pension costs	—	14,264	—
Other liabilities	—	5,510	—
Foreign currency translation adjustments	(6,009)	(1,919)	(5,943)
Funds provided by operations	10,000	37,287	16,270
Financing, Investment and Other Activities:			
Transactions in debt and capitalized lease obligations—Long-Term			
debt and capitalized lease obligations: Proceeds from sale of			
15% Senior Notes and 12% subordinated debentures, net of			
issue costs	120,530	—	—
Other increases	1,474	—	25,698
Repayments	(161,500)	(760)	(9,409)
Restructured debt	—	158,058	—
Debt replaced, including conversion of receivable sales of			
$23,919, and short-term bank notes payable of $9,028	—	(158,058)	—
	(39,496)	(760)	16,289
Net increase (repayment) in short-term bank notes payable	2,107	(3,982)	(2,016)
Net increase (repayment) in debt and capitalized lease			
obligations	(37,389)	(4,742)	14,273

EXHIBIT 4 (*continued*)
CONSOLIDATED STATEMENT OF CHANGES IN
FINANCIAL POSITION (Dollar amounts in thousands)

| | Year Ended October 31, | | |
	1984	1983	1982
Issuance of:			
Common stock	21,310	—	449
Common stock purchase warrants	6,663	—	—
Salaried pension assets reversion	39,307	—	—
Plant and equipment additions	(5,546)	(1,871)	(10,819)
Advances to unconsolidated companies	(2,882)	—	—
Other—net	269	1,531	848
Funds provided by (applied to) financing, investment and			
other activities	21,732	(5,082)	4,751
Increase in cash and temporary investments	$ 31,732	$ 32,205	$ 21,021
Cash Dividends	—	—	(2,369)
Increase in Cash and Temporary Investments	$ 31,732	$ 32,205	$ 18,652
Decrease (increase) in operating working capital (excluding cash			
items, debt and capitalized lease obligations):			
Accounts receivable	$ (23,908)	$ (5,327)	$ 42,293
Inventories	9,282	56,904	26,124
Refundable income taxes and related interest	11,289	(2,584)	(6,268)
Other current assets	259	10,008	(439)
Trade accounts payable	16,488	(1,757)	(3,302)
Employee compensation and benefits	698	(15,564)	(3,702)
Accrued plant closing costs	(3,888)	(14,148)	20,496
Other current liabilities	(3,181)	(15,927)	(3,030)
Decrease in operating working capital	$ 7,039	$ 11,605	$ 72,172

EXHIBIT 4 (*continued*)
CONSOLIDATED STATEMENT OF SHAREHOLDERS' EQUITY
(Dollar amounts in thousands except per share figures)

	Preferred Stock	Common Stock	Capital in Excess of Par Value of Shares	Retained Earnings	Cumulative Translation Adjustments	Total
Balance at October 31, 1981	$10,000	$10,085	$ 87,932	$120,005	$ —	$228,022
Cumulative translation adjustments through October 31, 1981					$ (1,195)	$ (1,195)
Issuance of Common Stock: 10,000 shares to Kobe Steel, Ltd.		10	91			101
38,161 shares under stock purchase and dividend reinvestment plans		39	309			348
Net (loss)				(76,531)		(76,531)
Cash dividends paid on:						
Preferred stock				(350)		(350)
Common stock $.20 per share				(2,019)		(2,019)
Translation adjustments, net of deferred income taxes of $128					(2,928)	(2,928)
Balance at October 31, 1982	10,000	10,134	88,332	41,105	(4,123)	145,448
Net (loss)				(34,630)		(34,630)
Translation adjustments, including deferred income taxes of $33					(899)	(899)
Balance at October 31, 1983	10,000	10,134	88,332	6,475	(5,022)	109,919
Issuance of:						
2,150,000 shares of common stock		2,150	19,160			21,310
2,000,000 common stock purchase warrants			6,663			6,663
17,500 shares of Series A $7.00 cumulative convertible preferred stock in discharge of dividends payable on preferred stock	1,750			(1,750)		—
Net income				15,176		15,176
Translation adjustments, net of deferred income taxes of $300					(5,874)	(5,874)
Other			178			178
Balance at October 31, 1984	$11,750	$12,284	$114,333	$ 19,901	$(10,896)	$147,372

EXHIBIT 4 (*continued*)
Financial Notes

Note 1

Summary of Significant Accounting Policies

Consolidation—The consolidated financial statements include the accounts of all majority-owned subsidiaries except a wholly-owned domestic finance subsidiary, a subsidiary organized in 1982 as a temporary successor to a distributor, both of which are accounted for under the equity method, and a wholly-owned Brazilian subsidiary, which is carried at estimated net realizable value due to economic uncertainty. All related significant intercompany balances and transactions have been eliminated in consolidation.

Financial statements of certain consolidated subsidiaries, principally foreign, are included, effective in fiscal year 1984, on the basis of their fiscal years ending September 30; previously, certain of such subsidiaries had fiscal years ending July (See Note 2). Such fiscal periods have been adopted by the subsidiaries in order to provide for a more timely consolidation with the Corporation.

Inventories—The Corporation values its inventories at the lower of cost or market. Cost is determined by the last-in, first-out (LIFO) method for inventories located principally in the United States, and by the first-in, first-out (FIFO) method for inventories of foreign subsidiaries.

Operating Plants, Equipment and Depreciation—Properties are stated at cost. Maintenance and repairs are charged to expense as incurred and expenditures for betterments and renewals are capitalized. Effective in 1981, interest is capitalized for qualifying assets during their acquisition period. Capitalized interest is amortized on the same basis as the related asset. When properties are sold or otherwise disposed of, the cost and accumulated depreciation are removed from the accounts and any gain or loss is included in income.

Depreciation of plants and equipment is provided over the estimated useful lives of the related assets, or over the lease terms of capital leases, using, effective in fiscal year 1984, the straight-line method for financial reporting, and principally accelerated methods for tax reporting purposes. Previously, accelerated methods, where applicable, were also used for financial reporting purposes (See Note 2). For U.S. income tax purposes, depreciation lives are based principally on the Class Life Asset Depreciation Range for additions, other than buildings, in the years 1973 through 1980, and on the Accelerated Cost Recovery System for all additions after 1980.

Discontinued facilities held for sale are carried at the lower of cost less accumulated depreciation or estimated realizable value, which aggregated $4.9 million and $3.6 million at October 31, 1984 and 1983, respectively, and were included in Other Assets in the accompanying Balance Sheet.

Pension Plans—The Corporation has pension plans covering substantially all of its employees. Pension expenses of the principal defined benefit plans consist of current service costs of such plans and amortization of the prior service costs and actuarial gains and losses over periods ranging from 10 to 30 years. The Corporation's policy is to fund at a minimum the amount required under the Employee Retirement Income Security Act of 1974.

Income Taxes—The consolidated tax provision is computed based on income and expenses recorded in the Statement of Operations. Prepaid or deferred taxes are recorded for the difference between such taxes and taxes computed for tax returns. The Corporation and its domestic subsidiaries file a consolidated federal income tax return. The operating results of Harnischfeger GmbH are included in the Corporation's U.S. income tax returns.

EXHIBIT 4 (*continued*)
Financial Notes

Additional taxes are provided on the earnings of foreign subsidiaries which are intended to be remitted to the Corporation. Such taxes are not provided on subsidiaries' unremitted earnings which are intended to be permanently reinvested.

Investment tax credits are accounted for under the flow-through method as a reduction of the income tax provision, if applicable, in the year the related asset is placed in service.

Reporting Format—Certain previously reported items have been conformed to the current year's presentation.

Note 2

Accounting Changes:

Effective November 1, 1983, the Corporation includes in its net sales products purchased from Kobe Steel, Ltd. and sold by the Corporation, to reflect more effectively the nature of the Corporation's transactions with Kobe. Previously only the gross margin on Kobe-originated equipment was included. During fiscal year 1984 such sales aggregated $28.0 million. Also, effective November 1, 1983, the financial statements of certain foreign subsidiaries are included on the basis of their fiscal years ended July 31. This change had the effect of increasing net sales by $5.4 million for the year ended October 31, 1984. The impact of these changes on net income was insignificant.

In 1984, the Corporation has computed depreciation expense on plants, machinery and equipment using the straight-line method for financial reporting purposes. Prior to 1984, the Corporation used principally accelerated methods for its U.S. operating plants. The cumulative effect of this change, which was applied retroactively to all assets previously subjected to accelerated depreciation, increased net income for 1984 by $11.0 million or $.93 per common and common equivalent share. The impact of the new method on income for the year 1984 before the cumulative effect was insignificant.

As a result of the review of its depreciation policy, the Corporation, effective November 1, 1983, has changed its estimated depreciation lives on certain U.S. plants, machinery and equipment and residual values on certain machinery and equipment, which increased net income for 1984 by $3.2 million or $.27 per share. No income tax effect was applied to this change.

The changes in accounting for depreciation were made to conform the Corporation's depreciation policy to those used by manufacturers in the Corporation's and similar industries and to provide a more equitable allocation of the cost of plants, machinery and equipment over their useful lives.

Note 3

Cash and Temporary Investments

Cash and temporary investments consisted of the following (in thousands of dollars):

	October 31, 1984	1983
Cash-in demand deposits	$ 2,155	$11,910
—in special accounts principally to support letters of credit	4,516	—
Temporary investments	89,336	52,365
	$96,007	$64,275

EXHIBIT 4 (*continued*)
Financial Notes

Temporary investments consisted of short-term U.S. and Canadian treasury bills, money market funds, time and certificates of deposit, commercial paper and bank repurchase agreements and bankers' acceptances. Temporary investments are stated at cost plus accrued interest, which approximates market value.

Note 4
Long-Term Debt, Bank Credit Lines and Interest Expense
Outstanding long-term debt payable to unaffiliated lenders was as follows (in thousands of dollars):

| | October 31, | |
	1984	1983
Parent Company:		
15% Senior Notes due April 15, 1994	$ 47,700	$ —
12% Subordinated Debentures, with an effective interest rate of 16.3%; sinking fund redemption payments of $7,500 due annually on April 15 in 1994–2003, and final payment of $25,000 in 2004	100,000	—
Term Obligations—		
Insurance company debt:		
9% Notes	—	20,000
9 7/8 Notes	—	38,750
8 7/8 Notes	—	40,500
Bank debt, at 105% of prime	—	25,000
Paper purchase debt, at prime or LIBOR, plus 1 1/4%	—	18,519
9.23% Mortgage Note due monthly to April, 1998	4,327	4,481
	152,027	147,250
Consolidated Subsidiaries		
Notes payable to banks in German marks	—	9,889
Contract payable in 1985–1989, in South African rands, with imputed interest rate of 12%	1,024	—
Other	—	36
	153,051	157,175
Less: Amounts payable within one year	644	17,799
Unamortized discounts	23,857	284
Long-Term Debt—excluding amounts payable within one year	$128,550	$139,092

EXHIBIT 4 (*continued*)
Financial Notes

Note 5

Harnischfeger Credit Corporation and Cranetex, Inc.

Condensed financial information of Harnischfeger Credit Corporation ("Credit"), an un-consolidated wholly-owned finance subsidiary, accounted for under the equity method, was as follows (in thousands of dollars):

Balance Sheet	October 31,	
	1984	1983
Assets		
Cash and temporary investments	$ 404	$19,824
Finance receivables—net	4,335	11,412
Factored account note and current account receivable from parent company	—	8,836
Other assets	4,181	661
	$8,920	$40,733
Liabilities and Shareholders' Equity		
Debt payable	$ —	$32,600
Advances from parent company	950	—
Other liabilities	71	1,429
	1,021	34,029
Shareholders' equity	7,899	6,704
	$8,920	$40,733

Statement of Operations	Year Ended October 31,		
	1984	1983	1982
Revenues	$ 1,165	$2,662	$ 9,978
Less:			
Operating Expenses	1,530	3,386	14,613
Provision (credit) for income taxes	(1,560)	(222)	180
Net income (loss)	$ 1,195	$ (502)	$(4,815)

Credit's purchases of finance receivables from the Corporation aggregated $1.1 million in 1984, $46.7 million in 1983 and $50.4 million in 1982. In 1982, Credit received income support of $4.0 million from the Corporation.

In 1982, the Corporation organized Cranetex, Inc. to assume certain assets and liabilities transferred by a former distributor of construction equipment, in settlement of the Corporation's and Credit's claims against the distributor and to continue the business on an interim basis until the franchise can be transferred to a new distributor. The Corporation recorded provisions of $2.5 million in 1983 and $2.3 million in 1982 and Credit recorded a provision of $6.7 million in 1982, for credit losses incurred in the financing of equipment sold to the former distributor.

EXHIBIT 4 (*continued*)
Financial Notes

The condensed balance sheet of Cranetex, Inc. was as follows (in thousands of dollars):

| | October 31, | |
	1984	1983
Assets		
Cash	$ 143	$ 49
Accounts receivables	566	428
Inventory	2,314	3,464
Property and equipment	1,547	1,674
	$4,570	$ 5,615
Liabilities & Deficit		
Loans payable	$4,325	$ 6,682
Other liabilities	338	620
	4,663	7,302
Shareholders' (deficit), net of accounts and advances payable to parent company	(93)	(1,687)
	$4,570	$ 5,615

The net losses at Cranetex, Inc. of $.2 million in 1984, $2.1 million in 1983 and $1.0 million in 1982 were included in Equity in Earnings (loss) of Unconsolidated Companies in the Corporation's Statement of Operations.

Note 6

Transactions with Kobe Steel, Ltd. and ASEA Industrial Systems Inc.

Kobe Steel, Ltd. of Japan ("Kobe"), has been a licensee for certain of the Corporation's products since 1955, and has owned certain Harnischfeger Japanese construction equipment patents and technology since 1981. As of October 31, 1984, Kobe held 1,030,000 shares or 8.4% of the Corporation's outstanding Common Stock (See Note 13) Kobe also owns 25% of the capital stock of Harnischfeger of Australia Pty. Ltd., a subsidiary of the Corporation. This ownership appears as the minority interest on the Corporation's balance sheet.

Under agreements expiring in December, 1990 Kobe pays technical service fees on P&H mining equipment produced and sold under license from the Corporation, and trademark and marketing fees on sales of construction equipment outside of Japan. Net fee income received from Kobe was $4.3 million in 1984, $3.1 million in 1983, and $3.9 million in 1982; this income is included in Other Income in the accompanying Statement of Operations.

In October 1983, the Corporation entered into a ten-year agreement with Kobe under which Kobe agreed to supply the Corporation's requirements for construction cranes for sale in the United States as it phases out its own manufacture of cranes over the next several years, and to make the Corporation the exclusive distributor of Kobe-built cranes in the United States. The Agreement also involves a joint research and development program for construction equipment under which the Corporation agreed to spend at least $17 million over a three-year period and provided it does so, Kobe agreed to pay this amount to the Corporation. Sales of cranes outside the United States continue under the contract terms described in the preceding paragraph.

EXHIBIT 4 (*continued*)
Financial Notes

The Corporation's sales to Kobe, principally components for mining and construction equipment, excluding the R&D expenses discussed in the preceding paragraph, approximated $5.2 million, $10.5 million and $7.0 million during the three years ended October 31, 1984, 1983 and 1982, respectively. The purchases from Kobe of mining and construction equipment and components amounted to approximately $33.7 million, $15.5 million and $29.9 million during the three years ended October 31, 1984, 1983 and 1982, respectively, most of which were resold to customers (See Note 2).

The Corporation owns 19% of ASEA Industrial Systems Inc. ("AIS"), an electrical equipment company controlled by ASEA AB of Sweden. The Corporation's purchases of electrical components from AIS aggregated $11.2 million in 1984 and $6.1 million in 1983 and its sales to AIS approximated $2.6 million in 1984 and $3.8 million in 1983.

The Corporation believes that its transactions with Kobe and AIS were competitive with alternative sources of supply for each party involved.

Note 7

Inventories

Consolidated inventories consisted of the following (in thousands of dollars):

| | October 31, | |
	1984	1983
At lower of cost or market (FIFO method):		
Raw materials	$ 11,003	$ 11,904
Work in process and purchased parts	88,279	72,956
Finished goods	79,111	105,923
	178,393	190,783
Allowance to reduce inventories to cost on the LIFO method	(34,081)	(37,189)
	$144,312	$153,594

Inventories valued on the LIFO method represented approximately 82% of total inventories at both October 31, 1984 and 1983.

Inventory reductions in 1984, 1983 and 1982 resulted in a liquidation of LIFO inventory quantities carried at lower costs compared with the current cost of their acquisitions. The effect of these liquidations was to increase net income by 2.4 million or $.20 per common share in fiscal 1984, and to reduce the net loss by approximately $15.6 million or $1.54 per share in 1983, and by $6.7 million or $.66 per share in 1982; no income tax effect applied to the adjustment in 1984 and 1983.

Note 8

Accounts Receivable

Accounts receivable were net of allowances for doubtful accounts of $5.9 million and $6.4 million at October 31, 1984 and 1983, respectively.

EXHIBIT 4 (*continued*)
Financial Notes

Note 9

Research and Development Expense

Research and development expense incurred in the development of new products or significant improvements to existing products was $5.1 million in 1984 (net of amounts funded by Kobe Steel, Ltd.) $12.1 million in 1983 and $14.1 million in 1982.

Note 10

Foreign Operations

The net sales, net income (loss) and net assets of subsidiaries located in countries outside the United States and Canada and included in the consolidated financial statements were as follows (in thousands of dollars):

	Year Ended October 31,		
	1984	1983	1982
Net sales	$78,074	$45,912	$69,216
Net income (loss) after minority interests	828	(1,191)	3,080
Corporation's equity in total net assets	17,734	7,716	7,287

Foreign currency transaction losses included in Cost of Sales were $2.7 million in 1984, $1.2 million in 1983 and $1.3 million in 1982.

Note 11

Pension Plans and Other Postretirement Benefits

Pension expense for all plans of the Corporation and its consolidated subsidiaries was $1.9 million in 1984, $6.5 million in 1983 and $12.2 million in 1982.

Accumulated plan benefits and plan net assets for the Corporation's U.S. defined benefit plans, at the beginning of the fiscal years 1984 and 1983, with the data for the Salaried Employees' Retirement Plan as in effect on August 1, 1984, were as follows (in thousands of dollars):

	1984	1983
Actuarial present value of accumulated plan benefits:		
Vested	$52,639	$108,123
Nonvested	2,363	5,227
	$55,002	$113,350
Net assets available for benefits:		
Assets of the Pension Trusts	$45,331	$112,075
Accrued contributions not paid to the Trusts	16,717	12,167
	$62,048	$124,242

EXHIBIT 4 (*continued*)
Financial Notes

The Salaried Employees' Retirement Plan, which covers substantially all salaried employees in the U.S., was restructured during 1984 due to overfunding of the Plan. Effective August 1, 1984, the Corporation terminated the existing plan and established a new plan which is substantially identical to the prior plan except for an improvement in the minimum pension benefit. All participants in the prior plan became fully vested upon its termination. All vested benefits earned through August 1, 1984 were covered through the purchase of individual annuities at a cost aggregating $36.7 million. The remaining plan assets, which totaled $39.3 million, reverted to the Corporation in cash upon receipt of regulatory approval of the prior plan termination from the Pension Benefit Guaranty Corporation. For financial reporting purposes, the new plan is considered to be a continuation of the terminated plan. Accordingly, the $39.3 million actuarial gain which resulted from the restructuring is included in Accrued Pension Costs in the accompanying Balance Sheet and is being amortized to income over a ten-year period commencing in 1984. For tax reporting purposes, the asset reversion will be treated as a fiscal 1985 transaction. The initial unfunded actuarial liability of the new plan, computed as of November 1, 1983, of $10.3 million is also included in Accrued Pension Costs.

In 1982 and 1983, the Pension Trusts purchased certain securities with effective yields of 13% and 12%, respectively, and dedicated these assets to the plan benefits of a substantial portion of the retired employees and certain terminated employees with deferred vested rights. These rates, together with 9% for active employees in 1984, 8% in 1983 and 7 1/4% in 1982, were the assumed rates of return used in determining the annual pension expense and the actuarial present value of accumulated plan benefits for the U.S. plans.

The effect of the changes in the investment return assumption rates for all U.S. plans, together with the 1984 restructuring of the U.S. Salaried Employees' Plan, was to reduce pension expense by approximately $4.0 million in 1984 and $2.0 million in 1983, and the actuarial present value of accumulated plan benefits by approximately $60.0 million in 1984. Pension expense in 1983 was also reduced $2.1 million from the lower level of active employees. Other actuarial gains, including higher than anticipated investment results, more than offset the additional pension costs resulting from plan changes and interest charges on balance sheet accruals in 1984 and 1983.

The Corporation's foreign pension plans do not determine the actuarial value of accumulated benefits or net assets available for retirement benefits as calculated and disclosed above. For those plans, the total of the plans' pension funds and balance sheet accruals approximated the actuarially computed value of vested benefits at both October 31, 1984 and 1983.

The Corporation generally provides certain health care and life insurance benefits for U.S. retired employees. Substantially all of the Corporation's current U.S. employees may become eligible for such benefits upon retirement. Life insurance benefits are provided either through the pension plans or separate group insurance arrangements. The cost of retiree health care and life insurance benefits, other than the benefits provided by the pension plans, is expensed as incurred; such costs approximated $2.6 million in 1984 and $1.7 million in 1983.

EXHIBIT 4 (*continued*)

Financial Notes

Note 12

Income Taxes

Domestic and foreign income (loss) before income tax effects was as follows (in thousands of dollars):

| | Year Ended October 31, | | |
	1984	1983	1982
Domestic	$1,578	$(35,412)	$(77,600)
Foreign			
Harnischfeger GmbH	432	(2,159)	(475)
All other	3,728	4,768	8,418
	4,160	2,609	7,943
Total income (loss) before income tax effects, equity items and cumulative effect of accounting change	$5,738	$(32,803)	$(69,657)

Provision (credit) for income taxes, on income (loss) before income tax effects, equity items and cumulative effect of accounting change, consisted of (in thousands of dollars):

	1984	1983	1982
Currently payable (refundable):			
Federal	$ —	$(7,957)	$(9,736)
State	136	297	70
Foreign	2,518	3,379	5,376
	2,654	(4,281)	(4,290)
Deferred (prepaid):			
Federal	—	2,955	2,713
State and foreign	(229)	(74)	(23)
	(229)	2,881	2,690
Provision (credit) for income taxes	$2,425	$(1,400)	$(1,600)

Unremitted earnings of foreign subsidiaries which have been or are intended to be permanently reinvested were $19.1 million at October 31, 1984. Such earnings, if distributed, would incur income tax expense of substantially less than the U.S. income tax rate as a result of previously paid foreign income taxes, provided that such foreign taxes would become deductible as foreign tax credits. No income tax provision was made in respect of the tax-deferred income of a consolidated subsidiary that has elected to be taxed as a domestic international sales corporation. The Deficit Reduction Act of 1984 provides for such income to become nontaxable effective December 31, 1984.

EXHIBIT 4 *(continued)*
Financial Notes

At October 31, 1984, the Corporation had federal tax operating loss carry-forwards of approximately $70.0 million, expiring in 1998 and 1999, for tax return purposes, and $88.0 million for book purposes. In addition, the Corporation had for tax purposes, foreign tax credit carry-forwards of $3.0 million (expiring in 1985 through 1989), and investment tax credit carry-forwards of $1.0 million (expiring in 1997 through 1999). For book purposes, tax credit carry-forwards approximately $8.0 million. The carry-forward will be available for the reduction of future income tax provisions, the extent and timing of which are not determinable.

Differences in income (loss) before income taxes for financial and tax purposes arise from timing differences between financial and tax reporting and relate to depreciation, consolidating eliminations for inter-company profits in inventories, and provisions, principally, for warranty, pension, compensated absences, product liability and plant closing costs.

During 1983 an examination of the Corporation's 1977–1981 federal income tax returns and certain refund claims was completed by the Internal Revenue Service, and as a result, a current credit for federal income taxes of $8.0 million was recorded in 1983, $3.0 million of which was applied to the reduction of prepaid income taxes.

In 1984, tax credits fully offset any federal income tax otherwise applicable to the year's income, and in 1983 and 1982, the relationship of the tax benefit to the pre-tax loss differed substantially from the U.S. statutory tax rate due principally to losses from the domestic operations for which only a partial federal tax benefit was available in 1982. Consequently, an analysis of deferred income taxes and variance from the U.S. statutory rate is not presented.

Report of Independent Accountants

Price Waterhouse
Milwaukee, Wisconsin
November 29, 1984

To the Directors and Shareholders of Harnischfeger Corporation

In our opinion, the financial statements, which appear on pages 18 to 34 of this report, present fairly the consolidated financial position of Harnischfeger Corporation and its subsidiaries at October 31, 1984 and 1983, and the results of their operations and the changes in their financial position for each of the three years in the period ended October 31, 1984, in conformity with generally accepted accounting principles consistently applied during the period except for the change, with which we concur, in the method of accounting for depreciation expense as described in Note 2 of this report. Our examinations of these statements were made in accordance with generally accepted auditing standards and accordingly included such tests of the accounting records and such other auditing procedures as we considered necessary in the circumstances.

Price Waterhouse

Cost Concepts and Analysis

Understanding Costs for Management Decisions

- *Precision Worldwide, Inc.*
- *Lille Tissages, S.A.*
- *Prestige Telephone Company*

A Brief Introduction to Cost Accounting

- *Hilton Manufacturing Company*

Understanding Costs for Management Decisions

"**C**ost" is a word used in many different ways in management and management decision making. Cost is a measure of something that has been given up (or will be given up) in the process of doing things. The utility and versatility of the concepts of cost are what make the collection, analysis, and presentation of cost information so useful in solving management problems.

Many problems can be "solved" by first measuring and then using "cost" as a central part of the overall criteria or analysis. Sometimes managers want to predict or accomplish an objective in the least expensive manner. At other times they may want to compare cost to revenue to predict or achieve the highest profit or smallest loss. The least costly decision may not be the one ultimately selected because added benefits that can be gained by incurring greater costs may outweigh the greater cost itself.

Costs are often predicted and analyzed before decisions are made and implemented. These anticipated cost data are frequently used to control operations or evaluate the effectiveness of decisions.

TYPES OF COST

Three types of costs—*current costs*, *opportunity costs*, and *sunk costs*—are frequently used in management decision making. Each can be used in several ways in cost analysis.

Current costs are measured as activities take place. In measuring current costs, the accountant attempts to determine what has been (or must be) given up in order to either implement a decision or carry out an activity. What is given up can take many forms. Physical effort, raw material, or fees paid in the form of money to others may all be required to implement a decision or produce a product or service. Each of these may represent a current cost of that activity. Management accountants usually measure each component of current cost in terms of a monetary equivalent. This is done to make the process of measuring, accumulating, and storing information both more feasible and more convenient.

Professor William J. Bruns, Jr. prepared this technical note as the basis for class discussion.

Copyright © 1997 by the President and Fellows of Harvard College, Case No. 197-117. To order copies or request permission to reproduce materials, call 1-800-545-7685 or write Harvard Business School Publishing, Boston, MA 02163. No part of this publication may be reproduced, stored in a retrieval system, used in a spreadsheet, or transmitted in any form or by any means—electronic, mechanical, photocopying, recording, or otherwise—without the permission of Harvard Business School.

Opportunity costs can be thought of as the cost of the second-best alternative. If cost is being incurred in producing product A, then it is not being incurred in producing product B. For example, if material is used in product A, it is not available for product B. In analyzing management options, it may be useful to think of the cost of product A as being what we gave up by not producing product B. Every management decision or option has an opportunity cost. Although opportunity costs are not always measured in financial terms and are rarely formally recorded in accounting records, they are important in management decision making and management accounting analyses.

The term "sunk" cost refers to expenditures of time, effort, material, and money that can never be recovered. In contrast to opportunity costs, which are rarely included in accounting records, sunk costs often are. The nature of sunk costs must be clearly understood by managers. Sunk costs are irrelevant in analyzing future courses of action or in making decisions about which future courses of actions would be most advantageous given organizational goals.

The effectiveness with which information about costs can be developed and used depends upon an understanding of definitions and communication of types of "costs." Understanding what has been given up, or what will be given up, or what has been given up that can never be recovered (and, therefore, can be ignored in considering a current problem) is the beginning of effective cost analysis.

COST VARIABILITY

The way in which costs change as activities change is important to determining the relevance of that cost in many decision problems. If the total amount of cost incurred because of a decision is not changed by that decision, that cost is *nonvariable*, *fixed*, or *nondifferential*. On the other hand, if the alternatives under consideration will result in changes in the amount of cost, that cost is *variable*, or *differential*, or *incremental*.

Good cost analysis almost always begins with an attempt to determine whether— and how much—a cost will vary with alternatives that might be chosen. Sometimes, determining a variable cost is very simple. If each unit of product or service requires a specified amount of material, it is quite easy to both predict and measure the amount of cost that will be associated with the decision to produce a certain quantity of that product. By the same token, if a monthly fee such as rent must be paid in order to utilize a production facility and the facility can be used for any of several quantities of product or service, than the rent is a cost that relates to a period of time rather than the volume of production. The terms *nonvariable cost* or *variable cost* refer to how the total cost changes as the quantity of product or service produced changes.

Whether a cost is variable or nonvariable often depends upon the time horizon of a decision or course of action with which management is faced. If a factory or office is owned or has been rented under a contract, the occupancy costs and/or rent paid for may be nonvariable for the life of the building or contract. On the other hand, if the capacity of the building is insufficient to provide for the quantity of production under consideration and additional space will be required, then additional occupancy costs become variable costs (or *differential costs*) in the analysis. It is not possible to make categorical statements about whether a cost is nonvariable without considering the time period involved.

A final complication in any discussion of cost variability arises because many costs do not fall neatly into one or the other classification—variable or nonvariable. In addition, some costs are nonvariable within ranges of activity. If a decision will move activity beyond that range, however, then the level of cost will change significantly.

ANALYZING COSTS IN SINGLE-PERIOD DECISIONS

When a management problem or decision involves a relatively short time period, the cost analysis process can be fairly straightforward. Since nonvariable costs will not change in a short period of time (remember that the definition of a nonvariable cost is one that does not change), attention need be given only to those costs that will change (or the *variable* costs). Once a decision criterion of minimizing costs or maximizing the difference between revenues or benefits and costs has been chosen, most analyses will lead quickly to indicated courses of action. The only serious questions are likely to involve how certain are the measurements and predictions of costs and whether they are truly variable or nonvariable.

In analyzing single-period decision problems, both managers and management accountants frequently use *contribution* analysis. The best decision will produce the most profit or make the highest "contribution" to covering *nonvariable* costs. Contribution analysis seeks to find the difference between the revenue or benefits and the variable costs that will result from a course of action.

For a unit of product or service, *contribution* is measured by the difference between the net selling price and the variable costs of producing a unit of the product or service. For a product line, it is measured by the revenue obtained by a given quantity of product or service delivered and sold to clients, less the total variable cost incurred in producing and delivering that quantity of product or service. Contribution is greater than profit because the nonvariable costs which are not changed as a result of the decision or action taken are excluded from the analysis. Contribution analysis is a simple, yet powerful method of making short-term decisions.

In spite of its power, contribution analysis has many limitations. Conclusions reached by analyzing contribution are dependent on judgments that have been made about cost variability over the time period under consideration. In addition, when contribution analysis is used as an input to decision processes, we necessarily make the assumption that the predicted costs will be those actually incurred. Finally, in many situations costs of various programs and activities interact, and it is difficult to separate these *joint costs*.

COST ANALYSIS OVER MANY PERIODS

As soon as a management problem or a cost analysis problem extends beyond a short period of time, a number of additional complications can come into play. Uncertainties about the future increase as the horizon moves away from our current knowledge and experience. The concept of cost itself tends to change, for a current cost is different from one that will be incurred in the future.

Managers and accountants have developed and utilize techniques for analyzing multiperiod decision problems. These techniques are based upon or utilize the concept of *interest*. The concept or *compound interest* relates a financial cost at one point in time to the financial cost at another point in time using a *rate of return*, an *interest rate*, or a *cost of capital* appropriate to either the organization or the particular class of problem(s). While there are several techniques for doing this, two that are particularly popular are called the *net present value method* and the *internal rate of return method*.[1]

In the net present value method of analyzing multiperiod problems, all costs (and benefits) at future times are related to their present value equivalents by using an interest rate equal to either the cost of capital or the expected earnings rate within the organization. The net present value of a future cost can be considered to be the amount that the cost now represents when consideration is given to the return that could be obtained between the present time and the time at which the cost will be incurred. Some students find it useful to think of this amount as the amount that we could pay someone now to take care of the cost in the future—assuming that the person we would pay now could earn a given interest rate on our deposit.

The internal rate of return method for analyzing multiple-period problems identifies the interest rate (or the cost of capital) that would make the various costs incurred and benefits received over the life of the project in question equal to each other in present value terms. In comparison to the net present value method, the internal rate of return method assumes that we know the costs to be incurred and the benefits to be received at the various points in time, and that we seek the interest rate that would allow us to treat them as equivalent. Both the net present value method and the internal rate of return method are based upon the same concepts and formulas, but technical differences in their application make them more or less useful in selected problems or to different managers.

Multiple-period problems require that costs be measured in terms of cash or their cash equivalents. Both the present value and internal rate of return methods depend upon the identification of the cash flows that will result from alternative courses of action. If a cost does not consist of cash expenditure or if benefits are not obtained in the form of cash, it is necessary to seek their equivalence in cash before these analytical methods can be applied.

Among the most frequent problems encountered in multiple-period analysis is the proper treatment of *depreciation*. The cash flow that relates to the cost of assets has usually been incurred in an earlier period. Therefore, when analyzing accounting costs in multiple-period cost analysis, it is necessary to "correct" for the effects of depreciation accounting. Depreciation is an allocation of a previous cash flow to an accounting period. But depreciation cannot be ignored. Depreciation often affects other cash flows, such as the determination of taxes due.

Multiple-period cost analysis is usually more complex than single-period analysis. In almost every case where decisions or analyses cover several periods of time, the number of variables to be considered will be greater than they are in short-term decision making.

COST AS A CRITERION FOR CHOICE

The concept of cost is a powerful one in economic decision making. If cost can be minimized for a given amount of output, or if more product or service can be

---

[1] Students who are not familiar with the use of compound interest in the analysis of multiperiod problems are referred to other references. Compound interest methods are appropriate whenever the planning or decision horizon extends beyond a single period.

obtained for the same amount of cost, economic efficiency will be enhanced. It is for this reason that managers in every organization seek an understanding of their costs and their cost of operations.

The process of cost analysis, however, must always proceed with some caution. The cost information utilized must be appropriate to the time period and the decision horizon of the problem at hand. The costs must be those that relate to actions that will be taken or have been taken. Careful analyses of costs that are irrelevant to the decision problem at hand are of little or no use.

Finally, cost analysis—taken by itself—will rarely lead to the discovery of new alternatives. For cost analysis to be effective as part of a total management system, there must be clear thinking about alternatives that could be taken or that might have been taken. This latter process should take place before, during, and after the cost analysis process. The effective manager or management accountant always brings imagination, ingenuity, and perseverance to every situation that requires information about costs.

Precision Worldwide, Inc.

In late May 2004, Hans Thorborg, the general manager of the German plant of Precision Worldwide, Inc. (PWI), scheduled an afternoon meeting with his sales manager, accountant, and development engineer to discuss the introduction by the French firm Henri Poulenc (a competitor) of a plastic ring substitute for the steel retaining rings presently used in certain machines sold by Precision Worldwide. The plastic ring, new to the market, not only had a much longer life than the PWI steel ring but also apparently had a much lower manufacturing cost. Thorborg's problem stemmed from PWI's large quantity of steel rings on hand and the substantial inventory of special steel that had been purchased for their manufacture. After a thorough survey, he had found that the special steel could not be sold, even for scrap; the total book value of these inventories exceeded $390,000.

For nearly 90 years PWI had manufactured industrial machines and equipment for sale in numerous countries. The particular machines involved in Thorborg's dilemma were made only at the company's plant in Frankfurt, Germany, which employed more than one thousand people. The different models were priced between $18,900 and $28,900 and were sold by a separate sales organization. Repair and replacement parts, which accounted for a substantial part of the company's business, were sold separately. As with the steel rings, these parts could often also be used on similar machines manufactured by competitors. The company's head office was in Toledo, Ohio, U.S.A. In general, plants outside the United States were allowed considerable leeway in administering their own affairs; the corporate headquarters, however, was easily accessible by telephone, email, or during executive visits to the individual plants.

In the late 1990s, competition had increased. Japanese manufacturers, with low-priced spare parts, had successfully entered the field. Other companies had appeared with lower-quality and lower-priced machines. There was little doubt that future competition would be more intense.

The steel ring manufactured by PWI had a normal life of about two months, depending upon the extent to which the machine was used. A worn-out ring could be

Professor William J. Bruns, Jr. adapted this case from "Industrial Grinders N.V." (HBS No. 175-246).

Professor William J. Bruns, Jr. adapted this case from "Industrial Grinders N.V." (HBS No. 175-246). HBS cases are developed solely as the basis for class discussion. Cases are not intended to serve as endorsements, sources of primary data, or illustrations of effective or ineffective management.

Copyright © 1997 President and Fellows of Harvard College, Case No. 197-103. To order copies or request permission to reproduce materials, call 1-800-545-7685, write Harvard Business School Publishing, Boston, MA 02163, or go to http://www.hbsp.harvard.edu. No part of this publication may be reproduced, stored in a retrieval system, used in a spreadsheet, or transmitted in any form or by any means—electronic, mechanical, photocopying, recording, or otherwise—without the permission of Harvard Business School.

Precision Worldwide, Inc.   4-7

replaced in a few seconds, and although different models of the machines required from two to six rings, the rings were usually replaced individually as they wore out.

The sales manager, Gerhard Henk, had learned of the new plastic ring shortly after its appearance and had immediately asked when PWI would be able to supply them, particularly for sale to customers in France, where Henri Poulenc was the strongest competition faced by PWI. Bodo Eisenbach, the development engineer, estimated that the plastic rings could be produced by mid-September. The necessary tools and equipment could be obtained for about $7,500. Eisenbach had initially raised the issue of the steel-ring inventories that would not be used up by September. Henk believed that if the new ring could be produced at a substantially lower cost than the steel ones, the inventory problem was irrelevant; he suggested that the inventory be sold, or if that was impossible, thrown away. The size of the inventory, however, caused Thorborg to question this suggestion. He recalled that the size of the inventory resulted from having to order the highly specialized steel in large amounts so that a mill would be willing to handle the order.

Henk reported that Henri Poulenc was said to be selling the plastic ring at about the same price as the PWI steel ring; since the production cost of the plastic ring would be much less than the steel, he emphasized that PWI was ignoring a good profit margin if it did not introduce a plastic ring. As the meeting concluded, it was decided that the company should prepare to manufacture the new ring as soon as possible but that until the inventories of the old model and the steel were exhausted, the plastic ring would only be sold in those markets where it was offered by competitors. It was expected that the new rings would not be produced by any company other than Henri Poulenc for some time, and this meant that no more than 10% of Precision Woldwide's markets would be affected.

Shortly after this, Patrick Corrigan, from the parent company in Ohio, visited Frankfurt. During a review of company problems, the plastic-ring question was discussed. Although the ring was only a small part of the finished machines, Corrigan was interested in the problem because the company wanted to establish policies for the production and pricing of all such parts that, in total, accounted for a substantial portion of PWI's revenues. Corrigan agreed that the company should proceed with plans for its production and try to find some other use for the steel; he then said, "If this does not seem possible, I would, of course, expect you to use this material and produce the steel rings."

A few days after Corrigan's visit, both Eisenbach and Henk came in to see Thorborg. Eisenbach came because he felt that since tests had indicated that the plastic ring had at least four times the wearing properties of the steel ring, it would completely destroy demand for the steel ring. He understood, however, that the price of the competitive ring was high, and he felt that the decision to sell the plastic ring only in markets where it was sold by competitors was a good one. He observed, "In this way we will probably be able to continue supplying the steel ring until stocks, at least of processed parts, are used up."

Henk still strongly opposed sales of any steel rings once the plastic ones became available. If steel rings were sold in some areas, he argued, while plastic rings were being sold elsewhere, customers who purchased steel rings would eventually find out. This would harm the sale of Precision Worldwide machines—the selling price of which was many times that of the rings. He produced figures to show that if the selling price of both rings remained at $1,350.00 per hundred, the additional profit from the plastic rings (manufactured at a cost of $279.65 per hundred versus the $1,107.90 per hundred for steel rings) would more than recover the value of the steel inventory, and do so within less than a year at present volume levels. Thorborg refused to change the decision of the previous meeting but agreed to have another discussion within a week.

Anticipating this third meeting and also having Corrigan's concern in mind, Thorborg obtained the data displayed in **Table A** from the cost accounting department on the cost of both plastic and steel rings.

Thorborg also learned that the inventory of special steel had cost $110,900 and represented enough material to produce approximately 34,500 rings. Assuming that sales continued at the current rate of 690 rings per week, without any further production, some 15,100 finished rings would be left on hand by mid-September. Thorborg then recalled that during the next two or three months the plant would not be operating at capacity; during slack periods, the company had a policy of employing excess labor (at about 70% of regular wages) on various make-work projects rather than laying workers off. He wondered if it would be a good idea to use some of this labor to convert the steel inventory into rings during this period.

QUESTION

What action should Hans Thorborg take? Why?

TABLE A

	100 Plastic Rings	100 Steel Rings
Material	$ 17.65	$ 321.90
Direct labor	65.50	196.50
Overhead[a]		
Departmental	131.00	393.00
Administrative	65.50	196.50
Total (cost)	$279.65	$1,107.90

[a] Overhead was allocated on the basis of direct labor cost. It was estimated that the variable overhead costs included here were largely fringe benefits related to direct labor and amounted to 80¢ per direct labor dollar or about 40% of the departmental amounts.

Lille Tissages, S.A.

Early in 2004, the marketing director and the finance director of Lille Tissages, S.A. met to prepare a joint pricing recommendation for Item 345. After the managing director had approved their recommendation, the company would announce the price in letters to its customers. In accordance with company and industry practice, announced prices were adhered to for the year unless radical changes in the market had occurred.

Lille Tissages was located in Lille, France. It was the largest company in its segment of the French textile industry; its 2003 sales had exceeded FF96 million. Company salesmen were on a straight salary basis, and each salesman sold the full line. Most of Lille Tissages' competitors were small. Usually, they waited for Lille Tissages to announce prices before mailing out their own price lists.

Item 345, an expensive yet competitive fabric, was the sole product of a department whose facilities could not be utilized on other items in the product line. In January 2002, Lille Tissages had raised its price from FF15 to FF20 a meter. This had been done to bring the profit per meter on Item 345 up to that of other products in the line. Although the company was in a strong position financially, it would require considerable capital in the next few years to finance a recently approved long-term modernization and expansion program. The 2002 pricing decision had been one of several changes advocated by the directors in an attempt to strengthen the company's working capital position so as to insure that adequate funds would be available for this program.

Competitors of Lille Tissages had held their prices on products similar to Item 345 at FF15 during 2002 and 2003. The industry and Lille Tissages volume for Item 345 for the years 1998–2003, as estimated by the sales director, are shown in **Exhibit 1**. As shown by this exhibit, Lille Tissages had lost a significant portion of its former market position. In the sales director's opinion, a reasonable forecast of industry volume for 2004 was 700,000 meters. He was certain that the company could sell 25% of the 2004 industry total if it adopted the FF15 price. He feared a further volume decline if it did not meet the competitive price. As many consumers were convinced

Professor William J. Bruns Jr. prepared this case. HBS cases are developed solely as the basis for class discussion. Cases are not intended to serve as endorsements, sources of primary data, or illustrations of effective or ineffective management.

of the superiority of the Lille Tissages product, the sales director reasoned that sales of Item 345 would probably not fall below 75,000 meters, even at a FF20 price.

During the pricing discussions, the finance director and the marketing director had considered two other aspects of the problem. The finance director was concerned about the possibility that competitors would reduce their prices below FF15 if Lille Tissages announced a FF15 price for Item 345. The marketing director was confident that competitors would not go below FF15 because they all had higher costs and several of them were in tight financial straits. He believed that action taken on Item 345 would not have had any substantial repercussions on other items in the line.

The finance director prepared estimated costs of Item 345 at various volumes of production (see **Exhibit 2**). These estimated costs reflected projected labor and material costs. They were based on past experience except for the estimates of 75,000 and 100,000 meters. The company had produced more than 100,000 meters in each of the last ten years, and earlier experience was not applicable because of equipment changes and increases in labor productivity.

QUESTIONS

1. Should Lille Tissages lower the price to FF15? (Assume no intermediate prices are being considered.)

2. If the department that produces Item 345 was a profit center and if you were the manager of that department, would it be to *your* financial advantage to lower the price?

3. Is there any possibility that competition might raise their prices if Lille Tissages maintains its price of FF20? If so, how do you take this factor into your analysis?

4. At FF15, will Lille Tissages earn a profit on Item 345? How do you decide?

EXHIBIT 1
Item 345, Prices and Production, 1998-2003

| | Volume of Production (meters) | | Price (French francs) | |
| | | | Charged by Most | |
Year	Industry Total	Lille Tissages	Competitors	Lille Tissages
1998	610,000	213,000	20.00	20.00
1999	575,000	200,000	20.00	20.00
2000	430,000	150,000	15.00	15.00
2001	475,000	165,000	15.00	15.00
2002	500,000	150,000	15.00	20.00
2003 (est.)	625,000	125,000	15.00	20.00

EXHIBIT 2
Estimated Cost per Meter of Item 345 at Various Volumes of Production (in French francs)

	75,000	100,000	125,000	150,000	175,000	200,000
Direct labor[a]	4.00	3.90	3.80	3.70	3.80	4.00
Material	2.00	2.00	2.00	2.00	2.00	2.00
Material spoilage	.20	.20	.19	.19	.19	.20
Department expense:						
Direct[b]	.60	.56	.50	.50	.50	.50
Indirect[c]	4.00	3.00	2.40	2.00	1.71	1.50
General overhead[d]	1.20	1.17	1.14	1.11	1.14	1.20
Factory cost	12.00	10.83	10.03	9.50	9.34	9.40
Selling & administrative						
expense[e]	7.80	7.04	6.52	6.18	6.07	6.11
Total Cost	19.80	17.87	16.55	15.68	15.41	15.51

[a] Any workers made redundant as a result of a decrease in the volume of sales of Item 345 could be economically absorbed in other departments.

[b] Indirect labor, supplies, repairs, powers, etc.

[c] Depreciation, supervision, etc.

[d] Thirty percent of direct labor, consisting principally of general plant administrative costs (plant supervision, plant services, etc.) and occupancy costs

[e] Sixty-five percent of factory cost.

Prestige Telephone Company

In April 2003, Daniel Rowe, president of Prestige Telephone Company, was preparing for a meeting with Susan Bradley, manager of Prestige Data Services, a company subsidiary. Partial deregulation and an agreement with the state Public Service Commission had permitted Prestige Telephone to establish a computer data service subsidiary to perform data processing for the telephone company and to sell computer service to other companies and organizations. Mr. Rowe had told the commission in 1999 that a profitable computer services subsidiary would reduce pressure for telephone rate increases. However, by the end of 2002 the subsidiary had yet to experience a profitable month. Ms. Bradley felt only more time was needed, but Rowe felt action was necessary to reduce the drain on company resources.

Prestige Data Services had grown out of the needs of Prestige Telephone for computer services to plan, control, and account for its own operations in the metropolitan region it served. The realization by Prestige that other businesses in the metropolitan region needed similar services and that centralized service could be provided over telephone circuits suggested that Prestige could sell computer time not needed by telephone operations. In addition, the state Public Service Commission had encouraged all public utilities under its jurisdiction to seek new sources of revenue and profits as a step toward deregulation and to reduce the need for rate increases which higher costs would otherwise bring.

Because it operated as a public utility, the rates charged by Prestige Telephone Company for telephone service could not be changed without the approval of the Public Service Commission. In presenting the proposal for the new subsidiary, Mr. Rowe had argued for a separate but wholly owned entity whose prices for service would not be regulated. In this way, Prestige could compete with other computer service organizations in a dynamic field; in addition, revenues for use of telephone services might also be increased. The commission accepted this proposal subject only to the restriction that the average monthly charge for service by the subsidiary to the parent not exceed $82,000, the estimated cost of equivalent services used by Prestige Telephone Company in 1999. All accounts of Prestige Data Services were

Professor William J. Bruns, Jr. prepared this case. HBS cases are developed solely as the basis for class discussion. Cases are not intended to serve as endorsements, sources of primary data, or illustrations of effective or ineffective management.

separated from those of Prestige Telephone, and each paid the other for services received from the other.

From the start of operations of Prestige Data Services in 2000 there had been problems. Equipment deliveries were delayed. Personnel had commanded higher salaries than expected. And most important, customers were harder to find than earlier estimates had led the company to expect. By the end of 2002, when income of Prestige Telephone was low enough to necessitate a report to shareholders revealing the lowest return on investment in seven years, Rowe felt it was time to reassess Prestige Data Services. Susan Bradley had asked for more time, as she felt the subsidiary would be profitable by March. But when the quarterly reports came (**Exhibits 1** and **2**), Rowe called Bradley to arrange their meeting.

Rowe received two reports on operations of Prestige Data Services. The summary of computer utilization (**Exhibit 1**) summarized the use of available hours of computer time. Service was offered to commercial customers 24 hours a day on weekdays and eight hours on Saturdays. Routine maintenance of the computers was provided by an outside contractor who took the computer off-line for eight hours each week for testing and upkeep. The reports for the quarter revealed a persistent problem; available hours, which did not provide revenue, remained high.

Revenue and cost data were summarized in the quarterly report on results of operations (**Exhibit 2**). Intracompany work was billed at $400 per hour, a rate based on usage estimates for 2000 and the Public Service Commission's restrictions that cost to Prestige Telephone should not exceed an average of $82,000 per month. Commercial sales were billed at $800 per hour.

While most expenses summarized in the report were self-explanatory, Rowe reminded himself of the characteristics of a few. Space costs were all paid to Prestige Telephone. Prestige Data Services rented the ground floor of a central exchange building owned by the company for $8,000 per month. In addition, a charge for custodial service based on the estimated annual cost per square foot was paid by Data Services, as telephone personnel provided these services.

Computer equipment had been acquired by lease and by purchases; leases had four years to run and were noncancelable. Owned equipment was all salable but probably could not bring more than its book value in the used equipment market.

Wages and salaries were separated in the report to show the expense of four different kinds of activities. Operating salaries included those of the six persons necessary to run the center around the clock as well as amounts paid hourly help who were required when the computer was in operation. Salaries of the programming staff who provided service to clients and maintained the operating system were reported as system development and maintenance. Sales personnel, who called upon and serviced present and prospective commercial clients, were also salaried.

Because of its relationship with Prestige Telephone, Prestige Data Services was able to avoid many costs an independent company would have. For example, all payroll, billing, collections, and accounting were done by telephone company personnel. For those corporate services, Prestige Data Services paid Prestige Telephone an amount based on wages and salaries each month.

Although Rowe was discouraged by results to date, he was reluctant to suggest to Bradley that Prestige Data Services be closed down or sold. The idea behind the subsidiary just seemed too good to give up easily. Besides, he was not sure that the accounting report really revealed the contribution that Data Services was making to Prestige Telephone. In other cases, he felt that the procedures used in accounting for separate activities in the company tended to obscure the costs and benefits they provided.

After examining the reports briefly, Rowe resolved to study them in preparation for asking Bradley to estimate the possible effects on profits of increasing the price to customers other than Prestige Telephone, reducing prices, increasing sales efforts and promotion, and of going to two-shift rather than 24-hour operations.

QUESTIONS

1. Appraise the results of operations of Prestige Data Services. Is the subsidiary really a problem to Prestige Telephone Company? Consider carefully the differences between reported costs and costs relevant for decisions that Daniel Rowe is considering.

2. Assuming the company demand for service will average 205 hours per month, what level of commercial sales of computer use would be necessary to break even each month?

3. Estimate the effect on income of each of the options Rowe has suggested if Bradley estimates as follows:

    a. Increasing the price to commercial customers to $1,000 per hour would reduce demand by 30%.

    b. Reducing the price to commercial customers to $600 per hour would increase demand by 30%.

    c. Increased promotion would increase sales by up to 30%. Bradley is unsure how much promotion this would take. (How much could be spent and still leave Prestige Data Services with no reported loss each month if commercial hours were increased 30%?)

    d. Reducing operations to 16 hours on weekdays and eight hours on Saturdays would result in a loss of 20% of commercial revenue hours.

4. Can you suggest changes in the accounting and reporting system now used for operations of Prestige Data Services which would result in more useful information for Rowe and Bradley?

EXHIBIT 1
Prestige Data Services Summary of Computer Utilization, First Quarter 2003

Revenue Hours	January	February	March
Intercompany	206	181	223
Commercial	123	135	138
Total revenue hours	329	316	361
Service hours	32	32	40
Available hours	223	164	143
Total hours	584	512	544

EXHIBIT 2
Prestige Data Services Summary
Results of Operations, First Quarter 2003

	January	February	March
Revenues			
Intercompany sales	$ 82,400	$ 72,400	$ 89,200
Commercial sales			
Computer use	98,400	108,000	110,400
Other	9,241	9,184	12,685
Total revenue	$190,041	$189,584	$212,285
Expenses			
Space costs:			
Rent	$ 8,000	$ 8,000	$ 8,000
Custodial services	1,240	1,240	1,240
	9,240	9,240	9,240
Equipment costs			
Computer leases	95,000	95,000	95,000
Maintenance	5,400	5,400	5,400
Depreciation:			
Computer equipment	25,500	25,500	25,500
Office equipment and fixtures	680	680	680
Power	1,633	1,592	1,803
	128,213	128,172	128,383
Wages and salaries			
Operations	29,496	29,184	30,264
Systems development and maintenance	12,000	12,000	12,000
Administration	9,000	9,000	9,000
Sales	11,200	11,200	11,200
	61,696	61,384	62,464
Materials	9,031	8,731	10,317
Sales promotions	7,909	7,039	8,083
Corporate services	15,424	15,359	15,236
Total expenses	$231,513	$229,925	$233,723
Net income (loss)	$(41,472)	$(40,341)	$(21,438)

A Brief Introduction to Cost Accounting

Organizations and managers are almost always interested in and concerned about costs. Control of past, present, and future costs is part of every manager's job. In companies that try to earn profits, control of costs directly affects the amount of profit earned. Knowledge of the cost of products or services is indispensable for decisions about pricing or product and service mix. In nonprofit organizations, control of costs influences the level of services that can be provided and the future survival of the organization.

Cost accounting systems can be important sources of information for managers. For this reason, effective managers understand the strengths and limitations of cost accounting systems and actively participate in the evaluation and evolution of cost measurement and management systems. Unlike accounting systems that support the preparation of periodic financial reports, cost accounting systems and reports are not subject to rules or standards such as generally accepted accounting principles. Managers are permitted to exercise as much creativity and ingenuity as they wish in the quest for information on costs. As a result, there is much variety in cost accounting systems used in different companies and sometimes even in different parts of the same organization.

This brief introduction to cost accounting will review the principal uses of cost data, provide some vocabulary for cost accounting, and present several of the questions managers have to answer in designing or using a cost accounting system. Its purpose is to provide the beginner with some vocabulary and ideas to use in learning about and exploring how cost management systems are designed and used by managers. While many of the references are to products and manufacturing environments, the vocabulary and concepts are equally applicable to services.

SOME USES OF INFORMATION ABOUT COSTS

Information about costs is used for two purposes in most organizations. Cost accounting systems provide information for evaluating the performance of an organizational

Professor William J. Bruns, Jr., prepared this note as the basis for class discussion.

unit or its manager. They also provide a means for estimating the costs of units of product or service that the organization may manufacture or provide to others.

Performance Measurement

Reports on the costs incurred by part of an organization—a department or a division, for example—are one means by which efficiency and effectiveness can be evaluated. By comparing *actual costs* to those that were expected—to *standard costs* or *budgeted costs*—the degree to which costs have been controlled can be judged. Deviations from expectations—*variances*—can be identified, evaluated, and discussed by managers. If needed, corrective actions can be taken or expectations can be modified to incorporate previously unexpected efficiencies.

Performance measurement reporting is usually periodic and systematic. Costs are assigned to parts of an organization that are identified as *cost centers*. When managers are held accountable for the costs incurred in a cost center, they are sometimes called *responsibility centers*. Performance reports provide information on the achievement of established objectives, efficiency of operations, and opportunities for cost control or cost reduction. Performance reports are used for both information and performance measurement and evaluation.

Product Costs and the Cost of Services

Inventory cost In manufacturing companies, product costs must be measured to determine the cost of items transferred from work-in-process to finished goods inventory. To satisfy the demands created by the *cost concept* used in financial reporting, a cost accounting system must measure all of the costs of the manufacturing process and assign some part of those costs to each unit of product. The costs of obtaining, maintaining, and managing the manufacturing facility need to be added to the costs of material and productive labor that each unit requires. The former costs are called *indirect costs*, and the latter are called *direct costs*. Generally accepted accounting principles require that inventory cost includes a "fair share" of total manufacturing costs, including indirect costs. In practice, there is considerable variation in how indirect costs are assigned to products.

Profitability analysis Information on costs is indispensable for analyzing the profitability of a product or product line. Product cost information allows managers to evaluate *contribution margin*—the difference between price and variable costs—and *gross margin*—the difference between price and total product costs. Information about sales, marketing, and distribution costs allows managers to evaluate the profitability of a product or product line. Without good information about costs, managers have no way to associate net income with actions or products about which they make decisions and over which they exercise control.

Product mix In companies that offer more than one product or service, information about costs is a key to managing the mix of products or services offered to customers or clients. With cost and profitability information, a manager can direct sales and marketing effort to the most profitable products. Unprofitable products can be eliminated, repriced, or bundled with more profitable products. The importance of product line decisions to future profitability requires confidence that product costs have been accurately determined.

Pricing Although prices are determined by market forces of supply and demand, product differentiation and marketing offer many managers some degree of latitude in setting prices. Product costs and trends in product costs often provide signals to managers that prices should be changed. In particular, a change in the cost of a critical material or component may signal the need to reconsider the prices asked for products.

Cost of service Many products require the seller to provide additional services to customers. In such cases, information about the cost of services is as important to managers as product costs. The same is true for managers of companies or organizations that provide only services. Unless the cost of service is measured, there is no way to know if providing the service is profitable or not and whether changes in pricing or marketing strategy are needed.

COST BEHAVIOR

Basic knowledge about cost behavior is a prerequisite for understanding, using, or designing cost accounting or cost management systems. The level of cost can be a function of either or both the *volume* of activity or *time* when the cost is incurred. Because prices of material, labor, and other resources change as time passes, and because time allows changes in manufacturing methods or service delivery, comparing costs at two points in time can be informative about efficiency. However, understanding the effect of changes in volume on costs is essential to measuring, analyzing, and using information about costs for both performance measurement and product costing.

Relation of Costs to Volume

If a company changes the amount of product or service it provides to customers or clients, its total costs will usually change as well. If more product is manufactured and sold, then we should expect the higher volume to cause costs to increase. However, in many instances, the increase in costs will not be proportional to the increase in product volume. To understand why, the concepts of *variable costs* and *fixed costs* must be understood.

Variable costs A cost which changes in strict proportionality with volume is called a variable cost. That is, if volume increases by 50%, a variable cost will increase in total by 50% as well. Materials used to create a product are a common example of a variable cost item. The total cost of materials to manufacture 20 units is double the cost to manufacture 10 units.

Nonvariable costs A cost that does not vary at all with volume is called a nonvariable, or fixed, cost. Over time the level of a fixed cost may change, but the change is independent of the volume of activity. Building rent is usually a nonvariable cost. The rent paid is independent of the number of units of product or service produced in the building or the number of customers served. Nonvariable costs can often be changed by management decisions, but they do not change simply because the volume of activity changes.

Semivariable costs Many costs include a combination of variable costs and nonvariable costs. The total amount of these costs varies in the same direction as volume, but less than proportionately with changes in volume. Sometimes semivariable costs can be separated into a fixed portion and a variable portion by isolating elements of the cost. The total cost of driving an automobile is semivariable with respect to the number of miles driven, but the cost of gasoline, oil, tires, and maintenance may be variable, whereas insurance and registration fees are probably fixed.

Chunky costs Often costs are assumed to be variable when they actually are incurred in chunks. Such costs, also known as *step-function costs*, are fixed for a range of volume of production but change in a chunk when volume drops below or exceeds the limits of the *relevant range* of volume. The costs of stockroom employees are often chunky. As volume of inventory or products increases, one stockroom employee may be able to handle material and finished goods until the volume level increases to the point where another employee must be added. The new staffing level will then be sufficient even as volume rises further until another "step" is reached. Chunky costs and costs that are not easily related to volume measures usually require special analysis and management.

ACCOUNTING FOR COSTS

Classifying Costs

The word *cost* is used many different ways in accounting and by managers. For clarity, other words are often attached to the word *cost* to enhance its meaning. In cost accounting, costs are usually classified into two categories: direct costs and indirect costs.

Direct costs Direct costs can be specifically traced to or are caused by a product, project, organizational unit, or activity. Materials specifically used in the manufacture of a product are an example of a direct cost. Labor specifically employed to provide a service would be another example. Many direct costs are variable costs, but nonvariable costs can also be direct costs if they can be traced directly to a project, organizational unit, or activity.

Indirect costs When a cost cannot be traced directly to a single product, project, organizational unit, or activity, it is classified as an indirect cost. The rental cost of a factory building making more than one product is an indirect cost with respect to each product. There is no feasible way to associate specifically an indirect cost with an individual unit or batch of products.

Indirect costs are included in *overhead cost*, or *burden*. To account for the full cost of manufacturing products, some portion of the overhead cost must be associated with each unit of product. The methods by which overhead costs are associated with products or services comprise the essence of most cost accounting systems.

Accounting for Direct Costs

A simplified cost flow chart for a manufacturing company is shown in **Exhibit 1**. Resources are acquired for cash or on credit and are classified as materials, payroll, or overhead. Payroll, which is classified as indirect cost, becomes part of overhead. In the production process, material, labor, and overhead cost become the cost of work-in-process inventory. When completed, work in process becomes finished goods and, later, cost of goods sold.

It is easy to understand the accounting for direct costs such as material and productive labor. As material is converted to product by the effort of production labor, the costs of material used and labor can be associated with products. As products are completed and transferred to finished goods and cost of goods sold, these direct costs are transferred with them. All the cost accountant has to do is keep track of how much material and labor cost is used in producing each unit of product. (Actually, this is a little more complicated than it may sound here, but this brief description captures the essence of the accounting process for these direct costs.)

Accounting for Indirect Costs

Accounting for indirect costs is more complicated than accounting for direct costs. Costs must be collected and associated with activities before they can be assigned to products. The relationship between expenditures or costs and products or services is often far from obvious. Assignment to activities is often based on arbitrary decisions about the possible relationships between the reason for an expenditure and an activity. For example, rent for a building that houses both manufacturing and sales activities might be assigned to each activity in the same ratio as the floor space occupied by each. Then, the manufacturing rent cost may be assigned to products manufactured using a measure of volume or some other measure of effort or activity.

Almost all cost accounting systems use a two-stage procedure for assigning indirect costs to products or other *cost objects*. First, costs are assigned to cost centers, or *cost pools*. Second, costs are assigned from each pool to products using *cost drivers*. The concept of a cost driver is based on the idea that products drive the consumption of resources.

The first question that the cost accounting system designer has to answer concerns how many cost centers to use. Using more cost centers than necessary adds complexity and cost to the cost accounting process itself. But using too few cost pools can create a risk that assigned costs will have little relationship to the activities and products that caused the cost to be incurred and resources to be consumed. In a manufacturing plant, the number of cost pools needed may be as small as one if machines, labor, and products are homogenous, or the number needed may be much larger if there is greater diversity in activities or products. In some manufacturing plants, each department, or even each machine, may be treated as a separate cost center.

The second set of questions the cost accounting system designer has to answer concerns how to assign costs to each cost center or cost pool. Expenditures for indirect costs may be assigned based on direct labor cost, floor space, head counts, or direct costs. More complex systems will attempt to implement as much direct charging to each cost pool as possible by using actual measures of the resources used by each cost center.

The third set of questions the cost accounting system designer has to answer concerns how to assign the costs collected for each cost center to the products that are manufactured by or pass through that center. Often the costs are assigned in proportion to the use of a resource that is easily measured. Each unit product may be assigned the same proportion of indirect cost as it consumes labor time, labor cost, machine time, or material cost, for example.

Given the number and complexity of choices facing the cost accounting system designer and the fact that there are no constraining "generally accepted principles of cost accounting," it should be obvious that there is great diversity in the cost accounting systems used by different organizations. A new manager or employee has no choice but to learn about the systems the company uses before using the cost information the system has produced. Every manager has to be continually alert to be sure the cost information available is the right information for the decision or task at hand.

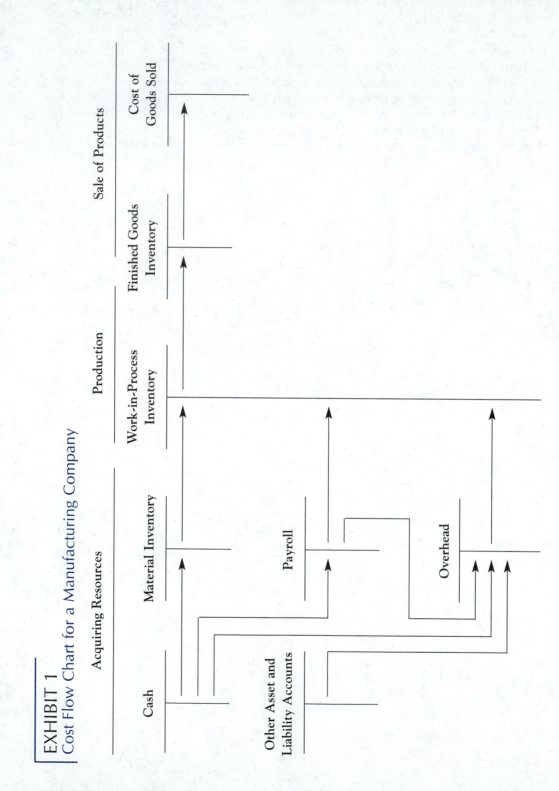

EXHIBIT 1
Cost Flow Chart for a Manufacturing Company

Hilton Manufacturing Company

In February 2004, George Weston was appointed general manager by Paul Hilton, president of Hilton Manufacturing Company. Weston, age 56, had wide executive experience in manufacturing products similar to those of the Hilton Company. The appointment of Weston resulted from management problems arising from the death of Richard Hilton, founder and, until his death in early 2003, president of the company. Paul Hilton had only four years' experience with the company, and in early 2004 was 34 years old. His father had hoped to train Paul over a 10-year period, but the father's untimely death had cut short this seasoning period. The younger Hilton became president after his father's death and had exercised full control until he hired Mr. Weston.

Paul Hilton knew that he had made several poor decisions during 2003 and that the morale of the organization had suffered, apparently through lack of confidence in him. When he received the 2003 income statement (**Exhibit 1**), the loss of almost $200,000 during a good year for the industry convinced him that he needed help. He attracted Weston from a competitor by offering a stock option incentive in addition to salary, knowing that Weston wanted to acquire financial security for his retirement. The two men came to a clear understanding that Weston, as general manager, had full authority to execute any changes he desired. In addition, Weston would explain the reasons for his decisions to Mr. Hilton and thereby train him for successful leadership upon Weston's retirement.

Hilton Manufacturing Company made only three industrial products, 101, 102, and 103, in its single plant. These were sold by the company sales force for use in the processes of other manufacturers. All of the sales force, on a salary basis, sold the three products but in varying proportions. Hilton sold throughout New England, where it was one of eight companies with similar products. Several of its competitors were larger and manufactured a larger variety of products. The dominant company was Catalyst Company, which operated a plant in Hilton's market area. Customarily, Catalyst announced prices, and the other producers followed suit.

Price cutting was rare; the only variance from quoted selling prices took the form of cash discounts. In the past, attempts at price cutting had followed a consistent pattern; all competitors met the price reduction, and the industry as a whole sold about the same quantity but at the lower prices. This continued until Catalyst, with its strong financial position, again stabilized the situation following a general recognition of the failure of price cutting. Furthermore, because sales were to industrial buyers and the products of different manufacturers were similar, Hilton was convinced it could not unilaterally raise prices without suffering volume declines.

During 2003, Hilton's share of industry sales was 12 percent for type 101, 8 percent for 102, and 10 percent for 103. The industrywide quoted selling prices were $9.41, $9.91, and $10.56, respectively.

Weston, upon taking office in February 2004, decided against immediate major changes. Rather, he chose to analyze 2003 operations and to wait for results of the first half of 2004. He instructed the accounting department to provide detailed expenses and earnings statements by products for 2003 (See **Exhibit 2**). In addition, he requested an explanation of the nature of the costs including their expected future behavior (see **Exhibit 3**).

To familiarize Paul Hilton with his methods, Weston sent copies of these reports to Hilton, and they discussed them. Hilton stated that he thought product 103 should be dropped immediately as it would be impossible to lower expenses on product 103 as much as 83 cents per hundredweight (cwt.). In addition, he stressed the need for economies on product 102.

Weston relied on the authority arrangement Hilton had agreed to earlier and continued production of the three products. For control purposes, he had the accounting department prepare monthly statements using as standard costs the actual costs per cwt. from the 2003 profit and loss statement (**Exhibit 2**). These monthly statements were his basis for making minor marketing and production changes during the spring of 2004. Late in July 2004, Weston received from the accounting department the six months' statement of cumulative standard costs including variances of actual costs from standard (see **Exhibit 4**). They showed that the first half of 2004 was a successful period.

During the latter half of 2004, the sales of the entire industry weakened. Even though Hilton retained its share of the market, its profit for the last six months would be small. For January 2005, Catalyst announced a price reduction on product 101 from $9.41 to $8.64 per cwt. This created an immediate pricing problem for its competitors. Weston forecast that if Hilton Manufacturing Company held to the $9.41 price during the first six months of 2005, its unit sales would be 750,000 cwt. He felt that if Hilton dropped its price to $8.64 per cwt., the six months' volume would be 1,000,000 cwt. Weston knew that competing managements anticipated a further decline in activity. He thought a general decline in prices was quite probable.

The accounting department reported that the standard costs in use would probably apply during the first half of 2005, with two exceptions: materials and supplies would be about 5 percent above standard; and light and heat would increase about 7%.

Weston and Hilton discussed the product 101 pricing problem. Hilton observed that especially with the anticipated increase in materials and supplies costs, a sales price of $8.64 would be below cost. He therefore wanted to hold the price at $9.41, since he felt the company could not be profitable while selling a key product below cost.

QUESTIONS

1. If the company had dropped product 103 as of January 1, 2004, what effect would that action have had on the $158,000 profit for the first six months of 2004?

2. In January 2005, should the company reduce the price of product 101 from $9.41 to $8.64?

3. What is Hilton's most profitable product?

4. What appears to have caused the return to profitable operations in the first six months of 2004?

EXHIBIT 1
Hilton Manufacturing Company, Income Statement for Year Ending December 31, 2003.

Gross Sales		$40,690,234
Cash discount		622,482
Net sales		40,067,752
Cost of sales		25,002,386
Gross margin		15,065,366
Less: Selling expense	$7,058,834	
General administration	2,504,597	
Depreciation	5,216,410	
Operating income		285,525
Other income		78,113
Income before interest		363,638
Less: interest expense		555,719
Income (loss)		$ (192,081)

EXHIBIT 2
Hilton Manufacturing Company, Analysis of Profit and Loss by Product, Year Ended December 31, 2003

| | Product 101 | | Product 102 | | Product 103 | | Total |
	Thousands	$ per Cwt.	Thousands	$ per Cwt.	Thousands	$ per Cwt.	Thousands
Rent	721	0.3383	603	0.5856	718	0.7273	2,042
Property taxes	240	0.1125	192	0.1862	153	0.1555	585
Property insurance	201	0.0941	153	0.1486	202	0.2047	556
Compensation insurance	317	0.1486	167	0.1620	172	0.1747	656
Direct labor	4,964	2.3282	2,341	2.2740	2,640	2.6746	9,945
Indirect labor	1,693	0.7941	814	0.7903	883	0.8947	3,390
Power	86	0.0403	96	0.0929	116	0.1171	298
Light and heat	57	0.0269	49	0.0472	39	0.0392	145
Building service	38	0.0180	30	0.0288	28	0.0288	96
Materials	2,935	1.3766	1,809	1.7572	1,862	1.8862	6,606
Supplies	201	0.0941	183	0.1774	135	0.1363	519
Repairs	68	0.0319	57	0.0557	39	0.0396	164
Total	11,522	5.4036	6,493	6.3059	6,986	7.0787	25,002
Selling expense	3,496	1.6397	1,758	1.7069	1,805	1.8286	7,059
General administration	1,324	0.6209	499	0.4850	681	0.6904	2,505
Depreciation	2,169	1.0172	1,643	1.5955	1,404	1.4223	5,216
Interest	201	0.0941	153	0.1490	202	0.2043	556
Total cost	18,711	8.7755	10,546	10.2423	11,078	11.2243	40,338
Less other income	39	0.0184	20	0.0192	19	0.0192	78
Sales (net)	18,672	8.7571	10,526	10.2231	11,059	11.2051	40,260
Profit (loss)	19,847	9.3084	9,977	9.6900	10,243	10.3784	40,068
	1,175	0.5513	(549)	(0.5331)	(816)	(0.8267)	(192)
Unit sales (cwt.)	2,132,191		1,029,654		986,974		
Quoted selling price	$9.41		$9.91		$10.56		
Cash discounts taken, percent of selling price	1.08%		2.22%		1.72%		

Note: Figures may not add exactly because of rounding.

EXHIBIT 3
Accounting Department's Commentary on Costs

Direct Labor: Variable. Nonunion shop at going community rates. No abnormal demands foreseen. It may be assumed that direct labor dollars is an adequate measure of capacity utilization.

Compensation insurance: Variable. Five percent of direct and indirect labor is an adequate estimate.

Materials: Variable. **Exhibit 2** figures are accurate. Includes waste allowances.

Power: Variable. Rates are fixed.

Supplies: Variable. **Exhibit 2** figures are accurate.

Repairs: Variable. Varies as volume changes within normal operating range. Lower and upper limits are fixed.

General administrative, selling expense, indirect labor, interest: Almost nonvariable. Can be changed by management decision.

Cash discount: Almost nonvariable. Average cash discounts taken are consistent from year to year. Percentages in **Exhibit 2** are accurate.

Light *and heat:* Almost nonvariable. Heat varies only with fuel cost changes. Light is a fixed item regardless of level of production.

Property taxes: Almost nonvariable. Under the lease terms, Hilton Manufacturing Company pays the taxes; assessed valuation has been constant, the rate has risen slowly. Any change in the near future will be small and independent of production volume.

Rent: Nonvariable. Lease has 12 years to run.

Building service: Nonvariable. At normal business level, variances are small.

Property insurance: Nonvariable. Three-year policy with fixed premium.

Depreciation: Nonvariable. Fixed dollar total.

EXHIBIT 4
Hilton Manufacturing Company, Profit and Loss by Product, at Standard, Showing Variations from January 1 to June 30, 2004.

	Product 101		Product 102		Product 103		Total Standard (thousands)	Total Actual (thousands)	Variance
	Standard per Cwt.	Total at Standard	Standard per Cwt.	Total at Standard	Standard per Cwt.	Total at Standard			
Rent	0.3383	337	0.5856	417	0.7273	365	1,119	1,021	+ 98
Property taxes	0.1125	112	0.1862	133	0.1555	78	323	307	+ 16
Property insurance	0.0941	94	0.1486	106	0.2047	103	302	278	+ 24
Compensation insurance	0.1486	148	0.1620	115	0.1747	88	351	348	+ 3
Direct labor	2.3282	2,321	2.2740	1,619	2.6746	1,341	5,281	5,308	− 27
Indirect labor	0.7941	792	0.7903	563	0.8947	448	1,803	1,721	+ 82
Power	0.0403	40	0.0929	66	0.1171	59	165	170	− 5
Light and heat	0.0269	27	0.0472	34	0.0392	20	80	83	− 3
Building service	0.0180	18	0.0288	21	0.0288	14	53	50	+ 3
Materials	1.3766	1,372	1.7572	1,251	1.8862	946	3,569	3,544	+ 25
Supplies	0.0941	94	0.1774	126	0.1363	68	288	288	—
Repairs	0.0319	32	0.0557	40	0.0396	20	91	88	+ 3
Total production cost	5.4036	5,387	6.3059	4,490	7.0787	3,548	13,425	13,206	+219
Selling expense	1.6397	1,635	1.7069	1,215	1.8286	917	3,767	3,706	+ 62
General administration	0.6209	619	0.4850	345	0.6904	346	1,310	1,378	− 68
Depreciation	1.0172	1,014	1.5955	1,136	1.4223	713	2,863	2,686	+177
Interest	0.0941	94	0.1490	106	0.2043	102	302	290	+ 12
Total cost	8.7755	8,748	10.2423	7,294	11.2243	5,626	21,668	21,266	+402
Less other income	0.0184	18	0.0192	14	0.0192	10	42	42	—
	8.7571	8,730	10.2231	7,280	11.2051	5,617	21,626	21,224	+402
Actual sales (net)	9.3084	9,279	9.6900	6,900	10.3784	5,202	21,382	21,382	—
Profit or loss	0.5513	550	(0.5331)	(380)	(0.8267)	(414)	(244)	158	+402
Unit Sales (cwt.)	996,859		712,102		501,276				

X = Fixed cost
— = Related cost

Note: Figures may not add exactly because of rounding.

Product Costing and an Introduction to Cost Management

Accounting for Indirect Costs

Activity Accounting—Another Way to Measure Costs

Standard Costs and Variance Analysis

Accounting for Indirect Costs

W hen resources are used in the process of creating a product or service, but a causal linkage between the use of resources and the product or service cannot be established, *indirect costs* are incurred. Indirect costs are not assigned directly to a cost object.

The goal in accounting for indirect costs is to select cost centers and bases of allocation that will relate resource consumption to products or services accurately. Achieving this goal is usually impossible. A more practical objective is to try to measure costs well enough that the information produced is good enough to improve the quality of decisions about pricing, product design, and product mix and to reduce the possibility of mistakes or errors.

In most cost accounting systems, indirect costs are budgeted in advance, and predetermined overhead allocation rates are calculated. Then, as production takes place, indirect costs are applied to (or absorbed into) cost objects. Determining a predetermined overhead rate involves selecting the *cost centers* (or *cost pools*) into which costs will be placed, estimating the total cost to be incurred in each cost center, and choosing cost drivers to allocate resource costs to cost objects.

Predetermined overhead rates are usually used, rather than actual overhead rates, for three reasons:

1. Predetermined overhead rates permit indirect costs to be applied to cost objects at the same time direct costs are applied, rather than waiting for the end of the accounting period;

2. Predetermined overhead rates provide anticipated product or service cost information that can be used in pricing or product-line decisions; and

3. Predetermined overhead rates reduce the amount of effort required to maintain the system because the overhead rates do not have to be recalculated each period.

Professor William J. Bruns, Jr., wrote this case as the basis for class discussion rather than to illustrate either effective or ineffective handling of an administrative situation.

THE ALLOCATION PROCESS

Even though overhead rates are almost always predetermined, it is easier to think about the process of allocating indirect costs to cost objects as if allocations were done during or after the production process has taken place. After production has taken place, there is no uncertainty about what resources were consumed and what was produced.

The production process, whether for products or services, consumes resources. To obtain or replenish those resources, cash must be expended. For example, supervisors of direct labor must be paid, along with landlords, insurance agents, and building service suppliers. The first step in allocating indirect costs is to assign these expenditures to cost centers. Some cost centers may not be directly involved in the process of production, but they provide services to production cost centers. The costs of these *service centers* need to be allocated to production cost centers so that they can be allocated to products. For example, the costs of a payroll department in a manufacturing plant might be allocated among the production cost centers served by the payroll department. Any costs of service centers not allocated to production cost centers will be treated as period costs, which may cause the measured full cost of cost objects produced to be understated.

Many different allocation bases are used to allocate different costs to cost centers. Some commonly used bases include payroll, number of employees in the cost center, space occupied or used by the cost center, value of materials processed in the cost center, the number of transactions within the cost center or with other cost centers, and the overall level of activity with the cost center.

Once all indirect costs are assigned to production cost centers, cost drivers need to be identified to assign the costs to products or services. Ideally, the cost drivers selected should allocate a fair share of the indirect cost to each unit. If all units of products or services are homogeneous, then a cost driver related to volume is usually appropriate. However, when a variety of products or services is produced, cost drivers such as labor hours, machine hours, number of setups, or transactions are often used. **Exhibit 1** is a schematic diagram for a cost accounting system for a manufacturing plant with a rented building, depreciation for building fixtures and three productive machines, and supervision.

Since overhead allocation rates are predetermined, the amount of indirect costs actually applied to products or services will almost never be equal to the expenditures on resources consumed. The difference between the actual indirect costs and those assigned to products or service arises because of a failure to predict indirect cost expenditures and activity levels perfectly, and is usually called an *overhead variance*. If small, overhead variances are usually charged as period costs. If large, further cost analysis may be justified, and the entire process of allocating indirect costs may be repeated after the fact to allow managers to figure out what is really going on as they create products or services.

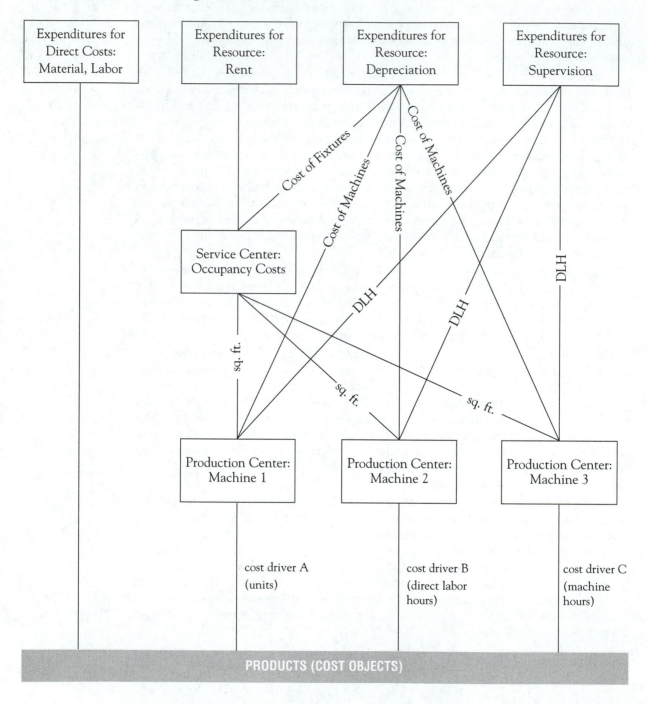

Seligram, Inc.: Electronic Testing Operations

We put in a piece of automated equipment a year ago that only fits the requirements of one customer. This equipment reduced the direct labor required to test his components and, because of our labor-based burden allocation system, substantially reduced his costs. But putting a $40,000 machine into the general burden pool raised the costs to our other customers. It just doesn't make sense shooting yourself in the foot at the same time you are lowering the company's cost of operations.

Paul Carte, Manager

INTRODUCTION

Electronic Testing Operations (ETO), a division of Seligram, Inc., provided centralized testing for electronic components such as integrated circuits. ETO was created as a result of a decision in 1979 to consolidate electronic testing from 11 different divisions of Seligram. ETO commenced services to these divisions in 1983. It was estimated that centralization would save Seligram in excess of $20 million in testing equipment investment over the next five years.

ETO operated as a cost center and transferred products to other divisions at full cost (direct costs plus allocated burden). Although ETO was a captive division, other divisions within Seligram were allowed to use outside testing services if ETO could not meet their cost or service requirements. ETO was permitted to devote up to 10% of its testing capacity to outside customers but chose to work mainly with other Seligram divisions due to limited marketing resources.

ETO employed approximately 60 hourly personnel and 40 administrative and technical staff members. Budgeted expenses were $7.9 million in 1988 (see **Exhibit 1**).

This case was prepared by Professor Peter B. B. Turney, Portland State University and Christopher Ittner, Doctoral Student, under the supervision of Professor Robin Cooper as the basis for class discussion rather than to illustrate either effective or ineffective handling of an administrative situation.

Testing Procedures

ETO expected to test between 35 and 40 million components in 1988. These components included integrated circuits (I.C.s), diodes, transistors, capacitors, resistors, transformers, relays, and crystals. Component testing was required for two reasons. First, if defective components were not caught early in the manufacturing cycle, the cost of repair could exceed the manufacturing cost of the product itself. Studies indicated that a defective resistor caught before use in the manufacturing process cost two cents. If the resistor was not caught until the end product was in the field, however, the cost of repair could run into the thousands of dollars. Second, a large proportion of Seligram's work was defense related. Military specifications frequently required extensive testing of components utilized in aerospace and naval products. By 1988, ETO had the ability to test 6,500 different components. Typically, however, the division would test about 500 different components each month and between 3,000 and 3,500 per year. Components were received from customers in lots; in 1988, ETO would receive approximately 12,000 lots of components.

ETO performed both electrical and mechanical testing (see **Exhibit 2**). Electrical testing involved measuring the electrical characteristics of the components and comparing these measurements with the components' specifications. For example, the specifications for an amplifier may have called for a 1-volt input to be amplified into a 10-volt output. ETO would deliver a 1-volt input to the component. By measuring the amplifier's output, ETO gauged its conformance with specifications.

Mechanical testing included solderability, component burn-in, thermal shock, lead straightening, and leak detection. Solderability involved the inspection of components to see if they held solder. Burn-in was the extended powering of components at high temperature. Thermal shock involved the cycling of components between high and low temperatures. Lead straightening was the detection and correction of bent leads on components such as axial components. Leak detection examined hermetically sealed I.C.s for leaks.

Components varied significantly in the number and type of electrical and mechanical testing procedures they required. This variation resulted in about 200 different standard process flows for the division. Process flows were determined by the different combinations of tests and specifications requested by the customer. Based on these combinations, ETO planners determined the routing of components between testing equipment and the type of tests to be performed at each station. I.C.s, for example, could follow six different flows through the facility. While some I.C.s only required electrical testing at room temperature (solderability and leak detection, for instance), others also required thermal shock and burn-in.

Each type of component required separate software development, and custom tools and fixtures were often required. Software, tools, and fixtures were developed by the engineering group, which was made up of specialists in software development, equipment maintenance, calibration and repair, tooling and fixturing, and testing equipment operation. Software engineers developed programs for specific applications. The programs were then retained in a software library for future use. ETO had 6,500 different software programs on file, of which 1,300 were programs developed in the past year. ETO also had an inventory of 1,500 tools and fixtures, of which 300 had been developed in the past year. The large number of tools and fixtures allowed the testing of components with a wide variety of leads, pin combinations, and mating configurations.

The testing facility was divided into two rooms. The main testing room contained the equipment used for electrical testing. The mechanical room contained the equipment used for mechanical testing, plus incoming receiving and the stockroom. A total of 20 people worked in the two rooms on each of two main shifts, and 10 people worked on the night shift.

Cost Accounting System

The cost accounting system measured two components of cost: direct labor and burden. Burden was grouped into a single cost pool that included burden costs associated with each of the testing rooms as well as the engineering burden costs relating to software and tooling development and the administrative costs of the division. Total burden costs were divided by the sum of testing and engineering labor dollars to arrive at a burden rate per direct labor dollar. The division costed each lot of components. Burden was calculated for each lot by multiplying the actual direct labor dollars associated with the lot by the 145% of burden rate. The resulting burden was then added to the actual direct labor costs to determine the lot's total cost. In 1988, the facilitywide burden rate was 145% of each direct labor dollar, of which more than 40% was attributable to equipment depreciation (see **Exhibit 3**).

Signs of Obsolescence

Several trends pointed to the obsolescence of the labor-based burden allocation process. Since the founding of the division in 1983, direct labor hours per lot tested had been steadily declining (see **Exhibit 4**). This trend was aggravated by an increased dependence on vendor certification. Vendor certification was a key component of Just-in-Time (JIT) delivery. With vendor certification, Seligram's suppliers did the primary testing of components. ETO then utilized statistical sampling to verify that the supplier's production process was still in control. Thus, whereas JIT led to an increased number of smaller lots being received by ETO, vendor certification reduced the number of tests performed. Early indications were that JIT deliveries would account for 30% of Seligram's shipments within the next five years.

In addition to declining direct labor content and fewer test lots, the obsolescence of the labor-based allocation system was intensified by a shift from simple inspection services to broader-based test technology. On complex parts requiring screening, environmental conditioning, and testing, the division was consistently cheaper than outside services. Where only elementary testing was required, however, low-technology outside laboratories were often cheaper, especially on large lots. The advantage that the division brought customers over the outside labs was that the latter provided essentially no engineering support, whereas ETO with its resident engineering resources was able to support such service on a rapid and cost-effective basis. The shift to more technically sophisticated services prompted a shift in the labor mix from direct to indirect personnel. The division expected to see a crossover between engineering head count and hourly head count early in the 1990s.

Finally, the introduction of high-technology components created the need for more automatic testing, longer test cycles, and more data per part. Digital components, for example, were currently tested for up to 100 conditions (combinations of electrical input and output states). The new generation of digital components, on the other hand, would be much more complex and require verification of up to 10,000 conditions. These components would require very expensive highly automated equipment. This increase in automation would, in turn, lead to a smaller base of direct labor to absorb the depreciation costs of this new equipment.

There were fears that the resulting increase in burden rates would drive some customers away. ETO had already noticed an increase in the number and frequency of complaints from customers regarding the rates they were charged for testing.

The division's accounting manager proposed a new cost accounting system to alleviate the problem. Under this new system, burden would be directly traced to two cost pools. The first pool would contain burden related to the administrative and technical functions (division management, engineering, planning, and administrative personnel). This pool would be charged on a rate per direct labor dollar. The second pool would include all other burden costs and would be charged based on machine hours. **Exhibit 5** provides the proposed burden rates.

Shortly after the accounting manager submitted his proposal, a consultant hired by Seligram's corporate management prepared an assessment of ETO's cost system. He recommended the implementation of a three-burden-pool system utilizing separate burden centers for each test room and a common technical and administrative pool. Burden would be directly traced to each of the three burden pools. Like the accounting manager's system, burden costs in the test rooms would then be allocated on a machine-hour basis. Technical and administrative costs would continue to be charged on a rate per direct labor dollar.

To examine the impact of the two alternative systems, ETO management asked that a study be conducted on a representative sample of parts. **Exhibit 6** provides a breakout of actual direct labor and machine-hour requirements per lot for the five components selected for the study.

Technological Future

In 1988, the division faced major changes in the technology of testing that required important equipment acquisition decisions. The existing testing equipment was getting old and would not be able to keep pace with developments in component technology. Existing components, for example, had between 16 and 40 input/output terminations (e.g., pins or other mating configurations), and ETO's equipment could handle up to 120 terminations. Although the 120-termination limit had only been reached a couple of times in the past few years, a new generation of components with up to 256 terminations was already being developed. Similarly, the upper limit of frequency on existing components was 20 MHz (million cycles per second), whereas the frequency on the next generation of components was expected to be 50 MHz.

The equipment required to test the next generation of components would be expensive. Each machine cost approximately $2 million. Testing on this equipment would be more automated than existing equipment, with longer test cycles and the generation of more test data per part. It was also likely that lot sizes would be larger. The new equipment would not replace the existing equipment but would merely add capabilities ETO did not currently possess. Additionally, the new equipment would only be needed to service the requirements of one or two customers in the foreseeable future. **Exhibit 7** provides a summary of the new equipment's economics and operating characteristics.

The impact of this new equipment would be an acceleration in the decline in direct labor hours per lot of components. At the same time, burden would increase with the additional depreciation and engineering costs associated with the new equipment. This would result in a large increase in the burden rate per direct labor dollar. As Paul Carte, manager of ETO, saw it, the acquisition of the new equipment could have a disastrous effect on the division's pricing structure if the labor-based allocation system remained in use:

> We plan on investing $2 million on a large electronic testing machine to test the chips of one or two customers. This machine will be very fast and will require little direct labor. Its acquisition will have a significant effect on our per direct labor dollar burden rate, which will result in an increase in charges to our other customers. It is clear that a number of customers will walk away if we try to pass this increase on. I am afraid that we will lose 25% of our customer base if we don't change our cost system.

EXHIBIT 1
Seligram Inc.: Electronic Testing Operations

1988 BUDGETED EXPENSES

Direct Labor		$3,260,015
Overhead		
Indirect Labor	859,242	
Salary Expense	394,211	
Supplies & Expenses	538,029	
Services[1]	245,226	
Personnel Allocations[2]	229,140	
Service Allocations[3]	2,448,134	
Total Overhead		$4,713,982
Total Budgeted Expenses		$7,973,997

[1] Includes tool repair, computer expenses, maintenance stores, and service cost transfers from other divisions.

[2] Includes indirect and salaried employee fringe benefits, personnel department, security, stores/warehousing, and holidays/vacations.

[3] Includes building occupancy, telephones, depreciation, information systems, and data control.

EXHIBIT 2
Seligram, Inc.: Electronic Testing Operations

TESTING CAPABILITIES

Internal Visual

Hermeticity Check

Wire Pull

Temperature Cycling

Solderability

Burn-In

EXHIBIT 3
Seligram, Inc.: Electronic Testing Operations

CALCULATION OF BURDEN RATE
Based on 1988 Plan

BURDEN RATE $\quad = \quad \dfrac{\text{TOTAL BURDEN \$}^4}{\text{DIRECT LABOR \$}}$

$\quad\quad\quad\quad\quad = \quad \dfrac{\$4,713,982}{\$3,260,015}$

$\quad\quad\quad\quad\quad = \quad 144.6\%$

EFFECTIVE RATE $\quad = \quad 145\%$

---

[4] Cost Breakdown:

	Variable	Fixed Depreciation	Other	Total
Total Burden	$1,426,317	$1,288,000	$1,999,665	$4,713,982

EXHIBIT 4
Seligram, Inc.: Electronic Testing Operations

D.L. HRS. PER LOT CHART

EXHIBIT 5
Seligram, Inc.: Electronic Testing Operations

PROPOSED BURDEN RATES
Based on 1988 Plan

Machine-Hour Rate	MACHINE HRS.	BURDEN $[5]
Main Test Room	33,201	$2,103,116
Mechanical Test Room	17,103	1,926,263
Total	50,304	$4,029,379

$$\text{Machine-Hour Rate} \quad \frac{\text{Test Room Burden \$}}{\text{Machine Hrs.}} = \frac{\$4,029,379}{50,304} = \$80.10$$

Effective Machine-Hour Rate = $80.00

Direct Labor Hour Rate

Total Engineering & Administrative Burden $ = $684,603
Total Direct Labor Dollars = $3,260,015[6]

$$\text{Burden Rate} = \frac{\text{Engr. \& Admin. Burden \$}}{\text{Direct Lbr \$}} = \frac{\$684,603}{\$3,260,015} = 21\%$$

Effective Burden Rate Per Direct Labor $ = 20%

[5] Cost Breakdown

| | | FIXED | | |
	VARIABLE	DEPRECIATION	OTHER	TOTAL
Main Test Room	$ 887,379	$ 88,779	$1,126,958	$2,103,116
Mechanical Test Room	443,833	808,103	674,327	1,926,263
Test Room Burden	$1,331,212	$ 896,882	$1,801,285	$4,029,379
Engineering & Admn.	$ 95,105	$ 391,118	$ 198,380	$ 684,603
Total Burden	$1,426,317	$1,288,000	$1,999,665	$4,713,982

[6] Includes all direct labor costs, including direct labor costs incurred in both test rooms as well as in engineering.

EXHIBIT 6
Seligram, Inc.: Electronic Testing Operations

Direct Labor and Machine-Hour Requirements
Actuals For One Lot

| PRODUCT | DIRECT LABOR $ | MACHINE HOURS | | TOTAL |
		MAIN ROOM	MECH. ROOM	
ICA	$ 917	8.5	10.0	18.5
ICB	2051	14.0	26.0	40.0
CAPACITOR	1094	3.0	4.5	7.5
AMPLIFIER	525	4.0	1.0	5.0
DIODE	519	7.0	5.0	12.0

EXHIBIT 7
Seligram, Inc.: Electronic Testing Operations

New Testing Equipment Economics and
Operating Characteristics

Cost:	$2 Million
Useful Life:	8 Years
Depreciation Method:	Double Declining Balance (First Year Depreciation Costs of $500,000)
Location:	Main Test Room
Utilization:	10% first year, rising to 60% by third year and in all subsequent years, based on 4,000 hours per year availability (2 shifts × 2,000-hour year)
Direct Labor Requirements:	Approximately five minutes per hour of operation; average labor rate of $30 per hour
Engineering Requirements:	$75,000 in installation and programming costs in first year
Estimated overhead (nonengineering depreciation)	$250,000 ($100,000 variable, $150,000 fixed)

Activity Accounting—Another Way to Measure Costs

Traditional cost accounting systems operate on the assumption that producing products and services is what causes costs to occur. For this reason, direct material, direct labor, and other direct costs are assigned to products, and all other costs are grouped as indirect and then allocated among the products that are produced, usually based on some measure of product volume. There is an implicit assumption that the indirect costs that must be allocated are necessary, or they would not have been incurred. Because the costs are necessary, each unit of product or service must bear its fair share of these costs.

These traditional assumptions work fairly well in situations where managers have successfully attained efficiency in organizational tasks related to a single product, homogeneous products, or services, or if indirect costs are small relative to direct materials and direct labor. In these situations, the assumption that costs should be allocated based on the volume of direct material, direct labor hours, direct labor dollars, units of product, or some other volume measure creates few significant problems. Because of the homogeneity of products or services, each unit of product or service gets what might be called its fair share of indirect costs. But in actuality, few manufacturing plants or organizations are as simple or homogeneous as the assumption demands. As product mix and product diversity increase, allocating indirect costs by volume alone may introduce distortions that allow high-volume products to subsidize low-volume products because the high-volume products carry more than their fair share of the actual indirect costs that are incurred.

In the last twenty years, increased attention has been given to another kind of cost accounting system. These *activity-based costs (ABC) systems* are built on the assumption that activities cause costs, and that products or services and customers are the reasons that activities must be performed. Therefore, for example, if a customer's special order requires us to order material, receive it, take it to the production line, prepare a check to pay the supplier, and prepare new product specifications for that special order, each of these activities and the cost of performing them should be measured and assigned to the units produced. The cost of the special order can be compared with the revenue generated to assess the profitability of the customer's

Professor William J. Bruns, Jr. prepared this note as the basis for class discussion.

order. *An ABC system attempts to trace the cost of each activity as closely as possible to the reason why organizational resources were consumed in support of the necessary activities.*

This approach, which is also called transaction-based costing, or activity accounting, focuses on what an organization does, the way time is spent, and the outputs of those processes. To do this requires at least four steps:

1. Identify activities;
2. Trace the costs of resources to the activities performed;
3. Identify activity measures (outputs) by which the costs of a process vary most directly; and
4. Trace activity costs to cost objects such as products, processes, and customers based on the usage of activities.

By this method, the cost of support departments, which might otherwise be simply accumulated as indirect costs and assigned based on volume in a traditional cost accounting system, are assigned to activities performed, such as setting up machines, receiving and handling material, and shipping finished products. Then, the expenses of each activity are assigned to products or customers based on their demand for the activities, such as the number of setups, the number of inbound material shipments, or the number of separate shipments to the customer.

ABC systems are similar to more traditional cost systems in that they capture costs, assign them to cost centers (activity centers), and then assign those costs to products based on the demand that the product or customer places on the activity itself. Some activities, such as machine setup, will occur each time a production run is initiated. Other activities, such as product engineering, may have nothing to do with how many units or batches of the products are produced.

ABC systems differ from more traditional volume-based systems because they focus on what causes a cost to occur rather than on simply allocating what has been spent. In many respects, you can think of ABC systems as abandoning the traditional ideas that a cost can be variable or fixed. Resources are consumed because something (activities) made a demand on them. The ABC system seeks to understand what that something (activities) is and to associate the costs of the resources consumed with whatever made the demand. The system creates the mechanism for tracing resource consumption to whatever caused spending to acquire the resource.

Proponents of introducing and using ABC systems usually concede that such systems are more complex and more costly than the traditional cost systems that they replace. However, they also feel that three benefits of using ABC systems outweigh the costs of designing, installing, and using such systems.

First, ABC systems produce more accurate product costs, particularly in circumstances where indirect costs are important in the total cost structure of the organization and where there is great diversity in products or services, the processes of producing them, or customers. With more accurate costs, the risk of poor decisions is reduced, and the revelation of competitive opportunity is likely to be more complete.

Second, focusing on the consumption of resources rather than merely allocating costs to product or services raises questions about why resources are being consumed in the way that they are. For example, if the cost of processing orders is high because each order has a special characteristic, the savings possible by producing a standard line can easily be uncovered with an ABC system. In addition, focusing on resources used can direct attention to reducing the cost (increasing the efficiency) of activities and business processes.

Third, the need for special cost analyses when confronted with usual situations is frequently reduced with more accurate cost information and management's improved understanding of what causes costs to be incurred.

You should be aware, however, that each ABC system will differ from others because every system must be closely tied to the technology and economic characteristics of the organization it supports. Although only a relatively small proportion of companies are using activity accounting systems to date, it is expected that many more will be experimenting with them in the future. Organizations that have developed and used such systems express enthusiasm for them, and managers agree that ABC developments have been one of the most exciting events in the development of cost accounting.

Destin Brass Products Co.

Every month it becomes clearer to me that our competitors either know something that we do not know, or they are crazy. I realize that pumps are a major product in a big market for all of us, but with the price cutting that is going on, it is likely that no one will be able to sell pumps profitably if they keep forcing us to match their lower prices. I guess we should be grateful that competitors seem to be overlooking the opportunities for profit in flow controllers. Even with the 12 1/2% price increase we made there, our sales representatives report no new competition.

Are the cost

Roland Guidry, president of Destin Brass Products, was discussing product profitability in the latest month with Peggy Alford, his controller, and John Scott, his manufacturing manager. The meeting among the three was taking place in an atmosphere tinged with apprehension because competitors had been reducing prices on pumps, Destin Brass Product's major product line. With no unique design advantage, managers at Destin had seen no alternative except to match the reduced prices while trying to maintain volumes. Moreover, the company's profits in the latest month had slipped again to be lower than those in the prior month.

The purpose of the meeting was to try to understand the competitive trends and to develop new strategies for dealing with them if new strategies were appropriate. The three managers, along with Steve Abbott, sales and marketing manager, who could not attend because he was away, were very concerned because they held significant shares of ownership in Destin Brass Products. Locally, they were a success story; the company had grown to be a significant business in Destin, Florida, better known for its white sand beaches and as "the Luckiest Fishing Village in the World."

THE COMPANY

Destin Brass Products Co. was established by Abbott, Guidry, and Scott, who purchased a moribund commercial machine shop in 1984. Steve Abbott had sensed an opportunity in a conversation with the president of a large manufacturer of water purification equipment who was dissatisfied with the quality of brass valves available.

Professor William J. Bruns, Jr. prepared this case as the basis for class discussion rather than to illustrate either effective or ineffective handling of an administrative situation.

John Scott was a local legend because of the high-quality brass boat fittings he had always manufactured for the fishing fleet along the Florida Gulf Coast. Roland Guidry had recently retired from the United States Air Force, where he had a long record of administrative successes. The three then selected Peggy Alford, an accountant with manufacturing experience, to join them.

John Scott was quick to analyze the nature of problems other manufacturers were having with water purification valves. The tolerances needed were small, and to maintain them required great labor skill or expensive machine controls, or both. Within weeks of forming the company, Scott and his shop crew were manufacturing valves that met or exceeded the needed specifications. Abbott negotiated a contract with the purification equipment manufacturer, and revenues soon were earned.

The company had grown quickly because the demand for water purification equipment increased, and Destin Brass Products became the sole supplier of valves to its customer. However, Abbott and Guidry both had greater ambitions. Knowing that the same manufacturing skills used in machining valves could also be used in manufacturing brass pumps and flow controllers, they created an engineering department and designed new products for those markets. Pumps were known to be an even larger market than valves, and flow controllers were often used in the same fluid distribution systems as valves and pumps. Moreover, by specializing in brass, the company could exploit Scott's special knowledge about working with the material.

Destin did no foundry work. Instead, components were purchased from brass foundries and then were precisely machined and assembled in the company's new modern manufacturing facility. The same equipment and labor were used for all three product lines, and runs were scheduled to match customer shipping requirements. The foundries had agreed to just-in-time deliveries, and products were packed and shipped as completed. Guidry described the factory to his friends as "a very modern job shop in specialized products made from brass."

THE PRODUCTS

Valves (24% of company revenues) were created from four brass components. Scott had designed machines that held each component in jigs while it was machined automatically. Each machinist could operate two machines and assemble the valves as machining was taking place. The expense of precise machining made the cost of Destin's valves too high to compete in the nonspecialized valve market, so all monthly production of valves took place in a single production run, which was immediately shipped to its single customer upon completion. Although Scott felt several competitors could match Destin's quality in valves, none had tried to gain market share by cutting price, and gross margins had been maintained at a standard 35%.

Pumps (55% of revenues) were created by a manufacturing process that was practically the same as that for valves. Five components required machining and assembly. The pumps were then shipped to each of seven industrial product distributors on a monthly basis. To supply the distributors, whose orders were fairly stable as long as Destin would meet competitive prices, the company scheduled five production runs each month.

Pump prices to distributors had been under considerable pressure. The pump market was large, and specifications were less precise than those for valves. Recently, it seemed as if each month brought new reports of reduced prices for pumps. Steve Abbott felt Destin had no choice but to match the lower prices or give up its place as a supplier of pumps. As a result, gross margins on pumps sales in the latest month had fallen to 22%, well below the company's planned gross margin of 35%. Guidry and Alford could not see how the competitors could be making profits at current prices unless pumps were being subsidized by other products.

Flow controllers (21% of revenues) were used to control the rate and direction of flow of liquids. As with pumps, the manufacturing operations required for flow controllers were similar to those for valves. More components were needed for each finished unit, and more labor was required. In recent months, Destin had manufactured 4,000 flow controllers in 10 production runs, and the finished flow controllers had been distributed in 22 shipments to distributors and other customers.

Steve Abbott was trying to understand the market for flow controllers better because it seemed to him that Destin had almost no competition in the flow controller market. He had recently raised flow controller prices by 12 1/2% with no apparent effect on demand.

THE MEETING

After the latest month's results had been summarized and reported, Roland Guidry had called Peggy Alford and John Scott into his office to discuss what changes they could or should make in their course of actions. The meeting had opened with his statement above concerning competition in pumps versus flow controllers. Guidry had a copy of the product profitability analysis (**Exhibit 1**) on his desk.

John Scott (Manufacturing manager): It really is amazing to me as well that our competitors keep reducing prices on pumps. Even though our manufacturing process is better than theirs, I truly do not believe we are less efficient or cost effective. Furthermore, I can't see what their motives can be. There are many manufacturers of pumps. Even if we or even several competitors were to drop out of the market, there would still be so many competitors that no monopoly or oligopoly pricing could be maintained. Maybe the competitors just don't realize what their costs are. Could that be, Peggy?

Peggy Alford (Controller): That does not seem likely to me! Cost accounting is a well-developed art, and most competent managers and cost accountants have some understanding of how product costs can be measured. In manufacturing businesses like ours, material and labor costs are pretty easily related to products produced, whether in the product design stage or after the fact. So, if anything, our competitors must be making some different assumptions about overhead costs or allocating them to products in some other way. Or, as you said Roland, maybe they have stupidly forgotten that in the long run, prices have to be high enough to provide product margins that cover corporate costs and produce return to owners.

Roland Guidry (President): Peggy, I know you have explained to me several times already the choices we could make in allocating overhead to products. In fact, last month you almost sold me on what you called a "modern costing approach," which I rejected because of the work and cost of the changeover. I also was worried about the discontinuity it might cause in our historical data. But I feel that I might need another lesson to help me understand what is happening to us. Could you try once more to explain what we do?

Peggy Alford: I would be happy to try again. We have a very traditional cost accounting system that meets all of our needs for preparing financial reports and tax returns. It is built on measurements of direct and indirect costs and on assumptions about our production and sales activity (**Exhibit 2**). Each unit of product is charged for material cost and labor cost; material cost is based on the prices we pay for components, and labor cost is based on the standard times for run labor times the labor pay rate of $16 per hour. Overhead cost is assigned to products in a two-stage process. First, the overhead costs are assigned to production—in our situation, we have only one producing department so we know all overhead costs are assigned correctly at the first stage. Then, we allocate the total overhead cost assigned to production on the basis of production-run labor cost. Every $1.00 of run labor cost causes $4.39 of overhead to be allocated to the product to which the labor was applied. You can see how this works in our "Standard Unit Costs" sheet, which I brought with me (**Exhibit 3**). This is a fairly inexpensive way to allocate overhead cost because we have to accumulate direct labor cost to prepare factory payroll, and we just use the same measurement in product costing.

Roland Guidry: All this looks familiar to me. But remind me again what the choices we discussed earlier were.

Peggy Alford: Well, one choice advocated by some would be to forego the overhead cost allocation altogether. Overhead costs could be charged each month as period expenses. Product profitability would then be measured at the contribution margin level, or price less all variable costs, which in our situation are direct material costs. We would still have to make some adjustments at the end of any period we held inventory to satisfy reporting and tax return requirements, but the effort to do that would be fairly trivial. The bigger danger would be that we would forget that all overhead costs have to be covered somehow, and we might allow our prices to slip.

John Scott: Yeah, the salesman's mentality in Steve Abbott would make that kind of direct cost accounting dangerous. He would be looking for marginal customers willing to pay marginal prices based on marginal costs. From the outset, we have succeeded in part because we insisted on trying to maintain a 35% gross margin on costs *including* allocated overhead.

Roland Guidry: John, the competitors are real and so are their prices. If we want to stay in pumps, we probably have to meet them head-on. Peggy, please go on.

Peggy Alford: The last time we discussed this, Roland, I showed you these revised standard unit costs (**Exhibit 4**). These are based on a more modern view of the proper way to allocate costs. I put these together in an attempt to allocate better overhead based on activities. First, I identified material related overhead, the cost of receiving and handling material, and allocated that to each product line based on the cost of material. The justification for this change is that material handling does not have any relationship to the labor cost of machining. Second, I took set-up labor cost out of the total overhead and allocated it to each product line. This is a small amount, but the cost of set ups also had no relationship whatever to the total labor cost of a production run. Finally, I substituted machine hours for labor dollars as a basis for allocating the remaining factory overhead. John [Scott] has really done wonders with our machines, but our expenses for machines are probably more than double the cost of labor. Therefore, it seems to me that machine hours better reflect use of an expensive resource and should be used to allocate overhead costs.

   The results of this proposal made sense to me and may contain a clue about why competitors are chasing lower prices in the pump market. The revised standard cost for pumps is more than $4.00 below our present standard and would show a gross margin percentage of 27% compared to our current 22%. Maybe our competitors just have more modern cost accounting!

Roland Guidry: And you said this modern approach would not cost much more to maintain once we adopted it?

Peggy Alford: No, it wouldn't. All I really did was to divide the overhead costs into two pools, each of which is allocated on a different measure of activity.

Roland Guidry: And, we could use the same numbers for financial reports and tax returns?

Peggy Alford: Absolutely.

(John Scott had been examining the revised unit costs and suddenly spoke up.)

John Scott: Peggy! This new method makes valves look more costly and flow controllers even more profitable than we know they are.

Peggy Alford: . . . or, thought they were! The profit for each product line will change if we change the way we allocate overhead costs to products.

John Scott: I realize that. But it seems to me that product costs should have more to do with the costs caused by producing and selling the product. That's usually true for material and maybe direct labor, but it is not true for most of these overhead costs. For example, we probably spend one-half of our engineering effort on flow controllers, but whether you use direct labor dollars or machine hours to allocate engineering costs to products, flow controllers don't get much of the engineering costs.

   I've been thinking about this a lot since last week when I attended an "Excellence in Manufacturing" conference in Tallahassee. One presentation was about "Cost Accounting for the New Manufacturing Environment." I couldn't follow all of the arguments of the speaker, but the key seemed to be that activity, rather than production volume, causes costs. In our operations, it is receiving and handling material, packing and shipping, and engineering orders that cause us to incur costs, not the length of any production run.

If I understood what this speaker was advocating, it was that whenever possible overhead costs that cannot be traced directly to product lines should be allocated on the basis of transactions—since transactions cause costs to be incurred. A product that required three times as many transactions to be incurred than another product would be allocated three times as much of the overhead cost related to those transactions than the other product would be allocated. Or said another way, a product that causes 3% of the total transactions for receiving components would be allocated 3% of the total cost of receiving components. At a basic level, this seems to make sense to me.

Peggy Alford: Recently I've been reading a lot in my professional magazines about this activity-based costing (ABC) . . . .

Roland Guidry: But, to cost products that way has got to be more expensive. It's more complex; also, who keeps count of transactions?

Peggy Alford: It can't be too hard. All overhead allocation is somewhat arbitrary. We could experiment with estimates to see how the product costs might be affected. The product costs for material, direct labor, and set-up labor will be the same as for my revised unit costs, and to allocate other overhead costs, we just need to estimate how many transactions occur in total and are caused by each product.

John Scott: I'd like to ask Peggy to put together an analysis for us. The managers at the conference from companies that have used these transaction-based costing systems really seemed excited about what they said they learned.

Roland Guidry: OK. Peggy, you and John get together this afternoon to put together the activity estimates you need. Get back to me as quickly as you can. Maybe we can figure out why the competitors think they should sell pumps regardless of price.

LATER

After lunch, Peggy Alford and John Scott met in Peggy's office. They discussed transactions and effort related to each type of overhead cost. The result was the overhead cost activity analysis shown in **Exhibit 5.**

REQUIRED

1. Use the Overhead Cost Activity Analysis in **Exhibit 5** and other data on manufacturing costs to estimate product costs for valves, pumps, and flow controllers.

2. Compare the estimated costs you calculate to existing standard unit costs (**Exhibit 3**) and the revised unit costs (**Exhibit 4**). What causes the different product costing methods to produce such different results?

3. What are the strategic implications of your analysis? What actions would you recommend to the managers at Destin Brass Products Co?

4. Assume that interest in a new basis for cost accounting at Destin Brass Products remains high. In the following month, quantities produced and sold, activities, and costs were all at standard. How much higher or lower would the *net income* reported under the activity-transaction-based system be than the *net income* that will be reported under the present, more traditional system? Why?

Gross Margin = Selling $ / Net Income
Net Income / Selling Price

Selling Price
Revised Standard unit + ABC
Net Income

EXHIBIT 1
Product Profitability Analysis

	Valves	Pumps	Flow Controllers
Standard unit costs	$37.56	$63.12	$56.50
Target selling price	$57.78	$97.10	$86.96
Planned gross margin (%)	35%	35%	35%
Last Month			
Actual selling price	$57.78	$81.26	$97.07
Actual gross margin	35%	22%	42%

$1 - (37.56/57.78) = 7$

EXHIBIT 2
Monthly Product and Cost Summary

Product Lines	Valves	Pumps	Flow Controllers	
Monthly production	7,500 units (1 run)	12,500 units (5 runs)	4,000 units (10 runs)	
Monthly shipments	7,500 units (1 shipment)	12,500 units (7 shipments)	4,000 units (22 shipments)	

Manufacturing Costs				Monthly Total
Material	4 components 2 @ $2 = $ 4 2 @ 6 = 12	5 components 3 @ $2 = $ 6 2 @ 7 = 14	10 components 4 @ $1 = $ 4 5 @ 2 = 10 1 @ 8 = 8	
Total material	16	$20	$22	$458,000
Labor ($16 per hour including employee benefits)				
Set-up labor	8 hours per production run	8 hours per production run	12 hours per production run	168 hours
Run labor	.25 hours per unit	.50 hours per unit	.40 hours per unit	9,725 hours
Machine usage	.50 hours per unit	.50 hours per unit	.20 hours per unit	10,800 hours

Manufacturing Overhead

Receiving	$ 20,000
Materials handling	200,000
Engineering	100,000
Packing and shipping	60,000
Maintenance	30,000
Total	$410,000
Machine depreciation (units-of-production method) $25 per hour of use	$270,000

EXHIBIT 3
Standard Unit Costs

direct labor

	Valves	Pumps	Flow Controllers
Material	$16.00	$20.00	$22.00
Direct labor	4.00	8.00	6.40
Overhead @ 439% of direct labor $ $(4.39 \times 4) \rightarrow$	17.56	35.12	28.10
Standard unit cost	$37.56	$63.12	$56.50

Overhead

Machine depreciation	$270,000
Set-up labor	2,688
Receiving	20,000
Materials handling	200,000
Engineering	100,000
Packing and shipping	60,000
Maintenance	30,000
	$682,688

Total run labor = 9,725 hours × $16 = $155,600

↳ *Total Direct labor*

Overhead rate $\dfrac{682,688}{155,600}$ = 439%

The calculations do not accurately reflect the amount of input that each unit Represents

Destin Brass Products Co.   5-27

EXHIBIT 4
Revised Unit Costs   Based on machine hours

	Valves	Pumps	Flow Controllers
Material	$16.00	$20.00	$22.00
Material overhead (48%)	7.68	9.60	10.56
Set-up labor	.02	.05	.48
Direct labor	4.00	8.00	6.40
Other overhead (machine hour basis)	21.30	21.30	8.52
Revised standard cost	$49.00	$58.95	$47.96

Material Related Overhead

Receiving	20,000
Materials handling	200,000
Total	$220,000

Overhead Absorption Rate

$$\frac{\$220,000}{\$458,000} = 48\% \text{ (materials cost basis)}$$

Other Overhead

Machine depreciation	$270,000
Engineering	100,000
Packing and shipping	60,000
Maintenance	30,000
Total	$460,000

Overhead Absorption Rate

$$\frac{\$460,000}{10,800 \text{ hours}} = \$42.59 \text{ per machine hour}$$

Part 5 *Product Costing and an Introduction to Cost Management*

EXHIBIT 5
Monthly Overhead Cost Activity Analysis   ABC

	Valves	Pumps	Flow Controllers
Receiving and Materials Handling:			
Receive each component once per run	4 transactions (3%)	25 transactions (19%)	100 transactions (78%)
Handle each component once per run	4 transactions (3%)	25 transactions (19%)	100 transactions (78%)
Packing and Shipping:			
One packing order per shipment	1 transaction (3%)	7 transactions (23%)	22 transactions (73%)
Engineering:			
Estimated engineering work-order percentage (subjective)	20%	30%	50%
Maintenance:			
Machine-hour basis	3,750 hours (35%)	6,250 hours (58%)	800 hours (7%)

Kanthal (A)

C arl-Erik Ridderstråle, president of Kanthal, was describing his motivation for developing a system to measure customer profitability.

Before, when we got an order from a big, important customer, we didn't ask questions. We were glad to get the business. But a small company, competing around the world, has to concentrate its sales and marketing resources. We needed an account management system if we were to achieve our strategy for higher growth and profitability. An account management system as part of the Kanthal 90 Strategy will enable us to get sales managers to accept responsibility for promoting high-margin products to high-profit customers.

HISTORY

Kanthal, the largest of six divisions in the Kanthal-Hoganas group of Sweden, was headquartered in Hallstahammar a town of 17,000 persons about 150 km. northwest of Stockholm. The company's history can be traced back to an ironworks founded in the 17th century to exploit the water power available from the stream running through the town. Kanthal specialized in the production and sales of electrical resistance heating elements. "We work for a warmer world," was its motto.

Kanthal had about 10,000 customers and 15,000 items that it produced. Sales during 1985 through 1987 had been level at about SEK 850 million.[1] Export sales, outside of Sweden, accounted for 95% of the total. Summary statistics for the past two years appear in **Exhibit 1**.

Kanthal consisted of three divisions:

Kanthal Heating Technology supplied manufacturers of electrical appliances and heating systems with wire that generated heat through electrical resistance. Prod-

Professor Robert S. Kaplan prepared this case as the basis for class discussion rather than to illustrate either effective or ineffective handling of an administrative situation.

Copyright © 1989 by the President and Fellows of Harvard College, Case No. 190-002. To order copies or request permission to reproduce materials, call 1-800-545-7685 or write Harvard Business School Publishing, Boston, MA 02163. No part of this publication may be reproduced, stored in a retrieval system, used in a spreadsheet, or transmitted in any form or by any means—electronic, mechanical, photocopying, recording, or otherwise—without the permission of Harvard Business School.

[1] In 1988, the Swedish kronor (SEK) was worth about US$0.16.

ucts included heating wire and ribbon, foil elements, machinery and precision wire. Kanthal's 25% market share made it a world leader in supplying heating alloys. Sales growth was sluggish in Europe and the United States but rapid growth was occurring in the Far East and Latin America.

Kanthal Furnace Products produced a wide range of heating elements for electric industrial furnaces. Its 40% market share gave it a dominant position in the large markets of the United States, Japan, West Germany, and the United Kingdom. A new product, Kanthal Super, was generating substantial growth because of its substantially improved performance over conventional materials, including longer service life, lower service costs, and higher operating temperatures.

Kanthal Bimetals was one of the few companies in the world with fully integrated manufacturing of thermo-bimetals for temperature control devices used in the manufacture of thermostats, circuit breakers, and household appliances.

Kanthal's manufacturing facilities were located in Hallstahammar, Brazil, the United Kingdom, West Germany, the United States, and Italy.

KANTHAL 90

Ridderstråle, upon becoming president in 1985, saw the need for a strategic plan for Kanthal.

The company had been successful in the past. We needed to use this base of experience to influence the future. We had to have a consolidated view to ensure that we did not sub-optimize in narrow markets or with a narrow functional view. Resources were to be allocated so that we could increase profits while maintaining a return on employed capital in excess of 20%.

The Kanthal 90 plan specified overall profit objectives by division, by product line, and by market. Currently, however, salespersons were compensated mostly on gross sales volume. Higher commissions were being paid for selling obviously higher-margin products, such as Super, and higher bonuses were being awarded for achieving sales targets in the high-margin products. But Ridderstråle wanted to achieve the additional growth planned under Kanthal 90 without adding sales and administrative resources to handle the increased volume anticipated.

We needed to know where in the organization the resources could be taken from and redeployed into more profitable uses. We did not want to eliminate resources in a steady-state environment. We wanted to reallocate people to generate future growth.

With our historically good profitability, and lacking any current or imminent crisis, we could not realistically consider laying off people at the Hallstahammar plant. But we wanted to be able to redeploy people so that they could earn more profit for us; to move people from corporate staff to divisions, from the parent company to operating subsidiaries, and from staff functions into sales, R&D, and production. Ideally, if we could transform an accounting clerk at Hallstahammar into a salesman of Kanthal-Super in Japan, we could generate a substantial profit increase.

Exhibit 2 shows the distribution of Kanthal's incurred costs. The existing cost system treated most sales, marketing, and administrative costs as a percentage of sales revenue. Therefore, customers whose selling price exceeded the standard full cost of manufacturing plus the percentage mark-up for general, selling, and administrative expenses appeared to be profitable, while a customer order whose selling price was below standard manufacturing cost plus the percentage mark-up appeared unprofitable. Ridderstråle knew, however, that individual customers made quite different demands on Kanthal's administrative and sales staff.

Low profit customers place high demands on technical and commercial service. They buy low-margin products in small orders. Frequently they order non-standard products that have to be specially produced for them. And we have to supply special selling discounts in order to get the business.

High profit customers buy high-margin, standard products in large orders. They make no demands for technical or commercial service, and accurately forecast for us their annual demands.

He felt that a new system was needed to determine how much profit was earned each time a customer placed a particular order. The system should attempt to measure the costs that individual customer orders placed on the production, sales, and administrative resources of the company. The goal was to find both "hidden profit" orders, those whose demands on the company were quite low, and the "hidden loss" orders, those customer orders that under the existing system looked profitable but which in fact demanded a disproportionate share of the company's resources to fulfill.

Ridderstråle pointed out the weaknesses with the present method of profitability measurement.

We distribute resources equally across all products and customers. We do not measure individual customer's profitability or the real costs of individual orders. In this environment, our sales and marketing efforts emphasize volume, more than profits. In the future, we want Kanthal to handle significantly increased sales volume without any corresponding increase in support resources, and to gain the share in our most profitable products.

Our current method of calculating product costs may show two customers to be equally profitable on a gross margin basis. But there could be hidden profits and hidden costs associated with these customers that we are not seeing (see **Exhibit 3**). If we could get more accurate information about our own manufacturing cost structure, as well as the costs of supplying individual customers and orders, we could direct our resources to customers with hidden profits, and reduce our efforts to customers with the hidden losses. We might end up with the same market share, so that our competitors would not even see this shift in our strategy, but our profitability would be much higher. To execute such a strategy, however, we need better information about the profitability of each order, each product, and each customer.

The biggest barrier we have to overcome is the notion that production overhead, selling, and administrative costs are "fixed." The definition of strategy is to recognize that all costs are variable. Our sales people must learn how to deploy resources to their most profitable use.

THE NEW ACCOUNT MANAGEMENT SYSTEM

Per O. Ehrling, Financial Manager of Kanthal, worked with SAM, a Swedish management advisory group, to develop a system to analyze production, sales, and administrative costs at the Hallstahammar facility. Over a period of several months, finance managers and the consultants conducted extensive interviews with all department heads and key personnel. The interviews were designed to elicit information about the nature of the activities being performed by support department personnel and the events that triggered the demands for these organizational activities. Ehrling described the philosophy of the new approach:

> In our previous system, indirect costs were either manufacturing costs that were allocated to products based on direct labor, or they were Selling & Administrative Costs, that were treated as period expenses and were unanalyzed. This treatment may have been correct 100 years ago when we had one bookkeeper for every 10 blacksmiths, but today we have eight bookkeepers for every three blacksmiths. This means that most of our costs today are indirect and our previous system didn't know how to allocate them.
>
> We wanted to move away from our traditional financial accounting categories. We found that most of our organizational costs could be classified either as Order-related or Volume Costs. Actually, we did investigate three additional cost drivers—product range, technical support, and new products. But the total costs assigned to these three categories ended up being less than 5% of total costs so we eliminated them.

Using the interview information, the project team determined how much of the expenses of each support department related to the volume of sales and production and how much related to handling individual production and sales orders (see **Exhibit 4**). The **manufacturing volume** costs, in addition to material, direct labor, and variable overhead, also included the costs of production orders to replenish inventory stocks. Only 20% of Kanthal's products were stocked in inventory, but these products represented 80% of sales orders so the cost of continually replenishing these products was assumed to be related to the volume of production. **Manufacturing order** costs therefore included only the cost of set-up and other activities that were triggered when a customer ordered a product not normally stocked. Manufacturing order costs were calculated separately for each major product group. The **sales order** costs represented the selling & administrative costs that could be traced to processing an individual customer's order. The S&A costs that remained after subtracting **sales order** costs were treated as **sales volume** costs and were allocated proportionately to the **manufacturing volume** costs.

For example, the Sales Department activities (see **Exhibit 4**) relating to preparing a bid for an order, negotiating with the customer about the order, and following-up with the customer after the order was delivered were classified as "order-related." All remaining activities, such as public relations and sales management, that could not be traced to individual orders were classified as "volume-related."

Follow-up interviews were conducted to corroborate the split of effort in each department between volume- and order-related activities. Sample calculations are shown in **Exhibit 5**.

Bo Martin Tell, controller of the Furnace Products Division, recalled the amount of tedious work required to collect all the numbers.

It took almost a year to develop a system to collect the data in the proper form. Even in production, we had problems identifying the costs that related to stocked and non-stocked orders.

INITIAL OUTPUT FROM THE ACCOUNT MANAGEMENT SYSTEM

Exhibit 6 shows a profitability report for a sample of individual orders from Swedish customers. Profit margins on these individual orders ranged from -179% to +65%. Previously, almost all of these orders would have appeared profitable. Similar reports were prepared to show total profitability by customer, by product group, or by all the orders received from customers in a country. For example, **Exhibit 7** shows, for a given product group—Finished Wire N, the sales volume and profitability of a sample of Swedish customers.

Leif Rick, general manager of Heating Technology remembered the initial reactions to the account management reports:

The study was a real eye-opener. We saw how the traditional cost accounting system had been unable to truly report costs and profits by market, product, and customer.

At first, the new approach seemed strange. We had to explain it three or four times before people started to understand and accept it. People did not want to believe that order costs could be so high; that order costs had to be treated as an explicit cost of selling. Most surprising was finding that customers thought to be very profitable were actually break-even or even loss customers. Salesmen initially thought the approach was part of a master plan to get rid of small customers. But people who have been working with the system now are convinced of its value and are beginning to take sensible actions based on the information.

Exhibit 8 shows the profits from Swedish customers, ranked by customer profitability. The results surprised even Ridderstråle. Only 40% of Kanthal's Swedish customers were profitable and these generated 250% of realized profits. In fact the most profitable 5% of the customers generated 150% of the profits. The least profitable 10% of customers lost 120% of the profits (see cumulative profitability chart in **Exhibit 9**).

Even more surprising, two of the most unprofitable customers turned out to be among the top three in total sales volume. These two customers had gone to just-in-time (JIT) delivery for its suppliers. They had pushed inventory back onto Kanthal which had not recognized the new demands being placed on its production and order-handling processes by the JIT approach. Moreover, further investigation revealed that one of these customers was using Kanthal as a back-up supplier, to handle small special orders of a low-priced item when its main supplier could not deliver. Because of the size and prestige of the two customers, Kanthal people had always welcomed and encouraged their orders. Ridderstråle now realized how expensive it had become to satisfy them.

The immediate problem was to devise a strategy for the large number of nonprofitable customers, particularly the very high volume ones. Corporate management had started a series of meetings with the general and sales managers of the operating divisions in Sweden to discuss how to handle these customers.

Also, while the account management system had been developed for the Swedish operating divisions, some overseas divisions remained skeptical about the value of the exercise. The account management system was seen as yet another intrusion of the headquarters staff into their operations. Ridderstråle knew he faced an uphill battle gaining acceptance for the account management system around the world.

EXHIBIT 1
Summary of Operations

	1986	1987
Invoiced sales (MSEK)	839	849
Profit after financial items	87	107
Return on capital	20%	21%
Number of employees	1,606	1,591

EXHIBIT 2
Cost Structure

Cost Component	Percentage
Materials	23
Production salaries and wages	19
Variable processing costs	5
Fixed processing costs	16
Subcontracted services	3
Selling and administrative	34
Total costs	100

EXHIBIT 3
Hidden Profit and Hidden Cost Customers

EXHIBIT 4
Order and Volume Costs

Type of Personnel	Order-Related Work	Volume-Related Work
Production		
Stock Replenishment	None	All activities
Production Planning	Order Planning Order Follow-up	Inventory Management
Operators	Set-up Start-up Expense	Direct Hours
Foremen	Order Planning Order Support	Machine Problems
Stock	Order Input Order Output	Order Handling
Transportation	Order Planning Order Handling	
Selling and Administrative		
Management	Offer Discussion Offer Negotiation	General Management
Sales	Offer Work Order Negotiation Delivery Follow-up	Sales-Unrelated to Orders General Public Relations Sales Management
Secretarial	Offer Typing	
Administration	Order Booking Order Adjustment Invoice Typing Customer Ledger Supervision	Accounting

EXHIBIT 5
Sample Calculation of Order and Volume Costs: By Product Group

Step 1. Calculate Selling & Administrative (S&A) Order Costs

Total Selling & Administrative Order Costs:		SEK 2,000,000
Total number of orders	2,000	
Stocked products	1,500	
Non-stocked products	500	
S&A order costs per order		SEK 1,000

Step 2. Calculate Manufacturing Order Cost for Non-stocked Products

Total Manufacturing Order Costs	SEK 1,000,000
(for non-stocked products)	
Number of orders for non-stocked products	500
Manufacturing order costs per non-stocked order	SEK 2,000

Step 3. Calculate Allocation Factor for S&A Volume Costs

Compute Total Manufacturing and S&A Costs:		SEK 7,000,000
Subtract Order Costs:		
Non-stocked products:	1,000,000	
Selling and Administrative Order Costs:	2,000,000	3,000,000
Total Volume Costs:		SEK 4,000,000
Manufacturing Volume Costs of Goods Sold (CGS)	3,200,000	
Selling & Administrative Volume-Related Costs	800,000	
S&A Volume Allocation Factor: S&A Volume Costs/		
Mfg. Volume CGS (800/3,200)		25%

Step 4. Calculate Operating Profit on Individual Orders for Non-stocked Product

Sales Value	SEK 10,000
Less: Volume Costs: Manufacturing Cost of Goods Sold	
(@ 40% of Sales Value)	4,000
Volume Costs: Selling & Administrative (@ 25% of Mfg. CGS)	1,000
Margin on Volume-related Costs	5,000
Less: Mfg. Order Cost for Non-stocked Product	2,000
Selling & Administrative Order Cost	1,000
Operating Profit for Order	SEK 2,000

EXHIBIT 6
Customer Order Analysis

Standard order cost: SEK572

Manufacturing order cost for non-stocked products: Foil Elements: SEK1508
                                                        Finished Wire: SEK2340

Country Customer	Order Lines	Invoiced Value (SEK)	Volume Cost (SEK)	Order Cost (SEK)	Non-Stocked (SEK)	Operating Profit (SEK)	Profit Margin
Sweden							
S001	1	1,210	543	572	0	95	8%
S002	3	46,184	10,080	1,716	4,524	29,864	65
S003	8	51,102	50,567	4,576	12,064	(16,105)	−32
S004	9	98,880	60,785	5,148	13,572	19,375	20
S005	1	3,150	1,557	572	2,340	(1,319)	−42
S006	5	24,104	14,889	2,860	4,680	1,675	7
S007	2	4,860	2,657	1,144	4,680	(3,621)	−75
S008	1	2,705	1,194	572	0	939	35
S009	1	518	233	572	0	(287)	−55
S010	8	67,958	51,953	4,576	12,064	(635)	−1
S011	2	4,105	1,471	1,144	0	1,490	36
S012	8	87,865	57,581	4,576	12,064	13,644	16
S013	1	1,274	641	572	2,340	(2,279)	−179
S014	2	1,813	784	1,144	0	(115)	−6
S015	2	37,060	15,974	1,144	3,016	16,926	46
S016	2	6,500	6,432	1,144	3,016	(4,092)	−63

Note: All financial data reported in Swedish kroner (SEK).

EXHIBIT 7
Finished Wire N Customer List

Customer #	Invoiced Sales (SEK)	Volume Costs (SEK)	Order Cost (SEK)	Non-Stocked Cost (SEK)	Operating Profit (SEK)	Profit Margin
33507	3,969	1,440	750	0	1,779	45%
33508	4,165	1,692	750	2,150	(427)	–10
33509	601	139	750	2,150	(2,438)	–406
33510	13,655	6,014	750	2,150	4,741	35
33511	2,088	350	750	2,150	(1,162)	–56
33512	1,742	637	750	0	355	20
33513	4,177	932	750	2,150	345	8
33514	7,361	3,134	750	0	3,477	47
33515	1,045	318	750	0	(23)	–2
33516	429,205	198,277	9,000	0	221,928	52
33517	31,696	13,128	3,750	0	14,818	47
A 33518	159,612	58,036	2,250	6,450	92,876	58
33519	48,648	17,872	9,750	12,900	8,126	17
33520	5,012	1,119	750	2,150	993	20
33521	4,933	2,170	1,500	4,300	(3,037)	–62
33522	17,277	7,278	1,500	0	8,499	49
33523	134	120	1,500	4,300	(5,786)	–4,318
33524	1,825	523	1,500	0	(198)	–11
33525	13,874	4,914	3,750	6,450	(1,240)	–9
33526	3,762	1,452	750	0	1,560	41
33527	64,875	18,559	3,750	8,600	33,966	52
33528	13,052	5,542	3,000	6,450	(1,940)	–15
33529	39,175	12,683	3,750	8,600	14,142	36
33530	383	87	750	0	(454)	–119
33531	6,962	1,865	750	2,150	2,197	32
33532	1,072	314	1,500	0	(742)	–69
33533	14,050	6,333	1,500	2,150	4,067	29
33534	820	244	750	0	(174)	–21
33535	809	181	750	2,150	(2,272)	–281
33536	1,366	316	750	2,150	(1,850)	–135
B 33537	155,793	65,718	21,750	49,450	18,875	12
33538	7,593	2,772	2,250	2,150	421	6
Total	1,060,731	434,159	84,000	131,150	411,422	39%

Note: All financial data reported in Swedish kroner (SEK).

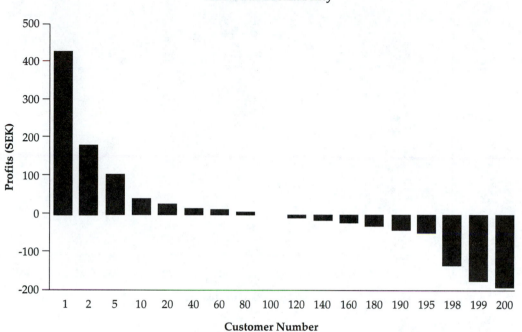

Customer Profitability

EXHIBIT 9
Cumulative Profitability by Customers

Cumulative Profits

Profits: % of Total

Cumulative % of Customers

Custom Research Inc. (A)

INTRODUCTION

Custom Research Inc. (CRI) had just passed its sixteenth birthday, but without much to celebrate. Profitability as a percentage of sales had been declining for several years and revenue growth had been flat recently. CRI partners Jeff Pope and Judy Corson had reached a turning point. They had just completed an extensive financial analysis and found that a large majority of their clients were clients who only did a few projects a year and while profitable, the small client project revenue did not add up to a big part of their total company revenue. They had started the company with, and continued to espouse, a "take all comers" philosophy as to prospective clients. "We've been operating under the presumption that there's no such thing as a 'bad' client. They all pay our bills," said Jeff Pope, "but we are now beginning to question this assumption." Should they stop working with these smaller clients? What would happen if they did? Could the company survive if they did not?

Furthermore, there were serious questions as to CRI's organizational structure. For example, staff members responsible for selling projects were also responsible for implementing project design, interviewing, and analysis. Did this structure make sense moving into the future? These were just a few of the questions senior staff were raising during a series of off-site meetings with Sam Marcus, currently Managing Partner—Brecker & Merryman, Inc., a New York management consulting firm.

Background

Judith Corson, fresh from completing a liberal arts degree at the University of Minnesota in 1964, decided she didn't want to be a "nurse or a teacher like everyone else." Through her sorority network, she was contacted by Norma Friedrichs, the manager of project administration in commercial research at The Pillsbury Company. Corson was promptly hired as one of three project directors in charge of project implementation of marketing research for Pillsbury.

Professor William J. Bruns, Jr. and Susan Harmeling (MBA '91) prepared this case. HBS cases are developed solely as the basis for class discussion. Cases are not intended to serve as endorsements, sources of primary data, or illustrations of effective or ineffective management.

Pillsbury, unlike a number of its competitors at this time, had a comprehensive internal research department. Marketing research analysts would request a study and Pillsbury's own internal research department would then implement the entire process from designing the methodology to composing the questionnaire to hiring interviewing services to tabulating results. Most other consumer products companies only had a group of in-house marketing research analysts who would contract their studies out to an independent research firm.

Corson led Pillsbury's new product marketing research implementation effort on and off for a period of 10 years (she had a stint in marketing research at Scott Paper in Philadelphia from 1967–1969 before returning to Pillsbury). In the late 1960s, Pillsbury established a central telephone interviewing capability in-house. Soon it became obvious that the peaks and valleys in Pillsbury's marketing research work volume made it impossible to staff this telephone facility. Operating as a stand-alone profit center funded by charging its time to various departments that needed its services, the marketing research department's problem of having a "single client" made it difficult to generate enough studies for the telephone center staff and therefore difficult to retain personnel.

In 1968, two marketing research analysts left Pillsbury to work for Johnson Wax. Without any internal marketing research department to turn to at their new firm, the analysts called Judy Corson to ask if she could continue to do studies for them. Her boss, Dudley Ruch, gave her permission to do so (and to seek other outside clients). Judy's outside research client business was soon profitable (enjoying 15%–20% profit margins while the company as a whole averaged approximately 4%–5%). This outside research group was able to supplement funding for developing new commercial research techniques.

After a few years, it became necessary to structure the outside research group's relationship to the company in a more formal way. Management demanded that the outside research group become a separate free-standing business—in essence, a line organization, paying corporate taxes to the firm. Seeing this as unfair (marketing research did their own accounting, HR etc.), Corson became increasingly frustrated with the status of her department. "We were paying corporate taxes, but we weren't getting any services in return!"

Furthermore, industry diversification was giving rise to a number of potential conflicts of interest that prevented Corson from accepting more outside business from other consumer research companies. For example, after Pillsbury bought Burger King, Corson was forced to turn down lucrative marketing research work from McDonald's. This prevented her from growing the outside research business as quickly as she wished.

In January 1974, when Dudley Ruch left Pillsbury to work for Quaker Oats and Corson had no one to report to, she decided it was finally time for a change. She approached Norma Friedrichs, her original boss, to ask her if she would like to go into business together. At that time, Norma was responsible for project implementation of all Pillsbury marketing research. They, in turn, asked Jeff Pope, a Pillsbury product manager who, prior to joining Pillsbury, had also done marketing research for an independent research company and KPMG, to join the team. Custom Research Inc. was founded in August 1974.

Immediately upon beginning the firm, the trio hired a lawyer to implement a Buy-Sell agreement which proved to be a wise first step—two years later, Norma

Friedrichs left the company and Judy Corson and Jeff Pope exercised the agreement buying out Friedrichs and becoming 50/50 partners in CRI.

The Industry

While the marketing research industry began as an in-house function of the larger consumer goods companies, CRI's experience was typical of the trend in the late 1960s and 1970s as companies began to contract with independent research firms. During this period, the industry was very fragmented, with a multitude of small, one or two person firms and a few well-established larger organizations.

In the recent decade, however, the trend was toward consolidation, with a few larger firms at the top able to complete all aspects of the research process from data collection to analysis and literally thousands of very small firms competing for data collection and tabulation business only. Furthermore, in a 1987 study of Counsel of American Survey Research Organizations (CASRO) Member firms, a large majority expected custom research spending to grow slowly or remain the same over the next few years. (See **Exhibit 1** for industry breakdown.)

The Marketing Research Study

A marketing research study typically includes the following steps:

1. **Study Design.** Establishes client's research and information needs, determines the limitations of available research tools and methods, and draws up plans for implementing the study. Includes development of detailed client questionnaire.

2. **Proposal.** Explains study design to client, offers cost and timing estimate within 10% of final cost to client.

3. **Data Collection.** Uses questionnaire to gather data necessary to determine what information a client needs to know about a new product idea, a price increase or other types of information. Typically done by outside interviewing services, either over the phone or in person (for example at shopping malls). Other data collection methods include mail.

4. **Tabulation.** Results from data collection stage are tabulated according to variables laid out during study design stage.

5. **Analysis.** Study results are analyzed for their relevance to client—should client develop the new product? Why or why not? What are the real implications of the study results?

At its inception, CRI did almost exclusively data collection and tabulation. The process went as follows: first, a research analyst from a client firm would request a study to test a new product idea with a certain number of consumers (e.g., the design stage was already completed by the client). CRI would receive the request and would, according to the size and scope of the study, develop a proposal with a cost and timing estimate for data collection and tabulation. At the beginning, clients would typically do the first step—study design—and the last step—analysis of the results—themselves. Later, in the early 1980s, as their client companies began to downsize, CRI began to perform the design and analysis functions as well.

(See **Exhibit 2** for a typical study request, results, and analysis.)

Organizational Structure

Once the proposal was accepted by a client, the CRI project manager would deploy staff to implement the study. Project managers were organized by industry into two main divisions. The first division included Business to Business (companies that sold products to other companies; i.e., auto parts suppliers, corporate service firms, etc.) and Medical (pharmaceutical, hospital supplies, etc.). This division accounted for only 25% of CRI's total revenues. Clients such as Johnson & Johnson were among CRI's first clients in the medical marketing research business.

The second division, representing the other 75% of CRI's business, was Consumer Research. Clients included Quaker Oats, Land O'Lakes and Johnson Wax. A third division, Corporate Services, provided support services to the research function, such as data tabulation, copying, shipping, etc.

CRI's project managers also served as salespeople—the company had not established an independent sales department. One reason for this structure was the nature of the business. As Judy Corson explained, "At CRI, salespeople must first be researchers—you must understand the methodology and the technology or you will not be taken seriously by the client. It normally takes five years to learn the business and there is no substitute for actually doing the studies."

Expanding Business, Declining Profits

From 1974 to 1990, CRI's customer base expanded steadily. With a number of large corporate clients, CRI had developed a reputation as one of the premier market research firms in the United States. However, during these years, a somewhat disturbing trend had developed. The results of an extensive profitability analysis completed in 1990 showed that while new bookings, closed sales, and overall operating profit were all on the rise, the crucial measure of profit as a percentage of sales was slowly declining. (See **Exhibit 3** for analysis.)

From its formation, CRI had used a detailed activity based costing system to assign costs to each marketing research study or project. Each employee or associate recorded time spent on each job using one of more than thirty different charge rates depending on the work done. Time spent on selling projects was charged first to a "zero" account and charged back later to jobs accepted. Using this system, CRI had a record of profitability for each research study or project.

As Executive Vice President Diane Kokal explained, profit as a percentage of sales was the main way that CRI measured its success:

> Working for a client that doesn't actually clear a profit is no fun. Obviously what you want is the highest possible profit margin, particularly in our business where the game is definitely not market share. The research business is a very fragmented one so market share is not such a meaningful measure. We knew we had to grow consistently but we also knew we must grow more profitably.

Jeff Pope further organized this data into a quadrant analysis that provided even more insight into the problem. Two thirds of all clients were in the "Low/Low" quadrant, meaning that they contributed less than $20,000 in margin contribution and less than a 20% profit margin (as a percentage of sales). Thus, these were either small clients or small projects or both.

Direction

The Steering Committee, made up of the two partners and the two executive vice presidents—Diane Kokal and Jan Elsesser—decided it was time to hire an outsider to facilitate the process of establishing the right direction for the future. They hired Sam Marcus, formerly of the Delta Group in New York, and the four members of the Steering Committee went off-site over a year for a series of one-day strategy meetings.

Questions were many. If a large percentage of clients contributed little or nothing to overall profit, should CRI neglect them? What would be the repercussions of such a strategy? What if the remaining clients experienced an economic downturn and cut back on their research budgets? Could CRI grow under this strategy? Jeff Pope thought CRI could focus on and grow the business of the larger more profitable clients.

What choices must be made if the Steering Committee were to terminate relations with some predetermined group of their existing clients? What criteria should they use to decide who to keep and who to drop? Should they in fact maintain all profitable clients and drop all unprofitable clients? Perhaps the choice was not that simple.

Furthermore, how exactly would they explain all this to their clients? Was it their responsibility to refer those smaller clients to someone else for service? What else did the Steering Committee need to address before making this very important decision about the company's future?

And finally, what about CRI's organizational structure? While it seemed to make sense that "doers" were also sellers, the research function was quite different, and in some respects, required very different skills, than did the sales function. Furthermore, while the project managers were out selling projects, they were unable to implement others and while directing research, they were unable to sell. This seemed rather inefficient. However, everyone agreed that it was crucial that CRI's salespeople all understand (and have experience in implementing) research projects.

EXHIBIT 1
Council of American Survey Research Organizations—Quarterly Bookings Report—Firms May 26, 1987

Size of Firm	(N)	1Q87	% Change	% Change vs. Year Ago
		115,139	*+2*	*—*
10mm and over	16	119,436	+6	+4
4mm to 10mm	21	33,892	+6	–4
		11,524	*–13*	*–1*
2mm to 4mm	16	10,955	–17	–6
		2,897	*–5*	*–22*
1mm to 2mm	9	2,697	–10	–28
		2,445	*–19*	*–32*
Under 1mm	14	3,035	—	–15
		165,897	*+1*	*–2*
TOTAL	76	170,015	+4	—

Italics —Represents analysis adjusted for outliers

Percent who said custom research spending by
their organization in the next 2 or 3 years would:

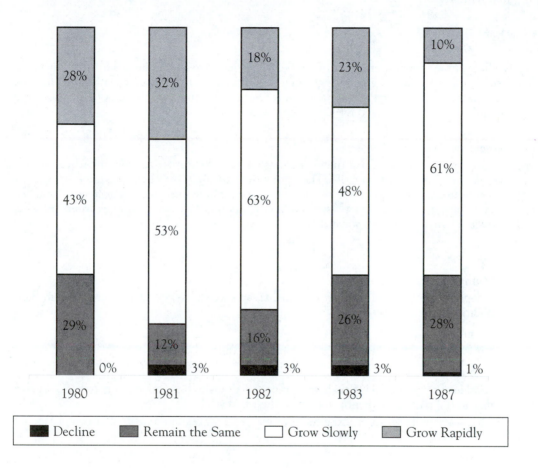

Decline   Remain the Same   Grow Slowly   Grow Rapidly

EXHIBIT 2

Mr. Joe Leim
Great Foods Company
2 White Pine Road
Jonesville, WV

Dear Joe:

Well, it's time for another wave of Pancake Mix Price Increase Awareness Study. This is the *second* of four waves. The following is our understanding of the study specifications for this study. Also included are the associated study costs and timing. Joe, please note that the costs did go up for this wave (and for each subsequent wave).

Background and Study Purpose
Due to current low supplies of the ingredients for pancake mix worldwide, the wheat futures market is extraordinarily volatile. The purpose of this study is to help you understand consumer awareness of pancake mix pricing increases and how these increases affect consumers' usage habits. You will conduct a series of four telephone surveys at six-week intervals. This study is the first of the four waves.

Specifications
Methodology
Telephone study conducted on weeknights, and weekends, using standard random digit dialing sampling procedures.

Locations
National (total U.S., excluding Alaska and Hawaii)

Quota
150 Head of Household (female/male if no female) who have bought any type of pancake mix in the past three months for use in their home.
Each wave will consist of 150 interviews for a total of 600 interviews after completing all four waves.

Sample
RDD sample will be provided by SSI.

Incidence
When the study was costed, incidence was estimated at 70%. However, during the Wave 1 study, incidence was falling out at 60%.

Questionnaire and interview length
Interview length is estimated at 6 minutes.

Coding
There is one open-end question.

Data Tables
We will provide data tables and a top line report upon completion of the study.

EXHIBIT 2 (*continued*)

Schedule and Budget

Schedule

We are operating under this timetable for Wave 2:

Sample at CRI	February 6
Final q'aire approved	n/a (same as Wave 1)
Data collection start	February 9
Data collection finish	February 16
Data tables and top line report to you	February 23

Budget

Joe, due to the lower than estimated incidence, the cost of each additional wave has increased from our earlier estimate. If the incidence should go up, we will adjust the costs accordingly. But, as of now, our projected costs for this wave of research (and each additional wave) will be within 10% of the following:

Data collection start	$6,400
Sample	$300
Data processing	$700
Total	$7,400

Did I get everything, Joe? If not, please let me know and I'll make the necessary modifications.

Best regards,

Norma Brennan
Sr. Research Associate

EXHIBIT 2 (*continued*)

Pancake Price Increase Awareness Study—Wave 2

Introduction (Base = All)

Good (morning/afternoon/evening). I'm (NAME) calling long distance from Custom Research Inc.

Today I'm collecting information for a marketing study about products used in the home.

(Are you/may I please speak with) the female head of the household (/lady of the house)?

IF THERE IS NO FEMALE HEAD OF HOUSEHOLD ASK: (Are you/may I please speak with) the male head of the household (/man of the house)?

Q1. Gender (Base = All)
RECORD GENDER.'
  'Female'/
  'Male'

Q2. Pancake Mix Bought Past 3 Months (Base = All)
In the past 3 months, has pancake mix of any type been bought for use in your home?
  'Yes'/
  'No'

> REFER TO Q2.　　　IF "NO", DISCONTINUE.
> ALL OTHER CONTINUE WITH Q3.

Q3. Usual Brand—Household Usage (Base = All)
In the past 3 months, what *one* brand of pancake mix was used most of the time in your home?

IF 2 OR MORE BRANDS: Was one of these brands used more often than the other(s), or were they both (all) used about equally?

IF 2 EQUALLY, ENTER BOTH.　 IF 3+, RECORD "NO USUAL."

RECORD ON BRAND LIST.'

EXHIBIT 2 (*continued*)

Q4. Next Brand—Household Usage (Base = All)

Thinking of the next time you buy pancake mix, as best as you can say, what *one* brand are you most likely to buy the next time you buy pancake mix?

IF RESPONDENT SAYS: "I buy what's on Sale/Coupon," RECORD "(50) Whatever on Sale/Coupon."

TWO OR MORE BRANDS: Would you be more likely to buy one of these brands than the other(s), or would you buy both (all) equally?

IF 2 EQUALLY, ENTER BOTH.   IF 3+, RECORD "NO USUAL".

RECORD ON BRAND LIST.'

Q5. How Often Will You Buy Pancake Mix (Base = All)

In the next three months, are you likely to buy pancake mix more often, about as often, or less often than you have in the past 3 months?'
   'More often'/
   'About as often'/
   'Less often'/
   'NK/Ref'/

Q6. How Much Will Buy Pancake Mix (Base = All)

Now thinking of the next time you buy pancake mix, are you likely to buy more, about the same number, or fewer boxes of pancake mix than the number you usually buy?'
   'More'/
   'About the same number'/
   'Fewer'/
   'NK/Ref'/

Q7. What Size Will Buy (Base = All)

The next time you buy pancake mix, are you likely to buy a larger size, the same size, or a smaller size of pancake mix than the size you usually buy?'
   'Larger'/
   'Same size'/
   'Smaller'/
   'NK/Ref'/

EXHIBIT 2 (continued)

Q8. Price of Pancake Mix Last Bought (Base = All)

Now thinking about the last time you bought pancake mix, was the price of the pancake mix higher than, about the same, or lower than the previous time you had bought the same brand and type of pancake mix?'

   'Higher'/
   'About the same price'/
   'Lower'/
   'NK/Ref'/

Q9. Price of Pancake Mix Increasing (Base = All)

Some people we've talked with recently mentioned hearing about an increase in the price of pancake mix. Have you seen or heard anything recently about pancake mix prices increasing, or not?'

   'Yes'/
   'No'/

REFER TO Q9.   IF "YES", CONTINUE WITH Q10.   IF "NO", SKIP TO DEMOS.

Q10. Cause of Increase in Pancake Mix Prices (Base = All)

What do you think is causing the increase in pancake mix prices?
PROBE AND CLARIFY FULLY.

DEMOGRAPHICS (Demos)   (Base = All)

My last few questions are for demographic purposes only.

Number in Household (Base = All)

In total, how many people live in your household, including children and yourself?
DO NOT READ LIST.'

   Resp sp 'One'/
   'Two'/
   'Three'/
   'Four'/
   'Five'/
   'Six'/
   'Seven or more'/
   'Refuse'/

EXHIBIT 2 (*continued*)

Household Income (Base = 18+ Years Old)
Is the total yearly household income over or under $50,000?
UNDER: Is it over or under $25,000?
OVER: Is it over or under $70,000?'
    'Under $25,000'/
    '$25,000-$49,999'/
    '$50,000-$69,999'/
    '$70,000 and over'/
    'Refuse'/

Education (Base = All)
What was the last grade of school that you, yourself, completed?'
IF NECESSARY, READ LIST.'
    'Grade School or Less'/
    'Some High School'/
    'High School Graduate'/
    'Some College'/
    'College Graduate'/
    'Post Graduate'/
    'Refuse (DO NOT READ)'/

Those are all of the questions I have for you today. Thank you for participating in this study. We value your opinion.

EXHIBIT 2 (*continued*)

Pancake Mix Price Increase Awareness: Waves 1 & 2
Market Research Department Report

Research Purpose: To track: 1) consumer awareness of pricing changes in the pancake mix category, 2) consumer perceptions for the reasons for the price increase, and 3) expected claimed habit changes due to pancake mix pricing volatility.

Success Criteria/Expected Results: Will be used with other data to aid brand management in decisions about product, promotion, pricing, and public relations responses to the pricing increases.

Initiated By: Brand management.

Locations of Data Collection: Continental United States.

Market Research Contact: Joe L.

Background: The wheat futures market is extraordinarily volatile with the spring futures increasing by over 50%, the second highest level ever. Unlike the most recent 1996 run-up, which was weather-related, this market is being driven by fundamental supply and demand issues as worldwide stocks of higher quality wheat are at critically low levels and estimates for this year's crop are 10% lower than last year. We expect continued volatility over the next three months. In an effort to understand consumer awareness of pancake mix pricing increase and how the price increase affects consumers' usage habits, we will conduct a series of four telephone surveys at six-week intervals.

Method/Test Description: Interviews were conducted via telephone. In order to track awareness of the price increases, perceptions of the causes and changes in claimed/expected behaviors over time, four waves of this study will be conducted at six-week intervals. A total of 600 heads of households (150/wave for four waves) who have bought any type of pancake mix in the past three months for use in their home, will be interviewed.

Key Dates: Wave 1 fieldwork—2/9/98 through 2/16/98. Wave 2 fieldwork—3/30/98 through 4/6/98.

Market Research Department Report

EXHIBIT 2 (*continued*)

Summary
Pancake Mix Increase Awareness: Waves 1 & 2

Research Purpose: To track: 1) consumer awareness of pricing changes in the pancake mix category, 2) consumer perceptions for the reasons for the price increase, and 3) expected claimed habit changes due to pancake mix pricing volatility.

The request states that the results will be used: with other data to aid brand management in decisions about product, promotion, pricing, and public relations responses to the pricing increases.

Respondents are: Heads of Household, age 18+.

Key data for Waves 1 & 2 are shown below.

	Heads of Household Who Purchased Pancake Mix in Past 3 Months	
	Wave 1 2/98	Wave 2 4/98
Base = Total Interviews	150	152
	%	%
Predicts Change in Habits (undup.)	30	24
Amount Planned to Buy in Next 3 Months		
More Often	4	5
About as Often	77	85
Less Often	18	11
Number of Packages Plans to Buy Next Time		
More	4	3
About the Same Number	87	87
Fewer	8	9
Size of Packages Plans to Buy Next Time		
Larger Size	8	9
Same Size	88	89
Smaller Size	3	1
Noticed Pancake Mix Price Increase (aided)	66	56
Price Compared to Last Bought Pancake Mix		
Compared to Previous Time		
Higher	41	43
About the Same Price	39	37
Lower	6	9
Reasons for Price Increase		
(Base = Noticed Price Increase)	(99)	(85)
Freeze/Frost/Bad Weather	25	29
Manufacturer Greed/Taking Advantage of Customer	10	11
Brand Usage		
Most Often Past Three Months Brand	42	43
Next Brand Will Purchase	39	39

Market Research Department Report

EXHIBIT 3
Fiscal 1990 Review—Custom Research Inc.—Confidential

Company Total—Fiscal 1990 Review[a]

	Actual	Plan	$ Difference	% Difference
Bookings[b]	$10,899.3M	$11,547.0M	$–647.7M	–6%
Closings[b]	10,297.0M	10,792.0M	–495.9M	–5%
Gross margins	1,677.6M	1,871.5M	–193.9M	–10%
General and administrative	729.8M	708.2M	–21.6M	–3%
Operating profit	$947.8M	$1,163.3M	$–215.5M	–19%
	9%	11%		–2%

[a] All data and numbers in **Exhibit 3** are disguised.

[b] "Bookings" refers to work under contract which in turn becomes work in progress. "Closings" is the revenue figure recorded once all costs are allocated. Typically, closings lag bookings by 5%–10% as this small percentage of booked business closes in the following fiscal year.

EXHIBIT 3 (*continued*)

New Bookings

Closed Sales (Completed Projects)

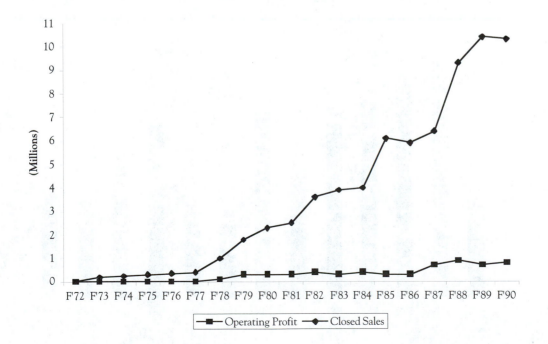

EXHIBIT 3 (*continued*)

Operating Profit—Internal P&L

Operating Profit as a % of Sales—Internal P&L

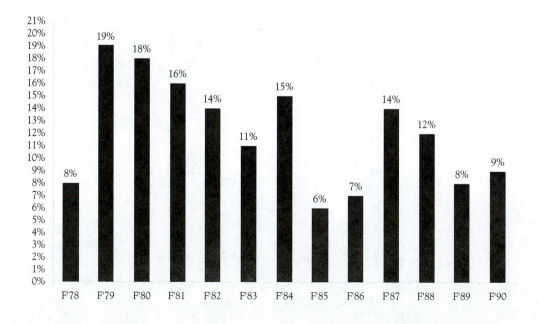

Part 5 *Product Costing and an Introduction to Cost Management*

EXHIBIT 3 (*continued*)

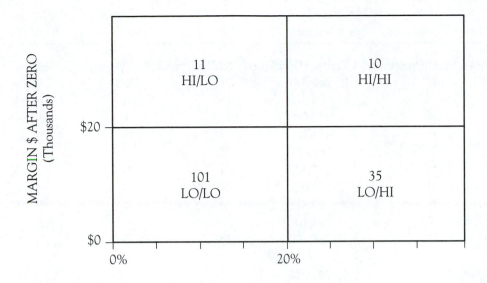

Number of Clients		$ Volume	$ Margin[a] After Zero	% Margin[a] After Zero	% of Total CRI Margin
10	HI-HI	$ 3,001K	$ 744K	25%	44%
11	HI-LO	2,919K	411K	14	25
35	LO-HI	1,094K	310K	28	18
101	LO-LO	3,283K	213K	6	13
157	TOTAL	$10,297K	$1,678K	16%	100%

[a] "$ Margin After Zero" refers to the profit margin after all direct project costs (salaries, data collection and tabulation, copying, shipping, etc.), as well as sales costs (e.g., all costs involved in selling the project) have been deducted. "Margin" refers to profit margin before sales costs have been deducted.

EXHIBIT 3 (*continued*)

Client I.D. Number	$ Volume	% Margin	% Margin After Zero	$ Margin After Zero
F-90 Closed Projects by Client—HI/HI (Over $20K/Over 20% Margin)				
30	$ 989,387	28%	26%	253,184
29	505,426	29	26	129,440
39	410,098	24	21	86,244
15	184,700	35	30	54,560
44	266,650	23	20	54,343
45	231,300	21	20	45,450
31	156,000	27	25	39,718
12	99,815	34	30	30,234
7	81,102	36	36	29,294
18	76,600	33	29	22,000
TOTAL 10	$3,001,078			$744,767
F-90 Closed Projects by Client—HI/LO (Over $20K/Under 20% Margin)				
46	$ 460,311	26%	19%	$ 88,518
60	206,125	19	16	49,531
61	281,962	22	16	45,255
54	252,269	22	18	44,904
71	276,608	15	12	32,640
78	293,600	10	10	28,685
73	232,300	20	12	26,877
68	189,358	23	14	26,529
79	258,535	22	9	24,406
76	223,681	13	10	22,592
67	144,500	15	15	21,155
TOTAL 11	$2,819,249			$411,092

EXHIBIT 3 (*continued*)

Client I.D. Number	$ Volume	% Margin	% Margin After Zero	$ Margin After Zero
F-90 Closed Projects by Client—LO/HI (Under $20K/Over 20% Margin)				
13	$ 61,250	32%	30%	$ 18,449
2	32,500	57	54	17,596
8	51,940	36	34	17,576
28	65,980	31	26	17,221
27	57,300	32	27	15,282
4	39,500	46	38	15,121
23	52,200	28	28	14,376
36	62,835	26	23	14,320
19	48,521	31	28	13,785
43	56,700	22	20	11,555
17	38,150	32	29	11,144
16	36,985	32	29	10,837
41	48,151	22	21	10,054
9	30,750	35	32	9,963
24	34,900	41	27	9,580
14	31,730	35	30	9,532
34	38,000	29	23	8,900
32	35,236	25	25	8,675
42	38,660	24	21	8,022
40	37,300	24	21	7,844
20	26,922	31	28	7,552
10	23,000	34	32	7,349
22	21,300	32	28	5,924
6	15,985	38	36	5,820
26	20,300	27	27	5,475
35	21,350	26	23	4,893
3	10,600	50	46	4,862
1	4,700	100	100	4,677
25	16,500	27	27	4,455
37	16,055	38	22	3,550
11	9,250	33	31	2,831
5	3,400	43	37	1,264
21	3,650	28	28	1,018
33	1,389	100	24	332
38	800	26	21	172
TOTAL 35	**$1,093,789**			**$310,006**

EXHIBIT 3 (*continued*)

Client I.D. Number	$ Volume	% Margin	% Margin After Zero	$ Margin After Zero
F-90 Closed Projects by Client—LO/LO (Under $20K/Under 20% Margin)				
72	$ 153,650	16%	12%	$ 18,438
66	113,780	19	15	17,067
83	186,680	17	9	16,801
59	102,501	21	16	16,400
84	203,320	14	7	14,232
47	57,900	24	19	11,001
55	59,789	22	18	10,762
82	115,925	16	9	10,433
64	57,165	24	15	8,575
49	42,100	24	19	7,999
70	62,800	22	12	7,536
63	45,850	24	16	7,336
80	74,547	11	9	6,709
58	40,650	21	16	6,504
52	35,600	23	18	6,408
56	36,660	28	17	6,232
87	110,885	7	5	5,544
69	38,494	16	14	5,389
57	31,284	23	17	5,318
53	29,000	26	18	5,220
65	29,300	20	15	4,395
75	27,500	22	11	3,025
50	15,600	27	19	2,964
62	18,000	20	16	2,880
92	91,900	12	3	2,757
81	30,600	21	9	2,754
85	36,500	13	7	2,555
96	47,250	10	5	2,363
134	38,600	30	6	2,316
123	45,000	20	5	2,250
77	19,100	22	10	1,910
48	9,685	29	19	1,840
157	31,950	6	5	1,598
125	30,150	17	5	1,508
91	36,675	17	4	1,467
155	35,800	16	4	1,432
120	22,994	26	6	1,380
74	12,350	15	11	1,359
51	7,600	26	17	1,292

Part 5 *Product Costing and an Introduction to Cost Management*

EXHIBIT 3 (*continued*)

Client I.D. Number	$ Volume	% Margin	% Margin After Zero	$ Margin After Zero
94	125,055	3	1	1,251
115	23,775	22	5	1,189
114	23,500	18	5	1,175
86	18,510	15	6	1,111
128	20,700	15	5	1,035
89	18,500	17	5	925
88	16,030	5	5	802
150	15,895	5	5	795
98	15,650	20	5	783
93	36,300	3	2	726
129	11,900	25	6	714
130	35,475	5	2	710
95	11,500	9	6	690
141	8,900	15	7	623
127	11,100	11	5	555
153	10,990	12	5	550
90	6,100	16	9	549
144	9,100	33	6	546
142	10,400	21	5	520
119	6,750	56	7	473
131	8,350	17	5	418
156	6,100	32	6	366
160	12,100	9	3	363
97	11,739	6	3	352
100	8,700	9	4	348
136	6,900	34	5	345
148	6,300	12	5	315
132	7,800	12	4	312
113	14,922	6	2	298
122	5,500	51	5	275
121	4,800	60	5	240
106	5,000	31	4	200
126	3,900	28	4	156
118	3,100	22	5	155
110	3,800	25	3	114
117	1,778	40	6	107
149	2,080	38	5	104
158	2,500	26	4	100
101	2,000	43	4	80
151	1,700	28	4	68

EXHIBIT 3 (*continued*)

Client I.D. Number	$ Volume	% Margin	% Margin After Zero	$ Margin After Zero
152	1,225	44	5	61
104	1,200	18	5	60
116	1,200	58	5	60
112	1,000	12	5	50
109	500	31	5	25
140	210	76	5	11
135	13,000	5	0	0
124	1,200	−1	−6	−72
139	7,800	4	−1	−78
111	2,000	−4	−9	−180
108	3,100	−4	−10	−310
147	3,900	−27	−32	−1,248
133	10,900	−5	−13	−1,417
159	9,800	−17	−19	−1,862
143	28,000	0	−7	−1,960
103	19,981	−3	−10	−1,998
138	12,100	−17	−22	−2,662
154	68,470	−2	−5	−3,424
102	43,180	−4	−9	−3,886
107	113,600	−1	−4	−4,544
99	54,450	−11	−12	−6,534
105	145,800	−5	−9	−13,122
TOTAL 101	$3,282,949			$213,357

Standard Costs and Variance Analysis

A *budget* is a quantitative expression of a plan of action. It serves as a goal that the organization strives to achieve. It is also used as a benchmark against which actual performance can be evaluated. Budgets span a specific period of time such as a month, a quarter, or a year. Organizations prepare a number of different budgets such as the sales budget, the production budget, the marketing costs budget, the cash budget, and the capital budget. This note will focus on budgets for product costs: direct costs (material and labor) and indirect costs (overhead), and their role in managing the overall costs of products and services.

Standard costs are developed based on the budgeted direct and indirect costs. A standard cost is a measure of how much one unit of product or service should cost to produce or deliver. A standard cost for a product will be made up of the costs of the components required to produce the product. For example, the standard cost of a leather jacket would include the cost of the materials (the leather, zipper, snaps, etc.), the cost of the labor (the time required to cut the pattern, stitch it, etc., at the production employee's wage rate), plus an allocation of the indirect or overhead costs related to it (the sewing machine depreciation, power, lights, etc.).

Once a standard cost is established, it provides a basis for decisions, for analyzing and controlling costs, and for measuring inventory accounts and cost of goods sold. Standard costs may be established using careful analysis of the product or service and the materials and process used to create it. Standard costs established in this way can be thought of as ideal costs. Other ways of determining standard costs, however, are also common. For example, last year's actual cost to produce a product or service can be used as the standard cost for this year.

Standard costs serve as benchmarks against which actual costs are compared. Differences between actual costs and standard costs are called *variances*. Actual costs may differ from standard costs because of price differences, quantity differences, errors or mistakes, or less than ideal conditions. Determining the reasons for variances may suggest corrective action or highlight that products are actually costing more or less than anticipated.

Lecturer Donella M. Rapier prepared this case as the basis for class discussion rather than to illustrate either effective or ineffective handling of an administrative situation.

Although the remainder of this note emphasizes standard costs and variances in a manufacturing setting, many of the same concepts can be applied to the delivery of services. The focus on manufacturing allows a clearer discussion of material, labor and overhead variances, which are often harder to conceptualize in service organizations.

DIRECT COSTS

Direct costs are costs, such as material and labor costs, that can be directly attributed to one unit of product. The standard cost for the direct costs of a product involve two components: a price component and a quantity component. The standard cost for a unit of production is the standard quantity to be used multiplied by the standard price per the unit of measure.

Example: Assume that our leather jacket should contain on average four yards of leather with a cost of $8.00 per yard, one zipper with a cost of $1.00, and two snaps with a cost of $0.25 each. Based on a time study recently done by management, a jacket requires an average of 5 hours of an employee's time to produce. Production workers are paid an average wage of $10 per hour including benefits. The standard cost for the direct costs (indirect costs will be discussed in the next section) would be as follows:

	Quantity	×	Price	=	Standard Cost
Materials:					
Leather	4 yards		$ 8.00		$32.00
Zipper	1		1.00		1.00
Snaps	2		.25		.50
Total material cost					$33.50
Labor cost	5 hours		10.00		50.00
Total direct cost					$83.50

Throughout the year, our leather jacket company will acquire leather, zippers and snaps and will hire and pay production workers. The actual amounts paid for these items, however, may not equal the amounts budgeted that formed the basis of the standard costs. For instance, the company may find leather at a lower price from a new discount supplier. A new machine purchased by the company may minimize the amount of material required for each jacket by reducing scrap material. Due to a significant order, the company might work its employees overtime which must be paid at time-and-a-half (150% of wage rate). The new machine might improve productivity so that it takes less than five hours to put a jacket together. These differences will give rise to variances between the actual and the budgeted standard costs.

An analysis of the year's results shows that the actual costs on average for the year for one jacket are as follows (no variances are assumed for zippers and snaps for simplicity):

	Quantity	×	Price	=	Actual Cost
Materials:					
Leather	3.5 yards		$ 7.50		$26.25
Zipper	1		1.00		1.00
Snaps	2		.25		.50
Total material cost					$27.75
Labor cost	4.8 hours		12.00		57.60
Total direct cost					$85.35

It is easy to see that jackets cost $1.85 more than budgeted. But without further analysis, a manager might miss potential opportunities for improving the business. For instance, a manager might miss the significance of the new supplier and the need to nurture this relationship. Or, without understanding the impact that the overtime pay has had, a manager might overlook the possibility of hiring additional workers instead of running overtime shifts. A manager might also misunderstand which department was responsible for savings, such as purchasing, and which was responsible for cost overruns, like production. Also, he or she would potentially miss the magnitude of the impact of the new machine and the possible opportunity to invest in additional machines.

In order to understand a variance, it must be broken into its component parts. An analysis of the materials variance is as follows:

Materials	Quantity	×	Price	=	Total
Leather:					
Budgeted	4.0 yards		$ 8.00		$32.00
Actual	3.5 yards		7.50		26.25
Materials variance					$ 5.75 favorable
Price variance	($8.00 – $7.50) × 3.5 yards			=	$ 1.75 favorable
Quantity variance	(4.0 – 3.5) × $8.00			=	4.00 favorable
Materials variance					$ 5.75 favorable

An analysis of the labor variance is as follows:

Labor	Quantity	×	Price	=	Total
Labor:					
Budgeted	5.0 hours		$10.00		$50.00
Actual	4.8 hours		12.00		57.60
Labor variance					$ 7.60 unfavorable
Price variance	($10.00 – $12.00) × 4.8 hours			=	$ 9.60 unfavorable
Quantity variance	(5.0 – 4.8) × $10.00			=	2.00 favorable
Labor variance					$ 7.60 unfavorable

The total variance is, thus, summed up as follows:

Standard cost	$83.50
Actual cost	85.35
Total variance	$ 1.85 unfavorable

Materials variance	$ 5.75 favorable
Labor variance	7.60 unfavorable
Total variance	$ 1.85 unfavorable

Formulas for analyzing variances can be expressed as follows:

Price variance $\quad = \ (SP - AP) \ \times \ AQ$

Quantity variance $= \ (SQ - AQ) \ \times \ SP$

Total variance $\quad = \ (SP \times SQ) - (AP \times AQ)$

Where:
   SP = **Standard price**
   AP = **Actual price**
   SQ = **Standard quantity**
   AQ = **Actual quantity**

Rather than worrying about whether to put standard or actual first in the formulas or about trying to keep track and understand whether a negative result is favorable or unfavorable, just think about whether the variance is good or bad. If the actual price is lower than the standard, it is a good or favorable variance; if the actual quantity is more than the standard, it is a bad or unfavorable variance, etc.

Note that by convention, price variance is computed using *actual* quantities, whereas quantity variance is computed using *standard* prices. This enables the purchasing agents to be assessed for price variations on quantities actually purchased. Production managers are assessed for quantity differences at standard prices, ignoring price fluctuations. While there are other ways of carving up the variances, this approach is the most typical.

A material price variance is often called a *purchase price variance*, and a material quantity variance is often called a *material usage variance*. A labor price variance is often called a *labor rate variance*, and a labor quantity variance is often called a *labor efficiency variance*.

INDIRECT COSTS

Direct costs vary in relation to the volume of units produced. Indirect or overhead costs, however, have elements that do vary directly with volume (variable overhead)

Part 5 Product Costing and an Introduction to Cost Management and other elements that do not (fixed overhead). The volume of production will fluctuate depending on many factors, for instance, demand for the company's products, labor shortages, etc. The effects of these variations in volume creates additional complexities in analyzing performance relative to an overhead budget.

Overhead Budgets

One approach to overhead budgeting ignores the volume considerations. This approach is called *fixed overhead budgeting*. Under a fixed budget approach, management determines the amount of overhead that should be incurred at the normal or most likely production level. This expense total becomes the budget against which cost performance is measured regardless of the level of production output actually achieved. An example would be as follows:

Allowed Overhead (in thousands)

Rent	$ 500
Depreciation	500
Supervision	1,000
Supplies	800
Power	800
	$3,600

Performance at the end of the year would be measured against the $3,600,000 total. This approach, however, by disregarding the true nature of the costs, may lead a manager to make some inaccurate conclusions about performance. For instance, assume that this budget is based on a "normal" production level of 160,000 leather jackets. Also assume that the power costs, representing in part the cutting and sewing machines, vary with the level of production. If 200,000 jackets are produced during the year, the power costs would exceed $800,000, say these costs total $1,000,000. Comparing this to the fixed budget, a manager might conclude that the warehouse supervisor did a poor job of managing the power costs, when in fact, the overspending relates solely to the extra 40,000 jackets produced.

The more conceptually sound approach to determining overhead standards is called *flexible budgeting*. A flexible overhead budget specifies allowable cost at each possible output level. Once a period is completed and the actual production volume is known, the budget standard is determined by reference to the flexible budget for the actual level of output. This is a direct parallel to the way a budget for direct material and direct labor is determined.

An example of a simplified flexible budget might look something like the following:

Flexible Budget

			"Normal"		Cost Behavior
Capacity Utilization:	40%[a]	60%	70%	80%	100%	
Labor Cost (piece rate):	$4,000	$6,000	$7,000	$8,000	$10,000	

Allowed Overhead						Cost Behavior
Rent	$ 500	$ 500	$ 500	$ 500	$ 500	Pure nonvariable or "fixed"
Depreciation	500	500	500	500	500	Pure nonvariable or "fixed"
Supervision	500	1,000	1,000	1,000	1,500	"Step" cost[b]
Supplies	400	600	700	800	1,000	Pure variable at 10% of labor
Power	600	700	750	800	900	Semivariable:
						$400 + 5% of labor
Total	$2,500	$3,300	$3,450	$3,600	$4,400	

[a] It is assumed that volume would never fall below 40% of capacity.

[b] A "step" cost is one which does not vary directly with production but does increase in lump-sum jumps when volume rises substantially. An example would be adding a second supervisor when volume rose to the level where a second shift was needed.

A flexible budget allows us to more intelligently analyze variable overhead spending.

Overhead Absorption

Now that our flexible overhead budget is established, we need a way to allocate the overhead to our products. The cost of a product should include all costs incurred in bringing the product to its completed form. Therefore, in addition to the direct labor and material costs, the standard cost of a product includes indirect costs, as well. But labor and material are easily measured and assigned to the products. It is much more difficult to determine how much rent, or supplies, or depreciation is consumed by a particular product.

Accountants resolve this dilemma by using an allocation method. This is termed *overhead absorption*, as the costs are *absorbed* into inventory. Overhead costs are first collected in *cost pools*. One pool might include all rent, another all costs related to inspection, another might be supervisory expenses. The cost pools are then allocated down to the products using a *cost driver*. For simplicity, in the remainder of this note, we will assume that all overhead is aggregated into a single pool. Assume that all of our overhead expenses for our leather jacket company are set forth in the table above and are accumulated in one cost pool for allocation to products.

In single-product firms, the overhead pool might be allocated on a per-unit basis, i.e., using units as the cost driver. The total budgeted overhead ($3.6 million using the example above) would be divided by the planned production volume (assume

200,000 jackets for this illustration). Then for every jacket produced, $18.00 ($3.6 million divided by 200,000) would be applied as overhead. The standard cost for a jacket under this method would thus be as follows:

Standard Cost:

Materials	$ 33.50
Labor	50.00
Overhead	18.00
Total standard cost	$101.50

In multiproduct firms, however, it is necessary to use an allocation method or cost driver other than number of units produced in order to more fairly apportion the overhead. For instance, if our company made leather gloves in addition to jackets, and the gloves could be manufactured in one-quarter of the time it takes to produce a jacket, it would be unfair to burden each pair of gloves with the same dollar amount of overhead as a jacket. Some other measure of capacity utilization must be used, such as labor hours, labor dollars, or machine hours. The choice of a volume measure in a particular business should be based on which variable best measures the level of capacity utilization for that business. For example, a machine depreciation cost pool might be allocated using number of machine hours per product as the driver. A supervision cost pool might be allocated using direct labor hours as the cost driver.

Since our jacket production process is fairly labor-intensive, we will use direct labor dollars as our allocation method. Using direct labor dollars, the standard overhead cost for a jacket would be $0.45 for every direct labor dollar ($3.6 million total budgeted overhead divided by $8 million budgeted labor cost). So for one jacket, $22.50 would be applied ($50.00 labor dollars per jacket multiplied by the $0.45 per labor dollar overhead rate). The total standard cost would be as follows:

Standard Cost:

Materials	$ 33.50
Labor	50.00
Overhead	22.50
Total standard cost	$106.00

This is the amount that would be accumulated as inventory throughout the year for every jacket produced. However, differences in planned versus actual volume will give rise to a *volume variance*.

Above we demonstrated how variable overhead would fluctuate with volume and therefore, could not be intelligently compared to a fixed or static budget. On the other hand, fixed overhead does not vary with volume. As indicated in our flexible budget above, rent and depreciation are the same amounts under all levels of production. But, let's think about the mechanics for a moment. If, throughout the year, $22.50 is allocated or absorbed into inventory for every jacket produced, what if the number of jackets is different than we planned? Certainly, if we produced the exact number planned, 160,000, the overhead absorbed would equal the actual overhead (assuming no spending variances).

Labor per jacket	$ 50.00
Overhead rate	× .45
Overhead/jacket	22.50
Number of jackets	× 160,000
Total overhead applied	$3,600,000

This would be equal to the total overhead planned. If, on the other hand, only 140,000 jackets were produced, the amount absorbed would be as follows:

Labor per jacket	$ 50.00
Overhead rate	× .45
Overhead/jacket	22.50
Number of jackets	× 140,000
Total overhead applied	$3,150,000

Let's assume that all of the $3.6 million overhead is fixed. At the end of the year, our accounts would show that $3.15 million of overhead was absorbed into inventory but our actual costs were $3.6 million. This gives us a variance of $450 thousand. What does this variance tell us? Does this tell us much about how we managed our overhead? Not really. The costs were fixed at $3.6 million and that's what was spent. It does indicate that at a lower level of production, our per unit cost is higher as our fixed costs are spread over fewer units, but this is to some extent, merely a function of the planned production chosen at the beginning of the year that we used to derive our overhead rate.

This variance, called a *volume variance*, is essentially just the mathematical difference that arises because overhead is applied as if it were a variable expense (a budgeted rate times a cost driver such as direct labor dollars), but it is actually fixed. The absorption rate is set to just absorb into inventory the planned overhead when the company operates at its normal volume. It is necessary to isolate the volume variance from the spending variance, which is much more managerially significant, because otherwise we would make inappropriate conclusions about our performance against the budget.

ANALYZING THE TOTAL OVERHEAD VARIANCE

Now that we have isolated the separate pieces of the overhead variance, the spending variance and the volume variance, let's work through an example. Assume the following:

Planned production	160,000
80% capacity	
$8 million direct labor dollars	
Actual production	140,000
70% capacity	
$7 million direct labor dollars	

Part 5 *Product Costing and an Introduction to Cost Management*

(in thousands)

Absorbed overhead	$3,150 ($7,000 labor dollars at $0.45)
Actual overhead	3,610
Unfavorable variance	460

Spending Variance

To analyze the spending variance, compare the actual overhead to the flexible budget at 70% capacity:

	Flexible Budget Allowance at Actual Volume of $7,000 Direct Labor Dollars	Actual Expense at Actual Volume	Spending Variance
Rent	$ 500	$ 500	—
Depreciation	500	600	$100U
Supervision	1,000	1,050	50U
Supplies	700	690	10F
Power	750	770	20U
Total	$3,450	$3,610	$160U

The difference between actual overhead incurred and the flexible budget at this level of output is the *overhead spending variance*. It measures cost control performance.

Volume Variance

To analyze the volume variance, compare the allowed overhead at 70% capacity to the absorbed overhead (in thousands):

Allowed overhead (70% capacity)	$3,450
Absorbed overhead	3,150
Unfavorable volume variance	300

The difference between the allowed overhead and the absorbed overhead at this level of output is the *production volume variance*. It results from the difference between planned and actual production volume. It is made up of under- or over-absorbed *fixed manufacturing overhead*. It does not include any variable overhead because items that vary directly with production are treated identically in both the absorption rate and in the flexible budget.

Total Variance

You will note that the sum of the spending variance and the volume variance is equal to the total variance. To express the variance analyses mathematically:

$$\begin{pmatrix} \text{Actual OH} - \\ \text{Allowed OH} \end{pmatrix} + \begin{pmatrix} \text{Allowed OH} - \\ \text{Absorbed OH} \end{pmatrix} = \begin{pmatrix} \text{Actual OH} - \\ \text{Absorbed OH} \end{pmatrix}$$

Spending Variance   +   Volume Variance   =   Total Variance

Plugging in our amounts from above (in thousands):

($3,610 − $3,450) + ($3,450 − $3,150) = ($3,610 − $3,150)

$160   + $300   = $460

Another way to look at the total variance is as follows:

Total variance   = Actual OH − Absorbed OH

Spending variance = Actual OH − Allowed OH

Volume variance = Allowed OH − Absorbed OH

To proof:

Spending variance   +   Volume variance   =   Total variance

CONCLUSION

The important questions that follow the calculation of variances concern *why* actual costs are different from standard costs. Variances provide clues for managers to investigate further. Sometimes the answers are obvious, but often they are not. For example, favorable material price variances may be caused by lower quality but cheaper material being used. This may lead to more labor time being spent by workers of high skill (and higher wages) leading to an unfavorable labor usage (quantity) variance. Skilled managers analyzing variances often try to weave clues together into a "story" to explain why the variances arose in order to make appropriate decisions to improve performance in the future.

Waltham Motors Division

When Sharon Michaels arrived at her office at Waltham Motors Division on June 4, 2004, she was pleased to find the monthly performance report for May on her desk. Her job as division controller was to analyze results of operations each month and to prepare a narrative report on operations that was to be forwarded to the corporate headquarters of Marco Corporation. Waltham Motors was a wholly owned subsidiary of Marco. The atmosphere at the division had been one of apprehensiveness throughout the month of May, and today would provide a chance to find out how well division management had compensated for the recent loss of a major customer contract.

THE CURRENT SITUATION

Waltham Motors manufactured electric motors of a single design that were sold to household appliance manufacturers. Originally a family-owned business, the division had been acquired in late 2003 by the Marco Corporation. Few changes had been made in either the company's operating procedures or systems because Marco's management had chosen to delay changing procedures and systems until it was able to observe how well those already in use at Waltham functioned. In April, Sharon Michaels, who had earned a master's degree in business administration in 2002, was transferred from the corporate headquarters controller's office to Waltham Motors. She was joined in late May by David Marshall, also from Marco, who was to be the new division manager.

Because of the lost contract, Michaels had asked the plant accountant to assemble the May figures as quickly as possible, but she was amazed that they were ready so soon. At headquarters, monthly results had rarely been available until several days after the end of each month. Even though the plant accountant had promised Sharon that he would be able to prepare the report in a single day with some overtime work, she was surprised that he had been able to do so.

Professor William J. Bruns, Jr. prepared this case. HBS cases are developed solely as the basis for class discussion. Cases are not intended to serve as endorsements, sources of primary data, or illustrations of effective or ineffective management. The case was updated by Susan S. Harmeling, MBA '91.

The division had prepared a budget for 2004 based on estimated sales and production costs. Because sales were not subject to seasonal fluctuations, the monthly budget was merely one-twelfth of the annual budget. No adjustments had been made to the May budget when the contract was lost in April.

THE PERFORMANCE REPORT

A glance at the performance report confirmed Michaels's worst fears. Instead of a budgeted profit of $91,200, the report showed the division had lost $7,200 in May. Even allowing for the lost volume, she had expected a better showing than indicated by the performance report. The plant accountant had attached the following memo to the report:

June 3, 11:00 P.M.

Sharon:

As promised, here is the performance report for May. (I told you smaller is better; we'll show headquarters how efficient our plant accounting department is!) I am sure you'll find the bottom line as disappointing as I did, but plant performance really looks good, and the crews there may deserve our compliments. Note how they are at or under budget on every single cost except for supervision. I suspect that the unfavorable variance in supervision was caused directly by the work involved in controlling other costs.

Because I worked late, I am taking a day off tomorrow. The other data you requested are as follows:

1. There were no beginning and ending inventories in work in progress or finished goods.

2. Per unit standard costs used in budgeting this year were:

   Direct material $ 6

   Direct labor   16

3. We are still using two hours per unit as standard labor time.

4. Actual material prices have been 5% less than expected.

5. Actual direct labor costs have been $8.20 per hour due to the increase in medical benefits granted last January.

A copy of the performance report is shown as **Exhibit 1**.

QUESTIONS

1. Using budget data, how many motors would have to be sold for Waltham Motors Division to break even?

2. Using budget data, what was the total expected cost per unit if all manufacturing and shipping overhead (both variable and fixed) was allocated to planned production? What was the actual per unit cost of production and shipping?

3. Comment on the performance report and the plant accountant's analysis of results. How, if at all, would you suggest the performance report be changed before sending it on to the division manager and Marco Corporation headquarters?

4. Prepare your own analysis of the Waltham Division's operations in May. Explain in as much detail as possible why income differed from what you would have expected.

EXHIBIT 1
Performance Report, May 2004

	Budget	Actual	Variance
Units	18,000	14,000	4,000
Sales	$864,000	$686,000	$178,000U
Variable manufacturing costs:			
Direct material	$108,000	$ 85,400	$ 22,600F
Direct labor	288,000	246,000	42,000F
Indirect labor	57,600	44,400	13,200F
Idle time	14,400	14,200	200F
Cleanup time	10,800	10,000	800F
Miscellaneous supplies	5,200	4,000	1,200F
Total variable manufacturing cost	$484,000	$404,000	$ 80,000F
Variable shipping costs	$ 28,800	$ 28,000	$ 800F
Total variable costs	$512,800	$432,000	$ 80,800F
Contribution margin	$351,200	$254,000	$ 97,200U
Nonvariable manufacturing costs:			
Supervision	$ 57,600	$ 58,800	$ 1,200U
Rent	20,000	20,000	—
Depreciation	60,000	60,000	—
Other	10,400	10,400	—
Total nonvariable manufacturing costs	$148,000	$149,200	$ 1,200U
Selling and administrative costs	112,000	112,000	—
Total nonvariable and programmed costs	$260,000	$261,200	$ 1,200U
Operating income (loss)	91,200	(7,200)	(98,400)U

Mile High Cycles

In 2005, Bob Moyer was reviewing production costs for Mile High Cycles. Located in Denver, Colorado, the company sold very high-quality, handcrafted mountain bikes to bicycle retailers throughout the country. Sales for the company were $13 million that year.

Bob Moyer had been an avid cyclist in college, racing for the Stanford University cycling team while completing his degree in mechanical engineering. After working for a few years as a design engineer for a company in Denver, Bob decided to start his own business. As a hobby, he had designed and built several prototypes of a mountain bike, which had been enthusiastically received by his mountain-biking friends. Approaching several friends and relatives for start-up money, Mile High Cycles was founded in 2003.

A mountain bike was a bicycle with 15 to 21 speeds, designed and built to take the punishment of riding on dirt trails and roads. The bikes were first made by avid cyclists who customized their 10-speed road bikes in order to ride on mountain trails and dirt roads. Some with framebuilding experience began to experiment making their own frames in order to handle better the additional demands of off-road riding. By 1992, several small companies had emerged selling bicycles specifically designed for riding under these conditions.

During the rest of the 1990s, mountain bikes had taken off in popularity, not only for use off-road but also for use in the city, where their sturdy construction could withstand the pounding from potholes and curbs. In addition, many casual cyclists preferred the mountain bike's more upright riding position in comparison to that of the hunched position of the 10-speed road bike. Sales of all bicycles in the United States had declined in 2003. However, over the same time period, sales of mountain bikes increased to more than 2.0 million units.

Bob Moyer had planned to produce 10,000 bikes in 2004, all of one model. Operations at Mile High Cycles consisted of three departments: frames, wheel assembly, and final assembly. In frames, steel tubing was cut to length for the components of the frame. Then the pieces were carefully welded together to form the completed

Professor William J. Bruns, Jr. and David J. Ellison prepared this case. HBS cases are developed solely as the basis for class discussion. Cases are not intended to serve as endorsements, sources of primary data, or illustrations of effective or ineffective management.

Part 5 *Product Costing and an Introduction to Cost Management*

frameset. This part of the process was quite time-consuming, requiring frequent inspection and measurement to ensure that the frameset was aligned perfectly. After welding, the frame was painted in one of 10 different color schemes and prepared for final assembly.

In wheel assembly, front and rear wheels were assembled from their key components: hubs, spokes, and rims. All of the components were purchased from an outside supplier. Mile High Cycles used a high-quality automatic lacing and truing machine to build its wheels. This machine would lace the spokes between the hub and rim and then automatically tighten the spokes to the appropriate tension. The machine was quite precise but would occasionally damage spokes during the insertion process. In such a case, the operator would replace any damaged parts and restart the machine. Each wheel would also be inspected and trued by hand in order to insure that the wheels were in perfect alignment.

In final assembly, the frame and wheels were combined with other purchased parts to create the final package that would then be shipped to bicycle dealers. In this area, the front fork and many other key components were attached to the frame, and the inner tubes and tires were mounted on the wheels. In order to minimize damage while shipping, some of the bicycles' components were left packaged for the bicycle dealer to assemble before selling the bike to the final customer. All of the components were purchased from outside suppliers and then were combined to form kits for the bicycles. Mile High Cycles carried an inventory of spare parts to replace any parts damaged during assembly or shipping, although such replacement was quite infrequent.

In reviewing his costs, Bob noted that he had produced 10,800 bicycles in 2004, 800 more than planned. Bob thought that operations during the year had done well to meet the additional demand, but he wondered if Mile High Cycles was doing a good job in managing its costs. **Exhibit 1** shows the planned material, labor, and overhead costs for 2004. **Exhibit 2** shows the actual material, labor, and overhead costs for that year.

QUESTIONS

1. Determine the direct cost and overhead variances. What might be causing each of the variances to occur?

2. Should Bob Moyer be concerned about Mile High Cycles's performance? Where should he be prepared to direct his attention? What additional information should he try to obtain?

3. Are there any purposes for which a total, per unit variance would be more useful than a series of functional variances? If so, for what?

EXHIBIT 1
2004 Production Budget

Budget based on 10,000 bicycles production

Frame assembly:

Steel tubing	$ 3,300,000	(110,000 lbs. @ $30.00/lb.)
Paint	25,000	(1,250 gals. @ $20.00/gal.)
Labor	$ 1,500,000	(100,000 hrs. @ $15.00/hr.)
Total frame	$ 4,825,000	

Wheel assembly:

Parts	$ 1,200,000	(10,000 kits @ $120.00/kit)
Labor	65,000	(5,000 hrs. @ $13.00/hr.)
Total wheel	$ 1,265,000	

Final assembly:

Parts	$ 3,500,000	(10,000 kits @ $350.00/kit)
Labor	105,000	(7,500 hrs. @ $14.00/hr.)
Total final assembly	$ 3,605,000	

Overhead costs:

Rent	$ 250,000	
Office staff	100,000	
Depreciation	100,000	
Other costs	750,000	(estimated to be 2/3 variable)
Total overhead	$ 1,200,000	
Total Annual Costs	$10,895,000	

EXHIBIT 2
2004 Production Costs

Actual production: 10,800 bicycles

Frame assembly:

Steel tubing	$ 3,572,100	(113,400 lbs. @ $31.50/lb.)
Paint	28,187	(1,375 gals. @ $20.50/gal.)
Labor	1,528,050	(100,200 hrs. @ $15.25/hr.)
Total frame	$ 5,128,337	

Wheel assembly:

Parts	$ 1,317,600	(10,800 kits @ $122.00/kit)
Rework parts	25,000	(spokes and rims)
Labor	74,250	(5,500 hrs. @ $13.50/hr.)
Total wheel	$ 1,416,850	

Final assembly:

Parts	$ 3,963,600	(10,800 kits @ $367.00/kit)
Rework parts	45,000	(miscellaneous parts)
Labor	116,000	(8,000 hrs. @ $14.50/hr.)
Total final assembly	$ 4,124,600	

Overhead costs:

Rent	$ 250,000
Office staff	100,000
Depreciation	100,000
Other costs	850,000
Total overhead	$ 1,300,000
Total Annual Costs	$11,969,787

Analysis for Capital Investment Decisions

PART 6

Basic Capital Investment Analysis

- *Riverbend Telephone Company*
- *Reto S.A.*
- *The Super Project*

Basic Capital Investment Analysis

Decisions about new investments in machines, a plant, or other assets are among the most important decisions that managers make for their organizations. In many cases, a decision to invest means that the organization will have to live with the effects of the investment for many years to come. Consequently, when new investments are considered it is of great importance that managers have all possible relevant information and that the information be analyzed with care in a meaningful manner.

Capital investment analysis always should begin with a careful search for alternatives. This is not always as easy as it first appears, because some alternatives may be more difficult to identify than others. Often investment alternatives have a sponsor who stands to gain if his or her alternative is selected, and other alternatives will be ignored or not mentioned by the sponsor. Or an investment perpetuates a traditional way of doing business when a more modern approach would prove more successful in the long run. All reasonable alternatives to any proposed investment need to be considered, and any that cannot be eliminated before formal investment analysis begins need to be studied and analyzed.

ESTIMATING CASH FLOWS

Once alternatives have been identified, the cash flows which will occur if each is accepted need to be determined. Usually the cash flows that result from making the proposed investment are compared to the alternative of doing nothing. For example, if the proposal is to acquire a new machine to replace one already owned, the cash flows that will take place if the new machine is acquired can be compared to the cash flows if no action is taken to determine the *differential cash flows* that are associated with the new machine. Only the differential *future* cash flows are of interest and concern. If there are several alternatives, a separate study of each will allow comparison to determine which is best.

Professor William J. Bruns, Jr. prepared this case as the basis for class discussion rather than to illustrate either effective or ineffective handling of an administrative situation.

TWO TECHNIQUES FOR EVALUATING CAPITAL INVESTMENT PROPOSALS

Two techniques are often used to help decide whether a capital investment should be made or not made. The *Net Present Value* (NPV) method uses an interest rate, cost of capital, or a desired rate of return to determine whether or not the present value of all future cash flows from the proposal is positive or negative. If it is positive, a decision to make the investment is supported. The *Internal Rate of Return* (IRR) method seeks the interest rate that will equate the present value of all cash outflows to the present value of all cash inflows. If this internal rate of return (or *yield*) exceeds the *hurdle rate* (cost of capital or desired rate of return), a positive decision to make the investment is supported.

Each of these techniques is based on the same algebraic formula. The difference lies in the unknown variable that is the focus of the solution. In NPV, the focus is on the net present value of all cash flows at a desired interest rate. In IRR, the focus is on the interest rate that will equate the present value of all cash outflows with the present value of all cash inflows. The formula looks like this:

$$\text{Net Present Value} = \text{Cash Flow (CF)}_0 + \frac{CF_1}{(1+i)^1} + \frac{CF_2}{(1+i)^2} + \frac{CF_n}{(1+i)^n}$$

where i is the desired rate of return.

If the Net Present Value is set to 0 and the equation is solved for i, i is the *internal rate of return*.

It is rare that anyone actually has to work with the formula above because it is built into all financial or business calculators, computer spreadsheet software, and many personal computers, and compound interest tables are widely available.

Each of these techniques requires the analyst to identify:

1. The amount of all cash outflows that the investment requires and their timing.

2. The amount of all net cash inflows that will result from the investment and their timing.

3. The criterion for acceptability of new investments of the type under consideration.

A SIMPLE EXAMPLE

Suppose that a proposed investment were $27,500 and the anticipated net cash flows were $9,000 each year (received at the end of each year) for five years.

If the desired rate of return is 15%, the NPV is $2,669.

If the desired rate of return is 20%, the NPV is ($584).

If the NPV is set to 0, the IRR is found to be 19%.

If the managers will make any investment that returns more than 15%, or if they find an IRR of 19% acceptable, they may make this investment. If they demand a return of 20%, the proposed investment is unacceptable.

SOME THINGS TO KEEP IN MIND

Cash flows, not earnings, are the focus of investment analysis. This means that the effects of income taxes and the deductibility of depreciation must always be considered if they affect cash flows. If the analysis begins with an estimate of the positive cash flows that will be obtained by making the investment, and these will be taxed, only the cash flow after taxes should be used in the analysis. However, if depreciation is deductible for tax purposes, that may shield some of the new positive cash flows from taxes.

If there is existing equipment that can be sold, the total net new investment required should reflect the sales price that the old equipment will bring. A trade-in of the old equipment has a similar effect, reducing the new investment required. Likewise, if there is a gain or loss on the sale of the old equipment that will add to or reduce income taxes, that must be taken into account in the amount of investment or future cash flows.

New investments may change the amount of working capital that is required, and working capital requirements should always be considered when analyzing investments. Even though additional working capital required because of a new investment will be recovered at the end of the new investment's life, the use of compound interest methods will make the present value of the recovered working capital a fraction of the investment in working capital required when the new investment is made.

A final consideration in investment analysis concerns pricing trends that may affect the amount of new investment required. It may be possible that the cost of the new investment will fall if the investment is delayed one year or more. When a price reduction seems likely, the benefits of investing now should be compared with the benefits of waiting to invest in the future. Sometimes the price reduction will be great enough to offset the cost of waiting to gain the benefits of the investment.

Effective capital investment analysis requires clear identification of strategies and competitive initiatives, ingenuity and imagination to uncover alternatives, and careful attention to factors that will affect current and future cash flows. Often early analyses will lead to new questions that can be answered only through study or research. But the objective should be held clearly in mind—managers want to make the best decisions possible based on the best information available, carefully analyzed. The future success of their organization depends on making the best investments at the most favorable times.

Riverbend Telephone Company

The Riverbend Telephone Company is independently owned and operates in the area between the west bank of the Short River and the state line. The company provides local telephone service to customers in several adjacent communities, and its lines connect with those of other companies to provide long-distance telephone service. Operating as a public utility, the Riverbend Telephone Company is subject to regulation by the State Public Service Commission, which periodically reviews service and must approve all changes in rates.

In recent years, the population of the area served by the company had grown rapidly as a result of a new bridge which facilitated daily commuting over the Short River to a nearby city. As a result of this growth, company personnel and equipment had been hard pressed to meet all demands for installation of new telephone lines and maintenance. For a time, the company had used an outside contractor to handle overload work, but several poor experiences had caused abandonment of that practice. By late 2004, it was obvious that the company needed at least one new maintenance truck and crew.

The need to obtain a new truck arose at a critical period for the company. Earlier, Riverbend had made heavy commitments to purchase telephone equipment needed to improve service. Recent payments for new equipment had strained the net working capital position of the firm. Stockholders were unable to provide additional resources and hoped to avoid selling additional shares which would dilute their ownership. Interest rates were quoted at 8% on short-term notes, and above 9% on long-term rates. Since the company had been earning only about 10% on net assets, the firm hoped to avoid unnecessary borrowing.

In November 2004, Warren Freeman, general manager of Riverbend, requested bids for the new trucks from four truck dealers. The lowest bid received was from the Reliable Motors Company, which quoted a cash price of $24,300, including all taxes and delivery charges. As an alternative, Reliable would lease the truck to Riverbend Telephone for five years at an annual rate of $7,200.

Professor William J. Bruns, Jr. prepared this case. HBS cases are developed solely as the basis for class discussion. Cases are not intended to serve as endorsements, sources of primary data, or illustrations of effective or ineffective management.

The truck which Riverbend Telephone Company needed was similar to several others which it already owned. At Mr. Freeman's request, the company accounting department used records to estimate the cost of operating the new truck. Those estimates are shown in **Exhibit 1**. The truck was expected to last for five years, at which time it could probably be sold for about $1,800. If the truck were purchased, it would be depreciated by the straight-line method because that was the only method allowed by the State Public Service Commission.

If the truck were leased, Riverbend Telephone would have to pay the annual lease charge on or before the first day of each year. In addition, they would be responsible for all costs of operation and maintenance of the truck except for tires which Reliable Motors would supply. The proposed agreement also made Riverbend responsible for all risks to the truck and property damage, collision, personal injury, fire, and theft. Finally, Riverbend would reimburse Reliable for all costs of vehicle registration and taxes.

Mr. Freeman was unsure how he should view the alternatives presented by Reliable Motors. Leasing the truck would reduce the immediate demands on Riverbend Telephone's financial resources. Still, the prospect of paying $36,000 over five years when the truck could be purchased new for $24,300 raised questions about how well he would be serving company stockholders if he leased rather than purchased the truck. On the other hand, the operating expenses and lease payments would be allowable expense deductions in calculating income for tax purposes. Since the company had been paying and expected to continue paying income taxes of 40%, an increase in expenses of $7,200 per year would not really cost that much.

The effect of his choice on Riverbend's rate of return earned on net assets was also important to Mr. Freeman. In 2004, the State Public Service Commission had allowed another telephone company to raise its rates to provide revenues to increase its rate of return to just above 11% on net assets. In an attempt to raise Riverbend's return without requesting higher rates, Mr. Freeman had not approved any new investments that would provide a rate of return on investment below 12% unless they were absolutely necessary. Since the truck had to be acquired and the choice was only whether it should be leased or purchased, Mr. Freeman was unsure whether his 12% return minimum made any difference in this case.

Mr. Freeman also wanted to consider how the State Public Service Commission might view leased assets in evaluating rates of return earned by utilities. Purchased assets were always included in total investment net of accumulated depreciation, and all operating expenses, including depreciation, were allowable deductions in determining annual income. While he was not able to ascertain exactly what the Commission might want, he reasoned that Riverbend could probably include all operating expenses and the lease payments among annual expenses in reports to the Commission, but he was unsure whether investment should be increased by the "fair value" of the leased asset before calculating return on net assets.

QUESTIONS

1. Should the company buy or lease the new truck? (Assume that Riverbend Telephone uses the straight-line method of depreciation for tax purposes as well as for reports to shareholders and the State Public Service Commission.)

2. If Riverbend Telephone purchased the truck and chose to depreciate it for income tax purposes only using the double-declining balance method, would this affect your decision to buy or lease? Assume that the annual depreciation would be:

Year	Depreciation
2005	$9,720
2006	5,832
2007	3,500
2008	2,100
2009	1,348

3. If the truck is leased, how should Mr. Freeman report investment and annual income for the Riverbed Telephone Company to the State Public Service Commission?

EXHIBIT 1
Estimated Operating Expense of Maintenance Truck

Type of Expenses	Year of Operation				
	1	2	3	4	5
Gasoline	$ 3,600	$ 3,600	$ 3,600	$ 3,600	$ 3,600
Repairs and maintenance	800	928	1,048	1,160	1,264
Tires	—	760	760	760	760
Insurance	2,400	2,400	2,400	2,400	2,400
Registration and taxes	848	720	600	488	384
Depreciation (straight-line method)	4,500	4,500	4,500	4,500	4,500
Total expenses	$12,148	$12,908	$12,908	$12,908	$12,908

Reto S.A.

I n December 2004, R. E. Torgler was trying to decide whether to add a new line of injection molded plastic products to those already manufactured and distributed by Reto S.A. In order to do so, the firm would have to buy new injection molding equipment; none of the existing equipment could be adapted to perform the necessary operations, and Torgler was anxious to retain control of manufacturing. Actually, new injection molding equipment of the type needed had been considered before, but a decision to purchase the equipment had been postponed because the product concept was judged to need additional development. But now the products seemed ready.

Sales of the new product were forecast at SFr. 2,000,000[1] per year, from which a sales commission of 15 percent would be paid to Reto's sales agents. Direct manufacturing costs were budgeted at SFr. 600,000 for materials and SFr. 900,000 for labor, leaving an annual cash flow before taxation of SFr. 200,000. The new equipment would cost SFr. 600,000, delivered and installed, and was expected to have an economic life of 10 years before it would become worthless.

Reto was able to borrow money at 8 percent, although it did not plan to negotiate a loan specifically for the purchase of this equipment.

QUESTIONS

1. Ignoring the effect of taxes, what is the "internal rate of return" (IRR) on the proposed investment? Assume the new equipment would be installed by January 1, 2005, and begin producing on that date.

2. The cost of the equipment can be deducted from annual cash flows before they are subjected to taxation. Assuming that the equipment will last 10 years, and that an equal amount of the cost of SFr. 600,000 will be deducted

---

Professor William J. Bruns, Jr. prepared this case. HBS cases are developed solely as the basis for class discussion. Cases are not intended to serve as endorsements, sources of primary data, or illustrations of effective or ineffective management.

---

[1] Actual sales were made in several different currencies, but for simplicity here all money measurements are stated in their Swiss franc equivalents. The approximate exchange rate at the time of writing the case was SFr. 1.30 = U.S. $1.00.

each year, and that the tax rate is expected to be 45 percent, what is the IRR on an after-tax basis?

3. Torgler has stated that Reto should be willing to purchase this machine as long as it yielded a return of 12 percent after taxation. Should he make the investment?

4. Actually, to stimulate industrial development, the tax rules allow up to one third of the cost of any such investment to be deducted from cash flows in the first year after the investment, and up to one-fifth of the remainder of the un-amortized investment amount can be deducted in the second year. Thereafter, annual deductions are computed on a straight-line basis such that no more than the original cost of the equipment is depreciated over its economic life. How, if at all, does this tax rule affect the attractiveness of the investment?

5. Reto has learned that investment in working capital (receivables and inventories, less payables) amounts to approximately 15 percent of sales. Will the additional SFr. 300,000 investment for the new line decrease the rate of return on investment to less than the 12 percent criterion Torgler has been using?

6. In late December 2004, Reto purchased the equipment, and the operating results turned out as forecast. A year later, Torgler learned that the manufacturer of the equipment had introduced new models which were more automated. The new equipment sold for SFr. 1,000,000 and would permit labor savings of SFr. 200,000 per year, thus doubling the net operating cash flow on the product. As a result of the technological advance, Torgler expected the one-year-old machine could be sold for only SFr. 200,000 despite the fact that its book value was SFr. 400,000. If Reto buys the new machine and depreciates it using allowed tax depreciation over 10 years, would the investment meet the 12 percent after-tax criterion?

7. If the one-year-old machine had no salvage value at all, would replacing it with the new machine still be desirable?

8. Torgler was loathe to throw away a nearly new machine and thought he might be better off to keep it one more year and then replace it. Would he be better off? How would you go about addressing this issue?

9. During 2005, the rate of inflation remained low, and it was expected that it would average about 4 percent for the year. Torgler wondered how Reto's analysis should reflect this rate of inflation, which he expected might continue for several years. Advise Torgler on this issue.

The Super Project

In March 1967, Crosby Sanberg, manager-financial analysis at General Foods Corporation, told a casewriter, "What I learned about incremental analysis at the Business School doesn't always work." He was convinced that under some circumstances sunk costs were relevant to capital project evaluations. He was also concerned that financial and accounting systems did not provide an accurate estimate of incremental costs and revenues, and that this was one of the most difficult problems in measuring the value of capital investment proposals. Sanberg used the Super project[1] as an example.

Super was a new instant dessert, based on a flavored, water-soluble, agglomerated[2] powder. Although four flavors would be offered, it was estimated that chocolate would account for 80% of total sales.

General Foods was organized along product lines in the United States, with foreign operations under a separate division. Major U.S. product divisions included Post, Kool-Aid, Maxwell House, Jell-O, and Birds Eye. Financial data for General Foods are given in **Exhibits 1, 2,** and **3.**

The $200,000 capital investment project request for Super involved $80,000 for building modifications and $120,000 for machinery and equipment. Modifications would be made to an existing building, where Jell-O was manufactured. Since available capacity of a Jell-O agglomerator would be used in the manufacture of Super, no cost for the key machine was included in the project. The $120,000 machinery and equipment item represented packaging machinery.

Lecturer Harold E. Wyman prepared this case as the basis for class discussion rather than to illustrate either effective or ineffective handling of an administrative situation. This case was made possible by the cooperation of General Foods Corporation.

[1] The name and nature of this new product have been disguised to avoid the disclosure of confidential information.

[2] Agglomeration is a process by which the processed powder is passed through a steam bath and then dried. This fluffs up the powder particles and increases solubility.

TABLE A
Dessert Market, August–September 1966 Compared with August–September 1965

| | Aug.–Sept.1966 | Change From Aug.–Sept. 1965 | |
		Share Points	Volume (%)
Jell-O	19.0%	3.6	40.0
Tasty	4.0	4.0	(new)
Total powders	25.3	7.6	62.0
Pie fillings and cake mixes	32.0	–3.9	(no change)
Ice cream	42.7	–3.4	5.0
Total market	100.0%		13.0

THE MARKET

A Nielsen survey indicated that powdered desserts constituted a significant and growing segment of the total dessert market, as shown in **Table A**. On the basis of test market experience, General Foods expected Super to capture a 10% share of the total dessert market. Eighty percent of this expected Super volume would come from growth in total market share or growth in the powders segment, and 20% would come from erosion of Jell-O sales.

PRODUCTION FACILITIES

Test market volume was packaged on an existing line, inadequate to handle long-run requirements. Filling and packaging equipment to be purchased had a capacity of 1.9 million units on a two-shift, five-day workweek basis. This represented considerable excess capacity, since 1968 requirements were expected to reach 1.1 million units, and the national potential was regarded as 1.6 million units. However, the extra capacity resulted from purchasing standard equipment, and a more economical alternative did not exist.

CAPITAL BUDGETING PROCEDURE

The General Foods Accounting and Financial Manual identified four categories of capital investment project proposals: (1) safety and convenience; (2) quality; (3) increase profit; and (4) other. Proposal procedures and criteria for accepting projects varied according to category (see **Exhibit 4**). In discussing these criteria, Sanberg noted that the payback and return guidelines were not used as cut-off measures and added:

> Payback and return on investment are rarely the only measure of acceptability. Criteria vary significantly by type of project. A relatively high return might be required for a new product in a new business category. On the other hand, a much lower return

might be acceptable for a new product entry which represented a continuing effort to maintain leadership in an existing business by, for example, filling out the product line.

Super fell into the third category, as a profit-increasing project. Estimates of payback and return on funds employed were required for each such project requiring $50,000 or more of new capital funds and expense before taxes. The payback period was the length of time required for the project to repay the investment from the date the project became operational. In calculating the repayment period, only incremental income and expenses related to the project were used.

Return on funds employed (ROFE) was calculated by dividing 10-year average profit before taxes by the 10-year average funds employed. Funds employed included incremental net fixed assets plus or minus related working capital. Start-up costs and any profits or losses incurred before the project became operational were included in the first profit and loss period in the financial evaluation calculation.

CAPITAL BUDGETING ATMOSPHERE

A General Foods accounting executive commented on the atmosphere within which capital projects were reviewed:

> Our problem is not one of capital rationing. Our problem is to find enough good solid projects to employ capital at an attractive return on investment. Of course, the rate of capital inputs must be balanced against a steady growth in earnings per share. The short-term impact of capital investments is usually an increase in the capital base without an immediate realization of profit potential. This is particularly true in the case of new products.
>
> The food industry should show a continuous growth. A cyclical industry can afford to let its profits vary. We want to expand faster than the gross national product. The key to our capital budgeting is to integrate the plans of our eight divisions into a balanced company plan which meets our overall growth objectives. Most new products show a loss in the first two or three years, but our divisions are big enough to introduce new products without showing a loss.

DOCUMENTATION FOR THE SUPER PROJECT

Exhibits 5 and **6** document the financial evaluation of the Super project. **Exhibit 5** is the summary appropriation request prepared to justify the project to management and to secure management's authorization to expend funds on a capital project. **Exhibit 6** presents the backup detail. Cost of the market test was included as "Other" expense in the first period because a new product had to pay for its test market expense, even though this might be a sunk cost at the time capital funds were requested. The "Adjustments" item represented erosion of the Jell-O market and was calculated by multiplying the volume of erosion times a variable profit contribution. In the preparation of this financial evaluation form, costs of acquiring packaging machinery were included but no cost was attributed to Jell-O agglomerator capacity to be used for the Super project because the General Foods Accounting and Financial Manual specified that capital project requests be prepared on an incremental basis:

The incremental concept requires that project requests, profit projections, and funds-employed statements include only items of income and expense and investment in assets which will be realized, incurred, or made directly as a result of, or are attributed to, the new project.

EXCHANGE OF MEMOS ON THE SUPER PROJECT

After receiving the paperwork on the Super project, Sanberg studied the situation and wrote a memorandum arguing that the incremental approach advocated by the manual should not be applied to the Super project. His superior agreed with the memorandum and forwarded it to the corporate controller with the covering note contained in **Appendix A**. The controller's reply is given in **Appendix B**.

EXHIBIT 1
Consolidated Balance Sheet of General Foods Corporation, Fiscal Year Ended April 1, 1967 ($ millions)

Assets

Cash	$ 20
Marketable securities	89
Receivables	180
Inventories	261
Prepaid expenses	14
Current assets	564
Land, buildings, equipment (at cost, less depreciation)	332
Long-term receivables and sundry assets	7
Goodwill	26
Total	$929

Liabilities and Stockholders' Equity

Notes payable	$ 22
Accounts payable	86
Accrued liabilities	73
Accrued income taxes	57
Current liabilities	238
Long-term notes	39
3-3/8% debentures	22
Other noncurrent liabilities	10
Deferred investment tax credit	9
Stockholders' equity	
Common stock issued	164
Retained earnings	449
Common stock held in treasury, at cost	(2)
Stockholders' equity	611
Total	$929
Common stock—shares outstanding at year-end (millions)	25.127

EXHIBIT 2
Common Stock Prices of General Foods Corporation, 1958–1967

Year	Low	High
1958	$24	$ 39
1959	37-1/8	53-7/8
1960	49-1/8	75-1/2
1961	68-5/8	107
1962	57	96
1963	77-5/8	90-1/2
1964	78-1/4	93-1/4
1965	77-1/2	89-7/8
1966	62	83
1967	65-1/4	81

EXHIBIT 3
Summary of Statistical Data of General Foods Corporation, Fiscal Year 1958–1967
($ millions, except employee and figures on a share basis)

	1958	1959	1960	1961	1962	1963	1964	1965	1966	1967
Income Statement										
Sales to customers (net)	$1,009	$1,053	$1,087	$1,160	$1,189	$1,216	$1,338	$1,478	$1,555	$1,652
Cost of sales	724	734	725	764	769	769	838	937	965	1,012
Marketing, administrative and general expenses	181	205	236	261	267	274	322	362	406	449
Earnings before income taxes	105	115	130	138	156	170	179	177	185	193
Taxes on income	57	61	69	71	84	91	95	91	91	94
Net earnings	$ 48	$ 54	$ 61	$ 67	$ 72	$ 79	$ 84	$ 86	$ 94	$ 99
Dividends on common shares	24	28	32	35	40	45	50	50	53	55
Retain earnings—current year	24	26	29	32	32	34	34	36	41	44
Net earnings per common share[a]	$1.99	$2.21	$2.48	$2.69	$2.90	$3.14	$3.33	$3.44	$3.73	$3.93
Dividends per common share[a]	1.00	1.15	1.30	1.40	1.60	1.80	2.00	2.00	2.10	2.20
Assets, Liabilities, and Stockholders' Equity										
Inventories	169	149	154	189	183	205	256	214	261	261
Other current assets	144	180	200	171	204	206	180	230	266	303
Current liabilities	107	107	126	123	142	162	202	173	219	238
Working capital	206	222	228	237	245	249	234	271	308	326
Land, buildings, equipment, gross	203	221	247	289	328	375	436	477	517	569
Land, buildings, equipment, net	125	132	148	173	193	233	264	283	308	332
Long-term debt	49	44	40	37	35	34	23	37	54	61
Stockholders' equity	287	315	347	384	419	454	490	527	569	611
Stockholders' equity per common share[a]	11.78	12.87	14.07	15.46	16.80	18.17	19.53	20.99	22.64	24.32
Capital Program										
Capital additions	28	24	35	40	42	57	70	54	65	59
Depreciation	11	14	15	18	21	24	26	29	32	34
Employment Data										
Wages, salaries, and benefits	$128	$138	$147	$162	$171	$180	$195	$204	$218	$237
Number of employees (in thousands)	21	22	22	25	28	28	30	30	30	32
Assets per employee ($ thousands)	$21	$22	$23	$22	$22	$23	$24	$25	$29	$29

[a] Per share figures calculated on shares outstanding at year-end and adjusted for 2-for-1 stock split in August 1960.

EXHIBIT 4
Criteria for Evaluating Projects by General Foods Corporation

The basic criteria to be applied in evaluating projects within each of the classifications are set forth in the following schedule:

Purpose of Project

a. Safety and Convenience:

1. Projects required for reasons of safety, sanitation, health, public convenience, or other over-riding reason with no reasonable alternatives. Examples: sprinkler systems, elevators, fire escapes, smoke control, waste disposal, treatment of water pollution, etc.

2. Additional nonproductive space requirements for which there are no financial criteria. Examples: office space, laboratories, service areas (kitchens, restrooms, etc.).

b. Quality:

Projects designed primarily to improve quality.

c. Increase Profit:

1. Projects that are justified primarily by reduced costs.

2. Projects that are designed primarily to increase production capacity for an existing product.

3. Projects designed to provide facilities to manufacture and distribute a new product or product line.

d. Other:

This category includes projects which by definition are excluded from the three preceding categories. Examples: standby facilities intended to insure uninterrupted production, additional equipment not expected to improve profits or product quality and not required for reasons of safety and convenience, equipment to satisfy marketing requirements, etc.

Payback and ROFE Criteria

Payback—return on funds projections not required but the request must clearly demonstrate the *immediate* need for the project and the lack or inadequacy of alternative solutions.

Requests for nonproductive facilities, such as warehouses, laboratories, and offices should indicate the advantages of owning rather than leasing, unless no possibility to lease exists. In those cases where the company owns a group of integrated facilities and wherein the introduction of rented or leased properties might complicate the long-range planning or development of the area, owning rather than leasing is recommended. If the project is designed to improve customer service (such as market-centered warehouses) this factor is to be noted on the project request.

If Payback and ROFE cannot be computed, it must be clearly demonstrated that the improvement is identifiable and desirable.

Projects with a Payback period *up to 10 years* and a 10-year return *on funds as low as 20%* PBT are considered worthy of consideration, provided (1) the end product involved is believed to be a reasonably permanent part of our line or (2) the facilities involved are so flexible that they may be usable for successor products.

Projects for a proven product where the risk of mortality is small, such as coffee, Jell-O Gelatin, and cereals, should assure a payback in *no more than 10 years* and 10-year PBT return on funds of *no less* than 20%.

Because of the greater risk involved, such projects should show a high potential return *on funds* (not less than a 10-year PBT return of 40%). Payback period, however, might be as much as *10 years* because of losses incurred during the market development period.[a]

While standards of return may be difficult to set, some calculations of financial benefits should be made where possible.

Source: The General Foods Accounting and Financial Manual

[a] These criteria apply to the United States and Canada only. Profit-increasing capital projects in other areas in categories c1 and c2 should offer at least a 10-year PBT return of 24% to compensate for the greater risk involved. Likewise, foreign operation projects in the c3 category should offer a 10-year PBT return of at least 48%.

EXHIBIT 5
Capital Project Request Form of General Foods Corporation

NY1292-A 12-63
PTD. In U.S.A.
"Super" Facilities   66-42
Project Title & Number

Jell-O Division   —   St. Louis
Division & Location

December 23, 1966
Date

New Request   ☒

Expansion-New Product
Purpose

Supplement   ☐ ☒ A ☐ R

Project Description

To provide facilities for production of Super, chocolate dessert. This project included finishing a packing room in addition to filling and packaging equipment.

Summary of Investment	
New Capital Funds Required	$200M
Expense Before Taxes	—
Less: Trade-in or Salvage, If Any	—
Total This Request	$200M
Previously Appropriated	—
Total Project Cost	$200M

Financial Justification	
ROFE (PBT Basis) - 10 Yr. Average	62.9
Payback Period April, F'68 Feb, F'75 From To	6.83 Yrs.
Not Required	☐
* Based on Total Project Cost and Working Fund of	$510M

Estimated Expenditure Rate	
Quarter Ending Mar. F19 67	$160M
Quarter Ending June F19 68	40M
Quarter Ending F19	
Quarter Ending F19	
Remainder	

Other Information		
Major ☐ Specific Ordinary ☐ Blanket ☐		
Included in Annual program Yes ☐ No ☐		
Per cent of Engineering Completed	80%	
Estimated Start-Up Cost	$15M	
Estimated Start-Up Date	April	

Level of Approval Required			
☐ Board	☐ Chairman	☐ Exec. V.P.	☐ Gen. Mgr.

For Division Use—Signatures	
Name & Title	Date

	Signatures	Date
Director Corp. Eng.		
Director B&A		
General Manager		
Exec. Vice President		
President		
Chairman		

The purpose of this form is to secure management's authorization to commit or expend funds on a capital project. Refer to Accounting and Financial Manual Statement No. 19 for information regarding projects to which this form applies.

New Request—Supplement   Check the appropriate box.

Purpose   Identify the primary purpose of the project in accordance with the classifications established in Accounting and Financial Statement No. 19, i.e., Sanitation, Health and Public Convenience, Nonproductive Space, Safety, Quality, Reduce Cost, Expansion—Existing Products, Expansion—New Products, Other (specify). Also indicate in the appropriate box whether the equipment represents an addition or a replacement.

Project Description   Comments should be in sufficient detail to enable Corporate Management to appraise the benefits of the project. Where necessary, supplemental data should be attached to provide complete background for project evaluation.

Summary of Investment

New Capital Funds Required   Show gross cost of assets to be acquired.

Expense Before Taxes   Show incremental expense resulting from project.

Trade-in or Salvage   Show the amount expected to be realized on trade-in or sale of a replaced asset.

Previously Appropriated   When requesting a supplement to an approved project, show the amount previously appropriated even though authorization was given in a prior year.

Financial Justification

ROFE   Show the return on funds employed (PBT basis) as calculated on Financial Evaluation Form NY 1292-C or 1292-F. The appropriate Financial Evaluation Form is to be attached to this form.

Not Required   Where financial benefits are not applicable or required or are not expected, check the box provided. The nonfinancial benefits should be explained in the comments.

   In the space provided, show the sum of the Total Project Cost plus Total Working Funds (line 20, Form NY 1292-C or line 5, Form NY 1292-F) in either of the first three periods, whichever is higher.

Estimated Expenditure Rate   Expenditures are to be reported in accordance with accounting treatment of the asset and related expense portion of the project. Insert estimated quarterly expenditures beginning with the quarter in which the first expenditure will be made. The balance of authorized funds unspent after the fourth quarter should be reported in total.

Other Information   Check whether the project is a major, specific ordinary, or blanket, and whether or not the project was included in the Annual Program. Show estimated percentage of engineering completed; this is intended to give management an indication of the degree of reliability of the funds requested. Indicate the estimated start-up costs as shown on line 32 of Financial Evaluation Form NY 1292-C. Insert anticipated start-up date for the project; if start-up is to be staggered, explain in the comments.

Level of Approval Required   Check the appropriate box.

Source: General Foods

EXHIBIT 6
Financial Evaluation Form of General Foods Corporation ($ in thousands)

NY 1292-C   10-64
PTD. In U.S.A.

Jell-O	St. Louis	The Super Project	67-89	
Division	Location	Project Title	Project No.	Date
				Supplement No.

Project Request Detail

Project Request Detail	1st Per.	2nd Per.	3rd Per.	4th Per.	5th Per.
1. Land	$				
2. Buildings	80				
3. Machinery & Equipment	120				
4. Engineering					
5. Other (Explain)					
6. Expense Portion (Before Tax)					
7. Sub Total	$ 200				
8. Less: Salvage Value (Old Asset)					
9. Total Project Cost*	$ 200				
10. Less: Taxes on Exp. Portion					
11. Net Project Cost	$ 200				

*Same as Project Request

Return on New Funds Employed—10-Yr. Avg.

	PAT (C ÷ A)	PBT (B ÷ A)
A—New Funds Employed (Line 21)	$380	$380
B—Profit Before Taxes (Line 35)		$239
C—Net Profit (Line 37)	$115	
D—Calculated Return	30.2%	62.0%

PayBack Years From Operational Date

Part Year Calculation for First Period	— Yrs.
Number of Full Years to PayBack	6.00 Yrs.
Part Year Calculation for Last Period	0.83 Yrs.
Total Years to PayBack	6.83 Yrs.

Funds Employed

Funds Employed	1st Per. F 68	2nd Per. F 69	3rd Per. F 70	4th Per. F 71	5th Per. F 72	6th Per. F 73	7th Per. F 74	8th Per. F 75	9th Per. F 76	10th Per. F 77	11th Per. —	10-Yr. Avg.
12. Net Project Cost (Line 11)	$200	200	200	200	200	200	200	200	200	200		
13. Deduct Depreciation (Cum.)	19	37	54	70	85	98	110	121	131	140		
14. Capital Funds Employed	$181	163	146	130	115	102	90	79	69	60		113
15. Cash	124	134	142	151	160	160	169	169	178	178		157
16. Receivables	207	222	237	251	266	266	281	281	296	296		260
17. Inventories												
18. Prepaid & Deferred Exp.												
19. Less Current Liabilities	(2)	(82)	(108)	(138)	(185)	(184)	(195)	(195)	(207)	(207)		(150)
20. Total Working Funds (15 Thru 19)	329	274	271	264	241	242	255	255	267	267		267
21. Total New Funds Employed (14 + 20)	$510	437	417	394	356	344	345	334	336	327		380

(continued)

EXHIBIT 6 (continued)
Financial Evaluation Form of General Foods Corporation ($ in thousands)

Profit and Loss	1st Per. F 68	2nd Per. F 69	3rd Per. F 70	4th Per. F 71	5th Per. F 72	6th Per. F 73	7th Per. F 74	8th Per. F 75	9th Per. F 76	10th Per. F 77	11th Per. —	10-Yr. Avg.
22. Unit Volume (in thousands)	1100	1200	1300	1400	1500	1500	1600	1600	1700	1700		1460
23. Gross Sales	$2200	2400	2600	2800	3000	3000	3200	3200	3400	3400		2920
24. Deductions	88	96	104	112	120	120	128	128	136	136		117
25. Net Sales	2112	2304	2496	2688	2880	2880	3072	3072	3264	3264		2803
26. Cost of Goods Sold	1100	1200	1300	1400	1500	1500	1600	1600	1700	1700		1460
27. Gross Profit	1012	1104	1196	1288	1380	1380	1472	1472	1564	1564		1343
Gross Profit % Net Sales												
28. Advertising Expense	1100	1050	1000	900	700	700	730	730	750	750		841
29. Selling Expense												
30. Gen. and Admin. Cost												
31. Research Expense												
32. Start-Up Costs	15											2
33. Other (Explain) Test Mkt.	360											36
34. Adjustments (Explain) Erosion	180	200	210	220	230	230	240	240	250	250		225
35. Profit Before Taxes	$(643)	(146)	(14)	168	450	450	502	502	564	564		239
36. Taxes	(334)	(76)	(7)	87	234	234	261	261	293	293		125
36A. Add: Investment Credit	(1)	(1)	(1)	(1)	(1)	(1)	(1)	(1)		—		(1)
37. Net Profit	(308)	(69)	(6)	82	217	217	242	242	271	271		115
38. Cumulative Net Profit	$(308)	(377)	(383)	(301)	(84)	133	375	617	888	1159		
39. New Funds to Repay (21 Less 38)	$818	814	800	695	440	211	(30)	(283)	(552)	(832)		

See Accounting & Financial Manual Policy No. 19 for Instructions.

This form is to be submitted to Corporate Budget and Analysis with each profit-increasing capital project request requiring $50,000 or more of capital funds and expense before taxes.

Note that the 10-year term has been divided into 11 periods. The first period is to end on the March 31 following the operational date of the project, and the P&L projection may thereby encompass any number of months from 1 to 12, e.g., if the project becomes operational on November 1, 1964, the first period for P&L purposes would be 5 months (November 1, 1964 through March 31, 1965). The next nine periods would be fiscal years (F '66, F '67, etc.) and the 11th period would be 7 months (April 1, 1974 through October 30, 1974). This has been done primarily to facilitate reporting of projected and actual P&L data by providing for fiscal years. See categorized instructions below for more specific details.

Project Request Detail   *Lines 1 through 11* show the breakdown of the Net Project Cost to be used in the financial evaluation. *Line 8* is to show the amount expected to be realized on trade-in or sale of a replaced asset. *Line 9* should be the same as the "Total Project Cost" shown on Form NY 1292-A, Capital Project Request. Space has been provided for capital expenditures related to this project which are projected to take place subsequent to the first period. Indicate in such space the additional cost only; do not accumulate them.

Funds Employed

Capital Funds Employed   *Line 12* will show the net project cost appearing on line 11 as a constant for the first 10 periods except in any period in which additional expenditures are incurred; in that event show the accumulated amount of line 11 in such period and in all future periods.

Deduct cumulative depreciation on *Line 13*. Depreciation is to be computed on an incremental basis, i.e., the net increase in depreciation over present depreciation on assets being replaced. In the first period depreciation will be computed at one half of the first year's annual rate; no depreciation is to be taken in the 11th period. Depreciation rates are to be the same as those used for accounting purposes. *Exception:* When the depreciation rate used for accounting purposes differs materially from the rate for tax purposes, the higher rate should be used. A variation will be considered material when the first full year's depreciation on a book basis varies 20% or more from the first full year's depreciation on a tax basis.

The 10-year average of Capital Funds Employed shall be computed by adding line 14 in each of the first 10 periods and then dividing the total by 10.

Total Working Funds   Refer to Financial Policy No. 21 as a guide in computing new working fund requirements. Items which are not on a formula basis and which are normally computed on a five-quarter average shall be handled proportionately in the first period. For example, since the period involved may be less than 12 months, the average would be computed on the number of quarters involved. Generally, the balances should be approximately the same as they would be if the first period were a full year.

Cash, based on a formula which theorizes a two weeks' supply (2/52nds), should follow the same theory. If the first period is for three months, two-thirteenths (2/13th) should be used; if it is for five months, two-twenty-firsts (2/21sts) should be used, and so forth.

Current liabilities are to include one-half of the tax expense as the tax liability. The 10-year averages of Working Funds shall be computed by adding each line across or the first 10 periods and then dividing each total by 10.

Profit and Loss Projection

P&L Categories (Lines 22 through 37)   Reflect only the incremental amounts which will result from the proposed project; exclude all allocated charges. Include the P&L results expected in the individual periods comprising the first 10 years of the life of the project. Refer to the second paragraph of these instructions regarding the fractional years' calculations during the first and eleventh periods.

Any loss or gain on the sale of a replaced asset (see line 8) shall be included on line 33.

As indicated in the caption Capital Funds Employed, no depreciation is to be taken in the eleventh period.

The 10-year averages of the P&L items shall be computed by adding each line across for the 11 periods (10 full years from the operational date) and dividing the total by 10.

Adjustments (Line 34)   Show the adjustment necessary, on a before-tax basis, to indicate any adverse or favorable incremental effect the proposed project will have on any other products currently being produced by the corporation.

Investment Credit   To be included on line 36-A. The Investment Credit will be spread over 8 years, or fractions thereof, as an addition to PAT.

Return on New Funds Employed   Ten-year average returns are to be calculated for PAT (projects requiring Board approval only) and PBT. The PAT return is calculated by dividing average PAT (line 37) by average new funds employed (line 21); the PBT return is derived by dividing average PBT (line 35) by average new funds employed (line 21).

Payback Years From Operational Date

Part Year Calculation for First Period   Divide number of months in the first period by 12. If five months are involved, the calculation is 5/12 = 0.4 years.

Number of Full Years to Payback   Determined by the last period, excluding the first period, in which an amount is shown on line 39.

Part Year Calculation for Last Period   Divide amount still to be repaid at the end of the last full period (line 39) by net profit plus the *annual* depreciation in the following year when payback is completed.

Total Years to Payback   Sum of full and part years.

To: J. C. Kresslin, Corporate Controller

From: J. E. Hooting, Director, Corporate Budgets and Analysis

March 2, 1967

Super Project

At the time we reviewed the Super project, I indicated to you that the return on investment looked significantly different if an allocation of the agglomerator and building, originally justified as a Jell-O project, were included in the Super investment. The pro rata allocation of these facilities, based on the share of capacity used, triples the initial gross investment in Super facilities from $200,000 to about $672,000.

I am forwarding a memorandum from Crosby Sanberg summarizing the results of three analyses evaluating the project on an:

I.   Incremental basis

II.   Facilities-used basis

III. Fully allocated facilities and costs basis

Crosby has calculated a 10-year average ROFE using these techniques. Please read Crosby's memo before continuing with my note.

* * * * *

Crosby concludes that the fully allocated basis, or some variation of it, is necessary to understand the long-range potential of the project.

I agree. We launch a new project because of its potential to increase our sales and earning power for many years into the future. We must be mindful of short-term consequences, as indicated by an incremental analysis, but we must also have a long-range frame of reference if we are to really understand what we are committing ourselves to. This long-range frame of reference is best approximated by looking at fully allocated investment and "accounted" profits, which recognize fully allocated costs because, in fact, over the long run all costs are variable unless some major change occurs in the structure of the business.

Our current GF preoccupation with only the incremental costs and investment causes some real anomalies that confuse our decision making. Super is a good example. On an incremental basis the project looks particularly attractive because by using a share of the excess capacity built on the coattails of the lucrative Jell-O project, the incremental investment in Super is low. If the excess Jell-O capacity did not exist, would the project be any less attractive? In the short term, perhaps yes because it would entail higher initial risk, but in the long term it is not a better project just because it fits a facility that is temporarily unused.

Looking at this point from a different angle, if the project exceeded our investment hurdle rate on a short-term basis but fell below it on a long-term basis (and Super comes close to doing this), should we reject the project? I say yes because over the long run, as "fixed" costs become variable and as we have to commit new capital to support the business, the continuing ROFE will go under water.

In sum, we have to look at new project proposals from both the long-range and the short-term point of view. We plan to refine our techniques of using a fully allocated basis as a long-term point of reference and will hammer out a policy recommendation for your consideration. We would appreciate any comments you may have.

APPENDIX A (*continued*)
Memos to Controller

To: J. E. Hooting, Director, Corporate Budgets and Analysis

From: C. Sanberg, Manager, Financial Analysis

February 17, 1967

Super Project: A Case Example of Investment Evaluation Techniques

This will review the merits of alternative techniques of evaluating capital investment decisions using the Super project as an example. The purpose of the review is to provide an illustration of the problems and limitations inherent in using incremental ROFE and payback and thereby provide a rationale for adopting new techniques.

Alternative Techniques

The alternative techniques to be reviewed are differentiated by the level of revenue and investment charged to the Super project in figuring a payback and ROFE, starting with incremental revenues and investment. Data related to the alternative techniques outlined below are summarized [at the end of this memo].

Alternative I. Incremental Basis

Method   The Super project as originally evaluated considered only incremental revenue and investment, which could be directly identified with the decision to produce Super. Incremental fixed capital ($200M) basically included packaging equipment.

Result   On this basis the project paid back in 7 years with a ROFE of 63%.

Discussion   Although it is General Foods' current policy to evaluate capital projects on an incremental basis, this technique does not apply to the Super project. The reason is that Super extensively utilizes existing facilities, which are readily adaptable to known future alternative uses.

Super should be charged with the "opportunity loss" of agglomerating capacity and building space. Because of Super the opportunity is lost to use a portion of agglomerating capacity for Jell-O and other products that could potentially be agglomerated. In addition, the opportunity is lost to use the building space for existing or new product volume expansion. To the extent there is an opportunity loss of existing facilities, new facilities must be built to accommodate future expansion. In other words, because the business is expanding Super utilizes facilities that are adaptable to predictable alternative uses.

Alternative II. Facilities-Used Basis

Method   Recognizing that Super will use half of an existing agglomerator and two-thirds of an existing building, which were justified earlier in the Jell-O project, we added Super's pro rata share of these facilities ($453M) to the incremental capital. Overhead costs directly related to these existing facilities were also subtracted from incremental revenue on a shared basis.

Result   ROFE 34%

Discussion   Although the existing facilities utilized by Super are not incremental to this project, they are relevant to the evaluation of the project because potentially they can be put to alternative uses. Despite a high return on an incremental basis, if the ROFE on a project was unattractive after consideration of the shared use of existing facilities, the project would be questionable. Under these circumstances, we might look for a more profitable product for the facilities.

In summary, the facilities-used basis is a useful way of putting various projects on a common ground for purposes of *relative* evaluation. One product using existing capacity should not necessarily be judged to be more attractive than another practically identical product which necessitates an investment in additional facilities.

Alternative III. Fully Allocated Basis

Method   Further recognizing that individual decisions to expand inevitably add to a higher overhead base, we increased the costs and investment base developed in Alternative II by a provision for overhead expenses and overhead capital. These increases were made in year five of the 10-year evaluation period, on the theory that at this point a number of decisions would result in more fixed costs and facilities. Overhead expenses included manufacturing costs, plus selling and general and administrative costs on a per unit basis equivalent to Jell-O. Overhead capital included a share of the distribution system assets ($40M).

Result   ROFE 25%

Discussion   Charging Super with an overhead burden recognizes that overhead costs in the long run increase in proportion to the level of business activity, even though decisions to spend more overhead dollars are made separately from decisions to increase volume and provide the incremental facilities to support the higher volume level. To illustrate, the Division-F1968 Financial Plan budgets about a 75% increase in headquarters' overhead spending in F1968 over F1964. A contributing factor was the decision to increase the sales force by 50% to meet the demands of a growing and increasingly complex business. To further illustrate, about half the capital projects in the F1968 three-year Financial Plan are in the "non-payback" category. This group of projects comprised largely "overhead facilities" (warehouses, utilities, etc.), which are not directly related to the manufacture of products but are necessary components of the total business activity as a result of the cumulative effect of many decisions taken in the past.

The Super project is a significant decision which will most likely add to more overhead dollars as illustrated above. Super volume doubles the powdered dessert business category; it increases the Division businesses by 10%. Furthermore, Super requires a new production technology: agglomeration and packaging on a high-speed line.

Conclusions

1. The incremental basis for evaluating a project is an inadequate measure of a project's worth when existing facilities with a known future use will be utilized extensively.

2. A fully allocated basis of reviewing major new product proposals recognizes that overheads increase in proportion to the size and complexity of the business and provides the best long-range projection of the financial consequences.

Alternative Evaluations of Super Project ($ in thousands)

	I. Incremental Basis	II. Facilities-Used Basis	III. Fully Allocated
Investment			
Working capital	$267	$267	$267
Fixed capital			
Gross	200	653	672
Net	113	358	367
Total net investment	380	625	634
Profit before taxes[a]	239	211	157
ROFE	63%	34%	25%
Jell-O project			
Building	$200 × 2/3 = $133		
Agglomerator	640 × 1/2 = 320		
	$453		

Note: Figures based on 10-year averages.

[a]   Assumes 20% of Super volume will replace existing Jell-O business.

APPENDIX B
Controller's Reply

To: Mr. J. F. Hooting, Director, Corporate Budgets and Analysis

From: Mr. J. C. Kresslin, Corporate Controller

Subject: Super Project

March 7, 1967

On March 2 you sent me a note describing Crosby Sanberg's and your thoughts about evaluating the Super project. In this memo you suggest that the project should be appraised on the basis of fully allocated facilities and production costs.

In order to continue the dialogue, I am raising a couple of questions below.

It seems to me that in a situation such as you describe for Super, the real question is a *management decision* as to whether to go ahead with the Super project or not go ahead. Or to put it another way, are we better off in the aggregate if we use half the agglomerator and two-thirds of an existing building for Super, or are we not, on the basis of our current knowledge?

It might be assumed that, for example, half of the agglomerator is being used and half is not and that a minimum economical size agglomerator was necessary for Jell-O and, consequently, should be justified by the Jell-O project itself. If we find a way to utilize it sooner by producing Super on it, aren't we better off in the aggregate, and the different ROFE figure for the Super project by itself becomes somewhat irrelevant? A similar point of view might be applied to the portion of the building. Or if we charge the Super project with half an agglomerator and two-thirds of an existing building, should we then go back and relieve the Jell-O projects of these costs in evaluating the management's original proposal?

To put it another way, since we are faced with making decisions at a certain time on the basis of what we then know, I see very little value in looking at the Super project all by itself. Better we should look at the total situation before and after to see how we fare.

As to allocated production costs, the point is not so clear. Undoubtedly, over the long haul, the selling prices will need to be determined on the basis of a satisfactory margin over fully allocated costs. Perhaps this should be an additional requirement in the course of evaluating capital projects, since we seem to have been surprised at the low margins for "Tasty" after allocating all costs to the product.

I look forward to discussing this subject with you and with Crosby at some length.

Measurements for Management Control

Control in an Age of Empowerment

- *Indianapolis: Implementing Competition in City Services*

- *Nordstrom: Dissension in the Ranks? (A)*

Responsibility Centers and Performance Measurement

- *Western Chemical Corporation: Divisional Performance Measurement (A)*

The Balanced Scorecard—Measures that Drive Performance

- *Wells Fargo Online Financial Services (A)*

Control in an Age of Empowerment

A fundamental problem facing managers in the 1990s is how to exercise adequate control in organizations that demand flexibility, innovation, and creativity. Competitive businesses with demanding and informed customers must rely on employee initiative to seek out opportunities and respond to customers' needs. But pursuing some opportunities can expose businesses to excessive risk or invite behaviors that can damage a company's integrity.

Consider the spate of management control failures that have made headlines in the past several years: Kidder, Peabody & Company lost $350 million when a trader allegedly booked fictitious profits; Sears, Roebuck and Company took a $60 million charge against earnings after admitting that it recommended unnecessary repairs to customers in its automobile service business; Standard Chartered Bank was banned from trading on the Hong Kong stock market after being implicated in an improper share support scheme. The list goes on. In each case, employees broke through existing control mechanisms and jeopardized the franchise of the business. The cost to the companies—in damaged reputations, fines, business losses, missed opportunities, and diversion of management attention to deal with the crises—was enormous.

How do senior managers protect their companies from control failures when empowered employees are encouraged to redefine how they go about doing their jobs? How do managers ensure that subordinates with an entrepreneurial flair do not put the well-being of the business at risk? One solution is to go back to the fundamentals of control developed in the 1950s and 1960s for machinelike bureaucracies. In that era, managers exercised control by telling people how to do their jobs and monitoring them with constant surveillance to guard against surprises. Although this approach sounds anachronistic for modern businesses, it is still effective when standardization is critical for efficiency and yield, such as on an assembly line; when the risk of theft of valuable assets is high, such as in a casino; or when quality and safety are essential to product performance, such as at a nuclear power plant.

However, in most organizations operating in dynamic and highly competitive markets, managers cannot spend all their time and effort making sure that everyone is doing what is expected. Nor is it realistic to think that managers can achieve con-

Robert Simons is the Charles M. Williams Professor of Business Administration at Harvard Business School in Boston, Massachusetts. His book *Levers of Control: How Managers Use Innovative Control Systems to Drive Strategic Renewal* was published in December 1994 by the Harvard Business School Press.

Reprinted by permission from *Harvard Business Review*, March–April 1995, 80–88. Reprint 95211. Copyright © 1995 by the President and Fellows of Harvard College.

trol by simply hiring good people, aligning incentives, and hoping for the best. Instead, today's managers must encourage employees to initiate process improvements and new ways of responding to customers' needs—but in a controlled way.

Fortunately, the tools to reconcile the conflict between creativity and control are at hand. Most managers tend to define control narrowly—as measuring progress against plans to guarantee the predictable achievement of goals. Such diagnostic control systems are, however, only one ingredient of control. Three other levers are equally important in today's business environment: beliefs systems, boundary systems, and interactive control systems.

Each of the four control levers has a distinct purpose for managers attempting to harness the creativity of employees. Diagnostic control systems allow managers to ensure that important goals are being achieved efficiently and effectively. Beliefs systems empower individuals and encourage them to search for new opportunities. They communicate core values and inspire all participants to commit to the organization's purpose. Boundary systems establish the rules of the game and identify actions and pitfalls that employees must avoid. Interactive control systems enable top-level managers to focus on strategic uncertainties, to learn about threats and opportunities as competitive conditions change, and to respond proactively.

DIAGNOSTIC CONTROL SYSTEMS

Diagnostic control systems work like the dials on the control panel of an airplane cockpit, enabling the pilot to scan for signs of abnormal functioning and to keep critical performance variables within preset limits. Most businesses have come to rely on diagnostic control systems to help managers track the progress of individuals, departments, or production facilities toward strategically important goals. Managers use these systems to monitor goals and profitability, and to measure progress toward targets such as revenue growth and market share. Periodically, managers measure the outputs and compare them with preset standards of performance. Feedback allows management to adjust and fine-tune inputs and processes so that future outputs will more closely match goals.

But diagnostic control systems are not adequate to ensure effective control. In fact, they create pressures that can lead to control failures—even crises. Whether managers realize it or not, there are built-in dangers when empowered employees are held accountable for performance goals—especially for difficult ones—and then left to their own devices to achieve them. For example, Nordstrom, the upscale fashion retailer known for extraordinary customer service, recently found itself embroiled in a series of lawsuits and investigative reports related to its sales-per-hour performance-measurement system. Used to track the performance of its entrepreneurial salespeople, the system was designed to support the service orientation for which Nordstrom is famous. But without counterbalancing controls, the system created the potential for both exemplary customer service and abuse. Some employees claimed that first-line supervisors were pressuring them to underreport hours on the job in an attempt to boost sales per hour. Settling those claims cost Nordstrom more than $15 million.

I recently conducted a study of ten newly appointed chief executive officers to understand better how they used measurement and control systems to implement their agendas. Within the first months of taking charge, many of the new CEOs established demanding performance goals for division managers and increased the rewards and punishments associated with success and failure in achieving those goals. In response to the pressures, several division managers manipulated financial data by creating false accounting entries to enhance their reported performance. The managers were fired, but not before they had inflicted damage on their organizations. In one memorable case, a retail company had been making inventory and markdown decisions based on the falsified data, a practice that resulted in significant losses. These are not isolated incidents. The Big Six accounting firms have observed a substantial increase in errors and fraud over the past five years as organizations downsize and reduce the resources devoted to internal controls. With the elimination of many middle management jobs, basic internal controls, such as segregation of duties and independent oversight, have often been sacrificed.

One of the main purposes of diagnostic measurement systems is to eliminate the manager's burden of constant monitoring. Once goals are established and people have performance targets on which their rewards will be based, many managers believe they can move on to other issues, knowing that employees will be working diligently to meet the agreed-upon goals. Yet the potential for control failures as the performance bar is raised and employees' rewards are put at risk underscores the need for managers to think about the three other essential levers of control.

BELIEFS SYSTEMS

Companies have used beliefs systems for years in an effort to articulate the values and direction that senior managers want their employees to embrace. Typically, beliefs systems are concise, value-laden, and inspirational. They draw employees' attention to key tenets of the business: how the organization creates value ("Best Customer Service in the World"); the level of performance the organization strives for ("Pursuit of Excellence"); and how individuals are expected to manage both internal and external relationships ("Respect for the Individual").

Senior managers intentionally design beliefs systems to be broad enough to appeal to many different groups within an organization: salespeople, managers, production workers, and clerical personnel. Because they are broad, beliefs statements are often ridiculed for lacking substance. But this criticism overlooks the principal purpose of the statements: to inspire and promote commitment to an organization's core values. Still, the statements achieve their ends only if employees believe, by watching the actions of senior managers, that the company's stated beliefs represent deeply rooted values. If employees suspect that managers are going through the motions of the latest fad, cynicism will set in.

Indeed, some managers adopt missions and credos not out of any real commitment but because they seem fashionable. However, managers who use their missions as living documents—as part of a system to guide patterns of acceptable behavior— have discovered a powerful lever of control. At Johnson & Johnson, for example, senior managers meet regularly with subordinates throughout the company to review and reaffirm the beliefs recorded in J&J's long-standing credo, which articulates clearly and passionately the company's responsibilities to customers, employees, local communities, and stockholders. Managers throughout the organization recognize the value that senior managers place on the exercise and respond accordingly. When problems arise, such as when J&J faced the Tylenol crisis, the strong beliefs system embedded in its credo provided guidance regarding the types of solutions to search for.

In the past, a company's mission was usually understood without reference to core values or formal beliefs; employees knew that they worked for a bank or a telephone company or a company that made shock absorbers. However, businesses have become much more complex in recent years, making it more difficult for individuals to comprehend organizational purpose and direction. Moreover, in many businesses, downsizing and realignment have shattered strongly held assumptions about the values and foundations of businesses and their top-level managers. Employees no longer know whom to trust. At the same time, their expectations for meaningful careers have risen as education levels have increased. Without a formal beliefs system, employees in large, decentralized organizations often do not have a clear and consistent understanding of the core values of the business and their place within the business. In the absence of clearly articulated core values, they are often forced to make assumptions about what constitutes acceptable behavior in the many different, unpredictable circumstances they encounter.

Beliefs systems can also inspire employees to create new opportunities: they can motivate individuals to search for new ways of creating value. We all have a deep-seated need to contribute—to devote time and energy to worthwhile endeavors. But companies often make it difficult for employees to understand the larger purpose of their efforts or to see how they can add value in a way that can make a difference. Individuals want to understand the organization's purpose and how they can contribute, but senior managers must unleash this potential. Effective managers seek to inspire people throughout their organizations by actively communicating core values and missions. As top-level managers rely increasingly on empowered employees to generate new ideas and competitive advantage, participants from all parts of an organization need to understand as clearly as possible their company's purposes and mission.

Beliefs systems can augment diagnostic control systems to give today's managers greater amounts of control. But they are only part of the answer. Think of them as the yang of Chinese philosophy—the sun, the warmth, and the light. Opposing them are dark, cold boundaries—the yin—which represent the next lever of control.

Harness Employees' Creativity with the Four Levers of Control

Potential	Organizational Blocks	Managerial Solution	Control Lever
To contribute	Uncertainty about purpose	Communicate core values and mission	Beliefs systems
To do right	Pressure or temptation	Specify and enforce rules of the game	Boundary systems
To achieve	Lack of focus or of resources	Build and support clear targets	Diagnostic control systems
To create	Lack of opportunity or fear of risk	Open organizational dialogue to encourage learning	Interactive control systems

BOUNDARY SYSTEMS

Boundary systems are based on a simple, yet profound, management principle that can be called the "power of negative thinking."[1] Ask yourself the question, If I want my employees to be creative and entrepreneurial, am I better off telling them what to do or telling them what *not* to do? The answer is the latter. Telling people what to do by establishing standard operating procedures and rule books discourages the initiative and creativity unleashed by empowered, entrepreneurial employees. Telling them what *not* to do allows innovation, but within clearly defined limits.

Unlike diagnostic control systems (which monitor critical performance outcomes) or beliefs systems (which communicate core values), boundary systems are stated in negative terms or as minimum standards. The boundaries in modern organizations, embedded in standards of ethical behavior and codes of conduct, are invariably written in terms of activities that are off-limits. They are an organization's brakes. Every business needs them, and, like racing cars, the fastest and most performance-oriented companies need the best brakes.

Human beings are inventive, and, when presented with new opportunities or challenging situations, they often search for ways to create value or overcome obstacles. But empowerment—fueled by inspiration and performance rewards—should never be interpreted as giving subordinates a blank check to do whatever they please. People generally want to do the right thing—to act ethically in accordance with established moral codes. But pressures to achieve superior results sometimes collide with stricter codes of behavior. Because of temptation or pressure in the workplace, individuals sometimes choose to bend the rules. As problems at Kidder, Peabody and Salomon Brothers showed, entrepreneurial individuals sometimes blur or misinterpret the line between acceptable and unacceptable behavior. At Salomon Brothers, a creative trader attempting to increase investment returns violated U.S. Treasury bidding rules and short-circuited existing controls; the aftermath of the scandal destroyed careers and impaired Salomon's franchise. Similar problems at Kidder, Peabody involving fictitious securities trades resulted in massive losses and ultimately led to the sale of the business. Clearly, the consequences of a misstep can be severe.

Boundary systems are especially critical in those businesses in which a reputation built on trust is a key competitive asset. A well-respected bank with a global franchise states as a part of its business principles that its three main assets are people, capital, and reputation. Of all these, it notes, the last is the most difficult to regain if impaired. To guard against damage to its reputation, the bank's code of conduct forbids individuals both from developing client relationships in "undesirable" industries, such as gambling casinos, and from acting as intermediaries in unfriendly takeovers, which senior managers believe could undermine the perceived trustworthiness of the company.

Large consulting firms like McKinsey & Company and the Boston Consulting Group routinely work with clients to analyze highly proprietary strategic data. To ensure that their reputations for integrity are never compromised, the firms enforce strict boundaries that forbid consultants to reveal information—even the names of

---

[1] My colleague, Professor Charles Christenson, coined this term in a 1972 Harvard Business School working paper.

clients—to anyone not employed by the firm, including spouses. They also clearly state in their codes of professional conduct that individuals must not misrepresent themselves when attempting to gather competitive information on behalf of clients.

Unfortunately, the benefits of establishing business conduct boundaries are not always apparent to senior managers. Too often, they learn the hard way. Many codes of conduct are instituted only after a public scandal or an internal investigation of questionable behavior. Over the years, General Electric has instituted codes of business conduct that prohibit activities relating to improper payments, price fixing, and improper cost allocation on government contracts. Each of those codes was instituted after a major crisis impaired the integrity of the business. For instance, when GE was forced to suspend its $4.5 billion business as supplier to the U.S. government in 1985, CEO Jack Welch responded by strengthening internal controls and issuing a clear policy statement that forbade the behaviors that had landed GE in trouble: improper cost allocations on government contracts. Similarly, senior managers at Wall Street investment firms did not pay much attention to business conduct boundary systems until the disclosure of improper behavior by a small number of employees at Salomon Brothers nearly destroyed the business. Again, senior managers at investment firms across the country scrambled to install compliance systems to avoid a similar crisis in their own firms.

Effective managers anticipate the inevitable temptations and pressures that exist within their organizations. They spell out the rules of the game based on the risks inherent in their strategy and enforce them clearly and unambiguously. Some behaviors are never tolerated: the firing of the manager who inflated his or her expense report by $50 is a familiar story in many organizations. On the surface, the punishment may seem too harsh for the crime, but the purpose of such punishment is to signal clearly to all managers and employees that the consequences of stepping over

Renew Strategy with the Four Levers of Control

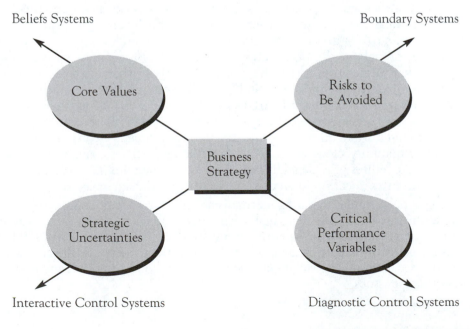

Beliefs Systems — Core Values

Boundary Systems — Risks to Be Avoided

Business Strategy

Strategic Uncertainties — Interactive Control Systems

Critical Performance Variables — Diagnostic Control Systems

ethical boundaries are severe and nonnegotiable. As performance-oriented organizations grow and become more decentralized, the risks of failure increase. Managers must rely more and more on formal systems in order to ensure that the boundaries are communicated and understood.

Not all boundaries concern standards of ethical conduct. Strategic boundaries focus on ensuring that people steer clear of opportunities that could diminish the business's competitive position. A large computer company, for example, uses its strategic planning process to segregate its product and market opportunities into what managers call *green space* and *red space*. Green space is the acceptable domain for new initiatives. Red space represents products and markets in which senior managers have decided they do not want to pursue new opportunities, although the organization could compete in those products and markets given its competencies. A British relief organization uses a similar system to monitor strategic boundaries; it maintains a *gray list* of companies whose contributions it will neither solicit nor accept. Managers at Automatic Data Processing (ADP) use a strategic boundary list that delineates the types of business opportunities that managers must avoid. The guidelines provide ADP managers with clarity and focus. This technique has contributed to 133 consecutive quarters of double-digit growth in earnings per share—a record unmatched by any other company traded on the New York Stock Exchange.

Working together, boundary systems and beliefs systems are the yin and yang that together create a dynamic tension. The warm, positive, inspirational beliefs are a foil to the dark, cold constraints. The result is a dynamic tension between commitment and punishment. Together, these systems transform limitless opportunity into a focused domain that employees and managers are encouraged to exploit actively. In combination, they establish direction, motivate and inspire, and protect against potentially damaging opportunistic behavior.

INTERACTIVE CONTROL SYSTEMS

When organizations are small, key managers and employees can sit around the same table and informally explore the impact of emerging threats and opportunities. But as organizations grow larger and senior managers have less and less personal contact with people throughout the organization, new formal systems must be created to share emerging information and to harness the creativity that often leads to new products, line extensions, processes, and even markets. Unfortunately, diagnostic control systems, which highlight shortfalls against plans, won't suffice. Instead, senior managers need sensing systems more like the ones used by the National Weather Service. Ground stations all over the country monitor temperature, barometric pressure, relative humidity, cloud cover, wind direction and velocity, and precipitation. Balloons and satellites provide additional data. These data are monitored continuously from a central location in an effort to identify patterns of change.

Managers need similar scanning mechanisms. Like weather-tracking systems, interactive control systems are the formal information systems that managers use to involve themselves regularly and personally in the decisions of subordinates. These systems are generally simple to understand. Through them, senior managers participate in the decisions of subordinates and focus organizational attention and learning on key strategic issues.

Making a control system interactive invariably demands attention from participants throughout the business. At Pepsico, for example, the weekly release of new Nielsen market-share numbers creates a flurry of activity as 60 or 70 people throughout the organization begin working on the data in anticipation of the inevitable scrutiny and queries of senior management. Senior managers schedule weekly meetings to discuss the new Nielsen information, to challenge subordinates to explain the meaning of changed circumstances, and to review action plans that subordinates have developed to react to problems and opportunities.

Interactive control systems have four characteristics that set them apart from diagnostic control systems. First, they focus on constantly changing information that top-level managers have identified as potentially strategic. Second, the information is significant enough to demand frequent and regular attention from operating managers at all levels of the organization. Third, the data generated by the interactive system are best interpreted and discussed in face-to-face meetings of superiors, subordinates, and peers. Fourth, the interactive control system is a catalyst for an ongoing debate about underlying data, assumptions, and action plans.

Interactive control systems track the strategic uncertainties that keep senior managers awake at night—the shocks to the business that could undermine their assumptions about the future and the way they have chosen to compete. Depending on the business, these uncertainties might relate to changes in technology, customers' tastes, government regulation, and industry competition. Because interactive control systems are designed to gather information that might challenge visions of the future, they are, by definition, hot buttons for senior managers.

A senior manager's decision to use a specific control system interactively—in other words, to invest time and attention in face-to-face meetings to review new information—sends a clear signal to the organization about what's important. Through the dialogue and debate that surround the interactive process, new strategies often emerge. Consider the case of a well-known hospital supply company. The company is a low-cost producer, supplying disposable hospital products for intravenous drug delivery such as plasma containers, tubing, and syringes. Even though efficiency, quality, and cost control are important competencies, these concerns do not keep managers awake at night. (They are well understood and can be managed effectively with diagnostic control systems.) Instead, senior managers worry that technological breakthroughs will undermine their ability to deliver products valued by the market. Accordingly, they use a project management system interactively to focus organizational attention on a dozen or so emerging technological issues. Senior managers meet monthly for several days to debate the impact of technologies—introduced by competitors or in related industries, or developed in-house—on their business. These meetings become intense as the managers challenge one another to assess the impact of new information and develop responses. From this dialogue, new strategies emerge.

Senior managers at *USA Today*, Gannett Company's daily newspaper, use a similar process to review information contained in a simple package of reports delivered each Friday. Three weekly reports give senior managers a picture of how they have done in the previous week and what conditions lie ahead for the upcoming few weeks. The data in the Friday packet range from year-to-date figures to daily and account-specific information. These data provide insight into changing industry conditions and the advertising strategies of key customers. They allow managers to look at the big picture and provide enough detail to identify specific vulnerabilities, opportunities, and the source of any problems that require proactive responses.

Each week, senior managers at *USA Today* schedule intensive face-to-face meetings with key subordinates to analyze and interpret the report data. Among the regular topics of discussion and debate are advertising volume against plan, committed future volume by issue, and new business by type of client. In addition to looking for unexpected shortfalls, managers also look for unexpected successes. From these meetings, significant innovations have been proposed to deal with unanticipated downturns and to capitalize on unanticipated opportunities. Innovations have included launching a new market-survey service for automotive clients, introducing fractional-page color advertising, selling exclusive inserts dedicated to specific customers and products, and using circulation salespeople to sell ad space in regional locations.

Of course, managers in other businesses choose different kinds of control systems to use interactively depending on the strategic uncertainties associated with their business strategies. For example, Johnson & Johnson uses its profit-planning system interactively to focus attention on the development and protection of innovative products in its various markets. Managers periodically reestimate the predicted effects of competitive tactics and new product rollouts on their profit plans for the current and the following year. The recurring questions posed by managers are: What has changed since our last forecast? Why? What are we going to do about it? The results are new ideas and action plans.

BALANCING EMPOWERMENT AND CONTROL

Effective managers empower their organizations because they believe in the innate potential of people to innovate and add value. For instance, the reason Nordstrom salespeople provide exceptional customer service is that they are selected and trained to act entrepreneurially. In turn, they have the freedom and motivation to tailor their service to each customer's needs. To unleash this type of potential, senior managers must give up control over many kinds of decisions and allow employees at lower levels of the organization to act independently. Good managers work constantly to help employees rise to their potential. In small organizations, managers do this informally. While eating or traveling together, they communicate core values and missions, the rules of the game, and current targets—and they learn about significant changes. As companies become larger, more decentralized, and geographically dispersed, senior managers are no longer in constant contact with all the employees who will identify and respond to emerging problems and opportunities. Nonetheless, the guiding principles of communication and control are every bit as important.

A large international construction company respected for its quality and customer service provides a clear illustration of how the control levers support one another. The company has more than 25 offices in the United States and abroad; as a result, project managers and employees make multimillion-dollar decisions far from the company's top-level managers. The senior managers who set the company's overall direction and strategy ensure that they have adequate control of their far-flung operations by using all four levers of control.

To communicate core values, they rely on a beliefs system. The company's widely circulated credo refers to the importance of responsibility, of collective pride in engineering quality, of financial success, and of integrity. It concludes with an overall objective handed down by the founder: "To be the best."

These inspirational beliefs are offset by clear boundaries. Managers are forbidden, for example, to work in certain countries where facilitating payments and bribes are required to do business, because these sorts of actions jeopardize the company's belief in integrity. The company also maintains a *turkey list* to communicate to managers the types of projects that the company has learned are not profitable and should be avoided. (For example, senior managers have learned from bitter experience to steer clear of sewage-disposal-plant construction.) The list is adjusted from time to time as managers learn where their competencies lie and where they don't.

Managers gain still more control by using a variety of diagnostic controls—among them profit plans, budgets, and goals and objectives. These control systems do not require very much attention from senior management other than the time spent setting annual goals and monitoring exceptions to see that events unfold according to plan. One control system, however, is used interactively. The project management system focuses attention on the strategic uncertainties that managers want everyone to monitor: the company's reputation in the trade, the shifting perceptions of customers, and the ideal skill mix required in various project teams. The new data are used as a catalyst to force regular face-to-face discussions in which managers share information and attempt to develop better ways to customize their services and adjust their strategies in a changing market.

Collectively, these four levers of control set in motion powerful forces that reinforce one another. As organizations become more complex, managers will inevitably deal with increasing opportunity and competitive forces and decreasing time and attention. By using the control levers effectively, managers can be confident that the benefits of innovation and creativity are not achieved at the expense of control.

Indianapolis: Implementing Competition in City Services

In November 1991, Stephen Goldsmith was elected Mayor of Indianapolis, Indiana. Indianapolis, with a population of 800,000, was the 12th largest city in the United States. As a Republican candidate, Goldsmith campaigned on the basis of neighborhood revitalization and making city government more effective by providing better services more efficiently, being more responsive to its people, and avoiding increases in property taxes. He was opposed by the existing bureaucracy, which wanted to maintain job stability and security, and the unionized city workers, who enjoyed monopolies over the provision of nearly all city services and were concerned about his threatened privatization of these services.

Goldsmith called for profound changes in the way the city was run. Skeptics argued that the city was in excellent shape. It had produced operating surpluses for several years, and its bonds were rated AAA—the highest possible by Moody's Investors Service, Inc. "Why fix what ain't broke?" they asked. Moreover, Goldsmith was following a popular Republican who had been mayor since 1976. The voters, however, seemed to agree with the 44-year-old Steve Goldsmith that the services provided the public for the taxes they paid were not returning a good value. Rising taxes and deteriorating public services were driving both companies and the citizenry to the suburbs.

COMPETITION AND COMPETITIVENESS

Newly-elected Mayor Goldsmith realized that drastic action was needed to stop this "flight of wealth." He also knew that he would have to move quickly while he still had the momentum and enthusiasm of his supporters and before coalitions could form to block his ideas. Although he had campaigned advocating "privatization," a policy of transferring city services to private contractors, he realized soon after taking office that public monopolies were likely to be only slightly less efficient than private monopolies. He was frequently quoted as saying that "if we had only one McDonald's in town, even with the best restaurant managers in charge, over time the price of the hamburger would go up while the quality deteriorated."

Professor William J. Bruns, Jr. and Professor Roger Atherton of Northeastern University prepared this case as the basis for class discussion rather than to illustrate either effective or ineffective handling of an administrative situation.

Goldsmith worked hard to put in place "the most comprehensive competition and competitiveness effort of any major city or maybe any governmental entity in the United States." In his presentations, he made it very clear that "we do not have a privatization effort in Indianapolis." Instead, he coined the term "marketization." His approach combined many existing ideas in an unusual combination. The application of competition to the public sector attracted so much local, national, and even international attention that it could help vault him into the governorship and perhaps even higher.

THE FIRST STEPS

Mayor Goldsmith created the Service, Efficiency, and Lower Taxes for Indianapolis Commission (SELTIC) in February 1992. SELTIC was comprised of nine entrepreneurs who volunteered their time to recommend ways to decrease costs, eliminate waste, and improve government services and make them more efficient. Each member led a group of private sector volunteers and some of the most enterprising employees in each city department. The commission and its 100 volunteers inventoried city assets to determine whether they should be sold and looked at city services, identifying about 150 that they recommended be opened to competition.

Goldsmith, soon after taking office, set up a separate Office of Enterprise Development and placed Skip Stitt, a 30-year-old lawyer, in charge, reporting directly to the Mayor. It was Skip's job to challenge all of the basic assumptions about city government—to ask why do we do things the way we do, why do we capture numbers this way, how could we do this service better, why are we in this business at all? In the Mayor's opinion, it was Skip's ability to confront a director directly that led to great debates and improvements in city government. Over time, the directors learned to challenge the assumptions that had built up over the years and stood in the way of making their departments more efficient. The Mayor commented that:

> It was Skip's job to torment everybody else in government until we reached the right equilibrium between the private side and the public side.

Stitt quickly recognized that if the city was going to use competition as a core strategy, the managers would have to know their real costs. At that time the city had no financial or accounting tools in place that would tell them their real costs. Stitt also realized they would need additional management tools if they were going to be successful in creating a more efficient and responsive government.

STRATEGIC TOOLS

Four new practices were developed which became known as the "Strategic Tools Initiative." Skip explained the first three of these as follows:

1. **Activity-based costing (ABC)** The city needed to know how much every service and activity cost. This tool was originally developed in a manufacturing environment, so that manufacturers who were making finished goods could determine what it cost to provide, to prepare, and to deliver each of the components. That way they could decide whether they should manufacture in-house or should buy them through out-sourcing (what we would call privatization in government) from another vendor. ABC was an important tool

for managing costs. It also facilitated continuous improvement. To the extent you could identify the cost of services, you could carefully and predictively compare yourself to other government providers, and even within the city we could compare the costs of snow removal services in one part of the city with the costs in another quadrant. ABC was particularly helpful as our in-house work force started thinking about competition. It allowed them to borrow the best ideas from other areas in the city and to implement best management practices in their own activities.

2. **Performance measures** Cost was not the only issue. Quality assurance required the city to develop performance standards for assessing how well city services were provided. Competitive contracting also required very clear standards from the city about how the contracts would be evaluated. It was important to know your expected outcomes to measure performance against other public sector and private sector entities. Performance measures were critically important so that we knew what it was we were doing, how well we were doing it, and how much we needed to do in terms of monitoring those services. These have also been helpful in our increasing emphasis on pay-for-performance.

3. **Popular budgets** By combining activity-based costing with performance measures, the city created a "popular budget" that explained to citizens what they were purchasing with every dollar of their budget. The focus was on such output measures as the miles of streets plowed or repaired, the number of park lawns mowed, or the number of police officers on the streets rather than the input measures as the number of plows purchased, labor hours used, or budgeted dollars.

One other strategic tool was developed: customer surveys. There was no point to being efficient delivering a service that was not wanted. City managers believed that regular customer surveys coupled with the popular budget, enabled them to make informed decisions about trade-offs between services.

THE RESULTS

By 1996 more than 60 city services had been moved into the competitive marketplace. The estimated cost savings from the public-private competition were substantial: $6.5 million in 1992; $12 million in 1993; and $27.6 million in 1994. Total predicted savings to the city are estimated to exceed $150 million. In addition, nearly $1 million of unused or underutilized city assets had been sold or not replaced. Some details are shown in **Exhibits 1** and **2**.

The new Mayor eliminated about 450 of 4,700 full-time employees in the first 16 months, including 160 mostly managerial-level employees within the first three months. He reduced city employment from 4,675 on December 31, 1991 to 3,641 on December 31, 1995. Excluding public safety, public employment in the city decreased 40% to the lowest level in 20 years. Some of the savings were used to enhance public safety and to pay for the largest infrastructure rebuilding program in city history. The 1996 budget of $439 million included operating expenses that were $26 million less than were incurred in 1992. The property tax rate had remained constant for eight consecutive years.

PUTTING ANALYSIS INTO ACTION: LOOKING FOR SMOOTH STREETS

A small cadre of young managers, selected by Steve Goldsmith, led the change in the delivery of city services. One of the most effective was Mitch Roob, a 30-year-old CPA who had earned an MBA at Notre Dame, and whom Goldsmith appointed director of the former Department of Transportation. It was Roob's job to bring competitiveness to the department that maintained the city's streets and alleys.

In 1995, Roob described how the effort began:

When the mayor ran four years ago he talked at length about the need to compete services and about privatization. He was endorsed by the regular Republican organization and opposed by AFCSME (the city employees' labor union). When he won, there was great concern on the part of organized labor that Steve Goldsmith's goal in life was to go after organized labor. There was great glee on the part of the Republican organization folks that they had secured their jobs for another four years. During the campaign, neither side had listened very well.

When Steve came into office and we decided to compete services, we looked at potholes. One of the reasons we chose potholes was that it had high public visibility. At about the same time we opened microfilming city records to competition. Does the public care about microfilm? No. They don't. Quite frankly, we wanted to make an early political statement. We did that with potholes. Other than snow removal and backed up toilets, there are very few things that the public cares about more than potholes. They hate potholes. So by competing street repair we could get the public's and the media's attention.

With the help of KPMG Peat Marwick we figured that it cost $425 a ton of asphalt to fix potholes. Having an outside firm estimate the costs through activity-based costing really helped because it made those costs credible. We did not know whether this was a good price or a bad price, so we had to find out. We told the people in street maintenance that they now had an opportunity to compete.

The union was very concerned about this. They thought they would lose this opportunity to compete and be out of their jobs, that this was just a polite way to fire all of them. So the union leadership came to us and said, "You've got too many managers. You've got 32 managers and 94 workers. You cannot expect us to be competitive if you keep that much overhead, so you've got to do something about it." That made sense to us. Just incidentally, about half of the managers were Republican-precinct committeemen. But we began eliminating managerial positions.

That action sent a pretty strong message to folks in the union. If management was willing to fire those who had supported them in the election, if we do not get the price right, what will they do to us? We intentionally wanted them to feel that way. This was a very charged environment. It was as stressful a time in my life as I have had.

Business theorists suggest that fear is a poor long-term motivator, and there seems to be a significant amount of anecdotal evidence that that is the case. However, fear is an extraordinary good motivator in the short term. We used fear to reorient our employees, and then after they began performing the way we wanted them to, we started to be really nice to them.

After we had scared the union guys, we worked with them to change their behavior, and we showed them what they could gain by working with us. We showed the union that they were in too many lines of business, and it was to all of our benefit to get out of some of them. We had to focus on the infrastructure management business.

We needed to show the union workers the advantages of preserving paved roads by sealing cracks earlier in their life at a cost of about $700 per mile in order to postpone patching or repaving them at a cost of $100 thousand a mile or replacing them at a cost of $1 million a mile because the cracks had not been sealed. To explain this, we had to put these concepts in terms of preventative maintenance on houses and cars, which they understood. Then, we told them that in the future we were going to buy the services to do the preventative maintenance. After we explained that we could go to either a private company or to them, they quickly saw that they should be more into the crack sealing business, and that they should invest in the technology to do better work faster. They came to believe that they could effectively compete.

We explained to them that if they could not do their work effectively and efficiently, we would get someone who would. We got them to behave the way we wanted them to behave, by treating them the same way we would have treated any other contractor.

When we did that, the union and management came back to us and said they could fill potholes more cost effectively than they did before. "We don't really need two trucks in every pothole crew. We don't really need to have eight people in a pothole crew. We could have only six people in a pothole crew. We could raise the crack sealing goal from two lane miles per day to three lane miles per day." Let's face it, necessity was the mother of invention. They felt the need to become competitive. When they did that, the $425 dropped to $307 for laying a ton of asphalt.

Once I had a group of lower level union officials come to me and ask me to remove an equipment operator from their crew because he was not very good. They did not want to be burdened with him because he did not work fast enough, and they thought they were going to lose bids because he slowed them down.

Another thing that affected what happened was that my predecessor was a pretty typical government manager with a military background, and he had managed as if he were still in the army. At first, crews were surprised to find me out on jobs working with them. Or they would be out working and I would be bringing them drinks. They soon felt that somebody cared about them more than the previous administration did. And I dealt fairly often with the guys right on the front line. I knew most of them by face, if not by name.

This was a style that worked well for me, but it probably also had the effect of undercutting the relationship that managers had with their workers. The managers were used to living in a command and control structure. They would often hear about my suggestions no sooner, and sometimes later, than their employees did. I destroyed their existing management paradigm, and I did not give them a new one.

Another thing that helped us was that we concentrated our work in the central city where most of our employees lived, instead focusing on the suburbs, as our predecessors had done. Our employees saw our commitment to their own neighborhoods. They saw their streets being resurfaced, and they were being paid to fix the streets where they lived.

Our relationship with the union started out as bad as it could be. These guys had supported Steve Goldsmith's opponent, and they were convinced that we were going to destroy them. They started off believing the worst in us. Actually, that was a really good place to start, because anything we did to show that we were not bad was seen as positive. Our relationship improved because it had started so low. The kinds of messages that we sent signaled that we all were in this thing together, and if they did not work with us, none of us would have jobs. We tried to encourage a we vs. them spirit in the sense of the public sector vs. private sector.

We had a sense of leadership that flowed from Steve Goldsmith through the rest of us. He had the vision and the willingness to inspire the rest of us to do things like being on the job at 2:30 a.m. on Christmas morning, giving hot chocolate to the drivers who were plowing streets in the middle of a snow storm. Those guys worked harder for us because they knew we cared about them.

Bob Larsen, a manager with the former Department of Transportation in 1995, described the changes from his perspective:

We've gone from 32 supervisors in February 1992 to six right now. When a bid comes up we have a meeting between the management and the union, and we decide whether or not to bid. If it is something that we do, we get a bid team together. We inspect the job and try to figure a way to do it.

We used to go out with five or six people patching or filling potholes. We do it with three people now. The teams are watching their mix of manpower and equipment because the costs are derived through activity-based costing. We have large trucks like tandem duals which you need only for snow. You do not need that large a truck out there to fill potholes. So they go out with a single axle, or a crew cab, or a one-ton dump truck.

Our performance measures in 1992 had crack sealing at two lane miles per day. We knew we could not win a bid at two lane miles per day, so we bid the contract at three lane miles per day. We won that bid. By adjusting our manpower and equipment to lower costs (see **Exhibits 3** and **4** for diagrams and changes in manpower and equipment), we actually averaged four lane miles per day and successfully completed the job at $20,000 under our bid. The Department of Transportation shared some of those savings with all of us in the form of an unexpected cash bonus. That really made an impression on our workers.

During the 1992 bid, I chewed our crews out if it took too long to get to the job site. In 1993 we had already cut back half of our supervision, and the crew leaders of the line employees took over.

In 1993 we put a class together on how to prepare bids. We put the class on for roughly 70 people, union and management, about half our work force. We started out with showing them what a company would have to do. For example, our license plate costs $5, while theirs would cost $258. They have to put so much money as a bid bond. Their average worker works 1,520 hours a year in private construction because of the weather; while we are still working, those guys are sitting at home. A lot of them don't have full medical and dental coverage. We have an outstanding plan. We let them in on the idea that if our guys get out there and do a good job, the work tilts toward the city worker.

After the bid team training, another manager came in and gave a one hour introduction to ABC that snowed the hell out of everybody. Now I sit down with two or three guys and we just talk about the assumptions and methodology. I take my laptop and get right in the back of a crew cab and say, "We have six guys on this job, what do we need six guys for?" They say, "It is a narrow road so we need a flagger," but I say, "Why can't the truck driver get out and wave his arms so that we can do the job with just five." Then, they see that the cost per ton goes down. They have been picking up these ideas.

We were successful on some of our bids, but we learned some lessons. We didn't have any historical data on concrete sealing, so when we bid the concrete we bid it just like an asphalt street. But concrete takes three times as much material, so it is going to take you longer to do it. So we lost some money on concrete work in 1993. But we made money on the asphalt contracts. The one bid on concrete on which we made money was one on which we had doubled our estimated labor time from 10 hours to 20, and then we added another hour just to be on the safe side. Our actual time was 19-1/2 hours to do 4.95 lane miles of concrete.

We had one contract in which a pothole team put in a bid assuming they were going to use a DuraPatcher. That is a machine that mixes the tak and stone in a hopper, which is cheaper. Instead of $22 per ton, you are putting out the material at $14 per ton. They had so many potholes that they went and grabbed a big tandem axle dual that is $55 an hour when they had put the bid in at $17.50 a unit. But with the bigger truck they were able to go out and do ten tons in seven hours instead of seven tons. They figured this out on their own; no one told them to do it.

By 1994 we had been able to train half the work force on how to calculate a bid, and to explain to them that everything we do is watched by internal audit, which wants to see all of the paperwork that goes with all of the contract work. Also all of the work is inspected. This schedule (**Exhibit 5**) shows the steps we used in preparing a bid.

All of our bids are based on costs that we keep up-to-date. (See **Exhibit 6**.)

There are still problems with ABC. If garbage goes in, garbage comes out. If there are errors in the ABC cost estimates, they foul up all of the ABC information that we use in bidding.

Once we win a bid, I prepare spreadsheets from the source documents that I get from the crew chiefs. I keep a running record on every bid, on a day-by-day basis. (See **Exhibit 7** through **Exhibit 10** for some of the daily reports used to monitor costs.) That was how I discovered that concrete was costing us too much. Sometimes if I think we are getting in trouble on costs, I go out to see the crews and to talk to them.

These reports show me and my boss where we stand. (See **Exhibits 11** and **12**.) She may ask whether she should be worried about being $1,000 down, and I can tell her yes or no, because I keep track of what is actually going on.

Ray Wallace, Stephen Goldsmith's special assistant, summarized his views on why the competitiveness effort had been so successful:

Our success really all comes down to competition. What our people needed was a tool to measure their efficiency so that they could compare their work to that of others. Anytime you can install competition into a process, it is going to bring out the best people have to offer. Once people knew that they had to win bids or lose their jobs, and that eventually they might share in savings, they began to look for ways to do their work better and at lower cost.

EXHIBIT 1
Highlights of the Indianapolis Competition Effort

What is the Indianapolis privatization effort?

Actually, Indianapolis does not have a privatization effort. It has a comprehensive effort to let private sector companies compete against government workers for contracts to provide services and manage assets. Regardless of whether the private sector or city government wins, the result is reduced costs and more responsive services for the taxpayers. Indianapolis is moving the provision of municipal services into the marketplace, and breaking up government monopolies.

Why is this necessary?

The environment in which cities operate is changing. Wealth and jobs are rapidly leaving our urban areas, chased out by crime, taxes, and other factors. In order for Indianapolis to remain successful in the next century, it must reduce the cost of providing government services so that it can keep taxes as low as possible.

What have these savings meant for the City?

Indianapolis has been able to balance the budget, cut the non-public safety work force by 40%, reduce the budget by $26 million, and use the approximately $150 million it has identified in savings to put more officers on the street and to undertake the largest infrastructure improvement program in the city's history—all without raising taxes. Indianapolis has enjoyed four consecutive years of record-setting job creation and now has one of the lowest unemployment rates in the country.

What are some of the successes of competition?

Private management of the Indianapolis International Airport will save $100 million over 10 years, helping to make Indianapolis one of the pre-eminent passenger and cargo hubs in the country.

Private management of the City's Advanced Wastewater Treatment plants is saving taxpayers $65 million over five years. The work force at the plants has dropped from 328 to 176, while the quality of the treated water leaving the plants has risen significantly.

Competitively bidding trash collection is saving taxpayers more than $15 million over three years. Collapsing the City's 25 trash collection districts into 11 districts and competing out contracts for them reduced the cost of providing trash collection from approximately $85 per household annually to about $68. City workers reengineered their work plans to win the maximum territory in the competition.

City workers reduced their budget, cut their work force, and increased their productivity to win a bid to maintain and service city vehicles. The agreement saves taxpayers $8 million.

In total, more than 60 services have been moved into the marketplace, with total savings to taxpayers of $150 million. Competition has improved services and made them more responsive in many areas throughout government.

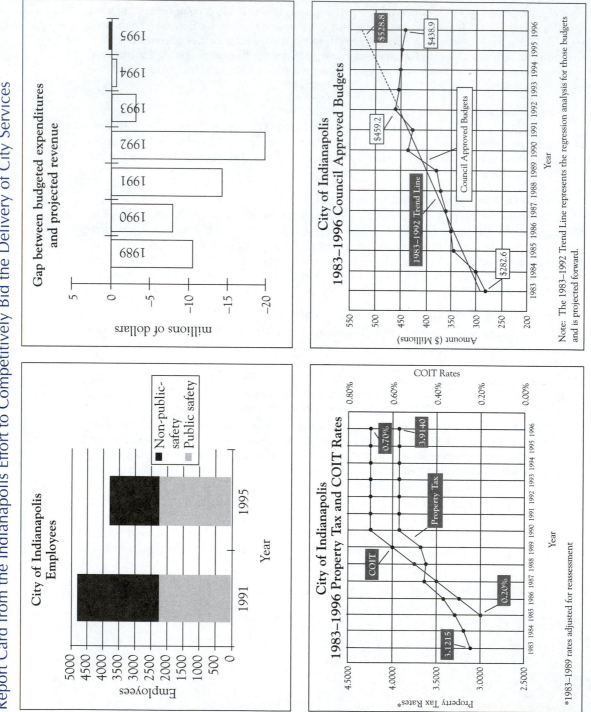

Gap between budgeted expenditures and projected revenue

(millions of dollars, by year: 1989, 1990, 1991, 1992, 1993, 1994, 1995)

City of Indianapolis Employees

(Employees, by Year: 1991, 1995; Non-public-safety, Public safety)

**City of Indianapolis
1983–1996 Council Approved Budgets**

$528.8
$438.9
$459.2
1983–1992 Trend Line
Council Approved Budgets
$282.6

Amount ($ Millions)

Year

Note: The 1983–1992 Trend Line represents the regression analysis for those budgets and is projected forward.

**City of Indianapolis
1983–1996 Property Tax and COIT Rates**

COIT Rates
0.70%
3.9140
Property Tax
COIT
0.20%
3.1215

Property Tax Rates*

Year

*1983–1989 rates adjusted for reassessment

EXHIBIT 3
The Old Way to Seal Cracks

DOT PLANNING CRACK REPAIR 1993	THE OLD WAY INSPECTION	LOCATION: ASPHALT	CONCRETE	MOVE IN/OUT	USE	UNIT COST	COST
JOB REQUIREMENTS							
TRUCK DRIVER		5	0		5	$30.00	150
LABORER		5	0		5	$20.00	100
CREW LEADER		1	0		1	$34.00	34
EQUIP OP					0	$33.87	0
OVERHEAD	0	11	0	0	11	$23.00	253
STAKE BED		0	0		0	$15.00	0
CREW CAB		1	0		1	$20.00	20
DOUBLE BOILER		1	0		1	$35.00	35
1 TON DUMP					0	$15.00	0
3/4 TON PU		0	0		0	$15.00	0
TRAILER					0	$18.00	0
ROUTER					0	$40.00	0
COMPRESSOR		1	0		1	$3.34	3.34
MINI PICKUP			0		0	$15.00	0
ARROW BOARD			0		0	$2.00	0
SINGLE AXEL DUMP		2			2	$16.55	33.1
CRUM RUBBER		200	0		200	$0.30	60
TOTAL COST							688.44

TRAFFIC CONTROL ⊗

⊗ ← BLOWER

← SINGLE-AXLE DUMP (SAD)

← COMPRESSOR

← SAD

← TACKWAGON

⊗ ⊗ ← BUCKET
⊗ ⊗ ← SQUEEGE

← CREW CAB W/ARROW BOAR

OLD WAY

11 MAN CREW
2 SAD's
1 CC
1 COMP.
1 T/WAGON

⊗ DENOTES MAN POWER

TRAFFIC CONTROL ⊗

Page 1

EXHIBIT 4
The New Way to Seal Cracks

DOT PLANNING CRACK REPAIR 1993	THE BETTER WAY	LOCATION:					
JOB REQUIREMENTS	INSPECTION	ASPHALT	CONCRETE	MOVE IN/OUT	USE	UNIT COST	COST
TRUCK DRIVER		3	0		3	$30.00	90
LABORER		2	0		2	$20.00	40
CREW LEADER		1	0		1	$34.00	34
EQUIP OP					0	$33.87	0
OVERHEAD	0	6	0	0	6	$23.00	138
STAKE BED		1	0		1	$15.00	15
CREW CAB		1	0		1	$20.00	20
DOUBLE BOILER		1	0		1	$35.00	35
1 TON DUMP					0	$15.00	0
3/4 TON PU		0	0		0	$15.00	0
TRAFFIC CONTROL		2			2	$15.00	30
ROUTER					0	$40.00	0
COMPRESSOR		1	0		1	$3.34	3.34
MINI PICKUP			0		0	$15.00	0
ARROW BOARD			0		0	$2.00	0
SINGLE AXEL DUMP					0	$16.55	0
CRUM RUBBER		200	0		200	$0.30	60
TOTAL COST							465.34

RENT TRAFFIC CONTROL TO SAVE $$$
No Overhead on Rental

BETTER WAY
⊗ 6 MAN CREW
1 SBT - Stake Bed Truck
1 CC - Crew Cab
1 COMP.- Compressor
1 T/WAGON- Tack Wagon

⊗ ← BLOWER

⊗ ← SBT

COMP. - Mounted Compressor on Truck } eliminated 1 Truck 1 Truck Driver

⊗ ← T.W.

⊗ ← WAND

⊗ ⊗ ← SQUEEGE - Eliminated 1 squeege

⊗ ← CC. w/A B

EXHIBIT 5

BID PREPARATION

BID NOTIFICATION
    MAIL NOTICE TO BIDDERS POST CARD RECEIVE TUESDAY OF 1ST WEEK
    NEWSPAPER APPEARS MONDAY 1ST WEEK AND 2ND WEEK

PICK UP BID ROOM 1522 CITY COUNTY BUILDING
    MAKE ADDITIONAL COPIES OF BID PACKAGE
    SAFE GUARD ORIGINAL BID PROPOSAL

ASSEMBLE THE BID TEAM
    MANAGEMENT REPRESENTATIVE
    UNION REPRESENTATIVE
    PEOPLE WHO WILL DO THE WORK

BID TEAM MEETING
    REVIEW BID PACKAGE
    DO WE BID
    IDENTIFY PROBLEMS
    ASSIGN JOBS

FIELD INSPECTION
    IS IT FEASIBLE?
    HOW DO WE DO IT?

PUT THE BID TOGETHER

SUBMIT THE BID BY THURSDAY OF THE 3RD WEEK

BID OPENS 10:00 AM

BE AT DCAM BOARD TO ANSWER ANY QUESTIONS

PRE-CON & TONICE TO PROCEED MEET CONSULTANT/INSPECTOR

CONTRACT SCHEDULE

TRACK COST

FINAL ACCEPTANCE

SUBMIT PO TO GET PAID

SET UP COMPLETE FILE FOR HISTORICAL DATA, INTERNAL AUDIT, & FINAL
ANALYSIS

EXHIBIT 6

OUTPUT COST SUMMARY

	1993	1994
BASE REPAIR	$ 29.11	$ 16.09 sq. yds.
BRIDGE CLEANING	$ 304.89	$ 298.16 ea.
CLEAN RIGHT-OF-WAY	$ 71.59	$ 4.87 hrs.
CONSTRUCT NEW SURFACE	$ 25.00	$ 44.67 sq. yds.
CURBS REMOVE/REPLACE	$ 18.00	$ 23.49 lin. ft.
DOUBLE BOILER SEALING	$1,815.00	$1,519.57 ln. mi.
HAND MOWING/BRUSH CUT	$ 77.00	$ 46.24 hrs.
HAULING TRASH/RUBBLE	$ 41.00	$ 41.18 cu. yds.
HUMP REMOVAL	$ 261.00	$ 234.40 ea.
INLET CLEANING	$ 38.00	$ 37.25 ea.
OTHER WORK	$ 30.00	$ 48.32 hrs.
PATCHING	$ 311.00	$ 211.19 tons
SIDEWALKS REMOVE/REPLACE	$ 108.00	$ 128.17 sq. yds.
SNOW CONTROL	$ 150.79	$ 86.53 hrs.
STRIP PATCHING	$ 166.00	$ 97.12 tons
TRACTOR MOWING	$ 48.00	$ 55.54 hrs.
UNPAVED ALLEY REPAIR	$ 1.93	$ 2.46 lin. ft.
UNPAVED BERM REPAIR	$ 3.19	$ 1.44 lin. ft.

EXHIBIT 7
FAX on Planned Work

To: MICHAEL FINGER, P.E.
PROJECT ENGINEER
UNITED SURVEYING, INC.

From: DAVID WALDROP
CREW LEADER

Date: *5-23-95*

Number of Pages: 1

Phone: 253-4996

Fax: 253-5385

FAX

Remarks: WE PLAN ON PATCHING ON WASHINGTON STREET STARTING AT ___*3800*___

THROUGH ___*?*___. WE PLAN TO START AT ___*9:30*___ HOURS.

THANK YOU.

David Waldrop

DISTRICT 1 - OPERATIONS DIVISION
DEPARTMENT OF PUBLIC WORKS
2001 DR. MARTIN LUTHER KING JR. STREET
INDIANAPOLIS, INDIANA 46202
PHONE: 317-327-5631 FAX: 317-327-5633
MANAGER MARK BENDER 327-5631
SUPERVISOR WILLIE HARRINGTON 327-5632
OFFICE ASSISTANT BECKY HARDIN 327-5630

EXHIBIT 8

Milestone Contractors, L.P.
2810 Columbia Avenue
Plant 14
Office: (317) 788-1040
Plant: (317) 923-1401

Milestone

SOLD TO: CITY OF INDPLS/D.P.W.
P.O.# UD 49029

NO. 02585

TIME	DATE	PLANT #	CUSTOMER #	TICKET #	TYPE MATERIAL	TRUCK #
10:02	05/23/95	14	22440	02585	#12 SURF	SA

PRODUCT #—NAME/LOAD #—ACCUMULATED TOTALS(TONS)		
03-#8 BIND	02-#12 SURF 003-0013.20	99-OTHERS

TRUCK WEIGHT IN TONS		
GROSS	TARE	NET
17.37	11.94	5.43

DRIVER _Harold_ RECVD. BY _____

ALL WEIGHTS ARE IN POUNDS UNLESS OTHERWISE SPECIFIED

NO.	TARE	1	2	3	4	5	6	7	TARE	ASPHALT	BATCH TOTAL

5.0 W. Wash 95.050

43 Country Club Rd. 2100

5-23-95

INSPECTOR'S SIGNATURE	_David Wallup_										10860
							LOAD TOTAL				

EXHIBIT 9
Daily Work Sheet

DATE: 5-23-95   WALDROP   DAILY WORK REPORT   TUESDAY–FRIDAY   MARTIN LUTHER KING

ACTY	LOCATION	LABOR	1	2	3	4	5	6	TOTAL
1 3 0 3	MLK Whitco - assfalt squ. Rail Tools	DW	4.0	6.0	1.0				
		HB	4.0	5.0	1.0				
		JC	4.0	5.0	1.0				
		VB				10.0	10 TM		
		RYAN							
2 3 0 0 6	W. Wash 3800–3400 E. Bowls	TOTAL							
3 3 0 0 6	Costn Club rd. 6100 Dispute	VEHICLE 1623 2039	4.5 4.0	5.0 2.0	1.0 1.0	4	5	6	
4 3 5 4 5	Leave								
5 9 9 9 9	0 loon 40 15	MATERIAL 5150 5210	5.50 16	5.0	.43	4	5	6	
6		NOTES:							

CREW LEADER David Wallac   MGR/SUPV _____   DATE ENTERED/INITIAL 5/30 Bb

EXHIBIT 10

DAILY WORK REPORT DATA

DPW OPERATIONS
STREET MAINTENANCE/MARTIN LUTHER KING
(c) De Lew, Cather & Company

DATE	MGMT UNIT	REF#	ACTIVITY	SUB-ACTIVITY	SYSTEM/ROAD CLASS
05/23/95	01	757	3875 PATCHING		

WORK REQUEST NO'S:

EQUIPMENT

CLASS/SPEC.	DESCRIPTION	HOURS ON JOB	CLASS/SPECF.	DESCRIPTION	HOURS ON JOB
1623	CREWCAB PU	0.5	2039	PATCHMAKER TRK	5.0

MATERIAL

CLASS/SPECF.	DESCRIPTION	QTY USED	UNIT OF MEASURE	CLASS/SPECF.	DESCRIPTION	QTY USED	UNIT OF MEASURE
5150	HOT MIX	5.0	TON	5210	TACK COAT	10.0	GALLON

ACCOMPLISHMENT

LOCATION	QTY
95-001	5.0

NOTES:

WORK UNIT: TONS

REG CLASS/B HRS SPECF.	NAME	OVERTIME CODE HRS	REG CLASS/B HRS SPECF.	NAME	OVERTIME CODE HRS
5.0 DW	DAVID WALDROP	5.0 HB	5.0 JC	JEFF CATT	

EXHIBIT 11

Sheet 1

CITY OF INDIANAPOLIS					
DEPARTMENT OF PUBLIC WORKS			3400-3800W		
OPERATIONS	WASHINGTON CHUCK HOLES WEST				
23-MAY-95					
REQUIREMENT	REG TIME			REG COST	TOTAL COST
CREW LEADER	5		$	20.00	$ 100.00
TRUCK DRIVER	10		$	17.00	$ 170.00
LABORER			$	14.00	$ —
OVERHEAD	15		$	14.85	$ 222.75
PATCHMAN	5		$	26.91	$ 134.55
CREW CAB	5		$	8.21	$ 41.05
1 TON DUMP			$	11.54	$
HOT BOX			$	9.32	$
HOT MIX	5		$	19.90	$ 99.50
SPECIAL MIX			$	23.07	$ —
TACK	10		$	.99	$ 9.90
DURAPATCH			$	17.05	$ —
COST PER TON	$155.55			MANPOWER	$ 270.00
				EQUIPMENT	$ 175.60
				MATERIAL	$ 109.40
				OVERHEAD	$ 222.75
					$ 777.75

EXHIBIT 12

Sheet 1

WASHINGTON STREET	COST PER TON	$160.00					
EMERGENCY RESPONSE	COST MOBILIZATION	$180.00			DATE AS OF	20-JUN-95	RFL
WASH-95-001 POTHOLE							
LOCATION	DATE/TIME NOTIFIED	DATE/TIME REPAIRED	TONNAGE	OUR COST	AMOUNT TO BILL	PROFIT (LOSS)	COST PER TON
2300-2900W	PATCHING	4/21/95	1	$ 150.18	$ 160.00	$ 9.82	$150.18
3800-4200W	PATCHING	4/26/95	4.07	$ 360.21	$ 651.20	$ 290.99	$ 88.50
4200-5000W	PATCHING	4/28/95	5.83	$ 767.87	$ 932.80	$ 164.93	$131.71
5000-4200W	PATCHING	5/12/95	2.41	$ 582.65	$ 385.60	$ (197.05)	$241.76
7000-8000E	PATCHING	5/10/95	0.5	$ 166.76	$ 80.00	$ (86.76)	$333.52
7000-8000E	PATCHING	5/11/95	3.53	$ 870.58	$ 635.40	$ (235.18)	$246.62
500-7930E	PATCHING	5/23/95	3	$ 681.19	$ 480.00	$ (201.19)	$227.06
3400-3800W	PATCHING	5/23/95	5	$ 777.75	$ 800.00	$ 22.25	$155.55
3400-3900W	PATCHING	6/6/95	3.03	$ 611.15	$ 484.80	$ (126.35)	$201.70
2900-1800W	PATCHING	6/7/95	4.02	$ 993.66	$ 643.20	$ (350.46)	$247.18
1800-3400W	PATCHING	6/8/95	1.41	$ 596.88	$ 225.60	$ (371.28)	$423.32
						$ —	#DIV/0!
						$ —	#DIV/0!
						$ —	#DIV/0!
						$ —	#DIV/0!
						$ —	#DIV/0!
			33.8	$6,558.88	$5,478.60	$(1,080.28)	$194.05

Nordstrom: Dissension in the Ranks? (A)

The first time Nordstrom sales clerk Lori Lucas came to one of the many "mandatory" Saturday morning department meetings and saw the sign—"Do Not Punch the Clock"—she assumed the managers were telling the truth when they said the clock was temporarily out of order. But as weeks went by, she discovered that on subsequent Saturdays the clock was always "broken" or the time cards were not accessible. When she and several colleagues hand-wrote the hours on their time cards, they discovered that their manager whited-out the hours and accused them of not being "team players." Commenting on the variety of tasks that implicitly had to be performed after hours, Ms. Lucas said, "You couldn't complain, because then your manager would schedule you for the bad hours, your sales per hour would fall, and next thing you know, you're out the door."[1]

Patty Bemis, who joined Nordstrom as a sales clerk in 1981 and quit eight years later, told a similar story:

Nordstrom recruiters came to me. I was working at The Broadway as Estee Lauder's counter manager and they said they had heard I had wonderful sales figures. We'd all heard Nordstrom was *the* place to work. They told me how I would double my wages. They painted a great picture and I fell right into it. . .

The managers were these little tin gods, always grilling you about your sales. . . . You felt like your job was constantly in jeopardy. They'd write you up for anything, being sick, the way you dressed. . . . The girls around me were dropping like flies. Everyone was always in tears. . . .

Working off the clock was just standard. In the end, really serving the customer, being an All-Star, meant nothing; if you had low sales per hour, you were forced out. . . .

I just couldn't take it anymore—the constant demands, the grueling hours. I just said one day, life's too short.[2]

Hilary Weston prepared this case from public sources under the supervision of Professor Robert Simons as the basis for class discussion rather than to illustrate either effective or ineffective handling of an administrative situation.

---

[1] Susan Faludi, "At Nordstrom Stores, Service Comes First—But at a Big Price," *Wall Street Journal*, February 20, 1990, p. A1.

[2] Ibid.

Despite employee grievances such as those of Lori Lucas and Patty Bemis, top management at the fashion specialty retailer acknowledged no serious problems with its management systems. Jim Nordstrom, co-chairman of the company with his brother John and cousin Bruce, explained management's position in a statement to the press:

> We haven't seen any complaints from the union. . . . If employees are working without pay, breaks, or days off, then it's isolated or by choice.
>
> A lot of them say, "I want to work every day." I have as many people thank us for letting them work all these hours as complain. I think people don't put in enough hours during the busy time. We need to work harder.
>
> A lot of what comes out makes it sound like we're slave drivers. If we were that kind of company, they wouldn't smile, they wouldn't work that hard. Our people smile because they want to.[3]

BACKGROUND OF THE CURRENT SITUATION

John W. Nordstrom founded Nordstrom in 1901 as a shoe store. Nearly a century later, by the end of 1989, the company had grown to become the nation's leading specialty retailer of apparel, shoes, and accessories. The company operated 59 department stores in six states and was implementing a national expansion plan that called for store openings in several additional states in the early 1990s. By the end of 1989, sales were approaching $3 billion and Nordstrom enjoyed one of the highest profit margins in its industry.

Nordstrom, which issued shares to the public in 1971, had always been run by members of the Nordstrom family, who still owned roughly half of the company. The third generation of Nordstrom family managers, who had been at the helm since 1970, upheld the management philosophy of the company's founder: offer the customer the best in service, selection, quality, and value.

Superior customer service was Nordstrom's strongest competitive advantage and consequently a major source of its financial success. The retailer had enjoyed nearly 20 years of uninterrupted (primarily double-digit) earnings growth before reporting a decline for the 1989 fiscal year. (**Exhibit 1** provides a history of Nordstrom's financial performance.) With sales per square foot of $380 in 1988,[4] Nordstrom was among the most productive in the industry, generating roughly double the 1988 industry average for specialty retailers of $194 per square foot.[5]

Throughout the 1980s, Nordstrom's salespeople were the envy of the industry in terms of their quality and productivity. The caliber of the company's sales clerks seemed to withstand the pressures of rapid growth as the company's work force expanded geographically and grew from 5,000 employees in 1980 to 30,000 in 1989. The clerks' "heroics" (as they called their exceptional customer service efforts) helped to build the store's alluring image, its extremely strong customer loyalty, and its lofty sales per square foot.

---

[3] Ibid.

[4] Richard W. Stevenson, "Watch Out Macy's, Here Comes Nordstrom," *New York Times*, August 27, 1989, p. 34.

[5] National Retail Merchants Association, *Financial & Operating Results of Department & Specialty Stores*, 1989 ed.

At Nordstrom's, it was common practice for sales clerks, or "Nordies" as they called themselves, to:

- drive to another Nordstrom store to retrieve a desired item in an out-of-stock size or color;

- drive to a customer's home to deliver purchases;

- call up a valued customer to alert her of newly arriving merchandise;

- help a customer assemble a complete outfit by retrieving items from several different departments; and

- write thank you notes to customers for their purchases.

Sales clerks were also known for performing such heroics as changing a customer's flat tire in the store parking lot; paying a customer's parking ticket if his or her shopping time outlasted the parking meter; lending a few dollars to a customer short on cash in order to consummate a purchase; and taking a customer to lunch.

By performing these extraordinary services—which were often performed outside of a sales clerk's scheduled time on the selling floor—sales clerks earned their customers' praise, gratitude, and loyalty. (**Exhibit 2** reproduces a typical customer letter.) In addition to customer loyalty, industrious clerks could earn over $80,000 a year. The average Nordstrom sales clerk earned $20,000 to $24,000 compared to the national average for all retail sales clerks of $12,000 a year.[6]

During the 1980s, more and more rivals such as R. H. Macy, Bloomingdales, and Neiman Marcus began to emulate Nordstrom's service-oriented strategy. According to one industry expert:

> All retailers in America have awakened to the Nordstrom threat and are struggling to catch up. Nordstrom is the future of retailing. . . . [It] is the most Darwinian of retail companies today.[7]

At the end of the decade, Nordstrom's much heralded reputation was formally acknowledged with the 1989 National Retail Merchants Association's Gold Medal—considered by many to be the most prestigious award in the industry.[8]

POLICIES, PRACTICES, AND MEASUREMENT SYSTEMS

In the mid-1960s, to support its high-service strategy and motivate its salespeople, Nordstrom had introduced an innovative commission system—revolutionary among specialty retail and department stores. Top management combined this incentive compensation system—which was driven by sales per hour (SPH)—with other distinctive policies to guide, motivate, and measure the performance of its sales staff. Although its established set of management systems and policies had proven very effective for over 20 years, problems began to emerge at the end of the 1980s.

---

[6] Faludi, op. cit.

[7] Stevenson, op. cit.

[8] Jean Bergmann, "Nordstrom Gets the Gold," *STORES*, January 1990, p. 44.

Sales-per-Hour Incentives

The following account[9] describes the mechanics of Nordstrom's commission-selling system as well as the explicit and implicit ways in which it affected employees:

> Interviews with a dozen current and former Nordstrom employees in California illustrate the contradictory pressures that workers can experience in a system that tries to give equal emphasis to service, profitability, and middle-managerial autonomy.
>
> Most of those interviewed said no manager ever formally told them to go off the clock, an order that would flatly violate state and federal fair labor standards laws. Rather, they said, it becomes clear to most Nordstrom salespeople soon after they are hired that the store's commission-selling program effectively penalizes any salesperson who insists on getting paid for every hour worked.
>
> The reason is that Nordstrom carefully evaluates salespeople on their sales-per-hour ratio. Each employee is given a target SPH ratio—a quota—based on his or her base hourly wage and store department. The actual SPH for the past two weeks—sales minus merchandise returned by customers, divided by hours worked—appears on each paycheck stub.
>
> If the actual SPH is higher than the target SPH, the employee is paid a 6.75% to 10% commission on net sales, depending on the department. If the SPH is below the target, the employee is paid the base hourly wage [roughly $9.00, with variations by department].[10] Failure to meet the target SPH often results in decreased hours or, in some cases, termination. Meeting or surpassing the target SPH means more working hours—including better hours when the shopping is heavier—and a better chance of promotion to a department manager job.
>
> Stories of some Nordstrom workers making $40,000 to $60,000 or more a year thanks to hefty commissions are widespread. But critics of the system say rank-and-file salespeople are often torn in this environment.
>
> To chalk up the most impressive SPH ratio, salespeople must be on the floor selling. But to carry out the Nordstrom credo of being a "team player" or a "Nordie," they also must be available to run themselves ragged meeting each customer's needs, which can take considerable time. Time also must be spent in routine merchandise stocking, store display activities or attending numerous sales staff meetings. These hours, if formally recorded, lower the SPH.
>
> Initially your feeling is, "I've got to punch in for every minute I'm there," said Joel Kirk, who worked as a salesman and a men's clothing manager for several years in Northern California before leaving Nordstrom last summer to return to college. "Then you find you're at the bottom on SPH, or near it. Then someone nudges you. It's there but it's not said. It's an underlying factor that everyone eventually realizes.
>
> "There is pressure on (department) managers to get people with the biggest SPH into the most hours. You're not told that if you don't (go off the clock) you'll get your

---

[9] Bob Baker, "The Other Nordstrom," *Los Angeles Times*, February 4, 1990, p. D1.

[10] Newly hired sales clerks began at an hourly rate of approximately $4.50 and in each of the four quarters of their first year, they received wage increases to bring them up to the maximum base rate for their department, which was roughly $9.00 per hour, depending on the department.

hours cut. It becomes an inferred thing. The more you sell per hour, the more hours you get," said Kirk, who spoke on the condition that his real name not be used.

As a result, critics of the system say, people making blue-collar wages and governed by hourly wage laws find themselves having to make time-management decisions usually reserved for white-collar "professionals" who are paid much higher weekly salaries and, in exchange, are expected to work some uncompensated hours.

Nordstrom says to salespeople, "This is your own business, treat it like your own business, but it's not said outright that you're going to have to do all these extra things," said Kirk, who emphasized that he has no hard feelings against the company. "They don't sit you down and say the calling of past customers for new business is important, the thank-you cards are important, taking things to the customer's house is important, running things out to a local tailor when Nordstrom's tailor is backed up is important."

To honor those who thrive, Nordstrom awards its top sellers annual membership in the company's Pace Setters Club, entitling them to 33% discounts on merchandise. The posting of SPH figures creates peer pressure that is regarded by retail analysts as a strong motivator.

However . . . dissident salespeople complain about intense competition between individual salespeople. Often cited is the court case in King County, Washington, where a jury last fall awarded $180,000 to a former Nordstrom saleswoman who claimed that she was wrongfully dismissed because co-workers wrote anonymous letters claiming that she stole from them by falsely crediting herself with their commissions.

Examples of Compensation Determination

The following two examples, one for a sales clerk generating $8,000 in weekly sales and one for a clerk generating $5,000 in weekly sales, illustrate the incentives built in to Nordstrom's SPH compensation system:[11]

Assumptions:

- Guaranteed base wage: $9.45 per hour
- Hours scheduled per week: 40
- Sales per hour (SPH) target: $140
- Sales per week target: 40 hrs. × $140 SPH = $5,600
- Commission rate: 6.75% (if sales *exceed* target)
- Overtime pay (O/T) for hours in 0.5 × average regular-time
  excess of 40 hours/week: hourly earnings

Example 1

A sales clerk who works 50 hours per week and generates weekly sales of $8,000.

1. If hours reported = 40, then
   SPH = $8,000/40 = $200, and
   Weekly earnings = .0675 × $ 8,000 = $540.

---

[11] These hypothetical examples are based on descriptions of Nordstrom's compensation system provided by multiple public sources, including the Washington State Department of Labor & Industries.

2. If hours reported = 50, then
SPH = $8,000/50 = $160, and
Weekly earnings = [.0675 × $8,000] + [premium for 10 hours O/T]
= $540 + [10 hours × .5 × $9.45] = $587.25.

As this example illustrates, a sales clerk would earn more for this week's work by reporting overtime hours; however, this option would result in a lower SPH. A low SPH could reduce a clerk's ranking among peers and could work against him or her when the supervisor assigns shifts.[12] As a result, a sales clerk may choose to sacrifice pay in the short term for better shifts and more hours in the future. The higher SPH also may improve a clerk's chances for promotion.

Example 2

A sales clerk who works 50 hours per week and generates weekly sales of $5,500.

3. If hours reported = 40, then
SPH = $5,500/40 = $137.50 (which is less than target), and
Weekly earnings = 40 hours × $9.45 = $378 (no commissions earned).

4. If hours reported = 50, then
SPH = $5,500/50 = $110 (which is less than target), and
Weekly earnings = 50 hours × $9.45 +[premium for 10 hours O/T]
= $472.50 + [10 hours × .5 × $9.45] = $519.75.

As in the first example, the sales clerk stands to gain financially by reporting all hours worked. If the clerk does so, however, the SPH drops substantially below his or her target level. According to employees' descriptions of the system, a substandard SPH can result in fewer scheduled hours, worse shifts, and—if such performance persists for several pay periods—termination, not to mention stressful peer pressure. Again, employees may opt to work off the clock rather than report all hours.

The lack of a clear distinction between "selling time" and "non-sell" work time exacerbated the pressures on employees. For example, an hour of extra work defined as "non-sell" (e.g., annual stock-taking) by Nordstrom entitled an employee to the guaranteed base wage with no effect on his or her SPH. If the same hour was considered selling time, his or her SPH would be affected negatively. Moreover, the clerk was considered to be fully compensated for all selling hours through commissions (assuming targets were exceeded) and was therefore not entitled to any extra pay for reporting the extra hour worked. (**Exhibit 3** reproduces an internal memo distributed by top management in an effort to clarify its system of differentiating between selling and non-selling time on the job.)

Additional Elements of the Management System

Although SPH monitoring was the heart of Nordstrom's distinctive management strategy, the SPH system was complemented by other organizational factors. For example, the composition of the sales force was well-suited to the competitive work environment. Nordstrom sales clerks tended to be young, often college-educated people looking for a career in retailing. They were willing to work hard in exchange

---

[12] Faludi, op. cit.

for the retailer's relatively high salaries and opportunities for rapid advancement.[13] The company's policy of promoting only from within also enhanced the overall level of Nordstrom experience within middle management and helped to motivate ambitious and hard-working employees.

The availability of desirable merchandise in appropriate colors and sizes was critical to Nordstrom's success. Department managers worked closely with buyers and often had direct buying authority. Since the sales-per-hour commission system rewarded turnover, Nordies were committed to working with their department managers to anticipate customer buying patterns and ensuring adequate stock.

Throughout the chain's rapid growth, top management endorsed a decentralized system of operations; department, store, and regional managers were relatively free to make their own decisions.[14] Moreover, they were eligible for bonuses tied to the achievement of their budget goals. Thus, decision-making responsibility and rewards were delegated directly to the front-line salespeople who were closest to the customer. At the same time, however, such decentralization limited top management's control over the application of sales force management systems. Such systems were originally centralized when the organization was much smaller. Without meaningful control over their use, however, these systems—which supported sales force scheduling, compensation, and promotions—could be vulnerable to abuse.

Another aspect of the Nordstrom's work environment that had both positive and negative ramifications was the role of group recognition and peer pressure. At monthly store meetings, managers read aloud customers' letters of praise. Sales staffs responded with applause and cheers. The salespeople who elicited such written praise were honored as "Customer Service All-Stars" and their pictures were usually displayed by the customer-service desk. The All-Stars also received added discounts on clothing and had their efforts documented in their personnel files.[15] The pressure to become an All-Star, however, could result in undesired behavior, such as "sharking"—the term Nordstrom employees used to describe stealing credit for sales made by other staff.

Competition was also promoted on the sales floor via various types of sales contests. For example, a free dinner might be awarded to the employee who generated the most multiple-item sales to individual customers. Such public fanfare helped to keep Nordstrom's sales clerks motivated and its incentive system alive on a day-to-day and hour-to-hour basis. Peer pressure was also strong among management ranks where an elaborate and very public goal-setting process transpired. Every year the company's managers gathered in large meetings where they individually proclaimed their store or departmental goals for the next 12 months. Then, immediately following each announcement, the boss of the particular manager stood up to unveil his or her previously hidden goal for that manager. Again, cheering and howling was a common accompaniment.

One last ingredient that helped to support Nordstrom's sales force management strategy was the use of automation: salespeople were able to track their performance on computer printouts available in back offices. The printouts listed individual sales by employee identification number so that clerks could compare their performance

---

[13] Stevenson, op. cit.

[14] Nordstrom's 1987 Annual Report.

[15] Stevenson, op. cit.

to both their own targets and their peers' performance. The ease of access to such information helped employees at all levels to determine precisely their achievement relative to their peers.

Nordstrom management believed their system worked. The company claimed that employees earned one of the highest base pay rates in the industry—as much as $10 an hour—and especially industrious employees could make as much as $80,000 a year. Moreover, Nordstrom's corporate policy of promoting only from within and its policy of decentralization combined to give managers unusual freedom to make decisions that would enhance customer service.[16]

FROM A LOCAL UNION DISPUTE TO CLASS ACTION SUITS[17]

In the second half of 1989, the same company policies and compensation systems to which much of Nordstrom's success was attributed became the target of a barrage of employee complaints, union allegations, law suits, and regulatory orders that tainted the company's reputation and blemished its financial performance. By the spring of 1990, the escalating accusations and events remained under dispute and it was not yet clear whether Nordstrom's change of fortune was temporary or long term.

In the summer of 1989, a discontent minority of Nordstrom's sales clerks chose to risk their reputation as "the most helpful and cheerful in the industry" and voice their grievances against the company. Angered by management's actions during contract negotiations, the United Food & Commercial Workers (UFCW) Local 1001 began a publicity campaign against Nordstrom, challenging the legality of the company's labor practices. Local 1001 was based in the state of Washington and represented roughly 1,500 of Nordstrom's nearly 30,000 employees. Local 367 represented another 200 sales clerks in the state. The Washington employees were the only unionized members of the Nordstrom work force; no other Nordstrom employees were unionized.

Representatives of Local 1001 complained that the company coerced employees to work "off the clock" without being paid. They maintained that Nordstrom neither recorded nor compensated employees for all the time they spent performing certain duties that were not directly related to selling—such as delivering packages to customers' homes, attending department meetings, writing thank-you notes to customers, doing inventory work, and general bookkeeping. Moreover, the union claimed that Nordstrom's use of sales per hour as a performance measure—for determining which employees were eligible for commissions (versus hourly wages), which were assigned the most and best shifts, and which were at risk of being fired—implicitly encouraged employees to work off the clock.

In an effort to quantify their claim, Local 1001's union officials distributed back-pay forms to the unionized sales clerks on which they could calculate and submit their individual claims. By late November 1989, the union reported to the press that they had collected $1 million in back-pay claims from several hundred sales clerks.

---

[16] Ibid.

[17] This section provides a chronological summary of the events that transpired between June 1989 and April 1990 as reported in the press.

In November 1989, Local 1001 filed a formal complaint with the Employment Standards Section of the Washington State Department of Labor & Industries. (**Exhibit 4** reproduces the Department of Labor summary of the complaint.) At the same time, members of the union also voiced their complaints through pamphlets, pickets, and the press, demanding that management reimburse employees the millions of dollars of back pay which they were owed.

Nordstrom management denied the allegations and dismissed them as a union ploy "to drum up support for their cause" at the bargaining table. (Contract negotiations had been at a stalemate since July 1989.) A company spokesperson said that the complaints were unsubstantiated and maintained that the company policy had "always been to pay employees for the time that they've worked."[18]

At the same time, the company was also forced to respond to a variety of charges filed against them by the National Labor Relations Board (NLRB).[19] The NLRB claimed that Nordstrom's bargaining tactics with the UFCW violated federal labor laws and that management had failed to provide the union with requested wage-related data and time card records.

The union complaints triggered a three-month investigation by the Washington State Department of Labor & Industries. On February 15, 1990, the department released its findings, which concurred with several of Local 1001's allegations. The administrative ruling stated that Nordstrom systematically violated state wage and hour laws in its failure both to record all hours worked and to pay sales clerks for performing certain services. The state regulatory agency ordered the company to bolster its record-keeping operations, to pay two years' of back pay to all Washington employees affected by the charge, and to pay employees in the future for time spent on such tasks as deliveries, meetings, and writing thank-you notes. The regulators did not specify the number of employees affected or the dollars involved in the back-pay reimbursements. (**Exhibit 5** reproduces the department's conclusions and its order.)

Local 1001 President Joe Peterson estimated that Nordstrom could be liable for as much as $30 million to $40 million in back-pay claims from its Washington employees alone, and for several hundred million dollars if the union followed through with a nationwide class-action suit on behalf of all Nordstrom employees.[20] By mid-February, the union said it had doubled its November "back-pay" collection and held individual claims totaling over $2 million from roughly 400 sales clerks in Washington, California, and Oregon. According to media reports, the sales clerks who submitted claims worked an average of 8 to 10 hours per week off-the-clock. Peterson asserted, "Nordstrom is doing a disservice to its reputation, employees and stockholders by continuing to deny that they have a culture. . . that requires employees to work without pay."[21]

In response, company co-chairman Bruce Nordstrom affirmed management's intentions to "fully comply with the law" and to review their record-keeping proce-

[18] Robert Spector, "Union Says Nordstrom Owes Workers Millions," *Footwear News*, November 6, 1989, p. 8.

[19] The National Labor Relations Board (NLRB) is an independent federal agency responsible for enforcing the National Labor Relations Act—a body of federal law that governs relations between labor unions and employers engaged in interstate commerce. In addition to conducting unionization elections, the NLRB investigates, prosecutes and remedies employers' and unions' labor practices that are in violation of the NLR Act. The agency operates out of 52 offices throughout the U.S. and employs nearly 3,000 people. Its leadership (a general counsel and five-member board) are appointed by the president.

[20] George Tibbits, *Financial News* (API newswire), February 26, 1990, time: 13:59 PST.

[21] Blackburn Katia, *Financial News* (API newswire), February 16, 1990, time: 17:21 PST.

dures and pay practices for any weaknesses.[22] Management announced that it was refining its time-keeping procedures to correct for any shortcoming. But, at the same time, Bruce Nordstrom denied that there was a "pattern" of abuse and maintained that complying with the law would "not alter our culture nor affect our continued commitment to customer service."[23]

As part of their efforts to illustrate their good intentions, Nordstrom management vowed to compensate employees for any past errors in its record-keeping and pay practices. To do so, they set up a procedure by which all employees nationwide could submit claims for back pay. The procedure offered employees the opportunity to collect a lump sum payment based on their choice of either length of service or their own detailed individual claims. In the former case, the payment was for $300, $700, or $1,000, depending on an employee's length of service. Initially, this back-pay offer was mailed only to current employees outside of Washington because management had to consult the State Labor & Industries Department and the local union before extending the offer to Washington employees.[24] Management was also designing a process by which former employees entitled to back pay could collect from the company. To fund the back-pay claims program, Nordstrom voluntarily established a $15 million reserve—which had a substantial effect on fourth quarter earnings.[25]

In addition to setting up the back-pay fund, management took steps to improve the existing system and restore its integrity. They first sent a memo to employees detailing company pay policies and reassuring sales clerks that they would be paid for all store meetings, inventory work, and deliveries. They also initiated several procedural changes, including the adoption of sign-out sheets. Under the new system, sales clerks who planned to do extra work at home or on the way home (i.e., deliveries) could punch out on the time clock at the end of their shift but also indicate on the sign-out sheet that they were doing work after hours. The next day they would submit a time sheet showing the amount of extra time worked.

Local 1001 President Peterson argued that this arrangement was placing the burden on employees to keep records, when it was Nordstrom's responsibility.[26] Peterson also criticized another Nordstrom policy: the classification of tasks performed off the sales floor into "selling" and "non-selling" activities. By continuing to classify certain behind-the-scenes tasks as "selling" duties, time spent writing "thank-you" letters and similar activities would remain in the denominator of sales-per-hour performance measures. Consequently, Peterson contended, employees would continue to feel pressure not to report all their hours spent on these tasks.

On February 27, 1990, Nordstrom became the target of another unhappy constituency. Immediately after fourth quarter earnings were released, three individual Nordstrom stockholders filed a suit against the company (for unspecified damages) in Seattle's King County Superior Court. They claimed to have suffered financial losses due to Nordstrom management's failure to disclose adequately their labor problems and the early claims for unpaid work. The suit requested that it be made a

---

[22] Bob Baker, "Agency Orders Nordstrom to Pay Back Wages," *Los Angeles Times*, February 17, 1990, p. D1.

[23] Francine Schwadel, "Nordstrom to Post Its First Decline in Annual Profit," *Wall Street Journal*, February 20, 1990, p. A16.

[24] Francine Schwadel, "Nordstrom Creates $15 Million Reserve for Back Wages," *Wall Street Journal*, February 27, 1990, p. A3.

[25] Although the $15 million provision was not made public until late February 1990, it was recorded as an expense against Nordstrom's 1989 fourth-quarter earnings (quarter ending January 31, 1990).

[26] Stuart Silverstein, "Nordstrom to Change Its Timekeeping Procedures," *Los Angeles Times*, February 24, 1990, p. D2.

class action suit on behalf of Nordstrom's more than 75,000 stockholders.[27] (See **Exhibit 6** for a history of Nordstrom's stock price.)

Within a two-day period, Nordstrom became the target of a second class action suit. On February 28, 1990, UFCW Locals 1001 and 367, together with five individually named plaintiffs employed by Nordstrom filed suit on behalf of approximately 50,000 current and former Nordstrom employees (union and nonunion) nationwide. The lawsuit accused the company of numerous violations of state and federal wage and hour laws and requested that the King County Superior Court order Nordstrom to improve its record keeping and award damages equal to twice the amount of unpaid wages (plus additional damages determined at trial and attorneys' fees). **Exhibit 7** reproduces the union's alleged "facts." Union officials had decided to launch the suit because they considered Nordstrom's response to the Washington State order, both the policy changes and the $15 million provision for back pay, inadequate.[28]

Reaction to the suit among employees was mixed. Many remained loyal to Nordstrom and came to its defense. Several employee-organized rallies took place outside stores in Seattle and California featuring signs and chants such as "We Love Nordstrom," "My Job is #1," and "I Love Being a Nordie." The demonstrators resented the local unions' assertion that the union spoke for all Nordstrom employees.

Nevertheless, the national publicity elicited by the suit brought into question the image and systems that Nordstrom's competitors had sought to emulate. According to one retail consultant, the company long considered the epitome of retailing excellence and superior service had actually enjoyed an unfair advantage by not paying fully for employees' work. If the apparent means of Nordstrom's success proved true, he believed, other retailers would probably become less eager to replicate the Nordstrom retailing model.

In the spring of 1990, Nordstrom management was defending itself on multiple fronts.

First, on March 16, 1990, Nordstrom's lawyers petitioned the court to void the Washington State Department of Labor & Industries' ruling (dated February 15) on the grounds that the department's investigation and release of findings had violated Nordstrom's constitutional rights to due process and equal protection. (The Labor & Industries Department subsequently filed a counter-claim in defense of its actions.) If Nordstrom and the agency could not resolve their differences directly, the agency would have to take Nordstrom to court to enforce its ruling.

Also, the NLRB maintained their charges that Nordstrom had illegally circumvented the union in communicating with its employees. If the agency could not persuade Nordstrom to settle out of court, it planned to bring its allegations before an administrative judge.

In addition to dealing with state and federal regulatory agencies, Nordstrom remained embroiled in the dispute surrounding both the shareholders' and the union's class action suits against it. In May 1990, 60 *Minutes*, the popular CBS news magazine show, televised a 20-minute segment on Nordstrom's incentive systems and related problems.

---

[27] *Financial News* (newswire), February 27, 1990, time: 20:27 PST.

[28] *Financial News* (API newswire), February 28, 1990, time: 21:30 PST.

According to the assistant director of the Washington State Department of Labor & Industries:[29]

> We're looking at what is likely to be the highest wage claim in the history of the state. These are employment practice patterns the company engaged in, not isolated incidents.

THE JURY WAS OUT

In Nordstrom's 1989 Annual Report, released in March 1990, the company's executive committee summarized its position:

> We are disappointed that there is now litigation regarding the payment of retroactive wages and related issues. Our policy has always been to pay our employees for the work that they perform, and this policy has not changed over the years. Employee initiative and enthusiasm has always been important in servicing the needs of customers, and we appreciate the efforts of our employees. They are the foundation of the Company's success. Some mistakes have been made in compensating our employees, and we are in the process of correcting them. We believe, however, that our sales employees are the highest paid in our industry. And we also believe that they will continue to provide the customer service that they have become known for because they enjoy selling for the Company and because they are rewarded for their efforts through commissions on their sales.

As of April 1990, there were no indications of emerging consensus among Nordstrom's 50,000 current and former employees as to the seriousness of the problem. While over a thousand employees had mailed in to Local 1001 back-pay claims (averaging $5,000 each),[30] hundreds of other fiercely loyal "Nordies" came to management's defense. Some loyalists expressed their sentiments by signing a petition to decertify the union and some participated in "pro-Nordstrom" rallies.

Confusion around the merits of Nordstrom's management systems and culture was evident in the contradictory claims of outspoken current and former employees. Some of these were negative:

> We have the sworn testimony of a supervisor. He said it was routine in this department that people would come in and do the markdowns in preparation for a sale on their own time, on their day off, off the clock. If they didn't get it done in time, he'd punish them by not scheduling them to work on the first day of the sale. This is no petty violation, and it goes far beyond customer service. It goes right down to the core of the business.[31]

* * * * *

> It was like a snake pit. They'd throw you into the arena, and the strong would survive.[32]

* * * * *

---

[29] Faludi, op. cit.

[30] Telephone interview with Joe Peterson, president of UFCW Local 1001, May 16, 1990.

[31] *60 Minutes*, (CBS news documentary on national television), May 6, 1990.

[32] Ibid.

The system fosters a lot of pettiness and jealousy. . . . It's fear that provides great customer service.[33]

Other comments, however, were positive:

I've never been asked to work overtime or make deliveries or do anything I didn't feel in my heart I wanted to do for many reasons. And my paycheck reflects that service I give. Everything I do, I'm compensated for in many, many ways.[34]

As the crisis escalated, national newspapers began printing letters to their editors which expressed opinions on the Nordstrom grievances. One letter challenged directly a basic assumption of the union grievance action:

When I worked at Nordstrom's Anchorage and Spokane stores, I was paid to the minute for all the time I was in the store as an hourly employee. When I was in management, I received a salary and bonus structure that rivaled that of many other professionals. The awards and sales incentives were fair and generous.

The people dismayed with the long hours required do not grasp a fundamental of retail: The shopkeeper must be available to the customer at the customer's whim, not to suit the employees' or owners' desires.[35]

When confronted by reporter Morley Safer during a *60 Minutes* interview on the problem, Bruce and Jim Nordstrom summarized Nordstrom management's beliefs:

The system is to have self-empowered people who have an entrepreneurial spirit, who feel that they're in this to better themselves and to feel good about themselves and to make more money and to be successful. That's the system.

[We have] expectations on our people. And when people apply for a job anyplace, they want to work hard and they want to do a good job. That's their intention. And our intention is to allow them the freedom to work as hard as they want to work.[36]

---

[33] Baker, op. cit.

[34] *60 Minutes*, op. cit.

[35] Letter to the Editor, *Wall Street Journal*, March 14, 1990, p. A19.

[36] *60 Minutes*, op. cit.

EXHIBIT 1
Nordstrom, Inc. and Subsidiaries Ten-Year Statistical Summary ($000, except per share figures)

	1990	1989	1988	1987	1986	1985	1984	1983	1982	1981
Operations										
Net sales	$2,671,114	$2,327,946	$1,920,231	$1,629,918	$1,301,857	$958,678	$768,677	$598,666	$512,188	$400,614
Total costs and expenses	2,491,705	2,129,514	1,757,498	1,489,679	1,214,478	886,167	694,838	550,353	468,513	364,059
Earnings before income taxes	179,409	198,432	162,733	140,239	87,379	72,511	73,839	48,313	43,675	36,555
Net earnings	$ 114,909	$ 123,332	$ 92,733	$ 72,939	$ 50,079	$ 40,711	$ 40,239	$ 27,013	$ 24,775	$ 19,655
Fully diluted earnings per share	1.41	1.51	1.13	.91	.65	.54	.54	.38	.35	.29
Stores and Facilities										
Company-operated stores	59	58	56	53	52	44	39	36	34	31
Total square footage	6,898,000	6,374,000	5,527,000	5,098,000	4,727,000	3,924,000	3,213,000	2,977,000	2,640,000	2,166,000

EXHIBIT 2
Sample Customer Letter

nordstrom

800 Tacoma Mall
Tacoma, WA 98409-7273
(206) 475-3630

10-23-89

Dear Mr. Nordstrom,

I shopped in your store October 7th. As always it was a fun experience. One of your employees, Anne Smith, was particularly nice. Your store did not have my size in a jacket I loved. Ms. Smith found out that I was from Oregon & wanted the jacket for a party on the 14th. She drove to South Center and picked it up (after work) and I came in later that evening and purchased it. She deserves recognition!

I supervise several employees and recognize outstanding employees when I see them. Ms. Smith went out of her way to see that the

October 31, 1989

Ms. Cheryl Johnson
1321 Lawnridge Ave.
Springfield, OR 97477

Dear Ms. Johnson:

Thank you for your thoughtful letter about the good service you received from Anne Smith in our Individualist department. I'm glad Anne followed through for you and located the jacket you wanted. Customer service is our number one priority at Nordstrom Tacoma Mall and salespeople like Anne help set a positive example for the rest of the store to emulate. It will be my pleasure to share your kind note with Anne and her department manager. I really appreciate your feedback.

Sincerely,

signed by Peter E. Nordstrom

Peter E. Nordstrom
Store Manager

PEN:cam

cc: Tracy Magnuson, Individualist Manager, Tacoma

Source: Washington State Department of Labor & Industries, ESAC Division, Nordstrom Investigation.

EXHIBIT 3
International Memo Differentiating "Selling" vs. "Non-Selling" Time

TO: ALL STORE AND DEPARTMENT MANAGERS
FROM: THE NORDSTROM FAMILY
SUBJ: EMPLOYEE COMPENSATION FOR TIME WORKED
DATE: AUGUST 1, 1989

The following information is offered as a review of some long-standing Company business practices. First of all, the Nordstrom policy of employee compensation is based on the premise that "all employees will be paid for time worked." Although it would be impossible to outline all examples of work activities, we'll attempt to review some common Company practices that warrant employee compensation.

"Hand carries"—merchandise that is picked up by an employee at one store and delivered to another. If done during regular work hours, employee remains on time clock. If effort is made going to and from work, the employee may be entitled to be paid for time over and above their normal commute time. ("Hand carries" that facilitate a personal sale are considered an extension of the selling process and regular "selling-time" would be paid. If the employee has been requested to pick up and deliver merchandise other than for a personal customer, their time would be compensated as "non-sell.")

"Home deliveries"—merchandise that is delivered to a customer's home, office, hotel, hospital room, etc. The same criteria as "hand carries" would apply.

Although there are many functions related to each employee's job, listed below are a number of activities that are part of the selling/customer service process. These efforts are to be performed at the workplace. Also, when work is performed outside the workplace (i.e., at home), then, depending on the circumstances, an employee may be entitled to compensation.

- Time spent locating merchandise from other stores via the telephone.
- Stock assignments, floor moves, and work parties, i.e., picking up "dead wood," "singles parties," "running hash," or any other merchandise-handling activity.
- Sales promotion activities and customer correspondence, i.e., Thank You notes, addressing sale notices, etc.
- MNS book documentation efforts.
- Customer Service Board, Human Resource Committee, and Safety Committee tasks and activities.
- "Personal Touch" department seminars and activities.
- Employee meetings that are mandatory. In addition, if the meeting is voluntary, then our people should never suffer criticism for not attending.

Again, this partial list does not pretend to encompass all possible job related functions. However, the intent is to reiterate and possibly clarify some compensatory work activities at Nordstrom.

Source: Washington State Department of Labor & Industries, ESAC Division, Nordstrom Investigation.

EXHIBIT 4
Summary of UFCW Local 1001 Complaint

February 15, 1990

Mr. Wayne Hansen
Lane Powell Moss & Miller
1420 Fifth Avenue, Suite 4100
Seattle, Washington 98101-2338

Dear Mr. Hansen:

On November 21, 1989, The Employment Standards Section of the Department of Labor and Industries received a complaint from Local 1001 of the United Food and Commercial Workers Union representing the employees of Nordstrom Inc. The basis of the complaint was:

1. Nordstrom employees are required or encouraged to attend store, department, and group meetings, outside normal work hours, without compensation, where the purpose of the meeting is to discuss work objectives and other work related topics.

2. Nordstrom employees are required or encouraged to locate merchandise at other stores, either by phone or in person, outside of normal work hours, without compensation. This would include deliveries of merchandise to customers' homes, called "hand carries."

3. Employees are required or encouraged to perform stock work outside of normal work hours, without compensation. This includes floor moves, sale set-ups, inventory preparation, mark downs and ticketing, and other merchandise handling activities.

4. Employees are required or encouraged to write customer correspondence including thank-you notes, as well as addressing advertising circulars, sales notices, and maintaining personal trade books, all outside of normal work hours, without compensation.

5. Employees are required or encouraged to work on "Make Nordstrom Special" projects outside of normal work hours, without compensation. This also includes Customer Service Book preparation and maintenance, as well as attendance at Customer Service Board meetings.

6. Employees' overtime rates are not adjusted upward when commission payments increase their gross earnings during weeks when overtime is worked.

On December 5, 1989, the Department requested certain records from Nordstrom Inc. A copy of one of those letters is attached. The investigation was assigned to the Seattle Service Location, and was coordinated by the Regional Supervisor, Cindy Hanson.

EXHIBIT 4 (*continued*)
Summary of UFCW Local 1001 Complaint

On December 11, 1989, the Department met with officials from Nordstrom Inc. and the company's attorneys. The majority of the records requested were provided at that time, with the remaining records being delivered on December 19, 1989.

Following is an overview of each allegation contained in the complaint; Nordstrom's position taken regarding the allegation; and the findings made by the Department. This overview is based on the complaint and documents submitted on behalf of the employees (See Exhibit 1); records provided by Nordstrom (See Exhibit 2); information obtained from the meeting with Nordstrom officials on December 5, 1989; and various telephone conversations with Nordstrom and employee representatives.

Source: Washington State Department of Labor & Industries, ESAC Division, Nordstrom Investigation.

EXHIBIT 5
Department of Labor & Industries Conclusion and Order

II. CONCLUSIONS

Based on the above findings of fact, the Department makes the following conclusions:

1. There is no indication that any of the voluntary meetings referenced in allegation 1 would meet the Department's position on unpaid training time (See Exhibit 3). An example given by Nordstrom at our meeting and the records received indicate that all meetings held are directly related to the employees' jobs. Therefore, the company is in violation of RCW 49.46.020 and RCW 49.46.130, where applicable, for not properly compensating its employees for all time spent in meetings. In addition, Nordstrom has not kept records of this time worked, in violation of RCW 49.46.070 and WAC 296-128-010.

2. Records reviewed indicate employees have made deliveries of merchandise to other stores, in person, outside of normal work hours. Certain hours worked by employees locating and delivering merchandise would be considered hours worked under Chapter 49.46 RCW. Therefore, the company is in violation of RCW 49.46.020 for failing to properly compensate employees for all time worked.

    In addition, Nordstrom has failed to record these hours of work performed by employees as specified in RCW 49.46.070 and WAC 296-128-010(6).

3. Nordstrom has failed to record the actual hours of work performed by cosmetic line managers as specified in RCW 49.46.070, WAC 296-128-010(6). Employees are required to perform inventory duties on their own time and the payment received for these hours worked by cosmetic line managers is not accurate or in accordance with the state overtime provisions as specified in RCW 49.46.130 and WAC 296-128-550.

4. Nordstrom permits the writing of thank-you notes by employees on their own time, without proper compensation, in violation of RCW 49.46.020. Nordstrom has failed to record actual hours of this work performed by employees as specified in RCW 49.46.070 and WAC 296-128-010.

5. Work performed by employees in preparing Customer Service Books and "Make Nordstrom Special" projects/books is considered time worked. In reviewing the documentation, the Department found nothing to substantiate the allegations that employees are encouraged or required to work on "Make Nordstrom Special" projects outside of normal work hours without compensation.

6. Nordstrom has not paid overtime to employees in violation of the state overtime provisions, as specified in RCW 49.46.130.

III.   ORDER

Based on the above findings of fact and conclusions of law, the Department of Labor and Industries hereby orders Nordstrom Inc. to immediately from this date forward:

1. Compensate employees for attending various store meetings, when the meeting is held in the interest of the employer or is directly related to the employees' job, pursuant to RCW 49.46.020 and RCW 49.46.130; and to

2. Comply with record keeping provisions pursuant to RCW 49.46.070 and WAC 296-128-010; and to

3. Compensate employees for all hours of work, pursuant to RCW 49.46.020; and to

4. Compensate employees for overtime hours worked pursuant to RCW 49.46.130; and to

5. Retroactively compensate all current and former employees who were not compensated for all hours worked, or who were not properly compensated for overtime hours worked, pursuant to RCW 49.46.020 and RCW 49.46.130.

BY:

Signed by Michael Pellegrini

Michael Pellegrini

Supervisor of Employment Standards

2-15-90

Date

cc: Joe Peterson, UFCW Local 1001
     Mark McDermott, Assistant Director, ESAC Division

Source: Washington State Department of Labor & Industries, ESAC Division, Nordstrom Investigation.

EXHIBIT 6
Nordstrom Stock Price History

		Monthly Close ($/share)
1989	January	32-4/8
	February	31-2/8
	March	33-2/8
	April	33-6/8
	May	34-4/8
	June	31-2/8
	July	35-6/8
	August	41-6/8
	September	39-4/8
	October	36-6/8
	November	37-4/8
	December	37-2/8
1990	January	33-4/8
	February	27-6/8
	March	31-4/8

III. Facts.

11. Nordstrom and Local 1001 have been parties to a series of collective bargaining agreements, the most recent of which expired on July 31, 1989. Nordstrom and Local 367 have been parties to a series of collective bargaining agreements, the most recent of which expired on July 31, 1989. The Unions do not bring the claims herein under these agreements.

12. Nordstrom has individual employment contracts with its employees, which contracts are formed from company-wide employment policies and practices. Under these employment contracts, employees are compensated as follows: Most sales employees are paid an hourly wage for time spent in selling activities ("selling time") and non-selling activities ("non-sell time"). In addition, employees may receive additional wages for selling time in the form of commissions based on sales of goods and services above each employee's sales quota. Each employee's sales quota is determined by dividing the hourly guaranteed wage rate by the commission rate applicable to the merchandise or services sold. For example, the sales quota for an employee who is guaranteed $9.75 per hour and has a commission rate of 6.75 percent is $9.75 per hour divided by 0.0675, or $144.44 of sales per hour. Some sales employees are paid an hourly wage plus a commission on sales of goods and services. Non-sales employees and some sales employees are paid an hourly wage.

13. Nordstrom has company-wide policies applicable to all employees, including employees represented by the Unions and unrepresented employees, the terms of which are included in individual employment contracts between Nordstrom and its employees. These policies require payment for all work Nordstrom has permitted to be performed for its benefit, including, but not limited to, the location and acquisition of merchandise from other stores; the delivery of merchandise to a customer's home, office, or other location; the performance of various stock assignments; the performance of sales promotion activities, including writing and addressing "Thank You" notes and addressing sale notices to customers; various customer service promotions, including "Make Nordstrom Special" projects, the preparation and maintenance of customer service books, and attendance at customer service board and other company meetings; and various other work activity all for the benefit of Nordstrom.

14. Nordstrom has consistently and routinely failed to pay wages to employees represented by the Unions, individual plaintiffs, and employees similarly situated, for activities for which compensation is required by individual employment contract or by law, including the activities identified in the preceding paragraph.

15. Officers, directors, and responsible managers of Nordstrom knew that employees were performing the work described in paragraph 13 above without being paid as required by individual employment contract or by law and yet continued to promote or permit these activities to continue.

16.   In failing to pay wages to employees as alleged in paragraphs 13 through 15 above, Nordstrom has acted willfully and with the intent of depriving employees of such wages.

17.   Nordstrom has failed to keep accurate records of the time worked by employees performing the activities alleged in paragraph 13 above.

18.   Nordstrom has discouraged employees from submitting claims for compensation for work performed "off the clock" and has subjected employees who submit such claims to reprisal and threat of reprisal.

19.   Nordstrom has compelled, coerced, or required employees to purchase clothing from Nordstrom to wear while working at stores operated by Nordstrom.

20.   Nordstrom has withheld from wages earned by employees the amount of commissions that were paid on merchandise that is subsequently returned, where such merchandise was not sold by the employee against whom the commission was charged.

21.   By its conduct alleged in paragraphs 13 through 20 above, Nordstrom has irreparably harmed employees represented by the Unions, the individual plaintiffs, and other employees similarly situated for which they have no adequate remedy at law.

Source: Washington State Department of Labor & Industries, ESAC Division, Nordstrom Investigation.

Responsibility Centers and Performance Measurement

Management control depends on measurement. Effective measurement of operations and performance requires assignment and acceptance of responsibility for performance. Performance measurements should meet three criteria: (1) they should be timely, informing when action can be taken; (2) they should be seen as fair; and (3) they should be congruent with the goals of the organization. Goal congruence assures that an improved measure of performance means the organization is nearer to achieving one or more of its objectives.

Measurements are used by managers for two reasons. First, measurements inform management about performance in the past, and they help managers answer questions about how they and the organization are performing. Second, they affect future behaviors by informing and motivating managers in the present and future.

Financial control of responsibility centers is achieved by measuring the dimensions of finance performance that managers can affect or control. Most responsibility centers can be classified by their focus on costs or expenses, margin or profit, or return on investment. Ideally, the financial measure should include any revenue or cost that managers can affect, even though they may not have complete control over revenues, expenses, or investments.

COST CENTERS AND EXPENSE CENTERS

When only the resources consumed in a responsibility center can be measured, it can be classified as a **cost center** or an **expense center**. Performance is measured by a financial measure of the resources used. Control is achieved by comparing performance to a reference point, which may be a standard, budget, or prior period expenditure. Service centers, such as an accounting department, are often managed as expense centers because it is easy to measure the cost of providing the service but hard to measure the benefit or value of the output of the center.

Professor William J. Bruns, Jr. prepared this note as the basis for class discussion rather than to illustrate either effective or ineffective handling of an administrative situation.

Copyright © 1993 by the President and Fellows of Harvard College, Case No. 193-101. To order copies, call (617) 495-6117 or write the Publishing Division, Harvard Business School, Boston, MA 02163. No part of this publication may be reproduced, stored in a retrieval system, used in a spreadsheet, or transmitted in any form or by any means—electronic, mechanical, photocopying, recording, or otherwise—without the permission of Harvard Business School.

A report for an expense center is shown in **Exhibit 1**. Actual expenses are compared to a budgeted amount. Control depends on the effective establishment of a reference point to which the actual expenses can be compared. Even then, however, no measure of the effectiveness or efficiency of the expense center can be made because the report does not show how well the accounting department performed, how good its services were, or how much more efficiently the department could have performed the service it provided.

FINANCIAL PERFORMANCE CENTERS

When both the inputs and the outputs of a responsibility center can be measured, a **financial performance center** or **profit center** can be created. As with cost centers, control is achieved by comparing actual margin or profit to an expected or budgeted margin or profit. Detail in the financial measurements provides information on problems and the need for management attention and action.

Exhibit 2 shows several possible performance reports for a financial performance center. The appropriate bottom-line measure depends on the extent to which costs or expenses are controllable or can be influenced by a manager. The broader a manager's responsibility, the more costs and expense are likely to be relevant. If a financial performance center supplies or is supplied by another in the same organization, a mechanism for determining **transfer prices** must be established as well. Some organizations go beyond income or profit as it is usually measured in accounting for financial performance centers by adding a charge to conventional expenses for the assets or resources that managers use to generate revenue and income. This **residual income** approach is thought to avoid some problems that can be encountered when an investment center is measured by return on investment.

Investment Centers

A manager of an **investment center** is held responsible for not only the inputs and outputs of that center but also for the amount of investment used to produce the outputs. A proper measurement of margin or profit needs to be selected, and the investment supporting the center needs to be measured. Investments can be measured by using their original cost, book value, current value, or replacement value. Control is best achieved by comparing expected return on investment to that achieved.

Two problems sometimes arise when investment centers are created. First, managers may be motivated to sell or dispose of assets that would have future utility to the organization, if doing so would give the appearance of improved financial performance. Second, managers may be reluctant to make new investments that would provide a return above the organization's cost of capital but below the current rate of return. Each of these two potential problems is illustrated in **Exhibit 3**.

Matching Performance Measures with Strategy

Because measurements motivate and affect the behavior of managers, care must be taken to be sure that the performance measures support the organization's strategy. An organization committed to superior service may find treating responsibility centers that interface with clients or customers as expense centers undermines its strategy. An organization committed to being a technological leader may find that charging a profit center manager for research and development costs leads to less effective research and development. The most effective organizations use a carefully selected mix of financial performance measures and continually evaluate their effectiveness.

EXHIBIT 1
Example of a Performance Measurement Report for an Expense Center

	Budget	Actual	Variance
Salaries	$3,070	$3,070	0
Overtime	0	206	(206)
Total	$3,070	$3,276	(206)

EXHIBIT 2
Profit Concepts for Financial Performance Centers

Summary of Activities in the Retail Division, July ($ 000s)

Revenue	$1,000
Direct division expenses	
Variable	700
Nonvariable controllable	100
Nonvariable noncontrollable	50
Indirect division expenses:	
Allocated corporate overhead	60
Required earnings rate	10%

Income Statements

Retail Division, July ($ 000s)	Division Contribution Margin	Division Controllable Income	Division Direct Income	Division Net Income	Division Residual Income
Revenue	$1,000	$1,000	$1,000	$1,000	$1,000
Less: Direct division variable expenses	700	700	700	700	700
Division contribution margin	$ 300				
Nonvariable controllable expense		100	100	100	100
Division controllable income		$ 200			
Nonvariable noncontrollable expenses			50	50	50
Division direct income			$ 150		
Indirect division expenses				60	60
Division net income				$ 90	
Capital charge (10%) on investment of $1,100	110	110	110		110
Residual income	$ 190	$ 90	$ 40		$ (20)

EXHIBIT 3
Examples of Performance Measures for Investment Centers

Measuring Investment for the Retail Division ($ 000s)

	Cost	Accumulated Depreciation	Replacement Value
Fixed assets:			
Land and buildings	$ 500	$ 200	$ 900
Store fixtures	100	25	150
Total	$ 600	$ 225	$1,050
Current assets:			
Cash	$ 50		$ 50
Receivables (net)	200		200
Inventories	250		275
	$1,100		$1,575

Investments

Gross historical	$1,100
Historical cost net of accumulated depreciation	875
Replacement value	1,575

Return on investment

$$\frac{Income}{Investment} = Return\ on\ investment$$

$$\frac{Division\ net\ income}{Gross\ historical\ cost} = \frac{\$90}{\$1,100} = 8.2\%$$

Residual income reports income as absolute dollar amount after a *capital charge*, or return, expected of all divisions. In most cases it encourages investments that are profitable (return more than capital charge rate) but below current rate of return.

Example:

A wholesale division currently earns $300,000 on an investment of $1,500,000 and has a rate of return of 20%. An investment of $500,000 can be made that will raise income $75,000.

	Return on investment	Residual income (capital charge = 10%)
Without investment	20%	$150
After new investment	18.75%	$175

Western Chemical Corporation: Divisional Performance Measurement (A)

The fact is that we really have not yet figured out the best way to measure and report on the performance of some of our foreign operations. Because of different ownership arrangements and the use of local financing, when we use conventional accounting principles and standards, we often get financial reports that seem to contradict what we believe to be the true results of operations. This creates problems within the company because people who are not familiar with particular operations see the reports and draw erroneous conclusions about how this one or that one is performing relative to others.

Now that you are beginning to get questions from shareholders and analysts about how some of these investments are performing, I realized that Cynthia and I had better brief you on what some of the problems are that we have with division performance measurement.

Stan Rogers, president of Western Chemical Corporation (WCC), was meeting with Samantha Chu, recently appointed director of Investor Relations, and Cynthia Sheldon, who had recently been appointed vice president and controller. Chu had that morning received an inquiry from a well-known chemical industry analyst who had some fairly specific questions about some of the company's investments in Europe and the Far East. When she questioned Sheldon, Cynthia suggested that they meet with Rogers to examine some of the issues that Rogers and Sheldon had been discussing, so that Chu could answer the analyst's requests more accurately.

The information on the financial performance of WCC's foreign operations was prepared by the same accountants who maintained the company's accounts and who prepared its quarterly and annual reports. A single database for all accounting had been established some years earlier in the belief that it could serve all accounting needs of both managers and those external to the company. A common chart of accounts and accounting policies was used throughout the company and in all of its subsidiaries.

Professor William J. Bruns, Jr. and Professor Roger Atherton of Northeastern University prepared this case as the basis for class discussion rather than to illustrate either effective or ineffective handling of an administrative situation.

A variety of new alliances and ownership arrangements had been used in recent international ventures to speed entry to new international markets and to minimize investment and risk. Because of these, Rogers had become convinced that some of the reports the accountants were preparing about some of the ventures could be quite misleading. It was for that reason that he and Sheldon were already discussing alternative ways to measure divisional performance, and that Sheldon thought Chu should be brought into their discussion before trying to answer the analyst's queries.

THE COMPANY AND INTERNATIONAL VENTURES

In 1995, WCC was a 75-year-old, *Fortune 300* chemical company. Its largest business marketed chemicals and chemical programs for water and waste treatment. Additional products and chemical services targeted manufacturing processes where the quality of a customer's product could be enhanced. The company was proud of its industry reputation for quality of its solutions to customer problems and exceptional service to customers. WCC had 4,900 employees and operated more than 35 plants in 19 countries. Financial information by geographic area is shown in **Exhibit 1**.

WCC manufactured in many different countries using a variety of ownership arrangements. Some plants were wholly-owned manufacturing sites, and others were operated as joint ventures with local affiliates. Three of these plants were useful illustrations as background for discussing the problems the company faced in measuring the performance of its international ventures. All had been constructed and had come on-stream in the 1991–1993 period.

A chemical plant on the outskirts of Prague in the Czech Republic was operated as a joint venture with a local partner. Total investment in the plant was between $35 and $40 million, including working capital. WCC retained a controlling interest in the joint venture and operated the plant. The company had invested about $5 million in the venture, and the balance of the investment had come from the venture partner and local borrowing.

A similar plant in Poland was 100% owned, and the total capital investment of $40 to $45 million including working capital had been funded by WCC. The venture itself had no external debt.

A third plant in Malaysia was also 100% owned. The plant was built to add capacity in the Pacific region, but the plant was considered part of the company's production capacity serving the global market. WCC had invested approximately $35 million in this Malaysian plant.

MEASURING THE PERFORMANCE OF THREE INTERNATIONAL VENTURES

Cynthia Sheldon had prepared some exhibits using representative numbers, and she began by explaining the income statement for the venture in the Czech Republic to Samantha Chu.

The first case is Prague. It is pretty much a classic situation. What I have put together here is a basic income statement for the facility for the first three quarters of 1995

(**Exhibit 2**). What this helps to show is how the difference between the ownership structures in Prague and Poland lead to apparent differences in reported income.

This is a nine-month year-to-date income statement for the joint venture. Earnings before interest and taxes of $869,000 is what we would normally report internally for a wholly-owned subsidiary, and that is what would be consolidated. As you proceed down the income statement, there is a charge for interest because we have the ability to leverage these joint ventures fairly highly, anywhere from 60% to 80%. This is interest on external debt—cash going out. We account for it this way because the venture has its own Board of Directors, even though we have management control and retain much of the ability to influence operations, which is not always the case. The fees of $867,000 are coming to WCC under a technical agreement that we have with the joint venture, as a percentage of revenues. In this case, we have put a minority interest line to get down to a net income for WCC. That is the actual income that we would report to the outside world.

We are reporting externally a loss of $646,000 on this business, when in truth, relative to our other businesses which are reported before interest charges and before fees, it is contributing to our corporate income. This report makes it appear that we are operating at a loss of just under $1.2 million, $532,000 of which is the share of our joint venture partner, and our share is the $646,000.

Stan Rogers described the investment:

In this business WCC has invested, in addition to its technical knowledge and technology, $5 million of its money. In addition, we do not guarantee the debt, which is off balance sheet so far as WCC is concerned. One other way that we can look at these businesses is to look at cash flows to WCC, and cash return on investment to WCC. When we do that, because of the $867,000 in fees which are paid to WCC, there is some return. Although the return is small, it is reasonable at this stage of development of a new business. This business, because of the fees, has been in a loss position, but because of the fees it has shown a positive cash return on investment to WCC.

Sheldon continued:

Our actual return consists of the fees paid to WCC, or $867,000, and our share of the reported operating losses, for a net income of $221,000. That is the return on our approximately $5 million investment. If the subsidiary were wholly owned with a total investment of approximately $40 million, we would be looking at the $869,000 income before interest and taxes, to which we might decide to apply a tax, on the investment of $40 million. That is how we measure the performance of wholly-owned divisions.

One of the reasons that this report appears as it does was that, a few years ago, then current management decided to work from a single data base and to have one group prepare both the external financial reports and the management reports for internal use. It was a fine decision, except for the fact that the external reporters did not have the interest or ability to report what was actually going on in the affiliates.

Now, let's look at the report for our subsidiary in Poland (**Exhibit 3**). This plant is 100% owned, so we do not report any interest or fees. The total capital investment was funded by the company and totaled about $40 or $45 million including working capital. There is no external debt or minority interest and no fees. The other charges include the amortization of interest that was capitalized during the construction of the plant. The cost of sales includes some profit from materials that are purchased from other plants, but the prices paid are reasonable if you compare them with competitors' prices. This is another interesting problem that we struggle with, since we are probably reporting $2 or $3 million in profits elsewhere because of these plant purchases. But consider how this would look if we were deducting interest on $30 million of debt, and fees of 8% of revenues as we do in the case of the Prague affiliate. We would then be showing a loss from the business of about $3 million. The accountants do not consider this, and their report makes it appear that the business was doing just fine.

Samantha Chu spoke up:

Your explanation implies that there must be some other measures of performance that tell you how these plants are performing. What are those?

Sheldon:

We use budgets and the original business plans. We look at the performance against those expectations.

Rogers:

Also, although we do not monitor cash flows to the degree that we ought to, we have in our head the cash contribution compared to the amounts that we have invested. In the Czech Republic we can look ahead and see that in the future we will have a 35% to 45% cash on cash return. Poland is draining cash out of us at a remarkable rate, and we have not yet figured out a way to stop it. There are still a lot of unresolved business problems. Compared to the original business plan we have not been able to generate the revenues that were forecasted and the costs have been higher. We do not present cash flow reports to our managers, so these analyses all have to be done in our heads. The information we would need to bring this about formally is all available, but we just have not asked anyone to do it.

What we have are three new plants built at about the same time, each having very complex and different financial reporting issues that lead you to have completely different views of the business. Cynthia, show Samantha the report on the plant in Malaysia and what happens when we introduce an economic value added (EVA) approach. . . .

Sheldon:

The third plant was built to supply a high margin part of our business. That part of our business is truly a global business in that we can actually ship our product from any of several plants to anywhere in the world. When the decision to build a plant in Malaysia was made we were running out of capacity. We made a strategic decision that we wanted to be located in Malaysia, but this was to be part of our production facilities to serve the global market. We do not usually build a separate plant to supply only the high margin products. The volumes sold and shipped tend to be small, and adding the technostructure of technical service and laboratories to a plant makes the economics somewhat unfavorable unless there are several other units in the same plant producing higher volume products to help carry the costs of these necessary add-ons.

Looking at the column labeled "Region of Manufacture," you can see the sales and profitability of the manufacturing facility in Malaysia (**Exhibit 4**). It sells $12 million worth of product, and you can see that with the costs being what they are, the plant is losing a lot of money. The capital charge that we show is an attempt to get a measure of the economic value added by the plant. As was the case with Poland, this report does not include any interest on the total investment of almost $35 million, or any fees.

The EVA approach uses a 12% capital charge based on the assets employed including working capital including accounts payable and fixed capital. Depreciation is included in cost of sales. I think the way we use EVA is very simple, exactly the way it is employed by other folks, but some get much more sophisticated about allocations, capitalized research and development, and the like. We do not do that.

In addition we have recently started to look not just at "region of manufacture" but also at "region of sale," primarily to get an understanding of whether or not a market is attractive. The second column labeled "Region of Sale" is all product being sold in Southeast Asia even if it is being manufactured outside, so it includes the cost of manufacturing product, shipping it, and delivering it to customers in the region. On that basis the earnings before interest and taxes are about $4 million. If we wanted to get down to economic value added, we would need to deduct taxes and a capital charge and the economic value added would still be negative but not so much so that we could not develop some reasonable strategies to fix it compared to the region of manufacture measure which is pretty daunting.

Stan Rogers interjected:

There is an incremental layer of complexity here in that this plant is starting to produce for the rest of the world because we are running out of capacity and are using this plant as the swing plant. Those shipments will show up in the Region of Manufacture numbers, but they will not show up in the Region of Sale numbers. We have not yet sorted this out, but my suspicion is that you cannot look at it this way and get an intriguing view—a solid view—of the business. We probably have to look at the whole system and analyze the incremental revenues and costs of the whole business.

The reason why I see this as another iteration of the same or complexity of the same problem, is that in Prague and Poland we had the different corporate structures that led to different accounting treatments of interest and fees, which gave us completely warped views on what was going on in the business. This presents the same challenge but adds the dimensions of region of manufacture and region of sale accounting and the need for total system analysis.

Samantha Chu broke the silence of the pause which followed:

Have you found a solution to the problem yet?

Rogers answered:

We understand it. We have not institutionalized a management reporting system that would lead someone who is intelligent but does not understand the background to understand what is really going on. We do not have a management reporting system in place that shows the relative performance of the three plants in a clear manner. On this basis the system does not work.

SOME POSSIBLE SOLUTIONS TO THE PERFORMANCE MEASUREMENT PROBLEM

Cynthia Sheldon began a discussion of some possible solutions to the division performance measurement problem:

> We are scratching away at a solution, perhaps using the concept of economic value added. We probably will also separate the people who are preparing the managerial reports from those who are concerned with external reporting, even though both groups will be working from the same databases. Until now, when we report to external public relations and to the chairman about the performance of the business, we have used external reporting standards and bases. I have concluded that to get away from that we have to have a separate group engaged with the businesses.

Stan Rogers chimed in:

> From a business standpoint we understand this we think. When we want to do a presentation we will do a one time analysis, pulling the numbers together that we think best reflect the situation. But we do not have a disciplined, repetitious reporting system that produces an analysis of how these businesses are doing in any other way than the way the external reporting system does it. That is an issue of priorities. We just do not have the time or resources to fix the system now. It is not that we do not understand the problem, or that we could not do it. I think we understand the problem, and we understand the intellectual underpinnings of a solution.
>
> I know that does not help you in responding to the analyst's questions today, so you will just have to respond very carefully.

Cynthia Sheldon continued:

> We are really just beginning to use EVA as a tool to get people to understand the issues. There is nothing wrong with using cash flow, return on net assets, and other familiar financial measures. There are always problems with any single financial measure, but right now in order to get people to focus it is easier to have one number and EVA is the most effective single number. We know that in order to make the business viable in our Southeast Asia region we have to go down a path of expanding the business. When you expand, EVA goes down, so if you focus on only that measure you risk saying that I do not want to do that. That is not the right answer. We are already seeing that kind of problem. But at least EVA gets people to focus on the cost of the capital associated with the income that they earn, and it gets more of a sense of cash flow, but we do not rely solely on it.

Stan Rogers summed up his feelings on the division performance measurement problems, echoing some of the conclusions of Sheldon:

> You know, I would say the same thing. There is not a planning department here that thinks about EVA and all that kind of stuff. We probably could use better numbers, but driving the business off any single number probably would not work.

QUESTIONS

1. What is causing the problems in measuring division performance at Western Chemical Corporation?

2. Are there alternative methods for measuring division performance that would avoid the problems that WCC management is having with the methods that they have been using?

3. Evaluate the approach to using economic value added (EVA) that WCC management is discussing and using experimentally. What are the strengths and weaknesses of this approach?

4. How should the performance of divisions of WCC be measured?

5. What should Samantha Chu tell the analyst if he asks specifically about the investments in the Czech Republic, Poland, and Malaysia?

EXHIBIT 1
Financial Information by Geographic Area

Western Chemical Corporation (WCC) is engaged in the worldwide manufacture and sale of highly specialized service chemical programs. This includes production and service related to the sale and application of chemicals and technology used in water treatment, pollution control, energy conservation, and other industrial processes as well as a super-absorbent product for the disposable diaper market.

Within WCC, sales between geographic areas are made at prevailing market prices to customers minus an amount intended to compensate the sister WCC company for providing quality customer service.

Identifiable assets are those directly associated with operations of the geographic area. Corporate assets consist mainly of cash and cash equivalents; marketable securities; investments in unconsolidated partnerships, affiliates, and leveraged leases; and capital assets used for corporate purposes.

Geographic Area Data (in millions)

	1994	1993	1992
Sales			
North America	$ 886.9	$ 915.1	$ 883.7
Europe	288.9	315.6	346.5
Latin America	72.2	66.4	60.7
Pacific	127.7	116.7	108.2
Sales between areas	(30.1)	(24.4)	(24.6)
	$1,345.6	$1,389.4	$1,374.5
Operating Earnings			
North America	$ 181.6	$ 216.9	$ 211.3
Europe	(10.2)	41.8	48.9
Latin America	9.3	11.4	10.0
Pacific	14.3	14.4	14.4
Expenses not allocated to areas	(20.3)	(21.6)	(24.3)
	$ 174.7	$ 262.9	$ 260.3
Identifiable Assets			
North America	$ 485.2	$ 566.6	$ 562.2
Europe	245.2	227.4	225.5
Latin America	66.9	45.4	42.7
Pacific	147.9	126.3	124.7
Corporate	337.0	246.7	395.5
	$1,282.2	$1,212.4	$1,350.6

EXHIBIT 1 (*continued*)
Financial Information by Geographic Area

Amounts for North America sales in the tabulation above include exports to the following areas:

(in millions)	1994	1993	1992
Latin America	$21.9	$19.2	$16.0
All other	7.3	13.0	12.0

The decrease in operating earnings in 1994 was mainly attributable to the pretax provision of $68 million for consolidation expenses. Of that amount, approximately $34 million was included in European operations.

EXHIBIT 2
Income from Czech Republic Joint Venture ($ in thousands)

	9/95 Year-to-Date
Revenues	$ 11,510
Cost of sales	(9,541)
Selling, technical expenses, and administrative expenses	(891)
Other income/Other charges	(209)
Income before interest and taxes	$ 869
Interest	(1,120)
Fees	(867)
Foreign exchange	(60)
Income (loss)	$ (1,178)
Minority interest	532
Taxes	—
Net income (loss)	$ (646)

EXHIBIT 3
Income from Poland Plant ($ in thousands)

	9/95 Year-to-Date
Revenues	$ 32,536
Cost of sales	(28,458)
Selling, technical expenses, and administrative expenses	(2,529)
Other income/Other charges	(121)
Income before interest and taxes	$ 1,428
Interest	—
Fees	—
Foreign exchange	34
Income	$ 1,462
Minority interest	—
Taxes	—
Net Income	$ 1,462

EXHIBIT 4
Income from Malaysia and Southeast Asia ($ in thousands)

	Region of Manufacture 9/95 Year-to-Date	Region of Sale 9/95 Year-to-Date
Revenues	$ 12,020	$ 36,052
Cost of sales	(12,392)	(26,648)
Selling, technical expenses, and administrative expenses	(3,775)	(4,845)
Other income/Other charges	(685)	(285)
Income before interest and taxes	$ (4,832)	$ 4,274
Taxes (40%)	—	(1,710)
Net income	$ (4,832)	$ 2,564
Capital charges	(3,600)[a]	(6,686)[b]
Economic value added	$ (8,432)	$ (4,122)

[a] $30,000 @ 12% = $3,600

[b] $110,000 @ 12% × [(36,052 − 12,020) / 102,800] + 30,000 @ 12% = $6,686

The Balanced Scorecard— Measures that Drive Performance

What you measure is what you get. Senior executives understand that their organization's measurement system strongly affects the behavior of managers and employees. Executives also understand that traditional financial accounting measures like return-on-investment and earnings-per-share can give misleading signals for continuous improvement and innovation—activities today's competitive environment demands. The traditional financial performance measures worked well for the industrial era, but they are out of step with the skills and competencies companies are trying to master today.

As managers and academic researchers have tried to remedy the inadequacies of current performance measurement systems, some have focused on making financial measures more relevant. Others have said, "Forget the financial measures. Improve operational measures like cycle time and defect rates; the financial results will follow." But managers should not have to choose between financial and operational measures. In observing and working with many companies, we have found that senior executives do not rely on one set of measures to the exclusion of the other. They realize that no single measure can provide a clear performance target or focus attention on the critical areas of the business. Managers want a balanced presentation of both financial and operational measures.

During a year-long research project with 12 companies at the leading edge of performance measurement, we devised a "balanced scorecard"—a set of measures that gives top managers a fast but comprehensive view of the business. The balanced scorecard includes financial measures that tell the results of actions already taken. And it complements the financial measures with operational measures on customer satisfaction, internal processes, and the organization's innovation and improvement activities—operational measures that are the drivers of future financial performance.

Think of the balanced scorecard as the dials and indicators in an airplane cockpit. For the complex task of navigating and flying an airplane, pilots need detailed information about many aspects of the flight. They need information on fuel, air speed, altitude, bearing, destination, and other indicators that summarize the current and predicted environment. Reliance on one instrument can be fatal. Similarly, the complexity of managing an organization today requires that managers be able to view performance in several areas simultaneously.

Robert S. Kaplan is the Arthur Lowes Dickinson Professor of Accounting at the Harvard Business School. David P. Norton is president of Nolan, Norton & Company, Inc., a Massachusetts-based information technology consulting firm he cofounded.

The balanced scorecard allows managers to look at the business from four important perspectives. (See the following exhibit, "The Balanced Scorecard Links Performance Measures.") It provides answers to four basic questions:

- How do customers see us? (customer perspective)
- What must we excel at? (internal business perspective)
- Can we continue to improve and create value? (innovation and learning perspective)
- How do we look to shareholders? (financial perspective)

The Balanced Scorecard Links Performance Measures

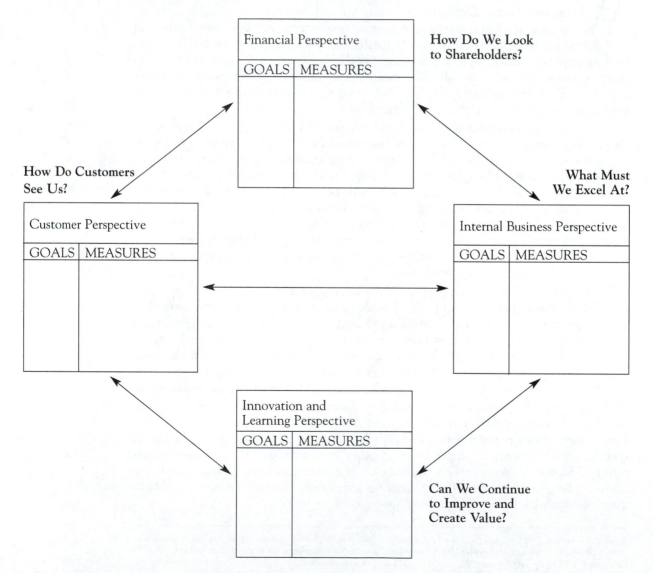

While giving senior managers information from four different perspectives, the balanced scorecard minimizes information overload by limiting the number of measures used. Companies rarely suffer from having too few measures. More commonly, they keep adding new measures whenever an employee or a consultant makes a worthwhile suggestion. One manager described the proliferation of new measures at his company as its "kill another tree program." The balanced scorecard forces managers to focus on the handful of measures that are most critical.

Several companies have already adopted the balanced scorecard. Their early experiences using the scorecard have demonstrated that it meets several managerial needs. First, the scorecard brings together, in a single management report, many of the seemingly disparate elements of a company's competitive agenda: becoming customer oriented, shortening response time, improving quality, emphasizing teamwork, reducing new product launch times, and managing for the long term.

Second, the scorecard guards against suboptimization. By forcing senior managers to consider all the important operational measures together, the balanced scorecard lets them see whether improvement in one area may have been achieved at the expense of another. Even the best objective can be achieved badly. Companies can reduce time to market, for example, in two very different ways: by improving the management of new product introductions or by releasing only products that are incrementally different from existing products. Spending on setups can be cut either by reducing setup times or by increasing batch sizes. Similarly, production output and first-pass yields can rise, but the increases may be due to a shift in the product mix to more standard, easy-to-produce but lower-margin products.

We will illustrate how companies can create their own balanced scorecard with the experiences of one semiconductor company—let's call it Electronic Circuits Inc. ECI saw the scorecard as a way to clarify, simplify, and then operationalize the vision at the top of the organization. The ECI scorecard was designed to focus the attention of its top executives on a short list of critical indicators of current and future performance.

CUSTOMER PERSPECTIVE: HOW DO CUSTOMERS SEE US?

Many companies today have a corporate mission that focuses on the customer. "To be number one in delivering value to customers" is a typical mission statement. How a company is performing from its customers' perspective has become, therefore, a priority for top management. The balanced scorecard demands that managers translate their general mission statement on customer service into specific measures that reflect the factors that really matter to customers.

Customers' concerns tend to fall into four categories: time, quality, performance and service, and cost. Lead time measures the time required for the company to meet its customers' needs. For existing products, lead time can be measured from the time the company receives an order to the time it actually delivers the product or service to the customer. For new products, lead time represents the time to market, or how long it takes to bring a new product from the product definition stage to the start of shipments. Quality measures the defect level of incoming products as perceived and measured by the customer. Quality could also measure on-time delivery, the accu-

Other Measures for the Customer's Perspective

A computer manufacturer wanted to be the competitive leader in customer satisfaction, so it measured competitive rankings. The company got the rankings through an outside organization hired to talk directly with customers. The company also wanted to do a better job of solving customers' problems by creating more partnerships with other suppliers. It measured the percentage of revenue from third-party relationships.

The customers of a producer of very expensive medical equipment demanded high reliability. The company developed two customer-based metrics for its operations: equipment uptime percentage and mean-time response to a service call.

A semiconductor company asked each major customer to rank the company against comparable suppliers on efforts to improve quality, delivery time, and price performance. When the manufacturer discovered that it ranked in the middle, managers made improvements that moved the company to the top of customers' rankings.

---

racy of the company's delivery forecasts. The combination of performance and service measures how the company's products or services contribute to creating value for its customers.

To put the balanced scorecard to work, companies should articulate goals for time, quality, and performance and service and then translate these goals into specific measures. Senior managers at ECI, for example, established general goals for customer performance: get standard products to market sooner, improve customers' time to market, become customers' supplier of choice through partnerships with them, and develop innovative products tailored to customer needs. The managers translated these general goals into four specific goals and identified an appropriate measure for each. (See the exhibit "ECI's Balanced Scorecard.")

To track the specific goal of providing a continuous stream of attractive solutions, ECI measured the percent of sales from new products and the percent of sales from proprietary products. That information was available internally. But certain other measures forced the company to get data from outside. To assess whether the company was achieving its goal of providing reliable, responsive supply, ECI turned to its customers. When it found that each customer defined "reliable, responsive supply" differently, ECI created a database of the factors as defined by each of its major customers. The shift to external measures of performance with customers led ECI to redefine "on time" so it matched customers' expectations. Some customers defined "on time" as any shipment that arrived within five days of scheduled delivery; others used a nine-day window. ECI itself had been using a seven-day window, which meant that the company was not satisfying some of its customers and overachieving with others. ECI also asked its top ten customers to rank the company as a supplier overall.

Depending on customers' evaluations to define some of a company's performance measures forces that company to view its performance through customers' eyes. Some companies hire third parties to perform anonymous customer surveys, resulting in a customer-driven report card. The J.D. Powers quality survey, for example, has become the standard of performance for the automobile industry, while the Department of Transportation's measurement of on-time arrivals and lost baggage

ECI's Balanced Business Scorecard

Financial Perspective

GOALS	MEASURES
Survive	Cash flow
Succeed	Quarterly sales growth and operating income by division
Prosper	Increased market share and ROE

Customer Perspective

GOALS	MEASURES
New products	Percent of sales from new products
	Percent of sales from proprietary products
Responsive supply	On-time delivery (defined by customer)
Preferred supplier	Share of key accounts' purchases
	Ranking by key accounts
Customer partnership	Number of cooperative engineering efforts

Internal Business Perspective

GOALS	MEASURES
Technology capability	Manufacturing geometry vs. competition
Manufacturing excellence	Cycle time Unit cost Yield
Design productivity	Silicon efficiency Engineering efficiency
New product introduction	Actual introduction schedule vs. plan

Innovation and Learning Perspective

GOALS	MEASURES
Technology leadership	Time to develop next generation
Manufacturing learning	Process time to maturity
Product focus	Percent of products that equal 80% sales
Time to market	New product introduction vs. competition

provides external standards for airlines. Benchmarking procedures are yet another technique companies use to compare their performance against competitors' best practice. Many companies have introduced "best of breed" comparison programs: the company looks to one industry to find, say, the best distribution system, to another industry for the lowest cost payroll process, and then forms a composite of those best practices to set objectives for its own performance.

In addition to measures of time, quality, and performance and service, companies must remain sensitive to the cost of their products. But customers see price as only one component of the cost they incur when dealing with their suppliers. Other supplier-driven costs range from ordering, scheduling delivery, and paying for the materials; to receiving, inspecting, handling, and storing the materials; to the scrap, rework, and obsolescence caused by the materials; and schedule disruptions (expediting and value of lost output) from incorrect deliveries. An excellent supplier may charge a higher unit price for products than other vendors but nonetheless be a lower cost supplier because it can deliver defect-free products in exactly the right quantities at exactly the right time directly to the production process and can minimize, through electronic data interchange, the administrative hassles of ordering, invoicing, and paying for materials.

INTERNAL BUSINESS PERSPECTIVE: WHAT MUST WE EXCEL AT?

Customer-based measures are important, but they must be translated into measures of what the company must do internally to meet its customers' expectations. After all, excellent customer performance derives from processes, decisions, and actions occurring throughout an organization. Managers need to focus on those critical internal operations that enable them to satisfy customer needs. The second part of the balanced scorecard gives managers that internal perspective.

Other Measures for the Internal Business Perspective

One company recognized that the success of its TQM program depended on all its employees internalizing and acting on the program's messages. The company performed a monthly survey of 600 randomly selected employees to determine if they were aware of TQM, had changed their behavior because of it, believed the outcome was favorable, or had become missionaries to others.

Hewlett-Packard uses a metric called breakeven time (BET) to measure the effectiveness of its product development cycle. BET measures the time required for all the accumulated expenses in the product and process development cycle (including equipment acquisition) to be recovered by the product's contribution margin (the selling price less manufacturing, delivery, and selling expenses).

A major office products manufacturer, wanting to respond rapidly to changes in the marketplace, set out to reduce cycle time by 50%. Lower levels of the organization aimed to radically cut the times required to process customer orders, order and receive materials from suppliers, move materials and products between plants, produce and assemble products, and deliver products to customers.

The internal measures for the balanced scorecard should stem from the business processes that have the greatest impact on customer satisfaction—factors that affect cycle time, quality, employee skills, and productivity, for example. Companies should also attempt to identify and measure their company's core competencies, the critical technologies needed to ensure continued market leadership. Companies should decide what processes and competencies they must excel at and specify measures for each.

Managers at ECI determined that submicron technology capability was critical to its market position. They also decided that they had to focus on manufacturing excellence, design productivity, and new product introduction. The company developed operational measures for each of these four internal business goals.

To achieve goals on cycle time, quality, productivity, and cost, managers must devise measures that are influenced by employees' actions. Since much of the action takes place at the department and workstation levels, managers need to decompose overall cycle time, quality, product, and cost measures to local levels. That way, the measures link top management's judgment about key internal processes and competencies to the actions taken by individuals that affect overall corporate objectives. This linkage ensures that employees at lower levels in the organization have clear targets for actions, decisions, and improvement activities that will contribute to the company's overall mission.

Information systems play an invaluable role in helping managers disaggregate the summary measures. When an unexpected signal appears on the balanced scorecard, executives can query their information system to find the source of the trouble. If the aggregate measure for on-time delivery is poor, for example, executives with a good information system can quickly look behind the aggregate measure until they can identify late deliveries, day by day, by a particular plant to an individual customer.

If the information system is unresponsive, however, it can be the Achilles' heel of performance measurement. Managers at ECI are currently limited by the absence of such an operational information system. Their greatest concern is that the scorecard information is not timely; reports are generally a week behind the company's routine management meetings, and the measures have yet to be linked to measures for managers and employees at lower levels of the organization. The company is in the process of developing a more responsive information system to eliminate this constraint.

INNOVATION AND LEARNING PERSPECTIVE: CAN WE CONTINUE TO IMPROVE AND CREATE VALUE?

The customer-based and internal business process measures on the balanced scorecard identify the parameters that the company considers most important for competitive success. But the targets for success keep changing. Intense global competition requires that companies make continual improvements to their *existing* products and processes and have the ability to introduce entirely new products with expanded capabilities.

A company's ability to innovate, improve, and learn ties directly to the company's value. That is, only through the ability to launch new products, create more value for customers, and improve operating efficiencies continually can a company penetrate new markets and increase revenues and margins—in short, grow and thereby increase shareholder value.

ECI's innovation measures focus on the company's ability to develop and introduce standard products rapidly, products that the company expects will form the bulk of its future sales. Its manufacturing improvement measure focuses on new products; the goal is to achieve stability in the manufacturing of new products rather than to improve manufacturing of existing products. Like many other companies, ECI uses the percent of sales from new products as one of its innovation and improvement measures. If sales from new products are trending downward, managers can explore whether problems have arisen in new product design or new product introduction.

In addition to measures on product and process innovation, some companies overlay specific improvement goals for their existing processes. For example, Analog Devices, a Massachusetts-based manufacturer of specialized semiconductors, expects managers to improve their customer and internal business process performance continuously. The company estimates specific rates of improvement for on-time delivery, cycle time, defect rate, and yield.

Other companies, like Milliken & Co., require that managers make improvements within a specific time period. Milliken did not want its "associates" (Milliken's word for employees) to rest on their laurels after winning the Baldridge Award. Chairman and CEO Roger Milliken asked each plant to implement a "tenfour" improvement program: measures of process defects, missed deliveries, and scrap were to be reduced by a factor of ten over the next four years. These targets emphasize the role for continuous improvement in customer satisfaction and internal business processes.

FINANCIAL PERSPECTIVE: HOW DO WE LOOK TO SHAREHOLDERS?

Financial performance measures indicate whether the company's strategy, implementation, and execution are contributing to bottom-line improvement. Typical financial goals have to do with profitability, growth, and shareholder value. ECI stated its financial goals simply: to survive, to succeed, and to prosper. Survival was measured by cash flow, success by quarterly sales growth and operating income by division, and prosperity by increased market share by segment and return on equity.

But given today's business environment, should senior managers even look at the business from a financial perspective? Should they pay attention to short-term financial measures like quarterly sales and operating income? Many have criticized financial measures because of their well-documented inadequacies, their backward-looking focus, and their inability to reflect contemporary value-creating actions. Shareholder value analysis (SVA), which forecasts future cash flows and discounts them back to a rough estimate of current value, is an attempt to make financial analysis more forward looking. But SVA still is based on cash flow rather than on the activities and processes that drive cash flow.

Some critics go much further in their indictment of financial measures. They argue that the terms of competition have changed and that traditional financial measures do not improve customer satisfaction, quality, cycle time, and employee motivation. In their view, financial performance is the result of operational actions, and financial success should be the logical consequence of doing the fundamentals well. In other words, companies should stop navigating by financial measures. By making fundamental improvements in their operations, the financial numbers will take care of themselves, the argument goes.

Assertions that financial measures are unnecessary are incorrect for at least two reasons. A well-designed financial control system can actually enhance rather than inhibit an organization's total quality management program. (See the insert, "How One Company Used a Daily Financial Report to Improve Quality.") More important, however, the alleged linkage between improved operating performance and financial success is actually quite tenuous and uncertain. Let us demonstrate rather than argue this point.

Over the three-year period between 1987 and 1990, a NYSE electronics company made an order-of-magnitude improvement in quality and on-time delivery performance. Outgoing defect rate dropped from 500 parts per million to 50, on-time delivery improved from 70% to 96%, and yield jumped from 26% to 51%. Did these breakthrough improvements in quality, productivity, and customer service provide substantial benefits to the company? Unfortunately not. During the same three-year period, the company's financial results showed little improvement, and its stock price plummeted to one-third of its July 1987 value. The considerable improvements in manufacturing capabilities had not been translated into increased profitability. Slow releases of new products and a failure to expand marketing to new and perhaps more demanding customers prevented the company from realizing the benefits of its manufacturing achievements. The operational achievements were real, but the company had failed to capitalize on them.

The disparity between improved operational performance and disappointing financial measures creates frustration for senior executives. This frustration is often vented at nameless Wall Street analysts who allegedly cannot see past quarterly blips in financial performance to the underlying long-term values these executives sincerely believe they are creating in their organizations. But the hard truth is that if improved performance fails to be reflected in the bottom line, executives should re-examine the basic assumptions of their strategy and mission. Not all long-term strategies are profitable strategies.

Measures of customer satisfaction, internal business performance, and innovation and improvement are derived from the company's particular view of the world and its perspective on key success factors. But that view is not necessarily correct. Even an excellent set of balanced scorecard measures does not guarantee a winning strategy. The balanced scorecard can only translate a company's strategy into specific measurable objectives. A failure to convert improved operational performance, as measured in the scorecard, into improved financial performance should send executives back to their drawing boards to rethink the company's strategy or its implementation plans.

As one example, disappointing financial measures sometimes occur because companies don't follow up their operational improvements with another round of actions. Quality and cycle-time improvements can create excess capacity. Managers

How One Company Used a Daily Financial Report to Improve Quality*

In the 1980s, a chemicals company became committed to a total quality management program and began to make extensive measurements of employee participation, statistical process control and key quality indicators. Using computerized controls and remote data entry systems, the plant monitored more than 30,000 observations of its production processes every four hours. The department managers and operating personnel who now had access to massive amounts of real-time operational data found their monthly financial reports to be irrelevant.

But one enterprising department manager saw things differently. He created a daily income statement. Each day, he estimated the value of the output from the production process using estimated market prices and subtracted the expenses of raw materials, energy, and capital consumed in the production process. To approximate the cost of producing out-of-conformance product, he cut the revenues from off-spec output by 50% to 100%.

The daily financial report gave operators powerful feedback and motivation and guided their quality and productivity efforts. The department head understood that it is not always possible to improve quality, reduce energy consumption, and increase throughput simultaneously; tradeoffs are usually necessary. He wanted the daily financial statement to guide those tradeoffs. The difference between the input consumed and output produced indicated the success or failure of the employees' efforts on the previous day. The operators were empowered to make decisions that might improve quality, increase productivity, and reduce consumption of energy and materials.

That feedback and empowerment had visible results. When, for example, a hydrogen compressor failed, a supervisor on the midnight shift ordered an emergency repair crew into action. Previously, such a failure of a noncritical component would have been reported in the shift log, where the department manager arriving for work the following morning would have to discover it. The midnight shift supervisor knew the cost of losing the hydrogen gas and made the decision that the cost of expediting the repairs would be repaid several times over by the output produced by having the compressor back on line before morning.

The department proceeded to set quality and output records. Over time, the department manager became concerned that employees would lose interest in continually improving operations. He tightened the parameters for in-spec production and reset the prices to reflect a 25% premium for output containing only negligible fractions of impurities. The operators continued to improve the production process.

The success of the daily financial report hinged on the manager's ability to establish a financial penalty for what had previously been an intangible variable: the quality of output. With this innovation, it was easy to see where process improvements and capital investments could generate the highest returns.

*Source: "Texas Eastman Company," by Robert S. Kaplan, Harvard Business School Case 9-190-039.

should be prepared to either put the excess capacity to work or else get rid of it. The excess capacity must be either used by boosting revenues or eliminated by reducing expenses if operational improvements are to be brought down to the bottom line.

As companies improve their quality and response time, they eliminate the need to build, inspect, and rework out-of-conformance products or to reschedule and expedite delayed orders. Eliminating these tasks means that some of the people who perform them are no longer needed. Companies are understandably reluctant to lay off employees, especially since the employees may have been the source of the ideas that produced the higher quality and reduced cycle time. Layoffs are a poor reward for past improvement and can damage the morale of remaining workers, curtailing further improvement. But companies will not realize all the financial benefits of their improvements until their employees and facilities are working to capacity—or the companies confront the pain of downsizing to eliminate the expenses of the newly created excess capacity.

If executives fully understood the consequences of their quality and cycle-time improvement programs, they might be more aggressive about using the newly created capacity. To capitalize on this self-created new capacity, however, companies must expand sales to existing customers, market existing products to entirely new customers (who are now accessible because of the improved quality and delivery performance), and increase the flow of new products to the market. These actions can generate added revenues with only modest increases in operating expenses. If marketing and sales and R&D do not generate the increased volume, the operating improvements will stand as excess capacity, redundancy, and untapped capabilities. Periodic financial statements remind executives that improved quality, response time, productivity, or new products benefit the company only when they are translated into improved sales and market share, reduced operating expenses, or higher asset turnover.

Ideally, companies should specify how improvements in quality, cycle time, quoted lead times, delivery, and new product introduction will lead to higher market share, operating margins, and asset turnover or to reduced operating expenses. The challenge is to learn how to make such explicit linkage between operations and finance. Exploring the complex dynamics will likely require simulation and cost modeling.

MEASURES THAT MOVE COMPANIES FORWARD

As companies have applied the balanced scorecard, we have begun to recognize that the scorecard represents a fundamental change in the underlying assumptions about performance measurement. As the controllers and finance vice presidents involved in the research project took the concept back to their organizations, the project participants found that they could not implement the balanced scorecard without the involvement of the senior managers who have the most complete picture of the company's vision and priorities. This was revealing because most existing performance measurement systems have been designed and overseen by financial experts. Rarely do controllers need to have senior managers so heavily involved.

Probably because traditional measurement systems have sprung from the finance function, the systems have a control bias. That is, traditional performance measurement systems specify the particular actions they want employees to take and then measure to see whether the employees have in fact taken those actions. In that way, the systems try to control behavior. Such measurement systems fit with the engineering mentality of the Industrial Age.

The balanced scorecard, on the other hand, is well suited to the kind of organization many companies are trying to become. The scorecard puts strategy and vision, not control, at the center. It establishes goals but assumes that people will adopt whatever behaviors and take whatever actions are necessary to arrive at those goals. The measures are designed to pull people toward the overall vision. Senior managers may know what the end result should be, but they cannot tell employees exactly how to achieve that result, if only because the conditions in which employees operate are constantly changing.

This new approach to performance measurement is consistent with the initiatives under way in many companies: cross-functional integration, customer-supplier partnerships, global scale, continuous improvement, and team rather than individual accountability. By combining the financial, customer, internal process and innovation, and organizational learning perspectives, the balanced scorecard helps managers understand, at least implicitly, many interrelationships. This understanding can help managers transcend traditional notions about functional barriers and ultimately lead to improved decision making and problem solving. The balanced scorecard keeps companies looking—and moving—forward instead of backward.

Wells Fargo Online Financial Services (A)

Mary D'Agostino, vice president and manager of finance, strategy, and planning for Wells Fargo's Online Financial Services group (OFS), headed back to her office, following a half-day workshop in December 1997 in which the team working on the balanced scorecard (BSC) initiative had debated, and ultimately agreed on, performance measures for the seven objectives underlying one of OFS's three strategic themes: to add and retain high-value and high-potential-value customers. She was struck by how differently the team was already thinking about the online banking business, and they hadn't even completed the scorecard. Whereas previously OFS had focused predominantly on financial measures to track performance—which was quite typical in the Wells Fargo culture—the team was now looking at performance from a multidimensional perspective. She was convinced that the new system would help OFS track the progress and impact of its recently defined strategy and communicate its performance both within OFS and to the rest of the bank. D'Agostino reflected on the new scorecard approach:

> This set of metrics gets at the core of the business case for OFS. We've never tracked and summarized the underlying drivers of our business on a systematic basis. The scorecard will take the mystery out of what is happening with our customers and our internal operations and it will be extremely useful to see the information on a monthly basis. We just don't get the same perspective from looking at our revenue and expense figures alone.

D'Agostino looked forward to next week's meeting in which the objectives and measures for the other two strategic themes would be discussed.

WELLS FARGO BANK

Wells Fargo Bank (Wells Fargo), headquartered in San Francisco, California, was the second-largest bank in California and one of the largest banks in the United States with almost $100 billion in assets in 1997 (see **Exhibit 1** for Wells Fargo financial information). Wells Fargo served 10 million households in 10 western states:

Senior Researcher Nicole Tempest prepared this case at the HBS California Research Center under the supervision of Robert Kaplan. HBS cases are developed solely as the basis for class discussion. Cases are not intended to serve as endorsements, sources of primary data, or illustrations of effective or ineffective management.

Arizona, California, Colorado, Idaho, Nevada, New Mexico, Oregon, Texas, Utah, and Washington. As of December 1997, the bank operated over 1,900 staffed retail outlets and 4,400 automated teller machines, including 1,295 ATMs it assumed through its $11.6 billion acquisition of First Interstate Bancorp in April 1996.

Wells Fargo was well known in the banking industry for its focus on innovation and cost management. In most cases the two were interrelated: innovations often enabled the bank to reduce operating costs. On the innovation front, Wells Fargo was one of the first banks in the country to offer extended weekday and Saturday hours, and it was a pioneer in pursuing nontraditional delivery channels, such as installing ATM machines in grocery stores. Such installations required less capital to build and cost less to operate than a standard freestanding branch. The bank was also a leader in testing new retail formats such as its one-stop-shopping banking center which included a full service branch, a Starbucks coffee outlet, a dry cleaner and a photocopying service all under one roof. Wells Fargo's focus on cost management was championed by Carl Reichardt, chairman from 1983 through 1994, who built an ambitious management culture with slogans such as, "Run it like you own it." The aggressive focus on costs caused the bank to exit businesses where the margins did not meet its targets; for example, the bank sold its home mortgage portfolio business in 1994 due to intense pressure on rates from regional savings and loans. Wells Fargo's acquisition of First Interstate was also an effort to gain efficiencies by enabling the bank to consolidate overhead and close over 300 redundant branches.

THE COMMERCIAL BANKING INDUSTRY

During the late 1980s, the commercial banking industry entered into a period of widespread consolidation as Congress, the Federal Reserve, and other government agencies lowered the barriers that had previously separated different parts of the financial services universe, blurring the lines between banks, brokerage firms, insurers, finance companies, and credit card issuers. Some of the most significant changes occurred when Congress passed legislation that allowed full-scale interstate banking in 1994 and when the Federal Reserve Board raised the limit on the amount of underwriting business a bank affiliate was permitted from 10% to 25% of revenues in 1996. By the mid-1990s, commercial banks could sell stocks and mutual funds, investment banks could offer lines of credit, and credit card issuers could sell insurance. Competition intensified even further due to a series of industry mergers and acquisitions initiated to increase profits through greater economies of scale. Some of the best known, long-standing names in the commercial banking industry merged or were acquired in the 1990s. These included Chemical Bank's $2.3 billion merger with Manufacturer's Hanover in 1991, BankAmerica's $4 billion acquisition of Security Pacific in 1992, Chase Manhattan's $10 billion merger with Chemical Bank in 1995, and Wells Fargo's $11.6 billion acquisition of First Interstate in 1996. In fact, of the 13 largest merger and acquisition (M&A) deals announced in 1997, 6 involved combinations of financial institutions, of which 3 were combinations of commercial banks, including NationsBank's $13.8 billion acquisition of Barnett Banks and Banc One's $7.3 billion acquisition of First USA (see **Exhibit 2** for the top 13 M&A deals announced in 1997). To succeed in an increasingly competitive environment, commercial banks were pursuing innovative ways to attract customers and reduce costs, many of which required significant investments in technology.

ELECTRONIC BANKING

The term *electronic banking* described two services that allowed consumers to access their bank accounts and conduct transactions using their computers. *PC banking* referred to customers using a bank's proprietary software or a personal finance software package such as Money or Quicken to access their bank's network via a modem. *Internet banking* allowed customers to access their bank account information through the Internet by connecting to their bank's Web site directly, using Web browser software, such as Netscape Navigator or Microsoft® Internet Explorer.

While only an estimated 250,000 U.S. households used electronic banking for account access or bill payment in 1994, the number had climbed to 4.5 million by 1997, representing 4.5% of all U.S. households. By the year 2000, industry experts projected that more than 17 million U.S. households would be using electronic banking (see **Exhibit 3** for projected usage of electronic banking).[1] Growth in electronic banking had been fueled by the growth in the installed base of personal computers in homes and in the workplace; between 1994 and 1996, the number of installed PCs in the U.S. had increased from 78 million to almost 95 million, a 10% compound annual growth rate. Moreover, personal finance was one of the leading uses for home computers, ahead of spreadsheets and work brought home from the office.

Internet usage in the United States had also grown rapidly between 1996 and 1997—increasing from an estimated 34 million adult users over the age of 16 to over 50 million by early 1997. By the end of 1997, 2,700 banks and credit unions had established Web sites on the Internet. However, the majority of these Web sites offered only standard, packaged marketing information; less than 6% offered customers direct account access.

WELLS FARGO ONLINE FINANCIAL SERVICES

In 1989 Wells Fargo introduced its first electronic banking product which allowed consumers to access their accounts through Prodigy's online service. Shortly thereafter, Wells Fargo introduced its own proprietary DOS-based system. However, by late 1994 only 20,000 customers were using the two services combined, prompting the bank to look for ways to improve its online banking offerings (Wells Fargo referred to all of its electronic banking services as "online"). The OFS group consisted of 75 people at the time, all of whom had come from other departments within the bank. In December 1994 Wells Fargo's corporate marketing group launched a Web site on the World Wide Web as part of its brand-building effort on behalf of the bank as a whole. The Web site initially provided only standard marketing information. Soon, however, customers were asking for direct account access. Karen Derr Gilbert, vice president of marketing for OFS, recalled:

> We took the customer feedback and asked our technology group, "can we do this?" By May 1995 we had balances and account histories available to customers through our Web site. It was phenomenal since it was an entirely customer-driven process.

---

[1] Online Banking Report, January 1998.

Wells Fargo was the first major U.S. bank to offer Internet access (see **Exhibit 4** for the launch dates of competitors' Internet offerings), and customer response was overwhelming—over 10,000 Wells Fargo customers accessed their accounts through the Internet service in the first two months of operation. Dudley Nigg, executive vice president of OFS at Wells Fargo, reflected on the decision to launch the Internet service:

> In recent years, banks have become far more consumer focused. The trend started about 15 years ago when banks began to offer longer hours and expanded services in response to consumer demand for greater convenience and greater access. We realized then that customers considered banking a chore, which led us to find ways to make it easier for them. We began to study which channels offered consumers the convenience they wanted. We began to look at convenience along a continuum, which included branch banking, telephone banking, and ATMs. Then we extended the continuum into the remote space. In 1994 an increasing number of customers saw the online channel as a very attractive medium, and we came to the conclusion that Wells Fargo should begin to aggressively offer banking as an option through that medium. Since then a couple of things have really allowed our Internet banking service to take off: first, the proliferation of PCs has given many more people access to online banking. In fact, we're playing catch-up—a lot more of our customers have PCs and Internet access than are currently banking online, so we are following behind a phenomenon that we don't have to lead; and second, the Internet has grown in importance far faster than any of us thought it would, especially out here on the West Coast.

By 1998, the Wells Fargo Internet service, accessed through the www.wellsfargo.com Web address (see **Exhibit 5** for Wells Fargo's home page), allowed customers to handle many of their banking needs online; for example customers could review their checking account and credit card balances, pay bills, transfer funds, conduct stock and bond trades, order checks, and request product information. Wells Fargo's Web site had generated significant praise from industry reviewers: Smart Money magazine named Wells Fargo "Best Online Bank" in 1996, the Online Banking Association named Wells Fargo's site "Best Overall Site by a U.S. Financial Institution" in 1996, and Financial Net News named Wells Fargo's site "Best of Banks" in 1997.[2] By early 1998 over 450,000 Wells Fargo customers used one of Wells Fargo's online banking services, and the company believed this number would grow to 1 million customers within two years. Wells Fargo's Internet service accounted for 350,000 of its online banking customers by early 1998 and it was projected to account for the majority of the growth going forward; the bank was enrolling close to 1,000 customers per day, and over 80% were Internet-based.

Given its first-mover advantage, by 1997 Wells Fargo had captured a significant share of all electronic banking users in the United States. Maintaining or growing that share would be a challenge as other banks, credit unions, brokerage firms, insurance firms and even nonfinancial institutions entered the electronic banking market. Wells Fargo's near-term strategy was similar to that of a "land rush": sign up as many customers as quickly as possible. Based on this strategy, early on Wells Fargo

---

[2] "Wells Fargo Goes the Extra Mile to Deliver Internet Banking to its Customers over the WebTV Network and AOL." Wells Fargo Press Release. June 17, 1997.

focused on designing its service to meet the needs of users of WebTV, Nokia Internet cell phones, and other Internet access devices, in an effort to meet customers wherever they were doing their banking.

THE WELLS FARGO ONLINE BANKING CUSTOMER

The Wells Fargo online banking service appealed to an attractive customer segment. The average user was 38 years old, had a median household income of $75,000 to $100,000, was in a wealth accumulation mode, and was a moderate to heavy borrower (through personal loans, credit cards, and auto loans). Their behavior as bank customers provided the foundation for three of the four elements driving the business rationale for OFS. First, the online customer stayed with the bank longer than average—the attrition rate for online banking customers was 50% below the bank's average. Second, the cross-selling opportunity was higher for online banking customers since they held, on average, one more product than the typical Wells Fargo customer. Third, online customers were more profitable to the bank since they carried higher balances on both deposits and loans. The fourth element of the OFS business case was not related to customer attractiveness, but rather to migrating Wells Fargo customers to a lower-cost service channel than branch banking, phone banking, and ATM operations. The American Banker's Association estimated that an online banking transaction cost $.01, whereas an ATM transaction cost $.27, a telephone transaction $.54, and a branch transaction $1.07.[3]

THE OFS ORGANIZATION

By 1998 the OFS group consisted of five functional areas, including operations, development, marketing, finance and planning, and human resources. (See **Exhibit 6** for the OFS organization chart). The operations group consisted of the most staff since it included the OFS call center, which handled customer service requests related to online banking. Within the call center there were three types of customer support agents: (1) technical support agents helped customers solve a wide range of more complicated technology issues, (2) phone support agents handled enrollment requests and basic technical inquiries, and (3) email agents responded to customer inquiries sent via email. Agents were paid on a continuum based on skill level and area of specialization. The goal was to migrate customers to email agents for support.

The OFS group was treated as a cost center. It attempted to recover its operating costs of servers, employees, and marketing programs by charging other bank departments for its services. OFS used two primary fee structures to charge back costs to product groups within the bank: one fee was charged for a service session, in which a customer logged onto the service for informational purposes only (no transactions); a second fee was charged for conducting a transaction. For example, if a checking customer logged onto the bank's Internet service to review account balances, OFS would charge that service session back to the checking division. The OFS group did not receive much resistance from other product areas in the bank for charging back costs for usage since online banking represented a less expensive serv-

---

[3] American Banker's Association/Booz Allen Hamilton Internet Banking survey. February 1996.

icing channel relative to the bank's other channels. The only direct revenue that OFS could count as its own was the small fee it charged for its bill-paying service when customers did not meet a minimum balance requirement, access fees from Money and Quicken users, and "bounty" fees it received from third parties, such as Internet service providers, for sourcing customers for them through joint marketing programs targeted at Wells Fargo customers. All other revenue generated from customer banking activities, such as new product sales or balance growth, was credited to the relevant product area of the bank. Under the cost recovery model, the OFS group was projected to break even in the year 2000.

THE NEED FOR A NEW APPROACH

The culture at Wells Fargo embraced financial metrics. The bank used traditional financial measures to track performance at all levels of the organization. The OFS management team, however, believed that financial metrics, alone, did not effectively measure or communicate its strategy. They were concerned that an over-reliance on financial measures could lead to short-term decision making, such as pressure to reduce costs, at a time when the online banking business required a long-term, strategic view of its role within the bank. The OFS group believed that online banking not only represented a tremendous cost-savings opportunity for the bank but also an effective customer acquisition and retention tool over the long term. The group felt that the potential future benefits of online banking warranted increased investment in its services—not an emphasis on cost containment and reduction. D'Agostino commented:

> Wells Fargo's culture embraces financial measures—how your P&L looks on an absolute basis, how it looks versus plan. However, if you only look at the business from a financial perspective you risk making poor decisions, especially in the online financial services business. We are considered a cost center and you wouldn't want to *invest* in a cost center, unless you could be sure of achieving significant efficiencies down the road. If you operate under this premise, you wouldn't develop new technologies or product offerings. Your goal would be to reduce costs.

In addition, more than almost any other area in the bank, OFS operated in a marketplace undergoing dramatic change on a daily basis. Technology-based companies often remarked that change occurred at Internet speed, which was 7 to 10 times faster than the normal pace of business operations. Due to the shifting competitive landscape in the Internet market, the OFS group found itself frequently changing the priority of its initiatives to take advantage of emerging technologies and opportunities, to address new competitive threats and keep up with customer demands. D'Agostino reflected:

> We're operating in an environment where new projects and opportunities come up continuously and our business environment and competitors are changing all the time. Alliances are constantly being forged and broken. Everyday, a newspaper story reports about a new technology, service offering, or way of doing business that affects us. We needed a tool to help us synchronize our strategy with what we were doing on a daily basis and translate that into measurable results. Such a tool would enable us to communicate with senior management, with other departments in the bank, and with our OFS employees.

As online banking grew in importance, the need for an objective set of measures linked to OFS's strategy escalated. Nigg recalled:

> In the early days the online channel was, more or less, viewed as an R&D effort. The objective was simply to understand the channel, develop it and see what we could do with it. By definition, an R&D effort is flexible. You need to give it freedom to evolve. Once you get 450,000 of your best customers onto a new channel, however, you can't afford to be haphazard—you need a certain degree of discipline.
>
> While we were very good at articulating the online vision at Wells Fargo, we often had difficulty translating that vision into effective execution. We needed a mechanism that would help us ensure that our plans closely supported our vision, and then we needed a set of clearly articulated, objective measures of performance. In the Internet space everything is new. And we needed a better way to identify what was working and what wasn't working to further our goals.

IMPLEMENTING THE BALANCED SCORECARD

The OFS group learned about the balanced scorecard approach during a discussion led by David Norton, a co-founder of the concept and a senior executive at Renaissance Worldwide, Inc. (Renaissance), a consulting firm based in Massachusetts. Nigg and his management team were impressed by the balanced scorecard's approach of integrating a set of multidimensional measures to assess a company's progress toward its goals. Nigg discussed the decision to implement the balanced scorecard:

> We looked at a number of tools, but focused on the balanced scorecard for two main reasons. First, the balanced nature of the scorecard appealed to us. Most of the tools we looked at did not put a premium on the balance between the various elements that make up success. They tended to be focused on one function—finance *or* operations *or* human resources. Secondly, the other tools did not put the same emphasis on quantitative measures for evaluating business performance as the scorecard. These two unique aspects of the scorecard led us to say "this makes sense."

With the decision made to implement this approach, Renaissance began working with OFS in September 1997 to develop OFS's balanced scorecard. Nigg assembled an internal OFS team to work on the project. The team consisted of the five functional heads from OFS and a cross-functional group of middle managers. D'Agostino was appointed the project leader. Nigg discussed the importance of middle management participation in the process:

> I don't think it would be possible for senior management to develop a robust balanced scorecard even if it wanted to. There's a level of depth and detail that you could never get from senior management. So from an operational standpoint it was essential to have middle managers participate in the process. It was also critical from a buy-in standpoint: having invented it, the team bought into the final product far more than they would have, had they not been as deeply involved in the process.

The first step in the process was to reaffirm the three strategic themes that had been developed by the OFS group, earlier in the year, during the strategic planning process:

- **Add and retain high-value and high-potential-value customers**

  We will grow the customer base by differentiating our offerings from the competition. In particular we will focus on continued leadership in product and feature development and superior customer service.

- **Increase revenue per customer**

  We will grow revenue per customer by continuing our third-party alliance programs and cross-selling both branded and nonbranded products.

- **Reduce costs per customer**

  We will reduce cost per customer by increasing the customer base to spread fixed costs and developing cutting-edge automated processes, support and self-help systems.

The team discussed whether the three themes accurately portrayed what OFS would need to do in the next three to five years to maintain its leadership position in the online financial services market. The team soon agreed that the three themes were a good statement of strategic intent. They then participated in a series of workshops to develop a comprehensive set of objectives linked to each strategic theme that looked at the business from the four balanced scorecard perspectives: financial, customer, internal business process, and learning and growth. The team was careful to screen each objective to ensure that it was an essential driver and that it was measurable. The team did not limit itself by whether the data required to measure the objective were currently available within OFS. Their primary concern was whether the objective lent itself to a quantifiable measure of any sort. The next step in the process involved developing a "linkage map" which mapped the interrelationships between each objective and the three strategic themes. This step in the process was both time consuming and controversial. Karen Gilbert, vice president of marketing, recalled:

> We spent weeks getting the linkage map right. We debated where every objective fit on the map. The discussions became heated at times. However, it was good for us to have a cross-functional discussion about each objective, because it helped everyone see how interrelated all objectives are. In the end it was a really useful process. Everyone benefited from the opportunity to talk as a group about the complex issues facing our business.

As they developed the linkage map, the team grappled with the issue of how to align the learning and growth objectives with a specific strategic theme. The learning and growth objectives were as follows:

- Attract and retain key OFS players and staff,
- Enhance OFS bench strength and succession planning,
- Increase managerial competency and functional technical competency at all levels,
- Continue development of the OFS organization and culture, and
- Deploy the scorecard and embed it in OFS.

The team believed that these objectives were necessary to achieve each of the three strategic themes. As a result, the team eventually decided to treat the learning and growth objectives as drivers behind all three themes, instead of aligning a sub-set of them under any one.

Once the team had completed the linkage map, it broke into sub-teams, assigned by strategic theme, to develop measures for each objective on the linkage map. While the sub-teams were cross-functional, members of OFS's marketing department played a greater role on the teams assigned to the first two themes, while members of the finance and operations departments focused more heavily on the third theme which focused on cost-reduction. The sub-teams met several times over the course of a two-week period to develop at least two measures per objective. The entire working team then reconvened to review and discuss the 41 measures that the three sub-teams had developed. The group debated each measure. Did it effectively measure the objective? Was it the best way to measure performance? Was it redundant with any other measure?

One of the key tenets of the scorecard approach was to limit the number of measures in order to focus the organization on the most important performance drivers. As a result, the OFS team worked to pare down the list of measures from 41 to 25. When the group could not reach agreement about whether a measure qualified for the final list, they voted on the issue.

Through this process, the team struggled with the measurements for the learning and growth objectives. The team felt it was difficult to *directly* attribute performance on the learning and growth objectives to the performance of the overall business. While they believed that the learning and growth objectives did impact the business, they felt the impact was more indirect than objectives from the other three scorecard perspectives. They also felt that it was difficult and potentially misleading to measure the learning and growth objectives, such as retention and employee competency, on a monthly basis as the other objectives were to be measured. Therefore the team made the decision to exclude measures from the learning and growth perspective from the scorecard, but agreed to review these measures on an annual basis.

The sub-team for the first strategic theme ("Add and retain high-value and high-potential-value customers") was the first to develop a comprehensive set of objectives and measures (see **Exhibit 7** for the linkage map and **Exhibit 8** for the objectives and measures). A team from the analytic and information management group within the OFS finance department then worked together to determine the best way to gather the data required for each measure. The team divided the data requirements into three categories:

1. the data were readily available in the correct format within OFS;

2. the data were available within Wells Fargo, but not currently accessible to OFS;

3. the data were not available within Wells Fargo.

Where the data were not accessible or available, the team recommended whether to hire someone on a full-time or part-time basis to gather the data, rely on an outside company to gather the data, or hire a consultant to set up a process to gather the data on a systematic basis.

Concurrently, another team from the finance department determined how to best communicate the scorecard results. The team decided to use visual icons as opposed to quantitative measures on the printed scorecard to show performance by month and relative to plan. Three icons were used to measure monthly results: (1) greater than 5% better than plan, (2) within 5% of plan, and (3) greater than 5% worse than plan (see **Exhibit 9** for a sample report structure).[4]

LOOKING AHEAD

The other two sub-teams were still developing the objectives and measures for the second and third strategic themes. The sub-team working on the "Increase revenue per customer" theme knew that they had to view revenue from both an OFS perspective and a Wells Fargo perspective. The largest component of OFS's internal revenue was the fees charged to other product areas within the bank, based on customer usage. However, OFS believed that outside revenue generated from third-party alliances also represented a potentially large opportunity for the department. The bank's primary means of generating revenue was from the spread it earned between the rate at which it could loan money and the rate that it paid depositors times the loans outstanding. Therefore, the higher the balances, the greater the bank's profits. In addition, the bank's potential to generate fee and interest income increased as the number of products a customer held increased.

The sub-team working on the "Reduce costs per customer" knew that one of OFS's most significant internal cost drivers was its staffed call center, which assisted customers with enrollment, technical problems, and other customer service issues. While customers could enroll online, the team knew that many customers would still call the center for enrollment. However, the goal was to reduce the number and length of calls into the center and to increase the share of calls handled by email agents. OFS also sought to increase the productivity per agent. Moreover, since routine transactions, such as ordering checks, issuing stop payments, and transferring money cost less to process through the online channel, the bank as a whole would lower its costs as customers migrated to the online service.

* * *

D'Agostino looked forward to the presentations by the two sub-teams to review and discuss the objectives and measures for the last two strategic themes.

---

[4] For the first few months of operation, the team recommended that the actual numbers be included along with the icons so that the department could familiarize itself with the numbers behind the icons. Over time the goal was to fully migrate to the visual icon format.

EXHIBIT 1
Wells Fargo Financial Statistics: 1995–1997 (in millions)

For the year	1997	1996	1995	% Change 1997/1996	%Change 1996/1995
Net Income applicable to common stock	1,130	1,004	990	13	1
Earnings per common share	$12.77	$12.21	$20.37	5	(40)
Dividends declared per common share	5.20	5.20	4.60	—	13
Average common shares outstanding	88.4	82.2	48.6	8	69
Profitability ratios					
Net income to average total assets (ROA)	1.16%	1.15%	2.03%	1	(43)
Net income applicable to common stock to average stockholders' equity (ROE)	8.79	8.83	29.70	—	(70)
Efficiency ratio	62.2%	69.0%	55.3%	(10)	25
Average loans	$64,625	$60,574	$34,508	7	76
Average assets	99,560	93,392	50,767	7	84
Average core deposits	72,996	70,890	36,624	3	94
Net interest margin	5.99%	6.11%	5.80%	(2)	5
At year end					
Investment securities	$9,888	$13,505	$8,920	(27)	51
Loans	65,734	67,389	35,582	(2)	89
Allowance for loan loss	(1,828)	(2,018)	(1,794)	(9)	12
Goodwill	7,031	7,322	382	(4)	—
Total Assets	**97,456**	**108,888**	**50,316**	**(10)**	**116**
Core deposits	71,397	81,581	37,858	(12)	115
Common stockholders' equity	12,614	13,512	3,566	(7)	279
Stockholders' equity	12,889	14,112	4,055	(9)	248
Tier 1 capital	6,119	6,565	3,635	(7)	81
Total capital (Tiers 1 and 2)	9,242	10,000	5,141	(8)	95
Capital ratios					
Common stockholders' equity to assets	12.94%	12.41%	7.09%	4	75
Stockholders' equity to assets	13.22	12.96	8.06	2	61
Risk-based capital					
Tier 1 capital	7.61	7.68	8.81	(1)	(13)
Total capital	11.49	11.70	12.46	(2)	(6)
Leverage	6.95	6.65	7.46	5	(11)
Book value per common share	$146.41	$147.72	$75.93	(1)	95
Common stockholders	42,629	42,277	27,885	1	52
Staff (active, full-time equivalent)	33,100	36,902	19,249	(10)	92
Physical distribution offices	1,935	2,007	975	(4)	106

Source: Wells Fargo 1997 Annual Report

EXHIBIT 2
Top M&A Deals Announced in 1997

TARGET NAME	ACQUIRER NAME	TRANSACTION VALUE in billions
MCI Communications	WorldCom	$34.6
Barnett Barks	NationsBank	$13.8
ITT	Starwood Lodging Trust	$13.0
Northrop Grumman	Lockheed Martin	$11.8
HFS Inc.	CUC International	$11.3
Morgan Stanley	Dean Witter Discover & Co.	$10.6
Hughes Aircraft	Raytheon	$9.5
U.S. Bancorp	First Bank System	$8.9
Salomon	Travelers Group	$8.9
First USA	Banc One	$7.3
MedPartners	PhyCor	$7.0
Great Western Financial	Washington Mutual	$6.8
U.S. Robotics	3COM	$6.5

Source: Securities Data
Fortune table

EXHIBIT 3
Online Banking and Bill Payment Users

Millions of U.S. households using online banking and/or bill payment each month

Online Banking Activity	1994	1995	1996	1997	1998	1999	2000	2001	2002	2003	2004	2005	2010
Total U.S. households	96.0	98.0	99.6	100	101	102	103	105	106	107	108	109	114
Mid-Range Forecast													
Account access & bill pay	0.1	0.3	0.8	2.0	3.5	6.0	10	13	16	18.5	20.5	22.5	31
Account access only	0.05	0.1	1.5	2.2	3.25	4.0	4.5	5.0	5.0	5.0	5.0	5.0	5.0
Bill pay only	0.1	0.2	0.2	0.3	0.75	2.0	3.0	4.0	5.0	5.5	6.0	6.0	6.0
Total online banking HHs	0.25	0.6	2.5	4.5	7.5	12	17.5	22	26	29	31.5	33.5	42
Household penetration	0.3%	0.6%	2.5%	4.5%	7.4%	12%	17%	21%	25%	27%	29%	31%	37%
Low-End Forecast													
Total online banking HHs	0.25	0.6	2.5	4.0	6.0	9.0	13	17	20.5	23	25	26.5	33
Household penetration	0.3%	0.6%	2.5%	4.0%	5.9%	8.8%	13%	16%	19%	22%	23%	24%	29%
High-End Forecast													
Total online banking HHs	0.25	0.6	2.5	5.0	9.0	15	22	28	33	37	40	42	50
Household penetration	0.3%	0.6%	2.5%	5.0%	8.9%	15%	21%	27%	31%	35%	37%	39%	44%

Source: Online Banking Report, 1/98

EXHIBIT 4
Internet-Based Online Banking Service
Among Top 10 U.S. Banks as of 3/17/98

(ranked by 1996 assets)

Rank	Bank	Internet-Based Account Access	Year of Introduction
1	Chase	no	—
2	Citicorp	yes	1997
3	Bank of America	yes	1996
4	NationsBank	yes	1998
5	J.P. Morgan	no	—
6	First Union	yes	1996
7	Bankers Trust	no	—
8	Wells Fargo	yes	1995
9	First Chicago NBD	no	—
10	Banc One	yes	1997

Source: Online Banking Report

EXHIBIT 5
Wells Fargo Online Home Page (June 8, 1998)

WELLS FARGO **Welcome**

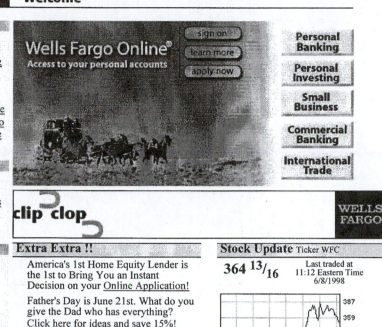

Quick Links:
- Online Banking
- Personal Banking
- Personal Investing
- Small Business
- Commercial Banking
- International Trade
- About Wells Fargo
- Wells Fargo in the Community

Features:
- Privacy Policy
- Press Releases
- Economic Reports
- Employment
- Wanted Posters

Tools & Tips:
- What's New
- Find Us
- Search Our Site
- Help
- Feedback

Search:
[   ] Go

Extra Extra !!

America's 1st Home Equity Lender is the 1st to Bring You an Instant Decision on your Online Application!

Father's Day is June 21st. What do you give the Dad who has everything? Click here for ideas and save 15%!

Shop with it. Bank with it. Pick up the tab with it. It's the Wells Fargo Express® ATM & Check Card.

Start banking online today with instant enrollment.

Take control of your finances. Use planning tools to reduce your debt or to reach your retirement goals early.

Pay your bills online for FREE. Find out how to qualify.

Should I convert my traditional IRA? Find the answers with the Roth IRA conversion analyzer.

Bank by television..with WebTV.

Stock Update Ticker WFC

364 13/16 Last traded at 11:12 Eastern Time 6/8/1998

Wells Fargo in the Community

Wells Fargo has a $45 billion, 10-year community reinvestment goal. Find out about Wells Fargo's Community Lending, Service and Investment programs.

This Date in History

June 8, 1871
Wells Fargo agent David F. Wagner sat in his Idaho City office expecting a treat. He read "FRUIT" on the label of the box sitting squarely on his desk. "Visions of strawberries and cream, pineapples,... (continued)

EXHIBIT 6
Online Financial Services Organizational Chart (as of 4/7/98)

Online Financial Services Group

Dudley M. Nigg
Executive Vice President
Group Head

Jeannie McCallister
Executive Assistant

Wendy Thomas
Vice President
Human Resources
- Sr. HR Consultant
- Sr. HR Consultant
- Sr. HR Consultant
- Sr. HR Consultant
- Project Manager

Karen D. Gilbert
V.P. Marketing
Product Management
- Manager Brand Mgmt, PR & Business Development
- Marketing Manager Internet Banking Functionality/ Personal Finance Sales
- Marketing Manager Internet Promotion/ Enrollment
- Sr. Distribution Channel Mgr. MS/Intuit
- Marketing Analyst

Mary E. D'Agostino
V.P. Finance,
Strategy & Planning
- Compliance Manager
- Finance Manager
- Financial Consultant
- Controller
- Analytical Marketing Manager

Sharon Osberg
Senior Vice President
Development
- Technology R&D
- Development/ Project Management
- Systems Development
- Manager Project Management
- Web Development Management
- Lan Administration/ Equipment Management

Dudley M. Nigg
Marketplace
Management

Regina Wallace
V.P. Customer
Service/Operations
- Manager Administrative Support
- Manager Strategic Planning/ Finance
- Manager 3rd Level Technical & Production Support
- Manager Alliance & Project Development
- Manager Global Services
- Manager Customer Care
- Customer Service Manager Westlake Texas

Source: Wells Fargo

EXHIBIT 7
Preliminary Linkage Map

EXHIBIT 8
Objectives and Measures for "Add and Retain High-Value and High-Potential-Value Customers"

BSC Perspective	Objective	Measure
Financial	Grow revenue	Revenue by product/service
		Number and % of active online customers; "active" defined as having logged on 1+ times in past 90 days
Customer	Add and retain high value customers	Number of incremental and total online customers
		Total bank profit per online customer
Customer	Manage attrition	Customer satisfaction ratio (as measured through customer satisfaction survey)
		Attrition rate among online checking customers
Internal business process	Maximize reliability	Weighted Internet availability (% of time that Internet servers and bill pay servers are up and running)
		Response time (how long customer has to wait to have data come up on screen)
Internal business process	Develop and implement cost effective marketing programs	Acquisition cost per enrolled customer
Internal business process	Continue leadership in superior product and features development	Weighted competitor index (rating based on competitor benchmarking)
Internal business process	Develop superior service capability	Bill pay claim ratio (% of claims on bills improperly handled through bill pay service)
		Telephone total service factor (% of customer service calls handled within 40 seconds)

EXHIBIT 9
OFS SCORECARD SUMMARY—THEME 1: Add and Retain High-Potential-Value Customers

Legend:
- (ribbon) = greater than 5% better than Plan
- (target) = within 5% of Plan
- (open circle) = greater than 5% worse than Plan

STRATEGIC OBJECTIVES	Measure	Business Proponent	1997 Baseline	1998 Target	Rolling 3 Months Dec	Jan	Feb	Actual YTD	Plan YTD	B/(W) Plan
GROW REVENUE	1. Revenue by product/service	K. Gilbert/ M. Baumli	$710	$940	(circle)	(ribbon)	(ribbon)	$768	$660	(ribbon)
	2. # and % of active online customers (AOL & INT)	K. Gilbert	104,000 / 48%	419,000 / 72%	(circle)	(circle)	(circle)	246,000	268,000	(circle)
	3. # of Incremental and total online customers	K. Gilbert	120,000 / 260,000	160,000 / 480,000	(circle)	(circle)	(circle)	28,000	41,000	(circle)
RETAIN VALUE CUSTOMERS	4. Profit (value) per customer and portfolio (BLENDED)	M. Baumli	$240	$280	(target)	QTRLY	QTRLY	$250	$258	(target)
MAXIMIZE RELIABILITY	5. Weighted Internet Availability	L. Gasparini	96.3%	98.9%	(circle)	(circle)	(circle)	94.2%	98.9%	(circle)
	6. Response Time (Open Net acct summary)	L. Gasparini	18.2 sec.	15 sec.	(target)	(ribbon)	(ribbon)	15.2 sec.	18 sec.	(ribbon)
EFFECTIVE MARKETING	7. Acquisition Cost per Enrollment	K. Gilbert	$28.16	$18.29	(circle)	(circle)	(circle)	$24.16	$21.80	(circle)
MANAGE ATTRITION	8. Customer Satisfaction Ratio	R. Wallace	TBD	TBD	TBD	TBD	TBD	TBD	TBD	
	9. Online Checking Attrition Rate	K. Gilbert/ R. Wallace	16.3%	11.0%	(target)	QTRLY	QTRLY	13.8%	14.2%	(target)
SUPERIOR LEADERSHIP	10. Weighted competitor index measurement	M. Baumli	TBD	TBD	TBD	TBD	TBD	TBD	TBD	
SUPERIOR SERVICE	11. Bill Pay Claim Ratio	S. Geraghty	2.6%	0.9%	(circle)	(circle)	(circle)	2.1%	1.6%	(circle)
	12. Telephone Total Service Factor	R. Wallace	78.2%	86.0%	(target)	(target)	(ribbon)	83.0%	82.0%	(target)

Note: All numbers have been disguised to preserve confidentiality.

Review Cases

- *Consulting Partners & Co.*
- *Adventurous Computer Games, Inc.*

Consulting Partners & Co.

The chairman's office just called with a special request. The Management Committee will be meeting this afternoon to discuss issues surrounding the National Training Center. The preliminary report on the Center's operations during 2003 has just arrived on his desk, and he is quite upset that the costs seem to be about one-third higher than he expected. Before he chairs the meeting this afternoon, he would like you to take a look at the costs and prepare an analysis of the performance of the Center last year. In addition, he has some idea that perhaps training costs should be treated as an asset in the firm's balance sheet. This would encourage partners to seek training themselves and to be more willing to release staff members for training. If training costs were capitalized (recorded to asset accounts), they would not be deducted from income immediately and they would not reduce the current year's distribution of income to partners. Finally, now that the National Training Center is up and running, he thinks we ought to pay some attention to establishing a management control system and performance measures that will allow us to determine the extent to which the Center is accomplishing its mission each year.

Robert Sampson, director of Human Resources at Consulting Partners & Co. (CPC) was speaking with Patricia Ryan, who had recently joined CPC as a specialist in personnel and human relations. Three-and-one-half years earlier, Ryan had earned a Master of Business Administration degree and accepted a position on the human relations staff of a Big 5 accounting firm. In November 2003, a headhunter called and she was convinced to resign her position and join CPC.

Sampson continued:

The chairman specifically asked that this assignment go to you. So whether you have time to take it on this morning or not, it's yours. His office has already faxed a copy of the summary report on operations for 2003 at the National Training Center (**Exhibit 1**). From my file, I found a copy of the proposal for the Center on which the July 2002 decision to establish a training center was based (**Exhibit 2**). The chairman's office also promised to fax his more specific questions as soon as they can get them typed up.

Professor William J. Bruns, Jr. prepared this note as the basis for class discussion.

THE FIRM

Consulting Partners & Co. was established late in 2001 by the merger of four separate consulting firms, each of which had been competing on a national basis. The concept of the merger was that a larger firm would be able to offer stronger and more diversified services on a nationwide basis in the United States and compete internationally with larger firms in the industry. The combined firms had nearly 1,400 partners and employed almost 10,000 personnel in 51 offices in the United States, and London, Paris, Frankfurt, and Mexico City.

Much consolidation and reorganization was made necessary as a result of the merger. In the cities where the newly merged firms each had offices, consolidation was inevitable. Real estate leases had to be negotiated or renegotiated to achieve economies of operation. Fortunately, the newly merged firm had sufficient operating capital that the restructuring could take place quickly, and the consolidation was mostly completed by mid-2003.

Even before the merger had taken place, the new firm had decided that required training for all professional staff would be one of the new firm's hallmarks. Initially, it was determined that all partners would be required to engage in a training activity for at least one week each year on average, and all other staff consultants would be required to spend two weeks each year in training. While such a requirement was not unprecedented in the professional services industry, CPC's standard would be a costly one: not only would the firm have to bear the cost of training, but during training, consultants would not be available to serve on assignments and to earn fees. Nevertheless, the partners in the new venture were convinced that professional training would provide a competitive edge until other professional service firms matched them.

Initially, the training requirement could be met in two ways. Consultants could choose to participate in professional development seminars run by universities or other training agents. Alternatively, individual offices of CPC could organize their own training sessions. The problem with the second alternative was that it was hard to achieve economies of scale within a single office without effectively shutting down that office during the time training was taking place.

Against that background, the Management Committee proposed to develop or purchase a training facility which would provide regular training for partners and staff of CPC on a cost-effective and firm-specific basis. Training would be based on CPC consulting principles and would be consistent with the culture that the new firm hoped to create and maintain. In early 2002, CPC learned that the entire campus of Sandown College in suburban Chicago was for sale, and a decision was made to purchase the property, renovate buildings, and establish the National Training Center.

THE NATIONAL TRAINING CENTER

In July 2002, CPC purchased Sandown College. Included in the $4 million purchase price was an administrative building, which housed several classrooms, several residence halls, and other incidental buildings. Half of the purchase price was allocated to the land, and half was allocated to the buildings. All buildings on the property were in substantial disrepair, as Sandown had struggled financially for several years before closing. In 2002, CPC had all buildings except the administrative and class-room building and one residence hall destroyed and immediately began renovating the two buildings which would become the National Training Center.

Each of the two buildings to be renovated was allocated half of the purchase cost of $2 million for the buildings, or $1 million each. The cost of renovations was great. A total of $7.5 million was spent renovating the residence hall, while renovations to the office and classroom building required an expenditure of just over $8 million. In both cases, the costs of renovation exceeded estimates because of unknown structural problems and the need for unexpected asbestos removal.

The proposal to create the National Training Center envisioned a permanent full-time staff devoted to training programs for partners and staff consultants, and a separate staff responsible for management and operation of the residence hall with its associated cafeteria. The capacity of the National Training Center would be 120 participants for the 48 weeks it would operate each year. Programs for partners would have space for 30 partners each week, while those for staff consultants could accommodate 90, usually in two sections of 45 each. While CPC would employ a professional training staff, they would also use external trainers from both professional firms and professors from universities with national reputations. Though the cost of external trainers was expected to be high, it would distinguish CPC's training effort from those of other professional service firms that did all of their own training in-house.

With renovations complete and the staff hiring nearly complete by the end of 2002, the National Training Center opened during the first week of January in 2003. Many on the professional staff had been reluctant initially to support the idea of a national training center. However, evaluations from participants in company-sponsored training programs held at the Center during 2003 were extremely positive. The renovations had resulted in comfortable accommodations, and the class-rooms were state-of-the-art classrooms with equipment for case discussions, multimedia presentations, and computer-based learning. As the year progressed word went out through the firm that the National Training Center was a great place to go to study with, and to get to know, other members of the professional staff of CPC.

The proposal on which the decision to establish the National Training Center had been based estimated an expenditure of $16.5 million for the purchase of Sandown College and building renovations. On a per-week basis, the forecasted cost of operating the National Training Center was estimated to be $784 dollars per week per participant, including the transportation cost of getting staff members from their home base to the National Training Center and back again. The decision to have the Center cover transportation cost was designed to minimize the reluctance of local offices to send people to the National Center instead of conducting their own training locally.

Robert Sampson had explained to Patricia Ryan that the costs of training had been a topic for lively discussion among the partners before the decision was made to establish the National Training Center. In addition to the out-of-pocket costs of training sessions, training incurs other kinds of costs. While they are participating in training sessions, staff consultants, partners, and principals are not working on client projects and are unable to bill clients for their time. In round numbers, the cost to the firm of this use of time is about $3,500 per week for a staff consultant and about

$7,400 per week for a partner or principal, based on estimates for 2003. In addition, staff consultants continue to earn their salaries while they are in training sessions.

Robert Sampson and Patricia Ryan had just had time to note that the cost per participant per week at the National Training Center shown on the report on operations for 2003 was $1,047—about 33% higher than that forecasted in the proposal. Sampson had just commented that it was no wonder the chairman wanted to figure out what was happening at the Center when the facsimile machine beeped its message that the chairman's questions had arrived. Ryan knew that it was time to get to work. This would be the first work that she had done directly for the chairman. She wanted to be as thorough and complete as she could be in the four hours that were available before she was to deliver her outline, notes, analysis, and conclusions to the chairman to study before the Management Committee met.

THE CHAIRMAN'S MEMO AND QUESTIONS

To: Patricia Ryan (and Robert Sampson)
          Office of Human Resources
From: David Li, Chairman
Date: January 18, 2004
Subject: Questions about the National Training Center

The first year of operations at the National Training Center is now history, and the Management Committee will be discussing the performance of the Center at our meeting this afternoon. I would very much appreciate your analysis and recommendations about three issues which concern me. First, I need some help in thinking about the proper accounting for the costs we are incurring because of the important role of training in the firm's strategy; it seems to me that we are creating something of great value to the firm and its future, and I think our balance sheet should reflect that value in some way. Second, the summary report on operations (copy faxed to Sampson this morning) concerns me a great deal; it looks to me that the costs of the Center are running about one-third higher for each participant than we forecast at the time the Center was proposed in 2002. Third, my concerns about the costs lead me to conclude that we should explicitly discuss establishing management control systems for the Center so that we can assess its effectiveness on an ongoing basis.

Questions on Accounting for Training Costs:

1. On January 1, 2003, the Statement of Financial Position for CPC showed the National Training Center at its cost to the firm, or $19.5 million. The investment that we had made by purchasing Sandown College and renovating our two buildings there was fully disclosed to our partners, all of whom took great pride in our decision to create the Center. Now, with a year's operations behind us it seems to me that we have created some valuable human capital and that our balance sheet should reflect the added value of the firm because of the training programs we have conducted at the Center. **I realize that if we were a firm subject to generally accepted accounting principles this would be difficult or impossible because our auditors would probably object, but CPC is a partnership and is privately owned by the partners only.** For this reason, application of the accounting principles of accrual,

matching, and realization all seem to me to support the idea that some or all of the training costs that we incurred in 2003 should be capitalized this year so that these potential expenses can be matched with the additional revenues we hope our trained professional staff will generate. Do you agree? Why, or why not?

2. Regardless of your answer to Question 1, which of the training costs incurred in 2003 are the best candidates for capitalization? If you suggest that some, but not all, of the training costs incurred in 2003 are good candidates for capitalization, what are the criteria that permit you to separate those that might be capitalized from those that should not be capitalized? Are there other costs incurred by CPC that are related to its training activities that should be capitalized?

3. If we adopt a policy of capitalizing some of the training costs that we incur at the Center, then we will have to adopt a policy for when those costs should be recognized as expenses. According to the presentation that Robert Sampson made to our partners at last year's Partners' Meeting, the average employment of a newly hired professional **as a staff consultant** will be just over three years; 30% will leave the firm before three years, and only 30% still will be with the firm at the end of the fourth year. Only about one in ten staff members is likely to become a partner or principal. At any one time, the average partner or principal will be a member of the firm for seven years from the current date. I am not sure how these data fit together with the idea that every staff consultant should spend two weeks in training each year and each partner or principal should average one week in training each year. If some training costs are capitalized, over what time period should they be matched with revenues? Please outline a possible accounting policy that I can present to and discuss with the Management Committee.

4. If we do adopt a policy of capitalizing some training costs, the operating income that we will report to partners will be higher for 2003 than if we do not capitalize some training costs. How, if at all, should this affect the cash payout to partners and principals for 2003? How will the capitalization of training costs affect the cash flows for the firm?

Questions on the Operations of the National Training Center:

5. Please analyze as completely as you can for me why the 2003 actual cost per participant of $1,047 per week exceeded the proposal estimate of $784 per week. I expect that there are going to be questions about this from the Management Committee, so the more clearly you can present and reconcile what we expected to what actually happened will help me very much. Do you have any possible hypotheses about why the differences occurred or what might have caused them?

6. I am not really very happy about the ways in which we are tracking the cost of training at the Center. Can you outline a system or ways we might do this better in the future?

Questions about the future Management Controls for the training activity:

7. At the present time we have no established management control system in place at the National Training Center or for the training activity in our firm.

Please outline your ideas for a management control system. What should be our objectives, how should we try to achieve them, and what should we be measuring to know that we are achieving them? Please be as detailed as possible in the time available to you.

8. One problem that we have had at the National Training Center is filling the available training weeks for partners and principals. Whenever I ask about this I am told that these people are reluctant to attend training at the Center because it means that those hours and days cannot be billed to clients, and billable time is part of the formula we use to distribute profits to partners and principals at the end of each operating year. Do you have any suggestions about changes to the firm's management control systems or incentive systems to encourage partners and principals to use the Center to its capacity?

Thank you for your help with this on such short notice. It is great to have you on our staff.

EXHIBIT 1

Consulting Partners & Co., The National Training Center Report on Operations—2003 ($ thousands except for cost per participant week)

Annual Costs:
  Training:

Training staff	$ 560	
Office staff	310	
Equipment and supplies	190	
Fees-external trainers	900	
Depreciation	400	
Other expenses	152	$2,512
Travel expenses		1,298
Residences:		
Managers and staff	$ 251	
Depreciation	425	
Cafeteria staff	142	
Maintenance and supplies	50	
Food and beverages	298	
		1,166
TOTAL ANNUAL COSTS		$4,976

Training in 1993:

Partner training	672 weeks
Staff training	4,080 weeks
	4,752 participant weeks
Cost per participant per week	$1,047

EXHIBIT 2
Consulting Partners & Co., The National Training Center Proposal—
July 2002 ($ thousands except for cost per participant week)

Purchase of Sandown College:

Land	$2,000	
Buildings	2,000	
		$ 4,000
Renovations:		
(actual = 7.5 mil.) Residence halls	$6,500	
(actual = 8.0 mil.) Offices and classrooms	6,000	
		12,500

Annual Costs-Training:

Training staff	$ 550	
Office staff	350	
Equipment and supplies	200	
Fees-external trainers	900	
Other expenses	150	
		$ 2,150
Travel expenses		1,620

Annual Costs-Residences

Residence managers and staff	$ 242	
Cafeteria staff	140	
Maintenance supplies	50	
Food and beverages	315	
		747
TOTAL ANNUAL COSTS		$ 4,517

Capacity is 120 participants for 48 weeks[a] = 5,760 participant
weeks. Cost per participant per week = $784.

[a] Thirty partners per week for 48 weeks; 90 staff per week for 48 weeks.

Adventurous Computer Games, Inc.

What a great year this has been. Getting our first product to market in time for holiday sales was the high point for all of us at Adventurous Computer Games, Inc. And to think we sold 65,400 units in a single quarter of a product we expected would sell 200,000 copies over a three-year lifetime. I think it proves that our way of developing product is the right way in today's competitive computer game market.

Bruce Caldwell, president and chief executive officer, of Adventurous Computer Games, Inc. (AdCom Games) had just opened a luncheon meeting discussion among company officers, two shareholders who held large blocks of AdCom Games common stock, and some prospective investors who had expressed interest in becoming shareholders. Company officers present included: Mary Sullivan, vice president and director of sales and marketing; George Thomas, vice president and director of product development, and Sybil O'Hara, treasurer and controller. All of the officers, shareholders, and investors were friends. The informal luncheon had been scheduled to allow everyone to bask in the euphoria of the highly successful introduction of the company's first computer game, *Secret Agent*.

Even though it was only the second week of 2004, O'Hara had prepared preliminary financial statements for the year 2003 (see **Exhibits 1, 2,** and **3**). Although the preliminary statement of net income showed a loss exceeding that of the prior year, O'Hara alerted everyone to the fact that some costs in developing computer software would have to be capitalized before the finalized financial statements could be prepared. She expected the capitalization of the software development costs would reduce the loss shown in the preliminary statement of net income and perhaps even eliminate it.

COMPANY BACKGROUND

Adventurous Computer Games, Inc. was founded early in 2002 by the four officers attending the January 2004 meeting. All four had worked previously at one or more competitors in the computer entertainment and educational software development industry. Thomas had convinced Caldwell, Sullivan, and O'Hara that with a carefully managed product development process they could develop computer games and entertainments rapidly to take advantage of trends in the developing computer game industry. Each new wave of products had to meet higher demands for quality graphics, animation, digitized artwork and video, and music and sound effects. Once a new trend was identified, developers had to move quickly to capitalize on it. Thomas concluded that the key was in streamlining the product development process.

The company was incorporated with only a production concept at its core. After each of the four officers had committed to personal investments of more than $100,000 each, they convinced others to join them in committing another $500,000 in exchange for shares of the newly formed company. Accomplishing this initial capitalization when the company had no products was evidence of the charisma and enthusiasm of the company founders and the high risk, high potential return of the computer entertainment industry in early 2002.

Development of the company's first product began in July 2002. By the end of the year, the company had 17 full-time officers and employees, had demonstrated the technological feasibility of its first product, *Secret Agent*, and had begun a detailed program design process to create new products. There were no revenues recognized in 2002, and a loss of $188,000 was reported for the year. However, the company ended 2002 with cash and cash equivalents of nearly $730,000, which officers hoped would sustain operations until the first product was completed and ready for sale.

CURRENT PRODUCTS AND PRODUCTS UNDER DEVELOPMENT

The complexity and ingenuity underlying computer games and entertainments had escalated rapidly in recent years. The most popular products featured high-quality graphics, animation, music, sound effects, art, and text to create interactive stories similar to cartoons or animated films. In these products, players typically guide a major character, and thus the flow and direction of the adventure, in order to solve problems, escape from perilous situations, experience different environments and interact with other characters. AdCom Games' first product, *Secret Agent*, and the other two products already under development, *The Wild West* and *World Search*, were typical. Briefly, the games could be described as follows:

Secret Agent In this game, the player assumes the role of an agent for the government of Plutonia. Another unknown agent is trying to steal secret communications codes which have allowed Plutonia to dominate its hemisphere for the last fifty years. The object of the game is to stop the theft.

The Wild West In this game, an assortment of characters is trying to seize a gold shipment being taken through outlaw territory by Wells Fargo. Unknown to Wells Fargo and their agent (die player), the shipment had been assembled from a series of thefts by dishonest and disreputable bankers. The object is to get the gold back into the hands of its rightful owners without complete knowledge of who those owners actually are, while under constant threat from the dishonest bankers and other outlaws who have learned of the shipment.

World Search Somewhere in the world a treasure of incalculable value has been hidden and everyone wants to find it. Pitfalls await unwary searchers, including the player, who may choose the wrong conveyance or who may choose the wrong route to the hiding place.

Secret Agent had been developed in just more than a year, and copies of the finished product were first shipped on October 1, 2003 to distributors and large retailers. George Thomas estimated that the first copies of *The Wild West* would be available for shipment by the end of the first quarter of 2004; and *World Search* was expected to be ready for shipment before October 1, 2004.

THE PRODUCT DEVELOPMENT PROCESS

The development of a computer entertainment such as a computer game began with the development of a concept to which tests of market feasibility, financial feasibility, and management commitment and ability could be applied. Sometimes ideas and concepts would come in the form of proposals from freelance game designers outside of the company. In other cases, the creative staff from within a computer game developer such as AdCom Games would initiate the development and apply these tests before deciding to proceed. Mary Sullivan and George Thomas spent much of their time brainstorming about, and considering the marketability of, different game concepts and situations. The tests of market feasibility and attractiveness were applied at every succeeding stage of the development process up to the product launch date to assure highest demand for the finished game. Unless a new game was judged to have high market potential, no further development effort would take place.

Beyond the concept and the ideas that underlie every computer software product lay the need to determine its technological feasibility. Although some detailed program design, and even some coding and documentation might begin before technological feasibility was established, questions about whether the concept behind a game could be captured in computer software had to be answered prior to extensive investment in the development of a product. A large part of the product development process which George Thomas incorporated into the development program at AdCom Games consisted of integrating and relating five steps of product development: technological feasibility, detailed program design, coding, testing, and documentation in instructions. Each product was controlled by a timeline chart that related these product development phases (see **Exhibit 4**).

The five basic activities involved in creating computer software products after market and financial feasibility had been established can be briefly described as follows:

Technological feasibility Establishing technological feasibility involves ". . . all planning, coding, and testing activities that are necessary to establish that the product can be produced to meet its design specifications including functions, features and technical performance requirements" (*Statement of Financial Accounting Standards No. 86*).

Detailed program design This is the most complete design level before coding and produces a detailed description of what the finished product will look like and what its design specifications will be.

Coding and testing These are the activities in the process that implement the detailed program design.

Documentation and instructions Preparation of the internal logic of coding and programs and instructions and user's guides.

In most of the computer game software industry, project teams were created and the teams themselves managed the integration of the product development process. While this group approach stimulated the creativity of everyone involved, George Thomas felt that it also enabled team members to spend too much time thinking about enhancement of the product and too little time writing the lines of code that would actually drive the product once it was installed on a player's computer. Once he reached this realization, Thomas conceived the idea of creating a Product Development Support Center upon which each project team could draw for the development tools, skilled programmers, and animation staff who would accomplish the myriad of details of creating code, testing, documenting and preparing instructions for each game. While the project team costs would be assigned directly to a product, the Product Development Support Center costs would be a cost to the corporation. In this way, a project team leader or member, immediately on deciding the scope of any design, coding, or documentation task, could assign it to someone in the Product Development Support Center, freeing the project team member to continue concentration on the creative elements of program development.

Company management felt that the Product Development Support Center concept had worked nearly perfectly in the development of *Secret Agent*. To create a product of the complexity of *Secret Agent* in approximately one year's time was amazing when compared to industry standards. Furthermore, Bruce Caldwell and George Thomas were convinced that the total cost of the product had been substantially less than it would have been had a larger product team been assigned to manage all steps in the product development process. **Exhibit 5** contains a summary of the costs of the Product Development Support Center in 2003 and **Exhibit 6** summarizes several measurements of software development activity in 2003 by quarters.

THE ACCOUNTING ISSUES

After fifteen minutes of animated conversation about company prospects and the enthusiastic reception which *Secret Agent* had enjoyed, Bruce Caldwell asked Sybil O'Hara to briefly summarize what she meant when she said that perhaps some software costs would have to be capitalized before final financial statements could be prepared. O'Hara began by briefly summarizing some theoretical issues and a brief history of accounting for computer software.

Until the mid-1980s, most computer software developers expensed the cost of developing software at the time the costs were incurred. Using analogies to research and development expenses, which had been expensed by most companies under accounting principles and under the guise of conservatism in most countries, software development costs were simply charged against whatever revenues were available in the period when the costs were incurred. In effect, that's what we did last year, because at the time we had no products or revenues with which to match our expenditures.

By 1983, however, some accountants and managers concerned with software development costs and expenses had become increasingly concerned about the mismatching that occurs if software development costs are expensed as expenditures are made, but revenues from software products are recognized in future periods as those products are delivered to customers. In the United States these concerns led the Securities and Exchange Commission (SEC) in April 1983 to propose a moratorium on accounting for the costs of computer software development. Companies that had been capitalizing those costs could continue to do so, but others were precluded from capitalizing costs of computer software if the policy of capitalizing such costs had not been disclosed previously. In August 1983 the SEC stated that the moratorium would be rescinded automatically after the Financial Accounting Standards Board (FASB) provided additional guidance on the subject.

Following the establishment of the moratorium by the SEC, the Financial Accounting Standards Board went through its rather tortuous and laborious process of considering whether some computer software development costs should be capitalized or whether all such costs should be expensed as are expenditures for research and development. In the end, they decided that all software development costs incurred after technological feasibility is established should be capitalized and then matched with revenues from the software use or sale over the expected useful life of the software developed. The FASB issued Statement of Financial Accounting Standards No. 86 which substantially reduced the diversity in accounting for computer software development costs by companies in the United States.

Last year this pronouncement did not affect us because we had no products that we had determined were technologically feasible until year end, but for 2003 we are affected because we have three products which are technologically feasible, and one from which we have recognized revenues. As a practical matter, what this means is that we have to decide how much of our costs relate to each product, how much cost should be capitalized, and how much of our costs should be expensed and matched with 2003 revenues. Whatever we decide will surely change the preliminary financial statements which I have given you today. Obviously, deferring and capitalizing some of our expenditures made in 2003 is going to improve both our balance sheet and our reported loss, but I haven't had much time to consider the appropriate way to approach this change and what effect it will have on our final financial statements.

The mood of the room had become somber as Sybil O'Hara had begun discussing the history and technical issues involving capitalization of software development costs. It was Bruce Caldwell who broke the silence.

Sybil, I sense that decisions we will have to make in the coming weeks are fairly important to us and our company and its future. Can you have someone put together a memorandum on some of the issues on which we will have to decide in the next few weeks and some estimates of what the possible effect on our final financial statements will be? Let's ignore any possible book tax effects of these decisions for the time being; we will have our tax accountant worry about those aspects later. I understand that we will still be able to expense development costs for tax purposes irrespective of how we decide to account for development costs in our financial records and reports.

Sybil readily agreed and the group discussion turned to a discussion of some of the twists and turns which the project teams were building into *The Wild West* and *World Search*.

The following morning Sybil O'Hara provided the following questions to the new MBA whom she had just added to her staff.

QUESTIONS

Part 1. Accounting for the Cost of Software Programs at AdCom Games

a. AdCom Games will need to develop a product costing system or some other procedures for deciding which of the product development costs that have been incurred should be associated with which products. On the surface, at least, it should be fairly easy to associate the project team labor cost with each product because each team works with only one product at a time. But what about the Product Development Support Center costs? (See **Exhibit 5**.) From day to day staff members from the Center move from project to project, working on the tasks assigned to them by the project team leaders, and we have intentionally kept no records of the time any staff member worked on any project. To have done so would possibly have undermined the very concept of the Product Development Support Center developed by George Thomas. Perhaps we could use some of the activity measures we keep by product to allocate the Product Development Support Center costs to products. Which costs should be allocated? On what basis? Please explain fully how you reached your recommendation.

b. Estimate the total product cost to date for each of our three products, *Secret Agent*, *The Wild West*, and *World Search*, using the product costing methodology you recommended above.

c. What future changes to our costing and product development accounting procedures would you recommend AdCom Games adopt in 2004? Why?

Part 2. Estimating what the Final Financial Reports for AdCom Games for 2003 will Show

d. If product development costs incurred after technological feasibility is established for each product are to be capitalized, how much cost should be capitalized in 2003?

e. The market life of *Secret Agent* was estimated to be three years when the product was introduced on October 1, 2003, and the total expected market for the product was estimated to be 200,000 units. How much of the total capitalized product development cost for *Secret Agent* should be matched with revenues in 2003? How will the Preliminary Statements of Income and Financial Position be affected by the adoption of the required accounting change?

f. There is a lot of latitude about whether "technological feasibility" has been established. AdCom Games could probably argue that technological feasibility for either or both *The Wild West* or *World Search* occurred one quarter earlier or one quarter later than shown in **Exhibit 4**—"Product Development Phases." Should we make such claims? How would our financial reports for 2003 be changed, if at all? What would you recommend? Why?

g. How will the Preliminary Statement of Cash Flows (**Exhibit 3**) be changed by the changes in accounting for software development costs in 2003, ignoring any possible effects on income taxes due or paid?

Part 3. Overall Evaluation and Conclusions

h. I would like you to give me your conclusions about what, if anything, AdCom Games is going to learn or gain from the effort to change from our practice of simply charging all software development costs to expense as they are incurred. Will the information available to management, shareholders, and prospective investors be improved by the capitalization of some software costs? If so, how? If not, why not?

EXHIBIT 1

Adventurous Computer Games, Inc., Preliminary
Statement of Income for the Year 2003, and Statement
of Income for the Year 2002, in Thousands of Dollars

		2003	2002
Net revenues		$1,640.5	$ 0
Manufacturing costs	$141.6		
Less: Inventories of Finished Product[a]	49.0		
		$ 92.6	0
Other costs and expenses:			
Product development:			
Project team labor		536.0	18.0
Product support center		797.0	54.7
Sales and marketing[b]		297.2	10.2
Interest		49.0	5.3
General and administrative		153.7	99.8
Total costs and expenses		$1,925.5	$188.0
Net loss for year		$ 285.0	$188.0

[a] In 2003, inventories of finished product included only the cost of preparation of discs, packaging, and game instructions for copies of *Secret Agent* which had been manufactured but not shipped to distributors.

[b] Sales and marketing expenses includes salaries of marketing staff and cost of advertising and point-of-sale displays.

EXHIBIT 2

Adventurous Computer Games, Inc., Preliminary Statement
of Financial Position for the Year Ended December 31, 2003,
and Statement of Financial Position for the Year Ended
December 31, 2002, in Thousands of Dollars

	2003	2002
ASSETS		
Current Assets:		
Cash	$ 43.0	$ 39.5
Short-term investments	—	690.1
Accounts receivable	781.0	0.0
Inventories of finished product[a]	49.0	0.0
Other current assets	17.0	13.6
Total current assets	$ 890.0	$ 743.2
Property and equipment (net)		
Computer equipment	243.0	171.0
Office equipment and leasehold improvements	171.0	183.0
	$ 414.0	$ 354.0
Software costs	0.0	0.0
Total assets	$1,304.0	$1,097.2
LIABILITIES AND OWNERS' EQUITY		
Current Liabilities:		
Notes payable to bank	$ 402.0	$ 197.5
Accounts payable	43.0	37.5
Accrued expenses	67.0	33.2
Accrued employee compensation	19.1	5.1
Other liabilities	49.0	7.5
	$ 580.1	$ 280.8
Long-term notes payable to shareholders	271.0	78.5
Stockholders' Equity:		
Common stock	325.4	325.4
Paid-in capital	600.5	600.5
Retained earnings	(473.0)	(188.0)
	$ 452.9	$ 737.9
Total liabilities and owners' equity	$1,304.0	$1,097.2

[a] In 2003, inventories of finished product included only the cost of preparation of discs, packaging, and game instructions for copies
of *Secret Agent* which had been manufactured but not shipped to distributors.

EXHIBIT 3
Adventurous Computer Games, Inc., Preliminary Statement of Cash Flows for the Year Ended December 31, 2003, in Thousands of Dollars

Cash flows from operations:

Net income (loss)	$(285.0)
Add depreciation	58.0
Reduction of short-term investments	690.1
Increase in accounts receivable	(781.0)
Increase in inventories	(49.0)
Increase in other current assets	(3.4)
Increase in notes payable to bank	204.5
Increase in accounts payable	5.5
Increase in accrued expenses	33.8
Increase in accrued compensation	14.0
Increase in other liabilities	41.5
Total cash flows from operations	$ (71.0)

Cash flows from investing:

Purchase of new computer equipment, office equipment, and leasehold improvements	(118.0)

Cash flows from financing:

Increase in long-term notes payable to owners	192.5

Net cash flows	$ 3.5
Cash, January 1, 2003	39.5
Cash, December 31, 2003	$ 43.0

EXHIBIT 4

Product Development Phases and Projections by Quarters (quarter) at December 31, 2003 (timelines show periods in which each development phase took place or was planned)[a]

Product/Development Phase	2002		2003				2004	
	Qtr. 3	Qtr. 4	Qtr. 1	Qtr. 2	Qtr. 3	Qtr. 4	Qtr. 1	Beyond
Secret Agent								
Technological feasibility								
Detail program design								
Coding								
Testing								
Documentation and instructions								
The Wild West								
Technological feasibility[a]								
Detail program design								
Coding								
Testing								
Documentation and instructions								
World Search								
Technological feasibility								
Detail program design								
Coding								
Testing								
Documentation and instructions								

[a] For example, AdCom Games' evaluation of technological feasibility for "The Wild West," began on October 1, 2002 and was determined to be complete on June 30, 2003.

EXHIBIT 5
2003 Product Development Support Center Costs in Thousands of Dollars

	Quarter 1	Quarter 2	Quarter 3	Quarter 4	Year 2003
Development tools	$15.0	$20.0	$25.0	$25.0	$85.0
Staff	58.2	132.3	170.1	214.8	575.4
Supervision	10.0	19.8	25.1	20.7	85.6
Depreciation	6.0	12.0	15.0	18.0	51.0
Total costs	$89.2	$184.1	$235.2	$288.5	$797.0
Staff headcount at end of quarter	10	20	25	30	

EXHIBIT 6
Activity Measures by Product

	2002		2003				2004	
	Qtr. 3	Qtr. 4	Qtr. 1	Qtr. 2	Qtr. 3	Qtr. 4	Qtr. 1	Beyond
Project Team Hours by Quarter:								
Secret Agent	—	1,000	2,500	1,500	1,000	—		
The Wild West			—	2,500	4,000	4,000		
World Search			—	2,000	4,000	6,950		
Lines of Code Written by Quarter:								
Secret Agent		—	500	1,000	500	—		
The Wild West			—	1,500	1,500	1,500		
World Search			—	—	2,500	3,500		
Cumulative Pages of Documentation:								
Secret Agent	—	25	50	65	70	70		
The Wild West			20	60	120	140		
World Search			—	35	110	160		
Project Team Labor Cost by Quarter ($ thousands):								
Secret Agent	—	$18	$45	$27	$18	—		
The Wild West			—	$45	$72	$82		
World Search			—	$36	$72	$139		

INDEX